The Big Myth

The Big Myth

How American Business Taught Us to Loathe
Government and Love the Free Market

Naomi Oreskes
Erik M. Conway

BLOOMSBURY PUBLISHING
NEW YORK · LONDON · OXFORD · NEW DELHI · SYDNEY

BLOOMSBURY PUBLISHING
Bloomsbury Publishing Inc.
1385 Broadway, New York, NY 10018, USA

BLOOMSBURY, BLOOMSBURY PUBLISHING, and the Diana logo are trademarks
of Bloomsbury Publishing Plc

First published in the United States 2023

The text from chapter 4 appearing on pages 100–105 was adapted from Naomi Oreskes,
Erik M. Conway, and Charlie Tyson, "Chapter 4: How American Businessmen Made Us Believe
that Free Enterprise was Indivisible from American Democracy: The National Association of
Manufacturers' Propaganda Campaign 1935–1940," in *The Disinformation Age:
Politics, Technology, and Disruptive Communication in the United States*, ed. W. Lance Bennett
and Steven Livingston (Cambridge: Cambridge University Press, 2020), 95–119.

A short essay adapted from chapters 4 and 5 appears in Naomi Oreskes and Erik M. Conway, "The
Magic of the Marketplace," in *Myth America: Historians Take on the Biggest Legends and Lies About
Our Past*, ed. Kevin M. Kruse and Julian E. Zelizer (New York: Basic Books, 2023), 129–40.

The opening passage of the conclusion appearing on page 415 was adapted from Naomi Oreskes,
"We Need Big Government to Save Us from the Pandemic," *Time*, April 17, 2020,
https://time.com/5823063/we-need-big-government-pandemic/.

ISBN: HB: 978-1-63557-357-2; EBOOK: 978-1-63557-358-9

LIBRARY OF CONGRESS CATALOGING-IN-PUBLICATION DATA IS AVAILABLE

2 4 6 8 10 9 7 5 3 1

Typeset by Westchester Publishing Services
Printed and bound in the U.S.A.

To find out more about our authors and books visit www.bloomsbury.com and sign up
for our newsletters.

The great enemy of truth is very often not the lie—deliberate, contrived, and dishonest—but the myth—persistent, persuasive, and unrealistic.

—JOHN F. KENNEDY, YALE UNIVERSITY
COMMENCEMENT ADDRESS, 1962

What is the cost of lies? It's not that we'll mistake them for truth. The real danger is that if we hear enough lies, then we no longer recognize the truth at all.

—JARED HARRIS AS VALERY LEGASOV, *CHERNOBYL*, "1:23:45" (2019)

I did not lie in Vienna, but I did not tell the whole truth.

—VALERY LEGASOV, REPORT TO THE SOVIET
ACADEMY OF SCIENCES, 1986

CONTENTS

LIST OF ABBREVIATIONS

AEI	American Enterprise Institute
AT&T	American Telephone and Telegraph
CAB	Civil Aeronautics Board
CEQ	Council on Environmental Quality
COLA	cost-of-living adjustment
EPA	Environmental Protection Agency
FBI	Federal Bureau of Investigation
FCC	Federal Communications Commission
FDIC	Federal Deposit Insurance Corporation
FEE	Foundation for Economic Education
FHLBB	Federal Home Loan Bank Board
FSLIC	Federal Savings and Loan Insurance Corporation
FTC	Federal Trade Commission
GAO	General Accounting Office (later called Government Accountability Office)
GDP	Gross Domestic Product
GE	General Electric Company
GM	General Motors Company
HDI	Human Development Index
HUAC	House Un-American Activities Committee
ICC	Interstate Commerce Commission

IMF	International Monetary Fund
MCA	Music Corporation of America
NAFTA	North American Free Trade Agreement
NAM	National Association of Manufacturers
NASA	National Aeronautics and Space Administration
NEA	National Education Association
NELA	National Electric Light Association
NIIC	National Industrial Information Council
NIRA	National Industrial Recovery Act
NLRB	National Labor Relations Board
OMB	Office of Management and Budget
OPA	Office of Price Administration
OWI	Office of War Information
PBGC	Pension Benefit Guaranty Corporation
PUHCA	Public Utilities Holding Company Act
REA	Rural Electrification Administration
SAG	Screen Actors Guild
SEC	Securities and Exchange Commission
TEPCO	Tennessee Electric Power Company
TVA	Tennessee Valley Authority

Will you leave these freedoms to your children?

Men have died to leave you these 4 symbols of freedom:

A Holy Bible — symbol of your right to worship as you wish. (First Amendment, U. S. Constitution)

A door key — your right to lock your door against illegal government force and prying. (Fourth Amendment, U. S. Constitution)

A pencil — freedom to speak or write what you think, whether you agree with the government or not. (First Amendment, U. S. Constitution)

And a free ballot — your right to choose the people who represent you in government — your protection against government tyranny. (Article I, U. S. Constitution)

In half the world today, these symbols and the things they stand for have been destroyed.

And Khrushchev says it can happen here. He boasts that our grandchildren will live under socialism.

Unthinkable? Yes — but only so long as America guards its freedoms well. Against threats that come from *inside* our country, as well as from the outside.

In these critical times you would think that all of America's energies and financial resources should be concentrated on strengthening our country's defense.

But there are some people who would weaken this effort through needless government spending. For example, they want to use billions of your tax dollars to put the government *deeper* into the electric power business.

Such spending is unnecessary because the *investor-owned* electric light and power companies can supply all the additional power a growing America will need.

Each time the government moves further into business — any business — it is another step on the road to socialism. And socialism is one thing Americans do *not* mean to leave to their children — or grandchildren, despite what Khrushchev says.

Selling the Big Myth: A 1950s advertisement—produced by a consortium operating under the name "America's Independent Electric Light and Power Companies"—promoting the electricity industry as the guardian of American freedom.

Introduction

This is the story of how American business manufactured a myth that has, for decades and to our detriment, held us in its grip. It is the true history of a false idea: the idea of "the magic of the marketplace."

Some people call it market absolutism or market essentialism. In the 1990s, George Soros popularized the name we find most apt: market fundamentalism.[1] It's a quasi-religious belief that the best way to address our needs—whether economic or otherwise—is to let markets do their thing, and not rely on government. Market fundamentalists treat "The Market" as a proper noun: something unique and unto itself, that has agency and even wisdom, that functions best when left unfettered and unregulated, undisturbed and unperturbed. Government, according to the myth, cannot improve the functioning of markets; it can only interfere. Governments therefore need to stay out of the way, lest they "distort" the market and prevent it from doing its "magic." In the late twentieth century, market fundamentalism was cloaked in the seemingly ancient raiments of received wisdom. In fact, it was more or less invented in the twentieth century.

Classical liberal economists—including Adam Smith—recognized that government served essential functions, including building infrastructure for everyone's benefit and regulating banks, which, left to their own devices, could destroy an economy. They also recognized that taxation was required to enable governments to perform those functions. But in the early twentieth century, a group of self-styled "neo-liberals" shifted economic and political thinking radically. They argued that any government action in the marketplace, even well intentioned, compromised the freedom of individuals to do as they pleased—and therefore put us on the road to totalitarianism. Political and economic freedom were "indivisible," they insisted: any compromise to the latter was a threat to the former—any compromise at all, even to address obvious ills like child labor or workplace injury. Why did we ever come to accept a worldview so impervious to facts? A worldview Smith himself, often thought of as the father of free-market capitalism, would have rejected? This book tells that story.

IN OUR FIRST book, *Merchants of Doubt*, we wanted to explain why intelligent, educated people would deny the reality of man-made climate change. At the time, most scientists thought they faced a problem of scientific illiteracy—that the "public" just didn't understand climate science. But through a series of accidents, we stumbled across the story of four physicists who laid the foundations for climate change denial as far back as the late 1980s. These men were prominent scientists—one was a former president of the U.S. National Academy of Sciences, another headed a major NASA lab—so it wasn't remotely plausible that they didn't understand the facts. We discovered they hadn't just rejected climate science but had fought settled science on a host of public health and environmental issues, starting with the harms of tobacco. Two of these four scientists had worked with tobacco companies. The seemingly obvious explanation for what they did—that they were industry shills motivated by money—turned out to be wrong. The right answer was ideology: market fundamentalism.

These men feared that government regulation of the marketplace—whether to address climate change or protect consumers from lethal products—would be the first step on a slippery slope to socialism, communism, or worse. This fear was rooted in their personal histories designing weapons systems in the Cold War. On behalf of the U.S. government, they had worked to build the atomic bomb, the hydrogen bomb, and the rockets and submarines to deliver those weapons. They saw the Soviet threat as serious, a threat they had helped to "contain." When the Cold War ended, they couldn't stop fighting. Instead, they found a new enemy—environmentalism—which they viewed as a back door to socialism, if not communism. As one of them put it, "if we do not carefully delineate the government's role in regulating . . . dangers there is essentially no limit to how much government can ultimately control our lives."[2] Today, tobacco control; tomorrow, goodbye to the Bill of Rights. Environmentalists, in their view, were "watermelons," green on the outside and red on the inside. The American way of life was at stake. So these men would do whatever they could to prevent government regulation of the marketplace, even if it meant fighting facts, challenging hard-won knowledge, and betraying the science they had helped to build.

Merchants of Doubt left us with a new question: Where did this ideology come from? After all, the United States had implemented all kinds of environmental, workplace, and public health safeguards both before and during the Cold War, and we had not succumbed to communism. Many European countries had even stronger regulations—particularly with respect to consumer products—and they were still democracies, too.

Between us we have been to all fifty states and lived in twelve, including wilderness Alaska and a dying mill town in northern New Hampshire. On our travels, we have found that market fundamentalism is widespread in "blue" and "red" states alike, and that some version of it underlies most climate change skepticism. Many people seem to take Ronald Reagan's view that "the government" is the problem, as it stands ready to steal both their money and their freedom. When asked why they hold these views—why they are skeptical that climate change is real or that government can do anything about it—they often point to articles they read in *Fortune*, *Forbes*, or the *Wall Street Journal*.

Even in supposedly liberal enclaves like Cambridge, Massachusetts, many people think climate change will be best addressed by technological innovation in the marketplace—despite the fact that even by 2010, the year our book came out, atmospheric CO_2 was climbing, Earth was getting hotter, and the market wasn't responding on any level commensurate with the threat. As one of our students put it, the most common answer, whether in Massachusetts or Montana, was "markets, markets, markets."

Thus emerged the question that informs this book and that we have spent the past decade studying: How did so many Americans come to have so much faith in markets and so little faith in government?

MARKET FUNDAMENTALISM IS not just the belief that free markets are the best means to run an economic system but also the belief that they are the only means that will not ultimately destroy our other freedoms. It is the belief in the primacy of economic freedom not just to generate wealth but as a bulwark of political freedom. And it is the belief that markets exist outside of politics and culture, so that it can be logical to speak of leaving them "alone."

We are all familiar with the idea that, as George Soros has summarized, "the doctrine of laissez-faire capitalism holds that the common good is best served by the uninhibited pursuit of self-interest."[3] That's the core argument Adam Smith made in 1776 and contented capitalists have accepted ever since. Market fundamentalists, however, depart from Smith by insisting there is no "common good," merely the sum of all the individual private goods. For this reason, they reject government's claims to represent "the people": there are only people—individuals—who represent themselves, and they do this most effectively not through their governments, even democratically elected ones, but through free choices in free markets.

Milton Friedman, America's most famous market fundamentalist, went so far as to argue that voting was not democratic, because it could too easily be distorted by special interests and because in any case most voters were ignorant. But rather than consider how special interests might be mitigated or how voters could be better informed, he maintained that true freedom was not expressed in the voting booth. "The economic market provides a greater degree of freedom than the political market," Friedman said in South Africa in 1976, as he encouraged the citizens of that country not to fuss over apartheid, but to preserve and expand their market-based economy.[4]

Friedman's argument works when we are talking about the freedom to buy, say, shoes of any type. But it fails when we consider the larger picture, including deceptive advertising, aggressive and misleading PR campaigns, and what economists call "external costs": costs that are invisible to or misunderstood by the shoe buyers, or that accrue to people who didn't buy those shoes at all. Pollution is an external cost. What happens when the shoe manufacturer dumps toxic chemicals behind the plant and hides that fact from its workers, investors, and customers? Friedman downplayed the problem by giving it the friendly label of "neighborhood effects," and claimed that any remedy would almost always be worse than the disease, because of the loss of freedoms or compromises to property rights typically associated with government regulations. In some cases, he may have been right. Regulations do compromise someone's freedom in order to protect the freedom (and welfare) of others. When it comes to pollution, the "freedom" of factories to dump toxic wastes has been rightly rejected. When it comes to climate change, the "freedom" of corporations to sell oil, gas, and coal jeopardizes the rest of us. This creates a fundamental dilemma for the fundamentalists. But rather than rethink their arguments, market fundamentalists protect their worldview by denying that climate change is real or asserting that somehow "The Market" will fix it, despite all evidence to the contrary.

FRIEDMAN HELD THAT capitalism and freedom are two indivisible sides of the same coin, but this "indivisibility thesis" predates him by decades. In the early twentieth century, it was promoted in the United States by a group of industrialists working under the umbrella of the National Association of Manufacturers (NAM). NAM and its allies used the thesis to argue against political reforms that today we take for granted, such as laws limiting child labor, establishing workers' compensation, and creating the federal income tax. In the 1930s, they aligned themselves with the electricity industry and used the thesis to argue against the Rural Electrification Administration, the Tennessee Valley Authority, and other elements of the New Deal. Mostly they lost these fights, in part because the thesis suffered a fatal flaw: it wasn't true. Electricity was a case in point. Markets had failed to bring electricity to millions of Americans who wanted it, but the government had succeeded, and rural Americans were better off economically and no less free. Indeed, they were arguably freer than before, because they now had electrical appliances that reduced manual labor and electric lights to lengthen the usable day.[5]

Because the indivisibility thesis had so little foundation in fact, American business leaders needed to find other ways to shore it up. One way was propaganda. In the 1920s, the National Electric Light Association (NELA) launched a massive campaign that included, among other things, the hiring of academics to rewrite textbooks and develop curricula to promote pro-market, antigovernment perspectives in emerging business schools and economics programs across the country. They also recruited experts to "prove" that private electricity was cheaper than public electricity, even when the available facts showed otherwise. In the 1930s, NAM reprised the effort, with a multimillion-dollar propaganda campaign to convince Americans that business and industry were working just fine, and that the real causes of the Great Depression were unionized labor's unreasonable demands, coupled with the government's excessive interference in business affairs and federal taxation that starved industry of the monies it needed to expand productive capacity. Well into the 1940s, NAM produced books, pamphlets, radio programs, lecture series, and documentary and feature films (and later television programs) designed to influence what newspapers had to say about the economy and American life, what teachers taught in the classroom, and, above all, what the American people believed.

A key part of the manufacturers' propaganda campaign was the myth of the Tripod of Freedom, the claim that America was founded on three basic, interdependent principles: representative democracy, political freedom, and free enterprise. This was a fabricated claim. Free enterprise appears in neither the Declaration of Independence nor the Constitution, and the nineteenth-century American economy was laced with government involvement in the marketplace. But NAM spent millions to convince the American people of the truth of the Tripod of Freedom, and to persuade Americans that the villain in the story of the Great Depression was not "Big Business," but "Big Government." They spread this myth to weaken Americans' confidence in government institutions that reined in abusive business practices and protected ordinary citizens.

Another strategy was to recruit sympathetic intellectuals to help give the myth credibility. For this, American businessmen relied on imports: the economists Ludwig von Mises and Friedrich von Hayek, leaders of the Austrian school of economics. In the 1940s, a group linked to NAM paid for Mises and Hayek to come to America, arranged for them to be hired at New York University and the University of Chicago, respectively, and worked assiduously to promote the economists' ideas, both in business circles and among the American people generally. This included publishing a dumbed-down version of Hayek's famous book *The Road to Serfdom* in *Reader's Digest* and a cartoon version of it in *Look* magazine. In the 1950s, Ronald Reagan would encounter that *Reader's Digest* version; decades later *The Road to Serfdom* would be promoted by right-wing radio hosts Glenn Beck and Rush Limbaugh and touted by influential Republicans including Senator Ted Cruz and House leader Paul Ryan.[6]

Businessmen helped create America's first libertarian think tank, the Foundation for Economic Education (FEE), established in 1946 by Los Angeles Chamber of Commerce manager Leonard Read to peddle pro-market, antigovernment ideology. They also funded the Hayek-aligned Mont Pelerin Society, a cadre of mostly European economists, cultural commentators, and political theorists promoting a renewed commitment to free-market principles under the aegis of what became known as neoliberalism.[7] And they would help Milton Friedman write his most influential book, *Capitalism and Freedom*—essentially a restatement of the indivisibility thesis—which would dramatically reshape the American cultural conversation in the 1970s and '80s. In 1988, Reagan would award Friedman both the Presidential Medal of Freedom and the National Medal of Science.

Few of Friedman's readers knew that the book's success was not the product of open competition in the marketplace of ideas: *Capitalism and Freedom* had been financed and nurtured by American businessmen, and it was the most public part of a much larger project. *Reader's Digest* notwithstanding, the people who had brought Hayek to America had quickly concluded that his approach was too intellectual and too European to break through to the public. The best way to get the book they wanted—the book they felt their countrymen *needed*—was to bankroll such an initiative at a reputable American institution. They chose the University of Chicago; the endeavor would be named the Free Market Project, sometimes also known as the Free Market Study. Friedman was its marquee star, but he was not alone. Chicago economist George Stigler would become a leading voice against government regulation and win a Nobel Memorial Prize in Economic Sciences for this work; he would also produce an edited version of Adam Smith's *Wealth of Nations* that expunged nearly all of Smith's caveats about free market doctrine, including his extensive discussion of the need for bank regulation, for adequate wages for workers, and for taxation for public goods such as roads and bridges.[8] Economist Aaron Director (Friedman's brother-in-law) developed the Antitrust Project, which should have been called the Anti-Antitrust Project. Monopolies, Director argued, represented economic natural selection in action: the fittest corporations were the ones that survived. One of Director's students was the jurist Robert Bork, who in the 1990s would successfully use these arguments against the U.S. Department of Justice's antitrust prosecutions, laying the groundwork for judicial resistance to strict antitrust enforcement that persists today.[9]

Market fundamentalism wasn't just about economics, however. It also involved religion and mass culture. The promoters of the Mont Pelerin Society and FEE overlapped with a movement called Spiritual Mobilization, designed to convince Christian clergy that unregulated capitalism was not merely compatible with Christian values but founded upon them.[10] Spiritual Mobilization was led by a Congregational minister named James Fifield, but its biggest donor was Sun Oil president J. Howard Pew—a leading figure in NAM—who also backed Billy Graham and Norman Vincent Peale. (Peale's parishioners included Fred and Mary Trump.)[11] Pew was also friends with libertarian journalist Rose Wilder Lane, daughter of Laura Ingalls Wilder, the author of the beloved Little House on the Prairie series. Or ostensible author, for while millions of American readers adored these books—sold as the true story of Wilder's childhood on the American frontier—the stories had in fact been crafted into parables of individual self-sufficiency and government superfluousness by her libertarian daughter.

One of FEE founder Leonard Read's writers was the émigrée Ayn Rand, who would split with Read because she found his libertarianism insufficiently stringent;

she would go on to infuse her bestselling novels, as well as their screenplay adaptations, with simplistic, unadulterated libertarian messages. Critics generally panned *The Fountainhead* and *Atlas Shrugged*; one reviewer called the latter a book "written out of hate."[12] But people loved them; Rand's hate evidently inspired subsequent generations of libertarians and millions of sales. One reason Rand's books sold so well, however, was that they were heavily promoted by sympathetic organizations, including FEE and the Ayn Rand Institute, whose mission is to "keep Rand alive."[13] The *New York Times* in 2007 reported that the Ayn Rand Institute was at that time donating four hundred thousand copies a year of its namesake's novels to Advanced Placement high school programs.[14] Supreme Court justice Clarence Thomas cites *Atlas Shrugged* as a major influence on his thinking. So does former longtime Federal Reserve Bank chairman Alan Greenspan, who described Rand's work as a "moral defense of capitalism."[15]

Rand's acolytes admire her as a philosophical purist who brooked no compromise. In truth, she was an architect of Hollywood censorship codes that involved serious breaches of freedom. Another erstwhile defender of liberty who endorsed censorship was Hollywood's own Ronald Reagan.[16]

Most Americans know that before becoming a politician Reagan was an actor, but fewer are aware that Reagan's flagging screen career was revived by a job with the General Electric Corporation (GE). Reagan hosted the popular television show *General Electric Theater*, where each week his voice and face reached into tens of millions of homes, promoting didactic stories of individualism and free enterprise. At the same time, he traveled across the country on behalf of GE—visiting factories, making speeches at schools, and doing the dinner circuit in communities where GE had a presence—promoting the corporation's stridently individualist antiunion and antigovernment vision.

Reagan's mentor in this work was GE executive Lemuel Ricketts Boulware, whose antiunion tactics were so extreme they earned a name: Boulwarism. (They would also earn GE several indictments for federal labor law violations.) And while Reagan helped GE promote the ideology of free markets and free choice, the company conspired to rig electricity markets (an offense for which it would be successfully prosecuted in the 1960s). Boulware's influence transformed Reagan's politics. He went into GE a New Deal Democrat and came out an antigovernment conservative Republican. GE transformed Reagan's political fortunes as well; he emerged from his time there with powerful backers in corporate America who helped him launch his career in elected office.

Reagan was known as the Great Communicator, and the success of American market fundamentalism was ultimately a triumph of public relations: its advocates built a myth and persuaded Americans of its truth. By the 1970s, what had begun as a self-interested defense of business prerogatives—one that was factually dubious and characteristically supported by gross distortions and misrepresentations of history—had been transmogrified into a seemingly intellectually robust body of thought. Meanwhile, a network of libertarian think tanks, heavily funded by industries selling dangerous products including tobacco and fossil fuels, had been established to promote these views in schools, in universities, and in American life writ large. Among other things, these think tanks distributed free of charge millions of copies of Hayek's and Friedman's (and Rand's) books. Meanwhile, progressive foundations mostly focused on specific issues—like saving whales or expanding access to education—not realizing that a larger ideological battle was under way.[17] The myth spread, influencing American presidents from Jimmy Carter and Ronald Reagan to Bill Clinton and Barack Obama and, most recently, Donald Trump.

THE MEN (AND a few women) in this story worked to ensure their ideas got widespread attention in academia, in politics, in Hollywood, and in religious life, regardless of whether their claims were *true*. Using various means at their disposal— from overt propaganda and disinformation to subtle forms of persuasion, from influencing what was taught in schools to what children saw when they went to the movies—they worked to change what Americans believed.

Americans in the early twentieth century were largely suspicious of "Big Business" and saw the government as their ally.[18] By the later decades of the century, this had flipped: many Americans now admired business leaders as "entrepreneurs" and "job creators" and believed it made more sense to count on the "magic of the marketplace" to solve problems than to engage government. Many Americans saw government as dead weight, taxation as unfair or even a form of theft.[19] That they accepted these claims is proof of this story's importance: propaganda and persuasion had *worked*. The people involved in this project were intellectually diverse and geographically dispersed, but they were also in important (and sometimes startling) ways interconnected. Theirs was not a conspiracy, but it was a network of people who knew each other, supported each other morally and financially, and used this mutual support to promote a singular myth.

LIKE ALL GOOD myths, this one had a kernel of truth. As any economist could tell you, markets can efficiently allocate resources. Markets are good for getting productive uses out of the inputs that create wealth. They are also good for amassing information. Markets reveal a lot about what people want, how far they are willing to go to get it, and how much they are willing to pay for it. If efficiency were our only goal, then market fundamentalism might make sense. But efficiency is a tool, not an end.[20] When asked about their values, Americans don't say "efficiency." What most people want are better lives. A pleasant place to live in a safe community, with good health care, education for their children, and recreation for themselves. Maximizing wealth by maximizing market efficiency distracts us from many of the things that matter most in our lives.

Prior generations understood that market values are different from society's values. As early as the first decades of the eighteenth century, it was clear that unconstrained economic activity could do damage, and by the end of the nineteenth century, Americans and Europeans had passed laws to mitigate some of capitalism's worst effects, especially the dreadful conditions in factories that the poet William Blake called "dark Satanic Mills." In 1802, the British Parliament passed the Health and Morals of Apprentices Act, which required that factories have windows, that youthful apprentices be given a basic education, and that those apprentices attend religious services at least once a month. The British Cotton Mills Act, passed in 1819, banned the employment of children under the age of nine. In Germany and the United Kingdom, systems were developed to compensate workers—or, where necessary, their widows—for workplace injury and death.

It was also clear at the time that unconstrained capitalism was commonly bad for capitalists themselves. In the nineteenth century, extreme business cycles and bank panics often drove otherwise solid companies to ruin. When banks failed, everyone lost their money. Cutthroat competition often became a race to the bottom in which few survived, and the market became dominated by a few players or even a single one. Powerful corporations engaged in anticompetitive practices and drove out rivals who might have offered better products at lower prices. By

1890, monopolistic behavior had become so common that the U.S. Congress passed the Sherman Anti-Trust Act, and Republican Theodore Roosevelt became one of America's most iconic presidents by building a reputation as a "trust-buster."

Around the start of the twentieth century, most Americans agreed that governments needed to step in to address the problems unregulated capitalism created. These included both market failures, such as bank collapses, and "social costs," such as the 146 garment workers—mostly women and girls—who perished in the Triangle Shirtwaist Factory fire in 1911 and the thousands of workers killed every year in railroad accidents, boiler explosions, and mine collapses. Early in the 1900s, the U.S. government established standards for occupational safety. In 1913, the Federal Reserve System was created to foster economic stability. In 1914, the Federal Trade Commission was established to prevent unfair and deceptive business practices. When banks failed during the Great Depression, the government created the Federal Deposit Insurance Corporation (FDIC) to protect people's savings. When the nation's water became so polluted that the Cuyahoga River in Cleveland caught fire, or the air in Los Angeles became so poisonous that people literally died from it, the government set standards for clean water and clean air. The Progressive Era, the New Deal, and the environmental movement all responded to market failures.

Reformers recognized that government had an essential role to play in sustaining markets, ensuring their fairness, and establishing the rules by which they operated. They were acknowledging that "The Market" doesn't exist outside of society but is part of society and, like society's other parts, must be subject to law and regulation. They were demonstrating that complaints about government "intervention" in the marketplace were incoherent, because they falsely implied that markets somehow could (and perhaps should) be beyond the reach of civil society. Nineteenth- and twentieth-century labor and environmental reforms reflected the widespread recognition that markets aren't magic, but need to be managed.

That's why we don't maim kids in coal mines anymore, and why it's now time to shut down coal mines altogether so future kids aren't clinging to survival in a world made close to uninhabitable by carbon pollution. Whether you call a better life "an externality"—as economists do—or a purpose beyond economic analysis, you end up in the same place. Markets are good for many things, but they are *not* magic. Just look around. Income inequality, the opioid crisis, the lack of affordable housing, retirees who can't afford to retire, the climate crisis: markets created problems that our market-based system has failed to solve. The only proven remedy is governance.

To accept market fundamentalism, one must ignore more than a century of history. Sadly, this is more or less what Americans have done in recent decades. As a result, we are hamstrung when we need to address serious challenges, from climate change to Covid-19. "Ill fares the land, to hastening ills a prey / Where wealth accumulates, and men decay," wrote Oliver Goldsmith in 1770, just six years before Adam Smith published *The Wealth of Nations*.[21] In the late twentieth century, wealth accumulated and our nation decayed, and today we find ourselves seemingly powerless to do much about it.

Consider one example of how market fundamentalism has entrapped even many moderates and progressives. When Pope Francis, in his 2015 encyclical letter *Laudato si'* (published as *Encyclical on Climate Change and Inequality*), questioned whether the challenges we face could be adequately addressed by market mechanisms, he was condemned from the right, the middle, and the left. Writing in the *New York Times*, conservative David Brooks all but labeled him a socialist for questioning market-based approaches to climate change, insisting that harnessing greed and self-interest would best address the problem.[22] That same day, also in the *New York Times*, economics reporter Eduardo Porter accused the pope of depriving "people of the . . . tools humanity will need to prevent climatic upheaval."[23] At the Harvard Kennedy School of Government, former Clinton administration official and now professor Joseph Aldy called the pope "out of step."[24]

Brooks argued that "within a regulated market, greed can lead to entrepreneurship and economic innovation." Sure, but the dominant trend in global capitalism for the past forty years has been *deregulation*. And often, for innovation to occur, we need governments to create markets, such as the markets for pollution control. Pope Francis argued it was unrealistic to think capitalism (at least as it is currently being practiced) would get us out of our predicament.

This raises a profound question: Is capitalism itself to blame for climate change, as critics such as Naomi Klein and Andreas Malm argue?[25] Or the opioid crisis? Or the lack of affordable housing? We argue no: the culprit is how we think about capitalism, and how it operates. The culprit is market fundamentalist ideology, which denies capitalism's failures and refuses to endorse the best tool we have to address those failures, which is democratic government. It also fails to acknowledge the role of other tools available to us, like corporate governance. Market fundamentalism touts the benefits and virtues of deregulation and the value of economic freedom to the near eclipse of other concerns.

We need a more realistic vision of what markets are and are not good at, of where they succeed and where they fail. We also need a historically informed conception of the role of governance in creating and managing markets, protecting markets from predatory practices, providing public goods, and addressing social costs of business. To do that, we need to understand how and why we came to put so much faith in markets in the first place.

Climate change *is* a market failure, because markets, acting legally, failed to provide what people need and created a problem that markets have proven unable to solve.[26] The invisible hand has disappeared completely. As one economist has written, carbon pollution is "free to emit but has costly consequences."[27] Since the price we pay does not reflect those costs, the market has failed to put an accurate price on fossil fuels. And if it's not the market's fault for failing to set prices correctly, then whose fault is it? Some conservatives would say government is to blame for wrongly subsidizing fossil fuels. That's partly true: we've many times argued that governments should eliminate fossil fuel subsidies. But even if that happened, it wouldn't be enough. We need to phase out the use of fossil fuels, and we've known this for decades, but the market response has been wholly inadequate. So if it is not the market that has failed, then what is left but the entire capitalist system? Which is, of course, what critics like Klein argue.

We think what's at issue is not capitalism *per se*. Contemporary conservatives, libertarians, and market fundamentalists are not really defending capitalism, even if they think they are. They are defending a certain *idea* of capitalism, a vision of growth and innovation by unfettered markets where government just gets out of the way. That capitalism is certainly not what Adam Smith imagined or advocated. To the extent that it once did (approximately) exist, it was a disaster: a world with little or no workplace safety, no constraints on pollution, no limits to the trees that could be cut down or the dangerous products that could be sold. If we were to try to return to an eighteenth-century vision of capitalism, cigarettes could be sold to children, who would smoke them during their factory breaks.

IDEAS DO NOT exist *ex nihilo*. They are developed, sustained, and promoted by people and institutions, and so this book is at once a social, cultural, political, and economic history. Although some economists appear, this book is not a history of economic thought. It is the history of the construction of a myth.

The late anthropologist Eric R. Wolf distinguished between tactical power—the power to choose between existing alternatives and make one of them win—and structural power—the power to create the alternatives from which people choose.[28] Conventional politics is all about tactical power; ours is a story of structural power. A group of individuals and institutions worked to make people believe they had to choose between "The Market" and "The State," between unconstrained capitalism and Soviet-style centralized planning. But there are all kinds of alternatives, and one important one is to see governments and markets as complementary, not as opposing camps. Adam Smith and other foundational thinkers understood their field of study as one integrated discipline—political economy—yet today we (wrongly) treat politics and economics as separate spheres.[29]

Market fundamentalism perpetuates a mistake in categories, conflating capitalism, which is an economic system, with democracy, which is a political system. We think that the properly framed choice is not *capitalism* versus *tyranny*; it is *democracy* versus *tyranny*, and *well-regulated capitalism* versus *poorly regulated capitalism*.

Whether its advocates were cynical or sincere, market fundamentalism has hobbled our response to a host of problems that face us today, threatening our well-being and even the prosperity that markets are designed to deliver. The rhetoric of the magic of the marketplace made meaningful alternatives disappear. We intend this book to recover a sense of possibility by examining how those alternatives were made to disappear in the first place. We ask who made the myth of the magic of the marketplace, why they made it, and how they made it stick.

We are academics, but this is not an academic intervention, because the big myth at the heart of this story affects us all, and severely. It powers the enormous wealth gap between the top one percent and the rest of us. It has been used to justify a sharp decline in the safety and stability of the work most of us do to get by. It has blocked the efforts we must take to reverse the heating of our planet and protect the very existence of the world as we know it. The big myth's expiration date is long past due. Our futures depend on rejecting it.

PART I

Foundations

Those things about which we cannot theorize, we must narrate.

—UMBERTO ECO, *THE NAME OF THE ROSE*

CHAPTER I

The Social Costs of Capitalism

Late nineteenth-century American capitalism was a deadly affair. Every year, thousands were injured, maimed, or killed in the course of their daily work. Miners died in explosions and roof collapses. Railroad workers were crushed between cars. Factory workers lost limbs in machinery. One estimate suggests that toward the century's end nearly half of all railroad workers sustained occupational injuries every year.[1] A young man born in America in 1899 would have been safer at age fifteen going to fight in World War I than going to work on the railroads.[2] The carnage was so great that contemporary commentators compared it to war, fought by an industrial army.[3]

The most dangerous trade was coal mining. In the mid-nineteenth century, 6 percent of workers in the Pennsylvanian anthracite mines were killed *every* year, with twice again that many injured or disabled. Over his career, a miner at a Scranton anthracite field was more likely to be killed, seriously injured, or permanently disabled than not. If he managed to reach his golden years intact, he might very well die of black lung disease.[4] Across the industrial landscape, workplace harms were pandemic. According to one estimate, in 1900 one in every thousand American workers was killed on the job, the equivalent now of 1.5 million people every year.[5]

When terrible injuries occurred, workers and their families were offered nothing. Widows and orphans were left to the generosity of family and friends, if they had them, or to charitable institutions. When mothers were unable to care for their children or find relatives to foster them, the children would land in orphanages, typically enclaves of malnutrition and neglect.[6] There was a racialized component as well: most industrial workers were immigrants, with little political power.

The industries responsible for this wastage of human life and potential paid no price for it. Nor did Americans consider it their collective responsibility. No state or federal government programs existed to help injured workers or the families of those killed. By the end of the nineteenth century, some workers—particularly skilled, unionized ones—had insurance through cooperative associations or benefits through mutual aid societies, but most did not. Private insurance was rarely available to workingmen precisely because of how common it was for them to die prematurely; many companies categorically refused to sell policies to workers in dangerous trades. The only policies that most insurers would offer them covered burial costs.[7]

In theory, a worker could sue his employer if he could prove negligence; in practice that rarely happened and almost never succeeded. Few laborers had the wherewithal to file a lawsuit and even fewer could prove that the daily practices of industrial capitalism constituted negligence.[8] Worse, the law often held the victim responsible. In the influential 1842 case *Farwell v. Boston and Worcester Railroad*, the chief justice of the Massachusetts Supreme Judicial Court ruled that employers were not liable when a worker was harmed by the negligence of a fellow employee on the grounds that "these are perils which the servant is likely to know, and against which he can as effectively guard, as the master."[9] If a worker was hurt on the job, it was his fault for not taking better care. Unless the injury was intentional, there was no legal remedy.[10]

The "accident crisis," as it came to be known, was one of the earliest problems to be recognized as a social cost—or "negative externality"—of capitalism. In 1920, British economist Arthur Pigou would develop an influential theory of social costs and suggest they should be paid for by a tax on the offending activity. To some extent this had already been done in Europe, where the first workmen's compensation systems were devised: Germany had created a workers' accident insurance program in 1884; England did so in 1897.[11] Employers paid into an insurance fund, which compensated workers injured or killed on the job. The system also created a positive incentive toward workplace safety: employers with high accident rates paid higher premiums.

The United States, however, had no such program, and not surprisingly had far higher rates of workplace injury. The 1872 report of the Massachusetts Bureau of Statistics of Labor, for example, noted that the average Lowell mill worker missed thirty-one days per year due to sickness or injury, far more than in similar mills in the United Kingdom, where greater safety precautions were taken.[12]

By the early twentieth century, several groups of academics, reformers, and businessmen had traveled to Europe to learn how other nations addressed the problem.[13]

American commentators linked the lower European injury rates to workplace insurance programs.[14] The question thus arose: Should a workmen's compensation program be developed in the United States? If so, who Should pay for it? Who *was* responsible for the social costs of industrial activity? The worker? The employer? The government?

Some employers accepted that workplace safety was their responsibility, if for no other reason than that killing large numbers of workers on the job was bad for morale. Steel magnate Andrew Carnegie, for example, donated $4 million to endow an accident relief fund for workers at Carnegie Steel.[15] With the rise of industrial engineering as a profession, the argument emerged that accidents were "wasteful" and "inefficient," and a scientific approach to industrial management should seek to reduce their occurrence. According to this line of thinking, it wasn't a matter of fault; improved efficiency would simply be better for all concerned. Industrial engineers and managers began to call for better practices to improve workplace safety and worker loyalty in the name of productivity.

But only a few companies followed Carnegie's lead or the industrial engineers' advice. Most business leaders and observers accepted accidents as part of industrial capitalism—literally the price of doing business. Except in most cases it wasn't the businessmen (or the consumers) who paid the price. It was the workers— mostly but not only men—who had no choice but to labor under hazardous conditions, and the partners and children left behind. This was the toll of laissez-faire capitalism. The free market had substantial costs tabulated not in dollars, but in human life.

In 1907, things began to change when President Theodore Roosevelt proposed the idea of a no-fault program: workers injured in the course of their duties would receive compensation irrespective of negligence or intent. Over the next decade, twenty-eight state and federal commissions investigated the issue, and by 1920, forty-two states had implemented some form of workmen's compensation.[16] (Mississippi was the most dogged holdout, waiting until 1948.) The laws passed were diverse: most paid benefits only for the death of a male breadwinner, offering nothing if a woman or a child died in the workplace. It would be some time before the United States had anything resembling a coherent or comprehensive program. But these laws had in common the idea of workmen's compensation as a form of insurance.

Work was dangerous. People would be hurt or killed on the job even when they were careful, and even when conscientious employers tried to create safer working conditions. Moreover, the pressures of capitalism made it hard for any employer to spend money on safety if his competitors were not also doing so, and the pressures of earning a living made it hard for laborers to leave a dangerous workplace. Workmen's compensation leveled the playing field, creating an incentive for all employers to improve safety and compensating victims when the inevitable happened. Workplace injuries were not eliminated, but they did decrease, and their consequences were mitigated. The "dark Satanic Mills" were no longer quite so satanic.

Workmen's compensation was one of many reforms implemented in the late nineteenth and early twentieth centuries to deal with the external costs of economic activity, to make capitalism safer and fairer—and at the same time more competitive. The Progressive Era saw laws passed to break up monopolies and prevent unjustifiable business practices, reduce import tariffs, limit child labor, improve working conditions, defend workers' right to bargain collectively, expand access to education, and ensure the safety of food and drugs. While some progressive reforms failed—most obviously Prohibition—many were very successful. Many things we now take for granted—the eight-hour workday, the right to be paid overtime, the five-day work week—were products of this time, the result of pressure brought to bear by unionized workers and their supporters in the progressive movement.[17]

These reforms were achieved through bitter struggle, and in those struggles we find the roots of what would become a century-long argument about the role of government—particularly the federal government—in addressing social costs and market failures. We also find the foundations of a powerful, damaging myth: that "The Market" exists as a thing unto itself, that it has agency and even wisdom, and that it functions best when left undisturbed.

AS SUPREME COURT justice Oliver Wendell Holmes Jr. wrote more than a century ago, "if there is any matter upon which civilized countries have agreed—it is the evil of premature and excessive child labor."[18] But in the early twentieth century, the United States waged a fierce battle over whether child labor was wrong, and who should decide. In fact, Holmes made his comment in a 1918 dissent to a Supreme Court decision that upheld the legality of child labor.

Holmes's comment was provoked by a legal challenge to the Keating-Owen Child Labor Act. This 1916 federal statute had banned interstate trade in goods made in factories, workshops, or canneries that employed children under the age of fourteen; products from mines and quarries that employed children under the age of sixteen; or goods and products from a factory, workshop, cannery, mine, or quarry where children between fourteen and sixteen worked more than an eight-hour day or more than six days per week.[19] Keating-Owen probably applied to fewer than 10 percent of working children at that time, but regardless of its modest reach, the Supreme Court deemed it unconstitutional on jurisdictional grounds: the federal government had no authority to regulate labor in the states.[20] Immoral products that crossed state lines could be regulated, but industrial practices—no matter how noxious—fell beyond the federal reach.[21]

The court's finding touched a highly contested issue: How much should government regulate industry, if at all? For progressives, it was self-evident that government had an obligation to protect workers with little power to protect themselves. Government also ought to protect the system against itself: against securities fraud, monopolistic practices, cutthroat competition, and other evils, to use the term of the day. Sending children as young as six years old—maybe younger—into mines, mills, and factories was for most progressives obviously evil. Children belonged in school and not on the shop floor.

Many corporate leaders, however, disagreed, believing that the federal government had no business interfering in business. The New York Stock Exchange, for example, fought financial regulation throughout the 1920s, and many other Progressive Era reforms were challenged in court.[22] Business leaders and social conservatives argued that child labor was a matter of *freedom*: the freedom to run an operation as its owner saw fit, and of fathers to decide what was best for their children.[23]

Before Keating-Owen, child labor had been defended by southern states hostile to federal power; by religious leaders who considered it the prerogative of the family; and by immigrant parents dependent on their children's wages.[24] (Some immigrants resisted compulsory schooling for the same reason.) However, the plaintiff in *Hammer v. Dagenhart*—the case that led the Supreme Court to overturn Keating-Owen—belonged to none of these categories.[25] He was Roland Dagenhart, who (supported by southern mill owners) contended that the Keating-Owen Act interfered with his sons' freedom to work with him in a textile mill.[26]

Dagenhart's sons—sixteen and fourteen years old—were in good health and, apart from the law, willing and able to work. Dagenhart himself was a man of "small means," for whom the boys' pay was "essential for the comfortable support and maintenance of the family." Dagenhart's lawyers argued that Keating-Owen infringed on his Fifth Amendment guarantee to liberty and property by denying him his sons' services until they reached the age of majority.[27] Judge James Boyd, who heard the challenge in North Carolina, agreed.[28]

Government counsel asked about the boys' rights, particularly if mill work prevented them from getting an education. What about *their* liberty if they were condemned from an early age to difficult and poorly compensated labor? Judge Boyd ruled that the government had no say in those considerations: "[T]he family is the nucleus around which the blessings of . . . liberty" gather, and the "right of the progenitor to regulate and control the habits of his progeny is not disputed."[29] The law viewed Dagenhart's children as his property, or at least prerogative, not unlike how the law had only recently viewed enslaved people. The minors' rights yielded to the perceived greater rights of the father. But just as the legal framework around chattel slavery had been rejected after the Civil War, the framework of children as property was under reconsideration, and would not long hold.

In its thirteenth annual report, in 1917, the National Child Labor Committee noted that many states had already passed laws limiting child labor. Six had passed provisions to make state law conform with Keating-Owen and four more had in some other way strengthened legal protections; others had raised the age limit for night messengers and strengthened provisions for compulsory education. Several states had also passed limits on working hours for women that pertained as well to minors. Progress was uneven, but the trend pointed toward keeping children in school and away from paid work. As the committee put it, "it is obvious to all right-minded poeple [sic] that a 12-year-old should not work 11 or 12 hours a day in a factory, or a 14-year-old child in a coal mine."[30]

The court had concluded that child labor was a matter best left to the states, but many manufacturers opposed state laws, too. Partly, it was a level-playing-field problem. In several cases prior to Dagenhart's, manufacturers had claimed that any state limits on child labor would disadvantage them relative to competitors in states without such limits.[31] As early as 1838, manufacturers in Pennsylvania had "expressed the fear that any . . . prohibition of labor, so long as it could apply only to Pennsylvania, must result disastrously to manufacturers in their competition with others not similarly restricted."[32] In New York, manufacturers had threatened to leave the state if child labor laws were passed, leading one observer to conclude that "it was this argument more than any other which proved fatal" to repeated efforts to pass such a law.[33] In South Carolina, one manufacturer went so far as to say that a proposed bill prohibiting employment of children under twelve might as well be "called a bill to discourage manufacturing in South Carolina."[34]

Competition among states could lead to a race to the bottom unless the U.S. government devised a cure, but the courts had ruled federal action unconstitutional. So a logical response was to amend the Constitution. In April 1924, the U.S. House of Representatives passed the Child Labor Amendment, granting Congress the power to "limit, regulate and prohibit the labor of persons under eighteen years of age."[35] The Senate approved the measure two months later and sent it to the states for ratification. Had it succeeded, it would have been the twentieth amendment to the Constitution. Given the level-playing-field argument, one might have expected American manufacturers to endorse it. Instead, they organized swiftly against it.

In an early example of what we would today call astroturfing, editors of the industry newsletter *Southern Textile Bulletin* organized a Committee for the Protection of Child, Family, School and Church. This was linked to a group called the Farmers' States Rights League, also industry-funded. The league and the committee took out advertisements in local newspapers alleging that the amendment would prevent boys from doing chores around the farm and girls from doing the dishes. This was untrue: the amendment by itself prohibited nothing and would have had no effect until such time as Congress might pass a law. Besides, previous congressional attempts to regulate child labor had always included broad, and sometimes blanket, exemptions for agriculture. In any case, the word *labor* was understood to refer to *paid* labor; not even the most zealous reformers had wanted to regulate household chores.

This example of fighting to sustain child labor with misleading claims was a sign of things to come. Over the next decade, opponents of the Child Labor Amendment spread false, misleading, and disingenuous arguments in a successful attempt to prevent ratification. A leader in that effort was the National Association of Manufacturers.

THE NATIONAL ASSOCIATION of Manufacturers (NAM) was founded in 1895 when six hundred manufacturers met in Cincinnati to formulate a plan for economic recovery from the Panic of 1893 and the depression that followed.[36] In its early years, NAM fought *for* government involvement in the marketplace in the form of protectionism: American businessmen wanted high import tariffs to make domestic goods more competitive. (They also argued for building the Panama Canal to facilitate the export of American goods.) However, as the nineteenth century gave way to the twentieth, NAM altered course and became known primarily for its opposition to unionization and federal taxation. It also reversed its position on the role of government in American business and industry. NAM now insisted that the federal government should stay out of its way and not regulate the workplace.

In 1903, NAM organized its Open Shop Department (later renamed the Industrial Relations Department) to counter an expanding union movement.[37] NAM argued that unions constituted a form of monopoly and should be considered illegal under the Sherman Anti-Trust Act. The organization played a major role in supporting business in the infamous 1908 Danbury Hatters Case (formally *Loewe v. Lawlor*, 208 U.S. 274), in which the Supreme Court overturned the lower courts to limit unions' latitude to strike and found that unions—even individual union members—could be held liable for damages resulting from certain kinds of boycotts.[38] (The ruling would be upended by the Clayton Antitrust Act of 1914, which affirmed the rights of workers to unionize, strike, and boycott.)[39]

In 1913, Congress investigated NAM for potentially illegal lobbying activities, including the surreptitious creation of so-called Workingmen's Protective Associations, ephemeral political clubs designed to support pro-business candidates.[40] (In one race, an association backed a socialist candidate in hopes of drawing away Democratic votes and electing the Republican.) President Woodrow Wilson described NAM's activities as a conspiracy of "special interests" that were creating an "invisible government" adverse to the American people. NAM admitted to an extensive lobbying campaign to support "legislation which it felt was beneficial to the welfare of manufacturers," but denied wrongdoing.[41] By the 1920s, NAM had become America's most prominent trade association; by the 1930s it would be spearheading the business opposition to the New Deal.[42]

In its opposition to child labor restrictions, NAM followed a playbook of rhetorical fallacies that market fundamentalists would lean on for decades to come, including slippery-slope arguments, ad hominem and straw man attacks, half-truths, misrepresentations, denial of documented evidence, and outright lies. One document is particularly illustrative. *An Examination of the Proposed Twentieth Amendment to the Constitution of the United States (Being the So-Called Child Labor Amendment)*—written by James A. Emery, NAM's general counsel, and issued by the office of the General Secretary of NAM in 1924—begins by dismissing child labor as a serious problem, given the relatively small number of children in the workplace as a percentage of the total labor force.[43] Of 12.5 million children counted in the 1920 census, 1 million were employed, 413,000 of them outside agriculture. Of those in agriculture, 88 percent worked on "the farms of their parents where they resided."[44] NAM concluded that the actual number of children employed in dangerous or unsafe non-farm labor was only 126,590—or about 1 percent of children in the country. Evidence suggested the numbers were dropping, so why did Congress need to amend the Constitution to protect such a small group?[45]

The issue for reformers, however, was not how large a *percentage* of children was in the workforce, but the fact that *any* children were working, and the appalling conditions under which many of them worked. Various reports and commissions had documented staggering rates of death and injury among children working in mills and factories.[46] In Massachusetts many children employed in textile mills were injured, crippled, or dead within just a few years of starting work.[47] NAM refused to accept these findings, insisting (without evidence) that "the nature and extent of the work done by children is grossly exaggerated."[48] They also alleged that reformers didn't really care about child labor at all, but were using it as an excuse to expand the federal government. The amendment, they asserted, was a power grab, intended to enable Congress to control the "labor and education of all persons under eighteen to an extent not now possessed by any State of the Union" under the "guise of protecting childhood."[49] In fact, the amendment said nothing about education.

NAM was making a slippery-slope argument: that it would be only a matter of time before the government would use the amendment to expand its power in noxious ways. NAM cited the federal income tax as a cautionary tale: the Sixteenth Amendment of 1909 had been "enacted in order that the Government might possess the power to levy an income tax during an emergency like war. No sooner was the power granted than it was exercised in peace, and to an unanticipated degree." This was a half-truth: the federal income tax was advocated as a general means to raise the needed revenue to support governmental functions broadly—in both war and peace—and a better one than the tariffs upon which the federal government had previously depended.[50] But NAM persisted, arguing that the proposed Twentieth Amendment, like the Sixteenth, would disturb the fundamental relationship between state and federal governments. Emery's pamphlet also marshaled James Madison, quoting *Federalist* essay number 45: "The power reserved to the several States will extend to all the objects, which in the ordinary course of affairs, concern the lives, liberties and properties of the people; and the internal order, improvement and prosperity of the State."[51] Labor was part of the ordinary course of daily life, and so (NAM argued) was best and most efficiently left to states.

This was an oft-quoted passage from the *Federalist Papers*, used by conservatives to argue against expanded federal power; in the years to come market fundamentalists would often turn to Madison as their favorite founding father.[52] But both Jefferson and Madison anticipated that the framework they offered might need adjusting in light of future realities, and they provided a system to do that. Despite NAM's protestations, it could hardly be thought unconstitutional to amend the Constitution. And given that business leaders had objected fiercely to state child labor laws—on the grounds that they placed unfair burdens on manufacturers in the states that passed them—industry's argument that the matter should be left to the states rang hollow.

Perhaps for this reason, NAM's pamphlet suggested that if any group should decide the question of child labor, it should be either local government or parents. The amendment would usurp "the duties of . . . parents and guardians and substitute the bureaucratic regulation of remote, expensive, and irresponsible authority for local and parental control." NAM declared its disapproval of this "revolutionary grant of power to the Congress . . . as repugnant to our traditional conception of local responsibility and self-government, tending to stimulate the growth of enlarged and extravagant bureaucracy, and serving to defeat the very humanitarian purpose which its disguise suggests."[53]

How could a law to protect children defeat its own humanitarian purpose? NAM quoted Reverend Warren Candler, a Methodist bishop, to argue the amendment would undermine parental authority. It would "discredit and dethrone parents and subvert family government, substituting for parenthood a paternalistic government at Washington and empowering the federal Congress to stand in loco parentis to all the children of the country [based] on the absurd assumption that Congress will be more tenderly concerned for children than their own parents."[54]

Researchers had established that desperate parents sent children to work in desperate conditions and that factory owners had no compunctions in hiring those children.[55] Which parents? The working poor, of course, which led NAM to allege that the child labor amendment was designed to flatten society and turn America into a classless society. "The proposal is socialistic in its origin, philosophy and associations," the 1924 document asserted, raising the specter of "centralization" as the federal government was interfering in "such ordinary [matters] as health, gambling, prize fights, physical training, censorship of the press, moving pictures and literature, the control of game birds, hunting and fishing reservations, labor contracts, maternity aid, and vocational training," alongside the "growing demand that the Congress shall regulate marriage and divorce." NAM implied that the entire Progressive vision of federal government efforts to improve citizens' lives was tantamount to Soviet-style central planning.[56]

NAM allowed that the word *socialistic* was sometimes used too loosely, but then proceeded to do just that, painting nearly all those who advocated against child labor as socialist sympathizers—or worse—and using the term *socialism* interchangeably with *communism*.[57] Admittedly the distinctions were not always clear, but one important distinction was that communists advocated revolution, whereas American socialists looked to electoral politics to achieve their goals. What was clear was that most progressives were neither communist nor socialist. NAM's claim hung on a single (and singular) example: Florence Kelley, Illinois's first chief factory inspector. Kelley was a pathbreaking lawyer, advocate of women's suffrage, and opponent of child labor. In 1907 Kelley had helped attorney Louis D. Brandeis prepare the original Brandeis Brief, in which he presented data on the adverse health effects of excessively long working hours.[58] (In later years, Kelley would help to establish the National Association for the Advancement of Colored People.)[59] NAM ignored these academic, intellectual, and legal credentials; to them she was simply "a socialist leader of marked distinction, a faculty instructor in the Rand School of Socialism [sic]" and "translator of those well-springs of modern socialism, Friedrich Engels and Karl Marx."[60] Kelley had produced important translations of Marx and Engels and likely was a socialist, but most supporters of the Child Labor Amendment were not. The fight against child labor was squarely in the center of the Progressive movement, whose leading lights included former Republican president Theodore Roosevelt. Indeed, many progressives took pains to distance themselves from socialism, lest their ambitions be discredited, as NAM was plainly trying to do.[61]

NAM was not content merely to tar child labor reform with a socialist brush but alleged a direct connection between the movement and Soviet communism. Invoking what he called "The Russian Conception of the Control of Youth," Emery's pamphlet pointed to the 1922 Fourth Congress of the Communist Internationale, which had declared its interest in the "complete transformation of the conditions of juvenile labor . . . [including] the abolition of wage slavery for all young workers up to 18 years of age."[62] If communists wanted to eliminate child labor, then clearly Americans who advocated the same must be communists. The Russians had also declared their intention to "nationalize" children, removing them from their families and educating them in state-run schools to be "real communists."[63] NAM's brochure dutifully engineered a false equivalence, quoting various progressives allegedly asserting that children belong not to their families but to society.[64]

The brochure concluded with the words of Utah senator William H. King, who (using a tactic that Senator Joseph McCarthy would later make infamous) insisted that Bolsheviks were behind the amendment, and that he knew precisely who they were but would not say: "Every Bolshevik, every extreme Communist and Socialist in the United States is back of the measure." King asserted that "one of the leading Bolsheviks in the city of Moscow" had given him "a number of names but I shall not mention them here . . . Of course this is a communistic, bolshevistick [sic] scheme, and a lot of good people, misled, are accepting it, not knowing the evil consequences which will result and the sinister purpose back of the measure."[65]

Once one recognized this Bolshevistic intent, NAM continued, it became obvious the amendment would not just regulate "the working life of children," but the life of "every person in the United States under eighteen years of age."[66] Here NAM was reiterating its claim that teenagers were not children; if the amendment aimed to protect them, too, that was merely proof of its nefarious intent, which could be achieved "only through an elaborate, and expensive bureaucratic system, inevitably tending to be top-heavy, irresponsible, unresponsive, remote from the subject of regulation, irritating in the circumstances of supervision, and by its operation lessening respect for obedience to the central authority. The theory of control and the social tendencies comprehended within the amendment are strangers to our soil and more in harmony with the philosophy and manifest desires of alien states."[67] The Child Labor Amendment was un-American.

In fact, nowhere in the proposed amendment was the right to nationalize American children suggested, and few if any American progressives would have advocated the removal of children from their homes. Quite the contrary: progressives tended to romanticize home, hearth, and the benevolence of maternal love and care. The suggestion that they wanted to hand over children to the state was absurd. But, along with NAM's other misleading claims, it likely had an effect, because by 1932, the Child Labor Amendment had stalled. By the end of that year, only six states had ratified, and the proposed amendment died.[68]

Throughout the child labor debate, NAM insisted that it was presenting the "facts," while others exaggerated and propagandized. To be sure, the exact numbers of working children and their ages were subject to debate, and no doubt some reformers could be overzealous and melodramatic.[69] But there was abundant evidence that significant numbers of children worked in mines, mills, and factories around the country—particularly (but not only) in the South, and often in dangerous conditions—and that many of these children were younger than thirteen years of age. There was also little doubt in most people's minds that a twelve-year-old was a child.

Perhaps the greatest misrepresentation in this debate was the implication that employers' destroyed credit for the decline in child labor. NAM persistently held that the proposed amendment was unnecessary because child labor was rare and getting rarer, as if manufacturers had seen the light of their own accord. During a later attempt by Franklin Delano Roosevelt's administration to revive the Child Labor Amendment, NAM responded with a February 1938 press release claiming that for "many years" the association had "advocated the elimination of child labor." They boasted that child labor now constituted less than 1 percent of the manufacturing workforce and offered their support to a bill pending in Congress "to eliminate undesirable child labor."[70] In fact, child labor had declined largely because of state laws mandating compulsory public education—the outcome of efforts by the very reformers NAM vilified as socialists and communists—and state labor laws that manufacturers had largely opposed. It was as if the tobacco industry, after decades of fighting tobacco control, now took credit for the decline in smoking.

IF THE MEN who ran NAM labeled anti-child-labor activists as advance agents of socialism, it was partly because they understood this fight to be one battle in a larger war over equality and human nature. They believed that men were inherently unequal: it was right and just for workers to be paid far less than managers and managers far less than owners. They also believed that in a free society some children would naturally enter the workforce. Child labor laws were (to their minds) socialistic because they enforced erroneous assumptions of equality—for example, that all children should go to school—rather than accepting that some children should work in factories.

NAM was influenced by pundits such as Columbia University president Nicholas Butler, who it quoted in a 1925 publication that opposed the Child Labor Amendment.[71] Blending the classic conservatism of Edmund Burke with contemporary social Darwinism, Butler believed liberty and equality were incompatible, and where they conflicted liberty must prevail. A review of his 1907 work *True and False Democracy* quoted Butler as having written: "Destroy inequality of talent and capacity, and life as we know it stops . . . The corner-stone of democracy is natural inequality, its ideal is the selection of the most fit. Liberty is far more precious than equality, and the two are mutually destructive." Not surprisingly, Butler was deeply anticommunist, believing it would "wreck the world's efficiency for the purpose of redistributing the world's discontent."[72] (In later years Butler would work to deny Ernest Hemingway the Pulitzer Prize for his novel of the Spanish Civil War, *For Whom the Bell Tolls*, on the grounds that it was too sympathetic to the antifascist forces.)[73] The men of NAM shared Butler's conviction that capitalism functioned *because of* inequalities. Like natural selection, it was propelled by differences of ability (and therefore of recompense). To them, this was no failing; on the contrary, it showed capitalism's consistency with the natural inequality of men.

In 1933, NAM secretary Noel Sargent returned to this argument in a forty-three-page lecture entitled "The Case Against Socialism, with Particular Analysis of the Views of Norman Thomas."[74] Thomas was America's most prominent and articulate socialist, one who made clear the distinction (frequently blurred by critics) between socialism and communism. A Presbyterian minister by training, in 1924 he had run for governor of New York and then in 1928 for president on the Socialist Party ticket. (Ultimately, he would run for president six times, including as a fourth-party candidate in the heated Truman–Dewey–Wallace race of 1948.) Thomas had strongly criticized the New Deal from the left, arguing that FDR was too focused on economic issues as opposed to moral ones, and that the New Deal had neglected some of the nation's most destitute citizens, such as southern sharecroppers.[75]

To his credit, Sargent engaged seriously with Thomas's arguments, recognizing that the "advocates of capitalism" had to "admit there are grave social evils" needing remedy. Sargent likewise conceded that capitalism's benefits were not equally distributed and that "under capitalism there have been, and are, many instances where individuals do not have that measure of justice or that standard of living that generally prevails." But he refused to countenance that these evils and inequities might be addressed through governance, much less that they reflected a fundamental flaw in capitalism as a system. On the contrary, he suggested that they reflected the reality of inequality: "Men are born unequal and remain unequal, and man-made laws cannot make them otherwise."[76]

The chief defect of socialism, Sargent argued, was its commitment to the doctrine of equality, particularly equality of income. The idea that all workers should be equally recompensed was both impractical and unethical: impractical, because if a worker knew someone working less hard or efficiently was paid the same, he would be resentful; and unethical because that more efficient worker had the right to be paid more. In any case, equality was a myth: even a Russian peasant knew that "God ... created men different."

Sargent dismissed in one sentence the disparities that made it possible for some men and women to become more skilled than others by insisting that "enough men have equal opportunities to demonstrate how unequal men are."[77] Nor did he acknowledge that extreme income disparities in the American industrial landscape drove hard-pressed families to put their young children to work, preventing even the most talented among them from developing their talents through education. Nor was there any acknowledgment of how long hours and dispiriting conditions robbed many workers of initiative. Instead, he invoked the "social selectionist" theory of nineteenth-century Yale sociologist William Graham Sumner and his student Albert Keller—who had also inspired Butler. They argued that just as variety was necessary for organic evolution, so it was for economic progress.[78] If there were "no [social] classes," Sumner wrote, "there would be no competition ... It is an error that society gains more by equality than it does by a class differentiation allowing of higher organization and greater efficiency."[79] Class was society's way of creating variation, competition, and therefore progress; excessive consideration for the poor was a form of "prejudice."[80] As one historian has put it, social Darwinism offered a justification not for a "jungle-like struggle" for existence, but a "more certain basis for order and authority," one that affirmed the rightness of the status quo.[81] In principle, Sargent claimed, capitalists accepted that "limitations may properly be placed upon [the] rights to possess and secure property." In practice, however, NAM opposed pretty much any limitations ever proposed.[82]

Sargent also drew on the work of conservative economist Arthur T. Hadley, author of an influential 1925 text, *The Conflict Between Liberty and Equality*. A classic laissez-faire economist, Hadley launched his academic career with an influential study of railroad administration and worked his way up the ladder to become president of Yale, serving from 1899 to 1921 (overlapping with Nicholas Butler at Columbia). As an undergraduate at Yale, Hadley studied with Sumner, absorbing his social Darwinist notions and applying them to economics.[83] Contrary to the popular association of equality with progressivism, Hadley contended that equality was fundamentally a conservative force, because a lack of difference would impede natural selection, and thus, progress. Hadley's belief that this held both for individuals and for corporations informed his stance against trust-busting: the big trusts were "winners" in the struggle for economic survival. Governments therefore should not interfere with this process; trust-busting ran counter to natural law and was doomed to fail.[84]

John Stuart Mill's famous definition of freedom—your right to do as you please so long as you do not harm others—was insufficient, Hadley argued, because one person's exercise of liberty necessarily interfered with another person's right to do the same.[85] "You always do interfere. The active exercise of liberty by one man operates as a restriction to the liberty of others."[86] How to resolve this? Hadley's answer was to privilege intelligence, defining liberty as "the power to use intelligence as a determining factor in our conduct."[87] The right to private property, for example, would be meaningless without the intelligence to use it wisely. The more intelligence you had, the greater your right to liberty.

Hadley's arguments were widely cited. One contemporary reviewer gushed: "What wonder then that a multitude of blind and foolish efforts [have been made] to solve the conflict of classes by legislation prohibiting and delimiting the individual's liberty to use his own mind and powers in solving the problems of life."[88] Quoting Hadley directly, he continued: "True equality . . . can never exist . . . unless the gifted minority are coerced and limited by the majority. Equality in achievement and reward can be secured only by compulsion, or in other words, at the sacrifice of liberty."[89] Floyd W. Parsons, the editor of *Coal Age* magazine, put it coldly: "[W]orkers have had hopes awakened that can never be satisfied."[90] (Parsons was a member of the plutocratic American Liberty League, a group that, like NAM, would play a central role in establishing market fundamentalism in the United States.)

With respect to child labor reform, these claims were nonsense. England had passed the first law restricting child labor in 1802 and more than one hundred years later still had private property, a capitalist economy, and a functioning liberal democracy. Germany in the mid-nineteenth century had also instituted child labor bans, along with other worker protections. Conservative chancellor Otto von Bismarck worked to satisfy some working-class priorities deliberately to undercut support for more radical reform.

Despite NAM's persistent invocation of the Founding Fathers, the Fifth Amendment guarantee of property, and the Tenth Amendment reservation of powers to the states, the Jeffersonian concept that "all men are created equal" eluded them.[91] Of course, Jefferson's ownership of enslaved people and his defense of a limited franchise cast those words in a different light, but NAM's spokesmen never even made it to that level of analysis; they simply asserted that men were created unequal, and therefore our economic system necessarily had to reflect that. Sargent insisted that "the capitalist maintains as a basic principle that men are of unequal ability and hence deserve and should receive unequal reward—in other words, that there are scientific, practical, and ethical considerations which both necessitate and justify inequality of pay and income."[92] Any suggestion that wages should be even somewhat less unequal, or workers somewhat more protected, was a step toward socialism. It made sense that poor children would work in mines, mills, and factories, because that was where they belonged.

This sort of logic would also characterize the debate over workmen's compensation.

IN CONTRAST TO its stance on child labor, the National Association of Manufacturers did not explicitly oppose workers' compensation.[93] Historian Robert Wesser credits this in part to the work of sociologist and progressive reformer Crystal Eastman.[94] In 1907–8, she undertook a comprehensive study of industrial accidents in Pittsburgh—a city with an industrial workforce of about a quarter of a million—and documented in graphic detail the killing and maiming of hundreds of workers in a single year. The vast majority of these accidents, she argued, were not the result of negligence, but simply part of the "nature of the modern manufacturing process."[95] In a follow-up study in 1910, Eastman found that 17 percent of NAM members already operated some form of accident relief system.[96] The following year, NAM published the results of its own study of accident compensation in Europe and, at its annual conference, endorsed the principle of workmen's compensation.

According to Wesser, many employers saw it as in their interest to do so. Historically, injured workers had found courts unsympathetic to their plight, but this was beginning to change. Some state courts had awarded injured workers significant monetary settlements. The potential cost—and its unpredictability—worried more than a few manufacturers; a no-fault system of fixed compensation for injuries would be easier for employers to manage. Workmen's compensation could also promote workplace harmony, an issue of increasing importance as unions became stronger and more forceful in their demands. New York's progressive Republican governor Charles Evans Hughes had argued that workmen's compensation could help to ease tensions between labor and management; when New York State held hearings on the issue in 1909 and 1910, several corporate executives testified to this point.[97] In 1914, Hughes signed a comprehensive workmen's compensation law, which Crystal Eastman had helped draft.

Yet despite NAM's professed support for workmen's compensation in principle, in practice it opposed the Hughes bill when it passed, condemning it as "alarming and drastic."[98] Other manufacturers also objected. Some continued to insist that if a worker was at fault, he should not be compensated. Others worried about the potential costs of any government-mandated scheme. Some raised the level-playing-field issue: match manufacturers testified in Congress that, yes, it was true that phosphorus poisoned the workers who handled it, but their firms could not justify the expense of safety precautions unless the law demanded it of their competitors in other states as well.[99] (In 1908, Congress had passed the Federal Employer's Liability Act protecting railroad workers injured on the job, which the courts allowed: railroads were interstate commerce, matches were not.)[100] An oft-repeated argument was that workmen's compensation undermined property rights by forcing employers to pay compensation without due process, and was, as one employer put it, an "entering wedge for socialistic doctrines."[101] During the debate in New York State, one member of the National Civic Federation—a group that championed a voluntary compensation system—characterized mandatory schemes as "socialistic perversions."[102]

Physicians also played a role in this debate. They opposed workmen's compensation because the standardized tables of coverage (this much for a leg, that much for an arm) were often accompanied by standardized fees and insurance companies might refuse to cover costs that exceeded published schedules.[103] To doctors, this raised the specter of socialized medicine, an argument that some applied as well to public parks, hospitals, transit systems, and even the Interstate Commerce Commission. It was not that these physicians objected to parks and hospitals, but that they objected to the government establishing and operating them.[104] Some physicians explicitly referred to workmen's compensation laws as a "species of socialism," particularly since the new American laws were modeled in part on those developed under social democracy in Germany. One member of the Industrial Accident Insurance Board worried in 1914 that importing a system of compensation from Europe would undermine the American national character via "the attempt to substitute the beneficence of the state for the individual ambition and farsightedness of the man himself."[105]

IN THESE DEBATES around child labor and workmen's compensation, NAM and its allies did not build their defense on the idea (prominent in later decades) that markets were always efficient. Few denied that industrial accidents were harmful and wasteful. Rather, their central claim was that permitting the federal government to address these ills would entail a harmful expansion of federal power and diminish freedom. Three themes emerged from these debates that would loom large in subsequent conservative thought about government's role in restraining the marketplace and accounting for the true costs of capitalism.

One theme was *freedom*—particularly freedom of contract, but also the freedom of parents to send their children to work if they deemed it necessary or appropriate and the freedom of owners to run their mines and mills as they saw fit. Another was *individual responsibility*—the idea that federal intervention would undermine individual initiative and accountability. A third was the *American way of life*—the idea that federal engagement in the marketplace was a step on the slippery slope to socialism. Often opponents of federal government intervention maintained that decisions about child labor and workmen's compensation belonged to families and factory owners, but if they were to be subject to law, those laws should be formulated by the states. No doubt some who made this argument believed it, but when state laws were offered, many who had claimed to support them in principle (including NAM) found reasons to oppose them in practice.[106] The net result was to preserve and protect the privileges of employers and industrialists at the expense of adult workers and children. The captains of American industry invoked high ideals to sustain low practices.

Opponents of child labor laws also began to use the word *freedom*, rather than *liberty*, which had been the more current term in the nineteenth century. *Liberty* had been commonly understood to involve the *responsible* exercise of freedom; *freedom* typically implied a condition with few or no constraints. By invoking freedom rather than liberty, they implied that governmental constraints were inappropriate. In doing so they laid the groundwork for a broader argument they would promote in the years to come about "economic freedom"—an expression that had rarely been used before.

The tension between equity and freedom highlighted in these debates resonated throughout the twentieth century into the New Deal, the civil rights movement, and environmental regulation. The arguments the "freedom" side invoked were neither wholly meretricious nor wholly untrue. Workmen's compensation did limit businessmen's freedom to run dangerous workplaces, just as child labor laws limited their ability to hire minors. But these laws also protected a worker's right to compensation if injured on the job, and a child's right to be a child. One set of rights was being pitched against another. Or we could frame the matter as one of competing freedoms: an employer's freedom to determine working conditions versus a worker's freedom from the fear and reality of dangerous workplace accidents; parents' freedom to send their children to work versus the children's freedom to develop their full potential.

LAWS EXIST TO prevent people from doing things that hurt other people. We do not see laws against murder and theft as infringing our freedom, because we take it for granted that there is no right to engage in such immoral activities. With issues such as abortion access or marijuana use—which are restricted to different degrees in different states—or, recently, mask mandates, debate continues in part because we lack consensus on their morality.

The debates over workmen's compensation and child labor were not dissimilar. Many Americans at that time, both liberals and conservatives, found it self-evident that child labor was an evil to be curtailed, but others were not convinced. Some legal scholars argued that constitutional amendments were only appropriate in crises. Yet, while the prevalence of industrial accidents was widely understood as such—that is why it was called the Accident *Crisis*—no constitutional amendment was put forward. It took decades before a federal system of workmen's compensation was emplaced.[107]

Opponents of workmen's compensation and child labor regulation repeatedly insisted that restrictions on business practices threatened American freedom, ignoring the fact that other industrialized nations had done more to protect citizens and that their economies worked as well as, if not better than, the American economy did. They had remained democracies. Their people were still free. The claim that restraining capitalism to protect workers threatened freedom was bogus, but the men advocating it had more money, power, and social position to deploy to propagate their views than their adversaries did. And so their arguments began to take hold. The competition between the rights of business and the needs of workers would never be a level playing field.

In his influential essays on liberty, first published in 1959, the philosopher and political theorist Isaiah Berlin argued that freedom is not an absolute good but needs to be weighed against competing considerations. Echoing a speech made by Abraham Lincoln during the depths of the Civil War, Berlin stressed that freedom for wolves can mean death to lambs. Lincoln had noted: "The shepherd drives the wolf from the sheep's throat, for which the sheep thanks the shepherd as his liberator, while the wolf denounces him for the same act as the destroyer of liberty . . . Plainly, the sheep and the wolf are not agreed upon a definition of liberty."[108] Almost a century later, Berlin reiterated: "Both liberty and equality are among the primary goals pursued by human beings throughout many centuries; but total liberty for wolves is death to the lambs, total liberty of the powerful, the gifted, is not compatible with the rights to a decent existence of the weak and the less gifted."[109] And in 1969, when he was revising his essay, he added: "The bloodstained story of economic individualism and unrestrained capitalist competition does not, I should have thought, today need stressing."[110] In fact, it did. It needed stressing when Berlin was writing, it needed stressing throughout the rest of the twentieth century, and it needs stressing again today.

CHAPTER 2

Power Plays and Propaganda

In the 1920s, a problem arose that struck at the root of American capitalism itself, a problem that seemingly could not be solved by tinkering around the edges or by making even moderate adjustments. It was the failure of the marketplace to supply electricity to rural customers.

The introduction of electric technology in the early twentieth century had revolutionized transportation and recreation. Cities installed electric lights that made for safe walking at night, and electric streetcars enabled the development of suburbs, amusement parks at the ends of their lines, and outings in the country. Electricity made Henry Ford's assembly line possible, along with countless other industrial innovations. It also transformed the American home, replacing dirty and dangerous gas lamps and paving the way for electrical appliances that made household labor less arduous.[1] By the early 1920s, many urban Americans had electricity in their homes, and with it a sense of satisfaction that the future was being realized before their eyes. Electric power was equated with personal power.[2]

Rural customers wanted electricity as much as their urban counterparts—and many observers argued that they needed it more—but electrical utilities had neglected them. By the mid-1920s, most rural Americans still did not have access. Urban electricity generation in the United States was mostly the work of entrepreneurs whose for-profit business made the required machinery—famously Thomas Edison and George Westinghouse—and the private utilities that put that machinery to work, including Edison Electric. Their companies and utilities were extraordinarily successful: Edison and Westinghouse became household words. As successful as these men and companies were, however, they had not found a profitable way to bring electricity to rural customers.

Outside the United States, the situation was different. In many countries, electricity was viewed not as a commodity—like corn or pork belly—to be bought and sold at a profit, but as a public good—like water or sewers—that demanded government engagement to ensure equitable distribution. In Germany, France, and New Zealand, electricity generation was developed as a public utility; in the United Kingdom, Parliament nationalized electrical generation.[3] Some American communities had established municipal utilities on these grounds, but most did not.

The contrast in results was stark: by the 1920s, nearly 70 percent of northern European farmers had electricity, but fewer than 10 percent of U.S. famers did.[4] In Pennsylvania, it was estimated that 90 percent of rural residents lacked access to an electricity grid.[5] Moreover, country folks who were fortunate enough to have access paid much higher rates—often double their urban counterparts—leaving many farmers unable to afford electricity even when it was offered.[6] As General Electric concluded in 1925, "the purchasing power of . . . 1.9 million [farmers] is too low to put them in the potential customer class."[7] Gifford Pinchot, the Progressive Republican governor of Pennsylvania, noted the irony that while private utilities had marketed and promoted electricity for its labor-saving capacity, the rural Americans who often labored longest and hardest had seen little electricity reach their homes.

Pinchot—best known for his earlier role as the first chief of the U.S. Forest Service—was typical of the era in asserting that the high U.S. standard of living was "mainly due to our use of greater quantities of power per inhabitant than any other people on Earth."[8] Lack of power, Pinchot thought, was the major factor holding back human progress. Power was the answer to scarcity, because "for the first time in history goods could be produced in abundance for all mankind."[9] Steam power in the nineteenth century had increased industrial productivity, but it had also brought conflict and inequity. Businessmen could harness steam in their factories, but ordinary working men and women received little direct benefit: after all, almost no one had steam power in their homes. It could even be argued that working men and women suffered from the advent of steam power, as the industrial labor it made possible was far more grueling than the cottage industries that it replaced. Fairly distributed, electricity would not just liberate people from drudgery, argued Pinchot, it would advance civil society. "Men can use steam power only where it is generated. That is why steam has concentrated vast numbers of people in industrial cities. In a steam-driven civilization the worker must go to the power, but in an electrically-driven civilization the power will be delivered to the worker. Steam makes slums. Electricity can replace them with garden cities."[10]

Electricity would advance democracy, because it could make energy available to all on equal terms. (Pinchot would no doubt have been proud when, in the 1930s, Americans could boast of using as much electrical energy as "all the rest of the world combined.")[11] But for that democratic advancement to occur, electricity had to be equitably distributed. It was fast becoming a necessity, and "the unregulated domination of such a necessity of life would give to the holders of it a degree of personal, economic and political power over the average citizen which no free people could suffer and survive . . . The situation is almost magical in its boundless possibilities for good or evil."[12] To ensure that electricity was harnessed for the former and not the latter, and that its benefits came to all Pennsylvanians, Pinchot proposed a plan to change the way electricity was distributed and sold in the state. He called it Giant Power.[13]

The industry might have worked with him to find a pricing structure that would enable utilities to deliver electricity to rural customers without going broke. Instead, electricity industry leaders organized one of the largest propaganda campaigns in the history of the United States.

IN CLASSIC ECONOMIC theory, markets work by matching supply to demand. If demand exceeds supply, then sellers may raise prices and demand will fall. Alternatively, entrepreneurs may be motivated to move into the market to increase supply and satisfy the existing demand at the same or perhaps a lower price. Conversely, if supply exceeds demand, sellers may cut prices to stimulate demand. In an ideal market, equilibrium is achieved—supply and demand match—and everyone is satisfied. This idea is so central to economic theory that it is conventionally referred to as the *law* of supply and demand.[14] It's a statement of an ideal type: how things would work in a perfectly responsive market.[15] In theory, if General Electric couldn't find a profitable way to supply rural electricity, then some other entrepreneur would. The market would be "self-correcting." It would find a way to meet any demand.

But electricity didn't work that way. The large amount of infrastructure required to produce electricity created nearly insurmountable barriers to entry for new players in the market, making competition infeasible. In these conditions of "natural monopoly," it would make sense either for the government to run the industry, or for the government to contract with a private entity to do so. In the eighteenth century the concept had been applied to mail delivery; many countries had decided it made sense to have a single, national postal service, either as part of or contracted by government. (The U.S. Constitution, for example, granted Congress the power to establish post offices and post roads.) In the nineteenth century, railroads became the quintessential natural monopoly, because it would be costly and inefficient to lay duplicate tracks along the same routes. In Europe, many countries established state-owned enterprises to build and run the railways; in the United States, the federal government created private monopolies by granting land to specific railroad companies for specific lines. (The Union Pacific Railroad, for example, owned most of the key routes through the American West, while the Atchison, Topeka, and Santa Fe owned most of the rest.)[16] Telegraphy was also viewed as a natural monopoly, and in the twentieth century telephone systems would be, too: Western Union and American Telephone and Telegraph (AT&T) would grow into huge corporations on the strength of their state-sanctioned monopolies.

Perhaps unsurprisingly, natural monopolies had all the problems associated with unnatural ones. The American railroads were notoriously corrupt and mismanaged, engaging in price-fixing, stock-watering, issuing false financial reports, and other shady practices. As historian Richard White has shown, railroad executives routinely bribed politicians and newspaper editors to tout the benefits of building lines into regions that they knew had no reasonable chance of long-term profitability; they also used false reports of unoccupied fertile lands to lure white settlers into areas already home to native populations.[17] Western rail lines greatly accelerated the destruction of ecosystems and the slaughter of Indigenous peoples.[18] Railroad magnates' actions also contributed to financial panics when their overvalued stocks collapsed.

Another problem involved so-called holding companies. In the 1920s, a typical American electrical utility was privately owned and served "a relatively small area from a single generating station in a single state."[19] Utilities often wanted to develop larger networks—and there could be economies of scale when they did—but this required substantial upfront investment, which small firms typically could not manage. Holding companies gained control of utilities by purchasing their stock on the open market, and then raised the capital needed to develop and extend trans-mission lines. They were able to do so because they were better known to investors than the myriad of small utilities that assembled under their aegis.[20] Large holding companies were also able to develop useful technical expertise; the rapid growth of holding companies in the 1920s was also a period of rapid growth of electricity use in manufacturing, which in turn led to significant productivity gains.[21] But there was a serious downside: holding companies engaged in various questionable financial activities, including the sale of highly inflated securities, which contributed substantially to the stock market crash that heralded the Great Depression.[22]

These dubious financial practices were widely acknowledged at the time (even if the environmental and cultural damage railroads caused was not), and most people understood that, in the absence of competition, natural monopolies had to be regulated. In a nineteenth-century case involving railroads, courts had held that under conditions of natural monopoly, states could regulate prices so long as they ensured industry players got a fair rate of return on the value of their investment. Regulatory commissions were created to adjudicate such matters. But "fair" was subject to interpretation, as was the value of the investment; in railway cases, judicial challenges to commission decisions were widespread, often blocking implementation for years.[23] Moreover, the whole framework of regulating prices for a fair rate of return rested on accurate information about operating costs, incentivizing railroads to exaggerate costs and hide profits. The same perverse incentives contributed to corruption in electrical utilities.

The term "regulatory capture" was not yet in vogue, but the phenomenon was. Most state regulatory commissions were heavily influenced, if not actually controlled, by the large holding companies, and commissions that tried to enact meaningful rate regulations were subverted by the companies' creative accounting methods. Holding companies stymied effective rate regulation by charging fees to the companies they operated that would be presented to the commissions as operating costs—costs that would then be passed on to consumers; the commissions had no way to distinguish these excess fees from real operating expenditures. As holding companies grew in size and power, concerns grew as well; some observers began to speak disparagingly of a "power trust" holding the American people hostage.

AS HEAD OF the U.S. Forest Service, Gifford Pinchot had championed efficiency as a cornerstone of resource management, a conviction he carried with him into the Pennsylvania governor's mansion. He was among the first to promote the idea of "sustained yield"—that one could both use and protect a resource, so long as the rate of use did not exceed the rate of regeneration—laying the foundations of the modern concept of sustainability. Unlike his one-time friend but later adversary John Muir, Pinchot believed that forests should not be set aside as preserves, but he also recognized that if forest management was left to the timber industry, the forests would be destroyed. (Pinchot knew the destructive practices of the timber industry firsthand: his father had made his fortune in home furnishings.) Pinchot's "wise use" framework was squarely in the mainstream of progressive reformers who sought not to take over American industry, but to curtail its excesses and shortsighted practices.[24]

When Pinchot was elected governor of Pennsylvania in 1922, he set out to bring efficiency and equity to electricity distribution. Encouraged by the new governor, the state legislature passed the Giant Power Survey Act, creating a Giant Power Survey Board and authorizing it to determine the feasibility of a project to provide electricity to all state residents at a fair price.

The Survey Board's report contrasted two concepts: Giant Power, organized and regulated by the state for the benefit of all citizens; and Super Power, owned and operated by the private sector for the benefit only of some. The term *Super Power* came from the title of a set of conferences in the early 1920s convened by the Department of Interior, and a report by the U.S. Geological Survey in 1921, proposing a "Superpower system for the region between Boston and Washington."[25] The idea was the development of one or more privately owned large generating stations and high-voltage transmission lines, to cover the entire region between Boston and Washington.[26] U.S. Commerce Secretary Herbert Hoover endorsed the concept and established a Northeastern Super Power committee to further the idea.[27] The Giant Power Survey Board agreed with Hoover that increased electrification was desirable, and long-distance transmission feasible, but concluded that the private sector should not undertake the work alone because their track record showed that most rural customers would be left unserved. The alternative, Giant Power, would be a public–private partnership.

Giant Power was not a government takeover of the electricity industry. Nor was it a proposal to build a state-owned enterprise. Under Giant Power, electricity would be generated at or near coal mines and fed into a common grid, with lines running across the state. The generation could be done by either private or public entities, so long as the entire system met two essential conditions: the pooling of supply, and the effective public regulation of the industry, with private utilities operating according to a set of publicly determined and transparent rules. No generator and no consumer would be privileged over any other, and all producers would have equal access to the grid. In some rural areas, farmers had attempted to create electricity cooperatives, only to find the grid operators refusing to supply them or charging extortionate rates, so a key element of Giant Power was that if farmers created cooperatives, providers could not turn away their business.

Pinchot compared the two options—Super Power versus Giant Power—to two elephants, one wild and one tame, saying that "the place for the public is on the neck of the [tame] elephant, guiding its movements, not on the ground helpless under [the wild elephant's] knees."[28] For an annual expense of less than 3 percent of their present construction costs, he noted, existing companies could have brought electricity to half of all Pennsylvania farms, but they had not. Their "almost complete failure to bring about rural electrification makes legislative relief imperative," he declared.[29] Rural electricity was a market failure. "For the safety and welfare of the people," the state would step in where the private sector had declined to.[30]

Pinchot's aspirations admittedly bordered on the utopian. "Giant Power," he explained, "is a plan . . . by which the drudgery of human life can be taken from the shoulders of men and women who toil, and replaced by the power of electricity."[31] In an address to the 1923 Annual Conference of Governors, he went further: "[L]ong distance electrical transmission is to be the basis of a new economic and social order."[32]

Yet, Giant Power was not radical. Like so many Progressive Era reforms, it sought "to adapt America to new conditions without challenging its basic institutions."[33] The Giant Power Survey Board emphasized on the first page of its report that "a scrupulous regard for investors' rights" would be essential to attract the necessary capital.[34] The plan was designed to "permit the [electric] companies to operate their business successfully, to pay a good but reasonable return on their invested capital, and to secure additional capital as need for new enterprises or for expansion."[35] Pinchot repeatedly stressed that he was not advocating public ownership. "If the people of the United States ever turn to the nation-wide public ownership of electric utilities," Pinchot predicted, "it will be because the companies have driven them to it." It would be their own fault, for having "opposed and prevented reasonable and effective regulation by the states and the nation."[36]

Giant Power did, however, involve planning. One of the tensions of this period was between two different kinds of planning, which conservatives typically (and sometimes deliberately) conflated: communist planning in a government-controlled economic system, and scientific planning, as advocated by managers following principles of the emerging field of industrial engineering. Rational, scientific planning, particularly in the workplace, but also in the use and distribution of resources, was a polestar for both Pinchot and his right-hand man, Giant Power Survey Board chair Morris Llewellyn Cooke.[37]

Trained at Lehigh University as a mechanical engineer, Cooke acquired a few years' experience in industry before becoming an assistant to Frederick Winslow Taylor, who was serving as president of the American Society of Mechanical Engineers. Taylor was the nation's leading proponent of scientific management of industrial practices; Cooke became a prominent advocate of "Taylorism" to increase industrial productivity, decrease waste, and reduce or even eliminate the need for layoffs, contributing to the prosperity of both workers and managers. Among other things, Cooke supported the eight-hour working day on the grounds that one simply could not work efficiently for longer.[38]

Taylorism was sometimes taken to excess, such as measuring and optimizing the precise distance between the sink and the stove in a kitchen without regard to the variation in size of people using that kitchen (and without allowing that there could be meaningful personal preferences in such matters). Unions often opposed Taylorism for giving managers undue control, and in its extreme manifestations Taylorism could border on the inhumane. But Cooke was clear about his beneficent intentions: science could improve life, and government should be rationally organized to "ensure the public welfare." Cooke rejected laissez-faire in large part because of its inefficiencies; he believed the federal government "must guide and direct the advancement of society."[39] Above all, government could defend the public interest against the "demands of particularistic groups," the electricity industry among them.[40]

Cooke's views on electricity were formed by his own experience in the electricity industry, which he found to be a distorting influence on the engineering profession and a "corrupting force in American life."[41] Utility executives evinced little concern for their customers, an attitude that had spread to many electrical engineers and professors of engineering.[42] Some of the latter, Cooke argued, were not so much university professors as "corporate employee[s] giving courses in universities."[43]

Cooke had witnessed various dishonest practices, such as utility employees posing as ordinary citizens at public hearings.[44] In 1924, Cooke accepted an invitation to speak about Giant Power to a group of engineers in Washington, D.C. When Cooke refused to allow the Pennsylvania Electric Association to vet the presentation, the invitation was withdrawn.[45]

Cooke was proud that Giant Power was a "revolutionary break with current practice," and not only in its technical aspects. "Giant Power signifies a social approach quite distinct from—even if not entirely unaffected by—financial considerations. Giant Power seeks to substitute the look-ahead for the regret after the event; to suggest a planned future as contrasted with a drifting policy."[46] Pinchot agreed, suggesting that electricity was "immeasurably the greatest industrial fact of our time. If uncontrolled, it will be a plague without previous example. If effectively controlled in the public interest it can be made incomparably the greatest material blessing in human history."[47]

Because Cooke and Pinchot put social considerations on par with—or perhaps even ahead of—financial ones, critics accused them of being "communistic," but neither man had sympathy for communism or socialism.[48] Rather, they advocated a more rational form of capitalism than what Americans at that time had, in which the needs of the people would be a primary consideration and in which engineering decisions would be made by engineers rather than financiers.[49] Cooke envisaged Giant Power as but one part of a "Great State . . . placing the government of our individual states on a plane of effective social purpose."[50] We might call it "*guidez-faire*": a form of capitalism in which government combated corruption, remedied market failure, and redressed social inequities.

What *was* radical about Giant Power was its reorganization of the entire system for generating and distributing electricity in Pennsylvania. Under Pinchot's plan, the Giant Power Survey Board would be authorized to construct and operate coal-fired power plants, to mine the necessary coal, to appropriate land for mining, and to build and operate transmission lines, or issue permits to others to do so. Private operators could still function—indeed, the system would need them—but they would have to play by the rules and rates the board established. The board could also buy electricity from operators in neighboring states, or sell to them. Farmers could create rural power districts and mutual companies, and if the board chose to it could subsidize them. After all, if the state could subsidize highways, then why not electricity transmission?[51]

The goals of Giant Power *were* socialistic in one important respect: the "chief idea" behind it was "not profit but the public welfare."[52] Its object was not "greater profit to the companies," but "greater advantage to the people."[53] To make this happen, "effective public regulation of the electric industry" was an essential condition.[54]

Cooke understood Giant Power would threaten entrenched interests and provoke self-serving opposition, so a major point of the Giant Power proposal was its empirical basis. Pinchot stressed that the report "proposes to deal with facts as it finds them," and its epigraph read, "Electrical development has brought the Commonwealth to the threshold of momentous changes in industry and transportation and in the life of the people . . . To act wisely in this situation facts must be our guide."[55]

This emphasis on facts—and the copious detail in the 480-page report itself—reflected an already incipient problem: industry pushback. The case for Giant Power rested largely on one piece of evidence the American electricity industry was starting to dispute: the Canadian government's success delivering electricity from Niagara Falls to farmers across Ontario.[56] Established in 1906, the Ontario Hydro-Electric Power Commission was the largest public power system in North America. It supplied electricity to nearly all the province's citizens at lower cost than the privately generated electricity available across the Falls on the U.S. side of the border.[57] And it was this key fact—that public electricity in Ontario was both more widely distributed and cheaper for the customer—that the American industry began to fight.

When the Giant Power Survey Board's report came out in 1925, industry leaders attacked both its contents and its sponsor. Immediately, they mobilized to prevent Pinchot's reelection. (He eked out a victory.) They also launched a disinformation campaign, using advertising, public relations, experts-for-hire, and academic influence to counter any suggestion that public management of electricity was desirable (much less necessary). Above all, the industry aimed to discredit the very idea that the public sector could do anything more fairly or efficiently than the private sector. The goal was to strengthen the American people's conviction that the private sector knew best, and to promote the idea that anything other than complete private control of industry was socialistic and un-American.[58]

Industries are of course entitled to their opinions, but this campaign was based on dubious and historically misleading assertions, misrepresentations, half-truths, and in some cases outright lies. To summarize the electricity industry's argument:

1. Private ownership works: electricity rates are fair, service is good, and the public is adequately protected by state regulation. Reports of industry corruption are untrue.
2. Private ownership alone gives opportunity for individual initiative, which is the cornerstone of our national success and prosperity.
3. Government involvement in electricity generation or distribution would be inappropriate, socialistic, even tyrannical.
4. Government involvement in activities that should properly be the domain of free enterprise will undermine individual initiative and ultimately destroy American prosperity.

Most of this argument was made not by the specific utilities or holding companies themselves, but by their trade organization: the National Electric Light Association (NELA).[59]

Created in 1885, NELA represented more than five hundred of the largest privately owned electrical utilities, accounting for more than 90 percent of U.S. kilowatt output.[60] In the early 1920s, NELA and its members, separately and together, had worked to stop the Muscle Shoals and Boulder (later renamed Hoover) Dam projects. A forerunner to what would become the Tennessee Valley Authority, the Wilson Dam project at Muscle Shoals, Alabama, was a proposal to generate hydroelectric power on the Tennessee River, use the electricity to run a manufacturing plant, and sell any excess electricity to local consumers. Although approved by both houses of Congress, it was heavily opposed by industry and vetoed by President Herbert Hoover. At the 1924 NELA convention, Hoover declared (in language Ronald Reagan would later echo) that it was essential to keep "initiative free from the deadening influence both of bureaucracy and of socialistic experiment."[61]

Hoover was not the antigovernment ideologue he is sometimes made out to be. Among other things, he endorsed building dams for flood control or to aid navigation—which he (and the courts) accepted as legitimate federal government functions. He also favored regulating the new electronic medium of radio.[62] But he rejected the idea of the government competing directly with the private sector. The argument was not one of practicality or economic efficiency, but of the proper function and limits of government. Announcing his Muscle Shoals veto, Hoover explained: "I hesitate to contemplate the future of our institutions, of our Government, and of our country if the preoccupation of its officials is to be no longer the promotion of justice and equal opportunity but is to be devoted to barter in the markets."[63]

One might concede part of Hoover's point: Why should the federal government compete with the private sector?[64] If the private sector were functioning well, then the answer would be that it shouldn't. But the private electricity sector had failed to serve a large share of potential customers and was probably overcharging many of the rest. If electricity were not viewed as a public good, this would not have been a matter for government. But people increasingly shared Pinchot's view of electricity as a necessity, viewing transmission lines as analogous to roads and bridges. Electricity executives insisted they were providing their product as cheaply and efficiently as possible and to as many people as they could, but the data said otherwise.

In 1921, Samuel Insull, the industrialist credited with building the electricity infrastructure of Chicago (and who would later see his entire enterprise collapse in the Great Depression), decided the industry needed to defend itself.[65] He concluded that there should be "a great campaign of education in the colleges and other institutions of learning."[66] In the 1920s, NELA did exactly that—except that both contemporary critics and later analysts would consider it not education, but propaganda. After holding hearings on the subject in the 1930s, the U.S Federal Trade Commission (FTC) concluded that NELA's effort was the greatest peacetime propaganda "campaign ever conducted by private interests in this country."[67]

The FTC hearings lasted six years—almost as long as the campaign itself—and created a "bookshelf" of reports: eighty volumes to be exact.[68] Fortunately, economic historians William J. Hausman and John L. Neufeld managed to summarize their findings in a single sentence: "[P]rivate utilities, led by [their] industry trade group, the National Electric Light Association ... mounted a large and sophisticated propaganda campaign that placed particular emphasis on making the case for private ownership to the press and in schools and universities."[69] Historian David Nye concurs: "The thousands of pages of testimony revealed a systematic covert attempt to shape opinion in favor of private utilities, in which half-truths and at times outright lies presented municipal utilities in a consistently bad light" and private utilities in a good light.[70] Historian Ronald Kline calls the campaign "underhanded" and "unethical."[71]

One contemporary observer was Judson King, director of the National Popular Government League, a civic organization dedicated to good government. King discussed the FTC findings' implications for educators, focusing on "the manner in which certain university professors have not only been used by the private power interests in the general propaganda, but also used to influence public opinion and Congressional action."[72] King described the effort as "breathtaking."[73]

The FTC found that industry actors had attempted to control the *entire* American educational system—from grade school to university—in their own economic interest. This effort focused on the social sciences—economics, law, political science, and government—but also included engineering and business. Its purpose was to ensure "straight economic thinking"—by which NELA meant capitalistic, free-market principles—and to supply young people and their teachers with "correct information." The goal was to mold the minds of the current generation and those to come.[74]

In King's analysis, the industry would deem the program a success when judges, lawmakers, members of public utility commissions, prosecuting attorneys, and engineers, "in short, all public officials—will be so trained as automatically to oppose genuine regulation, public ownership, honest valuations, equitable rates, etc.," and public opinion would be "created so that voters will elect officials who will approve such policies as benefit the industry."[75] This was achieved, the FTC concluded, through "false and misleading statements of fact, as well as opinions on public policy, found in reports and expert testimony of prominent university professors who are now discovered to have been in the pay of the private utilities."[76] This work had been advanced through NELA's seemingly beneficent "Committee on Cooperation with Educational Institutions." "It is astonishing to discover the extent of their success," King wrote.[77] King did not dispute the right of a university professor to be a consultant or "to state his honest opinion" on any subject. The issue was "for him to use, or permit others to use, his university title for palpable perversion of truth."[78]

The opinions NELA promoted were embedded in a larger argument that private property was the foundation not only of the American economy but of American life, so any attempt to interfere with the private operation of the electricity industry threatened to undermine that way of life. Opinions to the contrary were denigrated as "unsound," "socialistic," and fundamentally un-American. The FTC found that the "character and objective of these activities was fully recognized by NELA and its sponsors as propaganda," and that in their documents they "boasted that the 'public pays' the expense."[79] Ernest Gruening, a journalist at the time and later the long-serving territorial governor of Alaska, noted that when the presiding judge in the hearings asked if NELA had neglected any form of publicity, its director of public information replied: "Only one, and that is sky-writing."[80]

NELA organized lecture series aimed at colleges and universities, civic clubs, scout troops, women's clubs, school assemblies, church congregations, and other groups. NELA employees and their contractors wrote editorials and letters, met with newspaper editors in cities around the country to win them over to the industry perspective, and issued press releases and bulletins to provide fodder for articles with pro-industry slants. Sometimes these editorials resonated with the views editors already held, particularly in places such as Texas that were (then as now) generally hostile to the federal government. In other cases, the suggested editorials were linked—either explicitly or implicitly—to advertising revenues.[81] David Nye concludes that NELA spent up to a million dollars a year for at least several years in its efforts to influence politicians, business and civic leaders, newspaper editors, and the public.[82] In current dollars, that's about $15 million per year.[83]

In one incident, the industry ran into conflict with the Tennessee State Public Utilities Commission over taxation and permits. The Tennessee chapter of NELA, rebranded as the Tennessee Public Utility Information Bureau, dedicated $3,000— about $50,000 today—for an advertising campaign coupled with outreach to newspaper editors. Ads ran in more than one hundred papers in Tennessee, but it was the outreach, one NELA official boasted, that made the difference: the ads were placed "during a personal call upon the editors, at which time occasion was taken to discuss the matter with the editors and place before them the facts as we see them." The result? "Approximately 40 favorable editorials written on this matter," and only one or two unfavorable ones. "At a cost of less than $700 dollars we have been able to get our story in papers whose combined circulation is approximately 350,000."[84] After a similar campaign in Missouri, NELA boasted of "a splendid effect upon the editors . . . the newspapers are 99 per cent with the privately owned utilities."[85]

Between 1921 and 1927, papers across the country published 12,784 industry-sponsored editorials. Wire services were also a target: one executive crowed that the

Associated Press "sends out practically everything we give them."[86] Millions of pages of literature, "from single page fliers to bound volumes," were produced; one contemporary estimate placed the total page count at five million.[87] State utility commissions (let alone individual consumers) were not in a position to do anything similar on their own behalf.

To make them seem independent and credible, articles and editorials were often ghostwritten by academics. But despite their many authors, they carried a consistent message: municipal electricity was more expensive and less efficient than private sector electricity; state regulation was effective so there was no need for federal involvement; and generating power through the public sector—or even to advocate doing so—was socialistic. A characteristic editorial bore the title GOVERNMENT OWNERSHIP ADVOCATES SHADE FROM DEEPEST RED TO MAUVE. Red-baiting was pervasive. A "favorite method of attack," one defender of public ownership explained, was "to 'pin the red label.'" Advocates of the right of the people to own and operate public utilities "were labeled as 'Bolsheviks,' 'reds' or 'parlor pinks.'"[88]

NELA's defenders likened their activities to lobbying or PR. But unlike conventional lobbying, the academic campaign was not fighting or supporting a particular piece of legislation. And unlike conventional PR, the aim was not simply to create a positive impression of a particular business or even of the whole industry. Rather, the goal—expressed outright in numerous documents—was to change the way Americans thought about private property, capitalism, and regulation.

THE NELA ACADEMIC program had three major elements: First, recruiting experts to produce competing studies and offer alternative "facts" about the relative costs of private and public electricity generation. Second, rewriting textbooks to support the private electricity industry—including denying corruption charges and promulgating an ethical, trustworthy image—coupled with pressure on publishers to modify or withdraw textbooks that NELA found objectionable. And third, revising civics, economics, and business curricula in high schools, colleges, and universities—and establishing new programs, including at emerging business schools—designed to extol the benefits of laissez-faire capitalism. NELA also helped create and fund graduate programs in economics and business administration along lines congenial to the electric power industry where they did not previously exist. The expert-recruitment initiative was intended to undermine support for municipal electricity programs in the present; the other elements of the plan were intended to ensure the private electricity industry's future in the long run.

The arguments for and against public or private electricity had to account for their relative costs, which could be established factually. But NELA's intent, by its own admission, was not to support objective study of the matter but to "kill" the municipal ownership idea. As one document testified: "[T]he information we want is information showing the failure of municipal ownership, its inefficiency compared with private operation, and the fact that municipal ownership, in the last analysis, is more expensive."[89]

There were two aspects to this. The first was the price of private electricity. Under existing regulatory structures, utilities were entitled to a "reasonable" rate of return. This was generally thought to lie between 5.5 and 6.5 percent, but at least one study at the time showed that most companies made at least 7 percent; many made 8 or even 9. This meant companies were overcharging customers to the tune of millions or even tens of millions of dollars per year. The second was the cost of public electricity. Here, much of the debate surrounded the Ontario hydropower system. Nearly all independent observers affirmed that the Ontario Hydro-Electric Power Commission reached most province residents at a lower price than their U.S. counterparts were paying. A central task for NELA, therefore, was to fight this fact.

NELA took up the challenge by enlisting academics to produce studies "demonstrating" that Ontario Hydro-Electric Power was more expensive.[90] One expert hired to the task was E. A. Stewart, a professor of agricultural engineering at the University of Minnesota, who (ironically) had helped develop the Red Wing Project on Utilization of Electricity in Agriculture to test the feasibility and value of bringing electricity to American farmers.[91] His next, industry-funded study was promoted as "an impartial and scholarly survey of rural electrification" and was widely disseminated by NELA committees and discussed in their bulletins, press releases, and editorials. Its predictable finding was that Ontario hydroelectric power was more expensive than power generated privately in the United States.[92]

Stewart claimed his report had been vetted and approved by the engineering department at Ontario Hydro-Electric Power, but proponents of municipal power were skeptical and reached out to colleagues in Ontario.[93] It turned out that engineers there *had* checked the data and had alerted Stewart to various discrepancies, but the discrepancies had not been corrected. "Not only are the figures published in Stewart's report incorrect in many instances," the chairman of the Ontario

Hydro-Electric Power Commission stated, "but statements throughout the report are not in accordance with the facts."[94]

Nevertheless, newspaper articles and editorials around the country covered Stewart's report, and NELA members cited it as proof that public electricity was not as cheap as its proponents claimed. NELA committees (and their allies) sent out bulletins, letters, and editorials promoting Stewart's report. The *Boston Herald* published a full-page article, with an eight-column headline, entitled HERE IS THE TRUTH ABOUT ONTARIO HYDRO-ELECTRIC. Power officials were jubilant, writing, "We shall make good use of this."[95] Stewart himself went about "flogging his university credentials as proof of his scholarly objectivity."[96]

NELA found willing propagandists in faculties across the country. A professor at the University of Colorado was paid $1,692.33—about a full year's academic salary—for a survey of costs at municipally owned power plants in Colorado; not surprisingly, its conclusions were unfavorable to the municipal plants. An economics professor at the University of Missouri prepared a report—widely disseminated by Missouri Power and Light—based on data supplied by the industry, which by the latter's admission were "selected."[97] At the University of Iowa, an electrical engineering professor was paid to prepare a series of reports contrasting rates from public and private electrical facilities in the state; the findings favored the private side and NELA distributed the report "just as widely as we could legitimately."[98] The dean of the College of Engineering denied any conflict of interest, insisting that he could "see nothing reprehensible in such a practice so long as the employment did not interfere with university duties."[99]

Other reports addressed rural cooperatives. This was a delicate issue: farmers had created electricity cooperatives in response to the industry failure to supply them, so it was not necessarily in NELA's interest to call attention to them. As one executive wrote, "[I]f farmers can not get power from the companies, they may try to form 'power districts' of their own . . . It is a tricky business." NELA addressed this by declaring rural electrical cooperatives "alien" to the American way of life.[100] NELA even embarked on a program, in conjunction with Nebraska Agricultural College, to persuade farmers that electricity was not all it was cracked up to be. The idea—supported by the Nebraska Committee on Public Utility Information—was not to paint "too rosy" a picture of the benefits of electrification, lest farmers rush to rural cooperatives to obtain it.[101] Thus, the industry found itself, paradoxically, marketing *against* its own product.[102]

These NELA studies played a major role in public debate. Americans heard that academics had proved that public utilities could not generate electricity at lower cost than the private sector. It would be years before they learned these studies had been commissioned by the electricity industry and that their authors had been told what they needed to say.

PLEASED WITH THE results of their experts-for-hire campaign, NELA executives moved on to their second phase: rewriting American textbooks and, in effect, American history. The goal was to foster not just a positive view of the American electricity industry, but a positive view of capitalism and a negative view of government engagement in economic affairs.

The program began with a review of existing textbooks. The plan was to persuade publishers to discontinue textbooks the industry considered unacceptable; to contact authors and editors to suggest changes to textbooks that might be made acceptable with revision; and to recruit professors to write new texts resonant with NELA's point of view. The review included secondary- and university-level texts; its focus was civics, economics, and business. The secretary of NELA's Missouri Committee on Public Information concluded that most existing textbooks were "wholly valueless, and in many instances poisonous." He attributed this to the "fact" that "97 per cent of the textbooks used in the public schools affecting public utilities are written by socialists." The director of NELA's Texas Public Service Information Bureau took a more temperate tone but came to a similar conclusion: "All textbooks used in the schools are more or less erroneous on the utilities and generally on the fundamentals of economics. [NELA should recruit] some proper textbook-writer in preparing an honest textbook in civics for use in the high schools."[103]

NELA wanted to expunge any claim that the industry engaged in questionable financial dealings, or any suggestion that it unduly influenced the political process. J. B. Sheridan, chairman of NELA's textbook subcommittee, offered specifics: "Some of the textbooks state that the utilities are or were overcapitalized, have 'watered their stock,' and impose excessive rates upon their customers to enable them to make financial returns upon alleged capital investment which does not exist in fact."[104] (In the 1930s, investigators would conclude that the industry had done just these things; that the claims were in high school textbooks in the 1920s suggests these activities were already widely known or at least suspected.) NELA also objected to the characterization of their industry as "private"—*they* were the true public entities because they were owned by shareholders. (In fact, most of the shares held by the public did not carry voting rights.)

NELA officials objected to specific terms and phrases, including *over-capitalization, reasonable rates, natural monopolies, fair return, stock watering, abuses in rate making, weaknesses in regulatory practices*, and, in some contexts, even the word *taxation*.[105] They also objected to passages suggesting companies were corrupt, had overcharged their customers, had been insufficiently regulated, or perhaps should not be allowed to exist at all. Examples included:

> Franchises were . . . frequently secured by corrupting the city council . . . Privately managed public utilities have, therefore, been a very potent cause of municipal corruption.[106]
>
> Large campaign funds coming from hidden sources have led to serious corruption in the elections.[107]
>
> The reason why street-car companies in some cities cannot reduce fares is because the company has "watered the stock" [and so] fares are double what they by right should be.[108]
>
> [I]t has long been recognized that society must own or control enterprises which are natural monopolies. Among these are telephones, electric-light plants, street cars and railways.[109]
>
> The day has long passed when the people will tolerate silently the enrichment of a few who control a necessity or comfort of life. . . . [T]he spirit of a democratic people will not tolerate private monopoly, and their genius can be depended upon to eradicate it wherever it shows itself.[110]

One passage that NELA officials found particularly objectionable explained how industry malfeasance led people to see the necessity of government control of natural monopolies:

> In the past, public service corporations have often "watered" their securities; that is they have issued shares of stock and bonds beyond the real value of the property . . . In order to pay the interest on such securities, companies have frequently levied high charges and given poor service. When the

franchises which have made their high profits possible have been in danger they have at times bribed city officials, broken the laws, misled public opinion by controlling the newspapers through their advertising, and expended large sums of money to elect men to city councils, and even to State legislatures, who would vote for measures they wanted. In these ways they have menaced good government and have caused many people to become advocates of government ownership.[111]

NELA rated 105 textbooks as good, fair, bad, or very bad.[112] The bad books were labeled biased and socialistic; they needed to be replaced with more "objective" works.[113] In one allegedly "bad" book, written by distinguished Columbia University historian Charles Beard, three passages were singled out for opprobrium: one concluding that sentiment in favor of municipal ownership was growing as a reaction to political activities by utility companies; a second suggesting refrigeration would one day be considered a public good (because of its role in public health); and a third discussing the corruption of a politician by a streetcar company that had paid him to "accelerate public sentiment" in favor of a line extension.[114] With their ratings in hand, NELA representatives approached publishers and school boards.

Realizing that pressuring academics and publishers might be considered inappropriate, NELA urged its members to regard the program as "confidential," hoping "through quiet and diplomatic measures to have some of these inimical textbooks discarded" or at least revised.[115] NELA would work to gain cooperation from large publishers first, on the theory that once they were "straightened out and are working with us, the small publishers will naturally fall in line." One official reported making a "good start" with the largest schoolbook publishing house, "who printed over 12,000,000 books last year." This, he boasted, "will be a tremendous leverage on any other house should opposition occur."[116]

NELA found it relatively easy to pressure the publishers of high school texts; altering university textbooks proved to be more challenging. In the words of one executive, people connected with higher education were "touchy."[117] Some might object to private industry interfering with university and school textbooks, so "great care must be used to avoid going too far since if the public were to get the idea that textbooks were being used as propaganda for public-utility companies the reaction would be worse than the original misinformation." NELA officials urged their members to proceed with caution, and to handle requests "by tactful personal contact."[118]

In some cases, NELA's concept of tact was a bribe. One strategy was to approach textbook writers, suggest that their texts were outdated, and offer them money to write a new one. "This will give the boys a chance to . . . make some money, and we can show them individually just wherein the old textbooks are obsolete." Within a year, one textbook was "pretty nearly ready for the printers" and more soon followed.[119]

When a new text proved satisfactory, NELA or its members paid for copies to be widely distributed. In Missouri, for example, the St. Joseph Gas Company helped pay for copies of a new book to be sent to every high school principal in the state. NELA officials also contacted school administrators, librarians, and teachers, suggesting that they should abandon objectionable texts and adopt the new ones. This approach appears to have met with considerable success: "Where textbooks which were grossly unfair . . . were used in the high schools, we took the matter up personally with school officials, either through local [electricity] managers or directly [by NELA] . . . In nearly every instance [the targeted texts] were removed and placed on the library shelves for use as reference matter only."[120]

In addition to the approved textbooks, NELA sent hundreds of thousands of free copies of pro-industry pamphlets and newsletters to school districts. The Ohio public utility information committee wrote and distributed 200,000 copies of *Aladdins of Industry*. In Connecticut, NELA circulated a "public utility cate-chism," written in question-and-answer fashion. In Rochester, New York, a text-book entitled *The Story of the Public Utilities* was published cooperatively by the board of education and local utilities. (These materials were sent to public, private, and parochial schools.)[121] A brochure called *Niagara in Politics*, which denied the success of Ontario hydroelectric power, had a circulation of about 10,000, including 5,243 copies "placed in colleges and public libraries."[122] The minutes of one committee meeting reported that a NELA-approved book entitled *Prosperity Through Power Development*, based on papers from an industry conference, had been sent to more than six thousand libraries."[123]

IN 1928, THE National Education Association (NEA) reviewed the NELA "educational" activities, and found three central themes: that state regulation was adequate (and therefore federal regulation would be superfluous); that electricity rates were reasonable and had not increased disproportionately to other living costs; and that private utilities did a good job supplying their consumers at fair prices. In FTC testimony, NEA noted, the secretary of the Connecticut Committee on Public Service Information had admitted that industry statements were "intended to discredit municipal ownership." Witnesses also admitted that the goal was to influence children (as future voters) to reject any thoughts sympathetic to state ownership.[124]

Yet while witnesses at the FTC hearings admitted the ideological and political goals of the campaign, presentations to teachers were an entirely different matter. Cover letters to teachers insisted that the accompanying materials on offer were entirely fact-based. A cover letter sent in West Virginia, for example, stated, "The texts are authentic, accurate and strictly informational. The public services discussed in the booklets are important factors contributing to the home comfort and convenience of the people of West Virginia." In Nebraska, teachers were assured that what they were receiving contained "no advertising, no propaganda." In West Virginia, Missouri, and Kansas, cover letters contained testimonials by state educational officials.[125] These efforts were so successful that in 1927, NELA urged state committees that had not yet undertaken such efforts to do so.[126]

Not every effort was successful, of course. There were a few documented examples of professors rejecting industry approaches. A professor at Clemson College in South Carolina rebuffed an invitation to participate in the textbook survey, stating: "I consider the censorship of textbooks as one of the most objectionable and reprehensible of the practices of so-called big business." A series of pamphlets with titles including "The Romance of the Kilowatt" and the "Romance of the Trolley" fell flat. And some efforts triggered a backlash: when an industry-sponsored pamphlet was published by the Smithsonian Institution, an uproar ensued, leading the Smithsonian to withdraw the pamphlet and destroy the plates.[127]

Incidents like this may have contributed to the industry's realization that, for this work to be effective, the materials produced had to be perceived as objective. Thus, like the tobacco industry in later years, the electric power industry tried to create the appearance of authors' independence and to avoid the hard sell. "Be careful to avoid seeming to force material on schoolmen," one industry executive advised. "Get them to ask for it."[128] At the same time, industry representatives boasted about how easy it was to get professors to do their bidding. "Now the professor, if you please, gentlemen, regards himself as being inspired by Jehovah," a speaker at the 1926 NELA convention noted, but "the prophet is most amenable to inspiration."[129] In most colleges and universities, NELA found "a fine spirit of cooperation."[130]

Still, imposing a textbook upon a professor was not easy, and the attempt to alter college materials was less successful than the attempt to influence schools. In any case, books did not stand alone; they had to work in conjunction with courses. So a third component of the academic campaign involved direct intervention in university programs to develop curricula. Influencing what was taught in colleges and universities would be the ultimate "win" for NELA. As one executive put it, "The Colleges can say things that we can not say and be believed."[131]

NELA would consider its campaign a success when broad academic consensus formed around free-market principles and their crucial role in American prosperity and culture. If that occurred, future generations of citizens would hold the appropriate views, no further influence required. In a speech entitled "Government in Business," the president of the People's Gas Light and Coke Company of Chicago summarized what that consensus would entail: American prosperity would be attributed to the belief that "business has had here so little interference from government," and that prosperity "abounds because here in the United States individual initiative and enterprise and energy have had full play as no where else."[132]

In this context, NELA introduced two ideas that would prove crucial in nearly all later arguments about the virtues of free-market capitalism and the dangers of government action in the marketplace. The first was the allegation that government involvement in the marketplace was a departure from U.S. history. The second was the claim that *free-market capitalism was the embodiment of freedom, writ large*, and that *any* restriction on the freedom of *any* business would put us on a slippery slope to tyranny. As one NELA representative put it in a radio address:

> When we think of the freedom that is given to every man, woman and child in America to develop the spark of divinity with which he is endowed . . . it is almost unbelievable that there could be found those who would tear down this marvelous system. And yet, there are today subversive movements at work in our land, fathered and fostered by those who . . . would foist on America the shockingly, brutally lowering system of certain backward civilizations. Today, they are marshaling their forces in an attempt to

put the Government into the electric business . . . How long, my friends, will it be, after the electric industry is stifled before the same principles will be applied to the lumber business, under the guise of conservation, and reforestation, and the coal business and the grocery business, and every business, for that matter.[133]

The reference to forestry and conservation was clearly an attack on Pinchot; the rest was an attack on anyone who highlighted the limits—let alone the failures—of private enterprise. In NELA's view, everyone needed to understand that free-market capitalism, prosperity, personal liberty, and the American way of life were inter-linked. How better to do that than by ensuring this was taught in American colleges and universities? Curricula were the obvious and crucial next step.

State-based NELA committees (often with a phrase like "public utility informa-tion" in their names) played a major role in outreach to colleges and universities. Programs of "reciprocal relations" were established across the United States, including at the universities of Washington, Oregon, Ohio, West Virginia, Wyoming, Missouri, Illinois, and Oregon; Washington State University, Penn State, Harvard, Northwestern, and Purdue; state agricultural colleges in Nebraska, Colorado, and Missouri; and the Smithsonian Institution. The sums offered to support those rela-tions were substantial: in 1925, Northwestern received twenty-five thousand dollars; in 1928 Harvard received thirty thousand dollars.[134] At the University of Illinois, NELA sponsored a "utilities week" in which more than ten thousand people viewed an exhi-bition developed by the Illinois Committee on Public Utility Information and had the opportunity to hear an address by Chicago electricity magnate Samuel Insull.[135]

The focus was to influence—and, where necessary, create—courses and programs in business and economics whose curricula were organized around principles of free enterprise and private property as the foundations for economic growth, pros-perity, and freedom. The scant industry attention to electrical engineering curricula underscores this point: the goal was not to fund technological advances or ensure the next generation of American engineers, but to persuade the American people and government that public production of electricity (or anything else) was a bad idea. It was to persuade students that private ownership and management of busi-ness were "the American Way."[136]

The list of institutions known to have declined to participate is short: the University of Chicago, Princeton, Columbia, and the City University of New York.

Among the copious documentary records, only a handful of letters attest to a clear rejection of industry proposals. The dean of the business school at the City College of New York penned one of the few: he responded to an industry funding offer by politely noting that "we find no difficulty in getting very competent instructors in the City of New York and we have adequate material for the successful conduct of our courses."[137] But this was atypical: evidence suggests that most universities willing to work with NELA, and many were enthusiastic.

The "reciprocal relations" ranged from modifying specific courses to developing entire graduate programs. In Colorado, NELA built a for-credit course on electrical utilities for the state teachers' college. At least one administrator welcomed it, saying, "We want this thing to go big. . . . We should have more regular courses in public utilities."[138] Similar courses were offered at the Colorado Agricultural College and the Colorado School of Mines. At the University of Colorado, a correspondence course was developed conveying a "pertinent utility message" that had been "perfected by the Rocky Mountain committee on public utility information."[139]

NELA committees did not just provide financial support; they also supervised the topics covered and course materials used. At Penn State, a professor developing a utility economics course received a fifteen-page critique of his proposal. Among other things, he was asked not to use the word "profit"—because "in the utility business, in a sense, there are no profits"—and to remove any "sentences referring to bribery and corruption." Six weeks later, the official who had made the request was pleased to report these changes had been made.[140] At Missouri State University, a course taught by the dean of the School of Engineering included a lecture on "the Public Utilities and their Relation to the Public"; the local NELA committee considered it unsatisfactory. They asked the dean to revise it; he did, and eight thousand copies of the revamped lecture were printed and distributed to teachers around the state.[141]

IN LATER YEARS, industry funding of academic research would become routine; nowadays it is generally framed as philanthropy. These practices are by no means unproblematic, but in general, academics try to steer clear of overtly ideological funding, particularly when it comes to teaching.[142] But in the 1920s, industry funding of academia was not yet widespread, NELA was subsidizing teaching and curriculum development rather than research, and its goal was explicitly

ideological: to instill pro-market, antiregulatory convictions. And it worked:
NELA trumpeted that through its efforts "we have been able to substitute sound,
economic theories for biased, and in some cases, socialistic or communistic doctrines
that were taught in our public schools."[143]

Perhaps the best evidence of the self-interested character of these activities and
financial contributions is how NELA complained when it did not get what it
wanted. One NELA representative carped that, despite many tens of thousands of
dollars in payments to Harvard, "the Association . . . found itself somewhat in the
position of having got hold of something by the tail and not being able to let go and
not knowing quite where the two beasts were going." He concluded that "the association may need a [clearer] interpretation of the relations which should exist with
educational institutions," with a focus on what it meant for these relationships to be
"reciprocal."[144]

To be sure, faculty who worked with NELA were not marionettes. At Harvard,
NELA abandoned a few projects when the business school "insisted that the final
results should be published and should not become the exclusive property of those
who have donated the money."[145] But NELA generally had its way. On one occasion, NELA's public relations chairman compared academics to mules, noting that
"the individual mule in a team of twenty must be allowed to kick over the traces
once in a while if he will." Professors needed some latitude, or the "credibility of the
institution suffers," but there was little reason to worry if "occasionally a professor
breaks loose on stuff that does not please us."[146]

Despite its complaints about Harvard, NELA had an enthusiastic ally there:
Professor Philip Cabot, a Boston Brahmin banker and director of several public utilities, who joined the Harvard Business School (HBS) in 1924. HBS offered two
courses on public utilities, largely taught by guest lecturers from the local industry; a
donation from NELA permitted the school to hire Cabot to teach the topic full-
time. As part of a course on public utilities management and public utilities finance,
Cabot invited industry executives to speak, but there is no evidence he ever invited a
municipal electricity manager or advocate, much less a union representative.

Cabot also produced a set of case studies and, with NELA support, compiled
them into a 1927 textbook, *Problems in Public Utility Management*. Evidence from
the Harvard archives shows that his research expenses, and possibly his salary, were
covered by NELA, with the intent that his textbook would be used beyond
Harvard.[147] NELA's public relations chairman hoped the course would "result in

the compilation of a textbook of case method study of public utility management and operation, and it is obvious that such literature bearing the imprint of Harvard University would be quite generally adopted by other educational institutions."[148]

Cabot was neither an ideologue nor industry apologist, and during the Depression he would allow that America had "discovered by painful experience that free competition means cut-throat competition and that it is the wage-earner's throat that is cut. During the last two or three years this nation has been slowly bleeding to death because of its reverence for free competition."[149] Still, in the 1920s, he played a major role in ensuring that students at what would become America's leading business school would be presented with views and interpretations congenial to the electricity industry. Even in the 1930s, when he seemed to be rethinking the problems of competition, he continued to defend electrical utilities, affirming their right to set their own rates and not be subject to "strangulation by government regulation."[150] In a 1933 article, he argued that utilities must be "unshackled" and permitted to set their own rates in response to the "law of supply and demand," a bizarre position given the utility monopoly on supply and the relative inelasticity of electricity demand.[151]

CABOT WAS AN important NELA ally, but the champion of NELA's efforts to influence academic programs was Ohio State's dean Clyde O. Ruggles. In 1926, he undertook a tour of college and university economics departments in support of NELA aims. He also organized conferences and sought out faculty who might accept research funds.[152]

In 1928, Ruggles joined Cabot at Harvard Business School as Professor of Public Utility Management (later amended to Professor of Public Utility Management and Regulation).[153] While at Ohio State, Ruggles had corresponded at length with NELA executive director M. H. Aylesworth, among other things inviting him to deliver a guest lecture. Aylesworth spoke on rate regulation and suggested other guests for Ruggles to invite.[154] One was Benjamin Ling of the Ohio Committee on Public Utility Information (a NELA partner organization), who in turn wrote to another colleague encouraging him to support Ruggles "inasmuch as his ideas coincide with our own."[155]

At Harvard, Ruggles undertook a survey to determine how business schools could better prepare their graduates for careers in the electric utility industry. He completed the study with the support of NELA's Committee on Cooperation with Educational Institutions, comprising sixteen university professors and ten representatives from NELA's district offices; it was published by NELA in 1929. What became known as the Ruggles Survey was ostensibly an objective report on the state of business education; in practice, Ruggles promoted the idea that industry should be more involved in shaping academic curricula. Some respondents objected.[156] One professor, for example, suggested that the utilities' "cooperation" with academics was "rightly to be viewed with suspicion. Courses deal with problems many of which involve conflict of interests and public utility companies have demonstrated that they are not to be relied upon for an honest presentation of their side; their propaganda methods are far from ingenious."[157]

For his efforts, Ruggles was paid $1,250 each month during the year or so that he worked on the survey—a princely sum in 1929.[158] This became a point of contention in the FTC hearings, as well as the subject of an inquiry by the American Association of University Professors, which investigated Ruggles for ethics violations. He insisted he had done nothing wrong.[159] However, when the NEA considered the matter, he was one of two college professors singled out for disapprobation.[160] The NEA committee that reviewed the NELA campaign recommended the "Association strongly denounce the purpose and efforts of the utility service bureaus to carry propaganda into the schools."[161]

Ruggles's most lasting impact was in expanding and strengthening the Harvard Business School (HBS) along business-friendly lines. Founded in 1913, HBS in the 1920s was still relatively small and not particularly influential; the idea of a business school had not yet caught hold of the American imagination and many businesspeople failed to see the point. As part of a larger program to establish new programs and stabilize nascent ones, NELA gave Harvard at least $20,000 per year for several years; in 1927–28—the year of Ruggles's move—the figure was $30,000.[162] That same year, the graduate school at Northwestern received $32,500, and the University of Michigan, $12,349.

While the archival record does not reveal how these funds were spent, it is fair to assume that they were allocated in ways congenial to NELA's aims. We do know that these three institutions—Harvard, Northwestern, and Michigan—would become top-ranked business schools, educating hundreds of students every year, many of them future corporate leaders at home and abroad. (Today HBS boasts of its nearly fifty thousand alumni worldwide, not including graduates of its executive education short courses.) We also know that NELA's contributions were considered significant at the time: images of the checks as submitted into the FTC record were prominently displayed on the front pages of several newspapers, suggesting their scandalous nature.[163]

Such publicity would have been anathema to NELA, whose executives consistently tried to downplay their "educational" role, if not hide it. It is possible that some faculty did not realize their departments accepted funds from a donor with a specific political and ideological agenda; NELA certainly tried its best to make it seem as if the work being developed was the educators' own idea. The way to do that, one executive explained, was to recruit someone on the inside: "I feel that you will not get quite the results you wish if you go direct to the educators yourself. In this State [Colorado], while the idea originated in the committee, it reached the colleges and universities through a man high in educational circles who broached the subject, *without mentioning the public utilities as being interested.* Therefore, the colleges [could think that] on their own volition, [they] developed the idea and the committee [merely] volunteered to render all possible assistance."[164] At Harvard, Ruggles played that role.

In 1930, the HBS *Alumni Bulletin* discussed NELA's academic activities and the FTC investigation, concluding that the FTC disclosures "indicated clearly that the relation to educational institutions and educators of some of the member companies was improper." The *Alumni Bulletin* found that NELA's control of the flow of information stymied academic researchers who wanted to produce objective analyses: "Where information was desired upon intricate problems of finance or operation, the companies seem to have been disinclined to furnish it unless they knew in advance the conclusion at which the educator would arrive and the use of which he would make of it."[165] However, the *Alumni Bulletin* focused not so much on the hit to academic integrity, bad as it was, but on the consequences for future industry support of the school. Educators, it concluded ruefully, were "now afraid to develop any intimacy with a public utility corporation or to approve of its doings lest they be regarded as mere hirelings of the corporations."[166]

THE NELA PROPAGANDA campaign foreshadowed later efforts by the tobacco industry to fight the facts about their products and influence scientific researchers and educators to promote their point of view. Like Big Tobacco, the electricity industry organized ostensibly independent conferences that weren't, recruited academic researchers to lend credibility to misleading arguments, and funded favorable research. There was one major difference, though: the electricity industry had a good product. Used as intended, electricity did not kill people; it made their lives better. But the industry had failed to make it widely available to people who needed and wanted it, and in that sense had failed the American people. Like the tobacco industry, the electricity industry denied its failures, promoted disinformation, and, when confronted with adverse evidence, tried to change the subject to freedom.

On the surface, NELA lost its fight. David Nye concludes that the "public revulsion that the NELA hearings caused put [rural] electrification back on the public agenda . . . and prepared the way for New Deal utility legislation."[167] Jean Christie, the biographer of Morris Llewellyn Cooke, agrees that while Giant Power failed, his and Pinchot's outlook "entered into the New Deal which, on a national scale, carried out many" of their ideas.[168] (In 1935 Cooke became the head of the Rural Electrification Administration.)[169]

On the other hand, Giant Power was soundly defeated in Pennsylvania by conservative legislators who parroted the industry position that Giant Power "not only smelled of socialism but was 'pregnant with the vicious elements of confiscation.' It would lead not only to control of the electricity industry by one man—the governor—but also to America 'following Russia into the dismal swamp of commercial chaos and financial disaster.' "[170]

Moreover, while NELA was discredited and disbanded, it soon regrouped as the Edison Electric Institute, which exists today and remains a powerful political lobby. Its chairman since 2016, Thomas A. Fanning, has denied the reality of human impact on the climate—insisting that observed changes are merely natural variability—and the corporation that Fanning heads, the Southern Company, in Atlanta, Georgia, has until very recently been notorious in its opposition to greenhouse gas reductions.[171] Moreover, despite New Deal rural electrification, the United States today still has a predominantly private electricity system (about 90 percent) that is less strongly regulated than in many other countries. On average customers of publicly owned utilities pay about 10 percent less than customers of investor-owned utilities and receive more reliable service.[172] When attempts were made in the 1990s to deregulate the system entirely, it was a disaster for consumers.[173] The Enron company gamed the system before going bankrupt, and several of its executives went to jail for fraud, conspiracy, and insider trading.[174] Electricity deregulation also proved a disaster for the people of Texas: when the state's power grid failed in the face of an extreme winter storm in 2021, it left more than seven hundred dead and somewhere between $80 and $130 billion in damages.[175]

A century on from NELA's massive disinformation offensive, evidence suggests that the industry's taste for bullying persists. In 2014, the city of Boulder, Colorado, announced it would end its contracts with a private utility—contracts that were expiring—to form its own publicly held municipal utility. The private company served the city with a lawsuit, claiming in effect that Boulder had no legal right to do so—in effect, no freedom of contract. Fearing a protracted and costly fight against a deep-pocketed corporate adversary, the city settled out of court, agreeing to dissolve the municipal utility it had initiated.[176] Such is the power of the private sector in both the American marketplace and the minds of Americans.[177]

It is impossible to know just what happened to the textbooks that NELA promoted in the classroom and placed in libraries, or how the NELA-influenced university curricula evolved over time. But we have found no evidence of any systematic attempt to remove NELA-influenced textbooks from libraries in the wake of the FTC investigation, or that blackballed books were ever reinstated. Nor have we found evidence that any university department took steps to expunge NELA's influence. It is unlikely that any would have: a central part of NELA's strategy was to find, support, and reward faculty whose views already overlapped with its own, and to encourage them to believe they had developed their curricula entirely "on their own volition." Given this, the academic departments that accepted NELA funds would likely see no need for any response. They would have considered the matter one of academic freedom, believing their colleagues were in no way unduly influenced. But the result, at minimum, would have been a weighting of academic debate toward the industry's preferred views, and an anchoring of many academic programs in an antiregulatory intellectual framework.

It is also likely that the NELA campaign helped to squelch alternative perspectives that many intellectuals, particularly outside the United States, considered credible. As historian Michael Bernstein has shown, the economics profession in America is notable for its lack of diversity in intellectual orientation, both in contrast to other social sciences and in contrast to European economics departments. In American economics programs, market fundamentalism for a long time was the dominant order of the day, and in many quarters it still is.[178] NELA may have lost the battle over rural electrification, but it won the war of what would be taught in American business schools.

The NELA campaign not only falsely claimed that private sector electricity was cheaper and more efficient than public sector electricity, it built on arguments made in the debates over child labor and workmen's compensation that government involvement in the marketplace was an un-American infringement on freedom. In doing so, it helped to construct a key plank in the platform of American market fundamentalism and a key factor in the big myth of the Free Market: that the American way of life was inextricably linked to free-market capitalism, and that government engagement in the marketplace threatened that way of life. Perhaps most importantly, NELA pioneered a strategy of insisting that these claims were true, regardless of the facts.

CHAPTER 3

Fighting the New Deal

On October 29, 1929, the New York Stock Exchange collapsed. The Great Crash was the worst one-day loss in the exchange's history. Within weeks, 40 percent of its value evaporated. Wall Street—the icon of American capitalism—appeared to be in free fall. This was market failure on a grand scale, and it ushered in the worst depression in U.S. history.[1]

Herbert Hoover is often cast as a laissez-faire president who stood by haplessly, taking no meaningful action in the face of economic catastrophe.[2] But as commerce secretary for most of the 1920s (under President Warren Harding), he had warned against risky practices in the stock exchange—particularly buying on margin—and had suggested the need for government regulation.[3] However, like most of the American financial community, Hoover expected the market to recover after the crash and the real economy to follow. After all, it was hardly the first stock market crisis in U.S. history—the late nineteenth century had been rife with crashes and panics—and as a Republican who valorized individualism and a minimalist federal government, Hoover was loath to involve Washington in rescuing the economy. But as the stock market and the larger economy failed to "self-correct" and unemployment spread, many people urged him to do *something*. But what?

One place to start was overproduction. A robust economy was a good thing, but American farms and factories were producing more than Americans could afford to buy, leading to a death spiral of falling prices, bankruptcies, and foreclosures. Things were particularly grim in the agricultural sector: food prices had seen steep declines throughout the 1920s. During and after World War I, the United States had done a great deal to mechanize farming, increasing total production. European food production recovered from the war, too, leading to substantial food surplus and little demand for U.S. imports. As farm bankruptcies spread, demand for seeds, farm machinery, petroleum, and other products declined, too, in a cycle of falling prices and falling demand.

Hoover believed the problem could be solved through voluntary measures and "associationalism." Reasonable businessmen could see that overproduction was in no one's interest; Hoover thought they could be persuaded to restore profitability by limiting production, ideally by agreements reached in their trade associations, which by this time many industries had. But Hoover would neither *impose* production limits nor ask Congress for a law to do so—that smacked of centralizing planning. He waited for "The Market" to respond.

It did not. None of Hoover's efforts resolved the farm crises, much less the broader Depression, and in mid-1930 a drought decimated Midwestern farming and, with it, Midwestern banks. Congress passed the Smoot-Hawley Tariff Act of 1930, designed to help manufacturers by imposing stiff import duties, but America's trading partners retaliated, and one potential avenue to agricultural recovery—exporting surplus production—was cut off.

The financial consequences of declining farm revenues and increasing bankruptcies were very different from what they would be today. There was no federal crop insurance. Nor was there federal deposit insurance, so when a bank went bust its depositors lost their money. Farmers whose community banks failed had no way of financing the next year's plantings, so even if an individual farmer had managed to stay afloat, he might yet go under. By law, banking was entirely local. There were some state banks, but there were no national commercial banks, so the loss of a town bank due to farm failures undermined adjacent local businesses as well. A single year of drought could badly damage an agricultural region's economy; a multiyear drought was devastating. That's what happened in the early 1930s when the Dust Bowl hit the Great Plains. Over the course of Hoover's presidency, from 1929 to 1933, one quarter of American farmers lost their land.[4]

Congress attempted to provide loans for seed and livestock, but Hoover fought this, too, on the grounds that lending money to farmers was not a federal function. He similarly fought congressional efforts to support state- and privately run unemployment relief. Hoover had earned a reputation as a humanitarian for effectively leading famine relief in Europe after World War I, but his humanitarianism did not include the use of federal power, or federal funding, for public welfare at home. Instead, he saw federal emergency relief measures as socialist and un-American. In Hoover's worldview, relief should come from local governments and private charities.[5]

As the Depression worsened and Hoover refused to do more, political opposition mounted. In the 1930 midterm election, Republicans barely hung on to the

House of Representatives, and they retained control of an evenly divided Senate only by the vice president's tie-breaking vote.[6] Then, Republicans lost two special elections, and in 1931 Democrats controlled the House.

BY EARLY 1932, it was clear Hoover would face a strong Democratic challenge, but it was not clear who the challenger would be. The best-known potential Democratic candidate was the popular former governor of New York, Alfred E. Smith, but outside New York, Smith was a tough sell. He was Catholic; he represented the urban, largely immigrant working class; and he was "wet"—viewing Prohibition as an assault by the white Protestant majority on the heavily Catholic immigrant minority. Smith wanted the 1932 presidential election to focus on repealing the Eighteenth Amendment; his opponent Franklin Delano Roosevelt wanted to focus on the economy.[7] Roosevelt handily beat Smith for the nomination.

In his acceptance speech, Roosevelt pledged a "new deal for the American people."[8] A major element would be transparency in securities markets, responding to the stock market crash: "the letting in of the light of day on issues of securities, foreign and domestic, which are offered for sale to the investing public . . . Publicity is the enemy of crookedness."[9] The deal would also include large public works programs including soil conservation and reforestation to get Americans back to work, and emergency measures to reduce agricultural oversupply.

Under the New Deal, the federal government would not merely nudge the marketplace; where necessary, it would direct it. FDR knew his opponents would accuse him of promoting socialism, so he warned them that it was *their* approach that threatened the future of capitalism; his goal was not to promote socialism but to forestall it. If the New Deal foundered, "resentment against the failure of . . . Republican leaders to solve our troubles may degenerate into unreasoning radicalism."[10]

The campaign year witnessed increasing bank failures, crescendoing into a national crisis during the four months between Election Day and Inauguration Day (then March 3). Nevada had ordered its banks closed the week before the election to prevent runs. By March, nine more states had done the same; others severely restricted withdrawals. Hoover blamed Roosevelt for the crisis, because the latter refused to announce support for the former's policies, and both Hoover and

Roosevelt sought legal opinions on whether the president had the authority to declare a national bank holiday. They got the same answer: yes, under the Trading with the Enemy Act of 1917. Officials at the Federal Reserve Bank begged Hoover to do it and drafted a bill for congressional approval; he refused. At one A.M. on Monday March 6, 1933—only thirty-six hours after his inauguration—Roosevelt declared the bank holiday and sent the bill to Congress.[11] For a week in March 1933, all banking across the nation was suspended.[12]

Roosevelt's bank holiday began a wave of financial reform. His proclamation was ratified by an Emergency Banking Relief Act passed by Congress on March 9, backed by a promise from the Federal Reserve to provide banks with unlimited currency so withdrawal demands could be met. It was followed by the Banking Act of 1933 (often referred to as the Glass-Steagall Act), which separated commercial from investment banking, created the Federal Deposit Insurance Corporation (FDIC) to protect (small) depositors in commercial banks, and reorganized the Federal Reserve system. (The National Association of Manufacturers would oppose Glass-Steagall on the grounds that it would undermine good banking practices—as if bad banking practices hadn't necessitated the bill in the first place.)[13] Glass-Steagall also enabled the Federal Reserve to limit the interest rates that could be paid on deposits and prohibited interest-bearing checking accounts. As banks reopened, citizens began returning funds (and gold) to them.[14] Reform had restored people's trust in the financial system. The banking crisis had been resolved.

Other reforms included FDR's Securities Exchange Act of 1934, which mandated public disclosure of the financial underpinnings of new stock issues. A six-year-long Federal Trade Commission investigation of utility finance and a parallel Senate Banking Committee investigation of Wall Street culminated in the passage of the Securities and Exchange Act of 1935, which created the Securities and Exchange Commission (SEC) to regulate the nation's financial markets more broadly.[15]

Another area of reform was utilities. Like Gifford Pinchot and Morris Llewellyn Cooke, FDR considered electricity fundamental to national economic development, as well as to quality of life. But electrical utilities stood in the way. Or, more exactly, utility trusts. As states in the early twentieth century had attempted to regulate them, the utilities had turned themselves into holding companies with subsidiaries in several states, effectively immunizing themselves against either federal or state authority. FDR decided to rein in these "power trusts" through federal regulation.[16]

REGULATION WAS MADE politically palatable in part by the 1932 collapse of one of the most infamous trusts, the Middle West Utilities Company. Its founder was Samuel Insull, the Chicago-based industrialist who had financed Thomas Edison's pathbreaking Pearl Street Station—American's first central electricity generation plant—and then become president of NELA in 1897.[17] FDR shed no tears when the Middle West Utilities Company imploded. It gave him the opportunity to remind Americans that trusts like the Insull "monstrosity" were not just huge, but hugely corrupt.[18] Middle West Utilities had exercised "control over hundreds of thousands of operating companies, had distributed securities among hundreds of thousands of investors, and had taken their money to an amount running over one and a half billions of dollars—not millions, but billions!" FDR thundered. They had made "arbitrary write-ups of assets and inflation of vast capital accounts." And they had paid dividends out of capital, while hiding the facts from their investors, who "did not realize that sound subsidiaries had been milked and milked to keep alive the weaker sisters in the great chain." FDR concluded that "the 'new deal,' as you and I know it, can be applied to a whole lot of things. It can be applied very definitely, my friends, to the relationship between the electric utilities on the one hand, and the consumer and the investor on the other."[19]

FDR undertook two major utility reform efforts. The first was to revive the Muscle Shoals project (which the electricity industry had so fervently opposed) as a federally owned and operated utility, part of the new Tennessee Valley Authority (TVA). In some ways, the TVA was similar to Giant Power, and the TVA Act, signed in May 1933, generated a bitter fight between private utilities in the Tennessee Valley and the federal government, a fight that went all the way to the Supreme Court. (The government won.) It also made a public figure out of Republican Wendell Willkie, who led the utility industry campaign against the TVA and would challenge FDR for the presidency in 1940.[20]

The second of these efforts was the Public Utilities Holding Company Act (PUHCA) passed in August 1935. This law included what the utilities perceived as a "death sentence" clause: holding companies would have to prove to the SEC that they provided added value, and if they failed to do so, they would be broken up.[21] The PUHCA has been seen as less controversial than the TVA Act, perhaps because the holding companies largely dismantled themselves rather than waiting for the SEC to do it. But in both cases, utilities deployed the same argument: federal regulation of utilities was an unconstitutional infringement of property rights. At least in the 1930s, the Supreme Court did not agree. One of the lawyers who took the fight to the high court was Willkie.

Willkie had served as in-house counsel for Commonwealth & Southern Corporation, a utility holding company; in 1933 he became its president.[22] The company had utilities in several states, including Alabama Power and the Tennessee Electric Power Company (TEPCO), based in Chattanooga with hydroelectric holdings in eastern Tennessee.[23] The TVA was organized as a government-owned corporation that would take over ownership and operations of the Wilson Dam at Muscle Shoals, Alabama (built by the Army Corps of Engineers in 1918–24), build its own generating and transmission system throughout the seven states of the Tennessee Valley, and sell power directly to consumers and to other utilities. Willkie and the company he represented were in direct conflict with the new agency.

The TVA's arrangement differed from other federal hydropower developments of the era, such as the Hoover Dam, which was originally jointly run by Los Angeles's Department of Water and Power and Southern California Edison in an arrangement that avoided placing the government into direct competition with utilities. The federal government built and owned the Hoover Dam, while the utilities generated and sold electricity under long-term contracts. The TVA could have been developed on that model, but that was not what FDR wanted.

During his time as governor of New York, FDR had struggled with the question of how to set a "fair" price for electricity. Utilities charged residential use differently than they did industrial, and the rates they charged varied by locality. Roosevelt had advocated for creating publicly owned utilities as a yardstick enabling state governments to determine what a fair price actually was. Such benchmarks already existed in other areas of the economy, such as shipbuilding, where the U.S. Navy operated its own shipyards. The U.S. Army also operated powder works, which during World War I had pitted the agency against the DuPont Corporation. (Pierre du Pont had set prices higher than the Army believed justified.)[24] The TVA would be FDR's national yardstick for utility regulation.

The TVA's approach to pricing structures proved to be more innovative than that of the private utilities with which it was ostensibly competing. One of the three commissioners FDR appointed to run the agency, David Lilienthal, believed private utilities were sabotaging themselves by maintaining rates that were too high for most users. Lower rates would encourage higher consumption, which would lead to greater demand and higher profits. To test his theory, Lilienthal had the TVA offer lower rates than the local private utilities. He also negotiated agreements with electrical manufacturers to develop and market home appliances in the TVA catchment, and to offer consumer financing to make them affordable. Willkie's TEPCO cooperated with the appliance program, though not initially the experimental rate program. By the time the results of Lilienthal's experiments were reported, TEPCO had followed the model, developing a new rate structure that offer declining rates for increasing consumption. This "declining block rate" structure would dominate electricity pricing until the 1970s.

Lilienthal was right about rates, but that did not end the conflict between utilities and the TVA, waged both in the realm of public opinion and in the courts. By 1937, there were thirty-four lawsuits against the TVA, three of which made it to the Supreme Court. The Edison Electric Institute, reconstituted from the ruins of NELA, opined that the TVA was "palpably unconstitutional." The courts begged to differ: the TVA won all three cases.[25]

In a speech before the Economic Club of New York in January 1935—with Lilienthal in attendance—Willkie laid out a series of criticisms of the TVA that echoed the misleading NELA claims of the 1920s and presaged arguments that would be used in the future. He revisited the question of relative costs, claiming (again, falsely) that the electricity generated by the Ontario Hydro-Electric Power Commission was more expensive than privately generated electricity. He contended misleadingly that "private initiative [had] advanced electricity to its present place in our home and industrial life," obscuring the reality that government had stepped in where the private sector had failed.[26]

Willkie's "facts" were dubious at best, but he also made an argument on principles, some of which were fair enough. The first was that a government going into business could exempt itself from oversight. The TVA, he argued, had made itself unaccountable to the institutions that regulated private utilities, which was both unfair and unwise. "I favor the regulation of both public utility holding companies and government operations because I believe that human nature is often weak and when men are engaged in non-competitive work, the teachings of the preacher, the priest and the rabbi have not been sufficiently inculcated to impose the required restraint."[27] However, his argument was not in fact that government-owned or government-run utilities should be subject to comparable oversight, but rather that government should not be in business at all, because it could not be expected to regulate itself. This was misleading: "[T]he government" was not one thing; executive branch agencies had congressional oversight, both from Congress directly and from its audit branch, the General Accounting Office (since 2004 known as the Government Accountability Office). Congress wasn't necessarily *willing* to use its oversight powers, but that was true of the commissions that regulated private utilities, too.

The second argument on principle involved property rights. Willkie insisted that the federal government had no role in the marketplace, and that any involvement would threaten property rights and therefore the integrity of capitalism. "The traditional function of government has been to regulate rather than to absorb and commandeer private business, or stifle and strangle it by vieing [*sic*] with it as a competitor," he said. "Upon that condition and their belief in the Constitution of the United States and the decisions of the Supreme Court of the United States, our 300,000 security holders for whom I am Trustee, and more than four and a half million others have invested over $14,000,000,000 in the public utility industry in this country."[28] The TVA's "invasion" of the Tennessee Valley threatened this financial interest by placing the federal government in competition with existing utilities. This was disingenuous, because the lion's share of New Deal programs that Willkie and his conservative allies opposed did not involve the government commandeering private business, but *regulating* it, which, as Willkie noted, had long been accepted as a legitimate governmental function.

It wasn't just the direct competition that offended Willkie, it was government engagement in the marketplace, full stop. In another speech, Willkie claimed that the mere presence of the government stymied utility investment and thus economic recovery: "Utility properties cannot be expanded; rates cannot be reduced; capital expenditures cannot be made against the uncertainties of the threatened invasion of a business by government. Today, one billion dollars of utility property constituting 8 per cent of the entire electric utility property of the United States is rendered unable to finance itself without the assistance of holding company advances because of the mere existence of the Tennessee Valley Authority[.] This

Authority sits as a constant threat and potential invader of the territory of every operating utility company within transmission distance of it."[29]

The TVA *was* a departure from what the U.S. federal government had previously done, and some American public power advocates had taken their developmental model from European "statist" traditions. It was also true that some TVA commissioners, such as the first chair, Arthur Morgan, saw the agency as a utopian vehicle to support planned communities. But that idea garnered little support even within the TVA, much less within the Roosevelt administration, and went nowhere. Furthermore, Willkie's critique flew in the face of several key facts.[30]

Willkie knew perfectly well that other countries had been more successful in broad-based electrification, in part because they viewed electricity as a public good; if some Americans looked to the European model, it was because by many measures it worked better. Willkie also knew that Lilienthal believed the TVA's job was to foster business: the availability of large amounts of cheap power would encourage new private-sector firms and industries and help to expand the regional economy without government calling the shots. Lilienthal saw utilities as a form of infrastructure, similar to roads, bridges, and ports, which traditionally were publicly owned to encourage free commerce; the TVA was entirely consistent with this established federal government role. Rather than engage these arguments, however, and discuss how best to meet the needs of the American people, Willkie revived the tactics of Giant Power's opponents. He branded Roosevelt and Lilienthal "collectivists," contrasting them with traditional American "individualists" like Herbert Hoover and himself. By "collectivists," he implied socialists or communists.

The theme of (American) individualism versus (anti-American) collectivism would run steadily through corporate critiques of the New Deal. There was some truth in it: the advocates of the New Deal were concerned with questions of the common good, how to recover the economy and create collective prosperity. Yet corporate leaders would never admit their own organizations were collectivist, too. Publicly traded corporations, then as now, are owned by groups ("shareholders"), governed by groups ("boards of directors"), and operated by still other groups ("managers," "employees"). They are collective enterprises, but of a particular kind—collectives organized around the profit motive. Alfred Sloan's General Motors was a juggernaut of collectivism, even to the point of financing consumer credit to enable Americans to buy GM cars. DuPont had collectivized its workers into internal, company-supervised unions.

Privately, some New Deal opponents acknowledged this. "A good deal of individual enterprise persists [in America], but an increasing portion of business is corporate collective," one National Association of Manufacturers staffer wrote in 1943. "When we expect the reader to shudder as we warn him of 'creeping collectivism,' he may interpret the term quite differently. He is aware that business tends to be conducted more and more collectively—by corporations or other groups—and isn't greatly disturbed by this trend."[31] Corporate America had proved that collectivism could be a good thing. The contrast Willkie and his allies highlighted was not collectivism versus individualism, but for-profit versus nonprofit.

The TVA was not the only threat to Willkie's for-profit utilities, and possibly not the most serious. The PUHCA threatened utilities with financial regulation to prevent the kinds of abuse the collapse of the Middle West Utilities trust had revealed. This act is often counted as part of the "second New Deal," aimed less at relief than reform. Like the Sherman Anti-Trust Act, PUHCA was intended to foster competition by limiting corporate size. States had been unable to effectively regulate multistate utility companies, whose wealth and political power meant municipal governments could not fight them either.[32]

The FTC investigation of NELA's propaganda campaign had exposed this political power and its corrupting effects. But the utilities were not discouraged; on the contrary, they reprised dishonest tactics. To prevent passage of the PUHCA, for example, an avalanche of telegrams opposing the bill—more than ninety-seven thousand—descended on Congress in the days before a vote on the "death sentence" clause.[33] Most of the telegrams were fake. Congressmen trying to answer them were told by Western Union that the addressees didn't exist. Some names were pulled from telephone directories; other were taken by the Metropolitan Edison Company from the payroll of New York City's railway system. Western Union itself had paid its armies of delivery boys to gather signatures from regular clients.[34] The campaign was astroturf.

These shenanigans were exposed by another congressional investigation, this one led by Senator (later Supreme Court justice) Hugo Black, who documented more than one million dollars spent by five utilities.[35] Other groups had also lobbied against the bill, often through third parties. Several American captains of industry had contributed to nominally grassroots organizations that campaigned against passage, including the Crusaders (an anti-Prohibition organization whose board included Alfred Sloan), the American Taxpayers League (which had long combated the estate tax), the Sentinels of the Republic (an anti–New Deal, antisemitic, and anti-women's-suffrage group that had fought against child labor laws in the 1920s and was closely associated with the du Pont family), and the Farmers' Independence Council of America (ostensibly nonpartisan but closely associated with the Republican party).[36] The lobbying effort did not prevent the PUHCA's passage, but it may have helped to weaken the bill, earlier versions of which would have effectively rendered utility holding companies illegal.

This organized opposition may have influenced FDR, for the administration's next major effort to complete electrification of the United States departed from the TVA model. The Rural Electrification Administration (REA), headed by Morris Llewellyn Cooke, was authorized to make construction loans for wiring and generators, a model that the short-lived Public Works Agency had pioneered.[37] The initial plan called for loans to be made to cooperatives where utilities didn't exist. But the utility companies opposed even that, and often worked to undermine these cooperatives.[38] For example, they would discover where the REA was organizing new co-ops, then promptly string lines through the densest part of town to destroy the co-op's profitability.[39] Frustrated REA officials were hard pressed to condemn these tactics, given that they fostered electrification. On the other hand, they proved, *contra* Willkie, that private utilities *could* electrify rural areas, given motivation. These tactics also proved that utilities could raise more capital than Congress was willing to authorize for the REA; they just needed the spur of government competition to do it. Rural electrification wasn't so much a matter of couldn't, as wouldn't.

In 1936, Congress made the REA permanent, and by 1941, REA cooperatives controlled more distribution mileage than the five largest private utilities. By 1945 it had electrified about half of America's farms, and REA engineers cut the cost of transmission lines by more than half. REA's legal division also helped cooperatives understand state regulation and wrote a model bill to empower them; twenty-three states adopted the bill.[40] In the end, the REA succeeded where the private sector had refused even to try.

Willkie ultimately sold most of his holding company's assets in the Tennessee Valley to the TVA, and in 1940 he ran for president against FDR on an internationalist platform that supported U.S. intervention in the war in Europe. (The Nazi

invasion of France just weeks before the Republican convention helped secure
his nomination.) But Willkie's platform also included shrill anti–New Deal
language. Government engagement with the marketplace was not merely a one-
way ticket to socialism, candidate Willkie warned, but to darkness at noon.[41] "The
free-enterprise system, once lost, cannot be easily regained . . . we shall go down
into the totalitarian pit, and the next generation will struggle in darkness to rise
out of it," he declaimed. "It is getting late. In fact it is just about five minutes to
midnight."[42]

IN EARLY TWENTIETH-CENTURY debates over child labor, workmen's
compensation, and distributing electricity, the opponents of government action
repeatedly turned to the hobgoblins of socialism, communism, and collectivism
to discredit efforts to protect workers and consumers. In the 1930s, FDR's
opponents tried to convince people that—the 1929 crash and Great Depression
notwithstanding—the keys to American success and prosperity were private
enterprise, private property, and individual initiative. By 1934, lawsuits challenging the constitutionality of both the National Recovery Administration—
created by Congress in 1933 under the National Industrial Recovery Act (NIRA)
to encourage industries to establish codes of fair competition, including fair
wages—and the TVA were percolating through the court system, and utilities
were campaigning in Congress against what became the PUHCA. A key group in
these fights was the American Liberty League.[43] (In 1935, the Supreme Court
would find NIRA unconstitutional.)

One of the League's founders was John J. Raskob. He had started his career with
the DuPont Company, helping Pierre du Pont buy the family firm from his parents
in 1902. When the company took over General Motors in 1915 (after GM's president, William Crapo Durant, imperiled it through financial miscreance), Raskob
became GM's chief financial officer.[44]

In business history, Raskob is famous for his role in creating GM's revolutionary
auto financing arm, the General Motors Acceptance Corporation (GMAC), which
helped shape American car culture as we know it. He directed the corporation that
built the Empire State Building.[45] And he was a promoter of individual stock
ownership: Raskob believed public support was necessary for capitalism to thrive,
so all Americans should be (literally) invested in it.

Raskob was also interested in politics, particularly the fight against Prohibition. In 1926, with the support of the du Pont brothers—Pierre, Irénée, and Lammot—he breathed new life into the largest repeal advocacy group, the Association Against the Prohibition Amendment (AAPA).[46] Pierre du Pont served as president of the organization in 1927, and in 1928, Raskob stepped down from GM to become Al Smith's campaign manager in his bid for the Democratic presidential nomination on an anti-Prohibition platform.[47]

Aside from seeing Prohibition as fundamentally anti-Catholic and anti-immigrant, Smith viewed it as a violation of state, local, and property rights. Raskob agreed: many alcohol manufacturers and distributors had lost their businesses when the Eighteenth Amendment passed.[48] Pierre du Pont claimed the central issue was not property rights per se, but "the right of the majority to interfere with the liberties of a minority."[49] Chief among these was the liberty of a businessman to run a business.

The AAPA thrived despite Smith's loss in 1928 (and again in 1932). With wealthy backers from both the Republican and Democratic parties, it ran a major effort to shift public opinion in the wet direction. In February 1933, Congress sent a repeal amendment to the states, and by December the required thirty-six states had ratified. President Roosevelt announced repeal on December 5, 1933, the same day the final three states needed (Ohio, Pennsylvania, and Utah) voted in favor.

Between Prohibition's passage and its repeal, however, a lot had changed in American life. The Depression was in full force, and with it the New Deal response. Raskob's closest allies, the du Pont brothers, were patrician conservatives who had supported Roosevelt during the campaign but quickly turned against him. Raskob began organizing a new group to fight the "radical drift" of the New Deal and "to advocate the restoration and preservation of the fundamental principles of the Constitution."[50]

Raskob and the du Ponts were particularly incensed by the new National Labor Relations Board (NLRB).[51] Pierre du Pont had responded to labor unrest within his company by establishing in-house unions with limited authority. Negotiations were undertaken plant by plant, which helped du Pont maintain control. But decisions made in Washington were going against him. Labor organizations wanted company-wide, even industry-wide, collective bargaining rights, and they were getting them from the NLRB.

In June and July 1934, Raskob met with GM and DuPont executives to organize the effort to resist the New Deal, particularly what they viewed as its assault on property rights. Irénée du Pont suggested calling the organization the "Property Holders' Association," but that made its purpose a bit too transparent.[52] Alfred Sloan's preferred name was the "Association Asserting the Rights of Property," which was pretty transparent, too. Raskob thought the word *integrity* should appear in the name. A later draft of incorporation called it "The Union Asserting the Integrity of Persons and Property."[53] By the time it was publicly announced in August 1934, it had become the American Liberty League.

The group was founded to "defend and uphold the Constitution of the United States and to gather and disseminate information that will: (1) Teach the necessity of respect for the rights and integrity of persons and property as fundamental to every successful form of government, and (2) Teach the duty of government to encourage and protect individual and group initiative and enterprise, to foster the right to work, earn and save, and acquire property, and to preserve the ownership and lawful use of property when acquired."[54] For these propertied men, property rights were paramount, and there wasn't much that couldn't be framed in terms of the protection of those rights. Strikes deprived factory owners of the right to use their property as they wished. Securities were a form of property, so securities regulation was an infringement, too. The Tennessee Valley Authority placed the federal government in competition with private utilities, which infringed the property rights of those utilities by (potentially) reducing the value of their assets. But their argument went further: it wasn't *just* property rights that were at stake. It was freedom. It was the foundation of the nation.

Following Hoover and Willkie, these industrial barons insisted that any compromise of property rights would trigger a slide down a slippery slope. In June 1934, one GM executive hyperbolized that if present trends continued, "representative government will become mob government and not only will property rights be repudiated but what is equally if not more important, all of our other constitutional guarantees will also be lost, including free speech, the right of trial by jury, and the other provisions of the first ten amendments of the constitution."[55] This privileging of economic rights coupled with the slippery-slope argument—the idea that once property rights were compromised, other rights would ultimately be lost entirely—soon became a cornerstone of twentieth-century American conservative thought.

For the remainder of their lives, the du Ponts and Raskob would demand "restoration of Constitutional government."[56] By this they meant the Constitution as enacted in 1789, without the amendments that had been passed since then including, notably, the Thirteenth, Fourteenth, and Fifteenth. The Constitution they wished to "restore" was one that allowed voting rights only to property-holding white men—prior to Emancipation, prior to female suffrage. In 1948, Pierre du Pont would write to a friend that "it was a mistake to give negroes a vote, and it is also a mistake to give all white men and women a vote; that is, if we are to have good government."[57] Their ideal government was a plutocracy of propertied white men.

LIKE NELA IN the 1920s, the American Liberty League's task was to "educate" the public about the benefits of unregulated markets and business freedom. It launched an extensive propaganda campaign to convince Americans to oppose New Deal labor reforms, utility and financial regulation, and relief and fiscal policies—and, above all, to persuade people that these policies threatened their freedom. The league's principal vehicle was a series of pamphlets—135 in its first two years—sent to hundreds of newspapers, thousands of public libraries, and all members of Congress; occasionally they were presented as speeches. The pamphlets generated an enormous amount of what today would be called "earned media": news items, editorial comments, and radio time. The league estimated the pamphleteering effort gained it two hundred thousand news stories in its first two years.[58]

The league's leaders understood that they were engaged in a symbolic as well as a substantive conflict, and they strove to infuse traditional American symbols with meanings that suited their purposes. As FDR's 1944 "Four Freedoms" speech would underscore, freedom can be construed in many ways, including freedom from want and fear.[59] The league worked to a different understanding of the concept.

The U.S. Constitution placed life and liberty before property in its enumeration of the rights that could not be denied without due process of law. Liberty is apart from—and arguably larger than—property. It's not clear if that order was meant to imply priority, but it is reasonable to suggest that life was paramount, liberty next, and property third. Certainly, the founding fathers did not think liberty could be *reduced* to the protection of property. So the league needed to find a way to privilege property rights over other concerns. They did this by equating property rights with liberty—that liberty was property and vice versa—and by associating the symbols and language of American freedom with their specific interpretation. "Unless . . . the symbols of the old America are projected to [the public] through all the means at the hands of public education," league leaders wrote in an internal report, "there may be a real danger that the left wing projects symbols of greater belief and validity to them. If freedom and equal opportunity and property rights lose their meanings as words or ideas, and such phrases as 'redistribution of wealth' and 'New Deal' gain new and diverse meanings, they can carry great consequences for the present order."[60]

To hone its message, the league enlisted Edward L. Bernays, often considered the founder of modern public relations.[61] Bernays was a nephew of Sigmund Freud and author of the influential 1928 book *Propaganda*; he had also been a consultant to NELA. As its title suggests, Bernays's book codified persuasion as propaganda (and vice versa). Previously the word had been mostly understood in political terms—particularly wartime propaganda—but now it would be associated with various forms of cultural persuasion. In 1929, Bernays had mounted Light's Golden Jubilee, officially a celebration of the fiftieth anniversary of the light bulb but actually a drive to promote General Electric and advance NELA's goal of keeping electric power in private hands.[62] Bernays was also responsible for the infamous Torches of Freedom campaign, cynically (and fatally) encouraging women to smoke cigarettes as a symbol of feminist autonomy. A few years later, as part of a promotional effort for Lucky Strike, he would get the fashion industry to adopt forest green as the season's top color so the cigarettes' distinctive green packages would match the latest styles.[63]

The dominant theme of American Liberty League materials was "freedom"— the league was fighting for it while the New Deal threatened it—and a particular target was the Roosevelt administration's alleged "regimentation" of American life.[64] This critique focused on the Agricultural Adjustment Act (AAA) and the National Industrial Recovery Act (NIRA), both of which were passed in 1933.[65] The AAA endeavored to raise prices for agricultural products by limiting supply, and thereby help suffering farm families and restore the nation's agricultural economy. Because agricultural overproduction played a central role in triggering the Depression, the AAA permitted extreme measures, including empowering the administration to buy and destroy excess crops and livestock and to limit the amounts and kinds of crops and livestock that farmers could produce. No doubt it was heartbreaking for farmers to see good livestock put down and be told not to grow crops, but what offended the American Liberty League was not the damage to the farmer's pride, nor the waste of life, but Washington's "regimentation" of production and commerce.

Herbert Hoover made the same argument in his 1934 book *The Challenge to Liberty*. As the New Deal developed, Hoover's critiques became more severe: the new programs, even if not intentionally totalitarian, would destroy American liberty. "In our blind groping," Hoover wrote, "we have stumbled into philosophies which lead to the surrender of freedom. The proposals before our country do not necessarily lead to the European forms of Fascism, Socialism, or Communism, but they certainly lead definitely from the path of liberty." This was a slippery slope, for "a step away from liberty itself impels a second step [and] a second step compels a third . . . A few steps so dislocate social forces that some form of despotism becomes inevitable and Liberty dies."[66] Before the 1930s were out, the proposition that any compromise to economic freedom would *inevitably* lead to despotism—and that political and economic freedom were therefore *inseparable*—would become one of the fundamental tenets of market fundamentalism's big myth.

Like the league, Hoover used the word "regimentation" to name his fears of a totalitarian takeover. "For any plan of regimentation to succeed, it must have not only powers of rigid discipline, but adamant continuity." How could the government impose discipline on a large and diversified population, without suppressing freedom? It could not. In a democracy "such a course is impossible. Fascism and Sovietism have suppressed both free speech and representative government." And that was where the United States, under the New Deal, was heading.[67]

This understanding of "regimentation" was likely drawn from Bernays, who wrote in 1928 that propaganda *"regiment[s]* the public mind every bit as much as an army regiments the bodies of its soldiers."[68] In a pattern that would later become commonplace, Hoover accused his political opponents of precisely the same tactics that he and his allies were engaged in—in this case under the guidance of the world's foremost expert.

The notion of the military regiment, where power lies in the central command, captivated Hoover. "The first step of economic Regimentation is a vast centralization of power in the Executive," he declared, offering a laundry list of New Deal actions that he believed threatened liberty.[69] These included the use of federal power to set the value of currency, levy sales taxes, fix minimum prices, establish minimum wages, fix maximum hours and conditions of labor, and mandate collective bargaining. Whether or not this was a fair characterization of Roosevelt and the New Deal, it was breathtakingly hypocritical, because American business leaders had never objected to regimentation when they were the ones behind it.

"Scientific management"—a.k.a. Taylorism—as adopted by many leading industries in the early twentieth century was regimentation of the labor force using scientific techniques. Managers expected workers to perform the same task, in the same optimized way, every single time. There was no freedom here, no individual initiative, no "liberty" to innovate a new, possibly better technique. At best, Taylorism sacrificed workplace satisfaction for efficiency; at its worst, it destroyed craft skills and treated workers as automatons.[70] But for Hoover and the American Liberty League, it was easy to segue from decrying "regimentation" to painting FDR as a would-be, or even actual, dictator: fascist or communist, and sometimes both.[71] One member of the league protested, "We have now in fact, although not in form, a totalitarian socialistic state."[72] Said another, "Cannot you now understand that Roosevelt desires to pass laws utterly destructive of liberty . . . ? Neither Mussolini nor Hitler, nor Stalin of Russia, have gone so far."[73]

One may question whether seasoned businessmen such as Alfred Sloan or Pierre du Pont really believed that FDR wanted to make himself dictator of America. Roosevelt had made his own wealth on the stock market, after all—he was a businessman, too. Historians have concluded that the vitriol leveled at FDR reflects an aristocracy that felt itself to be under attack by one of its own—"*that man* in the White House."[74] To them, Roosevelt was a class traitor, a wealthy man who threatened the status quo that had enabled his (and their) own rise to power.[75]

IN PREPARATION FOR the 1936 election, the American Liberty League produced a pamphlet outlining a proposed congressional program. It would end deficit spending by transferring most relief spending to the states; cut taxes; reject "inflationary currency proposals and politically oriented banking measures"; and restore the gold standard.[76] All New Deal economic planning legislation would be defeated in favor of "withdraw[ing] the government from competition with private business." The PUHCA's "death sentence" provision would be repealed and "the socialistic activities of the TVA" curtailed; New Deal agencies should be investigated and abolished; and Congress would "reassert its responsibility for preserving the Constitution and the traditional form of government."[77]

But whose traditions were they defending? Not the traditions of American farmers or workers. The vast majority of the league's funds came from a handful of businessmen (thirty of them, during the 1936 election campaign, to be exact), making it easy for FDR in his convention speech to paint them as "economic royalists." The U.S. postmaster general, James A. Farley, would call them the "du Pont Liberty League."[78]

For the 1936 Democratic nomination, the league supported Al Smith, who by this time was now explicitly accusing FDR of socialism—and conflating that with Soviet communism. At a league dinner that year, Smith declared: "Just get the platform of the Democratic Party and get the platform of the Socialist Party and lay them down on your dining-room table, side by side," and you would see they were the same. Americans needed to oppose this: "There can be only one capital. Washington or Moscow. There can be only one atmosphere of government, the clear, pure, fresh air of free America, or the foul breath of communistic Russia. There can be only one flag, the Stars and Stripes or the flag of the godless Union of the Soviets."[79]

Only a few years before, Smith himself had been tarred as a socialist by the same reactionaries with whom he was now aligned. At that time, he had observed that plutocrats invoked socialism "to put a damper on progressive legislation" and undermine any reform they did not like. "Is that cry of socialism anything new? Not to a man of my experience. I have heard it raised by reactionary elements and the Republican party . . . for over a quarter century."[80] Now Smith had embraced that reaction.

In the end, Smith failed to unseat FDR, and in the general election the league threw its weight behind Republican Alf Landon, who won only two states. By 1940, the league was defunct. On one level, the league was an abject failure. If anything, its efforts to undermine Roosevelt backfired. One Roosevelt biographer argues that the conservative revolt drove his swerve to the left during 1935 and 1936: as his former business allies abandoned and vilified him, FDR was forced to seek allies in labor and social welfare organizations.[81] On another level, however, the league was extremely successful: It effectively articulated a set of arguments that would circulate and influence conservative thinking into the twenty-first century.[82] "Liberty" was now the watchword of American conservatism, and freedom would be defined above all as economic freedom. In the 1930s and into the '40s, a familiar group of free-market evangelists—the National Association of Manufacturers—would devote its considerable resources to developing these ideas into a new and more potent form.

CHAPTER 4

The Tripod of Freedom

The 1930s were not good for American business. Not in terms of profits, and not in terms of political influence. One group in particular worried about its political future: the National Association of Manufacturers (NAM). Since the crash of 1929, NAM had hemorrhaged members. In the early 1920s, the association counted more than five thousand companies as members; by 1933, that number had dropped to under fifteen hundred and resignations were averaging sixty-five a month.[1] The organization might have collapsed, but a new group of executives—mostly from large corporations and replacing the small businessmen who had led NAM in the 1920s—took over, with a bold idea to increase membership and their political power. They would do so not merely by fighting specific New Deal initiatives, but by framing the lessons people drew from the Depression experience. Like NELA and the American Liberty League before them, they intended to change how their countrymen thought about capitalism and its role in America.

The leaders of this effort were known as the "brass hats," a group of industrialists who were troubled that "radicals" and "demagogues" were supplanting genteel businessmen as leaders of the nation.[2] NAM already had a long history of working to prevent business regulation by state or federal governments and, above all, fighting unions.[3] Its leaders had pursued their goals through a news bureau, a speaker series, and requests that their members only advertise in outlets with antiunion views.[4] But the brass hats envisaged a broader and more aggressive program as a vital voice in public debate. This meant, above all, persuading the American people of the free-market system's virtues. Industry, NAM's new leaders argued, was responsible for American prosperity; business owners, CEOs, and industrial managers should be seen as heroes. The difficulty was that few people saw it this way, thus business leaders had a responsibility to "educate" them. After decades of journalistic muck-raking, trust-busting, and other attacks on Big Business, it was time for the public to hear *their* side.

NAM launched an ambitious campaign to win support for business. "The public does not understand industry, largely because industry itself has made no real effort to tell its story; to show people of this country that our high living standards have risen almost altogether from the civilization which industrial activity has set up," NAM's president declared.[5] He cited the tobacco industry propagandist, Edward Bernays—who was also advising the American Liberty League—as the sort of authority whose help NAM should (and later would) seek.

The program would also fight back against what the brass hats viewed as radicalism masquerading as reform. "The spirit of progressive-ness has gone wild. Radicalism in America . . . is dashing in higher and higher waves against the walls of constitutional government. The ultimate object of radicalism, of whatever complexion or degree or name, is to destroy the institutions of private property . . . The favorite and most conspicuous target of the radical is . . . the manufacturer," and so manufacturers needed to band together.[6]

NAM's "education" efforts centered around a massive campaign to persuade the American people that big business's interests were the American people's interests. Americans needed to see that the real threat came not from "Big Business," but from "Big Government." While NAM took care to call the campaign "public relations" or "education," its goals were overtly political and much of what was said was untrue.[7]

It took a few years for NAM's efforts to crystallize, but when they did, they proved more ambitious than the American Liberty League's assault on FDR and the New Deal, Wendell Willkie's defense of private utilities, and even the NELA propaganda campaign against Giant Power. In the words of historian Wendy Wall, NAM now "tried to convince the American public that their interests and those of the nation's largest corporations were virtually indistinguishable. Painting a picture of class harmony and consumer prosperity—guaranteed by business, not by government—they dubbed this image 'the American Way.'"[8]

NAM would attack federal taxation as not merely misguided, but as theft. It would try to shift workers' view of government from a "friend" offering a "helping hand during the Depression" to an obstacle to prosperity.[9] It would introduce the idea that the threat to American life was not "Big Business," but "Big Government." And, as historian Lawrence Glickman has shown, NAM made a subtle but significant rhetorical shift from championing "*private* enterprise" (or sometimes "competitive enterprise") to "*free* enterprise."[10] ("Private," one memo noted, was associated with selfishness, so rather than discuss private ownership, it would be better to say "business management.")[11] Capitalism was about *freedom*, NAM would insist, and the survival of American democracy was at stake. Democracy depended on capitalism, and the people who should be trusted to guide the ship were the captains of American industry.[12]

Historian Richard Tedlow credits NAM with bringing the field of corporate public relations into its modern form. NAM's attacks instilled in business leaders the conviction that "the cultivation of favorable public opinion was a matter of such importance that it should be delegated to a specific department staffed by experts."[13] But NAM's program went beyond touting a particular manufacturer or American manufacturers in general. It was designed to alter public thinking about major political and social questions—such as the role of government in the marketplace—and to construct a story of American life that placed free enterprise at its heart. And it did this with information that was often partial, and frequently misleading.

THE PROPAGANDA CAMPAIGN would be the task of two groups, the NAM Public Relations Advisory Committee, which had already existed for some time, and the National Industrial Information Council (NIIC), established in 1934. The latter was set up ostensibly as a statistical bureau to collect and distribute data about private enterprise to newspapers as well as members, but it played a major role in the propaganda campaign.[14] Extensive, multifaceted, and well funded, the campaign exploited a range of media: films and slide shows, newspaper advertisements, direct mail, billboards, posters, pamphlets, window displays, and more. One poster featured a picture of the Devil, labeled "Hidden Tax." A pamphlet entitled "At school—not at work" explained "How industry has freed our children from drudgery," taking credit for eliminating child labor when in fact NAM and its allies had fought its abolition.[15]

The two committees distributed "statistics" to newspapers (often published as "Industrial Facts"), as well as editorial features and columns via its *Six Star Service*, published under the rubric "You and Your Nation's Affairs."[16] NAM recruited and paid pro-business journalists and academic economists to write many of these items. The targeted audiences included schools, churches, and civic and women's groups; employee relations campaigns also targeted NAM members' workers. The key message, as one NIIC document summarized, was to promote the "system of free enterprise" and contrast it with its alternative: "a planned economy [that] leads eventually to totalitarianism."[17]

According to the Hagley Library, in Wilmington, Delaware (where the NAM archives are located), NIIC circulated "2 million copies of cartoons, 4.5 million copies of newspaper columns written by pro-business economists, 2.4 million foreign language news pieces and 11 million employee leaflets. It also displayed 45,000 billboards, which were seen by an estimated 65 million Americans daily, while its film series was viewed by approximately 18 million."[18] In 1933, the population of the United States was 126 million; these numbers suggest that at least half of all Americans were exposed to the NAM message.

Over the next two decades, NAM advanced the proposition that government was inefficient and badly run, but the private sector was efficient and well run. Terms used to discredit government included "wasteful public spending," "extravagant government," and "flagrant waste." In contrast, the "free-enterprise system" was associated with "prosperity" and "material progress." Americans had more—consumed more—than people in any other country thanks to the efficiency and creativity of business leaders working in the free-enterprise system. Technological progress was credited (solely) to the ingenuity and efforts of the private sector. "Where is the family spinning wheel?" one brochure asked rhetorically, before going on to explain that the progress of technology was the product of private initiative. The same brochure asserted that advances in science, in medicine, in education, and in recreation and culture were all the result of "our system" of "productive enterprise."[19] It was industrial productivity and enterprise capitalism that made social progress possible, yielding the cornucopia that was modern America.

NAM linked this to a broader argument referred to as the "Fight for Freedom!"[20] It produced copious materials on the "Perils of Centralized Government," the threat of "isms"—both socialism and communism, which NAM generally framed as indistinguishable—and the problem of "inequitable labor laws, and other threats to [business] freedom." Any government activity into the marketplace—whether through price supports to farmers, restrictions on child labor, or protections for collective bargaining—was a threat to freedom, a threat to the American way of life.[21]

One NIIC brochure summarized the campaign for NAM members. The plan was twofold. A short-range program would "attack the most urgent immediate threats to American enterprise . . . price controls, inequitable labor laws, and wasteful government spending." A second "continuing basic program, directed to all Americans on their own ground," would "counteract the 'opposition's' greatest asset—public misconceptions about industrial profits"—which were not nearly so large as most people supposed—and convince "the American people that the American enterprise system produces the greatest good for all people without destroying individual freedom." This would be done "through all effective media," meaning advertising, radio, speakers, newspaper publicity, newsletters of "farm-industry cooperation," home and industry conferences, a "trends in education–industry cooperation" newsletter, a youth program called "Tomorrow's Citizens," films, literature, and community relations programs. Everything was designed to "reach people in their own communities," through the efforts of NAM staff and the 330 industrial associations with which NAM was affiliated.[22]

Heading the effort in the 1940s was the chair of NIIC, Sun Oil Company president J. Howard Pew. The effort was enormous. NIIC boasted of a six-advertisement series that ran in 521 daily and 1,980 weekly newspapers, reaching nearly 44 million readers, followed by "a flood of press releases, 250,000 pieces of supplemental literature, 115,262 reprint posters, and 275 individually sponsored advertisements." *It's Your Business*, a fifteen-minute radio program, ran on 196 stations to reach nearly 12 million listeners. (Stations would often donate the time for this as a "public service.")[23] NIIC also counted a weekly clip sheet sent to 4,600 weekly and 500 daily papers, as well as 2,700 "house organs." Materials went to 1,750 editorial writers, business columnists, and radio commentators.

In 1940, NAM created a series of "16 beautiful posters which prove that the American way of life is the best way of life." Each poster told a story explaining why the "American economic system . . . is best suited to the needs of our great society," and they were made available "to schools, clubs and social agencies *without charge*."[24] The message of these posters was that:

1. America is the best country on Earth.
2. American business generates unprecedented prosperity.

3. Therefore, the interests of business and labor are the same; unions are not necessary and in fact mislead workers.

4. The real threat to workers' interest is taxation.

These themes were reprised in various forms for various audiences. One poster series was designed specifically for NAM members' factories, intended to complement pamphlets explaining to workers why a "Shorter Work Week Will Limit Earnings" and how the "Cost of Government Raises Your Taxes."[25] These posters and pamphlets argued that taxation of corporate profits was bad for workers, because it blocked management from using profits to expand factories (costing jobs) and because high taxes increased prices (hitting workers' pocketbooks). They also asserted that unionization protected lazy people, making it harder for management to reward hard workers. After the outbreak of World War II, NAM rolled back its previous isolationist messaging and launched a "National Defense Series"; posters were augmented by a radio program, *Defense for America*, glorifying American capitalism for giving workers sick leave and paid vacation and abolishing child labor—even though most of NAM's members had fought these innovations—and counting schools, hospitals, parks, roads, and bridges as part of the "real wealth of all Americans"—even while NAM bitterly fought the taxes that helped to make these public amenities possible.[26]

By 1946, NIIC estimated that its monthly "Program Notes" went to 59,000 women's clubs around the nation. Its *Trends in Education–Industry Cooperation* newsletter went to 36,500 education leaders. And its "You and Industry" materials—part of the "Tomorrow's Citizens" program—went out to a staggering 4 million teachers.[27]

EDWARD BERNAYS STRESSED that, for maximum efficacy, propaganda should be both continuous and, as much as possible, invisible. NAM followed this advice as it developed a program in "integration propaganda"—material designed to be integrated into a news story without the reader realizing its source or recognizing its intent. Tedlow estimates that in 1937 alone, NAM spent more than $793,000 on "public information" designed to work as integration propaganda (the equivalent of about $14 million today).[28] These expenditures constituted 55 percent of the organization's total income that year, and continued to rise in subsequent years.[29]

From the mid-1930s through the 1940s, NAM ran an "Industrial Press Service," sending a steady stream of materials to media outlets, particularly local and regional newspapers, in hopes that elements would be incorporated into stories. Outlets across the country received business news, statistics, graphics, opinion pieces by academics—particularly economists—and cartoons. Often these materials were offered in easy-to-use, camera-ready format but with no identification of their source, so while the editor would know the materials came from NAM, the reader would not.[30] One NAM pamphlet in 1938 boasted that 5,500 newspapers around the country "depended on this service."[31] A 1939 congressional investigation put the number higher: 6,252 weekly and small daily papers.[32]

NAM also pulled editors in with an early version of push-polling. In one case, editors of small weekly newspapers were surveyed to "see if they thought there was needless spending in their communities." From forty-seven states, 961 editors responded to the (leading) question: "What broad activities of government might now be reasonably curtailed?" Among the top answers: the Works Progress Administration, the Agricultural Adjustment Act and aid to farmers, and the Civilian Conservation Corps. NAM compiled the responses under the rubric of "Grassroots Criticism of Extravagant Government" in a 1941 report summarizing "Opinions Backed by Facts on Wasteful Public Spending," which it sent back to the editors to inspire stories and editorials.[33]

NAM also offered materials to major urban papers, including the *New York Times*. By the 1930s, the *Times* had established a reputation for accurate and objective reporting. Yet NAM had astonishing success seeding the *Times* with integrated messages aimed at political, business, and thought leaders. In an analysis of *New York Times* articles during the period 1937–39, historian Burton St. John found fifty stories that positively engaged with NAM themes. He identified three recurring themes consistent with NAM messaging: (1) an activist government is dangerous; (2) industry is best suited to lead the country; and (3) free enterprise is essential to democracy. These messages denied the federal government's role in economic recovery, attempting instead to bind Americans "to the pre-Depression ideal of the supremacy of the markets."[34] In 1937, the *Times* printed the conference platform from NAM's annual meeting in full, including the proposition "that heavy taxation, high federal deficits, state competition with private enterprise and intrusive labor laws all served as 'stop signals' that impeded the country's progress. All citizens needed to work together to remove these stop signals."[35] The *Times*'s articles on the conference reinforced this message of government inefficiency and the disadvantages of high taxation.

Any major newspaper might cover the annual meeting of a major trade organization. What stands out about the *Times*'s coverage is the amount of space given to the NAM meetings, the way in which the paper quoted large portions of NAM platforms verbatim without analysis or critique, and the lack of comment from other major organizations or influential individuals.[36] The *Times* cited NAM officials without remarks from representatives of labor organizations or the Roosevelt administration, even when the claims on offer were patently self-serving, such as a 1938 article quoting one executive declaring, "We have no selfish objectives."[37]

If the *New York Times* demonstrates NAM's success with highbrow editors and audiences, the *Uncle Abner Says* cartoon speaks to NAM's outreach to mass audiences. Presumably exploiting the beloved *Li'l Abner* comic strip—America's most popular cartoon of the period—*Uncle Abner Says* was a single-box cartoon, developed by NAM, featuring a grumpy old guy commenting cynically on government. "All shirk and no work makes Jack a sit-down striker," Uncle Abner grumbled, and "Seems t'me business could stand on its own feet a lot better if'n politicians would get off'n its back."[38] The cartoon—touted by NAM as a "daily feature" containing "homely homespun comments"—was developed originally as an insert for manufacturing plant publications, but was soon being printed (along with other NAM materials) in hundreds of regional and local newspapers. *Uncle Abner Says* ran regularly in an estimated 309 daily newspapers with a circulation of more than two million, with reprints reaching as many as five million.[39] One source described Uncle Abner as "one of America's most popular comic features."[40]

Uncle Abner's reach outstripped that of another 1930s reactionary icon: *Little Orphan Annie*, which during that decade was distributed to 135 daily and 100 Sunday papers.[41] The *New Republic* had dubbed the red-haired gamine "Hooverism in the Funnies," viewing her as part of a campaign to make "martyrs out of millionaires." Every day, this "idol of thousands of children" performed "heroic service in the cause of Andrew W. Mellon, Samuel Insull, and other persecuted philanthropists."[42] Curmudgeonly Uncle Abner was the antithesis of an adorable little girl, but his message was the same: industrialists were benevolent, they knew what they were doing, and government should leave them the heck alone.

The Uncle Abner cartoon contributed to NAM's program of shaping public opinion through print media, including bulletins to editors, prepackaged news stories, and the *You and Your Nation's Affairs* newsletter, which "popularized economics for the masses."[43] NAM insisted that it labeled the sources of all its "educational" materials, but at least in the case of the cartoons that was untrue: *Uncle Abner Says* was printed with only the signature of the cartoonist who drew them and no indication that NAM authored the captions, let alone that NAM had developed the series and supplied it free of charge. NAM's defense was that many other groups did this, too, and that the Uncle Abner series was just "one very small phase" of its much larger "educational" program.[44] But as one contemporary observer noted, "the comic strip is to the newspaper what the kettledrum is to the orchestra, 'the conductor from the rear,'" and the score they followed was largely Herbert Hoover's.[45] The "funnies" offered "facile optimism" alongside the determined conviction that unemployment is always "due to temporary mischance or to some personal weakness" and never to structural problems in American monopolistic capitalism. Uncle Abner differed from other cartoons only in being directly financed and commissioned by capitalists and being more heavy-handed in its messaging than most.[46]

FOR A HISTORIAN, it is always easier to show what people did than to prove what impact their actions had. The archives document NAM's activities in fine detail, but only rarely record how they affected and inspired others. However, one example of NAM's influence can be found in a 1949 sermon delivered by Walter R. Courtenay, a copy of was kept in NAM files as an example of effective outreach and shows how NAM propaganda was absorbed downstream.[47]

Courtenay was a Presbyterian minister in Nashville, Tennessee, and his sermon, entitled "The Road Ahead," was published in the *Presbyterian Tower*, a church newsletter. He took his title from a book of the same name by journalist John T. Flynn, one of the founders of the isolationist and antisemitic America First Committee, which sought to keep the United States out of World War II. With its telling subtitle, *America's Creeping Revolution*, Flynn's book—published that year—was a paranoid declensionist narrative of America's path to self-inflicted destruction. American socialists were operating "behind the mask" of unionism, national planning, demands for racial equality, and calls for World Peace.[48] Financed by American Liberty League cofounder John Raskob, excerpted in the *Reader's Digest*, and heavily promoted by NAM, Flynn's book outlined the alleged means by which New Deal policies were leading America down the slippery slope to socialism and, from there, to totalitarian communism.[49]

An essential element of the socialist agenda, Flynn asserted, was "The War on the South." In a blatantly racist chapter, Flynn characterized "the problem of the Negro and his position" as an "irritant." Socialists and communists deliberately focused attention on the South, he alleged, in order to discredit America as a whole. "First of all," he wrote, "the lurid and sensationalist stories about lynchings and hatreds and suppressions and oppressions have been outrageously exaggerated. It is a fact that almost all of the publicity about the outrages against Negros in the South has originated in the propaganda agencies of the Communist trouble-makers."[50] Give Black people equal rights, he warned, and in many areas of the South there would soon be "Negro supremacy."[51]

Such blatant racism troubled Reverend Courtenay not at all. Framing his Sunday service as a "defense of the free-enterprise system," Courtenay instructed his parishioners that *The Road Ahead* "ought to be read by every American, and certainly by every Christian." Most of the sermon focused on the "sickness of socialism." Following Flynn, Courtenay insisted that socialists would never *admit* they were socialists, but would instead "talk about welfare, pensions, insurance, socialized medicine, aid to education, aid to the farmer." (In fact, socialized medicine neither existed in America nor was it being proposed at that time.) Socialism in America was "already well advanced" as Americans were "being sold down a river."

The sermon culminated in an attack on government, which was "no longer our servant [but] our master." The state had "invaded" banking, electric power, and agriculture, and proposed to take over medicine, education, and "anywhere else it can interfere with free enterprise and democratic liberties." Courtenay implored parishioners to follow Flynn's advice and reject handouts, wasteful government spending, and, above all, planning. "I would personally rather see my nation die cleanly under the H-bomb than rot away under socialism," he declared. "A social planner in Washington differs not at all from one in Moscow or London."[52] Better dead than red.

Courtenay also implored his flock not to vote for the party of FDR. It was his "personal conviction that the Democratic Party has lost its soul to these men who seek the death of our American Way of Life. I do not see how any serious-minded person who wants the free-enterprise system and democracy continued can again vote for this party." Democrats were causing "the death of Uncle Sam," he concluded. "What are you going to do about it?"[53] Courtenay's jeremiad—preserved in the NAM archives—shows how NAM propaganda made its way through mouthpieces like Flynn to local leaders like Courtenay to be heard by ordinary Americans on an otherwise uneventful Sunday morning.

Ministers were a key target for NAM materials, but potentially even more important audiences were schoolteachers, college professors, and educational administrators. In 1939, NAM had considered a campaign—reminiscent of the 1920s NELA activities—to scrutinize textbooks and put pressure on publishers and educators not to use those NAM deemed inappropriate. That same year, a memo entitled "Improvement of American Educational Methods" argued that schools needed to do more to counter collectivism. Contra Flynn (and Courtenay), NAM leaders did not truly believe that socialism (much less communism) had taken hold in the nation. But in the absence of a better understanding of how business and industry worked, they feared, Americans—particularly young Americans—might turn to collectivism. It was crucial to reach educators in order to prevent this.

REVERENCE FOR "FREEDOM" pulsed like a steady drumbeat through NAM's published materials, but if they attempted to influence teachers and professors, might it not invite backlash—not to mention charges of hypocrisy—as an attack on "academic freedom"? One memo offered a defense—or at least a rationalization: "Academic freedom ends where academic license begins to undermine the vital concepts of representative democracy—with its inseparable commitments—free private enterprise and civil, especially religious liberty."[54]

NAM staffers weighed the pros and cons of an academic campaign. They expressed concern that many textbooks gave "a negative impression of the value of private enterprise by consistently understating its value."[55] One example was the widely used *Economics: Principles and Problems*, which concluded that centralized planning could not be done while still "leaving to individuals any semblance of present private property rights."[56] The paragraph at issue did *not* advocate centralized planning—in fact, it argued against it—but even this dispassionate consideration of the subject was a bridge too far. NAM didn't want central planning *discussed at all*.

Still, NAM staffers weren't sure that a textbook campaign was a good idea, primarily because "distributing a 'black list of banned books'" could backfire. It *would* be "an appropriate function" for NAM "to provide our members and other manufacturers with a suggestion how textbooks should be criticized and judged," one memo noted, but in the end rejected as "too dangerous for NAM to under-take."[57] Recalling NELA's disastrous textbook campaign, staffers were determined not to repeat its mistakes. "Some, including myself," one staffer wrote, "feel that our engagement in such a program might have consequences as serious [as] or even more so than those which resulted from the National Electric Light Association's efforts in the educational field more than a decade ago. You will recall, of course, the Senate investigation of this matter, and the fact that the bad reaction resulting from that organization's activities not only caused the organization itself to dissolve, but has left within the minds of educators a resentment toward business which persists even to this day."[58]

NAM settled upon what it thought was a more nuanced approach than the one NELA had pursued. In October 1940, it retained Dr. Ralph W. Robey—a professor of economics at Columbia University, business editor at *Newsweek*, and former member of the American Liberty League—to write abstracts of the major textbooks in economics, sociology, civics, and history used in American public schools—particularly high schools—and select quotations to document the texts' orientation with "respect to the private enterprise system." Robey and three assis-tants prepared abstracts of 563 textbooks, totaling more than 1,200 single-spaced pages. At NAM's behest, Robey offered his opinions to the *New York Times*: "A substantial proportion" of American textbooks displayed "contempt" for the free-enterprise system.[59]

Robey's public comments set off the very firestorm NAM had wanted to avoid. Some critics denounced the review as an inquisition; others lightheartedly suggested that educators ought to seek out and use the condemned books. In public, NAM distanced itself, suggesting that Robey's opinions were merely personal; the organiza-tion was only trying to find out what was being taught, not to pass judgment on it and certainly not to influence teachers. Rather than asking (or worse, demanding) that publishers withdraw or rewrite objectionable textbooks—as NELA had done—NAM simply "offered" Dr. Robey's findings to publishers for their information.

At the same time, however, NAM fed Robey's findings to its members, urging them to involve themselves in educational institutions in their communities.

They should "encourage educators to seek a better understanding of the private enterprise system" and impart that understanding to students as "an indispensable concept in the American way of life."[60] Some of these businessmen took it upon themselves to compile and disseminate blacklists of books that Robey had condemned.[61] And in 1944, NAM produced its own textbook, *The American Individual Enterprise System*, written by its "economic principles commission." Intended as a "Bible" of the free-enterprise system, the textbook was distributed free of charge to twenty-four thousand school libraries.[62]

In at least one community, these efforts provoked a backlash. In 1947, the North Dakota *Spectrum*, the student newspaper in State College Station, described a speech by DeWitt M. Emery of Akron, Ohio, president of the National Small Business Men's Association.[63] The occasion was a meeting of the Associated Industries of Fargo, at which Emery excoriated a textbook used at North Dakota Agricultural College (today North Dakota State University). The book was "communistic," he insisted, because it included a discussion of how communism was intended to work. The *Spectrum* lambasted Emery. Some faculty studied communism as an economic system, an editorial allowed, but "to conclude that one is a 'Communist!' because he has studied communism is like concluding that a physiologist is a 'Beri-Beri-ist!' because he has studied the diseases of malnutrition." Emery was "one of a flood of reactionaries preaching a doctrine of illogical thinking to the American public today." The country faced more danger from this kind of "name-calling" and irrationality than from communism itself. "Until the time when people learn to think and act—singly and collectively—according to the precepts of rationality, the world faces a danger of greatest magnitude." The textbook that prompted this exchange? NAM's old bugbear, *Economics: Principles and Problems*.[64]

RADIO WAS THE most important communications medium of the 1930s, reaching 83 percent of American families by the end of the decade.[65] It was through radio that most Americans got their news and entertainment, and listened to presidential "chats." NAM had experimented with a number of radio programs in the early 1930s, but it hit the jackpot with a hugely successful program called *The American Family Robinson*. The long-running series was the most expensive item in NAM's public relations budget and almost certainly the one that reached the most people.

Broadcast into the homes of ordinary Americans who might otherwise not have held strong views about business or free enterprise one way or another, it was likely NAM's most effective tool for preaching beyond the choir.[66]

The American Family Robinson was the brainchild of Harry A. Bullis, vice president of General Mills and the chairman of NAM's public relations committee. Each fifteen-minute episode was distributed free of charge to interested radio stations. The show was a central component of NAM's declared mission to help industry tell its own story.[67] One flyer explicitly called it "industry's own program."[68] From 1935 to 1940, it was syndicated by the World Broadcasting System, and nearly three hundred small independent stations broadcast the series.[69] NAM officials generally took care to label their activities "public relations," but occasionally they slipped: "Can the limitations on the use of radio be overcome," one memo asked, "so as to make sustaining programs as effective for propaganda as commercial programs have been made for advertising?"[70] *The American Family Robinson* showed the answer was yes.

The show followed the adventures of the Robinson family in the aptly named manufacturing town of Centerville. We meet Luke Robinson, the family patriarch and editor of the *Centerville Herald*; his wife, Myra, a radio host; their children, Betty and Bob; Betty's husband, Dick Collins; assorted relatives and friends; and other Centerville inhabitants. The town, like the rest of America, feels the effects of the Depression. In one plotline, even the *Herald*—a "sound business" if there ever was one, Myra declares proudly—verges on collapse.

Centerville's name emphasizes its ordinariness and by implication that of the Robinsons, a quintessential middle American family. The show's politics, however, are anything but centrist. Each episode has sustained stretches of dialogue arguing against "foreign," "visionary," "experimental," or "utopian" theories that involve tax increases or deficit spending. The program was so blatantly anti-Roosevelt that when NAM tried to pitch it to NBC, the network wouldn't touch it, as a script editor there reported, because the "definite intention and implication of each episode is to conduct certain propaganda against the New Deal and all its work."[71]

The program lifted its title from the Swiss pastor Johann David Wyss's 1812 novel *The Swiss Family Robinson*, which in turn borrowed from Daniel Defoe's *Robinson Crusoe*. Wyss's novel tells the story of a Swiss family, en route to Australia, who find themselves shipwrecked on a tropical island in the Pacific. Their new home (unlike Crusoe's) turns out to be an Edenic paradise, filled with succulent fruits and magnificent creatures. The family prospers. During ten years in isolation, they build something resembling a Swiss farm, with houses, fields, gardens, domesticated animals, and even a fishery. Through industry, the family colonizes the island; through hard work, they turn its untouched wildness into a microcosm of European civilization.

The Swiss Family Robinson began as a series of bedtime stories Wyss told to his four young sons to arouse curiosity about the natural world and inculcate Christian morals.[72] From its inception, *The American Family Robinson* was like the novel: episodic and didactic. Both the American and Swiss Robinsons cherish a work ethic. Both promise success through individual initiative. Government plays no role at all on the Robinsons' island, and no good role in Centerville.

But whereas labor is a source of pleasure in *The Swiss Family Robinson*—spinning flax, making candles, salting fish—in *The American Family Robinson* work reveals character and demonstrates patriotism.[73] And where *The Swiss Family Robinson* preaches Protestant piety, *The American Family Robinson* preaches free-market fundamentalism.

The show imparts its lessons through long stretches of dialogue or monologue that interrupt the plot. Often, the program's instruction takes the form of debates between the commonsensical editor Luke Robinson and his troublemaking socialist sponger brother-in-law Bill Winkle, nicknamed "Windy Bill." Eschewing honest work, Bill lives off the Robinsons' generosity, pursues get-rich-quick schemes, and runs for mayor representing the "Sociological-Economical Reform and Golden Age Reincarnationist Party."[74] His vocal support for "visionary wealth-sharing programs" annoys Luke and others in the town: one Centerville judge pronounces him a "pompous windbag" before throwing him in jail.

Bill always loses his arguments with Luke, Myra, Dick, and the other voices of realism and "sound business principles," who (in Luke's words) "seek to maintain our economic structure rather than sacrificing it to radical theories." Bill offers superficial caricatures of socialist critique of free markets, as in this exchange between a fluty-voiced Bill and the show's sonorous business hero:

BILL: That's business for you: the big fellas ganging up against the little fellas . . .
LUKE: That's just a childish defense for lack of initiative. Who are the big fellas, anyway? Why, they're the little fellas willing to work hard enough under the same rules as apply to you and me, and become big fellas . . .

BILL: Business has got to be taken out of the hands of businessmen.
LUKE: And put into the hands of theorists, who never met a payroll for workers on
    Saturdays, I suppose?

These arguments repeat across dozens of episodes, coupled with criticism
of "The Government." In one episode, Luke complains that the United States lost
billions "into thin air" during World War I because of too much government
control over the production of weapons, planes, and other matériel. Manufacturers,
not politicians, know how to produce military equipment, and industrialists can't
be incompetent or "they'd have been out of business long ago." Myra, too, swoons
over the arms industry: "I know the businessmen are doing everything possible for
national defense: we'll be secure, all right." The path toward national security is
simple: the government needs to back off and let the industrial system work.

Luke assures listeners that business leaders have our best interests at heart and
will see those interests served. He maintains that business leaders enable social
mobility in America, because men like Henry Ford started out as mere workers—
just like you and me. "Every big company was a small company once," one character
reminds us. The alternative position—that industrialists are not always competent
and government oversight might be needed—is pilloried as giving control of business to "theorists." Reforms that involve government regulation, spending, or tax
increases are unrealistic "theories," "experiments," and "loose talk." By contrast, the
claim that reducing taxes to stimulate business automatically produces economic
recovery is offered as unchallenged fact.

Often no debate is even allowed. Bill's pseudo-socialist position falls out
entirely, as the program features Myra and Luke affirming the need for "confidence" in private industry rather than "visionary pieces of legislation" such as the
"thirty-hour work-week." The program also inserts overt editorial content through
Myra's radio show or Luke's newspaper. When Myra hosts a letter-writing contest
inviting listeners to respond to the question "What will speed recovery?" most of
the letters read aloud on the show are endorsements of private industry. Then Bill,
hoping to win the cash prize, writes in under a fake name: "With all the money
that is stored in our beautiful Treasury building, we could all make a new start.
The government could divide it up. A home, a car, a swimming pool for everyone . . .
big grown-up children singing happily." Bill's proposal crystallizes the show's caricature of New Dealers as unrealistic utopians; the program paints socialists as

preposterous and implies that what Windy Bill really wants is pleasure and leisure for himself.

Much as the series depicts the *Centerville Herald* as a microcosm of American business and Centerville itself as a microcosm of America, the Robinsons are presented as a romanticized ideal of the American family. Their struggles are the nation's struggles, and the Robinsons weather their challenges, the show's narrator tells us, "like the true Americans they are."

The idea of "true Americans" underscores another important element of the show: it frames socialism as a foreign and multilayered threat. The "pink" socialist Windy Bill—lilting-voiced, perpetually unemployed, and frequently emasculated (in one episode a group of workers give him a scare by hoisting him up on a steam shovel)—is coded as an intrusion on the heterosexual nuclear family. He encroaches, unwanted, on Luke and Myra; at one point he tries to move in with newlyweds Betty and Dick. Like his literary ancestor Rip Van Winkle, another idler, Bill Winkle dreamily removes himself from the obligations work and family impose. When Bill arrives at Luke and Myra's house, he boasts of his culinary tastes and offers to "revolutionize" the Robinsons' dinner table. Luke and Myra rebuff him. "We're pretty simple folks," Myra says. The lesson is clear. The family—like the country—must protect itself from misguided reform, which includes insidious foreign theories, most obviously socialism.

In just a few years' time, NAM and its allies would literally import foreign theories and theorists—the Austrian economists Friedrich August von Hayek and Ludwig von Mises—as part of their effort to convince the American people that capitalism and freedom were two sides of the same coin. But *The American Family Robinson* recognized only bad "European" thinking: socialism, communism, and totalitarianism. "If this country's gonna switch from Americanism to socialism or totalitarianism or some other kind of foreign government," a character muses, we all might find ourselves working for a dictator, "instead of doing business the American way." At times the language veers into a militaristic register: Myra declares in one episode that the country is waging "a battle between the fundamental system we built up and a whole host of foreign invaders, all bringing every kind of artillery." In *The American Family Robinson*, "foreign theories" pose an existential threat.

Whatever the New Deal economic reforms might be—communist, socialist, or simply impractical—they are, above all, *un-American*. "We have to sit tight and let the theorists have their fun," Luke offers at one point, but on another occasion he warns us that European theories will achieve little except to threaten American prosperity. Not a single European country, Luke asserts, has "a system that works better than ours." European countries have low wages with "none of our American conveniences." (This was of course untrue; among other things, European farmers had the convenience of electricity before Americans did, a fact the NELA campaign attempted to suppress.)[75]

The program takes pains to link the American ideal of social mobility to the free-enterprise system. In one episode, Luke and his friend the Baron find themselves on a farm run by a Mrs. Whitcomb, who has firm ideas about foreign thinking.

BARON: I come from Europe, and I know the curse of class-consciousness. But I am happy to say there is less here than in some other countries.

MRS. WHITCOMB: There shouldn't be any of it. There's only one class: the American class. More buttermilk, you fellas? . . .

LUKE: I've always thought it's silly to speak of the working class, or the employer class, or even the farming class, when this is still the one country in the world where the classes are interchangeable. Where all the working men—say, the employees in a factory—know they stand a good chance of being employers.

This passage reprises a favorite NAM theme: that managers have the best interests of their workers at heart, so unions are at best superfluous and at worst foster class conflict and violence. Yet, while the characters rail against "foreign theories" that are "upsetting natural economic laws," the program reassures its listeners that the probability of America adopting a European-style system is slight. The majority of Americans are against the "trouble-making minority that's prejudiced against business and industry." Even Americans who might be inspired by Roosevelt's plan for "social security" prefer "security through employment." Decades before Richard Nixon's invocation of the "silent majority," *The American Family Robinson* claimed to represent the real voice of the people—the voice of Centerville.[76]

AND THEN THERE was film. Throughout the 1930s and '40s, the NAM Public Relations Advisory Committee worked with Hollywood to make movies promoting the free-enterprise system and "workplace discipline." These included newsreels, short films, and full-length feature films. Two widely distributed newsreels were narrated by the prominent journalist and radio announcer Lowell Thomas. Famous for inventing Colonel T. E. Lawrence's moniker "Lawrence of Arabia," Thomas was also a newscaster for J. Howard Pew's Sun Oil Company. In "Frontiers of the Future" and "America Marching On," Thomas celebrated the triumphs of American industry and enterprise capitalism; one archive describes the newsreels as "screen editorials."[77] When television became important in American life in the 1950s, NAM would revisit these themes in a program called *Industry on Parade*, produced by NAM in cooperation with NBC.[78]

One illustrative example of NAM's work in film is *Your Town: A Story of America*. The ten-minute fictional narrative—released in 1940 and designed to be run as a "short" in movie theaters before the feature film—revolves around a conversation between "Granddad" and his teenage grandson, "Jerry," over the role of industry in their town.[79] (Perhaps not coincidentally, their last name is Robinson.)[80]

The film begins with images of American symbols: a waving flag, the Statue of Liberty, Capitol Hill. "Yankee Doodle" plays as these words scroll down:

> Nowhere has progress been so great as in our country, with its system of representative democracy and private enterprise . . . Our duty to ourselves and to our country is to study the American way of life, to understand the institutions that have made this country great, and [with that] understanding to cherish and defend them.

The film cuts to a shot of a classic American town hall, then to an aerial view of tree-lined streets, and then to a two-story house with a white picket fence; the script describes it as "a cozy cottage." It is Granddad and Jerry's home.

Granddad is working in the garden as a police car bearing Jerry pulls up. "Hello, Mr. Robinson, got something for you," Officer Mike calls out genially. Jerry starts to speak, but Granddad cuts him off, asking the officer to explain. "Just a little ruckus down at the Manson factory," he replies. "One of those soapbox fellas gets up and starts yellin,' down with this and down with that, and down with capitalism and down with old man Manson." Jerry then relates what happened next: someone threw something, and a fight broke out. "Boy, was it swell!" he gushes. The officer recounts taking Jerry out of the melee and into protective custody, to deliver him safely to Granddad. Both thank the officer, who assures them "t'wan't anything" and happily drives away. But as the two walk back toward the house, it is clear Granddad is not impressed.

"So it was fun, eh, son?" he asks.

"Well, sure Gramps! Boy, I bet old man Manson's sore when he finds out. He thinks he's the most important guy in town. Well, guess we showed 'im."

Jerry starts to walk away, looking satisfied. Granddad stops him, saying, "Wait a minute, Jerry. Old man Manson may not be any more important than a lot of men . . ." But then, Granddad proceeds to explain why the factory owner *is* the most important man in town.

It is easy to criticize "established institutions" like the factory, Granddad opines. "Anybody can criticize, anybody can be destructive, but you want to know what you're talking about before you talk." As they walk through town Granddad explains that the man on the soapbox wasn't telling "the truth." The factory isn't just a building: "It's *your town*."

Granddad recounts what the town was like when he was a boy—just a scraggly place with a few farms, struggling because they had no one to sell crops to. But "there was a man who had a dream . . . his name was Manson." He found an investor and built a factory. A community grew around it, supporting diverse businesses. This was no theory, Granddad expounds: "I know, son, I was part of it all . . . and it was the factory payroll" that made it possible.

Jerry was part of it, too. The factory generated wealth that funded the hospital where he was born and the doctor who delivered him. There wouldn't be dentists or teachers without the factory payroll to circulate money for their salaries. A virtuous cycle ensued; wages "grew higher" and "hours grew less." People had more leisure time to enjoy the comforts they could now afford to buy. The local newspaper, too, owes its existence to the Manson plant, for how else could anyone buy the goods being advertised?

Suddenly Jerry gets it: "And they're the dollars that pay the reporters and the printers and all the other guys that work on the paper!" Granddad is relieved: "That's it, son. You can trace most everything you see in this town right straight back to the Manson plant." The schools, the fire department, the police, all of it comes, ultimately, from the wealth generated by the factory. It all happened "because of that man named Manson, and his dream . . ."

"That factory made your town, and when you're working against that factory, you're working against your own best interests," Granddad sums up. The same story applies across America: "Everybody's welfare can be traced back to manufacturing and industry . . . And that's why I say . . . The story of your town is the story of America." Granddad extends his hands, as if in benediction, as "My Country, 'Tis of Thee" plays in the background. "These are the blessings of peace and industry, that belong to all of us, and to our children, and our children's children," he concludes. "And we should guard them, and thank God for them, and for America, every day we live." As the music climaxes, the film cycles back through its opening symbols: first the Capitol, then the Statue of Liberty, and finally the American flag waving in the wind, with background voices singing "Let freedom ring!"

Like all good propaganda, the film was not entirely false. American prosperity did develop in large part through industrialization; many towns in the early twentieth century did rely on a single factory's payroll; and no doubt some manufacturers were benevolent. But *Your Town* also elided many things. It suggested that farmers could only succeed if a factory was nearby to create demand, ignoring the community-building role of agriculture itself. It omits government's part in providing infrastructure to ship goods from factories to markets. And most egregiously, it neglects to mention that unions fought for those higher wages and shorter hours, enabling the town's families to enjoy leisure time and buy the food raised by those farmers. Nor was there any discussion of what went on inside the factory, or what happened to people who got injured or who for whatever reason could not get jobs there. Or whether children worked there. Old Man Manson may have been benevolent, but many factory owners were not.

The film promoted the trope of heroic individualism. All that Granddad extols—prosperous farmers, happy people, doctors and lawyers and dentists and teachers, schools and hospitals, firefighters, and of course the affable policeman who looked out for Jerry—is possible because of one man's dream. Manson is a cipher for all American industry, and by the end of the short film, Jerry sees him as a hero and friend.[81] The national symbols that bookend the narrative reinforce the idea that capitalism and American freedom are inextricably linked.

We don't know what Americans thought about this film, but we do know that millions saw it. In 1940, NAM budgeted $51,000 for motion pictures (close to $1 million in current dollars), much of it for the distribution of *Your Town*. The film played in all forty-eight states, reaching 6.5 million cinemagoers.[82] It was also distributed free of charge to schools, libraries, and civic organizations, to whom it was presented as both educational and entertaining. In this respect, *Your Town* exemplifies integration propaganda: material and activities enmeshed with films, textbooks, and events, so as to appear to be something other than what they were.[83]

JUST AS NELA'S propaganda campaign attracted FTC scrutiny, the scale and scope of NAM's activities drew the U.S. Congress's attention. It was not the first time Congress had been interested in how the business community fought union-ization or the New Deal. A key leader in this was the progressive Wisconsin senator Robert M. La Follette Jr. For some time, La Follette had tracked the American Liberty League's attempts to undermine the Wagner Act (formally the National Labor Relations Act of 1935), which recognized the "inequality of bargaining power" between workers and employers. The act guaranteed private-sector workers' rights to unionize and engage in collective bargaining. It also established the National Labor Relations Board (NLRB) to hear worker complaints of unfair labor practices and provide oversight for union elections. The league insisted the act was unconstitutional and should be disobeyed; following this advice, corporate attor-neys throughout the country demanded that courts prevent union organizers from having their cases heard by the NLRB. In 1936, La Follette called several members of the league to testify in hearings on business resistance to labor organizing. But no formal action followed, and the corporate civil disobedience lasted until 1937, when the Supreme Court upheld the Wagner Act.

Companies used numerous tactics to undermine unions: La Follette's Senate committee documented corporate espionage, intimidation of union members and organizers, and management violence.[84] Manufacturers and mine owners hired strikebreakers to attack workers and picket lines, sometimes with the assistance of local police, and weaponized their facilities with tear gas, machine guns, and armored cars. Another tactic involved embedding spies in unions to report the leadership to management so they could be fired. (These company "stools," as in stool pigeons, were so common that they appear in Woody Guthrie's folk song "Union Maid": "She couldn't be fooled by a company stool, she'd always organize the guys.")

Employers also hired third-party allies specializing in industrial espionage, including the notorious Pinkerton National Detective Agency, infamous for its role in violent strikebreaking.[85] La Follette's star witness, an investigative reporter and researcher named Heber Blankenhorn, provided the committee with the names of more than two hundred such companies.[86] Blankenhorn testified that the three largest agencies, with combined revenues of $65 million, employed more than 135,000 "operatives," and that at least 40,000 "paid spies and stool pigeons" were embedded within unions.[87] In one case that reached the Supreme Court, Fruehauf Trailers had contracted with Pinkerton for a monthly fee of $175 to provide a union spy. The spy became the union's treasurer, and after reporting the organizers' names so they could be fired, he vanished with the union's funds.[88]

Blankenhorn had been involved with labor investigations since World War I, but he felt that these long-established tactics now represented a new kind of threat: "Espionage has ramifications outside the scope of the National Labor Relations Board. Involved is the problem of organized lawlessness. Most pertinent is the question whether there is any other breeding ground of crime so prolific as is a system of industrial espionage. Is it not industry's parasites and rogues who become the unreachable kidnappers and gangsters?"[89] Just as Al Smith's Association Against the Prohibition Amendment had argued that Prohibition created organized crime by driving a once-legal activity underground, Blankenhorn and the other NLRB leaders charged that business-funded antiunion activities produced violent lawlessness.

In 1938, La Follette again investigated industrial activities, this time with a focus on NAM and its propaganda campaigns, including the *Uncle Abner Says* comics and *The American Family Robinson*. As part of the investigations, NAM was served with several subpoenas.[90] NAM did not deny having spent money to promote its views but argued that the $750,000 it spent in 1938 was chicken feed compared to what the federal government had spent to promote the New Deal.[91] La Follette begged to differ. NAM propaganda "could not be said by any stretch of argument to contribute to a better understanding of our 'Industrial Economic Society' or to an easier adjustment of prospective recruits from schools and colleges for industrial employment." It was a "propaganda barrage," pure and simple.[92]

In 1939, La Follette introduced into Congress the Oppressive Labor Practices Act, designed to eliminate "certain oppressive labor practices affecting interstate and foreign commerce." This included the use of labor spies, strikebreakers and strikebreaking agencies, and armed guards off industry premises; industry stockpiling of munitions such as machine guns and tear gas; and other activities that

caused or provoked violence. NAM secretary Noel Sargent submitted a long statement denying that NAM had ever engaged in such practices or encouraged its
members to do so. NAM condemned the use of violence, he claimed, and recognized the "legitimate rights of labor to self-organization and collective bargaining."
But Sargent also reverted to whataboutism, reminding the congressional committee
that labor also used "strong armed and coercive" methods.[93] No doubt that was
true, but among the methods NAM offered as evidence of labor coercion were mass
picketing and sit-down strikes, scarcely comparable to the overt violence deployed
by Pinkerton guards and at times even by management directly.[94] Sargent also
argued that prohibitions on spying would constitute an infringement on free
speech. The proposed legislation was not so much a defense of workers' civil rights,
he concluded, but a massive attack on the rights of employers.[95]

Historian Richard Tedlow has summarized the NAM campaign: "Unnerved by
the impact of the depression, apprehensive of the growing strength of labor, enraged
at critics of the failures of business, and rejecting almost in toto the devices of the
new administration in Washington to find solutions to the problems it inherited in
1933," NAM leaders refused to engage in a serious attempt to identify the structural
weaknesses, errors, and abuses that had contributed to the Great Depression, and
honestly consider how they might be corrected.[96] Instead, they turned to propaganda, spending millions to persuade the American people of the greatness of business and industry, and that the fault lay entirely with government and unions
standing in the way of effective management.

LA FOLLETTE'S OPPRESSIVE Labor Practices Act of 1939 did not pass, but the
revelations about NAM and its members' behind-the-scenes efforts may have played
a role in inspiring the organization to adopt a new and more ambitious messaging
strategy. Even before 1939, NAM officials had concluded that their defense of
business—even if described as free enterprise rather than private enterprise—was
insufficient to persuade the American people. They were not breaking through.
Now, they concluded that they needed to link their cause to something "all
Americans held dear," something noncontroversial and incontrovertible. Their
answer: not free enterprise, but freedom itself. "Free enterprise [will not] be saved as
the result of appeals in the name of free enterprise alone," one NAM memo argued.
"Democracy and its preservation are the interest of every patriotic American today,"

so "[t]he public must be convinced that free enterprise is as much an indivisible part of our democracy and the source of as many blessings and benefits as are our other freedoms of speech, press, and religion."[97]

As historian Wendy Wall notes, this was not an easy argument for some businessmen to make, as many did not actually approve of majoritarian democracy. The American Liberty League had opposed the broad plebiscite; so had NAM secretary Noel Sargent, who believed that people receiving public funds should not be permitted to vote. (He conveniently ignored the issue of businessmen building their companies on government contracts.) Other conservative commentators in the 1930s agreed, offering reasons why majoritarian democracy—which they often equated with mob rule—was problematic.[98] Still, NAM staffers realized that if they could "emphasize effectively the inseparability of 'democracy' and 'free enterprise,' " enthusiasm and support for the former could carry the latter.[99] Late in 1939, they launched their new initiative to promote the "American System of Free Enterprise" by insisting it was one leg of a "tripod of freedom."

A tripod depends for its stability on all three legs, and NAM would now use this metaphor to insist that any compromise to economic freedom (which is to say, to business freedom) threatened other cherished freedoms. NAM put forth the "Tripod of Freedom" concept in a thirty-three-page Declaration of Principles adopted at its annual meeting on December 8, 1939. It began with a statement of what NAM held to be the "essential principles" of American society:

> In a world torn by war and dictatorship, Americans live at peace and in freedom. The best assurance that we shall remain free and at peace is our own internal unity and strength . . . Here, people have faith in constitutional representative democracy, in free enterprise, and in civil and religious liberty as inseparable fundamentals of freedom to be cherished and preserved.[100]

These fundamentals were the basis of America's prosperity, the foundation upon which it had achieved "the highest standard of living in the world . . . essential to America's greatness."[101] The source of prosperity was "individual business," pursued "on a plane of enlightened self-interest," and unimpeded by "outside authority" whether labor union, government bureau, or "economic dictator."[102] (The terms "self-interest" and "enlightened self-interest" appeared numerous times in the declaration.)

NAM recognized that society needed laws to protect from abuses, but any such laws had to be "framed as not to limit authority of management which would render it unable to fulfill its responsibilities." Hence the tripod of freedom: any compromise to business freedom threatened to put America on the path to totalitarianism.

The possibility of well-regulated enterprise capitalism was never discussed, and mixed economies and social democracies were rarely mentioned, except to dismiss them as socialism by another name. The sole alternative to free-enterprise capitalism, NAM insisted, was the "planned economy, with its political and economic dictatorship, requir[ing] controls which can be attained only by complete surrender of individual freedom and the concentration of both political and economic power in the hands of a single individual or political group." And totalitarianism was doomed to fail both socially and economically. It was inflexible and relied on too limited sources of information: "No one man, no one central authority . . . has the knowledge required to solve these problems . . ." But beyond that, planned economies lacked the discipline of the profit motive. Economic solutions require "the stimulus and inexorable tests of efficiency that only the profit motive and competitive effort can provide."

Time would vindicate the critics of Soviet economic management, but were the choices limited simply to "free enterprise" on the one hand and totalitarian central planning on the other? No European social democrat would have agreed with that premise, nor would most members of the Roosevelt administration. To counter this obvious complaint, NAM's argument needed one more element: the slippery slope. Even modest interventions in the marketplace (they argued) would ultimately lead to total government takeover of the economy. This was why free enterprise was inseparable from political democracy and civic freedom. As one went, so went the others. The document laid out eight objectives to which industry needed to commit itself, the last being "enlightenment of the public as to the obstacles which obstruct progress." The tripod of freedom campaign would be a major part of that "enlightenment."[103]

This now became the key concept in NAM materials. It appears in something like its purest form in a 1939 NAM statement to the National Association of

Broadcasters, regarding *The American Family Robinson*: The program's "avowed purpose" is "to present openly, and as effectively and attractively as radio will permit, the fundamental principle that freedom of speech and of the press, freedom of religion and freedom of enterprise are inseparable and must continue to be if the system of democratic government under which this country has flourished is to be preserved."[104] A pamphlet echoed:

> THE AMERICAN FAMILY ROBINSON seeks to emphasize the countless
> benefits which derive from living in a free country, with
>> CIVIL AND RELIGIOUS LIBERTY
>> REPRESENTATIVE DEMOCRACY
>> FREE PRIVATE ENTERPRISE.[105]

The key claim of the NAM statement to the broadcasters hinged on the word *inseparable*: that freedom of speech and of the press, freedom of religion, and freedom of enterprise are inseparable. (In a 1940 speech, NAM president H. W. Prentis Jr. explicitly connected it to the "religious concept common to Protestantism, Roman Catholicism, and Judaism—the sacredness of the individual.")[106] Elsewhere NAM would proclaim the "interdependence" of political, religious, and economic freedom. But the word that stuck—the word that echoed the American pledge of allegiance—was *indivisible*. A 1937 NAM memo had already summarized: "Free enterprise is as much an indivisible part of democracy and the source of as many blessings and benefits as are our other freedoms of speech, press and religion."[107] But this interdependence was also a vulnerability. "Throughout the ages, these institutions have gone hand in hand," Prentis declared. "They are inseparable. When one goes, all go."[108] Any government intervention in the marketplace would in time make America "just what you see in the dictator-controlled countries of Europe today."[109] Here lay the crux of what we call the indivisibility thesis: today, the eight-hour workday; tomorrow, the dictatorship of the proletariat.

DURING WORLD WAR II, NAM grew dramatically. By 1945 its annual budget was nearly $4 million, up from under a million per year in the 1930s. Its campaigns early in the war ignored the government's role in war production; later in the war, it began to actively denigrate it.[110] After the war, new threats loomed, including a full-employment bill that would have had the federal government guarantee jobs. NAM's leaders saw this as another step toward socialism. Working with more moderate business leaders, NAM was able to weaken the bill considerably; by the time it became law, the jobs guarantee was gone. NAM had even more success destroying the Office of Price Administration (OPA), which had been established in August 1941 to stabilize prices and ration scarce commodities in an effort to prevent inflation. OPA was due to expire in June 1946; NAM spent more than $3 million to convince the public that refusing to renew OPA was key to restoring prosperity.[111] As its defenders predicted, OPA's demise produced a spike in inflation, reaching 18 percent that December. Inflation would not return to single digits until late 1947.[112]

Meanwhile, NAM continued its shrill rhetoric. In October 1946, NAM president Robert Watson told an American Legion convention that "industry needs to be freed from shackles" of government and union control. If "America is to be strong," he told the legionnaires, "you must defend its industry. You must take from its throat the collectivists in Washington that choke it . . . If industry is to protect the American way of life, the authoritarian controls that prevent its functioning must be removed."[113] World War II was over, but NAM was still in battle mode.

Perhaps aided by a large wave of strikes during 1945 and 1946 that left unions relatively unpopular, the November 1946 midterms produced the first Republican-majority Congress since the 1928 election. NAM had dialed down its antiunion rhetoric after the La Follette investigation but had never accommodated itself to organized labor. Now it saw a huge opportunity: NAM used its PR machinery to spin unions as the real threat to America. Communities needed to be protected from union activists. The Wagner Act had violated employers' free speech rights by preventing them from propagandizing their employees (though they did it anyway, with materials NAM provided). NAM had never accepted the closed shop, and it wanted a new labor law permitting states to enact statutes allowing employees to refuse union membership. Such "right-to-work" legislation, of course, guaranteed no right to employment.[114]

In 1947, NAM put its weight behind a bill introduced by senators Robert A. Taft and Fred A. Hartley Jr. that banned many kinds of strikes, restored employers' propaganda rights, barred union donations to federal political campaigns, and allowed state "right-to-work" laws. In his 1950 PhD on the subject, political scientist Richard W. Gable quoted one senator describing NAM's role as "the most intensive, expensive, and vicious propaganda campaign" he had ever seen. Some observers claimed NAM actually wrote the Taft-Hartley Act. Gable concluded it "enacted into law...the labor principles of NAM [whose] suggestions were frequently conveyed to Congress through paid lobbyists, conferences with congressmen, direct testimony before legislature committees, and a vast _and_ intensive program of public relations."[115] Known formally as the Labor Management Relations Act, the Taft-Hartley Act passed Congress overwhelmingly twice, the second time with sufficient votes to override President Harry Truman's veto.

It is impossible to say exactly what effect all these activities had. By and large, in the 1930s NAM's arguments had struggled to gain purchase. Along with its allies, the American Liberty League and the U.S. Chamber of Commerce, NAM had tried to persuade people that the freedom of business was the foundation of prosperity, a hard sell with the economy only barely emerging from the Great Depression and business leaders defending practices that had at minimum contributed to—if not actually produced—that depression.[116] But available evidence suggests that, as the economy began to recover, the message had taken hold. In early 1941, a NAM survey found that 71 percent of respondents believed the disappearance of the free enterprise system would harm their personal liberty.[117] Later that year, NAM polling showed a majority of Americans believed it was industry—not government—that could best protect against the threats posed by the conflicts overseas.[118]

In 1950, NAM would be investigated yet again, this time for potential violations of the 1946 Federal Regulation of Lobbying Act. Inspired in part by utility company activities, the act was the first federal statute to regulate lobbying. According to historian Belle Zeller, one catalyst for the law was the problem of "propaganda from all over the country in the form of letters and telegrams, many of which have been based entirely on misinformation." (As we have seen, in the 1920s this was a NELA tactic.) It's not clear what inspired this second investigation of NAM, but the law required full disclosure of financial associations, something that NAM had not always done. Perhaps it was simply the sheer scale of their activities: legal documents revealed that in the late 1940s, NAM and NIIC spent $12,719,444.52 on activities intended to influence American public opinion, a figure that would be approximately $140 million today.[119]

It is unlikely that expenditures on that scale had no effect, particularly when coupled with lobbying of state and federal officials. What we know for sure is that, while the United States built a regulatory system and social safety net to prevent another Great Depression, NAM and its allies spent huge sums trying to stop it from doing so. They reached tens of millions of Americans—almost certainly half the population and possibly more—with billboards, brochures, lectures, films, and radio programs celebrating "free enterprise," disparaging government, and insisting that laws designed to regulate industry or help the unemployed were a step on the slippery slope to socialism, with no middle ground. This was the myth NAM had manufactured: American prosperity had been built of individual initiative, government involvement in the marketplace was destructive, and a system with anything less than complete economic freedom would soon brook no freedom at all.

AT THE END of his NAM-endorsed book *The Road Ahead*, author John T. Flynn provided a ten-point program to protect American capitalism:

I. We must put HUMAN FREEDOM ... first.

II. We must stop apologizing for capitalism.

III. Not one more step into socialism. Hold the line for the American way of life.

IV. Get rid of compromising leaders.

V. Recognize that this is a war, and we must fight it as such.

VI. Put an end to the orgy of government spending.

VII. Put an end to crisis government.

VIII. We must stop "planning" for socialism and begin planning to make our free system of private enterprise operate at its highest capacity.

IX. We must set about rebuilding in its integrity our republican system of government by returning government to the States and curbing the grasping hand of the federal government.

X. We cannot depend on any political party to save us. We must build a power outside the parties so strong that the parties would be compelled to yield to its demands.[120]

Flynn did not use the term *market fundamentalism*, but his ten-point program can be read in hindsight as its catechism. For the rest of the century, American businessmen would celebrate unregulated markets and corporate freedom, while

disparaging any protection of workers, consumers, or the environment as government encroachment, even "shackles."[121] They would insist that reforms intended to
address market failures or defend workers were alien, un-American ideas. They
would decry "excessive" government spending on social programs, while (with rare
exceptions) accepting an orgy of military spending from which they would often
benefit. Above all, they would develop and hone what in time became the mantra of
American conservatism in the second half of the twentieth century: limited government, low taxation, individual responsibility, personal freedom.

BY 1950, AMERICAN business leaders had constructed an intellectually
coherent—if historically and logically misleading—framework for market fundamentalism. Led by NAM, business leaders had fought child labor laws and workmen's compensation as unfair limits on business freedom. NELA enlisted academics
to help portray American business as efficient, even where it patently was not, and
insist that anything less than total business freedom was a step on the road to
socialism or worse. The American Liberty League added the fetishization of
freedom, and NAM pulled it all together under the indivisibility thesis and the
Tripod of Freedom.

By promoting a false dichotomy between laissez-faire capitalism and communist regimentation, market fundamentalists would make it difficult for Americans
to have conversations about crucial issues, such as appropriate levels of taxation
or the balance between federal and state authority, or even how to appraise the size
of the federal government objectively. And while they largely accomplished this by
building power structures outside the existing political parties, as Flynn advocated,
in the years ahead their arguments would often be advanced in cooperation with
Republican political leaders and by appeal to Republican voters.

While these business leaders clothed their claims in the guise of "freedom," they
had little interest in others' freedom. They used private espionage and strikebreaking to prevent workers from exercising their freedom to organize, and they
used their power and influence to suppress academic freedom by purging textbooks
they disliked and replacing them with commissioned texts. Throughout, they
rejected the idea that economic freedom might ever legitimately be circumscribed.
Building on NELA before it, NAM refined the playbook to ensure propaganda
would be taken as truth, that its prerogatives were defended as freedoms while

others' prerogatives were denied as socialistic.[122] Even today, NAM stands with the fossil fuel industry in its attempts to escape accountability for climate change caused by its products.[123]

The indivisibility thesis was meretricious, appealing to freedom but designed to protect business prerogatives. In a rare moment of candor, one 1944 NAM memo acknowledged this: "American industry does not cut a very convincing figure as the guardian of the people's freedom; we represent an economic interest, and it is a little out of character to appoint ourselves as spiritual advisers to the nation."[124] But by broadcasting its message through preachers' sermons, columnists' editorials, teachers' lessons, and radio characters' voices, NAM transmogrified a self-serving argument for business privilege into a seemingly virtuous defense of cherished American values.[125] NAM members didn't just manufacture cars and carpets; they manufactured a myth. They would spend the ensuing decades bolstering its intellectual credentials and embedding it in the bedrock of American culture, to the point where the myth would be mistaken for age-old truth.

PART II

Marketing

*It may be true that morality cannot be legislated but behavior
can be regulated. It may be true that the law cannot change the heart,
but it can restrain the heartless. It may be true that the law can't
make a man love me . . . but it can restrain him from lynching me,
and I think that's pretty important.*

—MARTIN LUTHER KING JR., UNIVERSITY OF CALIFORNIA,
LOS ANGELES, APRIL 27, 1965

CHAPTER 5

"A Stringent, Crystalline Vision of the Free Market"

The story NAM, NELA, and the American Liberty League told was a myth. The Tripod of Freedom was pure invention: the words "free enterprise" appear in neither the Declaration of Independence nor the Constitution. Nor was there any real evidence that if economic freedom were compromised, political freedom would be inevitably compromised, too. The argument rested on the implied claim that government "intervention" in the marketplace was a radical departure from American history. This claim was flagrantly false.

Since the nation's founding, both state and federal governments had been intimately involved in the marketplace. Historian Gary Gerstle has documented how, from the birth of the nation, state governments had "assumed the job of shaping decisively the contours of economic life."[1] Corporations were originally *products* of the state: throughout the first half of the nineteenth century, state governments used their right to charter corporations to influence and, at times, control the private sector. There was, in most states, no "right" to incorporate; businessmen had to plead their case to be granted the privileges of limited liability that incorporation entailed. Frequently, they argued that the proposed activity was in the public interest, and governments rarely approved such petitions without conditions. Some of these conditions might strike contemporary listeners as easily justified and understood, such as stipulating the cities through which a proposed rail line would run. Some, like the mandating of manufacturing standards, mirror functions now performed by the federal government. Others, however, are astonishing by today's standards, such as requiring a bank to lend money to a particular private venture.

Throughout the United States' early history, city and state governments authorized and helped finance transportation improvements to foster economic growth. States constructed canals, roads, and railways, mostly by chartering corporations such as New York State's 1817 Erie Canal Corporation.[2] "With the building of this canal," Gerstle observes, "New York moved from its earlier disposition to support private enterprises with subsidies and other incentives to 'direct funding and operation' by the state itself. This remained the model until the 1840s, by which time New York had constructed more than 600 miles of canals at a cost of more than $50 million."[3] Business leaders at the time applauded these efforts and rarely objected to state involvement in the economy when it created opportunities for them.[4]

Beyond infrastructure projects, nineteenth-century state and municipal governments involved themselves intimately in the marketplace. In 1837, the city of Chicago empowered itself to regulate manufacturing and commerce in just about any way it saw fit. Local authorities imposed sanitary guidelines on merchants and manufacturers, regulated the location of different types of businesses, and limited or prohibited entertainment activities (from "games of chance" to theatrical performances to "playing at ball or flying of kites") if they were deemed to impede social welfare.[5] America in the 1800s was not the laissez-faire dreamworld some suppose it to have been.

Some might argue that most late eighteenth- and nineteenth-century economic regulation occurred at the municipal and state—rather than federal—level; and that NAM—like the American Liberty League and other New Deal opponents—was mostly worried about the expansion of federal power. But the debate over child labor disproves that: there, NAM also opposed state laws it viewed as undermining private-sector license. Moreover, the story NAM told the American people was *not* just about restricting federal powers; it was about the importance of economic freedom on every level. In doing so, NAM obscured a rich and complex history of government interventions in the marketplace. Indeed, the American economic order was *built* upon such interventions.

One example of this is the creation of mass manufacturing itself. NAM's leaders would have been the first to insist that the nation's wealth was rooted in modern industrial technology.[6] But the impetus behind this innovation came from the federal government—via its military. Before the nineteenth century, every gun was handmade, so if a soldier's rifle jammed on the battlefield because of a broken part, he was defenseless until he could get another. For decades, blacksmiths and carpenters had tried and failed to make parts consistent enough to be interchangeable; the degree of precision and accuracy required would have been superhuman. In the early nineteenth century, the Army's Ordnance Department took up the challenge, experimenting with techniques invented (but never fully realized) in France.[7] The key was machining: using machines to make parts for other machines. It took nearly fifty years—what would have been an inconceivable period of research and development for a private corporation in the nineteenth century (or today, for that matter)—but once it was achieved, it revolutionized manufacturing. What we now call machine tools spread so rapidly through the American economy, and the world, that the technology came to be known as the "American System of Manufactures," then simply the "American System." It was critical to the development of the consumer goods that became emblematic of American industry and American life, including sewing machines, typewriters, adding machines, and automobiles.[8]

The "American System" is hardly the only case of federal action nurturing enterprise. The U.S. government's role in the promotion of railroads, for example—through land grants and the dispossession of Native Americans—has been well documented and well critiqued. Indeed, one of the most egregious elisions in NAM's mythos is the reality that American economic development rested on the violent expropriation of land from Indigenous people. None of this was the product of free enterprise; it was federal policy, enforced by state militias and the U.S. Army.[9] Bearing government-furnished land grants, (mostly) white settlers traveled on government-sponsored railroads to colonize territory cleared by government troops.

And of course, slavery refutes NAM's story on both the state and federal level. Slavery was, after all, an intensely regulated economic activity—most obviously in free states, where laws prohibited it. Some of these laws, as in Massachusetts, were on the books even before America became a nation. They were direct interventions in the marketplace—to bar a particularly noxious kind of market entirely. But slave states regulated this market, too: every one had a slave code, constraining both what enslaved people could do and what free men could do with those they held enslaved.[10] In most states, for example, it was illegal to teach enslaved people to read. Slavery's defenders typically invoked property rights to justify it—yet here, in the slave code, was a bald-faced restriction on what slaveowners could do with their (alleged) property. (Some states even banned literacy training for *free* Black people, an infringement on the rights of aspiring students and teachers alike.) It was also legal in many states to murder fugitive enslaved people; the owner would have to be compensated, but this nevertheless was an example (albeit monstrous) of the law sanctioning the destruction of someone else's property.[11]

The key point here is that a market for enslaved people didn't emerge simply because individual plantation owners insisted on their right to buy and sell other human beings. States claimed their prerogative to decide whether such a market would exist within their borders, and if so, what that market would look like. No less than railroads in the West, the building of New York's Erie Canal, or the regulation of kite-flying in Chicago, the history of slavery in America is proof of government intervention in economic life.

TO SPIN ITS tale of "The Market" that exists ex nihilo, outside of politics and culture, NAM had to skate over a mass of evidence to the contrary. Ironically, it also had to skate over its *own* history. NAM was created in the late nineteenth century to advocate for federal imposition of protective tariffs, and to encourage the U.S. government to build the Panama Canal—both policies benefiting American manufacturers. NAM's full-throated advocacy of "free enterprise" in the twentieth century was a reversal of its nineteenth-century position.

By supporting protective tariffs in the nineteenth century, NAM was not doing anything remarkable. One of the first laws passed after the ratification of the Constitution was the Tariff Act of 1789, designed largely by James Madison both to raise revenue and to protect fledgling domestic enterprise (and to hurt the British economy). Treasury Secretary Alexander Hamilton insisted on the need for tariffs: a new nation could not be politically independent if it was economically dependent, so it needed to shelter emerging businesses from international competition.[12] George Washington agreed, noting in his first congressional address that the "safety and interest" of a free people "require that they should promote such manufactories as tend to render them independent of others for essential, particularly military, supplies."[13] (He also argued in this address for "the advancement of agriculture, commerce, and manufactures by all proper means" as well as the "promotion of science and literature.")

In his 1791 *Report on Manufactures*, Hamilton argued for a range of tariffs to encourage industrial development, nearly all of which Congress adopted in 1792.[14] These tariffs played a significant role in the development of New England's textile industry, a bellwether for the United States' economic growth writ large. In the early nineteenth century, the term "American System" emerged to refer to a system with high protective tariffs, a central bank to standardize currency and promote industry, and federal spending on infrastructure (roads, bridges, canals) to support commerce.[15] By the late nineteenth century, tariffs were the main source of federal government revenue.

The United States was hardly alone in using protective tariffs to foster economic development. As economist Ha-Joon Chang has shown, most of today's rich industrial nations got rich with the help of protective tariffs. Until recently, at least some degree of protectionism was the norm; late twentieth-century neoliberals who demanded that poor nations commit to free trade were imposing a set of rules under which they themselves did not operate. They were, in Chang's words, "kicking away the ladder" their own countries had climbed.[16] In this respect the United States went further than most industrializing nations: from 1866 to 1883, purportedly to guard American wages, tariffs on imported manufactured goods averaged an astonishing 45 percent ad valorem.[17] Historian Paul Bairoch has gone so far as to label the United States "the mother country and bastion of modern protectionism," noting that this long history has been largely forgotten—or perhaps deliberately denied.[18]

These policies were clear examples of government involvement in economic life, and their greatest advocate was the Republican Party. The Tariff Act of 1890 was known as the McKinley Tariff, after its champion, Republican congressman (and later president) William McKinley, an "apostle of protectionism."[19] NAM's creation in 1895 as part of American industry's fight for protective tariffs was consistent with the Republican Party platform of 1896, which declared "allegiance to the policy of protection, as the bulwark of American industrial independence, and the foundation of American development and prosperity."[20] The party would continue to tout tariffs into the early twentieth century; when Woodrow Wilson abolished them and instituted the federal income tax in part to reduce the government's dependence on tariff revenues, he did so over Republican opposition.[21]

While historians continue to debate whether protectionist policies ultimately helped or hurt, there is no denying that they were a fact of nineteenth-century American economics. NAM's myth about the origins of American prosperity whitewashed the long history of protectionism from which manufacturers benefited, as well as the long history of government participation—on the local, state, and federal level—in markets. Americans may have been enterprising, but the enterprise in which they took part was not remotely "free."

None of this is to say that government actions in the marketplace were always good or effective: financial scandals frequently rocked state-chartered industries; railroads generated seemingly endless corruption, disruption, and destruction; and nothing could ever justify slave codes or the slaughter and dispossession of Native Americans.[22] It *is* to say that NAM's history was false. America was not founded on free enterprise. The U.S Constitution did not enshrine it alongside representative democracy. And the idea that state planning was "foreign" was laughable: if Washington, Madison, and Hamilton advocated for and implemented a visible government hand in economic life, what could be more American than that?

These historical facts did not discourage NAM. By 1944, the Tripod of Freedom had become the centerpiece of its propaganda activities. As one memo put it, "At the core of [our] strategy has been the idea of establishing free enterprise where it rightfully belongs—as one of the three great elements (along with the civil liberties of free speech, free press, and religious freedom, and the representative form of democratic governments) which . . . make up the American way of life."[23] It was a strategy of misrepresentation, promoted by a trade association with a history of questionable strategies and dishonest tactics.

In the 1940s, however, NAM was fighting an uphill battle to ingrain the Tripod of Freedom in the American mind. FDR had successfully framed the organization's position as "industrial dictatorship" and "economic royalism," in which the prerogatives and greed of the few trumped the rights and needs of the many.[24] When NAM and its allies argued for businessmen's freedom to set wages and working hours in their factories, but denied workers the freedom to unionize and engage in collective bargaining, many Americans were capable of seeing through the hypocrisy. Moreover, memories of the Depression were still vivid and bitter. As historian Wendy Wall has noted, in the wake of economic collapse the "narrative of capitalist-driven growth" seemed "questionable at best, a monstrous delusion at worst."[25] How could captains of industry claim they were best equipped to sail the ship of state when that ship had so recently crashed upon the rocks?[26]

With the Tripod of Freedom and the indivisibility thesis in place, NAM and its allies had a toolkit of potent rhetorical devices, but no blueprint of the structure those tools might build. This was all about to change, however, as American libertarians discovered and championed two émigré economists who granted their cause an intellectual legitimacy it previously had lacked. They were going to build a temple to the free market; Ludwig von Mises and his protégé, Friedrich von Hayek, would be its architects.

IN 1940, LUDWIG von Mises faced a predicament. The Nazi army was advancing across Europe. Mises was a nearly sixty-year-old economics professor of Jewish descent, and even his adoptive home of Geneva, in neutral Switzerland, felt unsafe. Other European academics were fleeing to the United States. But if Mises followed, he would need a job, and American demand for the services he could supply was decidedly limited.

As a young man in Austria, Mises had worked for the Vienna Chamber of Commerce, where his task was "to analyze existing and proposed legislation critically and to influence Austrian economic policy in a more pro-business, market-oriented direction."[27] In 1912, he had established his professional reputation with *The Theory of Money and Credit*, in which he argued (among other things) for free markets and the gold standard.[28] He followed it up with *Socialism*, published in German in 1922, which Friedrich von Hayek later described as "the definitive refutation of nearly every type of socialism ever devised."[29] An absolutist who sympathized with fascism, opposed laws restricting child labor, and doubted the virtues of public education,[30] Mises spent part of the 1930s as an economic adviser to Engelbert Dollfuss, the chancellor who ended the Austrian republic and established an authoritarian regime aligned with conservative Roman Catholicism and sympathetic to Italian fascism.[31]

All of this was a definite strike against Mises in FDR's America, where the theories of the British philosopher and economist John Maynard Keynes dominated government offices and university departments. Keynes argued that the state had to manage the marketplace, to smooth out otherwise crushing business cycles and attend to needs not met by the private sector. Laissez-faire capitalism had produced devastating social evils—brutal child labor, deadly working conditions, poor public health, low education levels, an impoverished elderly population, and so on—as well as serious economic problems, such as boom-and-bust cycles, widespread unemployment, and bank panics. In the century and a half since Adam Smith had laid out his vision of beneficent and efficient capitalism, the "invisible hand of the marketplace" had frequently been idle (as, indeed, Smith had warned it would). In 1924, even before the Great Depression hit America, Keynes could credibly declare that the world had come to "The End of *Laissez-Faire*."[32] By the early 1930s, with banks failing, millions out of work, and the global depression deepening, the invisible hand was AWOL. In his 1936 work *The General Theory of Employment, Interest and Money*, Keynes dismantled the notion that markets were rational and could be trusted to restore prosperity; rather, they required managing. The United States, under FDR, began adopting Keynesian strategies to address unemployment and stimulate demand.

Mises adamantly opposed government involvement in the marketplace. From his work flowed a strand of laissez-faire theory known as the Austrian school of economics; during the worst of the Great Depression, Mises and his acolytes advocated strongly *against* state action to stimulate demand. He was, as economic historian Karen Vaughn writes, "a staunch advocate of free markets at a time when enthusiasm for them had reached a nadir in American life."[33]

In 1936, when the English translation of *Socialism* appeared, American readers had a chance to consider Mises's ideas for themselves. The book was a frontal assault on the notion of the centrally planned economy. Mises built his argument on the premise that goods and services have no inherent value; they simply have a price, which tells us what buyers are willing to pay and what sellers are willing to accept. The worth of an item or service only exists insofar as it can be determined by the price system in a market economy.[34] To allocate resources effectively and make correct decisions about how much of a given good to manufacture or service to provide, Mises contends, economic planners would need to know the price of everything. But without markets, this is impossible. Even if you could sum up all the inputs—the materials, the labor, the factory operating expenses, and so on—to calculate the production cost of a thing, it still would not tell you the *value* of that thing, because something might be costly to produce yet be wanted by few, and vice versa.[35]

Mises also sniffs out a second problem: Socialism is premised upon cooperation but cannot attain it, because how can you divide labor when you don't know its value? "Without economic calculation, the economic system cannot achieve the complex coordination of the division of labor, and thus cannot realize the benefits of social cooperation."[36] Capitalism, in contrast, is premised on competition but yields cooperation.

Among the book's American admirers was a financial writer and *New York Times* editorialist named Henry Hazlitt, one of the most important conservative intellectuals of the mid-twentieth century who history has more or less forgotten. The financial editor of the *New York Evening Mail* during the 1920s, Hazlitt educated himself in economics and in the 1930s emerged as a leading critic of the New Deal, claiming (as did Herbert Hoover and other conservative antagonists) that it was a step toward authoritarianism.[37] Hazlitt joined the *New York Times* in 1934 as an editorial writer, penning both signed and unsigned columns on economic topics.[38] In 1938, Hazlitt reviewed *Socialism* in the *New York Times*, calling Mises's text "the most devastating analysis [of socialism] yet penned."[39] When Mises fled Europe, it was Hazlitt, working with colleagues at NAM, who ensured that the economist landed in America, and on his feet.

Hazlitt's support was essential; left to his own devices, Mises would almost certainly have seen his intellectual star fading. His admirers claim he initially failed to secure an academic job in the United States simply because his ideas clashed with the tenor of the times. But Mises had several additional strikes against him.[40] Despite his insistence that economics was a science, he came from a tradition that collected little or no data, and many claims he made were difficult if not impossible to test. Critics have also noted that his arguments were utterly rigid: historian Angus Burgin calls him "strident," and Vaughn describes Mises's writing as "imperious." He was intolerant of competing theories, and he fought battles that most other economists considered over. Moreover, aside from his methodological shortcomings and bullying manner, Mises's work had glaring errors.

Business leaders embraced his argument, in *Socialism*, that centrally planned economies were doomed to fail, but that book had a glaring problem: Mises collapsed *socialism* into *centralized planning*.[41] To be sure, centralized planning was an essential, almost sacramental feature of Soviet communism, with its vaunted five-year plans. But could socialism be equated with—and reduced to—centralized planning? Was socialism indistinguishable from communism in this regard? Most Americans in the mid-twentieth century did not think so.[42]

MISES'S USE OF the term *socialism* was misleading, at least in the American context, because no credible American political leader in 1944 was advocating central planning, not even the socialist leader Norman Thomas. As historian and theologian Gary Dorrien has stressed, American socialists took pains to differentiate and distance themselves from communists. As president of the American

Socialist Party, Thomas called himself a democratic socialist, and he not only believed in but participated in electoral politics, countering NAM's attempts to dismiss his ideas as undemocratic. In 1928, 1932, and 1936, Thomas ran for president on the Socialist Party ticket; previously he had also run for governor of New York State and mayor of New York City. Both Thomas and his predecessor in the party, Eugene Debs, were reformists who "defended liberty above other values and championed social democracy on moral grounds," striving in particular to protect workers, tenants, and African American sharecroppers.[43] Nor was Thomas an atheist scorning religion as the opium of the people: he was the son and grandson of Presbyterian ministers and had himself been ordained in 1911. He believed it was incumbent on Christians to "feed the hungry, shelter the homeless, comfort the afflicted, and build a just society," a view that was strengthened over seven years as a minister in a poor parish in East Harlem.[44] Socialism, for Thomas and his followers, was a *social* movement (as much as or more than an economic philosophy), linked to the ideal of the Social Gospel, and intended to improve the lot of the disadvantaged. It was in no way intended to strip individuals of their rights. On the contrary, Thomas was "allergic to authoritarianism of every kind."[45]

Leon Trotsky famously dismissed American socialists under Thomas as "a party of dentists"; Thomas welcomed that critique. The "future belonged to a democratic socialism that stuck to its core convictions about civil liberties, nonviolence, and economic democracy," he averred.[46] His party embraced neither centralized economic planning nor the notion of a revolutionary vanguard and dictatorship of the proletariat. Thomas's 1932 presidential campaign focused on many policies that became reality during the New Deal or in the following decades: agricultural relief, unemployment insurance, public works, low-cost housing, a progressive income tax. Indeed, one could argue that what defined his positions as socialist, and distinguished him from Democrats, like FDR, or earlier progressive Republicans, like Theodore Roosevelt, was his advocacy of the nationalization of banks, natural monopolies (e.g., railroads and utilities), and other essential industries (such as coal mines).[47] Precisely because Thomas was anti-Marxist, anti-Stalinist, and pro-democracy, critics had to work hard either to find fault in his views—or to misrepresent them.[48]

Actually, far more leading Americans in the 1930s and '40s were Nazi and fascist sympathizers than advocated central planning.[49] In the 1930s, the antisemitic, fascist-sympathizing Father Charles Edward Coughlin had an estimated thirty million listeners for his weekly radio broadcast, and in 1939, the Nazi sympathizer and open antisemite Charles Lindbergh was seriously put forward as a possible candidate for president by the America First Committee.[50] No American socialist had comparable status or media reach.[51]

In a rare moment of candor, NAM Secretary Noel Sargent had admitted that the opposite of socialism wasn't, in fact, capitalism. "Under capitalism, the means of production and distribution are privately owned and individuals may profit from their possession or operation, while under socialism they will be publicly owned and private profit forbidden. It would be accurate . . . to contrast 'socialism' with 'individualism' or 'commercialism.'" Sargent identified a key conceptual error in the indivisibility thesis: the failure to acknowledge that capitalism was an economic program, which could be linked with various forms of social and political organization. "[W]hen we compare socialism with capitalism we are discussing two economic programs, and are not discussing such questions as the relation of socialism to art, religion or forms of government. Capitalism may prevail under a democracy or under a dictatorship; socialism . . . in theory might exist full-fledged under a democracy."[52]

The argument about what socialism really was—and whether the New Deal was or was not socialistic—highlights a second flaw in Mises's work: it succumbed to the fallacy of the excluded middle. It rested on the false dichotomy of tyrannical totalitarianism on the one hand and unalloyed laissez-faire on the other. Between Stalinism and laissez-faire, there were myriad ways to understand economies and try to manage them (or not). Keynes and his followers rejected laissez-faire, but they were far from advocating communism in its stead. The heart of Keynesianism—and of a good deal of mid-century economic thinking—was to sort out the appropriate role of government in addressing business cycles, monopolies, and market failure. No wonder most American economists were not impressed by Mises, and few universities were interested in hiring him.

WHEN MISES FIRST arrived in the United States, he was kept afloat by funding from the Rockefeller Foundation, which had supported him in the 1930s at the Graduate Institute of International Studies in Geneva.[53] But by the early 1940s, the foundation, known for its desire to cultivate the best minds, had decided Mises was not, in fact, one of the best. The organization lost interest in him, and in Austrian economics generally. The market failures of the Great Depression, and the interventionist successes of the New Deal, made the Austrian school seem increasingly quaint, if not irrelevant.

Hazlitt stepped into the breach, first commissioning Mises to write articles for the *Times*, and, perhaps more importantly, introducing Mises to NAM.[54] Its backing helped sustain Mises, and provided life support for ideas which—given his extremism—might otherwise have withered away. Mises biographer Jörg Hülsmann recounts that "NAM immediately stepped in and offered to hire Mises as a consultant—'starting today.'" Mises became a member of NAM's Economic Policy Advisory Group and its Advisory Group on International Economic Relations with an "honorarium" of $3,000, soon increased to $3,600.[55] (This was a tidy sum at a time when the median American income was $956.)[56] Mises worked closely with Noel Sargent, the principal architect of NAM's 1930s propaganda campaign. And NAM was not Mises's only benefactor in the business community. He also began a long-lasting collaboration with an organization called the Foundation for Economic Education and its cofounder, Leonard Read, who would do much to promote libertarian economics in the United States.

Leonard Read was born and raised in rural Michigan. In 1925 he moved to Northern California, and then to Seattle to manage the Western Division of the U.S. Chamber of Commerce, where he worked closely with members of the Los Angeles Chamber of Commerce. In 1933, he met William Mullendore, a former Herbert Hoover aide who was now president and chairman of the board of Southern California Edison.[57] Mullendore was annoyed with the Chamber of Commerce for making too many concessions to the New Deal. Read asked to meet, hoping to convince Mullendore that the Chamber's positions were right. Instead, Mullendore convinced Read, who "came away as a newly baptized libertarian."[58] In 1939, Read moved to Los Angeles to become manager of the Los Angeles Chamber, at the time the largest of the local branches of the U.S. Chamber of Commerce.

In 1945, Read and Mullendore, along with David Goodrich of the B.F. Goodrich Corporation, hatched a plan to create a dedicated libertarian institute.[59] They assembled a network of funders among business executives, including Harold Luhnow, the director of the Kansas City–based William Volker Fund; Henry Ford II; GM executive Charles Kettering; media mogul William Scripps; and NAM leader and Sun Oil president J. Howard Pew.[60] They would christen it the Foundation for Economic Education (FEE), incorporated in 1946 with Goodrich as chairman, Read as president, and Hazlitt as vice president.[61] FEE would also be supported by Herbert Hoover; DuPont executive Jasper Crane; and Frank Donaldson Brown, the vice chairman of the board at GM (and a former employee at DuPont, where he had worked closely with American Liberty League cofounder John J. Raskob).[62] As funders, these businessmen were crucial to the task Read assigned himself: advocating for "a stringent, crystalline vision of the free market."[63] Ludwig von Mises was key to that vision.

Read was impressed by the "purity of Mises's opposition to any government power beyond the minimum necessary for the preservation of domestic peace and the market."[64] They were a good match: Mises's liberal purity harmonized with Read's political ambition, and the latter's writings and lectures became a vital part of FEE campaigns. Mises was "one of the first economists hired for lectures and seminars of FEE's premises and would eventually become its intellectual center for more than two decades."[65]

Around the same time, Read and Mullendore set up a company, Pamphleteers, Inc., to promote market fundamentalism and libertarian ideals under a series called *The Freeman*. Among the writers whose work they published were the Yale sociologist William Graham Sumner (who had influenced NAM's Noel Sargent) and a relatively recent émigrée novelist named Ayn Rand.[66] Read also began lecturing and published a handbook on how to market "free competitive enterprise" within the business community.[67]

Meanwhile, Hazlitt had arranged for Mises to continue contributing editorials to the *New York Times*, to give guest lectures, and, in 1944, to secure a teaching position at New York University.[68] Mises had offers from the University of Rochester and several other schools, but the imperious Viennese savant would "not settle for 'second-rate institutions.'"[69] Hazlitt and Read joined forces with Lawrence Fertig—an advertising executive, libertarian journalist, and NYU trustee—to arrange and pay for Mises to lecture at the NYU Graduate School of Business Administration.[70] In 1949, Mises's contract was not renewed, but now another private benefactor stepped in: Harold Luhnow, one of the founding funders of FEE. Luhnow's largesse enabled Mises to stay at NYU as a "visiting professor" for the rest of his career.[71]

Richard Ebeling—a libertarian economist, one-time FEE president, and passionate Mises admirer—admits that "it is doubtful that a vibrant and growing Austrian school of economics would now exist if not for Mises's relocation to the

United States," and that "the vision and the ideal of the liberal free market order might have been lost in . . . the rise of the interventionist welfare state."[72] Ebeling is probably right: wealthy businessmen underwrote Mises's American academic career, motivated not by the quest to advance economic science but by their determination to succor the Austrian school and sustain it as part of a political program. Financial and moral support from Hazlitt, Read, Luhnow, Fertig, and NAM helped keep Mises's political theory vital when it might otherwise have languished.[73] In his writings, Mises lionized competition and opposed government intervention in the marketplace, yet in his career he depended on allies in the commercial world, who staged an intervention on his behalf in the academic marketplace of ideas.

It is obvious why Mises needed this support, but why did these men need him? NAM leadership had already committed itself to a vision of American politics and economics consistent with Mises's views. In 1935, they had launched the *American Family Robinson* radio program with its message of the Tripod of Freedom; by 1938 they had developed the case for "free enterprise" to fight unions and protect business prerogatives; and in 1939 they had laid out the indivisibility thesis in their Declaration of Principles. Wendell Willkie had used these themes in his 1940 presidential campaign, insisting that America's core challenge was to preserve the "free-enterprise system," without which "we shall go down into the totalitarian pit."[74]

What, then, did Mises add? Hülsmann offers a credible answer: Mises's benefactors "needed intellectual leadership from people who were conversant both in the world of business and in the world of ideas. By February 1943, they had discovered what they were looking for in Ludwig von Mises."[75] Thanks to Mises, campaigns that in the 1930s had been exposed as unprincipled propaganda now could be reconstructed as a credible intellectual program. But while Mises was famous for his arguments against planning and interventionism—for the superiority of free markets over planned ones—he had not stressed the inseparability of political and economic freedom. For that, the men of NAM and FEE turned to Mises's protégé, Friedrich von Hayek.

HAD THINGS TURNED out differently, Friedrich von Hayek could very well have gone into sociology, and the history might have taken another path. After World War I, Hayek, who had been born and raised in Vienna, wanted to go to

Germany to study with the great sociologist Max Weber, author of some of the field's foundational texts, including *The Protestant Ethic and the Spirit of Capitalism*.[76] But the crippling inflation of Germany's Weimar Republic made this impossible, and in any case Weber died in 1920.[77] So, in one of history's more consequential contingencies, the twenty-two-year-old Hayek remained in Vienna, where in 1921 Mises hired him as a research assistant. Hayek assisted Mises's studies on money and banking; undertook a PhD in political science; and attended Mises's influential private seminar.[78] In later years, Hayek would say that "virtually all of his own contributions to monetary and business cycle theory, his critique of socialism and planning, [and] his analysis of competition and the market process" were "deeply influenced, if not directly inspired, by Mises's early writing in every one of these areas."[79]

What were these contributions? One was an argument against central banks. Following Mises, Hayek believed that the operators of a central bank, being fundamentally monopolistic, would suffer the same lack of information as socialist planners.[80] With Mises's help Hayek founded and served as director of the Austrian Institute for Business Cycle Research, which argued that economic upswings and downswings were inevitable when central banks set interest rates too low. Easy credit led to malinvestment and eventually to a bust.[81] If governments intervene to sustain the upward side of a cycle, Hayek insisted, it worsens the unavoidable downward side.

This work caught the attention of Lionel Robbins at the London School of Economics, and in 1931, Hayek was offered a post there; Robbins and Hayek would form the backbone of an anti-Keynesian position in British politics and economics.[82] They rejected Keynes's prescription for public spending and low interest rates to boost demand when markets failed to recover from the crash of 1929; Hayek and Robbins reviled this remedy as a further distortion of already distorted markets, a cure worse than the disease. It would be best to allow the private sector to respond, which, in time, they insisted, it would. (Herbert Hoover took essentially the same position in the United States, costing himself a second term as president.)

But what did it mean for markets to respond "in time"? By 1932, the U.S. unemployment rate was 24 percent, and inflation was running at 10 percent.[83] (In the United Kingdom, unemployment was lower—around 15 percent—because the country had already undertaken expansionist steps.)[84] How long would it take for markets to fix themselves? What about the pain people experienced in the meanwhile? The Austrians lacked answers to these questions. Decades later, even the dyed-in-the-wool libertarian economist Milton Friedman would disassociate himself from the Austrian school for this reason. In a 1998 interview, Friedman explained: "If you go back to the 1930s . . . you had the Austrians sitting in London . . . saying you just have to let the bottom drop out of the world. You've just got to let it cure itself. You can't do anything about it. You will only make it worse. You have [them] saying it was a great mistake not to let the whole banking system collapse. I think by encouraging that kind of do-nothing policy both in Britain and in the United States, they did harm."[85] As Friedman observed, while people went hungry Hayek and Robbins counseled patience, and when more people went hungry they counseled more patience.

Besides appearing inhumane, the Austrian position highlighted a contradiction in Mises's thought. He insisted that economics must be a value-free science, but the problems of the 1930s—especially how much suffering could be tolerated while waiting for markets to self-correct—raised profound political and moral questions. To argue that in the long run it would be better to allow markets to repair themselves was to discount the agony that many were experiencing in the present. One might argue the Austrians were implicitly adopting a utilitarian framework: privileging the greatest good for the greatest number of people and accepting current suffering so long as net harm was reduced. But any position grounded in a utilitarian calculus could hardly claim to be value-neutral. Mises and Hayek insisted on the *imperative* of value-neutrality, but their positions were anything but. The values they advocated—prosperity, freedom, and above all the right of individuals to decide for themselves what is best and right for themselves— may have been defensible, but they were values, and they were absolutely central to their "scientific" conclusions.

Still, until the mid-1930s their work was in the mainstream of technical argument, addressing properly economic topics such as banking, investment, monetary policy, the gold standard. Regardless of one's preferred moral framework, one can evaluate the impacts of alternative monetary policies based on empirical evidence. And even someone sympathetic to socialism could acknowledge that Mises had a point about the role of markets in generating information and the difficulty planners must encounter in the absence of that information. But in 1935, Hayek took up the argument that Mises began in *Socialism* and moved it in an explicitly political and normative direction.[86]

According to historian Douglas French, only a third of the participants in Mises's private seminar were economists; the rest were mostly philosophers and social theorists.[87] This intellectual milieu may help explain why—even though Hayek would build his career as an economist and eventually win the Nobel Memorial Prize in the subject—his most influential arguments were political.[88] Milton Friedman all but acknowledged this when he declared himself "an enormous admirer of Hayek, but not for his economics," which were "flawed" and often "unreadable." Nevertheless, Friedman gushed, Hayek had authored "one of the great books of our time": his 1944 work *The Road to Serfdom*, a book that would make Hayek a hero of the American right and the patron saint of free-market doctrine.[89]

The thesis of *The Road to Serfdom* is that capitalism and freedom are linked, and so if we wish to preserve political freedom, we must preserve economic freedom. Conversely, if we abandon economic freedom to centralized planning, whether in the name of fairness, efficiency, or equity, it is only a matter of time before we lose political freedom as well. Socialism was therefore not only bound to fail *economically* but also *politically*. Despite the best of intentions of even the most benevolent socialists, their actions inevitably strip individuals of freedom.[90] To Hayek, socialism is not merely irrational, it is dangerous. Wendell Willkie had argued that government control of the economy under FDR was a path into the pit of totalitarianism, from which future generations would struggle to emerge.[91] Hayek's point was essentially the same, but he gave the argument intellectual heft.

Hayek reasoned that the free-market system, based on private property, is the guarantor of our political freedom, because markets distribute power: individuals making free choices in the marketplace every day hold power in their hands and prevent its concentration in centralized government. In Hayek's free market, no planner can make choices on behalf of others and compromise their liberty. In his words: "[T]he system of private property is the most important guarantee of freedom, not only for those who own property, but scarcely less for those who do not. It is only because the control of the means of production is divided among many people acting independently that nobody has complete power over us, that we as individuals can decide what to do with ourselves."[92] Hayek's argument *is* the indivisibility thesis: political and economic freedom cannot be detached. Economic freedom protects political freedom.

To what extent should governments be involved in the functioning of markets? Hayek's answer: as little as possible. Left to their own devices, markets respond to demand, and in this responsiveness lie their efficiency and power. Planning may seem like a good idea; after all, we make plans for our lives, our careers, and our families. But government planning is different from personal planning for two reasons. First, centralized governments can never have the information they would need to plan effectively—economies are too dynamic and complex—so the information available to planners will always be too little, too late. At best the result is inefficiency; at worst, central planning leads to the tragic miscalculations that plagued the Soviet Union. Second, any attempt to control an economy necessarily implicates governments in the control of people, whom it must direct in service of the central plan. To execute their vision, planners need political power. Therefore, what starts as benevolent or well-intentioned planning necessarily ends as coercion; centralized planning becomes the road to serfdom. The Soviet Union's failures— both political and economic—did not stem purely from bad management; they were the inescapable result of the attempt to manage from above what should instead, in Hayek's view, be allowed to flourish from below.

Hayek's argument is not *exclusively* political; he does make an important economic point. Echoing Mises, Hayek holds that the marketplace should be understood as a means to process information; an item's price tells us what that item is worth to the people who either have or want it.[93] Still, Hayek's focus is more political than economic: for him, there can be no such thing as "democratic socialism" or even social democracy, because socialism—if it involves the government in the marketplace— however it begins, will end up undemocratic: "Our point . . . is . . . that planning leads to dictatorship because dictatorship is the most effective instrument of coercion and the enforcement of ideals, and, as such, essential if central planning on a large scale is to be possible."[94] This point was sufficiently important that he clarified it in the fore- word to the 1956 edition, in response to the complaint that he seemed to be suggesting that socialists *wanted* totalitarianism. What Hayek had argued in the book—he wrote, after having had time to absorb this critique—is that "the unforeseen but inev- itable consequences of socialist planning create a state of affairs in which, if the policy is to be pursued, totalitarian forces will get the upper hand."[95]

Hayek's focus on planning was perhaps an understandable response to the envi- ronment at the London School of Economics in the 1930s, where "planning was the word on everyone's lips." Students there could take seminars on "Economic Planning in Theory and Practice." The great sociologist Karl Mannheim, hired when he fled Frankfurt in 1933, insisted that "only by adopting a comprehensive system of economic planning could Britain avoid the fate of central Europe ... planning was inevitable; the only question was whether it was going to be totalitarian or democratic."[96] In 1937, Hayek's colleague Lionel Robbins complained that planning was "the great panacea of our age."[97] Hayek may also have been responding to the situation in Germany, where the Nazi government had taken over the economy to an unprecedented degree, which many German and Austrian liberals feared would continue even once the Nazis were removed from power.[98] Still, the essence of scholarship—historical or economic—is to look past the immediacies of time and place, which Hayek struggled to do.[99]

Historian Bruce Caldwell, one of Hayek's most astute interpreters, puts his argument this way: "Full-scale planning requires that the planning authorities take over all production decisions; to be able to make any decisions at all, they would need to exercise more and more political control. If one tries to create a *truly* planned economy, one will not be able to separate control of the economic from political control."[100] The key words here, of course, are "truly planned." Many modes of social democracy and social reform involve government *economic action* without government *planning* of the economy, much less a takeover of the marketplace.[101] Hayek, however, often elides this distinction. The words "truly planned" are Caldwell's, not Hayek's.

The most important example available to Mises and Hayek was Germany under Chancellor Otto von Bismarck. Already in 1944, it was widely accepted that the social reforms Germany had pioneered in the 1880s had had both the intent and the effect of undermining socialism: if industrial workers' legitimate grievances could be addressed—particularly the need for financial and physical security—radicalism would be less tempting.[102] Under Bismarck, Germany had created a system of social insurance against sickness, accidents, and disability, as well as a pension system. This had lessened the burden on employers to provide welfare assistance as "benefits" (as Henry Ford later would in the United States, creating pressure on other employers to do the same). The German approach involved no government direction of markets—quite the opposite. The system did place an obligation on businesses in that they shared the costs, but that obligation was equitable: it applied to all industrial employers. Otherwise, owners were free to run their businesses as they saw fit; in no sense did the government make decisions about *production*. Rather, the insurance system filled gaps that industrial capitalism left unfilled.[103]

Social reforms in the United States in the late nineteenth and early twentieth centuries took a different course, but they, too, did not implicate the federal government in socialist planning of the economy. Nor did they involve the elimination of competition. The Progressive Era in America—banking regulation, the prohibition of anticompetitive practices, the enactment of workmen's compensation and anti-child-labor laws—is best understood as a federal effort to establish the rules by which markets would operate. Theodore Roosevelt, American's most powerful progressive, was no socialist; his most famous legacy—trust-busting—was designed to protect competition, not disable it. The moral and intellectual centerpiece of his "square deal" was a level playing field, so monopolists and financiers would not be able to manipulate the system to their advantage. The New Deal went farther, but it was still a far cry from centralized planning, and many analysts, including conservatives such as the Hoover Institution's Seymour Lipset and Gary Marks, have credited Franklin D. Roosevelt with *saving* capitalism.[104] To suggest that either Bismarck's or Roosevelt's reforms were a step toward unfreedom is like claiming that road signs, stop lights, and speed limits are steps toward the elimination of driving.

TO AN EXTENT, Hayek acknowledges this; there is more to him than his doctrinaire acolytes allow. Belying its reputation today as the canonical libertarian text, *The Road to Serfdom* in fact makes considerable space for nuances that resist the stereotypical antigovernment platform. Among other things, Hayek allows that the "free" market is not really free—that it operates under a variety of constraints—and he does not oppose government involvement *per se*. He rejected the term *laissez-faire* as misleading: "The successful use of competition as the principle of social organization precludes certain types of coercive interference with economic life, but it admits of . . . and even requires" others.[105] Hayek was not suggesting that governments should simply do nothing, no matter the consequences: "It is important not to confuse opposition against planning with a dogmatic laissez-faire attitude. The liberal argument is in favor of making the best possible use of the forces of competition as a means of coordinating human efforts, not an argument for leaving things just as they are."[106]

What sorts of interventions *were* legitimate? Hayek specifies a surprisingly large number. They include paying for signposts on roads, preventing "harmful effects of deforestation, of some methods of farming, or of the noise and smoke of factories," prohibiting the use of "certain poisonous substances or to require special precautions in their use," limiting working hours, enforcing sanitary conditions in workplaces, controlling weights and measures, and preventing violent strikes.[107] He simply argues that if governments are to carry out such functions, they should do so equitably, and if doing so selectively limits the freedom of particular groups or individuals, then the justification for the intervention should be clear and compelling.

One way to understand Hayek's position on governance is to compare it to Adam Smith's view on taxation: Smith allowed that taxation was necessary for state functioning but insisted taxes be collected equitably and consistently. Similarly, Hayek insisted (again, not unreasonably) that the real issue is not *intervention*, but *favoritism*: "[W]ith respect to most of the general and permanent rules which the state may establish with regard to production, such as building regulations or factory laws: these may be wise or unwise in the particular instance, but they do not conflict with liberal principles so long as they . . . are not used to favor or harm particular people."[108] This is not an argument against having rules of the economic road. It is not an argument against all regulation, period. In fact, Hayek declares the idea of governance without action or intervention to be silly: "The question whether the state should or should not 'act' or 'interfere' poses an altogether false alternative . . . Of course, every state must act and every action of the state interferes with something or other."[109] The key question—one that Hayek never adequately answers—is how to evaluate the social costs and judge when government should act and when it should not.[110]

Hayek supported social security, workmen's compensation, and even a guaranteed minimum income. In *The Road to Serfdom*, he writes: "There is no reason why in a society which has reached the general level of wealth which ours has attained that . . . security should not be guaranteed to all without endangering general freedom." He distinguishes between "security against severe physical privation, the certainty of a given minimum of sustenance for all"—which he considered a legitimate government concern—and "the security of a given standard of life, or of the relative position which one person or group enjoys compared with others"—which he opposed, believing it would disincentivize work.[111] But that distinction aside, he was not as hostile to social welfare programs as he is often reputed to be. Elsewhere, in a passage that threatens to contradict the rest of his argument—and from the man who made his name as an opponent of Keynes!—Hayek allows that the state *should* address the vicissitudes of employment caused by business cycles, and even that doing so might require planning of a certain kind:

> There is, finally, the supremely important problem of combatting general fluctuations of economic activity and the recurrent waves of large-scale unemployment which accompany them. This is, of course, one of the gravest and most pressing problems of our time. But, though its solution will require much planning in the good sense, it does not—or at least need not—require that special kind of planning which according to its advocates is to replace the market . . . This might lead to much more serious restrictions of the competitive sphere, and, in experimenting in this direction, we shall have carefully to watch our step if we are to avoid making all economic activity progressively more dependent on the direction and volume of government expenditure . . . In any case, the very necessary efforts to secure protection against these fluctuations do not lead to the kind of planning which constitutes . . . a threat to our freedom.[112]

Endorsements of (some) social insurance and (some) state planning are not the only instances of *The Road to Serfdom* playing against type. Hayek also clearly states that governments at times need to supplement competition "where it cannot be made effective." It falls to the state "to provide services which, in the words of Adam Smith, 'though they may be in the highest degree advantageous to a great society, are, however, of such a nature, that the profit could never repay the expense to the individual or small number of individuals'" who undertook to provide them. These tasks, Hayek concludes, provide *"a wide and unquestioned field for state activity."*[113]

Still, Hayek declines to offer a framework for deciding which services should be supplied by the state and which could be left to the marketplace. He gives specific instances of warranted regulation but offers no evaluative criteria, other than the general notions of societal advantage and individual profit. Nor does he help us think through the problem of services, such as health care, that the private sector could theoretically provide but has not, in fact, provided—or at least not adequately or equitably. Instead, he evades the question by accusing social reformers of wanting to supplant competition entirely. "The question was no longer one of making competition work and of supplementing it but of displacing it altogether,"[114] he insists. That may have been true in Soviet Russia and some corners of Europe, but it was certainly not true in FDR's America. Like Mises, Hayek collapses the distinctions between social reform, social democracy, socialism, and even National Socialism (i.e., Nazism). He conflates all forms of *antiliberalism* with socialism and collapses socialism into fully fledged Soviet-style central economic planning.

In some ways, *The Road to Serfdom* is less an argument *against* socialism than it is a catechism *for* individualism. What is paramount for Hayek is the principle that people have the right to decide for themselves how they wish to live. Individualism, he explains, "does not assume, as is often asserted, that man is egoistic or selfish or ought to be. It merely starts from the indisputable fact that the limits of our powers of imagination make it impossible to include in our scale of values more than a sector of the needs of the whole society . . . From this, the individualist concludes that the individuals should be allowed, within defined limits, to follow their own values and preferences rather than somebody else's . . . It is this recognition of the individual as the ultimate judge of his ends, the belief that as far as possible his own views ought to govern his actions, that forms the essence of the individualist position."[115] In practice, this translates into a belief that the state cannot know—and should not presume to know—what individuals want. Therefore, "beyond a minimum of decency" as in the case of "calamities" and "genuinely uninsurable risks," the government should not attempt to provide for the needs of its people.[116]

In many ways, this is the crux of Hayek's argument: markets solve the information problem that dooms socialist planning, and markets are composed of individuals expressing their preferences, so individualism is the best social strategy.[117] It is a defensible point in some respects. Beyond clean air, water, and the basics of food, clothing, and shelter, different people have different preferences, and governments will be hard pressed to ascertain and reflect those preferences accurately. All else being equal, it is best for people to decide and provide for themselves. But key questions remain unanswered: How do we decide on those "defined limits"? What constitutes the "minimum" of decency? What distinguishes a legitimate intervention from an illegitimate one? On these inherently political questions, the voluble Friedrich von Hayek is oddly at a loss for words.

IN LATER YEARS, Hayek would become an icon to conservatives in the United Kingdom and the United States. It is said that when Margaret Thatcher was elected leader of the British Conservative Party in 1975, she cut off discussion of how Tories might cooperate with Labour compatriots by brandishing a copy of Hayek's 1960 book *The Constitution of Liberty*, declaring: "This is what we believe."[118] Libertarian think tanks such as the Cato Institute and the American Enterprise Institute have extensively promoted *The Road to Serfdom*. Fans of the book include some of the Republican Party's most inflexible ideologues—including former Speaker of the House Paul Ryan, former House majority leader Dick Armey, and Texas senator Ted Cruz, who claims to have read Hayek as a teenager—as well as talk-radio pundits Glenn Beck and Rush Limbaugh.[119] After Beck devoted one of his shows to Hayek, the next week *The Road to Serfdom* sold sixty thousand copies.[120] The book came in fourth in the right-wing *National Review*'s ranking of its favorite nonfiction books of all time.[121]

If market fundamentalism is a religion, its bible is *The Road to Serfdom*.[122] In 2020, none other than Fox News commentator Tucker Carlson made this point. The former Soviet Union, he argued, was a cult based on Marx's *Capital*, and American conservatism had its own cult based on *The Road to Serfdom*: "You read Hayek . . . You attend a couple of lectures at Cato and you think you're a libertarian and you've got the world figured out as kind of this seamless theory of everything. Next thing you know, you're arguing to privatize the sidewalks."[123]

Republican and conservative leaders' embrace of *The Road to Serfdom* has led a number of commentators, including the British journalist Nicholas Wapshott and Columbia University law professor Bernard Harcourt, to stress that Hayek was not remotely the unflinching free-marketeer that many believe him to be.[124] As we have seen, a close reading of his work bears this out: Hayek is not a heartless absolutist. *The Road to Serfdom* is not a brief against governance. It is a cautionary tale about the limits of information and the judiciousness that should follow from recognizing those limits. It is an argument against central economic planning, and against dirigisme of any kind, but it is not the book that many of its partisans seem to think it is.[125] How, then, did Hayek become the hero to 1940s American business leaders who opposed social security, and to American conservatives today who are rolling back environmental and workplace protection, contributing to deforestation, and refusing even to acknowledge many of the harms of industrial agriculture? How did he become the patron saint of all-out hostility to government?[126]

The fact is that the nuanced Hayek of *The Road to Serfdom* was not (for the most part) the Hayek who reached the American people. In the hands of ideologues, *The Road to Serfdom* was transmogrified from a complex and subtle argument about the risks of governmental control into an antigovernment polemic. That transmogrification began with the book's promotion in America by Henry Hazlitt and the National Association of Manufacturers.

THE INITIAL U.S. reception to *The Road to Serfdom* was negative: three major American publishers turned it down, seeing it as a very British book engaged in a very British argument. It was only through the efforts of University of Chicago economists—Aaron Director, Frank Knight, and Henry Simons—that the University of Chicago Press was prevailed upon to publish it.[127] (Political scientist David P. Ramsey says Director mounted a "prolonged lobbying campaign" to get the book published.)[128] Of course, even the best books need champions, but was this the best of books? The press didn't think so.[129]

"No one expected *The Road to Serfdom* to be a success," writes historian Kim Phillips-Fein.[130] But then the *New York Times* gave the book top billing, publishing Hazlitt's detailed appraisal on the front page of the review section. Calling it "one of the most important books of our time," Hazlitt began by situating Hayek in the philosophical pantheon. *The Road to Serfdom*, he declaimed, "restates for our time the issue between liberty and authority with the power and rigor of reasoning that John Stuart Mill stated the issue for his own generation in his great essay *On Liberty*."[131]

The comparison was odd, for Mill's utilitarianism grossly violated Hayek's dearly held individualism. Rather than engage these difficulties, however, Hazlitt reiterated Hayek's scolding of leftists, insisting they were to blame for the rise of European totalitarianism: "[F]ascism, and what the Germans correctly call National Socialism, are the end products not of 'nineteenth-century liberalism or of individualism, which represent their opposites, but of the growth of State control and State power, of national planning and of socialism' . . . Few are ready to recognize that the rise of fascism and nazism was not a reaction against the Socialist trends of the preceding period but a necessary outcome of those tendencies."[132] This claim made little sense: both Nazism and fascism were expressions of right-wing politics; communism and socialism were politics of the left. Perhaps Hayek was trying to say that it didn't matter where coercive doctrines placed themselves on the political spectrum; the effect of coercion would in the end be the same. But the historical reality was that socialists and communists had been among those most active in opposing fascism. That difficulty did not detain Hazlitt.

The *Times* headline described the book as an "economist's view of planning," and perhaps that was the problem: both Hayek and Hazlitt took extreme liberties with history. George Orwell, whose antifascist credentials were second to none, wisely suggested that while there was some truth in the "negative" part of Hayek's thesis—that collectivism can lead to tyranny—the solution was not a return to unfettered competition, for that would mean "for the great mass of people a tyranny probably worse, because more irresponsible, than that of the state."[133] Both Britain and Germany in the nineteenth century had seen what industrial tyranny looked like, and it was not attractive. There was warrant for the term "wage slaves."

Hazlitt ignored such concerns. Indeed, both he and Hayek disregarded the brutal power that many industrialists held. Hayek's view of workers as free agents—who, if they disliked a job, could simply move to another—was idealized to the point of offense. He wrote: "If all the means of production were vested in a single hand, whether it be nominally that of 'society' as a whole or that of a dictator, whoever exercises this control has complete power over us."[134] But that was precisely the problem in many corners of capitalism: many factory owners operated essentially as dictators, and few industrial workers in the late nineteenth and early twentieth centuries had the ability to act independently. In many Americans towns, the means of production *were* vested in a single hand: the local mining and manufacturing business.[135] Indeed, NAM had boasted of this in the film *Your Town*. Hayek clearly never comprehended the meaning of the term "company town," but millions of Americans did when, in 1946, American country singer Merle Travis released his famous song "Sixteen Tons." The lyrics tell of a man in a Kentucky coal mining town working under the truck and scrip system, whereby workers were paid in credit that could only be redeemed at the company store. In such a system, a worker could never accumulate the cash needed to break free—not even in death: "Saint Peter don't you call me 'cause I can't go / I owe my soul to the company store."[136]

Some nuances of Hayek's argument, including his critique of laissez-faire, did make it into Hazlitt's write-up, but these caveats would be mostly lost amid his gushing praise. Overall, reviews were mixed. John Maynard Keynes described *The Road to Serfdom* as a "grand book" with which he was "morally and philosophically" almost entirely in agreement, but he did not find in it an *economic* program and suggested that following Hayek's noninterventionist prescription "would only lead in practice to disillusion."[137] In a letter to Hayek, Keynes contended that, regarding the role of government, "you admit here and there that it is a question of knowing where to draw the line. You agree that the line has to be drawn somewhere, and that the logical extreme is not possible," yet "you give us no guidance whatever as to where to draw it."[138]

The diplomat Isaiah Berlin—later famous for his work on the forms and expressions of freedom—criticized "the awful Dr. Hayek." The great philosopher of science Rudolf Carnap told his colleague Karl Popper that he would not bother reading the book, because "it was praised mostly by the protagonists of free enterprise."[139] Even Frank Knight, who had reviewed the book for the University of Chicago Press, considered it "limited in scope and . . . one-sided in its argument."[140] Knight noted that the complexities of German history were given short shrift; certainly there was no straight line from Bismarck to Hitler.[141] Perhaps most important, the basic thesis—that planning would inevitably lead to tyranny—lacked empirical support.[142]

But while most academics looked askance at Hayek's book, business leaders wholeheartedly embraced it. As Hazlitt's review—with its opening comparison to John Stuart Mill—shows, it was the *political* component of Hayek's book that most attracted his fans. After all, the argument that Hazlitt, Pew, Read, and their NAM colleagues made against the New Deal had never really been an economic one. They had no basis to claim Hoover's volunteerist approach *worked*, and after the United States entered World War II, it became too hard to disentangle the effects of the New Deal from the war mobilization in which they actively and for the most part willingly joined. NAM's argument against the New Deal had always been that it was too dangerous *politically*. Now Hayek had explained why.

Hayek's book fit perfectly into the indivisibility thesis framework. The appeal of Hayek's argument to Hazlitt and his NAM allies is thus obvious: it offered a high-minded case for the position they already held. What in NAM's hands had looked like a raw defense of ruthless self-interest in Hayek's became a principled defense of government restraint. In the words of historian Kim Phillips-Fein, American business conservatives recognized the book as "an elegant, sophisticated statement of their world view."[143]

But to make it suit their purposes, they had some work to do. The nuanced Hayek who rejected laissez-faire and allowed for appropriate government intervention would have to be moved to the background, while the Hayek who conflated social reform with socialism and collapsed socialism into dictatorial central planning would have to be put front and center.[144] A key figure in doing so would be Harold Luhnow, one of the businessmen who had helped create FEE, bring Mises to America, and arrange Mises's job at NYU. In the spring of 1945, Luhnow paid for Hayek to come to the United States on a five-week book tour, which included an appearance in New York's Town Hall with an estimated audience of two thousand, and a radio broadcast.[145] On this tour, Hayek had the opportunity to make his own case directly to the American people. But that would soon change, as his business admirers began to make the case for him, and in their own way.

IN 1945, THE *Reader's Digest* published a twenty-page condensation of Hayek's text. The idea apparently came from Max Eastman, an ex-radical who had helped raise the money to send American journalist John Reed to the Soviet Union in 1917, an experience that led to the bestselling book *Ten Days that Shook the World*. In the 1920s, Eastman visited Russia, repudiated both communism and socialism, and became an editor at the *Digest* and a friend of Henry Hazlitt.[146] Eastman had received an advanced copy of *The Road to Serfdom* and proposed a condensation to editor in chief DeWitt Wallace. As an antiunion and anticommunist Republican and prominent opponent of the New Deal, Wallace likely took little convincing.[147]

The Road to Serfdom had done far better than the Chicago press expected, quickly selling seventeen thousand copies, but the *Reader's Digest* had a circulation of nearly nine million, and a million more copies of its adaptation of Hayek's book were distributed in pamphlet form.[148] A three-paragraph introduction, possibly written by Eastman, begins by quoting Henry Hazlitt's declaration that this was "one of the most important books" of the time, and distills Hayek's thesis: "[F]ascism and what the Germans correctly call National Socialism are the inevitable results of the increasing growth of state control and state power, of national 'planning,' and of socialism."

At twenty pages, the *Digest* version was bound to be far less nuanced than the original. But it was also bound to reflect what Eastman and Wallace considered the book's most important or effective aspect, and that was its focus not on socialism or communism as conventionally understood, but on *Nazi Germany*. Given that the word "socialism" appears eleven times in the condensed text, one might have expected a discussion of Soviet Russia and events there since 1917, or perhaps of China, given the recent ascendance of its Communist Party. But the words "Russia" or "Russian" appear a scant three times, and "China" or "Chinese" not at all. In contrast, the words "German," "Germans," and "Germany" appear *fifteen* times and "Nazi," "Nazis," and "Nazism" seven more. In fact, the *Digest* version of the text is primarily an account of the horrors of *totalitarianism*, with Nazi Germany as the prime example. (Italian fascism gets seven mentions.)

Obviously, those horrors were real, but the entire argument was a sleight of hand. The *right-wing* totalitarianism against which Americans were still fighting in the spring of 1945 is equated with left-wing socialism, which is in turn equated with central planning. Even though socialists (and communists) were prominent among the victims of fascism and in the resistance to it, National Socialism must be socialism, according to the *Digest*. (The Nazis' use of the term flummoxed people then as it does now.)[149] Nazism (they argued) could not be viewed as a distinctive pathology that happens to share the same word as part of its name, but as characteristic of all forms of socialism.

This was absurd. It was as if one insisted there was no difference between the Greek Orthodox and Orthodox Jews—since both are forms of orthodoxy—or between the American Republican party and the Republicans who battled Franco in Spain. Meanwhile, the specificity of Nazi terror disappears from the discussion: its infamous and virulent antisemitism, its equation of health with Aryan identity, its obsession with the *Volk* and blood purity, its imperialism, and the virulent, murderous ways in which the Nazi state victimized its own citizens. Americans in 1945 were of course by and large anti-Nazi, so it was clever rhetoric to wrap a critique of socialism in the shroud of Nazi terrors, to insist National Socialism was socialism, and from there to slip to the claim that "the forces which destroyed freedom in Germany" were also at work in the United States.[150] It was also disgraceful.

LIKE MISES, HAYEK used *socialism* as his term of art, but it was *communism*—specifically, Soviet communism—that embraced central planning, and in both theory and practice, there is a world of possibility between Soviet communism and laissez-faire capitalism. Yet Hayek, like Mises, reduced this spectrum of choice to two (and only two) "irreconcilable types of social organization."[151] "The difference between the two," Hayek claimed, "is the same as that between providing signposts and commanding people which road to take."[152] A nice metaphor, but it ignores the fact that we don't allow people to drive on the wrong side of the road, as well as the fact (acknowledged by Adam Smith) that someone had to build the road in the first place, and typically that someone was a government.

Many of the historical claims the *Digest* highlighted were dubious at best, such as Hayek's assertion that by the time Hitler came to power "liberalism was dead in Germany, and it was socialism that had killed it."[153] Others were patently false, such as the claim that "[t]he Rule of Law was consciously evolved only during the liberal age," or that only "since industrial freedom opened the path to the free use of new knowledge ... has science made the great strides which in the last 150 years have changed the face of the world."[154] Hayek's sense of history also reeks of Anglo-Saxon superiority, as when he insists that "the virtues which are [now] held less and less in esteem in Britain and America are precisely those on which Anglo-Saxons justly prided themselves and in which they were generally recognized to excel."[155] The preeminence the *Digest* version gives to claims that professional historians—in 1945 or today—could easily refute reveals the disregard Hayek's followers had for historical truth.

The *Digest* version of Hayek also played fast and loose with his prose. On its final page, the adaptation declares that "if we are not to destroy individual freedom, competition must be left to function unobstructed." The original passage from which this line was extracted put the matter very differently: "There can be no question that adequate security against severe privation, and the reduction of the avoidable causes of misdirected effort and consequent disappointment, will have to be one of the main goals of policy. But if these endeavors are to be successful and are not to destroy individual freedom, security must be provided outside the market and competition be left to function unobstructed."[156] In the original, Hayek *acknowledges* market failure, and allows that the solution to "severe privation" lies outside the marketplace (and therefore, presumably, in governance).[157]

In his talks, Hayek repeatedly emphasized that he was not against "government intervention per se." Bruce Caldwell notes that Hayek attempted on many occasions to make clear his desire for "a clear set of principles which enables us to distinguish between the legitimate fields of government activities and the illegitimate fields ... you must cease to argue for and against government activity as such."[158] And yet "government activity as such" was precisely what Hazlitt, Pew, Read, Lane, and Hayek's other American promoters attacked. While critiquing FDR for "selling" planning, they deliberately, and in an organized fashion, set out to sell its opposite: letting the chips fall, regardless of who gets hurt, and opposing all forms of government action to lessen privation. Also expunged were passages in which Hayek describes solidarity and altruism as natural human impulses and differentiates individualism from egotism.[159] In the hands of his American allies, Hayek's prose became propaganda.

Ironically, Hayek had understood propaganda's role in totalitarian states. "To make a totalitarian system function efficiently," he had noted, "it is not enough that everybody should be forced to work for the ends selected by those in control; it is essential that the people should come to regard these ends as their own ... This, of course, is brought about by the various forms of propaganda."[160] Yet, this is exactly what his supporters hoped to do in America: to make people regard the ends of businessmen as their own.

Later that same year, Hayek's book would be turned into an even more blatant piece of propaganda: a cartoon version of *The Road to Serfdom*, originally published in 1945 in the mass-market magazine *Look*, and then reproduced and distributed in booklet form by General Motors.[161] With only a trifle of text, "The Road to Serfdom in Cartoons" (described by one recent commentator as "The Road to Serfdom for Dummies") presents a simplified argument in eighteen pictures and captions:[162]

1. War forces "national planning."
2. Many want "planning" to stay ...
3. The Planners promise Utopias ...
4. but they can't agree on ONE Utopia
5. And citizens can't agree either ...
6. "Planners" hate to force agreement.
7. They try to "sell" the plan to all ...
8. The gullible do find agreement ...
9. Confidence in "planners" fades ...
10. The "strong man" is given power ...

11. The party takes over the country . . .
12. A *negative* aim welds party unity . . .
13. No one opposes the leader's plan . . .
14. Your profession is "planned" . . .
15. Your wages are "planned" . . .
16. Your thinking is "planned" . . .
17. Your recreation is "planned" . . .
18. Your disciplining is "planned" . . .

While Mises had primarily focused on Soviet-style planning, and Hayek on totalitarianisms of both the left and right, the *Look* cartoon—written in the aftermath of World War II—addresses Nazism, again misrepresenting national socialism as a form of (left-wing) socialism. The images are almost entirely of Nazis: men in Nazi-style uniforms, with boots, military-style caps, and black armbands, often on extended arms, speaking to loud crowds. Cartoon 12 explicitly states that the "early step of all dictators is to inflame the majority in common cause against some scapegoat minority. In Germany [it] was anti-Semitism." The accompanying illustration shows books being burned in front of a smashed store window. In cartoon 13, the crowd now has its arms extended; the Nazi-style leader orates onstage, while a soldier stands guard, wearing the exact same uniform, but carrying a rifle. The text reads: "Ability to force obedience always becomes the No. 1 virtue in the 'planned state.' All freedom is gone." In the final cartoon, a dissenter is placed before a firing squad.[163]

Conservative businessmen had originally organized to promote protective tariffs. They segued to a fight against collective bargaining and workplace protections. Now, they argued that if you opposed them—and in particular, if you sought government redress for your grievances—you supported the rise of Nazism. Or maybe you even were a Nazi. From collective bargaining to book burning and firing squads.

Some critics picked up on businessmen's promotion of *The Road to Serfdom*, dubbing Hayek the "darling of the Chamber of Commerce."[164] One left-leaning newspaper published an exposé on the hype: "Hayek's book—and the *Look* and *Reader's Digest* treatments of it—gave big business a wonderful opportunity to spread distrust and fear of the New Deal. Big business seized [that] opportunity."[165] Caldwell agrees that this campaign for *The Road to Serfdom* was crucial to its impact. "It is hard to imagine that Hayek's book would have become so widely known [and] remembered decades after its original publication had it not been for the *Reader's Digest* condensation. This allowed Hayek's message to reach many more people, and in at least one instance with dramatic effect: Antony Fisher, the founder of the [UK] Institute of Economic Affairs," which influenced Margaret Thatcher, "was inspired to wage the war of ideas after having read *the condensation* and then speaking with Hayek in his [London School of Economics] office in the summer of 1945."[166]

Most successful books owe at least some of their success to marketing and promotion, and—interestingly—Keynesianism was also sold to the public in cartoons.[167] But what the business community promoted was a flattened and propagandistic version of Hayek, in which his recognition of the realms of legitimate government action was made to disappear.

Still, that was not enough for these business leaders' purposes. What they needed, they agreed among themselves, was an *American* version of *The Road to Serfdom*. A book that would make the case for the indivisibility of free markets and free societies—of capitalism and freedom—in the American context. They would get it in 1962.

A KEY ELEMENT in the development and promotion of the indivisibility framework was the creation in 1947 of the Mont Pelerin Society (MPS, and spelled without an accent), named after the town of Mont Pèlerin, near Geneva, Switzerland, where its members first gathered.[168]

The society was the brainchild of Hayek and the economist Albert Hunold, a former socialist who in the 1920s became a follower of Mises and now headed the Swiss Watch Manufacturers' Association.[169] Their idea was to create a space for the principled and open discussion of what would soon come to be known as neoliberal thought, in a social context where its defenders felt isolated and even scorned. As historian and Herbert Hoover biographer George Nash has put it, "All across Europe, planning and socialism seemed ascendant."[170] Hayek and his colleagues wanted a forum from which to challenge that ascendancy in an intellectually rigorous way.

Theirs was to be a conference where participants could speak freely, undistracted by anxieties about how their views might appear from the outside, particularly given that they were not intending at this stage to influence politics. That would come in time, but first they needed to discuss and develop their views. Hayek insisted—ironically, given his passionate commitment to freedom—that theirs would be a "closed society," about which he would publicly say as little as possible.[171] (His colleague Karl Popper, who had just published *The Open Society and Its Enemies*, lost the argument for a more inclusive approach.)[172] Historian Dieter Plehwe observes: "One can readily appreciate the trickiness of attempting to square the circle of remaining closed and relatively secretive while striving to be cosmopolitan and open to opposing currents, all the while scrutinizing a political doctrine (liberalism) that was at least nominally pitched in favor of diversity, broad-mindedness, and open participation."[173] But Hayek insisted that, at least at the start, they needed privacy: "[T]his should be regarded as a private meeting and all that is said here in discussion off the record," Hayek cautioned.[174]

For similar reasons, Hayek did not "intend that any public manifesto should be issued." Even privately, he was nervous about defining a "creed," but he and other members nevertheless took a stab at it, and a draft statement in April 1947 proposed:[175]

1. Individual freedom can be preserved only in a society in which an effective competitive market is the main agency for the direction of economic activity. Only the decentralization of control through private property in the means of production can prevent those concentrations of power which threaten individual freedom.

2. The freedom of the consumer in choosing what he shall buy, the freedom of the producer in choosing what he shall make, and the freedom of the worker in choosing his occupation and his place of employment are essential not merely for the sake of freedom itself, but for efficiency in production . . .

3. All rational men believe in planning for the future. But this involves the right of each individual to plan his own life. He is deprived of this right when he is forced to surrender his own initiative, will and liberty to the requirements of a central direction for the use of economic resources.

4. The decline of competitive markets and the movement toward totalitarian control of society are not inevitable. They are the result mainly of mistaken beliefs . . .

5. The presentation of an effective competitive order depends upon a proper legal and institutional framework . . .

6. As far as possible government activity should be limited by the rule of law . . . Tasks which require that authorities be given discretionary powers should therefore be reduced to the indispensable minimum . . . In general an automatic mechanism of adjustment, even where it functions imperfectly, is preferable to any which depends on "conscious" direction by government agencies.[176]

7. The changes in current opinion which are responsible for the general trend toward totalitarianism are not confined to economic doctrine . . . Those who wish to resist the encroachments on individual liberty must direct their attention to these wider ideas as well as to those in the strictly economic field.

8. Any free society presupposes, in particular, a widely accepted moral code. The principles of this moral code should govern collective no less than private action.

9. Among the most dangerous of intellectual errors which lead to the destruction of a free society is the historical fatalism which believes in our power to discover laws of historical development which we must obey, and the historical relativism which denies all absolute moral standards and tends to justify any political means by the purposes at which it aims.

10. Political pressures have brought new and serious threats to the freedom of thought and science. Complete intellectual freedom is so essential to the fulfillment of our aims that no consideration of social expediency must ever be allowed to impair it.

These points make clear that their authors are not antigovernment, per se, nor anti-planning, per se (implicitly responding to the critique that "planning" is something private businesses do all the time). They are opposed to *government* planning because it undermines individuals' capacity to plan their lives. The reason for urgency, in the statement's authors' view, is that the slide into totalitarianism is not inevitable, but can be stopped by attending to "encroachments on individual liberty," particularly (but not only) in economic affairs. At the same time, they evince naïveté or willful ignorance about the lives of working-class people, as if an uneducated laborer had anything remotely resembling the freedom of choice of the boss who decides "what he shall make." (Indeed, the boss does not choose what *he* shall make, he decides what *his workers* shall make.)

The participants, however, could not agree on this draft, and so what the historian Dieter Plehwe calls the "oxymoronic Committee of Individualists" adopted a much shorter and weaker "Statement of Aims."

> The central values of civilization are in danger . . . The group holds that these developments have been fostered . . . by a decline of belief in private property and the competitive market; for without the diffused power and initiative associated with these institutions it is difficult to imagine a society in which freedom may effectively be preserved.
>
> Believing that what is essentially an ideological movement must be met by intellectual argument and the reassertion of valid ideas, the group . . . is of the opinion that further study is desirable inter alia in regard to the following matters . . .[177]

Some points were mostly anodyne, such as "the analysis and explanation of the nature of the present crisis." Others, progressives might have agreed with, such as "[m]ethods of re-establishing the rule of law . . . [so that] private rights are not allowed to become a basis of predatory power." One was deeply ironic: "Methods of combating the misuse of history for the furtherance of creeds hostile to liberty."[178]

But despite the exhortation for further study, this was not a scientific project, nor even an academic project at all. By their own admission theirs was an ideological project, an attempt to counter a belief system they rejected with one they could accept. The further study they proposed would attempt to crystallize their tenet that only through private property and a competitive system could freedom be preserved; they were unable to *imagine a society* organized differently and did not care to try. It was to be, in Plehwe's words, "a closed, self-referential system of thought."[179]

Plehwe suggests that the weakness of their Statement of Aims shows this "transnational band of participants did not have a very clear idea of where the project was headed in 1947."[180] If so, then it matters greatly that their financial support came from business leaders eager to direct the project in a particular way. The 1947 founding meeting of MPS included not just Hayek and like-minded intellectuals, but also like-minded journalists, politicians, and businessmen, such as Hazlitt, now writing for *Newsweek*; George Révay, representing *Reader's Digest*; and the "moneymen" who financed the meeting: Leonard Read, his FEE colleague Floyd A. Harper, and Harold Luhnow.[181]

By 1947 a network of businessmen supported the incipient MPS. Luhnow had persuaded Hayek to invite Jasper Crane, the DuPont executive who was one of the first trustees of FEE. Crane did not attend, but his colleague Loren B. Miller did; together Crane and Miller urged oil tycoon Harry Boyd Earhart to become involved. The deep-pocketed Earhart Foundation—founded in 1929 and dedicated to supporting free-market scholars though fellowships and professorships—became a major patron.[182] FEE sent the second largest delegation from the United States; the largest was the group of economists from the University of Chicago—including Milton Friedman, whose travel expenses (as well as those of other American participants) Luhnow helped to cover through the Volker Fund.[183]

Phillips-Fein notes that Hayek was reluctant to invite Jasper Crane for fear that journalists would use any businessman's presence to discredit the effort. Yet someone needed to foot the bill, and while Hayek worried about the optics of inviting businessmen—as well as the real possibility of being unduly pressured or influenced—Luhnow was reluctant to pay unless he *could* be in charge. His experience told him that it was "almost impossible to keep control of organizations of this sort."[184] Hayek tried to have it both ways, accepting Luhnow's money and inviting Crane but insisting that their names be omitted from the list of participants.[185] "I think you will agree," he wrote to Luhnow, "that any effort in the sphere of ideas, if it is to be effective, must avoid even the appearance of being dependent on any material interests, and for that reason we have been careful not to include in the list of persons originally invited, anyone, however sympathetic with our aims, who might be thought by the public to represent specific interests."[186]

Both Crane and Luhnow did represent "specific interests."[187] As historian Janek Wasserman has put it, "their interventions, despite professed objectivity and scientific neutrality, had ideological impacts that reinforced conservative values."[188] "Conservative values," however, can encompass a wide range of views; business patronage helped determine which forms of conservatism—which elements of the conversation that took place at Mont Pèlerin—would be nurtured and disseminated, while Hayek took care to keep their role in the background.[189] As political scientists Jacob Hacker and Paul Pierson have noted, "One thing big money typically lacks is credibility, which is why those who deploy it work so hard to cover their tracks."[190]

Historians have emphasized the diversity of views that, in 1945, offered potential foundations for twentieth-century neoliberalism. Quinn Slobodian, for example, identifies a group of "globalists," centered around Geneva, who did not see markets as self-regulating, autonomous entities and who envisioned an active role for the state in protecting them. Interestingly, he argues, the globalist project was antidemocratic, focused on "designing institutions—not to liberate markets but to encase them, to inoculate capitalism against the threat of democracy, [and] to create a framework to contain often-irrational human behavior."[191] These globalists did not see an inextricable connection between democracy and capitalism; on the contrary, they observed that the former often threatened the latter. Their version of liberalism was often an authoritarian one.[192]

Examples of alternative neoliberalisms abound. Economist Ralf Ptak reminds us that German "ordoliberals" endorsed a "social market economy" similar to what Bismarck pioneered and did not believe that "the free market" could flourish on its own; rather they emphasized the role of a strong state in "establishing and securing the capitalist market economy" within a democratic context.[193] Keith Tribe notes that even at the London School of Economics, British neoliberals differed in their degree of opposition to Keynesianism and the welfare state.[194] In the 1930s, the French organized what was arguably the first meeting on neoliberalism; François Denord emphasizes that these neoliberals were quite disunified, arguing about whether freedom was an end in itself or just a means to an end. (And if the latter, what was the end?)[195]

Running through all these strains was the question of what was central and essential versus peripheral and discretionary. Was the unifying principle individualism? Or was it the "use of the price mechanism as the best way to obtain the maximal satisfaction of human expectations"?[196] To what extent was neoliberalism a revival of traditional liberalism (with its emphasis on individual rights) or a different beast (with an emphasis on the centrality of markets)?[197] How did it differ from libertarianism? If neoliberalism didn't mean letting "cars circulate in all directions, if such is their will," as one French neoliberal put it—since that would obviously lead to traffic jams and accidents—then what did it mean?[198]

The 1947 Mont Pelerin Society roster encompassed diverse views: Angus Burgin stresses that many attendees were skeptical of political absolutes.[199] But what would ultimately dominate in the U.S. context was just that: a rigid, at times absolutist, market fundamentalism, expressed with little tolerance for complexities, ambiguities, or exceptions. It was an inflexible framework that insisted on the necessary and inextricable link between capitalism and freedom, viewed nearly any compromise to economic freedom as a threat to liberty, and paid little or no attention to counterexamples. When failures were noted, American market fundamentalists would find creative ways to insist that they weren't *really* failures or that any solution would be worse than the disease.[200] When the cars—going in all directions—did in fact crash, market fundamentalists would downplay the number of people injured, deny the crash had occurred, or say it was government's fault for building the road incorrectly or maybe even for building it at all.[201]

In the coming decades, the American version of this intellectual framework would replace *markets* with *The Market,* revered as a godlike force: powerful, mysterious, and omniscient, an entity whose will must necessarily be done, whom mere mortals should not attempt to second-guess.[202] In the early twenty-first century, NYU professor Jonathan Haidt, a regular on talk show circuits, would go so far as to suggest: "You're not crazy to worship markets. Markets really are amazing things."[203] Harvard divinity professor Harvey Cox would dedicate his book *The Market as God* to critiquing that view, showing how "current thinking ... assigns to The Market a comprehensive wisdom that in the past only the gods have known."[204]

In her nonfiction book *Payback*, Margaret Atwood concludes that somewhere in the twentieth century "people began substituting something called 'the Market' for God, attributing the same characteristics to it: all-knowingness, always-rightness, and the ability to make something called 'corrections,' which, like the divine punishment of old, had the effect of wiping out a great many people."[205] In this framework, it was easy to see the "invisible hand" as the hand of God. Though sometimes inscrutable, "The Market," like God, had the power to achieve good ends out of what on the surface might seem like bad means.

The deification of The Market involved a key step of illogic: viewing markets (or The Market) as autonomous, existing unto themselves, rather than as something created, sustained, and above all ruled by people, who might make conscious choices as to how they wanted those markets to operate, might nudge or adjust them when they were working well overall and fix them when they failed, and use government as the instrument to do that. As Hacker and Pierson have noted, to accept the pejorative language of government "interference"—as opposed to the neutral language of "action"—is to "endorse the zero-sum relationship between state and market that became prominent in the 1970s," but had not, in fact, been accepted before.[206]

While many if not most of the participants in the 1947 meeting at Mont Pèlerin recognized the necessary role of the state in protecting competition, American market fundamentalists would promote the myth of markets as autonomous. The state, they would argue, should stop "interfering," get out of the way, and leave markets to do their "magic."

Despite the post-hoc canonization of Hayek, the actual intellectual leader of this movement would be a different MPS member: Milton Friedman. Angus Burgin argues that many MPS founders later viewed "emboldened market advocacy" as a "violation of its original ideals," and they looked with both "admiration and disapprobation at the world that Milton Friedman had wrought."[207] How did this come to be? How did a complex and diverse set of approaches to the problems of business cycles, monetary theory, economic planning, and individual choice get reduced to market fundamentalism? What role did Luhnow, Crane, or Read play in all this?

The answer to the last question is: a big one, because American businessmen's participation in MPS helped channel the emerging intellectual framework in a specific way. Patrons rarely tell their protégés what to think or say; most patrons are not that crude, and few artists or intellectuals want to be pushed around. Rather, patrons seek out groups and individuals with congenial views and strengthen them with moral, logistical, and financial support.[208] They fund things that interest them, and so ideas that suit the rich are more likely to thrive than those that suit the poor. In this way, patronage by exceptionally wealthy individuals or organizations may act as a kind of unnatural selection, ensuring that the ideas they select come to the forefront of a cultural conversation, regardless of their actual fitness to explain the world.[209] And it was this process—not survival of the fittest, but selection by the richest—that helped to ensure that neoliberalism would be expressed in America primarily as market fundamentalism.

CHAPTER 6

The Big Myth Goes West

While millions of people encountered *The Road to Serfdom*—or a version of it—via its *Reader's Digest* adaptation, Friedrich von Hayek's book itself remained an aloof, erudite text. In that respect, it was ill suited to reach the widest possible American audience, and certainly would not have been appropriate for children. If libertarian ideas were to take root, they would have to reach the mass public—especially younger generations—through other channels. Indeed, years before Hayek's book saw the light of day, a more attractively packaged version of the free-market myth was already circulating with great success. It was partly the work of a largely forgotten journalist named Rose Wilder Lane.

In the 1920s and '30s, Lane wrote for leading magazines including *Reader's Digest*, the *Saturday Evening Post*, the *Ladies' Home Journal*, *Good Housekeeping*, and the popular California lifestyle magazine *Sunset*. She also published short stories, romantic fiction, several novels that sold well, and an admiring biography of Herbert Hoover.[1] Lane claimed to have been on "good terms" with Jack London, Charlie Chaplin, Henry Ford, Sinclair Lewis; with journalist and radio announcer Lowell Thomas; and even with Leon Trotsky.[2] She also alleged that she had nearly succumbed to the attractions of communism, as a young woman under the influence of the American journalist John Reed (author of the firsthand account of the Bolshevik Revolution *Ten Days that Shook the World*). But she saw the light, she insisted, on a 1920s trip to Europe, when she witnessed firsthand the disastrous results of "socialist/communist ideas." Soon, she had "figured it all out." "It" was the opposite of communism: a radical, crypto-anarchist individualism that saw government as the enemy of its people.[3]

Scholars have questioned Lane's representations: the details she offered to support her claim that she was once perilously close to becoming a communist were either hazy or demonstrably incorrect. In one case, she claimed to have witnessed the founding of the American Communist Party in Chicago, at a time when in fact she was in Mansfield, Missouri.[4] Her biographer acknowledged that this self-fashioning as a reformed leftist was a "fabrication" but dismissed this and other misrepresentations as insignificant on the grounds that Lane was merely "distorting her own personal history a bit."[5] They were not insignificant, however, because the narrative of the leftist who saw the light was part of her claim to intellectual independence and integrity. And Lane misrepresented others as well. It's doubtful that she was on good terms with Chaplin: as a result of "hack" biographies she wrote of him, London, and Ford, she was twice threatened with lawsuits.[6] In 1933, she wrote a commissioned piece for the *Saturday Evening Post* under the byline "A Grain Trader" that was frankly fraudulent.[7] The story, presented in the first person, purports to be a real-life account: "I saw it happen . . . I got the news . . . I drove to my office . . . It was the most striking thing I ever saw . . ." But Rose was never a grain trader, and her experience on a wheat farm ended at age eleven.[8]

Lane abhorred the Roosevelt administration, even describing, in a letter to her editor, a fantasy of traveling to Washington to assassinate the president before he could make himself a new Hitler.[9] (The American Liberty League had used similar rhetoric.) The *Saturday Evening Post* shared Lane's consistent and intemperate hostility to FDR, to intellectuals, and to leftists of all stripes, and in 1936 she penned a "Credo" for the paper, which FEE later republished as a pamphlet entitled *Give Me Liberty*. This personal manifesto began with a critique of Bolshevism and the failures of communist Russia, but it segued into a capacious attack on the very concept of government. "Government," as such, she argued, cannot exist. What can only exist is a man or a few men exerting power over other men.[10] "What is liberty?" Lane asks. What does it mean to be "truly free"? She answers that, in America, we are truly free, and our material success is the outcome of our embrace of freedom, manifested in and working through the "anarchy of individualism."[11] But we fail to understand this truth—that our success is the product solely of our individual autonomy and initiative. Instead, we succumb to the mistaken belief that we need government to do things for us, and so we yield to creeping collectivism, as manifested in the New Deal.[12]

But "Credo" is not Lane's most influential creation. At the time she was developing her philosophy, she was also helping her mother reconstruct her family history for a writing project. Her mother's name was Laura Ingalls Wilder. Through a complicated (and for many decades hidden) collaboration, the two of them would produce some of the most beloved American children's books of the twentieth

century, works of libertarian fiction that rival the novels of Ayn Rand in their
commercial appeal and ideological impact: the Little House series.

SET IN THE post–Civil War period and ending around 1885, the Little House
books were marketed as the true stories of Laura Ingalls Wilder's experiences. They
recount the Ingalls family's adventures in Wisconsin, the Kansas and Dakota terri-
tories, and Missouri. Decades of readers thrilled to these tales of settler life as seen
through the eyes of a young girl; the books have sold more than sixty million copies
in forty-five languages.[13] The finding aid for the Hoover Presidential Library—
which holds letters between Hoover and Rose Wilder Lane—describes the Little
House books as capturing "in eight volumes the essence of growing up on the American
frontier."[14] But while the stories had some basis in real events, they were heavily
manicured by Lane, who conjured libertarian mythos out of the Ingallses' much
more complicated reality.

Early twentieth-century accounts of the American West were almost always
infused with myths; the Little House series was not exceptional in that regard. One
was the myth of the West as empty or "free" land.[15] Frederick Jackson Turner's
famous 1893 essay, "The Significance of the Frontier in American History," posited
that the existence of "free land" in the West had served as a "safety valve" for the
industrializing east and its waves of immigrants. The frontier, a dynamic boundary
between "savagery and civilization," had shaped a unique American identity, one in
which vigorous and self-reliant people found a place for themselves in an expanding
land. For Turner, the frontier had "closed" by 1890—when the Superintendent of
the Census declared that "the unsettled area has been so broken into by isolated
bodies of settlement that there can hardly be said to be a frontier line"—a closure
that signaled a sea change in American identity and culture.[16] Also in 1890, Native
American armed struggle came largely to an end with the ignominious slaughter of
hundreds of Lakota men, women, and children on the banks of Wounded Knee
Creek in South Dakota, not far from a present-day Laura Ingalls Wilder museum.[17]

Another was the myth of the frontier as a locus of diligent, high-quality labor.
In fact, Turner had argued that early pioneers were an impatient bunch, many of
whom engaged in unsustainable farming practices, staying on the land for only a
few years before selling out and moving on. "The competition of the unexhausted,
cheap, and easily tilled prairie lands compelled the farmer either to go west and

continue the exhaustion of the soil on a new frontier, or to adopt intensive culture," Turner wrote.[18] It was a "bonanza economy," not one built on steady, slow develop-ment. A third myth was that these pioneers did it all on their own, with little or no help from government. The U.S. Army's role, for example, in displacing and killing the original inhabitants of these lands was swept aside for a narrative of hard work and just rewards. The facts of Laura Ingalls Wilder's biography reveal the gaps and distortions in each one of these myths.

Laura Ingalls was born in 1867 to Charles and Caroline Ingalls on their small farm near Lake Pepin, Wisconsin. She was the second of five children—four girls, and one boy who did not survive infancy. The family did not remain there long, moving first to Missouri in mid-1869, then later the same year to land within the Osage Diminished Reserve near Independence, Kansas. This spot was the location of Wilder's third (and most famous) novel, *Little House on the Prairie*; Charles Ingalls settled there to gain squatters' rights to the land. He was part of a broader pattern inspired by the federal government's involvement in railroad development: when the government released new land for settlement it was often snapped up by railroad companies, which then might resell it at a much higher price. Whites who had already squatted on the land, however, could claim it at the lower price. Of course, these lands were in most cases already occupied by Native Americans; in the Ingallses' case, the real dividends would pay off when federal troops removed the Osage people and the land was "legally" opened to settlement.

Congress passed the law enabling settlement of the Osage land in October 1870, and it was opened for purchase in the spring of 1871. But Charles had uprooted the family again. A rumor had spread that the federal government would be removing the settlers, not the Osage; meanwhile the buyer of his Wisconsin farm was no longer able to make payments, so Charles needed to repossess it.[19] The family moved back to Lake Pepin, arriving sometime in the spring of 1871. The first book of the series, *Little House in the Big Woods*, reflects this second period of life near Lake Pepin.[20]

In 1874, the family moved again. The previous year, declining agricultural prices had undermined railroad stocks, prompting a financial panic. Charles had borrowed money to buy equipment and seed and was now forced to sell the farm to pay his bills. In May 1874, they settled in a primitive dugout home adjacent to Plum Creek, near Walnut Grove, Minnesota. Charles filed a preemption claim on 172 acres near the railroad, for which he would eventually pay $431.[21]

The experience at Plum Creek was disastrous. A plague of Rocky Mountain locusts destroyed Charles's crops; adult Laura would recount the swarm graphically in her fourth book, *On the Banks of Plum Creek*.[22] Charles was forced to turn to wage labor, harvesting others' crops east of the Mississippi River (which the locusts had spared). When a prairie fire erupted while he was away doing wage work, neighbors helped save the house Charles had built for the family.

Charles Ingalls worked hard, but he was also unlucky. The locust plague "constituted the worst and most widespread natural disaster the country had ever seen," according to one recent account.[23] States provided little or no relief, and when they did, they often imposed harsh eligibility requirements, such as having to sell all one's livestock. Those who accepted relief were also subject to humiliation: newspapers and public officials decried relief as weakening "self-reliance" and fostering "indolence."[24] Charles moved the family out of the farmhouse and into Walnut Grove for the winter of 1875, but to receive some flour and seed he was forced to sign a mortifying pledge that he was without means. He sold the property for four hundred dollars and relocated the family to Burr Oak, Iowa.

This move took Charles out of farming for a time and marks a piece of Laura Ingalls's childhood that made it into no novel. Charles found work as a hotel manager, with his wife and daughters pitching in, but the arrangement did not work out, and Charles moved to running a feed mill.[25] By mid-1877, the family was again in debt, to their landlord and to the doctor who had delivered the youngest daughter; Charles and the family fled in ignominy in the middle of the night. They returned to Walnut Grove, which was still suffering the effects of the 1873 depression. Charles and the older girls took odd jobs, and Charles eventually built a house for the family on leased land. They were soon burdened again by medical debt. After several bouts of illness, Laura's older sister, Mary, lost her sight.[26] Family connections got Charles a new job later that year, handling payroll for a railroad crew in the Dakota Territory. In September 1879, he moved the family to a railroad camp in what would become South Dakota.

During the next few months, Charles would build a store to buttress a claim made on some land just before it went on sale in April 1880 (creating the town of De Smet). He promptly sold the store and built a larger one across the street. The family spent the next several winters living above it, while Charles tried again to make a go of farming on a homestead claim a mile south of town. He also rented space in the store to others. (Adult Laura picked up the thread of her childhood with the move to the Dakotas in the novel *On the Shores of Silver Lake*.) Things went reasonably well until the brutal winter of 1880–81. The last train into town arrived in early January 1881, and another couldn't make it through the snow until May. Food and fuel ran out. Eventually a couple of local boys took a sleigh to a farmer a dozen miles away to buy grain for the town. (Their successful return was chronicled in the novel *The Long Winter*.) Four years later, at age nineteen, Laura married one of those boys.

Laura and her new husband, Almanzo Wilder, moved to a house he had built on a tree claim near De Smet. Settlers often believed that trees would reduce winds and bring more rain, allowing previously arid areas to support agriculture. To "prove up" a tree claim, one had to plant forty acres in trees and maintain them for a decade.[27] Almanzo had begun this process. He also had a homestead claim on which he planted wheat for sale and oats for feed. But things did not go well for the newlyweds. The weather in their first summer of marriage was dry and the wheat did poorly. The second summer was worse: Almanzo harvested his oats successfully, but before he got the wheat in, a hailstorm destroyed it all. He had taken loans to buy machinery and equipment and now had no way to pay the debt. Laura and Almanzo wound up renting out the little house and moving to a shanty on the homestead claim. This was the shanty in which their daughter Rose was born in December 1886.[28]

The summer of 1887 was dry again, and Almanzo's yield was again poor. Meanwhile, in December, Charles Ingalls gave up his dream of farming independence and moved the remaining family back to De Smet.[29] In February 1888, Laura and Almanzo's own dreams were shattered by diphtheria. Laura recovered, but Almanzo lost much of the strength of his legs. (Laura blamed him for his own crippling, believing it the result of premature overexertion.) In his weakened state, Almanzo couldn't manage both properties, so they sold the farm and moved back to the house on the tree claim.[30]

The Dakota Boom, in which the Ingallses and Wilders participated, was unsustainable; the climate was too dry to support agriculture as practiced in the 1880s. In his famous study of the Great American Desert (what we now euphemistically call the Great Plains), geologist and explorer John Wesley Powell had pointed out that dry land farming wouldn't work in the arid climate, and for ranching one would need far more than the 160 acres provided under the Homestead Act of 1862. Irrigated agriculture might work, but that would require settlement to follow waterways (rather than the railroads). And it would require a cooperative model of development, to build the necessary irrigation systems.

Settlement boosters put Powell and his 1878 *Report on the Lands of the Arid Region of the United States* in their crosshairs. "In a campaign comparable to modern-day corporate denial of climate change, big business and the legislators in its pocket brushed Powell's analysis aside," Wilder scholar Caroline Fraser wrote.[31] Boosters also promoted a maximalist individualism: writing of the "failure" of Native Americans to advance economically, Massachusetts senator Henry Dawes commented in 1885 that "[t]hey have got as far as they can go, because they own their land in common . . . There is no enterprise to make your home any better than that of your neighbors. There is no selfishness, which is at the bottom of civilization."[32] Newspapers east and west also hyped settlement, with the predictable result that hundreds of thousands of people followed the Ingallses into Dakota Territory in the 1880s, filing claims on over 41 million acres.[33]

The Dakota Boom began to implode in 1889, and the implosion hit the Wilders. The De Smet area received half its usual rainfall that summer and a heat wave killed Almanzo's trees. That meant either abandoning the tree claim or buying it outright, since the trees' survival was required to "prove up" under the law. April 1889 also saw vast prairie fires.[34] In either July or early August, Laura had their second child, a boy who did not live long enough to name.[35] Then, in August, the house burned down: Laura had been feeding hay into the kitchen stove for fuel, walked away from it, and returned to find the house on fire. She saved Rose and the deed box; a neighbor saved some clothes and dishware. The Wilders moved in with a neighbor while Almanzo built another shanty on the tree claim. The following spring, Almanzo paid for the tree claim land and they left De Smet for the town of Spring Valley.

The next few years were peripatetic. From Spring Valley Laura and Almanzo moved to Florida for a year, and then returned to De Smet. This time, they lived in town and took on wage work. The ongoing drought was followed by the Panic of 1893, which bankrupted railroads and banks throughout the West. The Wilders joined the outmigration from the Dakotas in June 1894, abandoning the prairie for the Missouri Ozarks. Laura and Almanzo would spend the rest of their lives there, working odd jobs and slowly building up a farm; Laura also worked for many years as a federal farm loan administrator. They would not achieve any kind of financial stability until Laura began writing magazines pieces, and then, encouraged by Rose, her incredibly successful children's books. Under Rose's guidance, she would craft an "autobiographical" story far different from the one she had actually lived.

SOMETIME DURING 1929, the year of the Great Crash, Laura started working on a memoir, making notes from memory on yellow pads of paper. In May 1930, she delivered the pads to Rose, who went to work typing and editing.[36] Rose extracted the stories Laura had written about her family's second period in Lake Pepin and sent the manuscript to a New York couple who specialized in children's fiction. This piece of Laura's work, expanded at the publisher's request to contain more description of pioneer home life, became *Little House in the Big Woods*, published in 1932.[37] (The full-length memoir was rejected; it would not be published until 2015, as *Pioneer Girl*.)

Rose served as an editor for *Big Woods*, advising Laura on restructuring the manuscript around the seasons and the evening stories Charles Ingalls told, and suggesting what additional stories to include. Together, mother and daughter transmogrified Laura's memories of a disjointed life, beset with hardship and failure, into a positive and coherent vision of labor and loyalty rewarded.[38] *Big Woods* became about family, and the importance of discipline and obedience to parental authority. It also became a story of self-sufficiency—Charles poured the lead for his own bullets, threshed his own wheat, and slaughtered his own pigs—and the (alleged) independence it brought.[39] In this and later books, Laura and Rose depicted Charles Ingalls as a man of great skill and resourcefulness. Family life is happy, comforting, and harmonious. And Pa played a mean fiddle, to boot.

Wilder's next effort was to tell the story of Almanzo's childhood in upstate New York, which she began writing alone. Rose was simultaneously crafting some of her mother's other stories into a book of her own, *Let the Hurricane Roar*. Published in February 1933, Rose's *Hurricane* became a source of friction between the two: Laura didn't appreciate Rose's appropriation of her stories. But Laura's writing needed Rose's hand: when she submitted her second manuscript, the editors asked for a complete overhaul. Rose provided it, spending two months transforming the narrative into a celebration, in the words of historian Christine Woodside, of the "economics and freedom of farming."[40] *Farmer Boy* was published later that year.

One early story in *Farmer Boy* concerns a teacher whom local farmers hire for the winter. Bullies from "Hardscrabble Hill" harass the teacher, and the bullies plan (with the support of a parent of one of them) to assault him. (Wilder tells her readers that the teacher's predecessor had been beaten to death by these boys.) Almanzo complains to his father, who responds with a lecture on masculine self-sufficiency:

FATHER: Son, Mr. Corse hired out to teach the school . . . The school trustees were fair and aboveboard with him; they told him what he was undertaking. He undertook it. It's his job, not yours.

ALMANZO: But maybe they'll kill him!

FATHER: That's his business . . . When a man undertakes a job, he has to stick to it till he finishes it. If Corse is the man I think he is, he'd thank nobody for interfering.[41]

In the denouement, the bullies rush the teacher, but he's prepared with a whip, with which he defeats the assailants. It turns out that Almanzo's father provided the whip: in town he had heard that the lead bully's father was bragging about the upcoming assault. The story is thoroughly didactic: Corse knew what he was getting into. The community that hired him isn't responsible for his safety, only Corse himself is. Men shouldn't expect help in fighting their battles, even in the face of unfair odds. And some people are simply bad, such as the Hardscrabble Hill father bragging about his bullying son. Still, it's not for others to intrude; a man must stand up for himself.

Farmer Boy preaches economics, too. When a group of boys tease Almanzo for lacking money to buy lemonade, he asks his father for a nickel. Father hands him a half-dollar and asks Almanzo if he knows what it is. Almanzo knows it's a fifty-cent piece and gets treated to a lecture on what it represents: "It's work, son. That's what money is; it's hard work." Father then tells Almanzo the money is his to do what he wants: buy lemonade—or buy a suckling pig that he could raise and use to breed more pigs to sell for "four or five dollars apiece."[42] Almanzo buys the pig, marking him as the future farmer that readers already know he became.[43]

Throughout the book, the reader is instructed that America was made by hardworking farmers of Anglo-Saxon stock. The original inhabitants are mostly absent or depicted as inconsequential; other Europeans are painted as lazy, greedy, or both.

Spaniards only wanted gold, while the French were just traders "wanting to make quick money." The real Americans, Almanzo's father explains, were the ones who "wanted the land. It was farmers that went over the mountains, and cleared the land, and settled it and farmed it, and hung on to their farms." He continues the fantasy: "It's the biggest country in the world, and it was farmers who took all that country and made it America, son. Don't you ever forget that."[44] (Of course, several countries were larger.)

The book ends with what seems like a good offer: Almanzo can become an apprentice to the local wagon maker. His father considers it: the population is growing and so is demand for wagons, buggies, and related goods. But Almanzo's mother is horrified at the thought of him giving up farming:

> A pretty pass the world's coming to, if any man thinks it's a step up in the world to leave a good farm and go to town. How does Mr. Paddock make his money, if it isn't catering to us? I guess if he didn't make wagons to suit farmers, he wouldn't last long . . . Oh, it's bad enough to see Royal come down to being nothing but a storekeeper! Maybe he'll make money, but he'll never be the man you are. Truckling to other people for his living, all his days—He'll never be able to call his soul his own.[45]

Wilder tips her ideological hand: even a skilled craftsman is inferior to the independent yeoman farmer. Only the farmer can "call his soul his own."

Of course, Almanzo's family wasn't actually independent. They relied on the bank, the wagon maker, the itinerant cobbler, and of course the commodity traders. Father and mother sold potatoes, wheat, corn, and butter to merchants who arrived by train from New York. Independence was already a myth in the late nineteenth century, and by the time these stories were written Americans were even more *inter*-dependent. Most were now employees depending on wage income—Rose and Laura included.[46]

FOR THE THIRD and most famous book in the series, *The Little House on the Prairie*, Laura and Rose collaborated even more thoroughly. As before, Laura wrote the first draft and Rose overhauled it. But even more than before, they had to invent much of the story. Laura had been just three years old at the time of the events the book fictionalizes; she and Rose had to work together even to figure out where the house had been. (They missed the spot by dozens of miles, researchers later found.)[47] They wrote to people still in the region to glean details about the local Osage tribe and the actions of the government at the time. The published book contains idyllic scenes of the prairie and of constructing their home, as well as frightening scenes of a neighbor's near death while helping to dig a well, of Indigenous people demanding food, of surviving a prairie fire, and of an Osage war council, called off at what seems to the terrified three-year-old Laura the very last minute. The Osage leave instead, to the settlers' great relief, but the book still ends with flight, driven by fear that the federal government would drive them off "their" land.

Little House on the Prairie often uses neighbors to deliver ideological messages. One example is the farm wife, Mrs. Scott, who defends the right of settlers to take land previously occupied by Native Americans: "Lord knows, they'd never do anything with this country themselves. All they do is roam around over it like wild animals. Treaties or no treaties, the land belongs to folks that'll farm it. That's only common sense and justice."[48]

A popular source for the rationalization of land expropriation based on "improvement" was John Locke's 1690 *Second Treatise of Government*, often cited by Puritans like John Winthrop, and restated in 1889 by Theodore Roosevelt: "Let the sentimentalists say what they will, the man who puts the soil to use must of right dispossess the man who does not, or the world will come to a standstill." These sorts of arguments were commonplace in late nineteenth-century America, routinely invoked to justify expropriation of land from Indigenous people.[49] That said, it is doubtful that Laura recalled her neighbor saying these words.

A second economic theme related to labor. Charles Ingalls had little to no money, and he gained neighbors' help digging his well and erecting his roof by labor swapping: he worked for a few days for the neighbor, then the neighbor worked for him. He also aided a cattle drive for a few days, for which he was paid in barter—a cow, a calf, and a side of beef.[50] This reflected the communitarian character of frontier development: neighbors helping neighbors in a cash-poor and mostly debt-free economy. But Rose and Laura gave the story an individualist spin, emphasizing how—except for the precious nails he used in the roof and the glass windows he bought in town—Charles built everything himself from local materials. The implication was that the good life was a self-sufficient life. It was individualist, not communitarian.

Wilder's fourth book, *On the Banks of Plum Creek*, picks up with the Ingallses' brief return to Lake Pepin and subsequent migration to Minnesota. Rose helped polish this into a much more positive story than that told in the memoir *Pioneer Girl*. The book's theme became hope in the face of adversity. Nature replaced the Osage as the antagonist; Laura wrote graphically and emotionally about the fires and locusts that destroyed their crops on the homestead claim near Walnut Grove. The stories are beautiful in their horror, but they falsely end with success. In fact, after enduring two summers of locust assaults, the family fled for Burr Oak, Iowa. In the book, Charles finds his way home after a four-day blizzard, having made himself a snow cave to keep warm in. It's a story of hope and survival, not of giving up.[51]

By the Shores of Silver Lake, published in 1939, omits the failed Iowa sojourn entirely. It resumes with the family's return to Walnut Grove and traces their move to Dakota Territory. Readers of the novels wouldn't know they had left locust-, fire-, and blizzard-plagued Minnesota for Iowa or that they'd given up on farming and gone into the hotel business, however briefly. Laura knew it, of course. Her memoir contains stories from that period, which she clearly had not enjoyed: at the hotel she was witness to some of the worst of human behavior, including assaults. *Silver Lake* focused instead on positive homesteading stories.[52] In reality, most homesteaders failed, despite a good deal of government support. But Rose and Laura preferred to have her readers believe that the hardships had paid off, both financially and morally. The frontier, in this telling, built character, and character built America. The realities—expensive, brutal, and often bloody failures of frontier settlement, not to mention the genocide of Indigenous people—were not part of the story that Wilder and Lane wanted to tell. They would not let facts get in the way of their good story.

LAURA AND ROSE'S next book was *The Long Winter*, drafted in 1938. At the time, Lane was actively campaigning for the Ludlow Amendment, intended to keep the United States from getting involved in foreign wars without a national referendum. Her 1936 *Saturday Evening Post* essay "Credo," which professed her admiration for Italian fascism (among other things), was being widely republished, including in *Reader's Digest*. Herbert Hoover had lavishly praised it.[53] Rose embedded the principles of the "Credo" into *The Long Winter*.

Revising the manuscript in 1939, Rose again foregrounded the theme of heroic individualism. The winter of 1880–81 buried Dakota Territory in tens of feet of snow, making it impossible for trains to reach the frontier town of De Smet. Early in the book, an elderly Native American warns the townspeople that a harsh winter is coming; Charles Ingalls and Almanzo Wilder are among those who take him seriously and move to town to ride out the winter. Between January and May (when the trains start to run again), the seventy or eighty townspeople survive on grain stores, slaughter their animals, and finally benefit from the rescue mission undertaken by Almanzo and his friend, Cap Garland, financed by another townsman. Almanzo declares: "I'm free, white, and twenty-one . . . or as good as. Anyway, this is a free country and I'm free and independent. I do as I please."[54]

Almanzo and Cap set off in sleighs for a farm believed to have grain. Once there, they negotiate with the farmer, who had planned to keep all his winter wheat for the next year's seed. Almanzo starts the negotiation with the "full elevator price" of $0.82 a bushel. Ultimately the farmer gets $1.25 a bushel for sixty bushels. After all, it's a seller's market. When Almanzo and Cap return to town, they turn the wheat over to their financier, and, in what turns out to be a key issue in the story, they don't charge for their own time and labor (let alone the "risk premium" they could have claimed under free-market principles). The financier, a Mr. Loftus, then tries to charge the townsmen $3.00 a bushel. The angry townsmen enlist Charles to sort things out. Charles begins with an echo of Almanzo:

CHARLES: Don't forget every one of us is free and independent, Loftus. This winter won't last forever and maybe you want to go on doing business after it's over.
FINANCIER: Threatening me, are you?
CHARLES: We don't need to . . . It's a plain fact. If you've got a right to do as you please, we've got a right to do as we please. It works both ways . . . But your business depends on our good will. You maybe don't notice that now, but along next summer you'll likely notice it.[55]

Charles insists that the townspeople wouldn't have objected to the price if only Almanzo and Cap had been paid for their work—then it would have been fair. But Cap interjects: they "didn't make that trip to skin a profit off folks that are hungry." Loftus gives in and offers the wheat at cost. The scene ends with Charles commenting that they should ration the wheat "on a basis of how much our families need to last until spring."[56] One can almost hear the ghost of Karl Marx laughing between the lines—except the townsmen will still have to pay for their ration.

Here are two competing visions of capitalism. Loftus represents the unrestrained free market; the seller can charge whatever the market will bear. He admits that his game is to buy low and sell high, for "that's good business." Almanzo, Charles, and the townspeople represent a different vision, something closer to what today we might call corporate responsibility. They want a "fair price" that includes compensation for the young men. It's an anti-gouging sort of capitalism, but without government setting the "fair price." And this is key to the Wilder and Lane's vision. It's not that they naively deny that some capitalists can abuse the system. It's rather that victory is achieved by moral suasion—not government intervention. The market—represented by the townspeople—sets the fair price. Government is superfluous. As in all the Wilder books, government is either (falsely) absent, unnecessary, or malignant.

The penultimate book in the series, *The Little Town on the Prairie*, published in 1941, is still set in De Smet. The story is mostly about small-town life: Almanzo's courting of Laura, Laura's becoming a teacher, a Fourth of July. That local celebration becomes central as, during the speeches, Laura has a revelation about the Declaration of Independence: "This is what it means to be free," she realizes. "It means, you have to be good. 'Our father's God, author of liberty—' The laws of Nature and Nature's God endow you with a right to life and liberty. Then you have to keep the laws of God, for God's law is the only thing that gives you a right to be free."[57] This of course was *not* what Jefferson believed, nor most of the founding fathers, but it was consistent with libertarians' effacement of a key concept in American governance: that our freedoms are protected *not* by God, but by due process of law.

THE VIEWS OFFERED in the final book in the Wilder–Lane collaboration presage the full expression of Lane's radically individualist, antigovernment political philosophy. By the 1940s, Lane was working to develop an intellectual framework for twentieth-century libertarianism. In 1943, Lane published *The Discovery of Freedom: Man's Struggle Against Authority*. She was dissatisfied with it, but it had a big impact. It inspired Leonard Read to create the Foundation for Economic Education (FEE), and it helped earn Lane a place of honor among the three "founding mothers" of American libertarianism, along with novelist and screenwriter Ayn Rand and journalist Isabel Paterson.[58] William F. Buckley called them the "three furies."[59] Roger Lea MacBride—a libertarian publisher whom Lane ultimately designated as her heir—hailed the book as "a seminal individualist work."[60]

THE DISCOVERY OF Freedom is revelatory in two ways: in laying out Lane's philosophy explicitly and in illustrating her reckless disregard for facts. Lane writes in short, staccato sentences—her claims were as easy to read as they were categorical—and they were supported by numerous anecdotes and examples. Some of these examples were patently false. In one passage, she criticizes the amendment to the Constitution that allowed for the direct election of the U.S. president, an amendment that does not exist.[61] Others are self-contradictory: she declares that the American Revolution had no leader and seven pages later tells us that its leader was Thomas Paine.[62] Elsewhere, she argues that in a centrally planned economy *"costs automatically increase at an increasing rate* until the people can no longer pay them." Why? "Because the attempt to exercise a control of human energy that can not be exercised is a waste of human energy that must constantly increase." This is a tautology: Lane says costs must increase because they must increase.[63] Many of Lane's other claims are hard to judge because she cites no sources. The book has almost no references; for most of its 262 pages, it simply asserts.[64]

Amid this intellectual muddle, however, is a clear-enough animating argument: man is an individual. He is not, like a bee, part of a hive, or anything else. He is an individual, and he is free. Foreshadowing Margaret Thatcher, Lane believes there is no society. We may call the relationships between people society, but all that really exists, in her view, are the interactions between individuals. Anything else is fantasy.[65]

The problem, however, is that men don't *realize* that they are free. They wrongly believe that they cannot manage on their own, that they require a ruling authority—be it God, King, Country, Society, or "The Government." (Lane calls this "pagan superstition," implying a misguided faith in state authority.)[66] In yielding their power to authorities, men create conditions of waste: governments waste men's time, attention, and energy in the form of rules and regulations, and they steal the fruits of men's labor in the form of taxes. Poverty and suffering are the consequence of man's failure to recognize his own freedom, and his wrongheaded dependence on government. People are hungry and poor not because of limited resources, or inequitable concentration of wealth, but because of government waste. To the extent that America is prosperous, it is because our government interferes with our freedom less than most.

All economies—regardless of how they characterize themselves—are communistic, Lane holds, because they are controlled by governments that strip people of their individualism. All economies are planned economies, because people in positions of authority make decisions on others' behalf. And all economies are inefficient, which is why people end up without enough to eat.[67]

Lane's view of the world at first seems Hobbesian: nasty and brutish, full of famine and disease. Brushing aside evidence that many Indigenous peoples, including Native Americans, lived rather well before their social structures were destroyed by European settlers, Lane insists that throughout history, families have lived "in floorless hovels, without windows or chimneys." Workers walked "barefoot, in rags, with lousy hair and unwashed teeth."[68] Actually, Lane's view is the opposite of Hobbes's, for the brutality of life is found not in nature but in the commonwealth. People are not wretched because they cannot take care of themselves; they are wretched because of governments. People could take care of themselves perfectly well if only they were left alone to apply their energies efficiently. "Whenever men began to develop farming and crafts and trade," she asserts, "the Government stopped them."[69] Men left to their own devices would not squander their energies; they would find the way to take care of themselves, because they would have to.[70] Whereas Hobbes saw human wretchedness as warrant *for* government, Lane uses it to indict government.

Lane allows that government develops initially for good reason: as a police force to stop murder and theft. Using the American frontier as an example (and again eliding the Indigenous people who already lived there), she suggests that European settlers "lived in anarchy, and every man carried a gun," and since there was no government, "every man had to be able to defend himself."[71] This was a bother, and so men gathered up vigilance committees. Eventually they chose one among their number to be the sheriff, empowering him to protect them through force.[72] She summarizes: "This is the essential element of all Government: force, used with general consent."[73]

But governments are never content with just catching Bad Guys.[74] Lane insists that it is just a few steps from the sheriff to the planned economy.[75] "Instead of leaving industry to take its own course," she writes, governments have saddled businesses with "an interminable series of regulations . . . all inflicting serious harm."[76]

LANE'S DISTASTE FOR government includes democracy. The word, Lane notes, means rule by the *demos*—the people—but "the people," in her view, does not exist; there are only individual persons. So even democratic government is necessarily coercive.[77]

With breathtaking rhetorical audacity she asserts that America's Founding Fathers did not believe in democracy. As evidence, she gives us James Madison, quoting from the section of *The Federalist Papers*, essay 10, where Madison allows that a "pure democracy, by which I mean a society consisting of a small number of citizens, who assemble and administer the government in person, can admit no cure for the mischiefs of faction. A common passion or interest will, in almost every case, be felt by a majority . . . and there is nothing to check the inducement to sacrifice the weaker party or an obnoxious individual," so there will always be the risk—in a pure democracy—that the majority will run roughshod over minorities. So Madison concluded, "Hence it is, that such democracies have ever been found incompatible with personal security or the rights of property; and have in general, been as short in their lives as they have been violent in their deaths."[78]

To be sure, America's founders had a range of views about democracy, with some evincing more trust in the wisdom of ordinary people and others less. They also had divergent interpretations of the meaning of the word. Lane is right that Madison was concerned about factionalism and the risk that majorities could deny the rights of minorities. But Madison wrote the words in the *Federalist* 10 that Lane quotes so approvingly as he was in the process of establishing a government whose legitimacy was grounded in popular consent—in other words, a democracy. Madison was concerned that a passionate faction (like Lane and her associates!) could overwhelm the best interests of the union, but this was part of a larger argument not *against* democracy, but *for* the form of quasi-majoritarian representative democracy that he—and Washington and Jefferson and Franklin—were working to install.[79] Moreover, while Madison uses the phrase "such democracies"—making clear that he is talking about a particular form—Lane drops the qualifier, potentially leaving the reader with the false impression that Madison is against democracy of all types.

To bolster her claim that the Founding Fathers did not believe in majority rule, Lane follows the pattern established by the American Liberty League, NAM, and other business conservatives in resting her case on the Declaration of Independence, while eliding or disparaging the Constitution that actually created the American government. She insists that the founders said nothing about "The People," a move she can only make by ignoring the first three words of the Constitution.[80] The Constitution represents *The People* as an entity—it's not "We, these several persons"—creating the nation and its form of governance. Lane tries to square this circle by implying that the transition from the America of the Declaration of Independence to the America of the Constitution was a misguided compromise.[81] The events of 1776, she suggests, pointed the new nation in the right direction, but 1789 derailed it.

Lane is comfortable with the Bill of Rights, because it reversed a pattern established in England of viewing rights as something that a king grants to men and instead rests those rights in men themselves. She also approves of how the Bill of Rights articulates what the government may not do, and therefore can be viewed as much as a list of governmental prohibitions as individual rights.[82] The problem for Lane lies in the rest of the Constitution.

Because "The People" does not exist, the system the Constitution outlines (she argues) cannot work. Why? Because a person cannot assign their political rights to another person, any more than they could sign away their lives or their liberty. "Life is energy; liberty is the individual control of human-life energy. It can not be separated from life." To Lane this meant that you cannot designate another person to represent you, even if by voting.[83] If an individual's freedom cannot be delegated to anyone else, then representative democracy is impossible. Lane repeats this point throughout the book: whether pure or representative, democracy cannot work, because it always involves the usurpation of individual freedom.[84]

What is the alternative? Lane's answer is anarchism, with one exception: protecting private property. For Lane, the right to own property is the foundation of freedom.[85] But this is not an inalienable right, like life and liberty; it is a legal right that requires legal protection. In her view, guarding property rights is the only legitimate warrant for government. Lane is a *propertarian*.

Lane's animus to democracy is most visceral in her discussion of majority rule. "[T]here is no reason to suppose that majority-rule would be desirable, even if it were possible," she scoffs. "There is no morality or efficiency in mere numbers. Ninety-nine persons are no more likely to be right than one person is."[86] She writes approvingly of elements of the Constitution that deny direct election of members of government apart from the House of Representatives, and she scorns the tendency toward direct elections. Disparaging the valorization of voting as "an American superstition," she unequivocally disapproves of the expansion of the franchise: "Americans take it for granted that every human being has a natural right to vote. *Of course this is not true. No one has a natural right to vote.*"[87]

Lane allows that voting can be valuable "when voters have an opportunity to elect men who will repeal laws and reduce Government's areas of activities."[88] In other words, voting is only legitimate when it serves to reduce government, rather than to sustain or expand it. Alas, Lane concludes, a majority of voters cannot be counted on to do this, because they are too busy to pay sufficient attention to what their representatives are doing or to learn enough about the issues to make informed choices. Meanwhile, minorities will pressure the government to do more, rather than less.[89] And these minorities—"stupid men" and superstitious "reformers"—use the vote to force politicians to exceed their constitutional authority. This leads Lane to the position of praising governmental unresponsiveness. Elected officials for the most part do what they want and ignore their constituents, and this is good: "For why does anyone suppose that a majority of citizens *should* control their Government?"[90]

Lane argues that people should only be allowed to vote on issues in which they have a direct stake and would take the time to study. In her ideal world, "no one but automobile owners would vote for members of Highway Commissions or pay for highways." Ignoring the use of roads for collective endeavors such as emergency services, busing schoolchildren, or shipping food to markets, Lane insists it is an injustice that anyone who doesn't own a car should be compelled to pay a highway tax.[91] Then again, Lane rejects the idea that the government should have "interfered" with highways in the first place: she claims that the American Automobile Association, a "free mutual" undertaking, was already dealing with the relevant issues (an absurd claim, given that the government—not AAA and not the private sector—built the highways).

Lane sees only one bright light in the dim historical trend of expanding franchise and growing government: rebellion. Because governments are inefficient, people get fed up and periodically revolt. But in throwing off one kind of authority, they mistakenly substitute another. In this discussion, Lane reveals her stripes as she offers a counterfactual history of the Civil War and defends the Confederate secession. The war's cause, she insists, was not slavery, but tariffs.[92] The federal government had instituted tariffs to protect infant industries, but ordinary Americans fought them (she asserts), rightly seeing tariffs as taking money from some citizens to give to others. The protectionist maneuver "worked as all attempts to control productive human energy have always worked. It made everyone poorer."[93] Southerners fought back because they saw how tariffs hindered their ability to sell cotton on the world market, and they were well within their rights to secede (she insists) as this was a right that "all states had until then maintained."[94] But that was false: nowhere in the Constitution is the right to leave the Union. And Lane offers not one word about slavery, or the rights of Black men and women to be free. Her radical individualism had strict racial limits.

Even her admirers acknowledge that Lane's vision is Manichaean: the entire "history of mankind" is "understood only as the theater of two diverse forces, the authoritarians and the revolutionists, locked in an unending struggle for supremacy."[95] In Lane's paranoid vision, fellow citizens are a mob ready to strip landowners of their legal property rights, including the "right" to own other persons.

BY THE 1940S, Lane was part of a group of writers, intellectuals, and business leaders forming what Ludwig von Mises's biographer Jörg Hülsmann describes as "a seedbed of opposition, a network of leaders" preparing a counterattack against the New Deal and in favor of radical individualism and market fundamentalism.[96] They included J. Howard Pew, Henry Hazlitt, Lawrence Fertig (the ad exec responsible for installing Mises at NYU), Ayn Rand and Isabel Paterson, Leonard Read, DuPont executive Jasper Crane, University of Chicago economists Frank Knight and Henry Simons, and Mises himself.[97] After the 1943 publication of *The Discovery of Freedom*, Lane became a regular correspondent with Pew and Crane, and her position in their circle solidified.[98]

Lane's book debuted the same year as Isabel Paterson's *The God of the Machine* and Ayn Rand's *The Fountainhead*.[99] All three wrote books that sacralized property rights, celebrated (masculine) rugged individualism, and insisted that government's only legitimate role was the protection of private property.[100] All three disdained cooperation and altruism. Rand would sell the most books and in 1949 become famous after *The Fountainhead* was made into a Hollywood film starring Gary Cooper and Patricia Neal, but in the early 1940s Lane was more influential as a "behind-the-scenes operator."[101]

In 1945, in a new role as book review editor for the right-wing National Economic Council, Lane's stridency increased. She blasted Crane when he made an offhand remark about "restraint of trade by business." Crane implied that government intervention under antitrust statutes might occasionally be warranted; for Lane that was unacceptable.[102] While she aggressively opposed *government* monopolies, Lane believed that private monopolies existed only at our pleasure: "In a free economy . . . no monopoly can exist that does not anxiously serve and please the largest number of people."[103] Lane evidently persuaded Crane to toughen up; they continued to correspond for many years, with one colleague commenting that Lane was the person whose thinking had most influenced Crane.[104] Lane also worried that the emerging Mont Pelerin Society might not be "really reliable," because of the influence of Europeans not committed to radical individualism. In 1946, she advised Crane to hold off supporting the group until he was sure where it was heading.[105]

Historian Jennifer Burns has characterized Lane, Rand, and Paterson as "ideological enforcers"; nowhere is this clearer than in Lane's work with J. Howard Pew and Herbert Hoover.[106] During 1947 and 1948 Lane collaborated with them to get a particular textbook, written by the Keynesian economist and Stanford University professor Lorie Tarshis, banned from university curricula.[107] For Hoover, Pew, and Lane, Keynesian economics was nothing less than centralized planning, with all that implied according to the Austrian school view, now vividly expressed in Hayek's *Road to Serfdom*.[108] Lane and the others embarked on a campaign to pressure university presidents and donors to demand the book's removal. Pew brought it up at a lunch with Hoover and the president of Stanford, too. In an August 1948 letter, Pew recounted that he "spent at least a half hour denouncing the Tarshis book and expounding my views as to why and how such instructors should be eliminated" and praised Lane for "making a real contribution toward getting this book eliminated from our colleges."[109] As in the 1920s and '30s, the defenders of "freedom" had fought to suppress ideas of which they disapproved, and this time it worked: sales of the book plummeted. Economists took note. Burns concludes that the campaign "effectively stopped sales of Tarshis's textbook [and] left a lasting legacy for the way economists communicated with the public."[110] It also influenced what they taught the next generation.[111] Economist Paul Samuelson, whose textbook on Keynesian economics came out a year after Tarshis's, became the dominant voice instead—though he was attacked too. Forewarned was forearmed; Tarshis had written his textbook to be accessible to students and even non-students, while Samuelson, knowing what would come his way, wrote in a more technical, scientific, and defensible voice—"as if a lawyer were at my elbow," he recalled in 1997.[112] There's little doubt that the Tarshis affair had a chilling effect. As historian Michael Bernstein has noted, the field of economics in the twentieth century may not have been monolithic, but it was "remarkable the extent to which a prevailing doctrine [reigned] among its most influential and visible practitioners."[113]

By 1947, Lane's ideas had gone too far even for the man who most inspired them: Ludwig von Mises. (While *The Discovery of Freedom* had very few notes or citations, the influence of Mises in many points is plain.) In a letter to Mises, Lane explicitly laid out her hostility to democracy:

> "... as an American I am of course fundamentally opposed to democracy and to anyone advocating or defending democracy, which in theory and practice is the basis of socialism. It is precisely democracy which is destroying the American political structure, American law, and the American economy ... [114]

Mises did not agree; he saw Lane as neither liberal nor neoliberal, but as anarchist. In a private letter to a colleague, he explained that he disagreed thoroughly with the growing anarchism among some American conservatives, and attributed it to a psychological "reaction to the deification of the state."[115]

Lane's views were so extreme that at times Mises had trouble understanding them. Mises could not believe that any "rational man ever proposed that the production of security be trusted to private associations," only to discover that at least one woman did: Lane. She held that "the market place is the best way to protect life and property."[116] Mises was dumbfounded by this, noting that "in the absence of a [state] monopoly on the use of coercive force, 'everybody would have continually to defend himself against hosts of aggressors.'" Everyone would live in the Wild West, never free of the threat of violence. The principles Lane invoked were not enshrined in the Declaration of Independence, Mises wrote, but were "rather the principles that led a hundred years ago to the Confederate states to refuse to recognize the President elected by the majority. Whatever and whenever resorted to, these principles will lead to bloodshed and anarchy."[117] As, indeed, in the American Civil War they had, and which Lane endorsed.

ROSE WILDER LANE might be viewed as a footnote to history—influential only in extremist circles—except that she is revered as a founder of American libertarianism. FEE and other right-wing groups continue to promote her works. Above all, through the Little House books, tens of millions of impressionable children have absorbed her ideas.[118]

Some might argue that the libertarianism of the Little House books was more unconscious than intentional, and that the basic stories were true—that Rose simply influenced how the details were fleshed out.[119] But the stories were not true, not in their details and not in their overall framework. In the Ingallses' real lives, hard work didn't bring success. Nor were they rugged individuals: they relied on neighbors and community for their very survival, and their presence on the frontier was predicated on the federal government's removal of native Osage peoples and distribution of their land to white settlers. Yet in the books, the state scarcely appears, save in a negative light. Conspicuously, it fails to do the one thing Lane believed it should: perform its police function and protect white settlers.

Critics have noted that the Little House books offer a faulty portrayal not just of the background role of government in the Ingallses' lives, but also of a deeply personal and important element of Laura's life: her sister Mary's blindness. Mary lost her eyesight to an illness; she was able to attend the Iowa College for the Blind only because the government of the Dakota Territory covered her tuition.[120] And the school would not have existed were it not for the state legislators who funded it. It's a key omission, because it changes the way we understand the story. And it's far from the only example: throughout the stories, people of color are also expunged, leaving us with a dishonest story of "white self-sufficiency" instead of an honest story of government-sponsored settlements whose costs were borne by native peoples.[121]

Rose Wilder Lane died in 1968, having left her estate and her mother's copyrights to Roger MacBride, who brought the books—or, at least, a version of them—to the small screen, in a top-rated television series starring heartthrob actor Michael Landon as "Pa" Ingalls. Beginning in 1974, the show ran for nine seasons and aired over 200 episodes.[122] (It was so popular that one viewer was sure that it was "truly inspired by God.")[123] The adaptation was set in Walnut Grove, where the real Ingallses had lived first in a dugout; on television the dugout became a two-story frame house with glass windows and an enormous stone fireplace—more Little Mansion than Little House. It was, in the words of Caroline Fraser, less adaptation than "hyperbolic fantasy spin-off, wildly exaggerating the family's well-being."[124] On TV, the Ingalls didn't stoically survive calamity after calamity. They thrived. They prospered, both emotionally and financially. It was the narrative grafting of the postwar prosperity gospel onto late nineteenth-century frontier capitalism. Ronald Reagan reportedly cried while watching it.[125] Viewership peaked during the 1980–81 season, at an average of over 17 million weekly viewers, and the show of course helped to sell more books.[126]

Children's literature and middlebrow television were two avenues through which the myth of the free market could reach Americans, but the Little House franchise was hardly the only instance of individualistic, antigovernment ideas spreading surreptitiously through trusted channels. The Sunday sermon was another. Over the course of the 1940s and '50s, business leaders would infuse certain strains of Christianity with libertarian ideas. Their efforts would fundamentally transform the faith in America.

CHAPTER 7

A Questionable Gospel

With the publication and promotion of *The Road to Serfdom*, business leaders had found a way to wrap their ideology in academic respectability, but laissez-faire beliefs still faced another problem: Christianity. During the nineteenth century, mainline American Protestants had broadly embraced what was known as the "social gospel." Social gospelists were not socialists, but they did want to ameliorate the wretched conditions industrial capitalism had generated in many parts of the nation, as well as to address the Gilded Age's breathtaking—and to some observers shameful—concentrations of wealth. As such, many American Protestants supported economic reforms and legislation to improve the lot of the working classes. In the twentieth century, reforming Protestants took up the progressive causes of abolishing child labor and expanding compulsory education. They also took a leading role in Prohibition, most famously in the work of the Woman's Christian Temperance Union.[1]

The Christian argument for social welfare and economic equity was obvious. Jesus preached charity and urged his followers to love their neighbors as themselves, especially the poor. "It is hard for a rich man to enter the kingdom of heaven," he says in the Gospel according to Matthew. "Again I tell you, it is easier for a *camel* to go through the eye of a needle than for a rich man to enter the kingdom of God."[2]

American business leaders—including J. Howard Pew and other members of NAM and NELA, and the businessmen who brought Mises and Hayek to America—saw this as a serious challenge. Their insistence that letting business run free would achieve the best outcomes—not just for themselves but for all Americans—rang hollow amid the brutal realities of unfettered capitalism. To turn a blind eye to this suffering was not merely inhumane, it was un-Christian.

For their laissez-faire argument to be effective, business conservatives needed to find a way to counter its incompatibility with the teachings of Jesus. Having already done some heavy lifting to change how Americans thought about capitalism, their next step was to change how they thought about Christianity.

JAMES W. FIFIELD JR. was a Congregational minister in Los Angeles who rejected the social gospel in favor of Christian individualism; later he would call it Christian Libertarianism. Theologically, Fifield considered himself a liberal—he accepted evolution and the historicity of the Bible—but politically, his views aligned with NAM.[3] From the 1930s through the 1950s, Fifield would build an influential conservative movement, known as Spiritual Mobilization, whose goal was to convert mainline Protestant leaders and their parishioners into market fundamentalists.[4]

Fifield was born in Chicago in 1899 and briefly attended Oberlin College in Ohio before joining the U.S. Army during World War I. He returned to Oberlin to complete his undergraduate studies, then later earned a master's degree from the Divinity School at the University of Chicago.[5] He moved to South Dakota and then to the East Congregational Church in Grand Rapids, Michigan.

The trigger for Fifield's activism was the Oberlin Anti-Profit Resolution, passed by the Congregational Churches General Council meeting in Oberlin in June 1934.[6] While the suffering of the Great Depression had led many churches to adopt resolutions pronouncing capitalism's failures and calling for action, this one was frankly pro-communism. It advocated the "abolition of the profit system," "the inauguration of a thoroughly planned and organized social economy," and the elimination of "private ownership in the means of production and distribution wherever such private ownership interferes with the success of a planned social economy."[7] Fifield was appalled. In principle, one could be a communist and believe in God (which the Oberlin Congregationalists presumably did), but in practice communism was hostile to religion; Marx had pronounced religion a ruling-class ploy to keep workers complacent.[8]

Fifield met with Donald Cowling, the Congregationalist president of Minnesota's Carleton College, and William Hocking, an idealist Harvard professor of philosophy who had written extensively on religion, to discuss what to do. Hocking argued that the most important freedom is the "freedom to perfect one's freedom."[9] The three men decided to create an organization to combat what they labeled "pagan statism." They would call their new initiative the "Mobilization for Spiritual Ideals," soon shortened to Spiritual Mobilization.[10]

In 1935, Fifield accepted an offer to take the pulpit of the First Congregational Church of Los Angeles. The church had recently completed a major expansion and had a $750,000 mortgage to pay off. To expand membership, Fifield increased the number of weekly services and developed a church school and drama workshop. It worked: membership quintupled in the next five years and the debt was paid off in seven. At a time when many American churches were losing parishioners, Fifield's grew. But if he was energetic and entrepreneurial, he was also lucky: he had a wealthy congregation with several exceptionally prominent members, including Robert A. Millikan, the president of the California Institute of Technology, and Leonard Read.[11]

Fifield's message was not just spiritual; it was also economic and political. In 1938 he issued a pamphlet intended for broad distribution, "Christian Ministers and America's Future"; the Los Angeles Times took note and reported on it approvingly.[12] Much of what he had to say was similar (if not identical) to arguments already made by the American Liberty League, Ludwig von Mises, and NAM. Like Mises, Fifield asserted that Americans faced a choice between "democracy and capitalism" on the one hand and "dictatorship" on the other. Paralleling the business opponents of the New Deal, Fifield decried the growth of federal power. "Every concentration of power in our national government, especially in its executive branch, represents a reduction of freedom for the individual citizen and for the constituent States." What Fifield added was a harsh critique of his fellow religious leaders: he demanded the clergy lead a revival of "individual thought on a widespread scale" to prevent American descent into (echoing Wendell Willkie) "the abyss of totalitarianism."[13]

Every Saturday, the Los Angeles Times ran a religion section announcing upcoming sermons for the city's major churches; sometimes it also published summaries of them. In 1939 and 1940, the Times recapped Fifield's sermons alongside articles recounting his thoughts after traveling to Europe during the turmoil of 1939. Much of his message was fearmongering: the federal government was suppressing "individual thought," America was heading toward "Hitler paganism." But as historian James McKay notes, over the next few years Fifield would find a more positive message, moving toward the call for a return to "Freedom Under God."[14]

In 1940, Fifield embarked on a fund-raising drive organized around a "Service Pledge," asking people to rededicate themselves to "faith in God, democracy, freedom of speech, freedom of assembly, and freedom of worship."[15] The pledge was printed in advertisements designed for people to cut out and return with their names and addresses to the Spiritual Mobilization office. It also exhorted the faithful to mail the pledge to friends beyond Los Angeles. Fifield claimed the advertisement was reprinted in more than twenty other cities within the week; he told a *Times* reporter that he hoped "leaders of at least 30,000 churches in the country will urge their members to undertake this covenant to help meet the pagan challenge of the world."[16]

IN DECEMBER 1940, NAM invited Fifield to speak at its annual Congress on American Industry, held at New York's tony Waldorf Astoria hotel. This was the meeting at which NAM president H. W. Prentis introduced the Tripod of Freedom campaign; speakers also heard from J. Howard Pew, who spoke on "Preserving the Private Enterprise System."[17] Fifield's subject was "The Religious Foundation of True Americanism"; he shared the session with NAM attorney (and ex–Liberty Leaguer) James Emery, who propounded on the government's (alleged) strangling of America's defenses. A few weeks after the NAM meeting, Roosevelt gave his famous "Four Freedoms" speech, which enraged Pew, Fifield, and their community. Roosevelt's four freedoms were freedom of speech and expression; freedom to worship God in one's own way; freedom from want; and—perhaps most distinctly— freedom from fear.[18] The first two were consistent with what Fifield and Pew accepted, but the latter two were a direct confrontation. Freedom from want and from fear, in their view, would teach men to rely on Government rather than God. More than two years later, Fifield was still railing in his sermons against these ideas; in August 1943 he told Pew that this would be his theme for the year.[19]

Fifield embedded opposition to the Four Freedoms in his pamphlets, insisting in one that American fighting men "gladly abandon security and go forth to fight for freedom. Logically they conclude that freedom is more important to THEM than 'security.' As they reason further they decide that they do not desire freedom from want and freedom from fear!"

But while Fifield stressed the bravery of soldiers, willing to face fear and give up security, there was another aspect to his argument: Capitalism *needed* want and fear. What else would drive people to toil, and would keep workers showing up to dangerous, precarious, low-wage jobs? "Freedom from Want" was a threat, in Fifield's mind, because it implied government encroachment on a key church domain, namely charity. Fifield was not cruel—he understood that at times people needed help—but that was the job of the church, not the federal government. Fifield also understood that alms bound a congregation's poorer members to the church and helped maintain its social hierarchy. Making the poor dependent on socialized welfare transferred gratitude, loyalty, and obligation from church to state. Worse, it threatened to diminish God, as people would abandon Him for the greater (or at least more immediate) security of the state. In his August 1943 letter to Pew, Fifield encapsulated: "freedom from want and fear [are] unworthy objectives for our nation."[20]

SPIRITUAL MOBILIZATION WAS incorporated on July 29, 1942; Fifield hired a comptroller and recruited a board of advisers. One board member was Caltech president Robert Millikan; two others were Robert Gordon Sproul, president of the University of California, and Ray Lyman Wilbur, president of Stanford University. Donald Cowling also joined the board, along with Norman Vincent Peale, the soon-to-be-famous minister of the Marble Collegiate Church of New York City, and Eric Johnston, president of the U.S. Chamber of Commerce. Senator Albert Hawkes, Republican of New Jersey, rounded out the board, although he was listed not as a politician but as an industrialist.

While Fifield had originally based his work on myriad small donations, he now began to pursue large donors. His correspondence with Pew over the many years of their relationship mixed fund-raising with discussion of goals and objectives. Fifield's principal costs were in printing and distributing his pamphlets. For his first few years, his mailing list included some twenty-three thousand ministers.

In 1943, Pew increased his donations to Spiritual Mobilization, but first, he did some homework, hiring an economist named Alfred Haake to investigate the organization. Haake was convinced. "The basic issue today and for the coming generation, in terms of economics and politics[,] is 'Security v. Freedom,'" Haake wrote to Pew. "We must choose one or the other, for we cannot have both, and if we choose security, we not only lose freedom but fail to get security itself except at mere subsistence level. In terms of human life, the issue was 'Christ or Caesar,' or spirit vs.

materialism."[21] Security versus freedom was another way of reinscribing the dichotomy of communism versus capitalism, the insistence that if governments took steps to protect citizens from want or workers from abuse, totalitarianism lurked just around the corner. Fifield offered no evidence to back the claim, but it had emotional impact; Haake would join Spiritual Mobilization as director of the organization's Chicago office in 1945.

As part of his due diligence, Haake had interviewed Leonard Read, then still at the Los Angeles Chamber of Commerce. Read had reservations; he felt Fifield was not "down to earth" enough, not sufficiently specific in his instructions to his preachers, and that he resorted too much to emotional appeals. But Haake disagreed, explaining to Pew, "We do need to create an emotional attitude toward the encroachments of collectivism. It is an emotional attitude, now, that still holds many people to the pied piper of security who is leading us to disaster with his piping."[22]

Haake convinced Pew, who began helping Fifield raise money to expand Spiritual Mobilization. In 1944, Pew organized a meeting to introduce Fifield to other captains of American industry including Jasper Crane of DuPont, H. W. Prentis (president of Armstrong Cork as well as of NAM), and Harvey S. Firestone Jr. of Firestone Tires, who in turn solicited additional corporate sponsors.[23] With the largesse of these powerful and deep-pocketed corporate leaders, Spiritual Mobilization grew substantially. As Fifield drew on the support of corporate titans, his message began to shift away from free speech and freedom of religion and toward the centrality of free enterprise.

A key element in this shift was the promotion of *The Road to Serfdom*. Fifield worked with Pew to ensure that Hayek's book got wide attention in the United States. While Pew sent copies to his own circle of corporate leaders, he also footed the bill for Fifield to promote the book among key ministers.[24] In August 1945, former president Herbert Hoover gave a speech in Long Beach echoing the book (or the cartoon version of it); the speech was reported on the front page of the Sunday *Los Angeles Times* and Fifield republished it as a pamphlet mailed to his followers.[25] The pamphlet highlighted Hoover's claim that socialism was taking over Europe: "Whatever the particular name of these European systems may be, whether it be Communism, Socialism or the decoy term planned economy, they are all collectivist. They all have a common base in bureaucratic power over the liberties and economic life of the people. In the extreme form they leave little of free speech, free press, free assembly or independent justice."[26]

The Road to Serfdom had appeared when World War II was still being fought and the U.S. government's wartime production management infrastructure was still operating, so it was not unreasonable to worry that government control of the economy might become the new normal. When Hoover delivered his Long Beach speech, for example, the Office of Price Administration (OPA) still existed.[27] Moreover, some New Dealers had suggested that the OPA could not be dismantled quickly, lest that trigger inflation, and that other wartime controls might need to be maintained for the United States to avoid sinking back into a depression. But in Pew's and Fifield's hands, an understandable unease over the persistence of wartime emergency measures erupted into full-fledged paranoia that democracy was under siege.

"Things that matter most are in definite peril in America—constitutional government, free speech, free enterprise, free pulpit, free assembly, free press, the democratic process, rule by law instead of decree, and indeed the *sacredness* of private property and personal rights," Fifield wrote in a confidential memorandum to his followers.[28] Admittedly, in the Declaration of Independence, Thomas Jefferson placed the endowment of men's inalienable rights—life, liberty, and the pursuit of happiness—in their Creator. But the Declaration was the basis of the colonies' insurrection against Great Britain; it was not the basis of the new form of governance that was subsequently emplaced. Crucially, the Constitution defines property as a *legal* right, sustained by the rules of men, not God. It begins not with appeal to divine authority, but with "We the People." The rights it grants and protects are articulated by, agreed upon, and enforced by men, through their chosen form of governance. It took serious intellectual gymnastics to make the case that property rights were God-given.

Many other theologians criticized Fifield's arguments on this point. In 1944, a group of Unitarian ministers attacked Spiritual Mobilization for its efforts to vilify "the attempts that have been made to remedy the crying evils of our society."[29] In 1946, Reinhold Niebuhr—a leading public theologian, professor at Union Theological Seminary, and editor of the journal *Christianity and Crisis*—offered a thoroughgoing critique. What Spiritual Mobilization decried as "pagan statism" included "even the mildest forms of government control. If its standards are accepted, every nation beside our own is already caught in this paganism. Said a British Tory, not a British socialist, visitor to this country who had been given a leaflet of this organization: 'the uncritical identification of "Christian liberty" with a laissez faire economic program would not be possible in any modern nation except your own.'"[30]

Niebuhr argued that this difference between the United States and Europe derived from the idiosyncratic American definition of democracy as the separation of "economic process from political control." Political freedom, American business leaders insisted, relied on and was inseparable from economic freedom, no matter its social costs and consequences. Europeans, however, believed nearly the opposite: that there was "no way of avoiding totalitarianism if the ideal of political democracy becomes inexorably associated with economic insecurity." This was why Bismarck instituted social reforms in nineteenth-century Germany: moderate reform was the best way to stave off immoderate social upheaval. FDR believed essentially the same thing: that he was not ending capitalism but preserving it. Rejecting the false dichotomies between freedom and security and between democracy and totalitarianism, Niebuhr observed that Scandinavian governments, continental European governments, and Britain were all "seeking a middle way between too much planning and a too unregulated freedom, with the resultant economic insecurity."[31] They sought a just and workable balance. Fifield and his supporters refused to allow that such a balance could exist.

DURING 1947, FIFIELD concentrated on expanding his reach with clergy via a new pledge drive, "Perils to Freedom." He worked to get twenty-five thousand ministers to pledge to speak on the theme on Columbus Day that year, which happened to fall on a Sunday. Among the books he recommended as a resource was *The Road to Serfdom*.[32] Fifield claimed fifteen thousand of his pledgees sent their sermons back to him; one of them was Norman Vincent Peale.

Peale had got his start in politics on the losing side of the battle to preserve Prohibition. Like Al Smith, Peale viewed the Eighteenth Amendment as a means of sustaining the cultural hegemony of Protestant America over the largely Catholic immigrants of the late nineteenth and early twentieth centuries; unlike Smith, Peale considered that a good thing. But despite the failure to preserve Prohibition, Peale's own star rose. In 1932, he had been appointed senior minister at New York's Marble Collegiate Church (where he would serve for fifty-two years), and in 1935 he launched a successful weekly radio program, *The Art of Living*. From 1942 to 1945 he led the right-wing anti–New Deal Committee for Constitutional Government, and he launched a magazine, *Guideposts*. Peale biographer Carol George summarized *Guideposts'* editorial philosophy as "Americanism, free enterprise, and practical Christianity."[33]

Like Fifield's Spiritual Mobilization, Peale's *Guideposts* was kept alive in its early years by businessmen. Pew was a major benefactor; others included Eddie Rickenbacker of Eastern Airlines; Walter Teagle, formerly of Standard Oil of New Jersey; and media giant Frank Gannett. Industrial subscribers included R. J. Reynolds Tobacco and General Motors; the latter ordered thousands of copies to distribute to employees.

What message did Peale deliver to his parishioners on that Columbus Day Sunday in 1947? It was the Tripod of Freedom, transmogrified into catechism. "Our forefathers," Peale said, "formed this government on the following tripod of principles: First, it was to be a constitutional representative government. Second, we were to enjoy free private competitive enterprise, and third, it was to provide civil and religious liberty. If any one of those is weakened or broken the entire structure fails." Government was to "interfere as little as possible in the affairs of the people, acting only as an umpire to ensure that fair play and the rules of decency prevail and that life, liberty and property are protected." Against this vision of a nation defined by these indivisible freedoms, Peale juxtaposed "collectivism"—as filtered through Marx, Engels, and Stalin—which "under the guise of humanitarianism insists that government control the people for they do not know how to take care of themselves. This concept erases the philosophy of the greatness and sovereignty of the individual citizen under God as the arbiter of his own destiny."[34]

Some of our nation's founders may have believed in individual competitive enterprise, but they did not equate it with civil and religious liberty. Nor did they view it as a nonnegotiable component of the new nation they were creating, equivalent to, and on par with, representative government. On the contrary, it would be more than a century after the Constitution was written before the first federal law to foster competition and curb monopoly: the 1890 Sherman Anti-Trust Act. What the Constitution of 1787 did do was repair an error in the original Articles of Confederation, which granted the central government no authority over interstate trade. After independence, many of the new states raised trade barriers against each other—tariffs, road tolls, and the like—wreaking havoc on the nation's merchants (who included many founders). Still, when the Constitution handed control of interstate trade to a strengthened federal government via the interstate commerce clause, it guaranteed only a consistent regulatory framework, not free trade, let alone competition.[35]

As for property rights, historians, philosophers, and law professors have spilt oceans of ink on the topic. Suffice it to note that the First Amendment states that Congress shall make "*no* law respecting an establishment of religion, or prohibiting the free exercise thereof; or abridging the freedom of speech, or of the press; or the right of the people peaceably to assemble, and to petition the government for a redress of grievances." In contrast, the Fifth Amendment states that "No person shall ... be deprived of life, liberty, or property *without due process of law*; nor shall private property be taken for public use, *without just compensation*."[36] This is a huge difference: property rights can be compromised or even denied, under specific conditions.[37]

What Peale's parishioners heard was a plausible-enough story—bolstered by Peale's rhetorical skills—which enshrined property rights as equivalent to freedom of religion. But it wasn't true. It painted a picture of the federal government's role that the founding fathers (and most American historians) would barely recognize.[38] Like Fifield and Pew, Peale also elided the concept of *general* welfare—interpreting everything in individualist terms. In truth, the nation's founders were mindful that ensuring the general welfare might at times mean compromising the desires or even rights of individuals. Most parishioners presumably missed these distinctions, and even if they did not, they would have been unlikely to challenge their minister on a Sunday.[39]

Five years later, Peale would earn the title of "God's salesman" with the publication of *The Power of Positive Thinking*, which sold more than five million copies. The book combined Christian faith ("every problem can be solved and solved right if you pray"), pop psychology ("never think of yourself as failing"), and self-aggrandizement ("make a true estimate of your own ability, and then raise it 10 percent").[40] In 1977, Peale would officiate at the marriage of Donald and Ivana Trump.[41]

IN 1949, FIFIELD launched a new publication: *Faith and Freedom*. Its writers were a constellation of the right-wing intellectual firmament. Besides Pew, Read, Mises, and Hayek, they included Rose Wilder Lane and Henry Hazlitt. They also included Murray Rothbard, an Ayn Rand acolyte who argued that if the poor cannot feed their children, tough breaks; Clarence Manion, a conservative radio talk show host and former dean of the Notre Dame law school; and a rising young star of American conservative thought, William F. Buckley.[42]

Like the Spiritual Mobilization newsletter, *Faith and Freedom* was aimed at clergy, its purpose to connect the nation's Protestant ministers with laissez-faire economic thought. The unifying theme was Fifield's emerging doctrine of Freedom Under God. Like his earlier concept of pagan statism, the doctrine insisted that it was wrong to believe democratic government secured our freedoms. Freedom came from God, so the growth of the state could only come at the expense of freedom. Fifield also insisted that "individual dignity" was a Christian concept.[43] He would call it "Christian Individualism." Since the dignity of the individual flowed from God, Christians should look to God for sustenance. Welfare programs such as Social Security usurped God's role—or at least the role of his clerical agents on Earth.[44] Social Security was also morally wrong because it made people dependent upon the state, rather than on their Church and, above all, their faith. Any tax used to support it was "theft"—a word peppered throughout *Faith and Freedom*.[45]

A piece by Herbert Hoover in the inaugural issue offered a third argument for Christian Individualism: that the compassion of the welfare state was anti-Christian because it was coerced. Americans were no longer free to choose whether to be compassionate or not, and to whom, because, frankly, not everyone was worthy of compassion.[46] In 1952, Fifield added Hoover's criticism to Spiritual Mobilization's credo, which now read:

> Man, being created free as a child of God, has certain inalienable rights and responsibilities; the state must not be permitted to usurp them: it is the duty of the church to help protect them. Spiritual Mobilization's work and belief are based on a profound faith in God, the Author of Liberty, and in Jesus Christ, who never once advocated the use of the coercive powers of government to accomplish what he knew to be God's will for men.[47]

Christian individualism became Christian libertarianism, imbued with fear of state (but not corporate or religious) coercion.

Faith and Freedom was one means of promoting Christian libertarianism; Fifield also founded a weekly fifteen-minute radio program, *The Freedom Story*, which at its peak played on more than six hundred stations.[48] In 1957, Fifield tried to expand into television with a show called *Lighted Window*.[49] He discovered that what worked from the pulpit, or on radio, did not necessarily work on television; *Lighted Window* was a flop.[50] The failure hurt Fifield financially; Pew organized a partial rescue.

Spiritual Mobilization had probably already reached its pinnacle of success in 1951, when it organized a nationwide series of events around the 175th anniversary of the signing of the Declaration of Independence. With major funding from Pew, Fifield arranged the Committee to Proclaim Liberty to organize the enterprise. He assembled an impressive lineup: Herbert Hoover and General Douglas MacArthur, filmmakers Cecil B. DeMille and Walt Disney, and a B-grade Hollywood actor named Ronald Reagan. The committee also included the heads of the U.S. Chamber of Commerce, the National Association of Manufacturers, and other business leaders.[51]

The celebration's centerpiece was a reading of the preamble to the Declaration of Independence. As historian Kevin Kruse explains, restricting the reading to just the preamble allowed them to present the Declaration as a "libertarian manifesto, dedicated to the removal of an oppressive government." The full Declaration includes a "long list of grievances about the *absence* of government and rule of law in the colonies"; it critiques the British government for failing to do the job the colonists wanted—indeed, *needed*—done.[52] Fifield's partial reading served the economic interests of the corporate leaders supporting the Committee to Proclaim Liberty, with its sotto voce characterization of the New Deal as "oppressive government."

The Committee's efforts worked: On the Sunday before July 4, thousands of ministers preached freedom sermons, and a nationwide CBS radio broadcast of the show followed that evening. The committee had also arranged for the ringing of church bells across the nation on Independence Day, and city mayors and state governors issued proclamations of their own. Fifty thousand attended a rally at the Los Angeles Coliseum that included circus acts and a fireworks display. Fifield presided over the ceremony, while Gregory Peck did the dramatic reading of the Preamble.[53]

In the sort of jarring juxtaposition that sometimes happens in newspapers, the *Los Angeles Times* ran a set of op-eds advertising the Committee to Proclaim Liberty's efforts next to a piece on the demise of California's famed sardine fishery. The cause? "Overexploitation by commercial fishermen. The repeated and prophetic warnings were unheeded by the politicians who were controlled by commercial interests."[54] Unrestrained individualism hadn't worked out so well for California's fishing industry. One wonders if the page's editor noted the irony.

In 1954, Fifield turned over the daily operation of Spiritual Mobilization to an attorney named James Ingebretsen, who had served as the coordinator for the Committee to Proclaim Liberty. Fifield stepped down in 1959, penning a farewell message for the tenth volume of *Faith and Freedom*.[55] Handing the operation to a lawyer may have been a mistake: concluding that Ingebretsen didn't have the credibility to reach religious followers, Pew ceased his support. Other funders followed Pew's lead, and in 1961 Spiritual Mobilization shut down.[56] But that was by no means the end of the story: wealthy business conservatives would take the baton from Fifield and run with it.

ALTHOUGH HE REMAINED one of Fifield's most devoted backers through the 1950s, Pew was unsatisfied with Fifield's efforts. It isn't clear when Pew first had the idea to start another organization, but it was contemporaneous with an abortive effort by Fifield to step away from Spiritual Mobilization. In 1947, Pew, Fifield, and Jasper Crane had started working to have Norman Vincent Peale take over the organization; by 1949 they had nearly finished this deal. But then Peale lost interest after his book *The Art of Living* became a bestseller; separately General Motors committed to making the maximum legal donation for the next four years conditioned on Fifield's remaining in charge.[57] So Fifield stayed.

In 1946, Pew had been "shocked to learn for the first time, through polls taken for the NAM by Opinion Research Corporation, that ministers were by far the most important molders of public opinion of any American group."[58] He decided the time had come to create another group to market Christian libertarianism to American clergy: the Christian Freedom Foundation.

Like Spiritual Mobilization, the Christian Freedom Foundation had two major functions. It coordinated outreach to small groups of ministers through frequent conferences and meetings, and it published a journal to spread free-market theology. The first journal editor was a Quaker and retired businessman named Howard E. Kershner, who had been active in wartime children's relief programs and served in Hoover's National Committee on Food for the Small Democracies; Hoover had introduced Kershner to the Spiritual Mobilization leaders in April 1949.[59] The name of the new journal was *Christian Economics*.

The first issue, published in 1950, immediately came under fire from theologians. Robert McAfee Brown, who held a bachelor of divinity degree from the Union

Theological Seminary, had studied at Oxford, and was soon to complete his doctorate in the philosophy of religion at Columbia, published a lengthy criticism in Reinhold Niebuhr's journal *Christianity and Crisis*, Brown summarized the underlying assumptions of *Christian Economics* as:

1. Godless Communism is the major threat to civilization.
2. Socialism is a halfway house on the way to Communism; Britain has reached that point and America is not far behind.
3. Therefore, only a return to free enterprise, under God's sanction, will save America and/or civilization.[60]

Communism was admittedly its own kind of faith, and liberal theologians objected to that as much as conservatives did. Indeed, its totalizing faith was what made it terrifying: "Is not the real power of Communism derived precisely from the fact that it involves such total commitment, such a complete act of what can be called religious faith, on the part of its adherents?" Brown asked. The mistake Kershner and his allies made (Brown argued) was to equate Christian virtue with capitalist economics. The failures of capitalism were a large part of communism's appeal: "There is no realization of the fact that it might have been modern capitalism's tremendous exploitation of large groups of peoples, the disparities it produced between the 'haves' and the 'have nots,' which has driven millions . . . into the arms of the communists, not to mention the socialists."[61] Capitalism had not delivered broad and equitable economic security to the masses.

Theologically, the root of *Christian Economics*'s problem, Brown argued, was confusion about whether wealth was good or bad: "[T]he editors cannot make up their minds whether they are for, or against, what they call, in good Biblical terminology, Mammon." They criticize Mammon and demand readers turn from materialism to God, but they also celebrate American materialism. "[O]n the same page of the same issue, the American Way of Life is vigorously championed because it produces 40% of the world's wealth or Mammon, including 92% of the world's bathtubs." The so-called Christian economists resolved this contradiction with a gospel of success: *"religion brings material reward."*[62] This, Brown noted dryly, was a "questionable gospel."[63] Matthew (6:24) instructs that no one can serve two masters—God and Mammon—but Fifield and his friends seemed to be trying.

Brown levied his strongest criticism against the assumption that "the survival of the church depends upon the survival of capitalism." This claim came from an article Norman Vincent Peale contributed to *Christian Economics* and *Reader's Digest*, entitled "Let the Church Speak Up for Capitalism."[64] After arguing that the Protestant church's leadership and its seminaries were riddled with a "pink minority," Peale related a conversation with a theologian who had said that "Christianity has no stake in the survival of capitalism." Peale rejected this utterly. "I believe that Christianity has a considerable stake in the survival of capitalism. I intend to vote for it until I see a system more favorable to Christian progress."[65] To Brown, this was a dangerous claim:

> Now such a position, if really followed, must mean the death of the church. If the church cannot stand in judgment over all political systems, rather than being dependent on any one of them, the church had better close up shop, or at least give up any pretense to be preaching a prophetic Gospel. If there are areas of life upon which the searching and judging and renewing light of the Christian faith may not be thrown, then it is time to stop pretending that the Gospel is anything more than a sort of pious cloak for particular economic pressure groups.[66]

Peale was insisting that the Church should actively support, promote, and defend capitalism. Brown's response was that the Church, qua religion, should be independent of any economic or governmental system and should use its platform to critique those systems when they strayed from Christ's teachings. Brown also reminded his readers that both Gospel and church preceded capitalism, so the church clearly did not *need* capitalism. *Christian Economics* was advancing bad theology, bad economics, and bad history.

Throughout its run (which lasted until 1972), *Christian Economics* shared writers with *Faith and Freedom*—the journal of Spiritual Mobilization—which helped ensure a consistent message.[67] Kershner also collected lists of seminary students, giving them free subscriptions to *Christian Economics*, and sent copies to seminary libraries. He routinely spoke at seminaries and, in an activity reminiscent of the NELA educational campaign, helped formulate economics courses for their students.[68]

The circulation of *Christian Economics* peaked around three hundred thousand, about ten times that of Fifield's *Faith and Freedom* or Niebuhr's *Christianity and*

Crisis.[69] It became a major—perhaps *the* major—voice in 1950s American Protestantism. Through the efforts of Fifield, Pew, Peale, and their allies, much of American Protestantism would come to be increasingly aligned with pro-market, antigovernment ideology. Still, Pew wanted more. He found Kershner's magazine focused too much on economics and not enough on theology, and he considered Kershner's Quakerism too liberal.[70] So Pew tried again. This time, he leveraged evangelical leader Billy Graham.

Raised on a North Carolina dairy farm and ordained by the Southern Baptist Convention while still a young man, Billy Graham began to garner attention in 1947 with his first crusade in Grand Rapids, Michigan. Eventually known as "America's pastor," Graham became a national sensation in 1949 with a big tent revival in Los Angeles. Heavily promoted with the help of the Hearst newspaper empire, Graham's L.A. Crusade, scheduled to last three weeks, was extended to eight; he preached to around 350,000 people.[71] In 1950, he incorporated his Billy Graham Evangelistic Association; his first crusade on foreign soil was to London in the spring of 1954. Then came a tour of western Europe, a Scottish crusade in 1955, and an audience with Queen Elizabeth II.

Graham and Pew met in 1954 and began corresponding about the need for a rival to the *Christian Century*. Founded in 1884, that mainline Protestant publication was the principal liberal theological magazine of the day.[72] Pew and Graham shared the belief that liberal theology led to socialist politics and economics; spreading conservative theology would also spread conservative "economic and social philosophy."[73] Graham also thought that his revival meetings needed a durable follow-up. During the Scottish crusade, Graham wrote to Pew that "these campaigns that thrill and excite the clergy for a short period and show them what God can do with old-fashioned theology must be followed through with a periodical that will give them a reason for the hope that is in them."[74]

He and Pew were already well along in arranging for what would become *Christianity Today*. Graham's father-in-law, the surgeon L. Nelson Bell, had been tapped as the executive editor; the big question was what role Graham should play. Initially, Graham was reluctant to take a major role, but he changed his mind: "We have watched great universities, like the University of Chicago and Duke University, that started out to train young ministers for the gospel, degenerate into secular, pagan and socialistic institutions, due to the fact that the founding fathers lost control."[75] Graham wanted himself, Bell, and evangelical leader Harold Ockenga (the founding president of the National Association of Evangelicals and one of the founders of the Fuller Theological Seminary in Pasadena) to be the "theologically minded" inner circle of the magazine. Pew agreed to pay the costs for the magazine's first year while it developed reputation and circulation.[76] He would support it much longer.[77]

Bell sent Pew an "outline" of the magazine in March 1955, explaining its intended audience, messages, and editorial policy. Arguing that "the great majority of preachers have come from Christian homes [but] the home training has not been sufficient to meet the onslaught of liberal views in college and seminary," the magazine needed in effect to be "a theological seminary. The articles must be on a seminary level and not that of a Bible school."[78] Ministers needed material for sermons and homilies, and they should be made aware of important books. And the magazine should carefully avoid becoming a battleground between denominations (a principle that would later cause some conflict with Pew).

A few months later, Ockenga wrote a "Declaration of Principles for *Christianity Today*."[79] Echoing Fifield's Freedom Under God campaign, Ockenga wrote, "We believe that society is most Christian in which free, moral men rule themselves according to the laws of God and nature, vs all resort to legislative direction of work, income, speech, ballot, property and worship." He continued: "We believe that Christian Faith (theology) and the freedoms of man are interdependent vs all divorce of modern culture from Christian theology which results in legislative control and direction of individuals by use of force." Antistatism lies at the core of these principles, but Ockenga, like Peale, wasn't just rejecting the abuse of state power. He was rejecting the U.S. Constitution, which places governance in the hands of an elected legislature and separates Church and State; arguably, he was rejecting democratic governance itself.

Christianity Today launched in October 1956.[80] In its first three years, the magazine published articles covering theology, foreign policy, economics, and labor relations, presenting an unoriginal remix of individualism and the indivisibility thesis, but now leavened with Christian fundamentalism. Articles argued that freedom *originated* with Christianity; that a powerful central state is anti-Christian; and that labor unions are corrupt, malign influences on America. Repeatedly, they decried an alleged waning faith in freedom, in the face of godless communism and collectivism.

Two articles came from Irving E. Howard of the Christian Freedom Foundation. One, "Christ and the Libertarians," was more or less an advertisement for Spiritual

Mobilization, the Christian Freedom Foundation, and the Foundation for Economic Education.[81] The other, "Christian Approach to Economics," contended that both dominant economic philosophies—materialism (allegedly associated with Adam Smith and David Ricardo) and idealism (allegedly associated with socialists and welfare statists)—led inevitably to totalitarianism. Howard's point was to promote a third approach—Christian liberty, originating with God, not man—and to use it to rationalize the gross inequalities produced by American capitalism.

Howard insisted that inequality is both justified and necessary. "The problem of inequality is immediately solved," Howard announced, "by the fact of divine Providence. Inequality of talent, resulting in inequality of wealth, is in the plan of God. Justice does not demand absolute equality for God does not demand it." The quests for equality and security were "incompatible with freedom." When men lose faith in God, Howard continued, "they seek security in pensions and in government. Such people are candidates for a prison state." Here Howard echoed Fifield's argument in *Faith and Freedom* that state-provided social welfare would usurp the role of religion. For Howard, any "Christian approach to economics, if it is to follow the example of the Bible, must insist upon voluntarism and limit government to a police function."[82] In other words, all men are created *un*equal, capitalism is the logical reflection of our natural inequalities, and the state should do nothing but protect private property.

This was not a new argument. In 1933, NAM secretary Noel Sargent had made the point in a jeremiad against collectivist solutions to the Great Depression. Socialism was the wrong answer, he insisted, because it was based on a fairy tale, a "fairy-wand movement . . . semi-religious in character [with] the glamor of Hans Christian Andersen and the brothers Grimm."[83] The idea that all are worthy of equal recompense was patently false, Sargent intoned, as any reasonable person could see.[84] (In the 1960s NAM would oppose the Civil Rights Act, claiming it would lead to a flood of litigation, especially by women, who needed to be treated differently because of their "chemistry.")[85] Capitalism was based on the reality that men (and women) were equal neither in talent nor in effort. The profit system was "justified because of difference in quality and accomplishment" and offered the necessary "incentive to future effort and achievement."[86] Sargent defended wage inequality based on inherent inequality. "Men are born unequal and remain unequal, and man-made laws cannot make them otherwise. It is both untrue and cruel to tell men that they are equal and should be equally rewarded ... Scientific, practical, and ethical considerations ... both necessitate and justify inequality of pay and income."[87]

By the 1930s, many scientists had challenged these arguments. One was the great anthropologist Franz Boas, who had argued that while some simple traits, like eye color, were clearly inherited, others, like height, were a mixture of inheritance and social conditions, such as nutrition.[88] His protégée, the anthropologist Margaret Mead, demonstrated in her 1924 master's thesis that Italian American children's performance on IQ tests was strongly correlated with the length of time their parents had been in America and whether English was spoken at home.[89]

Catholic leaders had spoken out against eugenics—the movement to control reproduction among those deemed "less fit" by their social superiors—in part because it tended to target immigrants from southern Europe, who were disproportionately Catholic.[90] Perhaps for this reason Sargent felt compelled to make a religious argument for inequality. "The doctrine of equality of reward is contrary to sound ethics," he argued, since it would give the less efficient man rewards to which he was not entitled and deny to the man of "superior innate ability" rewards that he had fairly earned. Sargent invoked Matthew 20, the parable of the laborer in the vineyard, and Matthew 25, the parable of the talents.

Sargent either did not know his Bible or assumed his audience did not, because his use of these passages is idiosyncratic at best. Matthew 20 tells the story of a landowner who hires laborers throughout the day, promising to pay them all one denarius. At the end of the day, he pays them what he has promised, even though they had worked unequal hours. This, in Sargent's view, is clearly unfair, and he concludes that the Bible tells us the capitalist must pay more to the men who worked longer. But this is *not* the moral of Matthew 20. In the parable, the landowner defends his right to pay the men equally, framing it not as unfairness but as generosity. Matthew concludes, in one of the most famous of all New Testament passages: "So the last will be first, and the first will be last."[91]

Most theologians interpret the story in terms of God's original promise to the Israelites: they could resent God for welcoming latecomers as generously as he embraced them—his chosen people—or they could be happy that God extends his embrace to all nations. Similarly, Matthew 25—in which a rich man, going on a journey, entrusts his wealth (a talent in this case is a unit of money) to his servants in unequal portions—is generally interpreted *not* as a story justifying inequality, but as instructing us to make the best use we can of the gifts God has given us.[92]

To Sargent, any attempt to impose equality would necessarily be coercive. "True equality . . . can never exist in achievement unless the gifted minority are coerced and limited by the majority. Equality in achievement and reward can only be secured by compulsion, or, in other words, at the sacrifice of liberty."[93] His solution, like Rose Wilder Lane's, was disenfranchisement: "It is a perfectly suicidal policy to continue an electoral system which permits the recipients of public funds to vote . . . We should very carefully consider whether those who are in receipt of public funds of any kind except salaries, length of service of disability pensions, and war connected disability allowances should not be ipso factor dis[en]franchised."[94]

Missing in these discussions—both in the 1930s and again in the 1950s—was that labor leaders in America were not asking for *income equality*. They were just asking for a fairer share of the pie, and for the recognition that their labor played a meaningful role in the productivity and prosperity for which their managers took credit. But that was a concession that both secular business leaders and Christian individualists would never make.

ANTIPATHY TOWARD LABOR unions ran through nearly all Christian individualist thinking, and in "Christian Approach to Economics" Irving Howard took up NAM's "right-to-work" drumbeat. "Government has the right to limit a man's choices to protect the rights of other people, but beyond this a man should be free. No labor union has the moral right to deny a man the right to work."[95] In the same issue of *Christianity Today*, Harold Ockenga concurred: "Certainly one has the right to work where one wills. We are witnessing a tendency to deny this right to work in present society. Here a fundamental liberty is being taken away by force. Each man must possess the basic right of selling his labor power which is his own commodity. Once the laborer could be shut out from a shop, today unionized labor demands the closed shop."[96] The "right to work" was Orwellian rhetoric, developed by and for management to safeguard their ability to hire and fire at will. Despite what a naïve or literal person might think, the "right to work" did not include the right to employment. These Christians were not defending "the right to work where one wills," they were defending business prerogatives.

The animus against organized labor was also expressed in an article by the magazine's editor, Carl F. H. Henry, a longtime advocate for greater evangelical influence in American culture and politics. His piece focused on the Teamsters, at the time under investigation for racketeering.[97] Henry argued (reasonably) that all unions should be subject to the sort of independent oversight to which publicly traded corporations answered, but then he proceeded to blame liberal theology for the labor movement's poor moral standards. They were a product of "the liberal Protestant displacement of the gospel of personal regeneration by the social gospel: the task of the Church became that of organizing society, rather than of evangelizing it. But evangelical Protestantism was also at fault; in its concern for the purity of the gospel, it ironically gravitated toward social inactivism and neglected the exposition of Christian imperatives in labor and economics, and the state and culture."[98] The problem of corrupt unions was not to be solved with appropriate laws, but with Protestant evangelism. Labor leaders needed to return to the belief in "work as a divine vocation." Echoing Fifield, Henry concluded that a "democracy that prizes a citizenry under God must learn to prize business and labor under God as well."[99]

The Teamsters Union *was* corrupt. But *Christianity Today*'s criticism of corrupt unions was not matched by criticism of corrupt corporations or corrupt business leaders, much less corrupt ministers. Nor did its writers attempt to wrestle with the power imbalance between management and workers that had inspired the labor movement. Instead, workers were urged to accept their lower status as part of the natural order: "Writing to the Colossians, Paul has a word for workers and employers: 'Servants, obey in all things your masters ... not with eyeservice as menpleasers, but in singleness of heart, fearing God; and whatsoever ye do, do it heartily, as to the Lord, and not unto men.'"[100] Inequality was "divine providence." State intervention would contravene God's will. Moreover, the state could only address inequity through coercion—either by forced redistribution of wealth or by regulating wages, working hours, and working conditions—which undermined the rights of managers and property owners. Hayek had given intellectual respectability to a self-serving ideology, but *Christianity Today* went further, attempting to give not just moral respectability—but a Christian moral imperative—to what liberal theologians had long seen as patently immoral.

WHILE FIFIELD AND his network built Christian libertarianism, Leonard Read continued to strengthen the secular libertarian argument.[101] But while seemingly distinct, the two efforts were closely linked. Read belonged to Fifield's First Congregational Church, served as one of its trustees, and later joined the Spiritual Mobilization board. Read's mentor William Mullendore was on the boards of both Spiritual Mobilization and FEE; Jasper Crane and J. Howard Pew were advisers to and fundraisers for both. Frank Donaldson Brown, a corporate director at General Motors, was a Spiritual Mobilization board member and one of FEE's founders.[102]

As Spiritual Mobilization had worked to spread free-market gospel to mainline Protestant clergy, FEE worked to spread it into business circles and economics. In addition to its pamphlets, FEE organized lectures and speaking tours and acquired a magazine called *The Freeman* (like Read's pamphlet series). Launched in 1950 by Henry Hazlitt with funding from Pew, Hoover, and Crane, *The Freeman* had been rife with internal conflicts and lost hundreds of thousands of dollars; in 1954 Read bought it.[103] The reconstituted *Freeman* became Read's most successful outreach tool.

FEE was a secular organization, but its vision of the market was religious. Read's conception of the market as divine is articulated in his famous 1958 essay, "I, Pencil." Written in the imagined, first-person voice of a lead pencil, the essay follows the pencil's construction from the forests of California and the graphite mines of Ceylon to a factory in San Leandro, California. Millions of anonymous and unco-ordinated individuals have a hand in the making of this pencil. Yet no one of them actually knows how to make a pencil. "There isn't a single person in all these millions, including the president of the pencil company, who contributes more than a tiny, infinitesimal bit of know-how."[104] What accounts for the marvel of the pencil's existence? The answer is God.

> I, Pencil, am a complex combination of miracles: a tree, zinc, copper, graphite, and so on. But to these miracles which manifest themselves in Nature an even more extraordinary miracle has been added: the configura-tion of creative human energies—millions of tiny knowhows configurating naturally and spontaneously in response to human necessity and desire and in the absence of any human masterminding! Since only God can make a tree, I insist that only God could make me.[105]

God made the marketplace and the marketplace made the pencil; ergo God made the pencil. The invisible hand is the hand of God.[106]

A recurrent theme in Read's essay is that capitalism produces miracles, through the power of the marketplace. Indeed, the market is so powerful that it can be viewed as a miracle itself. The "astounding" fact is that there is no mastermind: "neither the workers in the oil field not the chemist nor the digger of graphite or clay nor any who mans or makes the ships or trains or trucks nor the one who runs the machine that does the knurling on my bit of metal nor the president of the company performs his singular task because he wants me . . . Indeed, there are some among this vast multitude who never saw a pencil nor would they know how to use one."[107] Without "anyone dictating or forcibly directing these countless actions," the pencil is created. This is "the invisible hand at work. This is the mystery" of the marketplace, the "miraculousness" of which the lowly pencil stands as proof: that somehow human activities "arrange themselves into creative and productive patterns in response to human necessity and demand—that is, in the absence of governmental or any other coercive mastermind." Read's use of the word "mystery" implicitly invokes Christian mysticism, as Christ as God's physical embodiment is often referred to as "the mystery of God." By the same token, for Read, the market is the physical embodiment of God's intention.

The pencil then shares its deeply held convictions about freedom. Understanding how the market operates, we must have "faith in free people," for "freedom is impossible without this faith."[108] Take the post office: Many of us believe the mail could not possibly be "efficiently delivered by men acting freely." We rightly perceive that any one person lacks the knowledge or capacity to deliver the mail, but from there we wrongly surmise that because "no individual possesses enough know-how to perform a nation's mail delivery," the government must step in. This is also a failure of awareness—"the unawareness that millions of tiny know-hows would naturally and miraculously form and cooperate" to do the job better than any government could—so we reach the "erroneous conclusion that mail can only be delivered by government 'masterminding.'"[109]

The lesson, Pencil admonishes us, is literally laissez-faire: Leave it be. "Leave all creative energies uninhibited. Merely organize society to act in harmony with this lesson. Let society's legal apparatus remove all obstacles the best it can. Permit these creative know-hows freely to flow. Have faith that free men and women will respond to the Invisible Hand. This faith will be confirmed. I, Pencil, seemingly simple though I am, offer the miracle of my creation as testimony that this is a practical faith, as practical as the sun, the rain, a cedar tree, [and] the good earth." [110] For Read, the "Invisible Hand" is not just a metaphor. It is the hand that made Creation. [111]

Read's essay has long been beloved of libertarians, and like many of their arguments this one was partly true. Read was right that manufacturing is a complex process involving many steps, and he was right that many people involved may have little or no knowledge of the larger effort in which they play a part. And it is impressive that the various steps in the process coalesce. But missing from his story are management and managers: pencils are made in factories, with foremen, production managers, procurement officers, and many others who ensure that the necessary components are gathered and assembled at the right place at the right time. *Contra* Pencil, this is not a mystical process. It is the result of organization, and the very thing Read and his colleagues abhorred when government was involved: planning.

Admittedly, government planning and corporate planning are not the same thing, and libertarians insisted that governments, being uniquely powerful, were uniquely threatening to freedom. But by the time Read wrote "I, Pencil," more than a few American corporations were as large and as powerful as some governments. The National Labor Relations Act of 1935 recognized that, noting the "inequality of bargaining power between employees who do not possess full freedom of association or actual liberty of contract and employers who are organized in the corporate or other forms of ownership." [112]

In 1977, the historian Alfred Chandler would coin a term for the sort of capitalism that yielded large-scale, organized manufacturing, typically in corporate form: *managerial capitalism*. But Read didn't need Chandler to enlighten him about the role of management; many of the founders and trustees of FEE— Donaldson Brown, Jasper Crane, and J. Howard Pew—were corporate managers. Orchestrating production—the very thing Read attributed to God—was their job, and their productive efforts involved enormous amounts of planning. [113]

As economist John Quiggin has noted, Read also ignored how the components of the pencil—the wood and graphite and paint— moved along railways and roads that were financed and managed by governments. "Reliance on the invisible hand to produce coherent railway networks was a failure wherever it was tried," Quiggin observed. [114] This should have been no surprise: as Adam Smith had observed, roads and bridges were a public good and therefore most likely to work best when supported by the state. In the twentieth century, large-scale transportation systems were almost always at least in part the result of government planning and action.

Market fundamentalists swept these truths aside. The Chicago economist Milton Friedman adored "I, Pencil" and would later write: "I know of no other piece of literature that so succinctly, persuasively, and effectively illustrates the meaning of both Adam Smith's invisible hand—the possibility of cooperation without coercion—and Friedrich Hayek's emphasis on the importance of dispersed knowledge and the role of the price system in communicating information that 'will make the individuals do the desirable things without anyone having to tell them what to do.'"[115] What Read left out—and Friedman chose to ignore—was that management was a force of coercion, and occasionally outright violence, in the lives of laborers. Corporate profits were easily converted into corporate power, exerted to enforce worker compliance—both directly, to suppress strikes, and indirectly, to influence law, politics, and culture.

AFTER FIFIELD'S RETIREMENT from Spiritual Mobilization, he faded from the scene, but his impact did not. Through the efforts of Spiritual Mobilization, *Christian Economics*, and *Christianity Today*—reinforced by FEE—the captains of American industry had found a way to turn Protestant theology on its head, from embracing the poor to celebrating the rich. They channeled corporate profits to promote as benevolent an economic system that often had been anything but, and to vilify government efforts to address that system's failures. By embedding capitalist propaganda into American Christianity, they ensured that millions of Americans heard their message weekly, in church, from their ministers and lay leaders—which is to say, from people the parishioners thought they could trust.

In his 2012 book *Masters of the Universe*, economic historian Daniel Stedman Jones refers to neoliberalism as "faith-based policy," because it has often proved impervious to evidence.[116] In its Christian libertarian expression, neoliberalism was not just metaphorically faith-based. It was literally so.

CHAPTER 8

No More *Grapes of Wrath*

In 1946, Eric Johnston—president of the U.S. Chamber of Commerce from 1941 to 1946 and a former board member of Spiritual Mobilization—became president of the Motion Picture Association of America. He immediately began redirecting Hollywood's mythmaking machinery. In a talk to screenwriters, Johnston said: "We'll have no more *Grapes of Wrath*, we'll have no more *Tobacco Roads*, we'll have no more films that deal with the seamy side of American life. We'll have no more films that treat the banker as villain."[1] Socioeconomic criticism was out, market fundamentalism was in.

Johnston was the vanguard of a movement that radically reoriented Hollywood's ideological compass. During the 1940s and '50s, libertarian moviemakers and their allies in business deployed censorship, intimidation, and overt propaganda to change the tone of America's screens and disseminate the myth of the free market. Alongside Christian libertarians such as Norman Vincent Peale and ideologues such as Friedrich von Hayek and Rose Wilder Lane, the soldiers of the Hollywood Right were the third great mid-century force embedding the indivisibility thesis and the Tripod of Freedom in American culture.

Pre–World War II mainstream American films had often been sympathetic to working-class interests. One factor was technological. After the release of *The Jazz Singer* in 1927, synchronized sound became the industry standard, and in the 1930s many silent film stars vanished from the screen. Captions in 1920s silent films had tended toward a formal English that was already being replaced by the vernacular of immigrant-filled urban areas. The "talkies" that now drew the largest audiences were diverse in both casting and dialect. They also depicted the vaudeville houses and bars where America's lower classes congregated, as well as the crime that often touched their lives in one way or another. Gangster films offered an alternative view of capitalism: "gangsters" were businessmen forced to operate outside the law.[2]

With changes in style and content also came new kinds of performers. A case in point is Will Rogers, the Cherokee comedian from Oklahoma. In the 1920s, Rogers was offered only bit parts as a drunk or petty criminal, but by the 1930s he was a major star, first in a syndicated radio show and then in film. As his work drew big audiences, Rogers took control of his career. Rather than hide his origins, he used them to create and reach new audiences. Rogers was a vocal defender of Roosevelt and the New Deal.[3]

The political economy of Hollywood was changing too, as the industry became strongly unionized. Stagehands had been unionized since 1893; Actors' Equity was founded in 1913, and the American Society of Composers, Authors, and Publishers (ASCAP) was founded in 1914. By the 1930s, Hollywood was following theater's lead. In 1933, the Screen Actors Guild (SAG) and Writers Guild of America (WGA) were founded, and in 1936 the Screen Directors Guild was formed (later to expand as the Directors Guild of America).

These transformations were reflected in the America depicted on screen: 1930s films often carried an anticorporate message. Wealthy men were depicted as corrupt; wealthy women were typically ditzy. Unions were generally a positive force; small producers and farmers were heroic icons of self-sufficiency and familial (or community) resilience. When the Western genre was revived in the '30s, it focused on "range wars" between small and large landholders. Plutocracy was a problem to be solved, not a fact to be accepted.

An important filmmaker in this genre was King Vidor, a founder of the Screen Directors Guild. In his 1934 picture *Our Daily Bread*, a young city couple are given land by family and told to "make it pay." They gather others into the effort, and the cooperative succeeds in saving their corn crop from the Dust Bowl.[4] The film depicts banks as villains—so much so that Vidor had to self-finance it.

Mostly known today as a director of Westerns, John Ford also focused in his early films on the experience of ordinary Americans.[5] One of these was the 1934 comedy *Judge Priest*, set in a small, Southern town. Will Rogers played the title character, a magistrate more in tune with the spirit of the law than its letter, who uses his authority to make his fellow citizens aware of their own intolerance. The judge's factotum was played by Stepin Fetchit (the stage name of Lincoln Theodore Monroe Andrew Perry), one of the first Black actors to have a Hollywood career. As an African American band plays "Dixie" before the courthouse, Rogers delivers a scathing antilynching speech.[6]

Ford's 1939 film *Stagecoach* centers two antiheroes: an outlaw who's broken out of prison, and a prostitute driven out of town by the Ladies' Law and Order League. Its villain is a corrupt banker—he robbed his own bank—who spouts NAM-like rhetoric: "America for Americans! The government must not interfere with business." Perhaps because of the political message, Ford had trouble getting backing for *Stagecoach*, but it proved a critical and commercial success.

Enter *The Grapes of Wrath*, the specter haunting Eric Johnston. It was Ford who made the award-winning adaptation of John Steinbeck's 1939 Pulitzer Prize–winning novel about California-bound migrants from the drought-devastated Great Plains. Millions of Americans made the journey between 1935 and 1939, as California politicians scrambled to keep them out. Los Angeles tried to have its police prevent migrants from entering the state at all, and California's oligarchic growers abused those who made it.[7] *The Grapes of Wrath* told this story through the eyes of the Joads, an impoverished family who, in the face of the Dust Bowl, abandon Oklahoma for California only to be exploited and rejected there, too.

Darryl F. Zanuck, the head of 20th Century Fox, had acquired the rights to the novel right away, though not without some trepidation on Steinbeck's part, particularly after the writer learned that Fox's largest shareholder was Chase National Bank; Steinbeck was concerned that his clear-eyed condemnation of American socioeconomic conditions might be watered down. To some degree, it was—Zanuck worked to ensure the film was not *too* anticorporate—although it turned out the head of Chase National Bank wasn't opposed; his wife had recommended the book to him and he thought it would make a "wonderful movie," too.[8]

A single scene early in the film exemplifies the kind of story Ford was trying to tell. The Joad family has been "tractored" off their land—driven off by the landowner who, now that he owns a tractor, no longer needs sharecropper labor. With no work to be had, they prepare to go west. The night before they depart, we see Ma Joad (Jane Darwell, whose performance earned her an Oscar) alone by the fire. As the folk song "Red River Valley" plays on the accordion, Ma goes through her memory box. We see souvenirs from a modest life. Several things go into the flames, including a newspaper clipping announcing the prison sentence of her son Tom (Henry Fonda).[9]

With this scene, Ford announces his film's central subject: the resilience of the American family. Steinbeck framed his novel as a story of class conflict: chapters following the Joad family alternate with short "counterpoint" chapters describing broader patterns of migration. Ford's film, by contrast, focuses tightly on the Joads, both thematically and in its visual language, as in the many shots in which the Joads are framed by a car window.[10] The film has a message, but is not a jeremiad. With its rangy performances and painterly lighting, Ford's direction won him his second Oscar.

Still, the film did not pull its punches. Among other things, it depicts police as the enforcers of oligarchic order. At the Joads' first migrant camp, police attempt to arrest a labor organizer and accidentally kill a woman bystander; most of the camp's occupants flee when a rumor spreads that police are coming to burn it down. In a second work camp, Tom Joad happens to be talking to his old friend Jim Casy (John Carradine)—a former preacher who has become the leader of a strike for higher wages—when police raid the camp and murder Casy. In the melee, Tom kills a police officer and the family is forced to flee again. In a third sequence, the family takes up residence in a camp run by the Department of Agriculture (whose superintendent looks rather like Franklin Roosevelt). Sheriffs send in ringers to start a riot—which would give them a pretext to shut the camp down—but the plot is foiled when a friendly grower warns the Joads, and the camp leaders organize to prevent the riot from happening. Here were two clear messages: police serve the capitalists, but solidarity works.

After a screening, Steinbeck told his agent that he thought Ford's film was "a harsher thing than the book, by far. It seems unbelievable but it is true."[11] Transforming description into imagery gave the story tremendous emotional power. Still, it was the book rather than the film that drew the most ire. It sold 429,000 copies in its first year of publication, but many local governments banned it. In Bakersfield, California, it was burned.[12] The House Un-American Activities Committee (HUAC)—which had been established by the U.S. House of Representatives in 1938 and would take extravagant aim at Hollywood during the Red Scare—heard testimony that *The Grapes of Wrath* was Stalinist propaganda derived from Communist Party notes.[13] Ford's adaptation was by and large spared these more paranoid attacks, but conservatives still condemned the film as sentimental crypto-Communism.[14] An unsigned review for *Time* magazine praised the movie's tragic power but suggested it would mostly move "pinkos who did not bat an eye when the Soviet Government exterminated 3,000,000 peasants by famine" but "will go for a good cry over the hardships of the Okies."[15] In a letter to the

Washington Post, one indignant filmgoer dismissed Ford's movie as "nonsense," demanding to know: "[W]hat better propaganda could we possibly dish up to make plausible the babbling of the Communists who want to wreck our constitutional form of government?"[16]

FORD'S LAST MAJOR prewar film addressed the social change wrought by industrial development. Through the eyes of a child, *How Green Was My Valley* depicts Welsh coal mining—and especially mine owners—as malevolent forces. The mine brings jobs but also accidents and death. It destroys families and the landscape. Unions are a corrective to corporate power (anticommunist unions, anyway— Ford at this time considered himself a social democrat). Released in October 1941, the film would win Ford his third Oscar for best director and his first for best picture, famously defeating Orson Welles's *Citizen Kane*. But the tenor of the film industry was about to shift.

During World War II, Hollywood became a vehicle of pro-war propaganda. The Roosevelt administration formed an Office of War Information (OWI) to ensure that films glorified the war effort and placed U.S. allies—including the Soviet Union—in a good light, while demonizing America's enemies.[17] Ford spent the war working for the Office of Strategic Services (forerunner of the Central Intelligence Agency). As an officer in the U.S. Naval Reserve, he developed war documentaries, including a lyrical take on the 1942 Battle of Midway.[18]

Director Frank Capra—fresh off the success of his 1939 populist classic *Mr. Smith Goes to Washington*—enlisted in the army after Pearl Harbor. He soon received an assignment from the top, meeting with General George C. Marshall himself. The war required that America "make soldiers out of boys," Marshall told Capra, who needed to know why they were fighting and dying.[19] Between 1942 and 1945, Capra answered the question with the seven-part series *Why We Fight*. It was in many ways a riposte to Leni Riefenstahl's technically dazzling 1935 Nazi propaganda film, *The Triumph of the Will*. Where Riefenstahl used aerial imagery, distorted lenses, and Wagnerian music to capture Nazi rallies in grand style, Capra employed confident voice-over narration and dizzying montage sequences to summon energy for the American war effort. *Why We Fight* argued against isolationism, intending to secure the enthusiasm of the troops, and later the public, for intervention. It was also a melodrama that cast Americans as heroes who would bring freedom to a Europe in the grip of Hitler and Mussolini.

Capra's documentaries occasionally overstepped OWI guidelines. The first film in the series explained that the German people had been seduced by Hitler because of their "inborn love of regimentation and harsh discipline."[20] Such remarks flouted the OWI's instructions that filmmakers focus blame on Axis countries' political elites, rather than the masses. The head of the OWI's motion pictures division complained that the agency had not been consulted about the film, but Roosevelt overruled him and insisted that *Why We Fight* be approved for wide distribution.[21] The films drummed up indignation at Hitler and the other Axis leaders, comparing these men to gangsters. They also worked to elicit sympathy for America's allies in trouble. (Asking Americans to sympathize with the Soviet Union was a delicate task: the film portrayal of Germany's invasion of the Soviet Union uses Tchaikovsky's music to indicate the beauty of Russian culture, but carefully avoids the word "communism.") By the war's end, some fifty-four million Americans had seen the films.[22]

Meanwhile, as the country ramped up war-related industrial production, FDR badly needed industrial peace, so the OWI demanded—and Hollywood made—films depicting labor–management comity. One of these was King Vidor's "industrial epic," released in 1944 as *An American Romance*. Produced by Metro-Goldwyn-Mayer (MGM) and distributed by Loew's Incorporated—but with heavy involvement by both NAM and the OWI—the film promoted efficient production and peaceful labor management relations.[23] Vidor had conceived it as a Horatio Alger tale, featuring an Eastern European immigrant, Stefan Dangosbiblichek—Dangos for short—who starts as a miner in the Mesabi Iron Range of Minnesota, ascends the iron workers' ranks, founds his own car company, is forced out by his bankers, and then, during the war emergency, is put in charge of an aircraft factory in San Diego. The film ends with an orgy of production, with a bomber rolling out of the factory every five minutes. Vidor meant it to be an individualist epic, not just an industrial one, but his vision was compromised by the demands of wartime censorship.

The draft script Vidor sent to the OWI was deemed unsatisfactory; reviewers perceived his screenplay to be inappropriately critical of both banks and unions. (Dangos is initially hired as a scab; later he teargasses his plant's autoworkers.) In the revised script, Dangos is forced out of his car company by his board, who eject him over his antiunion stance.[24] The film as released was not quite the "paean to rugged individualism" Vidor had wanted; it ended up more of the "celebration of management–labor co-operation" that OWI wanted.[25]

But it wasn't just the OWI controlling the narrative; NAM and MGM helped shape the story, too. In a test screening that included Louis B. Mayer of MGM, the film was judged to be too long, with extensive sequences of documentary footage that had been shot at industrial facilities.[26] Mayer ordered it cut by thirty minutes. NAM officials, however, loved it. The film that was finally released was a commercial flop, but NAM negotiated with Loew's to keep the movie—and its "wonderful free-enterprise" message—available for use, and distributed it for showings, financed and arranged by local manufacturers working with local theaters.[27] Screenings of *An American Romance* were part of the larger film program administered by NAM's National Industrial Information Council (NIIC), the same group that had spearheaded "integration propaganda" efforts in the late 1930s. NIIC estimated that through its efforts, in 1945 films representing the "enterprise economy at work" had been shown 14,892 times to 2,465,908 people.[28]

Both labor unions and management continued to act in ways that contributed to workplace unrest—in a few cases the federal government took over plants—but the overall success of wartime films was a reminder to corporate America that cinema—whether as overt propaganda, entertainment, or some amalgam—could be an effective tool against enemies, foreign and domestic.[29] That lesson was taken to heart by Ayn Rand.

BORN ALISSA ZINOVIEVNA Rosenbaum in St. Petersburg, Russia, in 1905, Ayn Rand came to the United States in the 1920s. Her father had owned a successful business before its confiscation in 1918 plunged the family into poverty. As a result, she hated communists and communism with white-hot fury. After attending film school in Russia—where she studied film as propaganda—she used family connections to emigrate to the United States in 1926 with an announced plan to return to Russia and build the Soviet film industry. Of course she never did. Instead, she moved to Hollywood, where she landed a job with De Mille Studios as a junior writer.[30] When that closed with the collapse of the silent film industry, she moved to RKO and eventually to Paramount, where her supervisor was Frances Hazlitt, wife of Henry Hazlitt.[31] A move to New York during the Depression brought her into the literary circle of the libertarian writer Isabel Paterson.[32] Though Rand initially supported Roosevelt, she soon convinced herself he was surrounded by Communists and became a critic. In 1940, she volunteered for Wendell Willkie in his bid to block FDR from a third term, hoping that Willkie would reverse the New

Deal. Rand considered starting an organization to fight the New Deal, but Paterson inspired her to focus on writing instead.[33]

Rand also was briefly involved with the Foundation for Economic Education (FEE). In the early 1940s, she offered to serve as an editor for FEE, but she soured on the organization over philosophical differences. FEE's early publications defended free-market capitalism for utilitarian reasons; Rand considered this a weak justification. Rand was also an atheist who categorically rejected any Christian basis for defending freedom and capitalism. But the immediate trigger for Rand's departure was a pamphlet Leonard Read published opposing rent control, written by two soon-to-be prominent neoliberal economists, Milton Friedman and George Stigler. The essay framed the problem not in terms of property rights—which Rand supported— but in terms of efficient economic policy; Friedman and Stigler had posed the question: which policies would produce the best housing stock for the nation? Rand found this unacceptably pragmatic. As she quit, she complained to Read's mentor William Mullendore about Read's having hired these two "red" economists.[34]

Rand had an astonishing disregard for facts and expertise. "I learned *from you*," she gushed to Isabel Paterson, "the historical and economic aspects of capitalism." Paterson was a novelist and literary critic with scant formal education and no training in history or economics, but Rand uncritically imbibed her positions.[35] After reading Hayek's *Road to Serfdom*, Rand accused him of socialism because he modestly acknowledged the rationale for social insurance, declaring him "real poison."[36]

In 1943, Rand published *The Fountainhead*, her first big commercial success. Warner Brothers bought the rights, and Rand returned to Hollywood to work on the screenplay. The following year, she joined the Motion Picture Alliance for the Preservation of American Ideals, established to "protect" Hollywood and the United States from communist and fascist "infiltration." Other members included Cecil B. DeMille, Walt Disney, Barbara Stanwyck, Ronald Reagan, John Wayne, and Gary Cooper. Despite having made left-leaning films, King Vidor and John Ford were members, too, signaling the already shifting political winds in Hollywood. The organization's statement of principles was individualistic, libertarian, and devoid of any acknowledgment of the challenges that many Americans faced: "We believe in . . . the freedom to speak, to think, to live, to worship, to work, and to govern ourselves as individuals, as free men; the right to succeed or fail as free men, according to the measure of our ability and our strength."[37]

Rand herself prepared a pamphlet in 1947 for the Motion Picture Alliance's "Screen Guide for Americans," aimed at influencing movie producers and directors.[38] Her premise was that communists had infiltrated Hollywood and were using films to propagandize the American people; the only solution was to fight fire with fire. "The purpose of the Communists in Hollywood is not the production of political movies openly advocating Communism," she insisted. "Their purpose is to *corrupt our moral premises by corrupting non-political movies*—by introducing small, casual bits of propaganda into innocent stories—thus making people absorb the basic premises of Collectivism *by indirection and implication*."[39] This was followed by a list of anticommunist, pro-industrial "Don'ts":

DON'T SMEAR THE FREE ENTERPRISE SYSTEM . . .

DON'T SMEAR INDUSTRIALISTS. *Don't* spit into your own face or, worse, pay miserable little rats to do it. You, as a motion picture producer, are an industrialist . . .

DON'T SMEAR WEALTH . . . Only savages and Communists get rich by force . . .

DON'T SMEAR THE PROFIT MOTIVE . . .

DON'T SMEAR SUCCESS . . . America is the land of the self-made man. Say so on the screen . . .

DON'T GLORIFY DEPRAVITY . . . *don't* place yourself and the audience on the side of the criminal . . .

DON'T DEIFY "THE COMMON MAN." . . .

DON'T GLORIFY THE COLLECTIVE.[40]

Rand thus laid out an openly propagandistic program: American films must glorify wealth, free enterprise, rugged individualism, and self-made men, and never suggest that wealth might ever be unfairly garnered or that opportunities were not equal. She authored books lionizing freedom of thought and expression—and wrote censorship codes denying free expression to other.

RAND'S "SCREEN GUIDE" became the FBI's manual for identifying "communist" propaganda. The 1946 film *The Best Years of Our Lives*, which won seven Academy Awards including Best Picture, was fingered by the FBI for its alleged anti-Americanism. Starring the dashing Dana Andrews, the movie follows the lives of three veterans returning from the war. One of them has lost his hands. The three men return to the same Midwestern town, where they struggle to reenter civilian life. "In working out their solutions [Robert E.] Sherwood [the screenwriter] and [William] Wyler [the director] have achieved some of the most beautiful and inspiring demonstrations of human fortitude that we have had in films. And by demonstrating frankly and openly the psychological blocks and the physical realities that go with prosthetic devices they have done a noble public service of great need,"[41] the *New York Times* wrote.

What was wrong with the film? One of the veterans has trouble getting a bank loan because he lacks collateral; this violated Rand's dictate that business not be criticized.[42] Under Rand's guidelines, it became "communist propaganda" to represent standard banking practice. Another film whose depiction of bankers drew the FBI's ire was Frank Capra's 1946 Christmas film *It's a Wonderful Life*, starring two of Hollywood's most reliable stars—Jimmy Stewart and Donna Reed—and destined to become one of the most beloved movies of all time.[43] Aided by the Motion Picture Alliance and other nongovernment anticommunist organizations, the FBI undertook internal film reviews to create evidence against "subversives" that could be used to pressure industry leaders. Any film that implied the American economic system didn't work as promised—or wasn't always fair—could find itself criticized as communistic.

HUAC'S FIRST CLOSED hearing on subversion in the film industry took place in Los Angeles in May 1947; it held public hearings in Washington that fall. The public headliner was Rand's testimony about a 1944 film, *Song of Russia*. The picture had been made during the war to promote comity with the Soviets, who had, after all, been America's allies during the war and whose soldiers had shed far more blood than Americans had. The film was *American* propaganda, not Soviet; it reflected the wartime U.S. interest. But HUAC's chair, Representative J. Parnell Thomas of New Jersey, decided that scrutinizing a specific film would help get his hearings going in the right direction. For this he turned to Rand.

Rand didn't seem to know that *Song of Russia* was a propaganda film. She contended that its depiction of Soviet peasantry as happy was subversive. They smiled too much. They appeared well fed. Pressed on this point by another congressman, she said: "If they do [smile], it is privately and accidentally. Certainly, it is not social. They don't smile in approval of their system."[44] The media responded poorly to her testimony; happy peasants several thousand miles away hardly seemed dangerously subversive. (And how could Rand possibly know what those peasants were thinking?) HUAC changed tactics, couching criticism in generalities instead. This proved more effective. A witness named Oliver Carlson testified against "social problem" films like *The Grapes of Wrath*. Critiques of the system, he asserted, "break the spirit of the American people." They serve "to make them think the American way of life is not good, that all politicians are opportunists, that businessmen in general are corrupt."[45] Such films needed to be suppressed.

HUAC tried to force witnesses to testify against their peers, leading to the infamous Hollywood blacklist. Ten people refused to testify about their alleged Communist Party membership and were cited for contempt of Congress. The "Hollywood Ten"—including brilliant screenwriters Dalton Trumbo and Ring Lardner Jr.—were fired by their studios and later imprisoned. Eric Johnston and other Hollywood leaders issued a statement that they would not knowingly hire communists; ultimately, the blacklist encompassed more than three hundred people, assembled largely via hearsay and guilt by association.[46] Ironically, the "subversives" Hollywood's anticommunist crusaders were most afraid of—the screenwriters—were the least hurt by blacklisting, because unlike actors and directors they could continue to work under pseudonyms or as ghostwriters.[47] Still, they were humiliated, shunned by colleagues, and lost considerable income.[48] For actors, work under a pseudonym wasn't an option, and at least one—Philip Loeb, previously a highly successful actor, director, and writer—took his life in despair.

Other important HUAC witnesses included Walt Disney and Ronald Reagan. Serving at that time as president of the Screen Actors Guild, Reagan testified ambiguously to nefarious "communist-like tactics" employed by some guild members. Disney, however, was unambiguous. A hardline reactionary well known for his antisemitic and anti-labor views, Disney testified to communist infiltration in the industry, blaming a 1941 strike at his studio on communist agitation and naming various industry figures—including one of his own animators—as communists.[49]

Hollywood didn't really need HUAC to help with suppressing social-problem films; studio owners could simply choose not to fund projects that challenged the capitalist order or even exposed its failings. Indeed, they could choose not to produce any film they didn't like. But HUAC provided political cover and perhaps helped to push some over the line from distaste or disagreement into censorship and repression. Whatever the mix of driving forces, during the HUAC years, the content of movies changed. A 1956 analysis found that in 1947, about 20 percent of Hollywood films addressed American social problems; by 1953, only 8 percent did.[50] A later analysis found that films depicting "big business as villainous or of the rich as a moral threat decreased from 20 and 50 percent, respectively, to less than 5 percent during the fifties."[51]

WITH HOLLYWOOD'S POLITICAL climate swinging hard right, King Vidor got a second chance to make his individualist epic by adapting Ayn Rand's *The Fountainhead*. The novel focuses on an architect named Howard Roark, who, like Rand herself, is an uncompromising individualist. He does not collaborate, cooperate, consult, or work with committees, because these would require compromise and undermine his own perfection. Teamwork, in Roark's ethos, produces mediocrity. In the narrative, Roark has agreed to design a public housing project on the stipulation that his design not be changed for any reason. But the housing committee slightly alters the construction, and the enraged Roark dynamites it. He stands trial and is acquitted. In the book and the film, Roark calls no witnesses. He defends himself, and the film ends with a monologue expounding the libertarian worldview.

Consistent with much libertarian thinking, *The Fountainhead* celebrates inequality. It idolizes an *übermensch*—a superman—who is utterly independent and unaccountable. Roark is unfettered, unbound by law or society. He could be the gunslinger of many a Western film; he has no family, no past, no interest in civic life, and no regard for convention or even law. In his address to the jury, he insists it was individualism that built America: "Civilization is the progress toward a society of privacy ... of setting man free from men."[52] The realities and complexities of familial, tribal, and national cooperation disappear.

Rand wrote the script for Vidor, fending off changes two other writers assigned to the project suggested. Like her protagonist, she required that Vidor film it exactly as she had written.[53] This created tension, as Vidor thought Roark's illegal act shouldn't escape punishment. He also found Roark's speech too long. Vidor wanted to change the ending, and to cut portions that didn't advance the storyline, but Rand objected; Jack Warner persuaded Vidor to shoot the scenes as she had written them.[54]

In the novel, Rand uses Roark to declare how she despises altruism: "The man who enslaves himself voluntarily in the name of love is the basest of creatures. He degrades the dignity of man and he degrades the conception of love. But this is the essence of altruism," Roark explains.[55] In the film, he goes farther: "The world is perishing from an orgy of self-sacrificing." In *The Long Winter*, Laura Ingalls Wilder and Rose Wilder Lane had their two heroes refuse payment for procuring food for the starving town; Rand would have none of it. Lane and Rand actually corresponded about this point. Lane accepted charity so long as it was *voluntary*; Rand rejected it *even if* voluntary.[56] She has Roark call "dependent" people parasites.

The Fountainhead was released in 1949, starring Gary Cooper as Roark and Patricia Neal as his love interest, Dominque Francon. Commercially, it was a flop, earning slightly less than its production budget. It was critically panned, too, with reviewers noting its lawlessness, its heartlessness, and its intellectual incoherence. The *New Yorker*'s reviewer called it "the most asinine and inept movie that has come out of Hollywood in years."[57] The *New York Times*'s influential Bosley Crowther wondered if Jack Warner had thought through the film's argument about a creator's right to destroy others' property, given that studios routinely altered films they produced.[58] (Vidor had made that point to Warner when he sought to change Rand's ending.) Other critics were barely more friendly. The *Hollywood Reporter* called the characters "downright weird." *Variety* labeled the film "cold, unemotional, [and] loquacious." *Cue* described it as "shoddy, bombastic nonsense." The *Daily Worker* called it "openly fascist."[59]

Critics also detested Rand's novel *Atlas Shrugged*, published in 1957. It was verbose, hectoring, "execrable claptrap."[60] *Time* magazine asked: "Is it a novel? Is it a nightmare?"[61] Even the right-wing *National Review* dismissed it as "silly" and "sophomoric."[62] A later film trilogy (released 2011–14) based on the novel was also a failure, panned by critics and avoided by moviegoers; the three films collectively earned a paltry $8.8 million at the box office.[63]

The *National Review*'s pan of *Atlas Shrugged* is particularly noteworthy because it was penned by the infamous ex-Communist Whittaker Chambers.[64] Until 1938, Chambers had been a spy for the Soviet Union, but he had turned tail as Stalin's

Great Purge swept up some of his fellow spies and friends. It was Chambers who wrote the critical review of *Grapes of Wrath* for *Time* magazine in 1940. In 1948 he became a household name for his role in the prosecution and conviction of former State Department officer Alger Hiss, accused of being a communist.[65] At Hiss's trial, no clear evidence was presented that he was or ever had been a communist, but there was evidence that he had lied about knowing Chambers; Hiss was convicted of perjury and served forty-four months in jail, although he always maintained his innocence. Hiss became a hero to the left, and Chambers a hero to the right. Chambers's 1952 memoir and exposé, *Witness*, became a bestseller.

William F. Buckley had hired Chambers as an editor at the *National Review* the same year *Atlas Shrugged* had started climbing the bestseller charts. Chambers's review of the novel highlighted a rift in libertarian thinking between Rand's atheism and his own Spiritual Mobilization religiosity. The book, he wrote, was a caricature, depicting a class war between free enterprisers and "looters." Among the latter, Rand included "Left-Liberals, New Dealers, Welfare Statists, One Worlders, or, at any rate, such ogreish semblances of these as may stalk the nightmares of those who think little about people as people, but tend to think a great deal in labels and effigies." (Generations later, presidential candidate Mitt Romney would reprise the theme, recasting it simply as "makers" and "takers.")[66] In the book, Rand's looters are society's incompetents; the only way the free enterprisers can win is by with-holding their creativity, their genius, and their organizational skills—a general strike of the competent. After society's inevitable collapse and the extinction of the looters, the free enterprisers "troop out of their Rocky Mountain hideaway to repossess the ruins."[67] Chambers suggested that *Atlas Shrugged* could "only be called a novel by devaluing the term."[68]

For Chambers, the root of the problem was Rand's godlessness. In the last line of the book, a character traces the sign of the dollar in the air, where the sign of the cross should be inscribed. "Like any consistent materialism," Chambers wrote, "this one begins by rejecting God, religion, original sin, etc., etc. . . . Randian Man, like Marxian Man, is made the center of a godless world," which ends with tyranny: "Hitler's National Socialism and Stalin's brand of Communism . . . From almost any page of *Atlas Shrugged*, a voice can be heard . . . commanding: 'To a gas chamber—go!'"[69]

Rand biographer Jennifer Burns observes that with *Atlas Shrugged*, Rand returned to "the language used by earlier defenders of capitalism," adopting an extreme, if not parodic, version of social Darwinism. Many conservatives agreed with Rand that men were not created equal—this was a trope in NAM's arguments against socialism, and a drumbeat within Spiritual Mobilization and its network. But most conservatives accepted a role for private charity, which many considered the desirable alterative to government social welfare programs. Rand did not. She believed the talented should reign unencumbered by altruism. In that sense, her view was less Darwin (who discerned a role for altruism in human evolution), and more Herbert Spencer (who coined the term "survival of the fittest").

What was at stake for Chambers and Buckley—as well as for *National Review* readers, most of whom associated atheism with communism—was the Christian case for free-market capitalism, the case that James Fifield, Norman Vincent Peale, and Billy Graham were carefully building. Rand was trying to sell a godless capitalism, which Buckley and Chambers liked no more than godless communism. As Burns puts it, Buckley's allies understood that capitalism was not perfect and there was a necessary place for "charity, humility, and equality" to blunt "the harsher edges of laissez-faire."[70] But charity should be Christian charity, not government relief.

These arguments mattered little to Rand's millions of libertarian followers. Despite the critical failure of the film version of *The Fountainhead*, Rand's book sales rose. *The Fountainhead* and *Atlas Shrugged* would become handbooks of late twentieth-century libertarianism. Michael Shermer—founder of *Skeptic* magazine and a recovered libertarian—has called Rand's philosophy of Objectivism as developed in the novels the "basis of a cult . . . the antithesis of reason and individualism."[71]

One reason her books sold well in the 1950s—and continue to sell well today—is that they were (and are) heavily promoted by conservative and libertarian think tanks. One of these is the Ayn Rand Institute, which, according to the *New York Times*, in 2007 donated four hundred thousand copies of her novels to high school Advanced Placement programs.[72] No doubt underfunded public high schools gratefully accepted that charity. Shermer explains the novel's attraction to younger readers this way: "Rand appeals to a lot of rudderless young adults who turn to her for guidance as religion continues its long decline in cultural influence."[73] Faith in one's personal superiority replaced faith in God.

AFTER WORLD WAR II, John Ford, like King Vidor, changed the sorts of films he made. Unlike Vidor, he didn't become a propagandist for American capitalism, but he never made another film like *Grapes of Wrath*. Ford's postwar oeuvre was mostly Westerns, which in some ways critiqued America's frontier myths, but in other ways reinforced them.

His first postwar Western, 1948's *Fort Apache*, inverts the story of Custer's Last Stand. A cavalry colonel named Thursday (Henry Fonda) has recently transferred west from a European posting. He sets out to make a name for himself by capturing Apache leader Cochise. One of his officers, Captain York (John Wayne), offers to meet with Cochise alone and convince him to come to the fort for negotiations under a flag of truce. York succeeds in gaining Cochise's trust, but Thursday, an anti-native bigot, breaks faith and takes the regiment out to ambush Cochise and his men. York protests, viewing the betrayal as a slight on his honor. York is reassigned to guard the wagons and survives the resulting slaughter; back at the wagon train, Cochise returns the company banner.

Ford makes both York and Cochise honorable warriors, but he is not quite done. In an epilogue, York—now the commander of Fort Apache—falsely tells reporters that the slaughter was Cochise's doing, not Thursday's. York protects his company's honor at the sacrifice of his own (though only a few of his men, and the audience, know that). York rationalizes the American genocide against the natives he once respected, and justifies the expropriation of their land. Ford would be criticized by generations of film scholars for this choice.

At one level, Ford was subverting one of America's foundational myths: its supposed innocence in the Indian wars. Ford also shows how lies can be rendered as true and national mythologies constructed. But film historian Richard Slotkin contends that Ford was up to something more. At the film's end, York is still the hero, surrounded by his men and his flags; *Fort Apache* can be read as an argument for continuing to believe in America's patriotic myths, even when we know them to be untrue. Victory in the Cold War, Slotkin argues, required an ideology "designed to build national solidarity in the face of the threatening advance of Soviet Communism—an ideology which . . . would ultimately rest on a deliberate and consensual falsification of history."[74] Ford offered that falsification.

Another filmmaker who took on the task of rebuilding American mythology was Cecil B. DeMille. Like *Fort Apache*, DeMille's *Ten Commandments* retells an old story with a new Cold War flavor: Moses is the founder of freedom and liberty, the stand-in for Christian America fighting Soviet Communism. DeMille explained, "The theme of this picture is whether men are to be ruled by God's law or whether they are to be ruled by the whims of a dictator like Ramses. Are men the property of the State or free souls under God?"[75] If that sounds familiar, it's because it echoed the arguments of Spiritual Mobilization, still operating in 1956. The film ends with words taken almost literally from the organization's 1951 Committee to Proclaim Liberty: "Go proclaim liberty, throughout all the lands, unto all the inhabitants thereof."[76]

DeMille was active in antiunion advocacy, creating an eponymous foundation to finance passage of "right-to-work" laws and make films promoting them. In 1944, he sued the American Federation of Radio Artists (he had a radio show and therefore had to be a member) to prevent its use of union funds for political purposes. He lost all the way to the Supreme Court, but the case brought him attention from businessmen, unsurprisingly—J. Howard Pew, A. C. Nielsen of the television viewership rating company, and Stephen DuBrul of General Motors. They funded his DeMille Foundation, which promoted not only state-level "right-to-work" laws but also a Constitutional amendment barring closed shops.[77] DeMille would claim he was a "voluntary unionist," opposed to being forced to join unions to have jobs. But his "voluntarism" didn't extend to allowing leftists to be union members, let alone hold jobs in the film industry. After World War II, DeMille attempted to conduct an anticommunist purge of the Screen Directors Guild. His efforts were stymied with support from John Ford—quite the complex character.[78]

DIRECT SUPPRESSION OF "subversive" anticorporate themes was one way that American business leaders sought to redirect film content and change the cultural landscape of postwar America. Another was through activities branded as "economic education." By 1952, businesses were spending more than $100 million per year on "free-enterprise" messages.[79] The private War Advertising Council, rebranded as the Advertising Council, was one vehicle; it continued to link private and public spheres in both the Truman and Eisenhower administrations—though far more comfortably with the latter. One campaign, "Our American Heritage," loaded a "Freedom Train" with documents and images to sell a business-oriented vision of

American freedom. In 1948 and 1949, the train visited more than 320 cities, while coordinated radio, newspaper, and billboard advertising ensured plenty of attendance at its stops.[80] Another Advertising Council initiative, the "American Economic System" campaign, was far larger and designed to promote free enterprise itself. More than eight hundred thousand copies of a pamphlet called *The Miracle of America* went to schools and businesses. Scholastic reprinted it in magazine form, and the U.S. Army distributed copies to its soldiers.[81] The Advertising Council's campaigns were mirrored by efforts by individual companies, industrial and trade organizations, and foundations. The National Association of Manufacturers developed a comic series, *Fight for Freedom*, in parallel with the Advertising Council's "American Economic System" campaign.

Many of these efforts were open and public, but some were clandestine. In 1939, the Alfred P. Sloan Foundation, which had been established by the GM CEO in 1934, had formed a partnership with New York University to make a series of live-action films on economic themes. But Sloan was displeased with the results; they were insufficiently ideological. After the war, Sloan tried again, this time using animation. Cartoons had been used for training, education, and propaganda during the war, and they seemed better to fit Sloan's goal. The cartoon series would be called Fun and Facts about American Business.

It came about circuitously. In April 1942, George Benson, the president of Harding College in Arkansas—a small, struggling conservative school operated by the Church of Christ—testified before the House Ways and Means Committee against New Deal spending, particularly the work of relief agencies. The *New York Times* covered his testimony, and he was soon asked to give many more lectures. A speech to the National Tax Foundation—which opposed federal taxation—gained him a meeting with Alfred P. Sloan, at the time still president and CEO of GM.[82] When the war intervened and film became tightly controlled, Benson launched his own enterprise, an anti–New Deal "National Education Program" at Harding College, with financial support from Sloan, J. Howard Pew, Charles White of Republic Steel, and other business leaders. The program combined lecturing, a syndicated column called "Looking Ahead," and a syndicated radio program to spread a message of economic freedom and evangelical faith.[83]

After the war, Benson approached Walt Disney about making cartoons to promote "free enterprise." Disney sent him to a cartoonist named John Sutherland, who had worked for Disney in the late 1930s and had spent the war as an independent producer making instructional films for the U.S. Army Signal Corps. Benson and Sutherland set to work. Their arrangement hid Sloan's role in funding the effort. The two would create the concept for each film; Benson would propose it to the Sloan Foundation. If the foundation agreed to the concept, it would provide the funds to Harding College, which would pay Sutherland's studio. There would be no direct link from Sloan to Sutherland, or vice versa. The completed film would name Sutherland's studio as the producer, and Harding College as the presenter. But while the name Alfred P. Sloan appeared nowhere on these films, his intent for them was clear. In a 1946 letter to Benson, he explained his goal to promote his economic worldview, because America's ability to produce goods depended on producing the right thinking. A way had to be found to "tell the simple economic truths to the masses of people."[84]

Given Sloan's ambition, the cartoons had to be suitable for theatrical release. That would not be cheap. The first nine-minute cartoon, *Make Mine Freedom*, from 1948, had a budget of fifty thousand dollars (more than half a million in 2021 dollars). A total of seven cartoons were released. (Two others were made, but MGM, their distributor, rejected them as excessively propagandistic.) It's unclear how much Sloan ultimately spent, but by the end of the project, Sutherland's fee alone had risen to eighty-three thousand dollars.[85] Production costs were also higher than originally expected, because the foundation frequently requested changes. At minimum, the Sloan Foundation paid something like half a million dollars, the equivalent of about seven million dollars today.

What stories did these cartoons tell? In *Make Mine Freedom*, a pink-suited travelling salesman named Dr. Utopia arrives in a small town selling a cure-all in the form of a bottle of "-ISM." The price of the bottle is signing away one's rights: "I hereby turn over to -ISM, INC. everything I have, including my freedom and the freedom of my children, and my children's children, in return for which -ISM promises to take care of me forever," the contract stipulates.[86] The town's leaders are ready to sign when John Q. Public jumps up off a park bench and calls the contract ridiculous. He recounts a story of "Joe" who invented a car, took money from his friends to develop and produce it, and created new, skilled jobs. Mr. Public dives into employment statistics (notably avoiding the mass unemployment of the Great Depression) and demands, logically enough, that they try -ISM before buying. The townsmen—only men are active characters in the film—sample Dr. Utopia's tonic and are treated to a Hayekian dystopia: property confiscation, state planning of everything, the crushing of dissent, mass imprisonment. -ISM isn't the road to serfdom, but it is the gateway drug.

Make Mine Freedom wasn't subtle. Members of a test audience in Los Angeles recognized the cartoon for what it was, some approving its confrontation with Soviet communism and others calling it fascistic. Still, MGM put it into wide circulation, expecting an audience of around thirty-five million. But if audiences didn't like the cartoons, then they wouldn't work, and a second offering in the series, *Going Places*, was rejected for mass circulation on the grounds that it wasn't entertaining. And there was another matter: How should these cartoons deal with the reality that competition and the profit motive didn't always work, and that the market didn't always "self-correct"? *Going Places* was supposed to extol the virtue of the profit motive through a story about manufacturing soap. Recalling the themes of NAM's *Your Town*, the cartoon shows how tax revenues from the soap factory fund schools and other amenities, workers come to trust the boss, and the stock market rewards everyone—until a factory owner conspires with his competitor to fix prices. A third competitor enters the market, undercutting them all, and their businesses collapse. But the narrator reassures the audience: "Ninety-nine times out of a hundred, competition works. When it doesn't, the government steps in to prevent monopolistic attempts."[87]

Going Places produced a rift among the backers and makers of the series. An initial version had treated the price-fixing arrangement differently, explicitly labeling it a monopoly and advocating government intervention to break it up. Sloan and Benson objected: they wanted the series to sell the self-regulating nature of industrial capitalism. Sutherland settled on the market-based solution of a third party undercutting the anticompetitive practices of the first two, but he wrote to Benson complaining that this didn't square with the historical record, noting the important antitrust actions against U.S. Steel and the motion picture industry itself.[88] This history suggested "free men must make laws to protect their freedom from combinations of more powerful men."[89] The collaborators' "vision of a self-regulating economy represented the way things ought to be," historian Caroline Jack has argued, not the way things actually were.[90] Like Leonard Read, Sloan wanted to sell a crystalline vision of capitalist theology. If the facts didn't match, too bad for facts.[91]

Benson, Sutherland, and the Sloan Foundation went their separate ways in 1952, but their effort to sell capitalism to the masses continued. Sutherland made PR films for business for the rest of his career. One, made for DuPont in 1954 and sponsored by the U.S. Chamber of Commerce, *It's Everybody's Business*, reiterated the indivisibility thesis while inventing new economic rights: "Our forefathers were constructing the foundations of a new nation, by interlocking inseparably the blocks of our political and economic freedom," the narrator intones. A stonemason carves the rights on actual blocks: they include freedom of worship, the right to go into business, the right of assembly, freedom to work in a job of your own choice, and the right to bargain with your employer without the intermediary of a union.[92] Benson went on to work against desegregation.[93]

WHILE THE SLOAN Foundation hid its sponsorship of Sutherland's animated propaganda, industrial giant General Electric had no qualms about putting its name on a branded television program. *General Electric Theater* was one of the most successful TV shows ever produced. Broadcast from 1953 to 1962, it logged more than two hundred episodes during one of the most important prime-time slots: Sunday evening at nine P.M. During its run, it was one of the most popular shows on American television, frequently ranked among the top shows in the coveted Nielsen ratings. In its 1956–57 season, it hit number three in the rankings, reaching an estimated 25 million viewers every week.[94] (The U.S. population was 169 million at that time, and about 60 percent were adults, so more than one in four adult Americans was watching weekly.[95]) Critics liked the show, too: the *Boston Herald* praised GE for not assuming that Americans were all "idiots."[96]

The show featured outstanding talents in well-written adaptations of novels, short stories, and plays. The list of performers who appeared is a Who's Who of 1950s Hollywood, an eclectic roster encompassing everyone from Rita Moreno to Charlton Heston, Boris Karloff to Harry Belafonte, Bette Davis to Groucho Marx.[97] Each episode, from the time he joined as host in 1954, was introduced by the popular and affable actor Ronald Reagan.

The program dramatically increased Reagan's visibility and influence. In the late 1930s and early 1940s, Reagan was a moderately successful actor, but not a star. During World War II, he had served in the First Motion Picture Unit, a division of the Army Air Forces, where he mostly made training films. After the war, he appeared in several trite pictures, such as the infamous 1951 comedy *Bedtime for Bonzo*, in which he plays a professor trying to teach morals to a chimp and score a win for the nurture side of the nature versus nurture debate. (Spoiler alert: he fails.) Reagan played a larger role in Hollywood as the president of the Screen Actors Guild (continuously from 1947 to 1952 and then again in 1959-60); *General Electric Theater* revived Reagan's acting career. More important, it laid the foundation for his political career, as his voice and face reached each week into tens of millions of American homes, and the seeds of his reputation as "the Great Communicator" were sown.[98]

While some episodes were simply dramas, comedies, or holiday specials, many had messages extolling the virtues of free-market capitalism and American individualism. Stories embedded themes about the centrality of hard work, individual achievement, and self-reliance. Get-rich-quick schemes typically came to naught, but hard work and perseverance paid off. Men who relied on others to solve their problems failed; men who took responsibility for their choices succeeded.

This didactic quality—and its pro-capitalist, individualist message—was no accident. The driving force behind the program was not a director, producer, or screenwriter, but the GE public relations department, which, working with Reagan, chose the scripts.[99] *General Electric Theater* was not just pitching electricity, it was pitching capitalism.

All television before the 1969 advent of national public television (and later, cable) was a medium for advertising, but this advertising was typically for products you could buy at a store. A handful of product categories generated more than 80 percent of network television revenues.[100] The nation's largest network advertiser in the 1950s was Procter & Gamble; among the top six product groups advertised on NBC in 1954 were soap and toiletries.[101] GE was different: while it did sell some consumer products—light bulbs, electrical appliances—most of its business was electricity and the equipment needed to generate it. The main product *General Electric Theater* sold was General Electric itself as a forward-looking corporation, electricity as both evidence and driver of progress, and capitalism as the American way of life. Put another way, the pitch—as one historian has put it—was not "merely hawking light bulbs, but . . . claiming credit for light itself."[102]

Each program began with an opening theme lauding General Electric as a literal and metaphorical engine of American progress: "In Research . . . in Engineering . . . in Manufacturing Skill . . . in the Values that bring a better, more satisfying life . . . At General Electric, Progress is Our Most Important Product." Each episode ended similarly: "From Electricity comes Progress! Progress in our daily living, Progress in our work, Progress in our national defense. Remember, at General Electric, Progress is Our Most Important Product."[103]

The viewer hardly needed to be admonished; after a few episodes, one could scarcely forget. Each week's drama was divided into two acts, separated by an intermission featuring a "progress report" about a new GE product or an improvement in an existing one. Flashbulbs, for example, illustrated how GE had helped to make indoor photography accessible to ordinary Americans—evidence of how "GE progress has literally brightened our lives."[104] Some intermissions were filmed on location in a factory, laboratory, or airplane hangar, because these were the "testing grounds of progress." One showed a test flight at Edwards Air Force Base of a military airplane that could reach forty thousand feet and stop and restart in midflight—all powered by a GE engine.

In later years, General Electric CEO Jack Welch would be famous (or infamous) for insisting that corporations existed to produce only one thing: value for shareholders.[105] But in the 1950s, the message from headquarters was different: by manufacturing light bulbs, electric ranges, televisions, and jet engines, GE was producing progress. It was protecting our present and building a future in which Christianity, competitive capitalism, industrial harmony, and individual enterprise would hold pride of place.

Many of the episodes in one way or another embedded these themes. Characters faced challenges mostly of their own making, as in the 1954 episode "I'm a Fool," in which James Dean plays a young man who learns the "consequences of telling a lie to impress a girl." Characters are redeemed when they acknowledge their own responsibility—something that they learn the hard way. In another episode, a man played by Harry Belafonte struggles to stand up to pressures put upon him by his mother and brothers. After considerable conflict, he does, but at no point is it suggested that his opportunities might be limited because of something over which he has no control: the fact that he is Black.

The episode called "No Hiding Place" stars Reagan himself as a young man named Victor who has lost his way because of alcohol.[106] The episode opens with his mother (Geraldine Page) lamenting that her son could have been a doctor or a lawyer but has ended up running a department store and squandering his earnings because of booze. "Hospitals, psychiatry, everyone's tried to help," his brother Eddie laments. True help finally comes in the form of religion: Victor hits bottom, first (sadly) finding himself on the street and then (happily) finding God. He declares he'll become sober and return to help other alcoholics, which he does.

The narrative turning point is Victor's acceptance of responsibility for his trouble: "Those were my hands reaching for that whiskey. Nobody ever poured a drink down me but me." Eddie objects, suggesting that many men drink, and it isn't really Victor's fault: with other men it is a habit, but with Victor it has been "a sickness." Victor rejects that excuse:

VICTOR: No, I don't buy that and I never did. I drank because I wanted to. I willed it. I wasn't born an alcoholic, I made myself one.
EDDIE: Then it comes down to personal will?
VICTOR: Right. My hands reaching for a drink. And that makes me my problem. And I'm the only one who can stop my drinking.

The drama concludes as Victor starts a program to teach alcoholics to will themselves not to drink.

Individualism and responsibility loom large thematically in many episodes, such as 1961's "Tippy-Top," starring Red Buttons and a very young (and adorable) Ron Howard. In this story, a lonely little boy (Howard) has only an imaginary friend for company: Tippy-Top, who is variously a sailor, a soldier, or a cowboy. The boy's mom is getting married, and her fiancé tells him that Tippy-Top isn't real. He is sad. Another boy also tells him Tippy-Top isn't real, and bullies him; the fiancé tells the boy he has to go back and confront the bully. The boy does; Tippy-Top tells him he's become a man now that he's solved a problem for himself.[107]

Self-reliance is also the theme of "We're Holding Your Son," also from 1961, in which the son of a successful businessman is arrested for grand larceny. Dad gets him probation and helps him out of some other scrapes; the boy ends up trying to steal a bottle of liquor on prom night and is caught. His dad finally stops trying to get him off easy. "Sorry I let you down, son," the dad apologizes, but the son realizes it was for his own good: "You know, Pop, you didn't let me down this time."[108] The boy straightens up when he has to stand on his own feet.

Only a few episodes dealt directly with communism, but several dealt with class distinctions and embedded messages about accepting one's place in the social order. In the 1954 episode starring James Dean, his character notices an elegantly dressed man and thinks he can woo a wealthy girl (Natalie Wood) by dressing and acting similarly. He puts on expensive clothes and affects an upper-class manner. He also takes on a name—Walter Matheson—which he thinks classier than his real name. He has dinner with the girl, but after she leaves town, he realizes that he does not have her address and she does not know his real name. By pretending to be what he was not, he lost any chance with her. The episode ends with him wishing he had never seen the fancy man and had never "got ideas in his head."[109] In a similar episode aired the following year, "The Clown," a trapeze performer played by Henry Fonda performs with his wife, who is frankly better than him—he keeps falling. He decides he wants to be a clown instead, and a sad one at that. His wife threatens to leave him if he does. He says, "That's what I do best, a man's gotta do what he does best." It turns out he is funny; he succeeds as a clown where he had failed as a trapeze artist.[110]

One episode that did directly address communism was "The Iron Silence," from 1961. The story takes place in occupied Hungary. One Russian character is sympathetic, but the rest are boorish, violent chauvinists. The didactic message comes in a conversation between two characters. One asks: "What about your duty to yourself?" The other replies: "A man's highest duty is to the state." Clearly, American viewers were expected to be repelled by that answer; more did not need to be said.[111]

UNLIKE FAILED MID-CENTURY onscreen efforts to transmit free-market ideology, *General Electric Theater* arguably succeeded as propaganda because it also worked as entertainment. The show was well produced; millions of Americans enjoyed it, and scores of actors did good work in it. More than sixty years later, many of its episodes remain interesting. A great deal of theater and literature is didactic; the fact that a story has a "moral" doesn't make it bad art. But the fact that *General Electric Theater* was well made doesn't mean it wasn't also propagandistic.

GE wasn't alone in exerting some creative control over a program it sponsored. Single sponsorship was common in radio and carried over into television in its early days. (The *Colgate Comedy Hour*, for example, was a variety show punctuated by advertisements for soap, scrubs, and dishwashing detergent.) Fearing controversy, sponsors frequently vetoed culturally or politically sensitive topics, such as sex, race, and trade unionism, and as a result early television tended to be anodyne. Sometimes script elements were vetoed or altered: For a *Playhouse 90* drama about the Nuremberg trials sponsored by the American Gas Association, advertising executives picked through the script and asked CBS to delete references to the Nazi gas chambers.[112] In 1955, Westinghouse objected to a *Studio One* program about atomic bombs while the company was promoting its contributions to the Atoms for Peace program. And one General Electric executive told the Office of Network Study (which was compiling a report about TV advertising) that GE was generally opposed to downbeat programs because they were at odds with its upbeat message of progress.[113]

By the late 1950s, however, television had become expensive, and few companies could afford to be the sole sponsors of a prime-time program. Even by 1953, when *General Electric Theater* launched, most programs had multiple sponsors, diluting the influence that any one sponsor could have. The shows with which *General Electric Theater* competed—the *Ed Sullivan Show*, *I Love Lucy*, *The $64,000 Question*, *Dragnet*—all had multiple sponsors. While Ed Sullivan may have censored Elvis Presley's sexy hips, his program had no message. Mostly, it was just entertainment, and the better the entertainment, the larger the audience and the happier the sponsors.

General Electric Theater was different. Going well beyond "a word from our sponsor," GE was the program's raison d'être, acting as producer, director, and sponsor rolled into one. Like the businessmen who financed Ludwig von Mises's professorship at New York University, General Electric was interested in promoting a particular vision of capitalism and what made for a good life. And that vision was asymmetric, focused on individual responsibility and enterprise, with little attention to the various domains in which individual effort was not enough, or the playing field was not level.

A host of different messages about American life—about racism, for example, or environmental damage from hydroelectric dams—were never offered on this show. Some might say that GE had the "right" to do this, or that other artists, other television programs, and other organizations could have developed offerings with different perspectives. Of course. But few, if any, others had the resources of General Electric.[114] Certainly, no union ever produced anything comparable, and if they had tried, General Electric executives would likely have attacked it as an inappropriate (or even illegal) diversion of members' dues.

Harvard law professor Yochai Benkler has demonstrated how disinformation and propaganda on the internet are asymmetric, with far more right-wing than left-wing claims.[115] This should not come as a surprise: propaganda is bound to be asymmetric, because its purpose is political, not analytical, and propaganda requires time, money, and access to outlets. As Edward Bernays—the theorist of propaganda—once wrote, "Those who manipulate [the views of] society constitute an invisible government which is the true ruling power of our country. We are governed, our minds are molded, our tastes formed, our ideas suggested, largely by men we have never heard of."[116]

As big winners in American capitalism, corporate Hollywood, GE, Alfred Sloan, and the Advertising Council had a good share of that ruling power, and they used it to mold minds and form tastes consistent with their preferred vision of American culture and their interpretation of freedom. Those had fared less well—who struggled to make ends meet in 1950s America, who lived under Jim Crow laws in the segregated South, faced systemic sexism or antisemitism, suffered from domestic violence, or watched helplessly as their local rivers became fatally polluted—might have taken a different view of matters. They might not have been so sanguine about the efficacy of individual initiative, or the glories of mass production and free markets. They might have wanted to see more "social problem films" like *Grapes of Wrath*, or films directed at the lives of immigrants or women or working-class people. But they did not have the resources to sponsor television shows or films or advertising campaigns, and they did not have the FBI helping them suppress dissent behind the scenes. On the contrary, if others held divergent views—and particularly, if they thought the government should do more rather than less to help, support, or protect them—corporate capitalists were determined to persuade them (and everyone around them) that those views were wrong.

CHAPTER 9

Steering the Chicago School

While Rose Wilder Lane, Ayn Rand, Leonard Read, and Ronald Reagan made the case for market fundamentalism to the masses, others continued to try to shore up its intellectual foundations. In *The Road to Serfdom*, Hayek had noted that from "the saintly and single-minded idealist to the fanatic is often but a step."[1] There were several steps—and two decades—between *The Road to Serfdom* and fanatical market fundamentalism, but Hayek's followers would get there, and throughout their journey their home base would be the University of Chicago. A key person in making that possible was Harold Luhnow.

A Baptist businessman born in Missouri, Luhnow had worked on a cattle ranch, studied agriculture, and run the wholesale furniture distribution company founded by his uncle, William Volker. In 1932, Volker had created an eponymous philanthropy focused on local charity and fighting machine politics in Kansas City, but by 1945 it was run by Luhnow and was mostly supporting free-market philosophy. A big part of that, now, would mean supporting and promoting Hayek, both the man and his ideas. Henry Hazlitt and his associates facilitated and underwrote Ludwig von Mises's career in America; Luhnow and his associates did the same for Hayek. Historian Kim Phillips-Fein has noted that Luhnow "was no intellectual."[2] But together with Leonard Read, J. Howard Pew, and DuPont executive Jasper Crane, Luhnow would play a pivotal role in funding and developing the intellectual movement called the Chicago school of economics. He would do it, however, not to foster economics, but to foster a market-oriented, antigovernment view of the world.

BEFORE LUHNOW'S ASSOCIATION with Hayek even began, the American was searching for an ideological standard-bearer. The idea originated with Crane, who had been closely associated with NAM in its fight against the New Deal but by 1945 had become disenchanted with NAM's approach. Like Leonard Read, Crane felt that NAM businessmen focused too much on the details of commerce and not enough on the vision of the society they wanted to build and sustain. They were also too willing, in his view, to compromise. The battle for a free society, Crane felt, needed to be carried forward by "a cadre of intellectuals and businessmen that would be *absolutely committed to the market.*"[3] Phillips-Fein quotes: "I have been wondering whether we ought to attempt to mobilize a few men who are *absolutely sound in the faith and will not compromise*, who are earnest in thinking, talking and writing for freedom, and who are resolved to uphold it at any personal sacrifice."[4]

Although Crane and Luhnow despised Karl Marx, they agreed with him that the point of philosophy should be not to study the world, but to change it.[5] They envisioned a project to move the public conversation, and thereby move American society—in the spirit of Marx, but in the opposite direction. The successful outcome would be an altered social contract that valorized and protected economic freedom above other considerations. But how would they do that? Well, Marx had written a book that had changed the world, so maybe they could find someone on their side to do the same.

The need was urgent because the changes effected by FDR were starting to be normalized, and many American businessmen were making peace with the New Deal. Historian George H. Nash has concluded that in the mid-1940s there was nothing in America that could even be identified as a conservative movement; libertarians were a "forlorn minority" and individualism was at its "nadir."[6] That might be an overstatement, but it is true that in 1943 no less a business-focused group than the U.S. Chamber of Commerce said "only the willfully blind can fail to see that the old-style capitalism of a primitive, free-shooting period is gone forever."[7]

Crane believed *The Road to Serfdom* might be the answer to their prayers, the "New Testament of capitalism" their project required.[8] With this in mind, Luhnow bet his chips on Hayek. Through the Volker Fund, Luhnow financed Hayek's U.S. book tour, arranged visits and lectures, and then provided backing and coordination for the first Mont Pelerin Society meeting in 1947. At the same time, Luhnow saw a snag: *The Road to Serfdom* was too dense and framed its argument too much in European terms. Americans needed an American version of the book.[9] If Hayek couldn't or wouldn't write it himself, he could perhaps lead a group that would. Luhnow put the idea to Hayek in 1945: "We are hopeful that you could bring together a group that would spell out in considerable detail but in language simple enough for the common man to understand, a complete plan for a workable society of free enterprise."[10] He offered financial support to hire the necessary research assistants, to see to it that Hayekian thought became their "intellectual weapon to curb the power of government in the postwar era."[11]

Historians Robert van Horn and Philip Mirowski believe it was Hayek who had the grand vision, and Luhnow was a somewhat reluctant sponsor. They wrote: "In August 1945 Hayek conceived of the *American Road* project at Chicago as a subordinate part of a larger and more comprehensive scheme—a political movement to counter the intellectual traditions that would, as Hayek thought, inexorably lead to the emergence of totalitarian regimes throughout the Western world." Luhnow, they argued, resisted that framework, stating that "experience has already proven in too many cases that it is almost impossible to keep control of organizations of this sort."[12]

Luhnow may have been skeptical of Hayek's desire to rescue Europe, but he was not reluctant to fund Hayek to rescue America. Moreover, he evidently thought he could keep adequate control of Hayek, because he now took steps to establish the Free Market Project, with Hayek at its helm, at the University of Chicago.[13]

IN LATER YEARS, Hayek claimed that he had been reluctant to work with these businessmen. Perhaps leery of being perceived as their tool, he reported that initially he demurred. (He would have similar misgivings over Jasper Crane's attendance at the inaugural Mont Pèlerin meeting.) According to Bruce Caldwell, Hayek worried that opportunistic businessmen would embrace his message of government reticence but in the next breath demand "that the government protect their industries from foreign competition." The history of NAM certainly validated that concern.[14] Van Horn and Mirowski argue, however, that Hayek was quite attracted by the opportunity Luhnow offered, and that it was Hayek who proposed the University of Chicago as the free-market project's home base.[15] He also had at least one conversation about who the right men would be to participate. One of them was the Chicago economist Henry Simons, who was well known for his 1934 *Positive Program for Laissez-Faire*: penned in the heart of the Great Depression yet unapologetically defending free-market policies.[16]

Simons and Hayek had already discussed establishing a think tank at Chicago promoting (or perhaps at this point, rescuing) the laissez-faire framework. Simons would call it the "Institute of Political Economy," but his intention was not so much academic as popular; he wanted to get the message out to Americans. To ensure that message would be consistent—and not mixed, as academic messages often are—it would be necessary to hire men whom they knew would not step out of "character as a libertarian." The two he had in mind were Aaron Director and Milton Friedman.[17] Director had studied at Chicago in the 1930s and then at the London School of Economics, where Hayek was teaching. Along with Simons, Director also played a major role in persuading the University of Chicago Press to publish *The Road to Serfdom*.

It was an obvious move to unite the Simons and Luhnow visions.[18] In May 1946, Hayek sent Luhnow his *Outline of Organization for the Proposed Free Market Study*. The two men agreed Chicago was the place for it, but negotiations with the university were stalled; the economics department balked at hiring Hayek. Perhaps this was just the usual academic resistance to external hiring suggestions, or perhaps *The Road to Serfdom* was viewed as insufficiently scholarly.[19] Some faculty saw Hayek as inadequately empirical; others rejected as extremist his openly "antistatist" views.[20] Historian Lanny Ebenstein notes dryly that "Hayek's views of economic activity and appropriate government policy during the Great Depression were not in accord with the facts."[21]

Simons himself admitted that his libertarian orientation was an academic outlier, "almost unrepresented among great universities, save for Chicago."[22] This was one reason Simons was eager to recruit Aaron Director to the Free Market Project, to shore up the libertarian wing, which at that time was not dominant.[23]

The project was almost certainly also opposed by faculty members of the Cowles Commission, an interdisciplinary study at Chicago grounded in math and statistics and addressing economic problems from a Keynesian perspective. (The commission was later pushed out of the university, as the economics department moved to the right, but it regrouped at Yale, where several of its members went on to win the Nobel Memorial Prize, including Joseph Stiglitz and Kenneth Arrow.)[24] With Chicago throwing up obstacles, Hayek and Luhnow approached Princeton, but that university was unwilling to accept monies whose use would be "specifically allocated by the donors."[25] Hayek complained about this to Chicago economist Jacob Viner, who responded that he thought that they would "run into the same situation at any of the respectable institutions."[26]

Viner evidently overestimated Chicago, because Luhnow refocused his attention there and soon succeeded.[27] He offered to pay the program director's salary as well as Hayek's, at least for the first year. The idea also emerged to situate the project in the Law School, and so a major part of the "Chicago school of economics" would develop outside an economics department.[28] Perhaps that made sense: Crane and Luhnow were not interested in answering economic questions such as the causes of inflation or the reasons for business cycles, or interrogating issues of wealth distribution.[29] Their goal—explicitly stated—was to lay out a political and social vision. And what arm of the state could be more important to influence in this context than the law?

Crane and Luhnow's vision focused on two key claims—axioms really, for they were taken as given without empirical confirmation. The first axiom was the primacy of free markets, or rather "The Free Market," which they insisted was "the most efficient organizer of economic activity." The project would be didactic, explaining "that the free market is systemic, rational, not chaotic or disorderly" and demonstrating its efficiency in "allocating resources to their best use."[30] The second axiom was the relationship between capitalism and freedom, with an emphasis on regulation as a "menace to the Free Market" and therefore to freedom, generally.[31]

Despite their theoretical commitment to competition in yielding socially optimal results, there would be no competition for the position of project director. Hayek stipulated (and Luhnow agreed) that the director would be Director (assuming the Law School agreed to hire him as a tenured full professor).[32] Within three years, the participants would produce "a semi-popular" book providing the blueprint for "an effective competitive system" of free enterprise.[33] The Volker Fund would cover all salaries, as well as the expenses of an advisory board "consisting of persons sympathetic to the purposes" of the project.[34] That board would include Leonard Read, as well as libertarian businessman Loren B. Miller, a driving force behind the Volker Fund's creation. The board would meet regularly in Chicago, ensuring that businessmen would not merely fund the project but also monitor it.

The Law School agreed to these terms, save for balking at tenure for Director given that Luhnow had only promised five years of funding. (Director agreed to come without tenure. He taught at the Law School from 1946 to 1975.)[35] Still, it took time to hammer out the details, particularly what to do with Hayek. In 1948, Luhnow met personally with University of Chicago chancellor Robert Maynard Hutchins and offered fifteen thousand dollars per year for ten years to cover Hayek's salary; evidently that did the trick.[36] Hayek was appointed in 1950, although not as a professor of economics, since the department would not have him. Instead, he joined the faculty as a professor in the Committee on Social Thought, with his salary paid by Harold Luhnow.

Academics often take funding from external patrons, including private citizens and foundations, and before World War II most external funding for basic academic research came from private patrons.[37] Still, it was highly irregular for a private individual to pay a particular professor's salary. Moreover, Luhnow did not simply provide the money: he had structured and shaped the project. He and Crane picked the people and the place. Open competition had not brought Ludwig von Mises to NYU, and open academic competition did not bring Friedrich von Hayek to Chicago or create the Free Market Project. Jasper Crane and Harold Luhnow did.[38] And while NAM and other conservative groups and individuals had long attacked socialism and communism as "foreign theories" and trade unionism as the product of "foreign influence," ideological alignment made such concerns melt away. Luhnow and Crane now literally financed foreigners to import foreign ideas and dress them up in American clothes.

IN PROMOTING AUSTRIAN economics in America, Luhnow and his associates aspired to use the discipline to promote an economic vision that feted the successes of capitalism and downplayed, even denied, its failures. Alongside this was a political vision introducing a new element in the big myth of market fundamentalism: economic freedom was now not merely one leg of a tripod, but the flagpole on which the flag of freedom flew. Put another way, their ambition was for Americans to understand freedom in singularly economic terms.

In time, the so-called Chicago school would come to include a variety of thinkers, who extended its vision well beyond what Luhnow and Crane financed. It would be strongly identified with the University of Chicago's economics department, despite their rejection of Hayek. It would also be closely associated with the Mont Pelerin Society: Friedman would serve as its president, and Director would also play a major role.[39] Still, the ideological center of the Chicago school would continue to be Luhnow's Free Market Project and the key participants it had brought together: Aaron Director, Milton Friedman, and later George Stigler, who was hired in 1958 with funding from drugstore magnate Charles Walgreen Jr.[40] (Henry Simons died by suicide in 1946.)[41] Over the following decades, a huge amount of work in economics would come out of Chicago, much of it deeply influential. For some people, "Chicago" would become synonymous with "economics." But it was a very particular kind of economics. By the late 1950s a "specific and radical neo-liberalism" had emerged at Chicago, one that Dieter Plehwe notes "differed markedly both from the liberalism of the older generation of Chicago-based scholars like Simons and Knight, and from the Austrian economics and philosophy that Hayek promoted."[42]

As it evolved, the Chicago school reformulated the traditional concerns and commitments of classical liberalism. It also largely brushed aside Hayek's caveats about the need for "minimum standards." As Bruce Caldwell puts it, Chicago economics ditched Hayek's argument for "a clear set of principles which enables us to distinguish between the legitimate fields of government activities and the illegitimate fields of government activity." Above all, the Chicago school abandoned Hayek's admonition: "You must cease to argue for and against government activity as such."[43]

The complex history of the Chicago school is beyond the scope of this book, but three efforts—derived from Luhnow's intervention—stand out in terms of shaping the national conversation about capitalism and the role of governments in markets.[44] The first is George Stigler's Americanization of Adam Smith. The second is Aaron Director's development of an intellectual program to challenge the premises of anti-trust law. And the third is Milton Friedman's fulfillment of the promise of a bible of American market fundamentalism. *The Road to Serfdom* had come out of Europe and would serve as the ideology's Old Testament. In America, Milton Friedman would write the New Testament.

GEORGE STIGLER WAS first to move the ball of laissez-faire revivalism down the field. A classmate of Milton Friedman, Stigler had earned a PhD in 1938 under the direction of Frank Knight—often considered part of the "first generation" of Chicago economists. (Knight was also instrumental in getting *The Road to Serfdom* published.) After graduate school, Stigler taught at Iowa State, the University of Minnesota (where he was again a contemporary of Friedman), and Columbia University before returning to Chicago in 1958. He was a founding member of the Mont Pelerin Society, served as its president from 1976 to 1978, and would win the Nobel Memorial Prize in Economic Sciences in 1982 for his work on economic regulation.[45] (Stigler coined the term "regulatory capture," arguing that many if not most regulations would fail to achieve their goals because vested interests would manipulate the system to their advantage.)

In the 1950s, Stigler took on the task of producing an edited version of Adam Smith's foundational work, *The Wealth of Nations*. At more than a thousand pages, the original 1776 text was not something a professor could assign in its entirety to undergraduates (nor for that matter to most graduate students). Stigler had to pick and choose the most salient parts.[46] His treatment does an impressive job encapsulating Smith's central antimercantilist argument that commerce and wealth can arise from individuals' actions without the guidance of a monarch or other central authority; in Smith's famous words, "It is not from the benevolence of the butcher, the brewer, or the baker that we expect our dinner, but from their regard to their own interest."[47] Yet, at the same time, Stigler expunged the passages where Smith acknowledged the limits of that view, just as *Reader's Digest* expunged the passages where Hayek qualified his views.

Conspicuous among the topics elided (or omitted entirely) are Smith's arguments *for* the necessity of regulation when self-interest fails, and the necessity of raising funds for public goods that markets by themselves either do not provide or cannot sustain. To be sure, Smith advocated open trade and competition, but he also acknowledged the need for restraints on the marketplace to protect public safety. He also identified the problem of wages that were sometimes inadequate, and the necessity of taxation to pay for public goods such as education and infrastructure. That Adam Smith is nowhere to be found in Stigler's Chicago version.

Consider this passage on banking from book 2, chapter 2, of *The Wealth of Nations*:

> To restrain private people, it may be said, from receiving in payment the promissory notes of a banker, for any sum whether great or small, when they themselves are willing to receive them, or to restrain a banker from issuing such notes, when all his neighbours are willing to accept of them, is a manifest violation of that natural liberty which it is the proper business of law not to infringe, but to support. Such regulations may, no doubt, be considered as in some respects a violation of natural liberty. *But those exertions of the natural liberty of a few individuals, which might endanger the security of the whole society, are, and ought to be, restrained by the laws of all governments, of the most free as well as of the most despotical. The obligation of building party walls, in order to prevent the communication of fire, is a violation of natural liberty exactly of the same kind with the regulations of the banking trade which are here proposed.*[48]

Adam Smith, the hero of capitalism, here insists on the necessity of regulating banks. (He may also be fairly read as endorsing the necessity of building codes.) His explanation is clear and simple: *Restraints on liberty are justified when the actions of a few individuals endanger the rest.*

Smith spends many pages explaining his argument for bank regulation; chapter 2 is entirely dedicated to the issue. The discussion is not merely theoretical; it is based on problems that had already arisen in the banking system. In the late eighteenth century many banks issued promissory notes as a form of currency; this system depended on the "fortune, probity, and prudence" of the banker to produce gold and silver when demanded in exchange for those notes.[49] Anticipating the modern notion of reserves, Smith allowed that the banker does not have to stockpile gold and silver in exact proportion to the notes he has issued; he need only stockpile enough to meet demand as it arises. "By this operation, therefore, twenty thousand pounds in gold and silver perform all the functions which a hundred thousand could otherwise have performed." A good thing. But it only works if the banker is honest and carries adequate reserves, which had proved to be something one could not assume.

In Smith's native Scotland in the previous twenty-five to thirty years, the number of banks issuing paper money and promissory notes had grown substantially. Many of these banks also offered lines of credit—often on "easy terms . . . of repayment"— which helped stimulate economic activity.[50] Then, as now, credit gave businesses room to maneuver.[51] The merchant in Edinburgh, where such accounts were available, could do more than a comparable merchant in London, where they were not, and the Scottish economy boomed. But many of these banks did not carry adequate reserves, and if people realized this, it could lead to a run on the banks. In a worst-case scenario, banks might collapse and depositors would go bankrupt.

There was another problem: Because paper money was of no use abroad, British merchants with excess paper were returning it to the Bank of England, which was obliged to buy gold and silver to redeem it. This drove up the price of these metals, forcing the bank to pay higher costs to make coinage of the same market value. A shilling was still a shilling, but the silver needed to make it cost more, so the bank lost money. "[T]he Scotch banks . . . paid . . . dearly for their own imprudence and inattention: but the Bank of England paid very dearly not only for its own imprudence, but for the much greater imprudence of almost all the Scotch banks."[52] Through the fault of *others*, British bankers were suffering. Scottish liberty was doing financial harm in England.

Smith stressed that he was not against banks: overall "the judicious operations of banking can increase the industry of the country."[53] The problem, he made clear, was that many bankers did not act judiciously, which leads to his conclusion: some things just need to be regulated. The proliferation of paper money in excess of reserves, for example, could be curtailed by regulating the circulation of paper to dealers (as opposed to consumers), or by limiting paper money to large denominations. (He suggests that ten pounds would be an appropriate lower limit and certainly not less than five pounds.)[54] And it is this suggestion—about restraints on the use and denominations of paper money—that leads to his acknowledgment that such restraints might be criticized as a violation of liberty.

Smith anticipated the objections that Mises, NAM, Hayek, the Mont Pelerin Society, the Chicago school, and diverse latter-day conservatives would all make: that regulations are an infringement of liberty. And so they are. Smith—the hero of libertarians, the father of free-market economics, the patron saint of self-interest— spent a significant section of his most famous work discussing banks and banking precisely *because* it illustrated an essential and nonnegligible point: *that regulations do infringe liberty, but they are necessary when the "natural liberty of a few individuals . . . endanger[s] the security of the whole society."*[55] The image of Smith as someone who insists on the comprehensive self-sufficiency and self-correcting character of markets, and the adequacy of self-interest and the profit motive in driving productive behavior, is simply incorrect.[56] Jacob Viner put it this way: "The modern advocate of laissez-faire who objects to government participation in business on the grounds that it is an encroachment upon a field reserved by nature for private enterprise cannot find support for this argument in the *Wealth of Nations.*"[57]

What does Stigler do with Smith's long, detailed, and thoughtful analysis of the need for banking regulation? Nothing. Smith's discussion of the problems of late eighteenth-century banking and the need for banking regulation is entirely omitted from Stigler's version of the volume.

The Wealth of Nations is admittedly an enormous and complicated book, and any reduction of it to barely more than one hundred pages will inescapably invite critique. But considering how central money and its relation to value is to Smith's framework, and particularly his prominent treatments of money, wealth, and value in Books I and IV, Stigler's omission of Smith's critique of paper money and crisp articulation of the necessity of banking regulation is more than a little lacuna. And considering that liberty is arguably the motivating concept in the neoliberal defense of market economics, it is astonishing that Stigler omits Smith's discussion. For Smith does not merely *acknowledge* the problem, he *solves* it. Hayek had insisted that he was not antigovernment, but merely wanted a "clear set of principles" by which to distinguish when regulation was justified. In 1776, Smith had given it; in 1957, Stigler expunged it.

BANKING IS NOT the only area in which Smith discusses the warrant for regulation. In book 1 of *The Wealth of Nations*, Smith takes up the topic of wage regulation with a degree of vigor that would surprise most contemporary readers. In a chapter entitled "Of the Wages of Labour," Smith suggests that power imbalances between workers and their masters might make it appropriate to level the playing field, particularly considering that existing laws were biased in favor of masters. Wages could be understood as a contract between two parties—whose interests "are by no means the same. The workmen desire to get as much, the masters to give as little, as possible. The former are disposed to combine in order to raise, the latter in order to lower, the wages of labour." So far so good.

The problem is that under nearly all circumstances, the masters have the advantage, because they control the workplace. Moreover, they are more likely to be able to manipulate the situation to their advantage, as "being fewer in number, [they] can combine much more easily: and the law, besides, authorizes or at least does not prohibit, their combinations, while it prohibits those of the workmen. We have no acts of Parliament against combining to lower the price of work, but many against combining to raise it." The reason is simple: the ruling classes tend to pass laws that protect their own interests. Moreover, Smith notes, in any conflict, the masters, having more assets, can hold out longer than the workers.[58] So they are multiply advantaged: by their intrinsic position, by their assets, and by the legal protections that they have granted themselves.

Even where owners don't combine formally, Smith notes, they "are always and everywhere in a sort of tacit, but constant and uniform, combination, not to raise the wages of labour" and sometimes "enter into particular combinations to sink the wages of labour." These activities typically are conducted with "the utmost silence and secrecy." On the rare occasions when workers organize to fight back, their activities "are always abundantly heard of" and often met with demands for legal action to prevent or punish them.[59] Two centuries before American conservatives, businessmen, and the Chicago school in the twentieth century decried unionization as a form of restraint on trade, Smith noted that workers were far less likely than owners to be able to manipulate the marketplace.

Could wages ever be set so low that workers would struggle to survive on them? In theory no, because in a rational system workers would reject starvation wages. But in practice they often had no alternative. Wages were sometimes so low that workers' children did starve; the situation was so bad—and so common—that laborers routinely tried to rear "at least four" children in order that two would survive. Wages also varied from year to year in ways that did not correspond to price variation, so laborers had years of plenty and years of want for reasons beyond their control, and in the latter, children perished.[60]

Smith believed many workers were better off in 1776 than previously, given the lower cost of "an agreeable and wholesome variety of food."[61] He noted that where there is high demand for labor, wages will increase sufficiently that most families will be able to rear children to adulthood. In this way, labor, no less than other commodities, would respond to the forces of supply and demand. "It is in this manner that the demand for men, like that for any other commodity, necessarily regulates the production of men.[62] This seems pretty cold-blooded, as Smith implies that infant mortality is the unavoidable (and possibly acceptable) result of the interplay of supply and demand. Yet Smith absolutely affirms that workers are entitled to a minimum standard of decency: "No society can surely be flourishing or happy, of which the far greater part of the members are poor and miserable. It is but equity, besides, that they who feed, cloath and lodge the whole body of the people, should have such a share of the produce of their own labour as to be themselves tolerably well fed, cloathed and lodged."[63] If one were not persuaded by arguments of equity, Smith offers the practical argument that well-fed workers are better workers.[64] "That men in general should work better when they are ill fed than when they are well fed, when they are disheartened than when they are in good spirits, when they are frequently sick than when they are generally in good health, seems not very probable."[65] Thus he concludes that when a *regulation, therefore, is in favour of the workmen, it is always just and equitable, but it is sometimes otherwise when in favour of the masters.*"[66]

As a result of these passages, Smith was considered to be a friend of the poor, and in the 1790s he would be invoked by British advocates of minimum wage regulation.[67] Economist Amartya Sen finds that a full reading of Smith reveals him as someone who was "deeply concerned about the inequality and poverty that might survive in an otherwise successful market economy."[68] Smith's rejection of mercantilism and defense of free trade were *not* a defense of the impoverishment of laborers or a rejection of the idea that the government might set appropriate standards for wages. What does Stigler do with this? He omits it.

STIGLER'S EDIT OF *The Wealth of Nations* also undermines a key passage on taxation and the provision of public goods. In book 5, Smith identifies four major domains that market forces might not adequately address: defense, justice, public works and institutions, and the "expense of supporting the dignity of the sovereign." Some of these can pay for themselves, as when tolls cover the costs of building and maintaining roads. Even courts of law can to some extent be financed by court fees (although, as Smith notes, that creates a significant risk of corruption). But there are definite limits to how much these activities can be made self-financing.

The clearest example—which even most libertarians accept—is the expense of a standing army. But Smith argues that the other domains, too, are "beneficial to the whole society, and may therefore, without injustice, be defrayed by the general contribution of the whole society."[69] Nor was his list exhaustive; other activities that benefit society as a whole may rightly be undertaken by governments and paid for by the public. Smith discusses various means to cover these costs—including rents from sovereign lands, and government functions that raise their own revenue, such as the post office—before working his way around to taxation. He does not oppose it, but articulates four principles, or "maxims," regarding how taxes should be applied:[70]

1. The subjects of every state ought to contribute towards the support of the government, as nearly as possible, in proportion to their respective abilities.

2. The tax which each individual is bound to pay, ought to be certain and not arbitrary. The time of payment, the manner of payment, the quantity to be paid, ought all to be clear and plain to the contributor, and to every other person.

3. Every tax ought to be levied at the time, or in the manner, in which is most likely to be convenient for the contributor to pay it.

4. Every tax ought to be so contrived, as both to take out and to keep out of the pockets of the people as little as possible, over and above which it brings into the public treasury of the state.

Smith then delves into a detailed examination of different tax policies around Europe and elsewhere. The whole discussion, running to seventy pages, conveys that while Smith is not enamored of taxes, he is by no means offering a general treatise against them, much less a polemic. For Smith, taxes are both legitimate and necessary—he just wants them to be levied in a manner that does not create undue or unfair burdens.[71]

So long as the system is fair, transparent, and certain, Smith has no problem with it being *progressive*. Indeed, he believes that "a very considerable degree of inequality . . . is not near so great an evil as a very small degree of uncertainty."[72] In essence: take what you need but no more, and do it in a civilized, consistent way. Don't be arbitrary, don't make the process vexatious, and as far as possible don't waste money on the system of taxation itself. Twenty-first-century readers who consider Smith the anti-Marx may be surprised to see Smith suggest that the appropriate way to raise revenues is by "all the different members contributing, as nearly as possible, in proportion to their abilities."[73]

Stigler is fairer to book 5 of *The Wealth of Nations* than to book 2. While the latter vanished completely, the former's 199-page argument gets twenty-six pages. Stigler follows Smith's outline dutifully—until he gets to taxation. The parts where Smith describes means of government financing *other* than taxation (such as tolls on roads and bridges or profits from government enterprises) remain, but Stigler tosses the parts where Smith concludes that some taxes are justified. And Smith's defense of progressive taxation is entirely gone. A student reading Stigler's condensation might easily get the impression that Smith believed that *all the legitimate governmental expenses could and should be self-supporting*, and that *taxation plays no valid role*.

Again, any volume as slim as Stigler's will be the result of choices, more and less defensible. But it seems fair to summarize the situation this way: Smith was a good scholar and an astute thinker who considered potential objections to his theory and even granted that some of these objections had merit. He recognized that the market alone would not attend to all of society's needs, and he provided well-reasoned frameworks for economic regulation and taxation. That Smith is missing from Stigler's volume.[74]

Stigler would have been well aware of these arguments, because they had been highlighted by his own mentor, economist Jacob Viner. In a 1927 paper inspired by the 150th anniversary of *The Wealth of Nations*, Viner had noted that in numerous instances "Smith supported government restrictions on private initiative."[75] Smith was "not a doctrinaire advocate of laissez-faire," Viner continued. "He saw a wide and elastic range of activity for government, and was prepared to extend it even farther if government, by improving its standards of competency, honesty, and public spirit, showed itself entitled to wider responsibilities."[76] Viner even wondered if Smith had not undermined his own argument "by demonstrating that the natural order, when left to take its own course, in many respects works against, instead of for, the general welfare."[77]

Viner resolves the problem by understanding *The Wealth of Nations* as "a specific attack on certain types of government activity" that operated against national prosperity, such as international trade restrictions and the apprenticeship systems that limited where and how men could work. "Smith's primary objective was to secure the termination of *these* activities of government."[78] To be sure, Smith adopted a presumption against government regulation, but that presumption could be challenged by evidence of adverse outcomes, as it was in the cases of banking transgressions and wage inequity.

There is, furthermore, an exception in Stigler's book that proves the rule: Smith's discussion of the regulation of school fees and professors' salaries. Smith clearly carried a grudge against academics, because in this discussion his otherwise temperate tone and prolix style becomes crisp and dyspeptic.[79] Professors were not only generally paid a fixed salary irrespective of the quality of their teaching, Smith complained, they were also typically shielded from competition. "Rivalship and emulation render excellency," but there was little of that in education, because schools operated as virtual monopolies in their regions and professors as monopolists in their subject.[80]

Most professors were "indolent" and "indifferent," showing up to "attend upon [their] pupils" only the set numbers of hours to which they were formally obligated. The college was set up "not for the benefit of students, but for the interest, or more properly speaking the ease, of the masters. Its object is, in all cases, to maintain the authority of the master and whether he neglects or perform his duty, to oblige the students in all cases to behave to him as if he performed it with the greatest diligence and ability."[81] Smith here assumes that most everyone is lazy and will necessarily be as "careless and slovenly" as "authority will permit."[82]

His solution to the education problem is to introduce competition into the educational environment, to highlight and condemn the factors that bind students to colleges irrespective of the quality of education being offered, and to condemn scholarships attached to particular colleges. Students should be free to go wherever is best for them, and to study with whomever they find most inspiring. Most pointedly, Smith criticizes any regulation that prohibits the members of a college from leaving and going elsewhere "without leave first asked and obtained of that which they meant to abandon."[83]

Smith defenders might note that this particular discussion is scarcely central to the overall thesis of the book, but that is just the point. This ill-tempered portion, frankly peripheral to Smith's major concerns, is one that Stigler includes. Indeed, the *only* appearance of the word *regulation* in Stigler's version of *The Wealth of Nations* is a hellish one, where students are prisoners of the academic institutions they attend, stuck in classrooms with boring and pretentious dons and no means to escape.[84] In short, Stigler preserves a discussion that is peripheral to Smith's main thesis but in which regulation is detrimental, while excising several much more important passages in which Smith frames regulation as potentially beneficial or even essential.

STIGLER'S EDITED VOLUME was published in a series presenting great works with little or no historical context. But it is odd that a scholar known for his interest in the history of economic thought would make scant effort—in this book and elsewhere—to situate Smith in the intellectual climate of his times.[85] This may not be an accident, for when one places Smith in context, one must acknowledge that he was no conservative, and certainly no libertarian.

As historian Emma Rothschild has noted, in his day Smith was considered a politically seditious radical, reviled by conservatives such as Edmund Burke.[86] Many scholars point out that in Smith's "other" book, *The Theory of Moral Sentiments*, published in 1759, he argues that self-interest is but one part of our instinctual apparatus; another equally important part is our capacity for empathy.[87]

Morality is rooted in concern for others, which is as much a part of our nature as self-interest is. To understand Smith's philosophy as a whole is to understand how we counterbalance self-interest in economic activities with morality in guiding society.[88] Yet this is precisely what Stigler and his Free Market Project colleagues failed—or refused—to do. Nor did they account for how it was that Smith went from being reviled by conservatives to being beatified by them.

Amartya Sen offers perhaps the best evidence that Smith was not the ideologue the Chicago school made him out to be. A few years before Smith died, Sen remarks, philosopher Jeremy Bentham complained that Smith had failed to adequately appreciate the *benefits of markets*! (Among other criticisms, Bentham singled out Smith's discussion of banking regulation.)[89] Economist Craig Freedman has dryly concluded that Stigler "reduced Smith's economics to fit a pattern contiguous with his own views."[90]

Stigler was not alone in constructing out of Smith "a mouthpiece for the unalloyed virtues of the market." According to Sen, Smith's makeover as "an uncomplicated champion of pure market-based capitalism" was already well under way in the nineteenth century.[91] But it was in the twentieth century that he was "canonized," and the Chicago school—underwritten by Luhnow and the Volker Fund—played a major role.[92]

In 1935, when arguing against the New Deal, Henry Simons had said that what his generation needed more than anything, "especially the so-called brain-trust," was an understanding of Adam Smith.[93] Two decades later, George Stigler would make it easy for anyone to read Smith, but harder to understand him. The reader of Stigler's Smith would get little sense of Smith's concern for those who markets failed to serve, of the need for regulation when self-interest impeded the common good, or the rather wide space Smith found for government activity. What the reader would get was a stick-figure version of Adam Smith saying everything could be left to self-interest and government plays no useful role.

How much impact did Stigler's presentation have? The likely answer is *a lot*. Croft Classics published his edited volume in a small, inexpensive edition intended for teaching. Large numbers of American students and their teachers probably encountered Smith through Stigler's version of him. And students reading only this version of Smith would never have known that he offered—again in the words of Sen—"a balanced argument for supporting a society with multiple institutions in which the market would play its part without being hostile to the important role of other institutions, including those of the state."[94] Perhaps most important for conservatives (or anyone, really), they would not know that Smith had, *avant la lettre*, offered a solution to the problem that vexed Hayek and is at the root of all questions of democratic governance: how to decide when infringements on liberty are warranted and when they are not.[95]

ACCORDING TO THE terms of the Free Market Project, Aaron Director was to take the lead on producing the American *Road to Freedom*. He never did.[96] Nor did Hayek, who went on to write about other things and in 1962 returned to Europe. Director became the head of a different initiative: the Antitrust Project. The title was misleading, for its focus was anti-antitrust: Director and his students argued against the need for antitrust regulation and enforcement. Discarding other possibilities or considerations, they started from the premise that "the existing structure is the efficient structure."[97] Director's arguments would play a leading role not only in the development of arguments for deregulating monopolies such as airlines and telecommunications in the 1970s and '80s, but in undermining antitrust enforcement in the United States entirely.

As an undergraduate at Yale, Director had come to believe that the "public" were too stupid to make good decisions, a belief he shared with Rose Wilder Lane, J. Howard Pew, and other antidemocratic conservatives. But unlike them, Director became a highly educated economist and was able to merge his antidemocratic orientation with a sophisticated defense of markets as a better venue for decision-making than the voting booth. This view would greatly influence George Stigler and Milton Friedman. By 1953, Director had taken the lead of the Antitrust Project, which continued through 1957. His commitment to free-market ideals was so absolute that students described it as a religious faith, his persuasion of them akin to religious conversion.[98]

Historian Dieter Plehwe characterizes the tenor of the Antitrust Project as a "corporations can do no wrong" perspective. That may go too far, but Plehwe is right to highlight that, for all its glorification of competitive capitalism, the Chicago school was oddly sympathetic to private monopoly. And as he suggests, Antitrust Project writings often read as apologia for corporate America.

By definition a monopoly is anticompetitive, and in the late nineteenth and early twentieth centuries monopolies were widely seen as a threat to democracy as

well as to capitalism. That was a major motivation for the passage of the Sherman
and Clayton antitrust acts in 1890 and 1914, respectively. But members of the
Antitrust Project, particularly Friedman and Director, generally saw "unregulated
private monopoly [as] relatively benign phenomenon." These men warned gravely of
the risks of concentrated public power in the form of "the state," but were perfectly
comfortable with concentrations of private power in corporations.[99] There was only
one federal government, they reasoned, but there were many corporations, so no
one corporation could ever wield the singular power that the government could. Or
so they claimed. But where did the evidence for this view come from? Certainly not
from American history, so perhaps that is why the Chicago economists repeatedly
misrepresented it.

Director's most famous student was Robert Bork, known today mainly for being
rejected by the U.S. Senate to serve on the Supreme Court, after Ronald Reagan
nominated him in 1987 to replace the retiring Lewis Powell. (The seat would ultimately be filled by Anthony Kennedy.) But Bork should really be remembered for
his role in undermining the structure of American antitrust jurisprudence.[100]

Bork studied at Chicago with Director, and both men would participate in
archconservative Barry Goldwater's 1964 presidential campaign.[101] Bork then
taught at Yale Law School, served as solicitor general under Richard Nixon, and
then as the American Enterprise Institute's director of legal research before being
appointed by Ronald Reagan to the federal bench in 1982. During the Watergate
crisis, Bork also briefly served as acting U.S. attorney general. After two superiors
resigned rather than fire the special prosecutor, Archibald Cox, Bork fired Cox.
Bork claimed that, in gratitude, Nixon promised him a Supreme Court nomination. That opportunity never arose, but when Reagan had the chance, he nominated
him.[102] The contentious confirmation hearings focused on Bork's position that the
Constitution recognized no right to privacy, but Bork's career had been built on the
argument against antitrust enforcement that he developed under Director.

Both classical and neoclassical economics saw competition as central to the workings of markets. Director and Bork departed radically from that view. Constructing an
economic analogue to Darwin's theory of natural selection, Director would argue that
monopolies were often the appropriate outcome of competition, in which the "best"
company survived. Government attempts to break up monopolies were therefore
undoing the work that competition had done. It was misguided to think the existence
of a monopoly proved that anything had gone wrong. Bork would add to this

argument by suggesting that what mattered was not competition, but *price*. So long as prices were low, it didn't matter how they were achieved.[103]

This became known as the Consumer Welfare Standard, although the term is misleading, since prices are not the only thing that matters to consumers, and the term appears nowhere in any antitrust statute.[104] Bork came to his views by misrepresenting (or at least misreading) the history of the nation's antitrust statutes and ignoring the concern that motivated their passage: the concentration of corporate power. In a 1966 review published by the University of Chicago's *Journal of Law and Economics*, Bork argued that the Sherman Anti-Trust Act had been aimed only at fostering lower prices for consumers.[105] Bork was a brilliant jurist, and the paper was well written and smartly argued. Indeed, it was so brilliant that many people believed it, even though it was false.[106]

A little more than a year earlier, the great American historian Richard Hofstadter had reviewed this history, reminding readers that Congress had had three goals in passing the Sherman Anti-Trust Act: one, an economic goal of fostering competition; two, a political goal "to block private accumulations of power and protect democratic government;" and three, a social goal built on the belief that competition built moral character.[107] The act's sponsor, Republican senator John Sherman of Ohio, had been clear on these points. Although the Senate was a conservative body, Sherman noted, "it has always been ready to preserve, not only popular rights in their broad sense, but the rights of individuals as against associated and *corporate wealth and power*."[108] Sherman elaborated: "The popular mind is agitated with problems that may disturb social order, and among them all none is more threatening than the inequality of condition, of wealth, and opportunity that has grown within a single generation out of the concentration of capital into vast combinations to control production and trade and to break down competition."[109] These concentrations of power threatened to confer kingly prerogatives, which undermined the very basis of democracy. "If we will not endure a king as a political power, we should not endure a king over the production, transportation, and sale of any of the necessities of life," he declared.[110] This was not a theoretical argument; concentrated private power had become a threat to American values, American democracy, and the American way of life—not to mention American capitalism itself.[111] Congress used its appropriate legislative power to combat the growth of corrosive private power. The Sherman Anti-Trust Act thus empowered the federal government to break up concentrations of private power.

In its early years judicial interpretations of the act led to its being used mostly against unions—clearly not Sherman's intent—but that changed under the "trust-busting" administration of Theodore Roosevelt, and with the passage in 1914 of the Clayton Antitrust Act, which further specified which sorts of illegal activities were at issue. Also in 1914 came the creation of the Federal Trade Commission, authorized to investigate, identify, and forbid anticompetitive practices.

The intent of these acts was clear: to prevent corporations or other private groups from undermining capitalism by undermining competition, but also, and crucially, to prevent them from undermining democracy. As legal scholar Timothy Wu puts it, "antitrust represented a democratic choice of economic structure and a check on the political and economic power of the monopolies."[112]

Under Teddy Roosevelt and his successor, William Howard Taft, the federal government prosecuted several corporations, most famously Standard Oil. But within a few decades, the Chicago school was turning the facts of history on their head, arguing that state power was the real threat, both to democracy and to capitalism. They made this case in part by insisting that monopolies were not necessarily bad. Milton Friedman would argue that "the great threat to freedom is the concentration of power," but not all forms of power concentration alarmed him equally. Like Director, he was vexed by state power and conspicuously comfortable with corporate power.[113] Friedman cavalierly swept monopolies aside as mere market "imperfections," and as typically better than the alternatives. Where monopolies did arise, he saw them as products not of corporate malfeasance, venality, or greed, but of bad governance.[114] Friedman was complacent about corporate power, if not downright sympathetic to it; Bork took this sympathy and ran with it.

Ignoring the actual history of antitrust legislation, Bork elided concerns about inequality, private power, and the defense of democracy and told a story in which Congress had limited itself to concerns about "consumer welfare," defined solely in terms of short-run prices. Quoting Wu again: "Robert Bork's attack on antitrust was really laissez-faire reincarnated . . . with a slightly less overt worship of monopoly—but with much the same results."[115] It would fall to Milton Friedman to complete the reincarnation.

CHAPTER 10

The American *Road to Serfdom*

If market fundamentalism were a scientific theory, by the early 1960s it would have been viewed as refuted.[1] The European experience disproved its central premise—that compromises to economic freedom would necessarily compromise political freedom. European social democracies had taken steps toward what was increasingly called "the mixed economy," in which many markets were largely private, others were regulated to some degree or run as natural monopolies, and some industries were fully nationalized. At the same time, these countries—France, Germany, Belgium, the Netherlands, and the Nordic nations—had strengthened their democracies as they emerged from the rubble of World War II. Germany had recovered from the Nazi catastrophe with a system of *soziale Marktwirtschaft*— literally "social market economy," sometimes called "social capitalism"—which combined a market-based capitalist economy with government policies to protect competition alongside a generous welfare state. The Scandinavian countries had built particularly robust welfare states, with ample provisions for education, health, unemployment insurance, retirement, housing, childcare, and more. The United Kingdom largely recovered from rationing and other war traumas and experienced considerable economic success, while also creating its expansive National Health Service.[2] In Britain, university tuition was not only free, but qualified students were *paid* to attend (a benefit that persisted until it was phased out by Margaret Thatcher).

Social democracy was the middle way whose existence both Mises and Hayek denied. Their followers might say it was too soon to tell—that these nations might yet slip into tyranny—but the available evidence showed social democracies moving in the direction of more political freedom, not less.

The market fundamentalists doubled down. While social democracy thrived overseas, Chicago school economist Milton Friedman released *Capitalism and*

Freedom, the most full-throated articulation and defense of the indivisibility thesis yet penned, and the one that would become most influential.

FIRST PUBLISHED IN 1962, *Capitalism and Freedom* would sell more than half a million copies, see numerous editions, be translated into eighteen languages, and be accessible to just the audience that Harold Luhnow and Jasper Crane had envisaged. The Foundation for Economic Education (FEE) has described the book (evidently without irony) as "much more accessible to intelligent undergraduates than Hayek's, which was intentionally addressed to intellectuals." Friedman, says FEE, was "the best communicator of the political-economic ideas of the classical liberal tradition of the last century."[3] (FEE did much to promote him and his book.)

Capitalism and Freedom appears on virtually every list of conservatives' top one hundred or even top ten books, but its impact has been wide and deep. It was named a top-one-hundred book by *Time* magazine, the *Times Literary Supplement* (London), and others. Friedman would become not only the most influential economist of his generation, but one of the most influential public intellectuals. In 1966, he became a regular columnist for *Newsweek*, and he would go on to write hundreds of opinion pieces for mass media.[4] In the 1970s, he spoke frequently in London at the Institute of Economic Affairs, where he was credited with shaping Thatcher's policies, which in turn influenced Ronald Reagan; Friedman became an adviser to both leaders. (He also advised Chilean economists affiliated with the dictator Augusto Pinochet.)[5] In 1976, he would be awarded the Nobel Memorial Prize in Economic Sciences. In the 1980s, he had his own television program, *Free to Choose*, a ten-part series produced by the Public Broadcasting Service. (Rose Director Friedman co-authored the companion book.) And he had the rare distinction of earning both the National Medal of Science and the Presidential Medal of Freedom, awarded to him by President Reagan.

Who supported the work that became Friedman's most significant book? In the preface to *Capitalism and Freedom*, he says it was based partly on lectures he gave at "Volker conferences" at Claremont College, the University of North Carolina, and Oklahoma State—as in the Volker Fund, run by Harold Luhnow. The preface implies that any connection to the Volker Fund was incidental, but in later years Friedman would describe Volker support as "extremely significant." As for the Free Market Project and Luhnow himself, the book mentions neither directly.[6]

In the first chapter Friedman does acknowledge the role of rich men's money in advancing his work. In fact, he celebrates it. Under socialism, he alleges, all opposing views are crushed, but under capitalism anyone with money can support whatever ideas suit them—including outlier ones—and so influence society. Rather than see this as a problem requiring redress—that philanthropy is a game of winners where wealthy individuals buy outsized influence while common folks struggle to make their voices heard—Friedman embraces it as a *benefit* of inequality:

> One feature of a free society is surely the freedom of individuals to advocate and propagandize openly for radical change in the structure of society. [But for] advocacy of capitalism to mean anything, the proponents must be able to finance their cause . . . Radical movements in capitalist societies . . . have typically been supported by a few wealthy individuals . . . This is a role of inequality in wealth in preserving political freedom that is seldom noted.[7]

In a capitalist society, "it is only necessary to convince a few wealthy people to get funds to launch any idea, however strange."[8] In this manner, "a free market capitalist society fosters freedom."[9]

It is hard not to read Henry Hazlitt, J. Howard Pew, Jasper Crane, and Harold Luhnow into these passages: a few individuals who used their wealth to "advocate and propagandize openly for radical change in the structure of society." To most Americans at the time, these ideas were strange indeed, discredited by the experience of the Great Depression and the success of the New Deal. But with the help of the Chicago school, and particularly Friedman, these strange ideas would be normalized.

No doubt Friedman saw wealth inequality as a benefit because it had been a benefit to *him*. After all, he had convinced a few deep-pocketed men to support him. But Friedman had mastered the art of making a self-serving argument appear principled; he insisted that in a capitalist society, *any* individual could find a way to have a voice. In reality, however, ideas that failed to appeal to the wealthy would often fail to find support.

It's an old socialist joke that capitalist societies run on the golden rule: he who has the gold makes the rules. What Friedman added was that the man with the gold could pay clever people—like himself—to defend those rules with all their strength. Hayek had recognized this problem in 1956, when he explained why he did not consider himself a conservative: "A conservative movement, by its very nature, is bound to be a defender of established privilege and to lean on the power of government for the protection of privilege."[10] Adam Smith had made a similar argument explaining why workers were generally disadvantaged relative to their masters. But in Friedman's vision, this was not a problem at all, because the wealthy would defend freedom. In theory, anyone could be a benefactor to men of ideas, but in practice only the wealthy were positioned to do so. In this and many other ways that Friedman would rarely acknowledge, the rich are a good deal freer than the poor. Nothing in unregulated capitalism is a level playing field.[11] As Anatole France put it, "the law in its majestic equality forbids rich and poor alike from sleeping under bridges."[12]

To be sure, Harold Luhnow didn't tell Friedman (or Stigler or Simons or Hayek) what to think; he didn't *pay* them to hold the views they did. Nor did Henry Hazlitt pay Ludwig von Mises. Patronage doesn't generally work that way.[13] It's rather that patrons find people whose views they like, then support and sustain them. Aaron Director had argued that monopolies were the companies that outcompeted the others, ignoring the anticompetitive practices those businesses often used to achieve their dominance. Similarly, Friedman thought of philanthropy as a form of economic natural selection—except there was nothing particularly "natural" about it. The marketplace of ideas was not free: it was very expensive. The rich could buy the ideas that they wanted, and an awful lot was for sale at the Chicago school.

CAPITALISM AND FREEDOM begins with a restatement of Hayek: that "the great threat to freedom is the concentration of power."[14] But not just any concentration of power. What worries Friedman is government, because governments (he argues) can become all-powerful in a way that individuals, families, or corporations cannot. Happily, there is a solution to this threat: the economic system we call capitalism. Like Hayek before him, Friedman argues that capitalism is a bulwark against tyranny, because the market distributes power among many hands and prevents its concentration in government. As his title suggests, capitalism and freedom are two sides of one coin, and his central object is the inextricable link between them (and, conversely, between socialism and subjugation). In the words of one reviewer, each specific problem in the book was "deduced from a general formulation that the most important thing in the world is 'freedom' [which in] turn . . . is said to depend above all upon limiting the functions of government as closely as possible."[15]

Friedman's "major theme" is "the role of competitive capitalism—the organization of the bulk of economic activity through private enterprise operating in a free market—as a system of economic freedom and a necessary condition for political freedom." His "minor theme is the role that government should play in a society dedicated to freedom and relying primarily on the market to organize economic activity."[16] And that role is tightly circumscribed. Rather than focus on socialism—or rather communism, but labeled socialism—as Hayek did, Friedman focuses on the threat that government, per se, poses to freedom. Friedman sees government not as a means to ensure the blessings of liberty but as a clear and present danger to them.

Friedman situates himself in the tradition of classical liberalism, which emphasizes, in his words, "freedom as the ultimate goal and the individual as the ultimate entity in society."[17] But where classical liberals centered political and civic freedom—or freedom of thought and association—Friedman insists on the primacy of economic freedom, because without that, all other freedoms will soon be lost. He views the organized pursuit of happiness, welfare, equality, or security as subservient to freedom, and even in conflict with it.

Departing from the long history of philosophy, religion, and sociology, Friedman surmises that the basic problem of human organization is not moral or social but economic: "how to co-ordinate the economic activities of large numbers of people."[18] He recognizes that people are interdependent, and that any society has to "reconcile this widespread interdependence with individual freedom": neoliberalism does not mean cars get to drive in any direction.[19] But Friedman views the problem in black-and-white terms, and like Mises and Hayek before him perpetuates the fallacy of the excluded middle: "Fundamentally, there are only two ways of coordinating the economic activities of millions," he proclaims. "One is central direction involving the use of coercion—the technique of . . . the modern totalitarian state. The other is voluntary co-operation of individuals—the technique of the market place."[20] Markets spread power around rather than consolidating it in the state apparatus. "By removing the organization of economic activity from the control of political authority, the market eliminates this source of coercive power. It enables economic strength to be a check to political power rather than a reinforcement."[21]

One can see the merit of this point, but still reject its Manichaean framing. In Friedman's dualistic vision, either the government organizes (nearly) all activity or (nearly) everything is left to the invisible hand. The idea of social democracy or even well-regulated capitalism is not taken seriously. As he puts it, "A society which is socialist cannot also be democratic."[22]

Friedman rejects what he sees as the prevailing intellectual view that "the material aspects of life" are less important than certain "higher values"—by which he presumably means political, social, religious, and civic freedom. For him, the value of economic freedom is twofold: indirect, in preserving political freedom, and direct, in permitting citizens their right to do as they please. The latter is just as important as the former. Friedman invites the reader to imagine a citizen of the United Kingdom who cannot act on his desire to vacation in the United States because of currency controls that restrict his access to American dollars. That British citizen is "denied of an essential freedom no less than the citizen of the United States who was denied the opportunity to spend his vacation in Russia."[23]

This is why Friedman hates taxes, which he views not as a necessary function of government in supporting public goods—as Adam Smith did—but as the denial of the individual's right to spend his money as he sees fit. Likewise, Friedman opposes all compulsory insurance and retirement schemes, including Social Security. "The citizen of the United States who is compelled by law to devote something like 10 per cent of his income to the purchase of a particular kind of retirement contract, administered by the government, is being deprived of . . . part of his personal freedom."[24] He similarly opposes licenses, fair-trade laws, and farm quotas. In Friedman's worldview, medical licensing is not a reasonable means to protect patients; it is an unfair usurpation of the doctor's right to practice his chosen profession, a deprivation of "an essential part of his freedom."[25] And, like Hayek and NAM and J. Howard Pew, Friedman explicitly advances the indivisibility thesis. "The kind of economic organization that provides economic freedom directly, namely competitive capitalism, also promotes political freedom because it separates economic power from political power and in this way enables one to offset the other."[26] In the preface to the 2002 edition he goes further, making the thesis into a historical claim: "Competitive capitalism and freedom have been inseparable."[27] For Friedman, capitalism and freedom go hand in hand, they always have, and they always will.

ONE OF THE mysteries of *Capitalism and Freedom* is how a man who believed economics should be a "positive" science could make so many claims that are immune to empirical confirmation or refutation. The answer may be that many of Friedman's themes are not a matter of what is true or false, but a matter of world-view, a worldview that valorizes individual freedom above all else. Put another way: in contrast to the American founding fathers, who put life before liberty, Friedman's radical individualism puts liberty before life.

Liberty, for Friedman, is individuals deciding for themselves what they want. There is no whole greater than the sum of its parts; the "nation" and "society" are theoretical abstractions. He wrote,

> To the free man the country is the collection of individuals who compose it, not something over and above them ... [He] will ask neither what his country can do for him nor what he can do for his country. He will ask rather "What can I and my compatriots do through government" to help us discharge our individual responsibilities, to achieve our several purposes, and, above all, to protect our freedom? And he will accompany this question with another: How can we keep the government we create from becoming a Frankenstein that will destroy the very freedom we establish it to protect?[28]

This claim about the relationship between nation and citizen is neither true nor false; it is an opinion, a point of view that anyone who has served in the military—or honored those who have died for their country—could easily reject.

Because government is a threat to liberty, Friedman would rather it be decentralized. Dispersed power can be escaped: "If I do not like what my state does I can move to another. If I do not like what Washington imposes, I have few alternatives in this world of jealous nations," he writes.[29] The best government is therefore the most local. The great mistake of twentieth-century progressives was to believe that "power should be located in favor of the state instead of the city, of the federal government instead of the state, and of a world organization instead of a national government."[30]

The Dutch have a term for this: *machtsafstand*, generally translated into English as "power distance." (This leads to the concept of power distance index, a measure of the degree to which people without power accept and expect that power is distributed unequally, and thus one way to measure inequality and its social effects.) The concept of power distance suggests, as Friedman argues, that local governments may be more aware of, and therefore more responsive to, local citizens. But Friedman goes much further. He sees markets as an *alternative* to government. The first substantive chapter of *Capitalism and Freedom* is entitled "The Role of Government in a Free Society," but by the third paragraph, Friedman is discussing markets. In his view, they govern the world—or should, at least, because they create choice, while state power destroys it.

Governments demand yes-or-no answers, and enforce them. The number of separate groups or preferences that can practically be represented "is narrowly limited, enormously so by comparison with the proportional representation of the markets."[31] For Friedman, markets are more democratic than even ostensibly democratic government, so we should look to markets to solve our problems. The best government is the one that governs least, most locally, and with most deference to the marketplace.

In fairness, Friedman is not opposed to government, per se. "The existence of a free market does not of course eliminate the need for government," he writes. On the contrary, government is essential both as a forum for determining the "rules of the game" and as an umpire to interpret and enforce the rules. But what the market achieves "is to reduce greatly the range of issues that must be decided on through political means," and thereby foster wide diversity in people's life choices. The market is, in "political terms, a system of proportional representation. Each man can vote, as it were, for the color of the tie he wants and get it; he does not have to see what color the majority wants and then, if he is in the minority, submit."[32] This in turn encourages social harmony: "The widespread use of the market reduces the strain on the social fabric by rendering conformity unnecessary with respect to any activities it encompasses."[33] There is no limit, at least in principle, to the options the marketplace can offer us.

Friedman allows (albeit begrudgingly) that some matters cannot be handled well—or at all—by markets. "Absolute freedom is impossible,"[34] he acknowledges; we need laws—for example, against murder and theft. But in a revealing line, he notes that "however attractive anarchy may be as a philosophy, it is not feasible in a world of imperfect men." Like Rose Wilder Lane's, Friedman's ideal government would come as close to anarchy as the imperfection of men allows.[35] The problem, as political philosophers have long noted, is that freedoms conflict, and when they do, "one man's freedom must be limited to preserve another—as a Supreme Court justice once put it, 'My freedom to move my fist must be limited by the proximity of your chin.'"[36] Friedman does acknowledge this.

But the reader eager for a nuanced answer to the problem of competing freedoms will be left hungry. Friedman deals with it through one example—murder—which he agrees must not be allowed, and then moves on quickly to his real interest, economic freedom. There, he finds, the central problem is defining "free enterprise"—whether it means the freedom to set up an enterprise and compete in the marketplace, or includes the freedom to fix prices and keep out others. This is related to the definition of property rights. How far do my rights go when I own property? Do they allow me to prevent someone from flying an airplane over my backyard? Or to demand that he pay for the privilege to do so? Could he demand that I pay him for refraining? In Friedman's view, firm lines must be drawn to contain this slipperiness: "a well specified and generally accepted definition of property is far more important than just what the definition is."[37] The most important goal of government is to define the meaning of property rights, and then enforce that definition.

Any system that privileges property will inevitably privilege the rich, but if this bothers Friedman, it doesn't detain him. As for workers, the manager's "freedom" to exploit them is not discussed, only the "particularly acute" problem of labor unions, which juxtaposes the "freedom to combine and freedom to compete." It is striking that Friedman's discussion of competing freedoms—arguably *the* most important question of social organization in a democracy—lasts all of two paragraphs. Then he is on to the government's role in issuing currency, finally concluding that the only real role for government is "the maintenance of law and order . . . the enforcement of contracts voluntarily entered into, the definition of the meaning of property rights, the interpretation and enforcement of such rights, and the provision of a monetary framework."[38] Environmental stewardship, workplace safety, fair-labor practices, preventing fraud in banking or other sectors, public health, the enforcement of voting rights, or even the protection of competitive markets (for example, through antitrust statutes) do not appear.[39]

While Friedman's list of what governments should do is very brief, his list of what they should not do is long and yet still "far from comprehensive." It includes minimum wage laws, rent control, regulation of radio and television, public schools, public housing, subsidized mortgages backed by the federal government, national parks, toll roads (unless private), and—perhaps most significant, revealing his extremism relative to Smith and Hayek—Social Security and any other form of public pension program. He would also eliminate military conscription and banking regulation.[40]

Though enforcing the "rules of the game" could be understood to include combating monopolistic or other anticompetitive practices, preventing pollution, or a host of other things, Friedman is emphatic that it does not. He addresses this under the category of things that could "conceivably be done through the market but [are] difficult to do that way," because "strictly voluntary exchange is either exceedingly costly or practically impossible." He divides these into two classes: monopoly and other market "imperfections," and what most economists would call "external costs" (but Friedman labels "neighborhood effects"). His response to these problems is that, while they may be real, any government intervention to address them is likely to be a cure worse than the disease. The net result of this vision, in the words of historians Robert van Horn and Philip Mirowski, is that the role of government is "reduced to a skeleton."[41]

Monopolies are a potential stumbling block for Friedman, as they deny the very volunteerism that makes markets guarantors of freedom. Anticompetitive practices deny actors their freedom to enter the marketplace, and they remove consumer choice. Friedman admits this is bad, but he blames the situation on *government*, insisting that most cases of private monopoly result from government action of one form or another. The solution is to avoid government involvement in the market in the first place. In rare cases of true collusion, existing antitrust statutes may need to be enforced, but Friedman doubts that true collusion occurs very often, if ever. Like Aaron Director, he assumes that monopolies earned their position through their superior performance.

Other economists might point to natural monopoly as a market "imperfection": a situation in which competition is either impossible or likely to be grossly inefficient, such as electricity and telephone service. Friedman rejects the term "natural monopoly"—he prefers to call them "technical monopolies"—and argues that there are three types: private monopoly, public monopoly, or public regulation. "All three are bad," he declares, "so we must choose among evils." Here, Friedman appeals to the authority of Chicago school progenitor Henry Simons—who in earlier work concluded that public regulation was the worst option—and the German economist Walter Eucken, who came down hardest against public monopoly. That left only private monopoly, which Friedman endorses on the grounds that "public regulation and public monopoly are likely to be less responsive" to changing conditions.[42]

Friedman had a point about the historic rigidity of regulatory structures. Times had certainly changed since railroads were first regulated in the nineteenth century, yet many old rules were still in place. (President Jimmy Carter's administration would soon deregulate railroads, along with trucking and aviation.) Less defensible was Friedman's discussion of "neighborhood effects"—a misleading euphemism for pollution.

Friedman defines neighborhood effects as circumstances where "the actions of individuals have effects on other individuals for which it is not feasible to charge or recompense them ... An obvious example is the pollution of a stream." Friedman's use of the idiosyncratic and friendly term *neighborhood* effect—rather than more common negative terms such as *external costs*, *negative externalities*, *damages*, and *nuisance*—signals his attitude. While recognizing these effects are real, he brushes them off, reasoning that because they are hard to quantify and impossible to remedy without infringing someone's freedom, in most cases they should be tolerated. Because freedom is paramount, the potential benefit that comes from addressing pollution (or other external cost) is likely to be incommensurate with the cost of the loss of freedom.

> It is hard to know when neighborhood effects are sufficiently large to justify particular costs in overcoming them and even harder to distribute the costs in an appropriate fashion. Consequently, when government engages in activities to overcome neighborhood effects, it will in part introduce an additional set of neighborhood effects by failing to charge or to compensate individuals properly. Whether the original or the new neighborhood effects are the more serious can only be judged by the facts of the individual case, and even then, only very approximately. Furthermore, the use of government to overcome neighborhood effects itself has an extremely important neighborhood effect which is unrelated to the particular occasion for government action. Every act of government intervention limits the area of individual freedom directly and threatens the preservation of freedom [overall] ... *[Therefore,] we shall always want to enter on the liability side of any proposed government intervention, its neighborhood effect in threatening freedom, and give this effect considerable weight.*[43]

Friedman insists as *a matter of principle* that the benefits of addressing external costs, such as pollution, have to be weighed not only against the monetary costs imposed on the polluter, such as installing scrubbers on smokestacks, but also the loss of freedom to the polluter and the cost of chipping away of freedom, overall. And this last effect he wants to give "considerable weight," even though, unlike the disease burden of pollution, for example, it cannot be measured. In truth, it cannot even be proven to occur.

And what exactly is the "freedom" that is being lost, in the case of pollution? Friedman's position seems to imply that if pollution arises from my use of my property, it is part of my property rights, and therefore I have an implicit right to pollute. Should we consider pollution a *right*? Does an air pollution regulation deny a manufacturer his "freedom" to dump garbage into the atmosphere? Does a water pollution statute deny his "right" to release toxic chemicals into a lake or river?

Friedman's answer is yes: if I own a factory, then my right to operate it as I see fit encompasses the right to pollute, and that right is "extremely important" and has to be given "considerable weight."[44] Limiting this right *might* be justifiable if we could document, definitively, the local harms, if we could precisely quantify those harms and show how they are distributed, and if we could prove that government action would redress them. Typically, however, that cannot be done—at least not to Friedman's satisfaction—so we are left to conclude that an indefinite benefit of government action must be weighed against a definite loss of freedom, with the definite loss dominating the calculus.

It is true that some environmental values—like peace and quiet—are hard to quantify, and environmental control devices—like industrial chimney scrubbers—do cost money. But notice the asymmetry: the loss of freedom is taken as given, but the harm to health or well-being or damage to *other* people's property must be proved and quantified. (Friedman does not even consider losses imposed on plants and non-human animals.) The child whose asthma was probably (but not positively) caused by local air pollution necessarily has a weaker case than the factory owner who would not merely incur monetary costs should government regulation force him to clean up his act but also lose a portion of his freedom. The smoker who died of lung cancer has a weaker case than the cigarette manufacturer. The default assumption is always against regulation.

And there is a second asymmetry: the child who has died from pulmonary disease has lost her freedom too—as have the citizens who have lost their ability to breath fresh air or swim in an unpolluted lake—but their losses go unaccounted.

This combination of foregrounding the difficulty of assessing external costs and privileging property rights results in Friedman's essentially shielding polluters from responsibility for the harms of their activities. And since polluters typically hold positions of privilege, it becomes a powerful form of status quo bias. The thumb on the scales will almost always favor the polluter who stands to lose his "freedom," and not the victim of that pollution, whose well-being— because it is hard to pin down and typically not tied to specific property rights—is not as "considerable."[45] No wonder conservatives constantly harp on the uncertainties in environmental science: in this framework, uncertainty always mitigates against action.

FRIEDMAN'S ARGUMENTS ABOUT concentration of power and benefits of markets have some force. The book is powerfully written, its prose admirably direct, and, as Crane and Luhnow had hoped, it spoke in a register that made sense to an American audience with examples drawn neither from Soviet Russia nor Nazi Germany but from American public schools, toll roads, and national parks. But there are also some glaring problems and lacunae. The most obvious, as Van Horn and Mirowski stress, is that economic freedom becomes not a means to an end but an end in itself.[46] Friedman claims to be advancing a view that respects individual desire, but in reality what most people want above all is *not* economic freedom. As Thomas Jefferson suggested, what people need first and foremost is life, for without life there is no liberty and no pursuit of happiness. To the extent that economic freedom supports the pursuit of happiness, then it makes sense to valorize and protect it. But to prioritize it *over* happiness—as well as health, well-being, justice, equity, tranquility, and all the other values that Friedman declares secondary—flies in the face of everything we know about human desire. In fact, it's worse than that: given that pollution kills, Friedman's vision of economic freedom can cost some people their lives.[47]

Since Plato (and maybe before), politics has been understood as a means for people to achieve their ends. But for Friedman, politics is appropriate only for dealing with matters that *markets cannot solve*. Government becomes so skeletonized as to be in many respects *unable* to act even when warranted, thus—in a self-fulfilling prophecy—confirming Friedman's belief in its inefficacy.[48] Moreover, while Friedman cites many examples of failures of governance, he brushes aside market failures as inconsequential.

Perhaps the underlying problem is that Friedman holds to a utopian vision of rational, voluntary cooperation: in the marketplace, I buy from you if and only if I want to, and you do the same in selling. "The possibility of co-ordination through voluntary cooperation rests on the elementary—yet frequently denied—proposition that both parties to an economic transaction benefit from it, *provided the transaction is bi-laterally voluntary and informed*," he professes.[49] But this is precisely the problem of pollution, workplace injury, and all the other adverse outcomes that Friedman dismisses as "neighborhood effects": they are rarely entirely voluntary and typically are not fully informed (and sometimes not informed at all).

By definition, negative externalities are "external" to the transaction: the affected people are bystanders who did not agree to the transaction or perhaps did not even know it was taking place. Or, they were participants, but did not know that the effects at issue might occur or did not have the power to demand appropriate advance compensation. Few people willingly agree to be hurt by a dangerous drug, killed by an unsafe consumer product, or have their communities seriously polluted. The assumption of volunteerism flies in the face of facts, especially when companies hide evidence of their products' risks; when these products' adverse effects are evident only after the fact; or when citizens' objections are overruled by people with greater power (often on the grounds of the property rights that Friedman invokes). The assumption of free choice is also dubious: it has long been true that many workers accept jobs in dangerous trades because there are few if any alternatives. Friedman is right that governments often fail to live up to their ideals and their interventions may fail to achieve their intended results, but he is wrong in refusing to acknowledge that markets fail to live up to their ideals and fail to achieve their intended results.

Consider his treatment of discrimination. Friedman allows that discrimination is wrong, but he dismisses it as inconsequential on the grounds that people can get other jobs. At the time that he was writing, however, Jim Crow segregation prevailed in a large part of America, and across the country women, African Americans, and ethnic minorities were routinely excluded from not just some jobs, but entire professions. (Hence, the folk song "No Irish Need Apply.") Similarly, when he insists that state government is necessarily less oppressive than federal because a person can always move to another state, he ignores such historical realities as Oregon's legal prohibitions barring Black residents for nearly a century. Before the passage of the Fourteenth Amendment, many state governments were more coercive than the federal government, so moving to escape discrimination was not necessarily an option. (Many of the founding fathers, for example, thought that while the federal government should not pass any law establishing religion, it was fine for a state government to do so.)[50] Even after the Fourteenth Amendment, racial, religious, and gender discrimination persisted in most American states; Friedman insisted that the marketplace was a better guarantor of freedom than the government at the very time when restrictive covenants and other forms of discrimination kept Jews like him from living in many American neighborhoods.

Friedman similarly argued that capitalism protected freedom of thought, using Hollywood as an example.[51] It was true that the Hollywood Ten had been persecuted for their views, he acknowledged, but they suffered no real harm because commercial incentives led the studios to employ them, albeit using front men and pseudonyms. Dalton Trumbo even won two Academy Awards. The power of the profit motive made the blacklist ineffective. The Hollywood Ten's "fundamental protection was the existence of a private-sector economy in which they could earn a living."[52]

Except that wasn't true. Trumbo was an exception, in part because Kirk Douglas went to bat for him. Most blacklisted writers found themselves unemployed, suffering serious loss of income and, in some cases, their entire careers. For those who could continue to work, was it not humiliating to "win" an award under a politically enforced charade? Even Trumbo had to use a pseudonym on the smash hit *Roman Holiday*.[53] And in most professions, pseudonyms weren't an option. The aerospace industry, for example, imposed loyalty codes and restrictions, driving many people not just out of particular jobs, but out of their professions.[54]

WHILE FRIEDMAN ACKNOWLEDGED his debt to Hayek and frequently referenced Adam Smith, he was far more extreme than either of them. Smith made the case for regulating banks and Hayek recognized the need for social insurance; Friedman not only rejected social security, he rejected the idea of "social responsibility" altogether.

One might argue that social insurance would be superfluous if corporations sufficiently compensated their workers or contributed adequately to private philanthropy in their communities. But Friedman rejects that idea, too, declaring that corporate social responsibility is "a fundamental misconception."[55] The only obligation of business is to "use its resources and engage in activities designed to increase its profits so long as it stays within the rules of the game, which is to say engages in open and free competition, without deception or fraud." Doing otherwise is not only beyond their remit; it is misguided and undemocratic, because who are they to decide what the "social" interest is? "Few trends could so thoroughly undermine the very foundation of our free society as the acceptance by corporate officials of a social responsibility other than to make as much money for their stockholders as possible." It falls to the rest of us "to establish a framework of law such that an individual in pursuing his own interests is, to quote Adam Smith again, 'led by an invisible hand to promote an end which was no part of his intention. Nor is it always the worse for the society that it was no part of it. By pursing his own interest, he frequently promotes that of the society more effectually than when he really intends to promote it.'"[56]

As we have seen, Adam Smith's understanding of self-interest and its limits was more complex than Friedman makes it out to be. Setting that aside, Friedman's frequent invocation of Adam Smith raises a fundamental question, relevant to the entire Chicago school: who made Adam Smith God? Friedman quotes Smith as if he had *proved* a system of natural laws, and therefore one need only offer an apt quotation to bulletproof any point. But what, exactly, does a quotation from Adam Smith demonstrate? Like most Enlightenment philosophes, Smith believed in a natural order, but *The Wealth of Nations* is a *treatise*, not a statement of the results of scientific investigation. The invisible hand is a metaphor, not a scientific fact or law. So while framed with the trappings of academic inquiry, *Capitalism and Freedom* is in fact a laundry list of assertion and opinion.[57]

Friedman justifies his views on social responsibility not with empirical evidence from history or social scientific research, but with the assertion that society will be best served if decisions about social responsibility—whether it is funding the opera or sustaining public schools—are made by individuals (and not corporate directors). "Can self-selected private individuals decide what the social interest is?" he asks. Like Margaret Thatcher after him, he believes there is no "society as a whole," so in a real sense there is no social interest. When Friedman speaks of the responsibilities of "the rest of us," he means the rest of us acting *as individuals*. There is no social interest that can be defined apart from the summation of citizens' discrete and singular interests.

By Friedman's logic, a corporation engaging in philanthropy usurps the individual prerogatives of its shareholders, because it acts on behalf of a collective interest that does not exist. "The Corporation is an instrument of the stockholders who own it. If the corporation makes a contribution, it prevents the individual stockholder from deciding how he should dispose of his funds."[58] There should be no *organizational* support of philanthropy—no support from government, but no support from private corporations either. There should only be support from *individuals*.[59] This position accounts for Friedman's extreme skepticism of government: he doubts that any government can effectively reflect the will of its people.[60]

FRIEDMAN DESCRIBES HIS work as characterized by one major theme—competitive capitalism as a system of economic freedom essential to the preservation of political freedom—and one minor theme, the role of government in such a system. There is also a third argument that is worth addressing, because it has discernibly influenced American business leaders from Wall Street to Palo Alto. It is the claim that government is not a force for creativity or innovation, only the market is.

This claim takes on a transhistorical sweep when Friedman proclaims that "the great advances of civilization, whether in architecture or painting, in science or literature, in industry or government, have never come from centralized government." The truth of this claim might hinge on one's understanding of the word *centralized*, but even allowing for a range of plausible interpretations, it's just false. In the United States alone, there are numerous examples that refute it, starting with the development of the technology of interchangeable parts, financed by the U.S. Army. Railroads, rockets, jet engines, digital computers, nuclear power, and nuclear weapons all came to be via massive federal government support. Or think about the lunar landing: financed, supported, managed, and directed by the U.S. government's National Aeronautics and Space Administration (NASA). Any historian of technology can list a score of major technological advances, from aviation to the internet, that were largely the product of organized government.[61]

When it comes to history, Friedman exhibits a reckless disregard for fact, making one astonishingly erroneous claim after another. Perhaps the most outrageous is this: "Columbus did not set out to seek a new route to China in response to a majority directive of a parliament."[62] Never mind that Spain had no parliament in 1492; Columbus was directed by a *monarch*—the ultimate form of centralized government.

Friedman attributes all the advances of civilization to "individual genius," working in a social climate that permitted "variety and diversity." Among others he cites Albert Einstein, Niels Bohr, and Boris Pasternak. Einstein and Bohr may have been geniuses, but historians of science have shown that they did not work alone. And Pasternak lived and worked in Soviet Russia!

The most serious flaw in the book, however, is that its central thesis is demonstrably false: capitalism and freedom are not indivisible. Capitalism did not bring freedom to the four million souls who lived under American slavery. Nor did it bring freedom to the millions of African Americans in the Confederate states who had been emancipated in 1863 only to be subjected to Jim Crow segregation after Reconstruction ended in 1877. Or the free Blacks who were forbidden from living in Oregon from the 1840s until the passage of the Fourteenth Amendment.[63]

A few years after the publication of *Capitalism and Freedom*, the economist Paul Samuelson tried to test the indivisibility thesis. Comparing Norway, Sweden, the United Kingdom at two points in its history (1948 and 1960), and the United States at three (1928, 1953, and 1960), Samuelson generated a graph indicating no clear relation between economic and political freedom. To the extent that the analysis suggested any relation, it was a negative one: when or where economic freedom increased, political freedom decreased.[64]

Of course, it's not at all clear how to measure either economic or political freedom, and Samuelson acknowledged that his graph had no numbers. His point, explained further in an article in 1983, was that Hayek's views—affirmed by Friedman and his Chicago cohort—were not supported by evidence. "I was taught at the University of Chicago that business freedoms and personal freedoms have to be strongly linked, both as a matter of brute empirical fact and of cogent deductive syllogism." Neither was true; the "paradigm could not fit the facts."[65] Samuelson stressed that the experience of Sweden offered strong refutation: you could reduce economic freedom and still sustain a full suite of political liberties. Within a few years, the experiences of Chile and China proved the inverse was true: you could increase economic freedom dramatically without gaining much, if anything, in the way of political freedom. Yet, Friedman never altered subsequent editions of his book.

Friedman at times hedges against the tight interweaving of "capitalism and freedom" that is very title of his book (just as Hayek at times hedged against the "inevitability" aspect of his thesis). "History only suggests that capitalism is a necessary condition for political freedom. Clearly it is not a sufficient condition," Friedman writes at one juncture. "The relation between political and economic freedom is complex and by no means unilateral."[66] And yet, repeatedly he returns to the refrain that if not sufficient for freedom, capitalism is certainly necessary for it: "Historical evidence speaks with a single voice on the relation between political freedom and a free market. I know of no example in time or place of a society that has been marked by a large measure of political freedom, and that has not also used something comparable to a free market to organize the bulk of economic activity . . . Capitalism is a necessary condition for freedom."[67]

One could argue this point at length, but one clear refutation comes from the world of Adam Smith himself, when British society had extended political freedom to many of its members but had not (yet) organized the bulk of economic activity through free markets. That, of course, was why Smith wrote his most famous book: to urge it to do so.[68] At least some people were, in fact, free, before capitalism came to be.

LIKE THE NOVELS of Ayn Rand, *Capitalism and Freedom* became a huge success despite these evident flaws, and despite being poorly received by critics. The book was not reviewed by the *New York Times* or the *Washington Post*.[69] Even though reactionary anticommunist and Republican partisan Henry Luce was running *Time*—and likely would have enjoyed Friedman's book—that magazine did not review it either. Among papers that did, the *Chicago Tribune* found it was "easy to poke fun at." The questions it raised were important ones, the reviewer allowed, but "our answers will not be Professor Friedman's."[70]

Academic reviewers were even less sympathetic; some found the book hard to take seriously. Writing in *Business History Review*, Harvard history professor Oscar Handlin accused Friedman, like other laissez-faire thinkers, of constructing models in which the "tie between theory and actuality has practically disappeared," and of writing in a tone that was "bitter, dogmatic, and petulant."[71] A reviewer for the journal *Ethics* allowed that Friedman was "clear," "systematic," and "earnest," but that his accounting of the United States from 1914 to the present "is such an unremitting catalogue of political errors that one wonders how we have managed to survive . . . From this point of view most of the political problems of our day receive short shrift. They appear either as the unfortunate consequences of our previous interferences with the operations of the market or as regrettable necessary evils."[72]

In the *Annals of the American Academy of Political and Social Science*, Leon H. Keyserling, a lawyer and economist who had headed President Truman's Council of Economic Advisers, said the book "sheds no light on economic problems as such." The overall formulation was either "inconsequential or misleading," and nearly all of Friedman's claims might be equally valid if turned on their heads. "Dr. Friedman says that 'by relying primarily on voluntary cooperation and private enterprise in both economic and other activities, we can ensure that the private sector is a check on the powers of the governmental sector and an effective protection of freedom of speech, of religion, and of thought.' In the American context, there is at least equal merit in the opposite proposition that centralized government power is essential to prevent private action, or decentralized state or local action, [from] impairing freedom of speech, religion, or thought."[73]

Predictably, the *Wall Street Journal* lauded it for presenting the "case for true liberals" and commended the argument that property rights are "human rights," but even the *Economist* gave it a mixed review.[74] It praised Friedman himself as "brilliant," suggesting that the book would make "ideal reading for politicians of either party . . . because it challenges the reader to sort out his own ideas fundamentally." But the reviewer was not convinced. Few readers, for example, would share Friedman's "generalized distrust of government" or be impressed by his proposal to "deprive the monetary authorities of all discretionary powers and instead to follow, come what may, the simple rule of increasing the stock of money at a constant rate year in and year out." Friedman was woefully unrealistic in suggesting that "all people who are neither children nor insane are responsible. A little experience of social problems," the reviewer wrote, "would teach him that the dividing line is blurred [and] that prisons, asylums and cash are insufficient to look after the poor and weak. Professor Friedman does not really face this issue."[75]

Keyserling concluded his review describing the book as a "set of prankishly employed theorems, which seeks to place roadblocks across the desires of free people." It was "nonsense," but fortunately not dangerous, but "only because too many free people have too much good sense to listen to it."[76] In short, reviewers recognized *Capitalism and Freedom* as a deeply flawed book, jammed with arguments that might make sense in principle but fail in practice, dismissing the realities of inequality, discrimination, and unequal access to resources and opportunity, and hanging on easily refutable historical claims. In hindsight, the most apt reviewer may have been the academic who recognized it as a "radical book" that was "likely to win a niche in American intellectual history . . . Future intellectual historians will find this book indispensable when they tell how Chicago gave its authority and intellectual luster to doctrines that otherwise have usually been served by lesser champions."[77] *Capitalism and Freedom* won more than a niche. It sold fabulously and has never gone out of print. How did this radical and incredible—which is to say, not credible—book sell so well?

FRIEDMAN'S *NEWSWEEK* COLUMN no doubt played a role in elevating his visibility, as did the hundreds of opinion pieces he would go on to write. He was willing to take positions that were not only unpopular, but often inflammatory: in 1967— the very height of the campaign for civil rights—he argued that "Negros" in America had made great strides not because of the civil rights movement, the weakening of Jim Crow segregation, the 1964 Civil Rights Act, or the 1965 Voting Rights Act, but because of "their own efforts" and "the opportunities offered them by a market system." (The implication was that, for Friedman, "their own efforts" did not include Black Americans' activism to push these acts through the democratic process.) In fact, he argued, discrimination was largely the fault of liberals, who had "awakened the sleeping giant of racial prejudice among the whites in the North" and encouraged "unrealistic and extravagant expectations" among Black Americans.[78] Thanks to these provocative columns, Friedman became a major public intellectual, and then a celebrity. He spoke regularly in business circles, was interviewed in *Playboy* in 1973, and appeared on the *Phil Donahue Show*.[79] The *New York Times* later referred to him as a "regular on the talk-show circuit," perhaps the first economist to earn that distinction.[80]

Still, in the 1960s, Friedman was considered an extremist, allied with the failed presidential candidacy of Barry Goldwater and—to most people—the receding tide of institutionalized racism. So how did this racist extremist become ascendant in the 1970s?[81] Clearly one part of the answer has to be his winning the Nobel

Memorial Prize for Economic Sciences in 1976. But most people who win Nobels—whether the original ones in the natural sciences or the Memorial one in economics—do not become household names. The Foundation for Economic Education describes Friedman as a genius at both "science and self-marketing"—and certainly the second part of that claim is true—but also credits the 1977 PBS series *Free to Choose*, and its producer, Bob Chitester, for making the economist a star.[82]

Chitester was not a famous producer at the time. He was the founding manager of the local TV and radio stations in Erie, Pennsylvania, WQLN and WQLN-FM. A libertarian, radical individualist, and fan of Christmas, classical music, and the poetry of Robert Frost, Chitester adored Friedman and his work and wanted to promote him widely. In the introduction to the PBS series, a narrator concedes that many viewers will be "appalled" by Friedman's views, but Chitester was convinced that people would be convinced, if those views were presented appropriately.

Friedman made the project his primary focus for the better part of four years. As one libertarian historian has noted, the "Friedmans, in their autobiography, described how Chitester proposed not only a television series, but a full-fledged marketing campaign to explain the benefits of capitalism and political freedom to the world."[83] It would include a lecture series, audio and video cassettes of the episodes, a college-credit companion course, resource materials for high schools, and an expanded edition of *Capitalism and Freedom*. Chitester also created a foundation, known as the Free to Choose network (still active today), focusing on creating documentaries and other "entertainment" to "build support for personal, economic, and political freedom." (Among other things, it offers a two-minute condensation of Friedman's life's work.)[84]

The project was a giant success. Its first episode, "Power of the Market," recorded at the University of Chicago, garnered fifteen million viewers. In 1980—nearly two decades after it was first published—the revised edition of *Capitalism and Freedom* became the number one nonfiction book of the year. Episodes of *Free to Choose* are still available today on YouTube and Amazon Prime; the latter describes the programs as helping "millions to understand the close relationship between ... human freedom and economic freedom."[85]

The program itself, however, was hardly free: it cost more than $2.5 million to produce.

Unlike most PBS programs, which routinely (and sometimes ostentatiously) declare whose support made them possible, *Free to Choose* was mum on its sponsors.

Most of the money came from fifteen corporate funders and conservative foundations. The former included PepsiCo, W. R. Grace, General Mills, General Motors, Firestone, Getty Oil, and the Whittaker Corporation (a major military contractor). The latter included the extreme right-wing Sarah Scaife Foundation (created by Richard Mellon Scaife and soon to become active in climate change denial), the John M. Olin Foundation (dedicated to "encouraging the thoughtful study of the connections between economic and political freedoms" and a major funder of the Federalist Society and the law and economics movement), and the Lakeview Fund (later merged with other funds founded by Lila and DeWitt Wallace of the *Reader's Digest* to form the Wallace Foundation). *Reader's Digest* was itself a funder, as was the National Federation of Independent Business.[86]

The first episode featured Friedman explaining how markets work both to stimulate economic activity and to preserve and protect human freedom. In the middle, the episode breaks from footage of factories and Freidman on the road in Asia, to offer us the professor, in suit and tie back at the university. Friedman holds a pencil, looks at it thoughtfully, and asks, What brought together the thousands of people who cooperated to make this? It was "I, Pencil" all over again. (Leonard Read was thanked in the program acknowledgments.) "There was no commissar, sending out . . . orders from some central office," Friedman says. "It was the magic of the price system. The impersonal operation of prices, that brought them together, and got them to cooperate to make this pencil, so that you could have it, for a trifling sum. That is why the operation of the free market is so essential, not only to promote productive efficiency, but even more, to foster harmony and peace among the peoples of the world."[87] There were nine more episodes like this to come.

To Chitester's (or PBS's) credit, several episodes ended by offering discussants the opportunity to raise critical points. One of these was the democratic socialist Michael Harrington, whose book *The Other America*, published the same year as *Capitalism and Freedom*, was a stinging indictment of poverty in the United States. Harrington said that he admired Adam Smith, but that the world had changed since 1776, witnessing the rise of multinational corporations with a "tremendous tendency towards monopoly and concentration." Friedman's ahistorical invocation of an outdated eighteenth-century theory, Harrington argued, particularly his "mystical belief in the invisible hand of the marketplace," did not make sense in the modern world. Whatever Friedman's intent, the book could only have the "practical political effect" of rationalizing "conservative power in America."[88]

After allowing Harrington and the other commentators their say, the episode ended with a voice over the credits announcing that in the next episode, Friedman would explain "what goes wrong" when governments try to control the economy. Overall, the series gave prominence to conservatives supporting Friedman; it also helped to promote libertarian thinkers who at the time were not as well known, such as the African American conservative Thomas Sowell. (Sowell had received his PhD at Chicago under George Stigler and in 1969 had characterized Black student protesters at Cornell as "hoodlums."[89])

By the 1980s Friedman was advising President Reagan and being lauded as one of the country's most powerful public intellectuals. A 2020 retrospective in the *New York Times* called his economic theories "among the most consequential" of the twentieth century, "still hold[ing] sway over large parts of corporate America."[90] To be sure, Friedman was smart, articulate, at times even witty, and he used his talents to great effect. In hindsight, one corporate leader concluded that Friedman had "brainwashed . . . a generation of C.E.O.s."[91] *Brainwashed* is a fighting word, but the people who supported Friedman's work believed that they were, indeed, in a fight.

ONE PART OF the answer to Friedman's fame and influence is that, by the 1970s, the Keynesian framework was breaking down, people wanted answers to what had gone wrong, and Friedman had one. As PBS put it in promos for *Free to Choose*, Friedman offered "solutions for the ills of our time . . . his view of the way we live now and where we are headed."[92] In the 1960s, most Americans still had a lot of faith in the capacity of government to address ills and even achieve great things, like righting the wrongs of segregation and putting astronauts in space. But by the 1980s, after the traumas of Watergate, urban riots, American's humiliation in Vietnam, stagflation, and the Arab oil embargo, to many Americans things were looking a bit grim. With the Great Depression in the rearview mirror and most of the architects of the New Deal dead and gone, it was perhaps easy to forget the lessons of the 1930s. And the Chicago school, of course, was determined to deny—or at least reinterpret—those lessons.

Whatever negative things one might say about Friedman's answer to America's problems, it was, as Leonard Read had long advocated, crystalline and clear. It may have been wrong, but it wasn't ambiguous. And it didn't hurt that many newspaper editors and television producers found his message congenial. Business leaders were happy to be told they need worry about nothing other than making profits; white people to be told that discrimination was someone else's problem; and industrialists that pollution was just a trifling "neighborhood" effect. Whether his motivations were cynical or sincere, Milton Friedman served his audience's interests well. He was saying what many powerful people wanted to hear.

With the publication of *Capitalism and Freedom*, Luhnow, Crane, Read, and Pew, along with their allies in the National Association of Manufacturers, the American Enterprise Institute, and the Foundation for Economic Education, had their wish fulfilled. They now had the American version of *The Road to Serfdom*, their New Testament of market fundamentalism. Above all, they had what appeared to be a serious academic argument to transform their cruel and self-interested "opposition to unions and the welfare state from reactionary politics to good judgment in the public mind."[93] They had taken a self-interested and essentially unsubstantiated ideology—one with scant empirical foundation and bucketloads of available historical refutations—and transmogrified it into respectable academic theory. What had begun in the 1930s as self-interested propaganda had been reconstructed as respectable intellectualism.[94] And it would profoundly influence American politics and culture from the 1980s onward.

PART III

Mainstream

*I remember one striking moment at dinner . . . you began to talk
about freedom and I thought, I'm interested in that, so I turned
away from Mick Hucknall's hot girlfriend to listen to you, and there
you were talking about the freedom of the market as if that was what you
meant by liberty, which couldn't have been true, because you're a Labour
prime minister aren't you? So I must have misunderstood, or perhaps this was
a New Labour thing, freedom = market freedom, a new concept, perhaps.
Anyway, quite the surprise.*

—SALMAN RUSHDIE [TO TONY BLAIR], *JOSEPH ANTON*

CHAPTER 11

A Love Story about Capitalism

By the 1960s, corporate leaders, neoliberal economists, and libertarian intellectuals had for more than thirty years been selling a story in which businessmen were the heroes and government the villain. Markets were efficient; individual initiative was all that was needed to succeed; and racism, discrimination, corporate violence, monopolistic practices, dangerous working conditions, and abusive child labor played only an incidental role. "Economic freedom" meant the freedom of business owners to run their shops as they saw fit, but not the freedom of workers to unionize. Above all, it was a story in which political and economic freedom were indivisible, so any government action in the marketplace—even if well intentioned and seemingly warranted—would put us on the slippery slope to socialism, or worse. In effect, American manufacturers had been manufacturing a myth.

But despite a very hard sell, for the most part Americans weren't buying. FDR had been beloved, elected and reelected four times. In 1948, his vice president and then successor, Harry Truman, won reelection in his own right. When Dwight Eisenhower was elected in 1952—the first Republican president since Herbert Hoover—it was as a centrist determined to negotiate a middle ground between excessive power in either state or private hands.[1] Eisenhower not only supported Social Security, but expanded it. He wrote to his brother that "should any political party attempt to abolish social security, unemployment insurance, and eliminate labor laws and farm programs, you would not hear of that party again . . . There is a tiny splinter group, of course, that believes you can do these things," but "their number is negligible and they are stupid."[2]

Most Americans accepted a vigorous role for the federal government because history had demonstrated the need. Within living memory, the federal government—not the private sector—had pulled the country out of the economic morass of the Great Depression. Washington had also mobilized the nation's industrial capacity to win World War II. After the war, the federal government became a major investor in science and technology, using defense dollars to drive technological innovation.[3] Businessmen loved to take credit for American prosperity, but often that prosperity had been nurtured by state support and shared with workers only under duress. None of this is to say that the federal government's efforts always worked well; the results of federal programs were always mixed and no doubt officials could overreach. The point is that ordinary Americans—especially working- and middle-class Americans—saw government as their ally because, for most of the twentieth century, it was.[4]

At century's end, however, the picture was different. Deregulation was the word of the day, the federal government was in seemingly permanent retreat, and free-market principles reigned effectively unchallenged in American politics. Many people and organizations had a hand in this shift, as we will see in the chapters to come. But the person who did the most to articulate an alternative vision to the public was Ronald Reagan. Using the ideological tools market fundamentalists had honed over decades, he changed the national narrative. Reagan framed government not as an expression of the will of the people, but as an outside threat, interfering where it did not belong. Not all state action was "interference," of course; Reagan and his allies had no objection to government intrusion into the bedroom or the family planning clinic. But the corporate boardroom was off limits. In the 1920s, Americans had hated "Big Business"; Reagan would persuade us to hate "Big Government."

He didn't frame it as a tale of loathing, however. Perhaps that was key to his success. Channeling the spirit of *Little House on the Prairie*, of Hollywood Westerns, and of *General Electric Theater*, Reagan narrated the American story as a parable of individual success in a free-enterprise system—a love story about capitalism.

Reagan also reframed a set of important questions about the role of business in America—particularly the complex relationships between industry on the one hand and workers and customers on the other—as a matter of the *size of the federal government*. After all, why was government "big" when it protected worker safety or curtailed industrial pollution, but not when it restricted reproductive rights? And why does the size of government even matter, as opposed to its efficacy? The answer, to a great extent, is that this was the story the American Liberty League, NELA, NAM, and their allies had been promoting since the 1930s. It was the ideology that Hayek, Friedman, and the Chicago school had made respectable: the power of markets, the threat of government, and the inseparability of political and economic freedom.

For decades, advocates of market fundamentalism had been obsessed with storytelling: How could the power of narrative overcome natural resistance to unpalatable ideas? Their success was mixed. Jasper Crane and Harold Luhnow had fretted that Hayek was too highbrow for an American audience and had promoted a simplified version in *Reader's Digest*, then in a literal cartoon. Rose Wilder Lane had helped produce beloved children's novels, but how many people had read *The Discovery of Freedom*? Ayn Rand's *The Fountainhead* was free-enterprise canon, but King Vidor's adaptation was a commercial flop. Luhnow's Volker Fund had supported Milton Friedman, but in the 1960s his account of the free-market myth was still mostly known only to academics and conservative intellectuals. Reagan—the Hollywood actor, the charming television host—would tell the story much more effectively.[5] And he learned how to do that when he worked for General Electric.

Reagan joined GE in the 1950s to jump-start both the company's faltering efforts at television production and his own faltering acting career; the consequences of this choice. went much further.[6] Hosting *General Electric Theater* contributed to his education in right-wing politics, but that was only half his job. The other half was spent as the face of a massive PR program designed to convince GE's workers and their communities of the greatness of American capitalism. To understand how Reagan became the foremost advocate of market fundamentalism ever, it is essential to understand GE during his tenure there. For much like a washing machine or a Soft White lightbulb, the Ronald Reagan who burst onto the political scene in the 1960s was one of the company's products.

GE WAS ONCE a forward-looking company: its research laboratory in Schenectady, New York, was home to Irving Langmuir, who won the 1932 Nobel Prize in Chemistry, and the lab created many innovative products, from improved lightbulbs to better submarines. GE's factories were also well run, and many of its workers well paid. Its chief engineer in the 1920s was a socialist, and its chairman in the 1930s advocated for a national pension system and helped craft Social Security.[7] But GE was also deeply problematic. It had been a leading member of NELA and continued to support the group after it was dissolved in 1933 and reconstituted as the Edison Electric Institute.[8]

In the 1930s GE was prosecuted for antitrust violations, and it would not be the last time the company's anticompetitive business practices came under scrutiny. In 1960, a federal grand jury returned twenty-one indictments against GE, Westinghouse, and twenty-seven other corporations involved in electricity generation and transmission for conspiracy to fix prices, rig bids, and suppress competition in their industry. Of the twenty-one indictments, General Electric was implicated in all but one. (Only Westinghouse fared worse; it was indicted in all twenty-one.) Indictments were also returned against forty-five individuals, sixteen of whom were executives or managers at GE.

The firms were accused of conspiring to set prices for a variety of items essential to electricity generation and transmission—from simple porcelain insulators to sophisticated turbines. The value of these items was over $1.7 billion; the IRS estimated this to represent about one seventh of total annual electrical industry receipts.[9] After long and complicated negotiations, the parties all pled either guilty or nolo contendere on all counts.[10] (GE and Westinghouse pled guilty on all seven counts that the government considered most serious.) The corporate defendants were fined $1,721,000—an amount equivalent to about one tenth the value of the rigged sales—and individual defendants paid an additional $136,000. Thirty-one of them were given jail sentences of thirty days.

As is characteristic of corporate crime cases, most of those sentences were suspended, but seven defendants went to jail.[11] The lion's share of the imposed fines fell on GE officers (Westinghouse was next) as did the jail terms: five of the seven men who went to jail were managers at either GE or Westinghouse. These were the "Big Brothers" of anticompetitive activities; the others were a "score of small fry."[12] The industry was an oligopoly, dominated by these two companies, and this structure, combined with illegal collusion and the "clandestine character" of their schemes, made these activities not just an infraction but a genuine "menace to the competitive business system."[13]

While modest fines and mostly suspended sentences may seem like a slap on the wrist for a multibillion-dollar fraud affecting millions of Americans, at the time they were considered extremely strong. The presiding judge described them as necessarily "onerous," given the character and magnitude of the violations.[14] An article published in the *University of Chicago Law Review* noted that these were the most severe penalties handed down in the seventy-year history of the Sherman Anti-Trust Act.[15] Their "exceptional severity" had been justified by "the magnitude and reach of the conspiracy, coupled with their persistence and flagrant character, . . . their 'public impact,' [and] the measures of concealment employed."[16] These were not small or accidental infractions, and because of GE's role in the Tennessee Valley Authority, the cheated customers included the federal government. For this reason, Attorney General Robert F. Kennedy suggested that the industry's actions represented a "serious threat to American democracy."[17]

Kennedy made a point of saying these men were "not gangsters. They were respected and highly regarded members of their communities."[18] But the evidence presented in court showed they had behaved like gangsters: assigning each other code names and numbers; sending communications to their homes rather than their offices, in plain envelopes with no return address; and destroying all communications after reading. "It is indisputable," one analyst wrote, "that these conspirators knew what they were doing, and knew that their arrangements for fixing prices and for sharing the market in agreed propositions violated the law."[19] They broke the law because they believed it was "good business"—which is to say, good for profits.

These illegal, anticompetitive activities took place in the late 1950s, at precisely the time when *General Electric Theater*, with Ronald Reagan as its host, was touting the virtues of the competitive free-enterprise system. *General Electric Theater* promoted the myth that the company was on the side of the American worker and consumer, when in fact it was working to sustain a world that was safe for corporate profits, even if that meant abusing workers and breaking the law. For price-fixing was not GE's only illegal activity during the period when Reagan worked for them; GE was also prosecuted for labor law violations. The company had not always been aggressively antiunion, but its wages and benefits trailed the auto and steel industries' and its pay scales were highly discriminatory against the large number of women in its workforce.[20] After a major successful strike in 1946 by the powerful United Electrical, Radio and Machine Workers of America that garnered strong popular and political support, the company altered its position on union labor.[21] It adopted a combative stance toward the workers' unions, began to work aggressively on behalf of right-to-work laws, and in the 1950s moved several facilities to right-to-work states, mostly in the South.[22]

The leading architect of these antiunion policies in the 1950s and beyond was GE executive Lemuel Ricketts Boulware. Born in Springfield, Kentucky, Boulware had served as an infantry captain in World War I, and then as operations vice chairman of the War Production Board during World War II. He then worked in various positions in sales, marketing, and accounting before joining GE in 1945, in its employee relations division. In 1956 he became vice president of employee and public relations, a post he held until he retired in 1961. But *relations* might be too kind a word to describe his treatment of GE employees. So would *negotiation* when reporting his method of working with labor unions. Boulware did not negotiate; he stipulated. When he died, the *New York Times* described his approach as conducting "extensive research of all issues" and then offering a "fair, firm offer" that was not subject to future concessions. Union leaders characterized it as "telling the workers what they are entitled to and then trying to shove it down their throats."[23]

By his own account, Boulware adopted a "take-it-or-leave it" approach to labor "negotiations," in which GE would put an offer on the table. This strategy—which union leaders considered a deliberate attempt to undermine their authority—came to be known as Boulwarism.[24] In 1961, Boulware's antiunion activities spurred the International Union of Electrical, Radio and Machine Workers to file a complaint with the National Labor Relations Board. At issue were GE's collective bargaining practices. Under the law, companies were required to negotiate in good faith with the unions representing their workers, and not attempt to evade or otherwise undermine them. GE's process, union leaders argued, did just that.

From the company's perspective, the process began with "research": GE would review data regarding worker salary and benefits, the costs of manufacturing, the sales prices for GE products, and other information it deemed salient. Then, based on its reading of these data—and crucially, its own interpretation of salience—the company would present what was essentially a nonnegotiable offer. The only exception GE allowed was when "new information" came to light, but only the company could provide that information. No action by the union—no data, no argument, and certainly no strike—would induce the company to change its offer if the company deemed the requested changes to be "incorrect."[25] The union argued that this violated the good-faith expectation. The law also required that if a company claimed it was fiscally unable to meet union demands—if, for example, the wage demands would bankrupt the company—data demonstrating the financial case had to be supplied on request; GE had repeatedly failed to do this. Most egregiously, while involved in formal negotiations with national union leadership, GE had several times attempted to negotiate separately with local representatives, a clear violation of Taft-Hartley (the Labor Management Relations Act of 1947). Even GE's defenders admitted this was a "divide-and-conquer" strategy.[26]

Like GE's collusion with its industry peers to fix prices, these offending activities were neither incidental nor accidental. An article in the *Duke Law Review* explained: "By means of intensive year-round research, GE attempts to determine what is 'right' for its employees . . . On the basis of facts derived from its own sources and from initial bargaining sessions with the unions, the company presents a 'firm, fair offer' to all unions." This was obviously paternalistic; what made it illegal was that under the law, "a negotiator who enters sessions with a 'take it or leave it' attitude" violates the Taft-Hartley Act "although ostensibly he may go through the *form* of bargaining."[27] It was not enough just to show up at the table; GE's approach was not bargaining, but fiat.[28] After several years of hearings and re-hearings, the National Labor Relations Board decided in the workers' favor.[29] The Second Circuit upheld this ruling on appeal, and the Supreme Court then declined review, so the finding held: GE had engaged in a clear, censurable pattern of bad faith.[30]

This unilateral strategy was undergirded by a broad-based "communication" program designed to support GE's corporate practices. From 1947 to the early 1960s, GE ran what the presiding judge in the hearings called a "coordinated and massive campaign" to "educate" the company's 250,000 employees—as well as members of the communities in which it operated—about the virtues of free enterprise, the vices of socialism, and the omnipresent threat of "government encroachment." Like NAM in the 1930s and '40s, GE claimed the real threat to worker prosperity was not low wages, but "burdensome" federal taxation. Under Boulware's leadership, GE sought to convince employees, their families, and their community leaders that corporate managers were a more reliable steward of workers' well-being than their elected union representatives. If GE could persuade its employees that it had their best interests at heart, then managers could simply run their business as they saw fit—precisely what NAM had argued should be the case in all American business. There would be no need for collective bargaining—indeed, no need for unions at all.

IT'S OFTEN SAID that conservatives resent liberals, journalists, and "the government" telling them what to think, but the GE public relations program was designed to do just that. Like NELA and NAM and GM's Alfred P. Sloan before him, Lemuel Boulware didn't frame it that way, of course. People who didn't appreciate the free-enterprise system were ignorant and needed to be educated.[31] They were "economically illiterate."[32] Boulware presented his program in a 1940 speech at Harvard Business School entitled "Salvation Is Not Free." Imbued with the syntax and cadences of evangelism, the speech began with the premise that the American people simply did not understand "how we got this standard of living that's the envy of the rest of the world."[33] The answer was the free-market system, in particular its incentive structure, without which people would not be motivated to work their hardest and do their best. Prosperity, in Boulware's view, came from the pressure to compete.[34]

Echoing NAM, Boulware warned that our "enlarged government" was threatening the stability of the system. The chief culprit was taxation, which drained funds needed for productive investment. Presaging the supply-side economics that Reagan would later promote, Boulware griped that the government was "unfairly" taxing the "income and savings of the very people who would finance more arm-lengthening equipment and methods" that led to productivity gains.

Reprising the indivisibility thesis, Boulware held that not just free markets but "our free persons" were at stake.[35] However politicians might characterize their intent, prevailing policies were an "attack from within on the very free economic and political system our officials are sworn to defend and protect."[36] He asserted that government involvement in the marketplace necessarily meant planning and—shades of Hayek—because that planning was bound to fail, there would arise the "inevitable necessity ... of having to shut off free choice and free speech in order that their planning failure" not be unmasked.[37]

Americans not only lacked appreciation for how capitalism worked but also how corporate America worked for *them*. "Too many of our employees and too many of their friends and representatives ... not only do not respect us but do not like us. They do not understand or appreciate what we are trying to do." Boulware submitted that they had come to believe in "magic," the magic of getting something for nothing, an "escape from the rules of arithmetic." They could not see that business *had* produced a kind of magic, "a fantastic fairyland of well-being." It was what Reagan would soon call the "magic of the marketplace."

In Boulware's view, businessmen had failed to make the case to the American people; he counterfactually claimed that corporate leaders had been "silent" in public when "confronted with union and other economic and political doctrines contrary to our beliefs."[38] It was high time they spoke up. For Boulware, the missing ingredient in the business response was politics: "private and public political action by managers, farmers, stockholders, bond holders, insurance policy holders . . . and any other upstanding citizens with an interest in keeping the value of money honest, the standard of living rising, and the freedom of choice, speech, worship and movement really free."[39] Again echoing Hayek, Boulware insisted that the business community had to reject any step in the direction of socialism, even social welfare. "We have got to get just as aroused and just as active about all kinds of socialists as we are about the communist brand of socialist." British socialism was just "communism" with better manners, and "in not so much of a hurry"; for that reason it was even more dangerous, because it threatened to slip under the radar.[40] It was imperative that the business community begin to "preach . . . the alternative to socialism" or risk ending up "silenced and enslaved."[41] It was time, Boulware thundered as he approached the crescendo of his speech, for the American worker to be "born again" with a new understanding of the threat of socialism and the promise of the free-market system. Without that understanding, we would become impotent witnesses as "our free markets and our free persons" perished.[42]

The GE public relations program was Boulware's call to arms in action. It worked on several fronts. One component, reminiscent of NAM's integration propaganda efforts, was a "managed news program"; the PR department worked to place articles and encourage editorials favorable to the company and capitalism in local newspapers where GE operated. As Reagan became an increasingly visible spokesman for the company, press releases would be circulated encouraging coverage of his speeches and other events.[43] Since GE was generally the biggest local employer—as well as the biggest advertiser in local papers—obtaining favorable coverage was not hard.

A second component consisted of publications the company produced itself. These included magazines, newsletters, bulletins, and pamphlets that viewed the news of the day through the GE lens, updated workers on contract negotiations (such as they were), or presented Boulware's views on government, the economy, and other matters.[44] One example was the GE *Works News*, distributed on Fridays so that workers would take it home, where it might also be read by family members. To ensure broad appeal, the newsletter would include items of local interest, such as company bowling league standings or photos of the latest Miss GE pageant, alongside antiunion jeremiads and news of Reagan's latest appearance. Individual plants and facilities had their own weekly newsletters. GE corporate produced a glossy monthly magazine, *Monogram*, which often covered Reagan and *General Electric Theater*, and *The General Electric Forum*, which focused on national defense.[45]

GE also mailed publications directly to workers' homes, where they and their families could read articles with overtly antiunion headlines, such as "Show how employees not represented by unions get their wage and benefit improvements without the possible delay of waiting for union acceptance" and "Why the company has no choice but to 'take' a strike rather than be forced beyond what is right." (Union rebuttals did not appear.) One article about GE's role in building advanced weapons systems interrupted itself to remind workers that their "balanced best interests" did not necessarily include large wage increases.[46] (It did not, however, dwell on how GE relied on "Big Government" contracts for this work.)[47]

These diverse missives were unified, consistent, and unequivocal. As one Reagan biographer notes, "Boulware left little to chance. Test pages were often distributed in advance" and employees were surveyed to ensure the right messages were being conveyed.[48] Some of the articles were factual, such as reports on company earnings and plant expansions, but others were propagandistic, such as "How Big are General Electric Profits—Are They Too Big?" (no, obviously) or "Let's Learn from Britain" (enumerating the alleged failures of British "socialism").

Perhaps the most important GE publication—because of its reach—was the *Employee Relations News Letter*. Initially it was sent to all GE supervisors and employee relations managers—about fifteen thousand in all—to ensure unity in the managerial ranks. However, it was soon expanded into a broad program of political outreach, with copies sent to clergymen, local politicians, media, schoolteachers, university professors, and others whom GE hoped to influence. Suggested reading lists reinforced the message, pointing newsletter recipients to complementary materials. The echoes of Mises's and Hayek's views in Boulwarism were no coincidence: managers were instructed to read the *Wall Street Journal*, the *National Review*, and the columns of Henry Hazlitt, William F. Buckley Jr., and Lawrence Fertig (the libertarian advertising executive and journalist who had maneuvered to get Mises hired at NYU).[49] Boulware also had a deal with Leonard Read to republish material from the *Freeman*, and it was during his time at GE that Reagan became a regular reader. In later years he would mention Hayek and Hazlitt as major influences.[50]

The newsletter was the most aggressively Boulwarian element of the GE communications program, designed to "help the supervisor and his employees to avoid the wrong course and take the right one" and "overcome the otherwise damaging power of anti-business forces." Like many later conservative commentators, GE would accuse its opponents of having a hidden agenda, charging union leaders, for example, with claiming to pursue better conditions for their members while in reality "seeking to cut down the usefulness of business."[51] Also like many later conservatives, Boulware measured his success in part by how much it infuriated his opponents; the idea that their fury might be inspired by his distortions and misrepresentations does not seem to have indisposed him.[52]

In addition to a panoply of propagandistic publications—an "avalanche of materials" in the words of one historian—GE also sponsored employee book clubs.[53] Intended to address "economic illiteracy" among GE employees and their families, the clubs were structured to meet each week for sixteen weeks, with assigned texts in economics, usually with an Austrian school slant. Hazlitt's primer, *Economics in One Lesson*, and Fertig's *Prosperity Through Freedom* were both on the reading list. Another was Wilhelm Röpke's *Economics of the Free Society*; its author was an orthodox Misesian, "a stalwart advocate of capitalism and free trade, and a fierce critic of . . . every manner of government interference with the economy."[54] One of Boulware's favorites was John T. Flynn's American Liberty League–financed and NAM-promoted polemic, *The Road Ahead*.

The book clubs also served as an information source for GE: managers used the reactions of their employees—and particularly their spouses—to gauge how the "educational" program was going.[55] Most important, in the words of historian Kim Phillips-Fein, by using "the work of thinkers like Hayek [and] von Mises," the book clubs "helped to legitimate GE's anti-unionism, by recasting it from old-fashioned reaction to a blow struck for freedom against tyrannical control."[56]

From informal book clubs with reading assignments, the next logical step in GE's educational program was formal school. The company established its own university—the GE Management Development Institute—complete with leafy campus and ivy-covered buildings in Crotonville, New York. One estimate put its 1959 enrollment at thirty-two thousand, far more than most large public universities at that time. (Although presumably most of these students were managers who attended for short courses, not four-year programs.)[57] *Fortune* magazine called it "the Harvard of corporate America."[58] A major player in the school was Ralph J. Cordiner, who in the late 1940s had been personal assistant to GE's CEO Charlie Wilson; Cordiner would serve from 1950 to 1958 as GE's president and from 1958 to 1963 as chairman and CEO. He taught a course called New Frontiers for Professional Managers, in which he professed the Boulware program. He also developed a set of management principles that went by the acronym POIM—Plan, Organize, Integrate, Measure—proving that corporate executives had no objection to planning when it was in their hands!

Cordiner's principles were frequently described in religious terms: they were "commandments" and a set of volumes describing them in greater detail were the "gospel."[59] One commandment was pure Boulware: corporate managers had a responsibility to be politically engaged in fighting high taxes, union power, the expanding federal government, and public hostility to "big business."[60] The Crotonville campus mainly targeted executives and upper-level managers, but classes were also offered at GE plants, where workers could receive instruction on company time. An estimated fifteen thousand supervisors received copies of the *Supervisor's Guide to General Electric Job Information*, which encouraged them to visit plants to see the principles in operation.

As with all serious propaganda, the creators intended for the targets to think they had come to these conclusions themselves. Like the young woman of the 1920s who wore green and smoked Luckies, believing she was liberated and fashion-forward, the GE worker would come "of his own free will to want to do what we recommend."[61] It was a sales job: just as a customer would be guided to choose GE products, employees would be guided to accept the GE vision of corporate capitalism.

GE bosses thus not only managed factories, they also attempted to manage their workers' reality. If the rank and file didn't agree with the company line about capitalism and corporate profits, they were told they suffered from "economic illiteracy" and needed to be further educated. Or, as Lemuel Boulware admitted in a moment of candor, to be "re-educated."[62] In a 1959 cover story about GE, *Time* magazine noted that a key tactic of Boulwarism was the "steady barrage of propaganda . . . aimed at winning the worker" over to the company point of view.[63] The editors of *Time*—prominent in the '50s for their anticommunism—knew propaganda when they saw it.[64]

APART FROM BEING frequently featured in the *Monogram*, Ronald Reagan played little or no role in GE's publications and book groups. He did, however, play a central role in its external public relations efforts.[65] In his 1949 Harvard speech, Boulware lamented that the defenders of capitalism too often appeared to be "coldly against everything" and "never seem to be willing or able to speak up warmly and convincingly to prove that what we are doing is for the common good."[66] Reagan would solve that problem. Hosting, acting in, and helping to choose the scripts for *General Electric Theater* was one part of Reagan's job with GE. The other part was going on the speaking circuit, first to GE facilities and then more widely to the communities in which GE operated. During his tenure at GE, Reagan spent a quarter of his time visiting GE facilities and delivering lectures on the company's behalf.

Because it was illegal under Taft-Hartley for corporations to participate directly in partisan politics, Boulware always insisted that his own advocacy, though political, was not partisan. But as Reagan biographer Thomas Evans notes, the politics GE promoted were conservative Republican politics, and this was no less true of Reagan's work for them than of other parts of the communications program. Reagan had come to GE as a Democrat—he sometimes noted that he had voted for FDR four times—and as the president of a union, albeit an extraordinarily elite one. Soon he would be promoting the political positions of Boulware and GE.

By his own estimate, Reagan spent the equivalent of two years—largely between 1954 and 1956—on the road. GE had 136 factories in twenty-eight states; Reagan visited most if not all of them, and addressed a very large proportion of GE's quarter of a million employees.[67] A typical day entailed giving a formal speech at a GE factory, meeting informally with workers and managers, attending a reception, signing autographs, and flirting with female employees.[68] Sometimes he would meet with schoolchildren and their teachers, and attend an evening event or deliver the after-dinner speech at a Rotary or Lions club. (These visits would be written up in the local GE newsletter, and often in local newspapers as well.)[69] As Reagan's facility with people became evident, GE sent him to increasingly prestigious venues, such as local executive clubs and Chamber of Commerce banquets.[70]

Reagan was nothing if not energetic. His schedule would be packed with events, as many as fourteen in a day. If he had time at night, he would study up for the next day. Between events he would travel by train or car, during which time he would read some more, often tracking GE book group selections: the historian George Nash suggests that in this way Reagan read the *Reader's Digest* version of *The Road to Serfdom*.[71] What emerged from this activity was a powerful conservative ideology blended with a set of stories gleaned from his travels. We do not know what GE workers really said to their corporate spokesman and resident television star, but we do know what Reagan later claimed they said: he began to gloss what he had heard as "complaints [about] government interference in [their] daily lives."[72]

On the lecture circuit, Reagan also learned he could talk about things far beyond his expertise—education is one documented example, transportation another—supporting them merely with a few good stories, so long as the speech was well delivered.[73] This may also be where he developed his use of "factoids"—numbers and anecdotes that illustrated a point but may or may not have been true—because Lemuel Boulware did this, too.

While accusing others of magical thinking, Boulware routinely made claims with no evidence. He asserted that lower tax rates would lead the wealthy to reinvest in their factories, without acknowledging the possibility that they might actually spend their added wealth on yachts, Fabergé eggs, or real estate in Pacific Palisades.[74] On one occasion, plucking numbers from who knows where, he claimed that the problem facing American business could be solved through education, because the vast majority of people were sensible and would see reason if presented with facts: "A few husbands will fall for harlots, but about 99.44 percent of the time the wife ... triumphs over the mistress."[75]

By the late 1950s, Reagan had adopted this style. He had also begun to hone what would become his substantive message: the threat of "government encroachment," particularly through excessive taxation. In a brilliant rhetorical stroke, he would maintain that this was not *his* message—and certainly not GE's—but what he was hearing from the American people. "People wanted to talk about and hear about encroaching government control," he told his audiences. He asked for *their* suggestions "as to what they themselves could do to turn the tide.[76] And, taking these suggestions, he began to fill his speeches with stories of government run amok.

Reagan's themes coalesced in 1959 in a speech delivered at the GE plant in Schenectady, New York, coinciding with a major, but secretive, decision by GE executives to delve deeper into American political affairs—including electoral politics—and convert the company into "a giant political force."[77] The plan was to expand GE activities in a number of domains, including encouraging the company's employees to view political activity as part of their jobs and use their influence to shift the views of their families, friends, and neighbors. GE salesmen and managers would be instructed to sell GE's worldview along with its products.[78] J. J. Wuerthner, manager of public affairs in GE's Syracuse facilities, published *The Businessman's Guide to Practical Politics* and organized a two-day seminar for managers, called Political Primer for Management. The seminar was advertised not only to GE managers, but to local divisions of GM, Chrysler, and other companies as well.[79]

Reagan also made an increasing number of appearances before civic groups, including some extreme right-wing ones, such as the racist John Birch Society and the radical right Christian Anti-Communism Crusade.[80] In 1959, he sent a copy of what was now emerging as "The Speech" to Vice President Richard Nixon. Entitled "Business, Ballots, and Bureaus," it summarized Reagan's two major themes: the federal government encroaches on American citizens with excessive taxation, and people were "fed up" with the situation. Nixon replied: "You have done an excellent job of analyzing our present tax situation and the attitudes that have contributed to it."[81] As Reagan delivered the speech in Schenectady and elsewhere, GE newsletters across the country reported it under the headline REAGAN SEES A LOSS OF FREEDOM THROUGH STEADY INCREASE IN TAXES.

Thomas Evans recognizes the coverage of Reagan's speech as a concrete example of what the courts held to be GE's "massive, coordinated" campaign of proselytizing its employees.[82] And yet he takes Reagan's claims at face value, asking, "Why did GE workers become concerned about 'government encroachment'?" And "[How] is it that Reagan's pronouncements in the late 1950s fit so closely into the philosophy set out by Lemuel Boulware ten years before?"[83] The answer to the first question is obvious. We don't know if Reagan's claims were true, but to the extent that any workers were worried about government encroachment, it is likely because Boulware's propaganda had succeeded. For years GE employees had been "educated" to hold this view. They were bombarded with this message, hearing it repeatedly from the men who paid their salaries and partly controlled their fate. No doubt some workers recognized it as propaganda and resisted, but likely others were at least somewhat persuaded.

As for the second question—how did Reagan's views come to align so closely with those of the captains of industry who employed him?—Reagan claimed it was the result of a "self-conversion," based on his immersion in Middle America.[84] Perhaps. But Reagan was also being paid to follow a script, and in that process he came to believe in its truth.

Reagan began his work with GE by immersing himself in Boulware's policies. He understood that the audiences he met were "receiving a constant stream of Boulware's messages" and he "didn't want to be at a loss to discuss it."[85] At first this was a role he needed to play. But as Kurt Vonnegut wrote in his 1962 novel, *Mother Night*—about a man who pretends to be a Nazi propagandist and later cannot prove he wasn't one—"We are what we pretend to be, so we must be careful about what we pretend to be."[86] (Or, as the theorist of ideology Louis Althusser put it, quoting Pascal: "Kneel down, move your lips in prayer, and you will believe.")[87] Reagan began by playing a part, one that he may or may not have believed in, but he played it night and day, and after ten years he was living it. In this sense, "Reagan's story at GE is, to a startling degree, the story of . . . Lemuel Boulware."[88]

By the time Reagan entered electoral politics, not only had he been exposed to the American people, but they had been exposed to him: according to one survey, in 1958 Reagan was one of the most recognized men in the country.[89] Theater professor Tim Raphael concludes that through his work for GE, Reagan "achieved a visibility . . . far greater than he ever had as a movie star."[90] When he launched his campaign for governor of California, Reagan's experience on the lecture circuit probably had put him in direct touch with more Americans than any candidate running for state office at that time. Reagan and his audiences had established a rapport, a "mutual fandom," that would serve him well in public office.[91] By the time he became president, "there were only a handful of people whose image had circulated for as long or as widely through the communications media . . . the Reagan brand was an unparalleled political asset."[92]

Most people think of revolutions as overturning ruling classes, empowering those who have been disempowered. The Reagan Revolution was the reverse. As president, Reagan would promote the interests and ideology of some of the most powerful people in America. He would ingeniously sustain the impression that the rich and powerful were somehow victims of an unfair system, he would work to reverse more than half a century of progress for ordinary people, and he would do it all in the name of "freedom." To paraphrase an earlier corporate leader, Reagan would convince us—despite a century of evidence to the contrary—that what was good for GE was good for America. No matter how Reagan became so closely aligned with his corporate sponsors' views, it is clear that the ideas Reagan held for the rest of his life were developed by, at, and for GE.[93]

GENERAL ELECTRIC THEATER was canceled in 1962, and Reagan's formal association with the company ended. The reasons for Reagan's departure are still debated. One version has him being fired for criticizing the Tennessee Valley Authority—a major GE customer—as a telling example of a "government boondoggle."[94] Another version ties it to a federal antitrust investigation of the Music Corporation of American (MCA), involving a sweetheart deal with the Screen Actors Guild when Reagan was its president. Reagan was called to testify before a grand jury, where he claimed to have forgotten nearly all specifics of the deal; a few months later, MCA was formally indicted.[95] GE was already implicated in one antitrust suit, and it surely didn't want the negative publicity of a second suit, particularly one involving its most famous employee.

Whatever the reason, the end of his association with GE freed Reagan for the political career that followed, and he was ready. His key themes had been market tested and endorsed by the same powerful people who would support his aspirations.[96] The 1959 Schenectady Speech became "The Speech," a verbal assault on "Big Government" that formed the basis of his star-making appearance at the 1964 Republican convention, endorsing Senator Barry Goldwater as the nominee for president.

American market fundamentalism got its first major political airing since Herbert Hoover during the 1964 presidential campaign. Beginning in 1960, Clarence Manion, the conservative Catholic former dean of the Notre Dame law school—an erstwhile America Firster turned radio star—chaired a committee to recruit and fund Barry Goldwater for the Republican nomination. In 1962, he was joined by William Baroody Sr., president of the American Enterprise Institute.[97]

Goldwater had been representing Arizona in the U.S. Senate since 1952, but came to national notice in 1958, when Senate hearings on union corruption gave him a platform to promote his "right-to-work" position.[98] In 1959, when Goldwater denounced the Supreme Court's 1954 decision in *Brown v. Board of Education of Topeka*, he became a star among segregationists.[99]

Goldwater ran as a rigid Cold Warrior, decrying federal power and alleged "moral decay," and validating white resentment. He gained the nomination in a contested convention (his principal opponent was the "establishment" Republican Nelson Rockefeller) and lost the presidency in a landslide.[100] But the baton had in many ways already passed to Ronald Reagan, who had been Goldwater's most popular campaign surrogate. During his years at GE, Reagan has honed a message similar to Goldwater's, and he was now laying the foundations for his own political career on anti-federal-government and pro-business-freedom grounds.

Reagan's themes could be found in Barry Goldwater's 1960 book, *The Conscience of a Conservative*, in part because they drew on many of the same sources.[101] Goldwater argued that both the Republican and Democratic parties had given up their commitment to states' rights, "our chief bulwark against the encroachment of individual freedom by Big Government."[102] But Reagan's experience, personality, and practice at delivering the message made him a better campaigner for Goldwater than Goldwater himself.

Reagan's endorsement speech, "A Time for Choosing," offers a vivid picture of his mature political personage, fusing the ideology of the men with whom he had spent the previous decade and the rhetoric with which he would propel himself into office. It is a powerful speech, brilliantly delivered with pregnant pauses and well-timed jokes. (Unlike many politicians, Reagan knew how to wait for a laugh line to land.) Watching it helps reveal how Reagan became America's strongest exponent of conservative philosophy. It also illustrates how conservative ideology shaped Reagan, how a man who had once believed in the power of government to improve people's lives transformed into the political leader who most fully positioned government as the enemy against which the American people had to fight.

The speech begins with Reagan challenging the Democratic claim that their policies had brought peace and prosperity. One third of our income went to taxes, Reagan noted; the government was massively in debt; and there wasn't enough gold in the coffers to back up the money being printed. Worse than that, our freedom was being compromised by the government that claimed to protect us. Deploying his trademark anecdotes and factoids, Reagan painted a frightening picture of assaults on freedom emanating not from Moscow, but from Washington. A farmer who had his lands seized and sold at auction. Another farmer who was told by a bureaucrat how to plant his crops. A woman who divorced so she could get government benefits that would be denied if she were married. And urban renewal that "takes from the needy and gives to the greedy."

In a line borrowed from Hayek, Reagan said that "the government can't control the economy without controlling people," and cannot do that without "force and coercion." Every new government program, and every expanded existing program, was a threat to freedom. Echoing Rose Wilder Lane, Reagan insisted that, because government is inefficient, its expansion threatens our prosperity. "Outside of its legitimate functions," Reagan said (without enumerating what those functions were), "government does nothing as well or as economically as the private sector." Both freedom and prosperity therefore rested on limiting government.

Like Mises, Hayek, and Milton Friedman, Reagan focused particular ire on planning. But since the United States did not actually have a planned economy, Reagan had to segue from economic planning to any "plan" to address societal ills. Social Security, urban renewal, farm aids, welfare: these were not *programs*, they were *plans*, and they had failed, because, after all, if they worked, then why were people still in need? Why were workers still unemployed? In a deft sleight of hand, the failures of capitalism were painted as failures not of the system, but of the government programs developed to remedy them. The lovers of planning, Reagan continued, would never admit this. On the contrary, they would double down: "The more their plans fail, the more the planners plan." These programs threatened our liberty, because they entailed an ever-increasing "level of government activity in our lives." Well-meaning liberals might argue that a small loss of liberty was worth a large gain in prosperity, but that was meretricious. The reality was that we were on the road to socialism, hurtling toward a loss of both liberty and prosperity.

Reagan was also serving at the time as spokesman in the American Medical Association's fight against the creation of Medicare, demonizing it as "socialized medicine." President Lyndon B. Johnson signed Medicare into law in 1965, but the combination of the work for the AMA and the Goldwater endorsement—televised as part of a prerecorded television program that shamelessly stole its title from FDR, *Rendezvous with Destiny*—put Reagan on the national stage, where he remained for the rest of his life.

The arguments Reagan served his national audience were not new. They had been used in the early 1900s to oppose child labor laws and workmen's compensation; in the 1920s to oppose Giant Power; in the 1930s and early '40s to oppose nearly all aspects of the New Deal; and by GE in the 1950s to undermine union power. The argument against Medicare was the same as conservatives had used when FDR tried to add health care to the Social Security Act. They were all variations on the theme of the road to serfdom: today health care, tomorrow total-itarianism. "Pretty soon your son won't decide when he's in school, where he will go or what he will do for a living," Reagan insisted, "he will wait for the government to tell him."[103]

In the 1964 speech, Reagan cited an apocryphal quotation from socialist leader Norman Thomas, alleging that Thomas had said Goldwater would, if elected, stop the advance of socialism in America. Reagan repeated the theme in the fight to block Medicare, alleging that it was socialism by the back door. "Under the name of liberalism," Reagan claimed that Thomas had said, "the American people would adopt every fragment of the socialist program." There is no evidence that Thomas ever said this, but it was a familiar trope.[104] In the 1940s and '50s, most Americans had seen it for the self-interested corporate story it was. In the mid-1960s, however, the argument would begin to stick, as ordinary Americans began to wonder if perhaps the federal government *had* gone too far. But perhaps more important, Reagan (like Goldwater) linked it to white anxiety about civil rights. When he announced his run for governor of California in 1966, one of his key issues would be the question of racial discrimination in housing, and he would use the issue to segue from the threat of "government encroachment" to the threat of "minority encroachment," enabled by the federal government's forcing the issue of civil rights.

FEW PEOPLE LAUNCH a successful career in politics by running first for an office as high as governor of one of America's largest states. But by 1965, Ronald Reagan was very famous, having held a place in the public eye for three decades.[105] And now—having given him a public platform, a political ideology, and the opportunity to refine both the message and its delivery over thousands of speeches—GE executives would give him the wherewithal to run for office.[106]

In later years, Reagan would assemble a forceful coalition of business leaders, social conservatives, evangelical Christians, and disaffected blue-collar Democrats, but this was not how he launched his political career. Reagan's "kitchen cabinet" was a handful of very wealthy white men—business executives all—spearheaded by his old associates at GE: Ralph Cordiner, Lemuel Boulware, and J. J. Wuerthner. They were all Goldwater Republicans and party insiders: Cordiner had served as chair of the Republican finance committee, and Wuerthner had close ties to Richard Nixon.[107] While Goldwater went down to a crushing defeat—winning only his home of Arizona and five states from the former confederacy—Republicans garnered many state-level wins. Nearly all those wins were in states with GE factories or other facilities.[108] Over the previous decade, GE had moved a number of its facilities to "right-to-work" states, mostly in the South; these states formed the backbone of the Goldwater coalition and what would become an emerging pattern of southern Republicanism.[109]

In addition to direct financial support, the GE executives shepherding Reagan into electoral politics introduced him to other wealthy individuals—in real estate, banking, retail sales, publishing, and the hospitality industry—and arranged for him to work with a campaign management consultancy. Reagan was ignorant in many policy domains, so the team embarked on a crash course to educate him in "seventeen major categories," including transportation, education, and water, and to polish his message so he would come across as "a reasonable guy" offering a "positive program" and not as an extremist.[110] The professional team included thirty-one staff members. Presidential historian Arthur Schlesinger Jr. later said that one of the most stunning aspects of Reagan's ascendance was "the revival in the United States of conservatism as a respectable social philosophy."[111] Reagan's kitchen cabinet did much to catalyze that revival. But despite their efforts to fashion Reagan's respectability, many of his political moves were deeply disreputable.

One of Reagan's tactics in the California gubernatorial campaign was to redeploy an argument Goldwater had made for the right to refuse to sell property to minorities. (Milton Friedman had also supported the right of a seller to refuse to sell on any grounds, including race.)[112] Throughout California, many communities had discriminatory covenants preventing property purchases by non-whites and Jews.[113] Courts had invalidated these covenants in 1948 and again in 1953, but they persisted. The state was divided on the issue: in 1963, the legislature passed the Rumford Fair Housing Act, which prevented segregation in residential rental properties, but a year later the law was repealed via a ballot proposition (Proposition 14) that amended the state constitution. The repeal was framed as a matter of property rights. "I have never believed that majority rule has the right to impose on an individual as to what he does with his property," Reagan said in November 1966. "This has nothing to do with discrimination. It has to do with our freedoms, our basic freedom."[114]

Reagan lost that fight: in 1967, state and federal supreme courts ruled that Proposition 14 violated the Fourteenth Amendment guarantee of equal protection under the law. But he had found an argument that enabled him to signal to his intended audiences. Goldwater and Reagan would always deny racial animus, but Reagan nevertheless reprised the implicit racist themes of the American Liberty League: that property rights necessarily entailed the right to use and dispose of property however its owner saw fit. That argument also echoed the nineteenth-century insistence that, because enslaved people were property, abolition was an infringement of property rights.[115]

Reagan would lose the campaign to maintain the right to discriminate but win the governor's mansion. His two terms in office would keep him in the public eye, but they would also expose a fundamental contradiction (at least to those paying attention). Reagan continued his rhetorical assault on government, while expanding California's government enormously, more than doubling the state's budget.[116] Personal and corporate income taxes also rose, along with taxes on gas, cigarettes, and inheritances.[117] Former U.S. deputy assistant secretary of the treasury Bruce Bartlett has noted that, as governor, "Reagan presided over an astonishing expansion of taxes."[118] Biographer Garry Wills credits his administration for streamlining what had been a mess, but nevertheless acknowledges that Reagan "had committed the very sin he inveighed against—[big] government."[119] These realities would be swept aside by the force of Reagan's rhetoric and his persuasive personality.

IN NOVEMBER 1977, THE future president would deliver the Ludwig von Mises annual lecture at conservative Hillsdale College in Michigan. The speech presaged Reagan's priorities as president. Laden with the unverifiable anecdotes that were now a hallmark of his speaking style, it positively rang with the rhetoric of the American Liberty League, NELA, NAM, and GE. It foregrounded arguments that would have warmed the hearts of Lane, Mises, Hayek, and the Chicago school. And to his general argument about the threat of "government encroachment," Reagan now added a new threat to property rights: environmental protection. "Free enterprise is becoming far less free," he declaimed. "Property rights are being reduced and even eliminated in the name of environmental protection. It is time that a voice be raised . . . pointing out that profit, property rights, and freedom are inseparable and you cannot have the third unless you continue to be entitled to have the first two."[120] It was the Tripod of Freedom all over again, although two of its original legs—representative democracy and civil liberties—had been replaced with profit and property.

The Mises lecture concluded with a concept (borrowed from Lemuel Boulware) that would emerge as a conceptual centerpiece: "Will we, before it is too late, use the vitality and the magic of the marketplace to save this way of life, or will we one day face our children, and our children's children, when they ask us where we were and what we were doing on the day that freedom was lost?"[121] With this slogan—"the magic of the marketplace"—Reagan decoupled his ideology from Adam Smith and even Hayek.

What Reagan carried forward from Mises, Hayek, and other twentieth-century neoliberal thinkers was an unfalsifiable reverence for markets and hostility to government. Sometimes that reverence bordered on the mystical; it was a short step from Leonard Read's "mystery" of the marketplace to Reagan's "magic." This mysticism underpinned Reagan's pivot from deregulating specific markets—which in the late 1970s Jimmy Carter was already doing with trucking, aviation, and natural gas—to demonizing governance, broadly. It also underpinned one of the most disturbing (and ironic) aspects of the Reagan legacy: the rejection of information.

The idea that market economies run on information—specifically, prices—was central to Mises's and Hayek's thinking. But market *failures* were also a source of information, as were external costs; it was this information that had motivated government statutes to protect workers, consumers, and the environment. Having absorbed Mises's insight about the importance of prices as information, Reagan reframed them as the *only* source of information in a market economy. He had also absorbed the neoliberal hostility to government but thrown away the caveats that both Hayek and Adam Smith had allowed. Smith, after all, had clearly explained the need to regulate banks and suggested the legitimacy of minimum wage laws; Hayek had specifically mentioned pollution as an area that required government response.

"The magic of the marketplace" was not just a throwaway line. Reagan would use it again and again, and when he became president in 1981, it became his catchphrase. But first would come the presidency of James Earl Carter Jr., the Democrat who launched the Reagan Revolution.

CHAPTER 12

The Dawn of Deregulation

By the 1970s, there was a case for revisiting regulation. The world had changed since the crash of 1929: energy markets were now thoroughly international; aviation was no longer a fledgling industry in need of nurture; banking and securities had become much more complicated; and technological innovation was about to radically reshape telecommunications. Both Democrats and Republicans began to consider which areas merited reconsideration.

This was at least partly enabled by the election of a new class of Democratic representatives who increasingly understood their constituencies more as "consumers" than "workers." One of the loudest voices for market-oriented reforms in the Democratic Party was Senator Edward M. ("Teddy") Kennedy of Massachusetts, who made transportation reform something of a personal crusade. His brother John F. Kennedy, when he was president, had made a brief and abortive effort to deregulate transportation. In a special message to Congress in 1962, JFK had called for ending what he called "segmented" regulation of transportation—trucks and railroads by the Interstate Commerce Commission, airlines by the Civil Aeronautics Board —in favor of a more comprehensive approach, while contending that "greater reliance should be placed upon competitive forces which have hitherto been blunted by excessively detailed and cumbersome regulation."[1] But Congress hadn't gone along. Now, Teddy Kennedy found an ally in President Jimmy Carter, who had been elected on a "good government" platform. The two would push laws through Congress removing the New Deal–era price and service regulations from commercial air travel, trucking, and railroads; Carter would also target the nation's vast energy sector for sweeping reform, motivated by the decade's twin crises in oil and natural gas.

Carter entered office in 1977 facing a host of challenges. American's confidence in the federal government had been undermined by the Vietnam War and Watergate. Antifeminists were proposing a Human Life Amendment to ban abortion and trying to prevent passage of the Equal Rights Amendment, which only a short while before had seemed destined for success.[2] Violent crime was rising, as were terrorist bombings.[3] The nation was experiencing an "energy crisis"—really two crises—in oil and in natural gas. The biggest issue, however, was the troubling economic development known as "stagflation."

Historically, inflation was associated with economic expansion, so while inflation was bad, the growth it was linked to was generally viewed as good. Conversely, low inflation was associated with stagnant economies. Ideally, one wanted a growing economy without too much inflation, and the Federal Reserve Bank worked to achieve this Goldilocks position by adjusting the federal funds target rate (the rate that banks charge each other for short-term loans).

In the 1970s, however, inflation and growth became decoupled, with the highest unemployment rates since the end of World War II (peaking at 9 percent in May 1975) alongside double-digit inflation. Hence, stagflation: a stagnant economy with high inflation. Richard Nixon had implemented wage and price controls— hardly a traditional Republican response, but reflective of how serious the situation was perceived to be. After Nixon's resignation in 1973, Gerald Ford declared inflation to be "public enemy number 1," but his "Whip Inflation Now" program focused on voluntary measures. (When it failed to produce rapid results, the acronym WIN was turned upside down to read NIM—"No Immediate Miracles.") In any event, the focus on inflation left unemployment unaddressed. One possible answer was to spend money on jobs programs, but that would increase the debt, also perceived as inflationary. The Keynesian economic framework under which policymakers since the 1930s had been operating seemed to be failing.[4]

The intellectual fulcrum of the Carter administration's sweeping reform efforts was a Cornell University economics professor named Alfred E. Kahn. The son of Russian immigrants, Kahn was born in New Jersey in 1917, graduated from New York University, and completed a PhD in economics at Yale University. He liked to claim he was the last student of Harvard University economist Joseph Schumpeter, who was not actually his adviser but was one of his dissertation readers.[5] Schumpeter is best known today for his theory that technological change drives economic growth through "creative destruction," from which Silicon Valley's taste for "disruption" derives. At the same time, Schumpeter thought it was important to understand the role that institutions—governments, for-profit and nonprofit corporations, etc.—play in economic life. He was among the last, too. After World

War II, microeconomics—the study of individual and business decisions—swept the field, refocusing it on mathematically rigorous studies of prices.[6] (Even macroeconomics became highly mathematicized.) Kahn was a quasi-institutionalist, interested in how (government) policy innovation could help create and sustain competition. He was particularly interested in regulation.

Prior to joining the Carter administration, Kahn had published a magnum opus, *The Economics of Regulation*, analyzing several industries. The first volume, *Principles*, focused on utilities, and Kahn argued for changing the way regulators set utility rates. In the 1930s, the Tennessee Valley Authority had used a rate structure that gave larger consumers lower rates to encourage consumption. This "declining block rate" worked well, from a particular point of view: it encouraged rapid expansion in the industry at a time when the driving idea was to bring electricity to people who didn't have it. However, it also embedded expectations of continual expansion, and the notion that utility managers' central problem was how to finance the next wave of power plant construction.[7] But endless growth wasn't necessarily efficient, and it didn't provide the lowest costs. The declining-block-rate structure had encouraged overconsumption, which in turn produced excessive capital demand (to finance new power plants), as well as excessive pollution.[8]

Kahn wanted to change the pricing system to allow the price of electricity to vary with demand. Electricity would be priced highest during peak demand and lowest during periods of lowest demand. This would be a more efficient use of capital, because it would reduce the need for "peaker plants"—plants built solely for the purpose of supplying peak demand. Because peakers typically only ran for a few hours a day, they were very inefficient: much of the day, they simply sat idle. This was not a good use of investment, and it raised the cost of electricity. If you could reduce the need for peaker plants by reducing peak demand, you could lower overall costs.

Kahn also argued for including "social costs"—such as pollution—in the marginal cost calculation: "For an item such as electricity, pricing below marginal social cost would have not only the usual result of encouraging excessive consumption; it would also lead to the additional construction of expensive, polluting power plants, all the while driving the electricity company toward bankruptcy."[9]

One of Carter's first acts as president was to appoint Kahn as chairman of the Civil Aeronautics Board (CAB), where he would lead the effort to dismantle airline price regulation before spearheading the administration's anti-inflation efforts. Carter, Teddy Kennedy, and Kahn would succeed at sweeping reforms and phase out most of the remaining New Deal–era price controls. In doing so, they showed that it was possible for government to learn from experience, respond to evolving technologies, and make midcourse corrections, while neither being trapped in an obsolescent paradigm nor forgetting the lessons of the past.

In hindsight, the Carter era gives us a glimpse of what could have been: a future in which some of the excesses of the New Deal were corrected, without swinging the pendulum too far in the other direction. But it also shows how antiregulatory, antigovernment ideology had seeped even into Democratic thinking, laying the ground for the excessive pendulum swing that did, in fact, follow. It's become commonplace to identify our recent decades of business-friendly deregulation and the resulting skyrocketing inequality with the so-called Reagan Revolution. But that revolution started with Jimmy Carter.

CARTER, A NAVY veteran, peanut farmer, and former governor of Georgia, was not a market fundamentalist. In many ways he was a traditional moderate Democrat. But he came into office at a moment of intersecting crises, among them the persistent stagflation he had inherited from Nixon and Ford. In hindsight, it's evident that stagflation had several causes. Oil shocks were an obvious one: since the cost of energy is embedded in just about everything, the 1973 oil embargo imposed by the Organization of the Petroleum Exporting Countries (OPEC) drove up prices across the economy. Another was the transformation of international trade. Since 1945, West Germany and Japan had rebuilt themselves into formidable competitors, and the American "balance of trade" had become persistently negative.[10] U.S. policy throughout the postwar period had been to encourage reindustrialization among allies, with the United States as the primary destination for their exports, but foreign competition was now hurting U.S. manufacturers and workers. Nixon's abandonment of the gold standard in 1971 (a response to the trade imbalance) also encouraged inflation.[11] And union demands played a role: workers had come to expect annual increases in wages and benefits, sometimes tied to productivity increases, but often not. This contributed to a cycle of cost-push inflation: increased costs pushed up consumer prices, which led workers to demand better wages, which led to increased costs, and so on.

During the 1976 presidential campaign, Ford and Carter both promised reme-dies. Ford, who had been challenged on the right by Ronald Reagan and only narrowly won the Republican nomination, promised tax cuts, smaller government, and balanced budgets.[12] Carter, running mostly as a traditional New Dealer, proposed to lower unemployment with youth programs and a job guarantee, but he pledged tax cuts and a balanced budget, too.[13] Carter also raised hopes of stimu-lating the economy through deregulation. In several respects, his speech accepting the Democratic Party nomination reflected arguments that NAM and other New Deal opponents had been making since the 1930s: "As . . . a businessman, I see clearly the value to our nation of a strong system of free enterprise based on increase[d] productivity and adequate wages. We Democrats believe that competi-tion is better than regulation." Like Eisenhower in the 1950s, Carter was seeking a middle way, hoping "to combine strong safeguards for consumers with minimal intrusion of government in our free economic system."[14]

The New Deal had a mixed legacy on regulation. Roosevelt initially embraced cartelizing the nation's economy under the National Industrial Recovery Act of 1933; then, after NIRA's failure, he pursued price regulation in finance, airlines, trucking, natural gas, and utilities. Later in his presidency FDR also tried trust-busting to foster competition. Eisenhower, Kennedy, Johnson, and Nixon had mixed records on regulation and antitrust enforcement, too, but none had sought wholesale changes in the New Deal framework. Candidate Carter was signaling a shift toward competition, hoping that softening New Deal constraints would improve productivity and lower prices, without losing important worker and consumer protections.

UPON INAUGURATION IN January 1977, Carter's immediate task was to deal with the two energy crises. The obvious crisis was the nation's dependence on imported oil. Long gas lines, displayed across the country on the nightly news, reminded Americans that the United States imported more than a third of the oil it used and was vulnerable to shortages, supply cutoffs, and other disruptions that would drive up prices. Nixon had responded to the embargo with price controls and rationing; the latter was extremely unpopular and triggered truckers' strikes.[15] Carter came into office under pressure to do something to help the United States achieve "energy independence."

The less obvious crisis involved natural gas. The 1938 Natural Gas Act had authorized the Federal Power Commission to set prices for gas carried in interstate pipelines and sold in interstate markets, but it couldn't set prices for gas sold within a producer state. Over time, prices in producer states became higher than outside them. In response, producers hoarded gas, refusing to sell it at the regulated rates. Regulators imposed minimum sales requirements, so that nonproducing states didn't run out. But as the nation's population moved south and west, regulators couldn't keep up—they needed consumption data to set those prices and allocations, and data collection and analysis was always too slow. Also, to encourage production, regulators had developed a two-tiered pricing system with higher prices for "new" gas. This was intended to stimulate investment, and thereby increase production, which would help keep prices down. But underinvestment persisted. This was part of the inspiration behind candidate Carter's promise to do something about natural gas regulation; it would also lead Milton Friedman, in 1977, to use his *Newsweek* column to attack gas regulation.[16]

The winter of 1976–77 was harsh and triggered gas shortages. Carter had his staff prepare a complex energy bill designed to encourage conservation, reduce oil imports, stimulate new production, foster increased coal use in electricity generation, and finance energy research, including the development of synthetic fuels or "synfuels" from coal. (The issue of climate change also came up and would spur two important studies in 1979, offering a cautionary note on coal.)[17] It did not propose to decontrol natural gas prices.

Many of Carter's ideas made sense, but he presented them—particularly conservation—in a negative light. In a major speech in April 1977 promoting his energy reform proposals, he painted a particularly gloomy picture: "Because we are now running out of gas and oil, we must prepare quickly for a third change—to strict conservation and to the renewed use of coal and to permanent renewable energy sources like solar power." The cornerstone of his plan was conservation—"a clear difference between this plan and others which merely encouraged crash production efforts"—but prices were part of the problem, particularly prices that were "artificially low" and encouraged profligacy. "[P]rices should generally reflect the true replacement cost of energy. We are only cheating ourselves if we make energy artificially cheap and use more than we can really afford."[18] Price controls induced both overconsumption and underinvestment, which had led the nation to the energy precipice, so his proposals combined price decontrol to encourage investment with taxes to discourage consumption.

After considerable congressional back and forth, a bill emerged that was far less ambitious than Carter had wanted.[19] His expansive conservation effort was reduced to grants for insulating low-income housing and public buildings and subsidies for low-income consumers; the proposed taxes on heating oil and gasoline had been dropped entirely. The coal expansion plan was weakened; oil price decontrol had disappeared completely. Instead, Carter used administrative authority granted by the Ford administration's Energy Policy and Conservation Act of 1975 to remove oil price controls, beginning in June 1979. To compensate for the resulting price increases, he gained congressional approval of a windfall profits tax.[20] Meanwhile, a separate bill, the Natural Gas Policy Act, passed in 1978, would phase out gas price controls by 1985—after Carter's hoped-for second term in office.[21] Until then, an even more complex set of regulations, dividing natural gas production into eleven different categories, all priced differently, would govern the gas market.

The fundamental political problem for the decontrol advocates was regionalism. Price deregulation had winners and losers. Representatives of gas-producing states wanted full decontrol immediately—and at the time these were mostly Democrats. Representatives from gas-consuming states did not, because it would harm their consumers and feed inflation, and these included both Democrats and Republicans. But Carter and his economic and energy advisers were united in support for price decontrol, even though it might be inflationary in the short term.

While the Natural Gas Policy Act didn't solve the natural gas crisis immediately, it did stimulate investment in production and helped to resolve the maldistribution of resources. A recession in 1980–83 crushed consumption, and prices fell. By the time the recession was over, the world had changed again: foreign policy in the Persian Gulf states had been transformed by the Iranian Revolution of 1978–79 and then the Soviet invasion of Afghanistan in 1979, and the resulting Carter Doctrine—which included the permanent stationing of U.S. military forces in the Gulf. There would be no more oil embargoes. In fact, an oil glut would drive prices down throughout the 1980s.

AVIATION WAS ANOTHER regulated market ripe for reevaluation. Both fares and routes for commercial airlines had been regulated by the Civil Aeronautics Board (CAB) since 1938. For constitutional reasons, CAB's authority extended only to interstate airlines, not intrastate ones; by 1976, there were two significant scheduled passenger airlines operating successfully outside its authority: Pacific

Southwest Airlines in California and Southwest Airlines in Texas. Both offered lower fares than regulated airlines flying the same routes. Federal regulation had produced stable growth in the industry, but not low prices and often not high profits, either. It had produced higher wages for workers in the regulated part of the industry, which was mostly unionized, but that meant higher prices for consumers. There was growing sentiment in the Democratic Party for regulatory reform that might yield lower prices.[22]

In February 1975, Teddy Kennedy had held hearings on airline regulation. Kennedy's views were guided by special counsel (and later Supreme Court justice) Stephen Breyer.[23] The hearings foregrounded consumer welfare, with Breyer arguing the potential consumer benefits of increased competition through decreased regulation. Kennedy noted that in the "transportation area alone, studies have estimated the cost to the public of Federal regulation to be $8 to $16 billion each year. That is an unreasonable price at any time. It is wholly unacceptable under our present economic conditions."[24] (In today's dollars, that's as much as $74 billion.) Kennedy noted that in "the past 14 months, the [Civil Aeronautics] Board has granted direct fare increases of over 16 percent. It has eliminated special fares for children and vacationers, producing an average fare increase of more than 20 percent."[25] After wondering whether the task of regulation was so complex and difficult that it inevitably resulted in higher prices, Kennedy offered the alternative of reform "accomplished by returning the determination of prices to the market-place and the laws of supply and demand."[26] In May, the senator introduced a bill to reform airline regulation, and transportation deregulation soon became part of candidate Carter's proposed platform: "The present patchwork scheme of rail, truck, and airline regulation at the federal level needlessly costs consumers billions of dollars every year. However valid the original purpose of promoting fledgling industry and protecting the public from the tyranny of monopoly or the chaos of predatory competition, the present system has, more often than not, tended to discourage desirable competition."[27]

Carter and Kennedy represented a new generation of Democrats who no longer thought that institutional regulation of prices and services was an appropriate solution to economic troubles. But their arguments for deregulation were not antigovernment; on the contrary, their pro-consumer orientation sat easily alongside traditional Democratic programs like Social Security and Medicare. One could be pro-market *and* pro-government, allowing businesses to operate more freely in many domains without sacrificing the good that government did in other domains. At least, that was the idea.

Business leaders today often whine about "excessive regulation," but the regulated air carriers in the 1970s—as well as their unions—were happy with the status quo. Having operated in an environment of nearly perfect protection—CAB always granted fare increases whenever a major carrier got into trouble, so regulated airlines were very safe businesses—none of the majors wanted to lose the shelter of CAB rules. Meanwhile, the unions believed (correctly, as it turned out) that workers would pay the price of deregulation. If consumers were going to see permanently lower prices, airlines would have to cut costs, and wages were their largest budget line item. Both labor and management defended the status quo.

Kahn and the White House domestic policy staff embarked on a campaign to persuade Congress to deregulate the airlines.[28] An odd bedfellows alliance of consumer, business, and conservative groups backed the effort, including NAM and Ralph Nader's Aviation Consumer Action Project.[29] While airline unions remained universally opposed to deregulation, some industry executives defected and became supporters. Pan Am saw an opening to gain access to domestic markets, which CAB had denied it in the past; United Airlines saw an opportunity to expand routes and strengthen its domestic dominance.[30] But most airlines remained opposed, some for prescient reasons. Frank Lorenzo of Texas International prophesied that the outcome of deregulation would be a "couple of very large airlines. There will be many small airlines that will start up here and there, but they will never amount to a very significant amount of the transportation market."[31]

In October 1978 Congress passed and Carter signed the Airline Deregulation Act, which required that the CAB utilize market forces to the maximum extent possible, automatically grant entry to new carriers, and allow mergers unless they were deemed anticompetitive. The law enacted a new program of subsidies to support rural routes, but only for a period of ten years. The CAB would administer that program until the board itself was phased out in 1985; its remaining regulatory responsibilities would be transferred to the Department of Transportation.

Viewed from the price perspective, deregulation was enormously successful: after adjustment for inflation, average fares dropped by half. Not surprisingly, air travel increased: in 1976, the airline trade association counted more than 233 million passengers; in 1987, the number was nearly 450 million.[32] This in turn supported a large increase in industry employment. Kahn had argued that deregulation would generate more jobs, and he was right.[33] The major scheduled airlines had employed a little more than 300,000 people in 1977, a figure that soared to more than 450,000 by 1987 and peaked in 2001 at more than a half million. But Frank Lorenzo proved right about consolidation. Only three of the sixteen CAB-regulated major passenger airlines of 1977 still exist: United, American, and Delta. The only minor airline that has managed to climb into the top ranks is Southwest, which operated in Texas in the mid-1970s under the regulation of the Texas Aeronautics Commission, not CAB.

Airlines have always operated on thin margins, and as the increasingly deregulated U.S. economy returned to the boom-bust cycle of the nineteenth century, airlines became super-cyclical—hit harder in the "bust" part of the cycle than many other industries, and barely returning to profitability at the end of an expansion before the next bust hit.[34] After deregulation, several legacy airlines—Pan Am, Eastern, Continental, Northwest—went bankrupt or were swallowed up; many upstarts disappeared as well. Service quality declined, too. It got so bad that Barry Goldwater wrote to Kahn to complain, receiving a characteristic response: "When you have further doubts about the efficiency of a free market system, please do not hesitate to convey them to me. I also warmly recommend some earlier speeches and the writings of one Senator Barry Goldwater."[35] The free-enterprise system Goldwater championed might be efficient, but it was not comfortable.

Workers suffered the most. As union leaders predicted, wages sank; a 1996 analysis found a 10 percent decline.[36] As aviation became more competitive, airlines used bankruptcy proceedings to terminate union contracts and, in several instances—United, U.S. Airways, Pan Am, and Eastern—dumped their retirement obligations onto the Pension Benefit Guaranty Corporation (PBGC), which had been created in the Ford administration to absorb the pension commitments of failed manufacturers.[37] This tactic saved United billions between 2005 and 2010, but at a large cost to retired employees who found themselves with much smaller pensions than they had been promised and, of course, to taxpayers.[38] There was also a large cost to the environment, as air travel expansion has contributed dramatically to greenhouse gas pollution.

And airlines didn't stay competitive, thanks in many ways to the Chicago school arguments gaining traction in American jurisprudence. The influence of Aaron Director and Robert Bork would be evident when, in 1999, the Clinton administration filed an antitrust case against American Airlines. The Justice Department accused American of attempting to monopolize routes through predatory pricing and of using its reputation for such tactics to discourage would-be market entrants.[39]

The case concerned American's behavior when a newcomer, Vanguard Airlines, offered lower fares on certain shared routes. In response, American lowered its prices. When demand increased on those routes, American moved planes from other routes to offer more flights. So far so good, but the government was poised to demonstrate that the airline had lost money through this tactic; the "clear implication is that American deliberately adopted a strategy of sacrificing profits" in the short run to kill a competitor—the very definition of predatory pricing. Once Vanguard was forced out, the added American flights were "promptly withdrawn," and American raised prices back up.[40] This outcome would seem to have harmed consumers, but the judges involved granted summary judgment on the grounds of insufficient evidence. In doing so, they invoked a Chicago school argument that made it almost impossible ever to have sufficient evidence.

The original presiding judge in district court, John Thomas Marten—a Clinton appointee—cited a 1981 paper by University of Chicago Law School graduate Frank H. Easterbrook, who had worked as deputy U.S. solicitor general under Robert Bork and had been appointed to the U.S. Court of Appeals for the Seventh Circuit by Ronald Reagan.[41] Easterbrook's influential paper—which had been cited previously by the Supreme Court—argued that it was difficult to separate predatory pricing from vigorous but legal competition, and that government involvement threatened to inhibit the latter. This would cause prices to rise: the exact opposite of what government antitrust enforcement was intended to achieve. Echoing Milton Friedman, Easterbrook concluded that the cure would be worse than the disease. He also insisted (without citing evidence but with ample irony) that predatory pricing schemes were rare because the costs of being caught were high.

Citing the Supreme Court's prior use of Easterbrook, Judge Marten asserted: "Predatory pricing schemes are rarely tried, and even more rarely successful, and the costs of an erroneous finding of liability are high." This of course assumed that antitrust prosecutions occurred and were successful, which, if the judges followed Easterbrook's logic, would no longer be the case. This contradiction did not detain the judge, who continued: "The mechanism by which a firm engages in predatory pricing—lowering prices—is the same mechanism by which a firm stimulates competition . . . It would be ironic indeed if the standards for predatory pricing liability were so low that antitrust suits themselves became a tool for keeping prices high."[42]

Lowering prices is of course only one means of stimulating competition; higher quality or greater variety are others and might be more important in many markets. The judge's argument was also speculative: no one knew how often firms engaged in predatory pricing. After all, who would freely admit to an illegal practice? How could we know if it was rare or not? And if the practices were rare, then why did American Airlines have a *reputation* for predatory pricing? Ignoring these difficulties, Judge Marten concluded that, while he did not doubt predatory pricing occurred—or even that it had anticompetitive consequences—it was impossible for a *judge* to tell the difference.[43]

The U.S. Court of Appeals for the Tenth Circuit heard the case on appeal. In his decision, Judge Carlos Lucero, another Clinton appointee, cited Easterbrook explicitly in the text of his decision, as well as Bork's argument that antitrust prosecutions were not necessarily in the public interest. In fact, the judge relied on the *theoretical* arguments of the Chicago school to decide the *factual* merits of the case,

> Scholars from the Chicago School of economic thought have long labeled predatory pricing as implausible and irrational. Frank Easterbrook, a leader of the Chicago School, once concluded that "there is no sufficient reason for antitrust law or the courts to take predation seriously" . . . Chicago scholars argued that lowering prices could only be pro-competitive and any prohibition on such conduct could ultimately deter firms from engaging in conduct that is socially beneficial . . . In two seminal antitrust opinions, the Supreme Court adopted the skepticism of Chicago scholars, observing that "there is a consensus among commentators that predatory pricing schemes are rarely tried, and even more rarely successful."[44]

By accepting at face value the Chicago argument that predatory pricing schemes were extremely rare, the judge not only raised the standard of proof for the government, he also made it next to impossible for the government to successfully prosecute a predatory pricing case.

The man who had initiated airline deregulation was not happy. The American Airlines case was the first airline antitrust suit since the industry had been deregulated in 1978; in 1999 Alfred Kahn discussed it in a *New York Times* interview, rejecting the claim that "unfettered competition is all the safeguard the flying public needs." Contra the Chicago school's assertions, not only did predatory pricing exist, Kahn said, but the airline industry was "particularly susceptible to it." Unlike a factory, which cannot easily move, an airline can easily increase capacity to thwart a competitor and then move out of that market once the would-be competitor is crushed. This was precisely what American stood accused of, and Kahn affirmed that recent developments in the industry were "a cause for real concern."[45]

Kahn acknowledged that there could be "an element of validity" to concerns that the case against American might hurt consumers, if fear of antitrust enforcement made airlines hesitant to lower fares. But he doubted that was the dominant effect. "Right now," he concluded, "it's too much on the side of permitting very deep pinpointed [discounted] fares temporarily, until the competitors are driven out." With antitrust enforcement "attenuated," the industry had been emboldened and was now confident that "no one can ever bring a successful suit against them."[46]

Kahn was particularly appalled by an attack on the government case by Bork, published in the *Wall Street Journal* in May 1999. In a tone dripping with condescension, Bork wrote that the government case was based on a "discredited, anticonsumer theory of monopolization." What the government called "predation" was just "good business sense." If the government had its way, Bork wrote, it would "transform antitrust from a guarantor of free markets to a comprehensive regulatory regime dictating prices and asset allocations, turning the large firms ... into a semicomatose group of quasipublic utilities. However delightful that might be to inefficient competitors, it would harm consumers by establishing a domestic form of protectionism." Bork accused the government of proposing "a radical revision of the law."[47] This was projection: it was Bork who had offered a radically revisionist history of antitrust statutes. Now he was playing the socialist card, too, accusing the government of seeking to prop up inefficient firms. Bork had no evidence for this; if anything, it was his camp that might be accused of defending inefficiency, by siding with lugubrious incumbents against potentially nimble upstarts. In any event, Bork was scarcely objective: he was representing American Airlines in the case.

Characterizing Bork as more scornful than serious, Kahn offered a point-by-point rebuttal, published in the *Wall Street Journal* a few weeks later. Bork had mischaracterized the factual allegations, obscured critical aspects of the government's case (which actually accorded with what Bork himself had said should be the test of predation), and "ignores the distinctive, if not unique, characteristics of the airline industry." Kahn reiterated that he was in favor of lowering costs for consumers, "[b]ut no purpose is served by simplistic dismissals" of the genuine threat posed by "predatory responses" to competition.[48] But the simplistic dismissal won.

Looking back on this period, Kahn lambasted the rationale that had gutted antitrust enforcement as a triumph of "eighteenth-century" liberalism. Actually, it was an inversion of traditional liberalism. Before, anticompetitive practices were assumed to do harm. After all, the whole point of markets is that they foster beneficial competition. Now it was assumed that because markets "naturally" worked efficiently, harm to consumers was all but impossible.[49]

CARTER'S DEREGULATION OF the trucking industry followed a similar path as airline deregulation. Since the late nineteenth century, railroads had been regulated by the Interstate Commerce Commission (ICC), which included transport of agricultural products. The Motor Carrier Act of 1935 added trucking regulation to the ICC's docket, but with an important exemption: the transport of "unprocessed" agricultural products. This was meant to enable farmers to haul their own products by truck to markets and railheads, but over several decades U.S. secretaries of agriculture had pushed to widen the exemption to cover all kinds of agricultural products, regardless of who was transporting them.[50] The result was a patchwork of regulations with little logic.

Why was trucking regulated, anyway? Trucking was not a "natural monopoly" like railroads or electricity, where the costs of entry were so great that competition was infeasible. It was rather the opposite: the costs of entry were so low that there was a threat of too much competition, and of a race to the bottom that drove everyone out of business. Congress in the 1930s intended the Motor Carrier Act to limit entry into the industry through the issuance of operating certificates that permitted specific kinds of cargo on specific routes, enabling truckers to compete profitably against both railroads and each other. It would also offer consumers an alternative to the railroads, which were infamous for price-fixing and other anticompetitive practices.[51] By controlling one industry (trucking), the Motor Carrier Act's authors hoped to create competition in the larger realm of commodity transport.

Whether the Motor Carrier Act was a good idea or not, by the 1970s there were at least three reasons to reexamine it. One was minor in 1935 but had become major by 1970: the agricultural exemption. Another was infrastructure: the interstate highway system had made trucking more profitable and, in many regions, faster and more efficient than railroads. A third was technology: larger, faster vehicles helped profitability. These forces had combined to break the railroads' oligopoly over transport after World War II, so many of the original arguments for supporting the trucking industry no longer held.[52]

Regulated trucking had accumulated a variety of inefficiencies. Because the ICC granted routes and cargoes to specific operators, regulated carriers could sometimes transport steel but not aluminum or plastic. Or they were permitted to haul a load in one direction but not the other. This "deadheading," which caused trucks to return empty, was obviously inefficient. Worse, because some agricultural products were exempt but not others, independent truckers might be able to carry apples to a cannery but not applesauce from it. This led to byzantine workarounds, including a practice called "trip-leasing" in which an independent trucker would contract for a nonexempt cargo from a regulated carrier.[53] Another oddity was that rates within the regulated trucking sector were set not by ICC directly, but by regional "rate bureaus," which tended to do their work in private. This practice would have been illegal under the nation's antitrust laws, but trucking was exempt.[54] In theory, the rate bureaus prevented rate discrimination, but since the processes were shrouded, no one knew if they did. While the ICC had authority to investigate rate bureaus' decisions, it received so many challenges that it could act on only a few.

Still, the Motor Carrier Act had achieved Congress's original goal: it had raised the incomes of truck drivers and truck company owners and helped to establish and sustain a profitable industry. Trucking companies had gained "monopoly rents"— income higher than they would otherwise have had in the absence of regulation—and truckers could boast middle-class incomes. But in 1977, boosting wages was no longer a primary goal, even among Democrats. Moreover, many truckers themselves now wanted deregulation. Whether they worked in the regulated or exempt sectors, were unionized or independent, few of them liked the myriad federal and state regulations they faced. As a farmer, Carter was particularly sympathetic to this concern.

There was one more issue motivating reform. By the 1970s, the Teamsters Union was seriously corrupt. Teamsters president Jimmy Hoffa had been prosecuted and convicted for jury tampering, attempted bribery, conspiracy, and mail and wire fraud, and in 1967 had been sentenced to thirteen years in prison. Many teamsters had concluded that union leadership was not working in their interest, and wildcat strikes erupted in 1970 and again in 1976.[55] Independent truckers also struck, largely to protest inflation and the fuel crises, in 1973, 1974, and again in 1979. One historian of trucking culture explained, "when truckers came to feel betrayed by arbitrary government regulations and the undemocratic Teamsters Union, radically libertarian politics came to the fore."[56]

In a 1979 special message to Congress, Carter enumerated the pathologies of trucking regulation with a litany of anecdotes about what was, and wasn't, exempt: frozen dinners were exempt, unless chicken or seafood; crab shells were exempt but not oysters; raisins coated with honey, exempt, but coated with chocolate, not; wine was regulated as a foodstuff, but not beer. He excoriated the rate bureaus for price-fixing, which was "normally a felony, punishable by fines up to $100,000 and imprisonment up to three years for individuals, and up to $1 million for corporations."[57] While Congress had made this legal, it was anticompetitive and cost consumers $5 billion a year. Testifying before the House Subcommittee on Surface Transportation, Kahn argued that reform would "free the trucking industry from the straitjacket of government regulation and restore it to the free enterprise system."[58]

When he signed the new Motor Carrier Act of 1980, Carter declared that it would "bring the trucking industry into the free-market system where it belongs."[59] This was only slightly exaggerated. The bill removed the rate bureaus' antitrust exemption, allowed carriers to set rates within a range without ICC interference, and eliminated many of the certificate restrictions that had been created over the decades—particularly the routing restrictions that had led to empty carriages and inefficient routes. It also removed antitrust enforcement from the ICC and gave it to the Federal Trade Commission, while consolidating safety regulation in the Department of Transportation. The legislation still required the ICC to certify the "fitness" of new entrants to the business—meaning their ability to operate safely and carry appropriate levels of insurance—but also granted the ICC substantial authority to license new entrants if it would "improve the competitive climate."[60] Overall, the act did what many advocates believed was most important: it used government to support competition rather than suppress it. New entrants to the trucking business flooded in.

Did trucking deregulation work? As with airlines, it depends on your perspective. The administration's primary goal was to lower prices, which deregulation did. According to one major study, the elimination of monopoly rents accruing to both owners and truckers saved consumers somewhere between $4.3 and $14.9 billion, while annual efficiency gains to the nation's economy were estimated at between $1.5 to $4.9 billion.[61] (These broad ranges illustrate the difficulty of determining the actual impacts of deregulation.) Traffic density and productivity also surged, restoring profitability.[62] Coupled with parallel changes implemented in the railroads at the time, the cost of shipping declined, lowering the cost of many consumer goods.[63] As a contribution to combating inflation, trucking deregulation was a success.

On the other hand, the overall efficiency gain was small. The U.S. Gross Domestic Product (GDP) in 1979 was $2.6 trillion, so even the high-end estimate of $4.9 billion wasn't much. Trucking jobs increased, but unionized jobs decreased: Teamsters Union membership plummeted and wages dropped.[64] One history of trucking deregulation offers its interpretation in its title: *Sweatshops on Wheels*. And large numbers of trucking companies went out of business: most of the regulated carriers that had existed in 1979 vanished through either acquisition or bankruptcy.[65]

Part of the problem was that, while Congress removed price and entry regulations, it did not apply the Fair Labor Standards Act—the law that sets maximum work hours and overtime rules—to trucking, so the work week of truckers expanded while compensation shrank.[66] Kahn had not expected this outcome. In congressional testimony, he had brushed this worry aside on the grounds that trucks were easily transferrable from areas with excess capacity to others with insufficient capacity. "It is inconceivable to me," he had confidently declared, "that cut-throat competition could become a way of life in the trucking industry."[67] He was wrong. Trucking was once a route from high school to a middle-class lifestyle. After deregulation, that route still existed, but it was a far bumpier ride.

MEANWHILE, A CRISIS was brewing in the nation's financial regulatory system, and Carter again turned to deregulation as a solution. The most jeopardized component of the financial system were the savings and loan associations—also known as thrifts—which could only provide home mortgages. The rules under which they operated were strict: Thrifts were only allowed to operate in a single area, the interest rates they could pay on savings accounts were capped by law, and they could only offer fixed-rate, fixed-term mortgages. Deposits were insured, and they had a separate regulator from the other two major kinds of banks (commercial and investment). Over the first two postwar decades, thrifts funded the housing boom that produced modern suburbia.

But by the late '70s there were problems. The existing rules allowed thrifts to pay higher interest rates on deposits than commercial banks, which had produced pressures to deregulate interest rates, if not fundamentally restructure the system. This problem had long been recognized, but until the 1970s, efforts to address it got no traction. Another problem involved "creative destruction." Innovation in banking and financial markets created volatilities in a system that previously had been stable. In 1961 Citibank introduced "certificates of deposit" (CDs) that were uninsured (and therefore unregulated) but made them available only to depositors with millions of dollars. These CDs typically carried variable interest rates; when those rates were higher than the regulated thrifts could pay, they drew funds out of the thrift system. This happened twice during the 1960s, temporarily reducing the funds available for housing. Neither event was seen as a crisis, but a third instance in 1969 led the Nixon administration to consider deregulation. Congress, however, wouldn't go along, and financial restructuring bills failed in 1973 and 1975.[68] The problem continued to brew.

At the same time, ordinary citizens began to eye the high interest rates commercial banks paid on CDs, and the Gray Panthers, a senior citizens' activist group, sued the government, demanding access to CDs for small depositors.[69] Regulators gave them what they wanted; this led to a huge outflow of funds from thrifts and a credit crunch in housing. Now the thrifts perceived themselves to be the victims—of arbitrary decisions by banking regulators—and they sued, too. In April 1979, the U.S. Court of Appeals for the District of Columbia agreed with them.[70]

Congress took the opportunity to give commercial banks and their allies the restructuring they wanted. The House of Representatives initially sought only to ratify what the financial regulators had done and avoid the political drama of true reform. Neither the Senate Banking Committee nor the Carter administration agreed; they were willing to risk the drama. Carter asked for the interest rate caps imposed under the Banking Act of 1933 to be removed, permitting interest on deposits to "rise to market-rate levels." To ensure banks and thrifts could actually pay those rates, he also asked Congress to allow federally chartered institutions to offer variable-rate mortgages, consumer loans, and interest-bearing checking accounts for all depositors. Declaring that pro-market reforms would benefit consumers, Carter wrote in a special message to Congress: "These steps will bring the benefits of market rates to consumers, promote a steadier flow of mortgage credit and improve the efficiency of the financial markets."[71]

Carter got most of what he wanted. The Depository Institutions Deregulation and Monetary Control Act of 1980 created a committee supervise the elimination of deposit interest rate caps over a six-year period, after which the committee would disband. The act extended the authority to offer interest-bearing checking accounts to all kinds of depository institutions and raised the insurance limits on federally insured accounts from forty thousand dollars to one hundred thousand.[72] Thrifts were authorized to offer consumer loans and to hold commercial paper and corporate securities up to 20 percent of the value of their assets. The act also removed geographic limitations on real estate loans.

The law did not, however, authorize all kinds of banks to provide variable-rate mortgages. Instead, it required an interagency task force to make recommendations to "provide balance to the asset-liability management problems inherent in the thrift portfolio structure."[73] In plainer language: if interest rates on deposits could vary but mortgage interest rates could not, it would be impossible for thrifts to stay solvent. This task force report was due by June 1980, but nothing would be done to resolve this structural problem until late in the decade. Congress kicked the can down the road, and it would wind up costing taxpayers dearly.

THE GROWING POWER of the business lobby, and the concomitant waning of labor influence in American politics, is nowhere more visible than in the 1978 Revenue Act. During the preceding decades, American tax policy had become more progressive, with higher rates for higher earners and lower, or zero, rates for lower-income people. But industrialists hated this, and the relatively new (and, until 1978, relatively moderate) Business Roundtable, a group designed to mobilize CEOs, revived an old NAM argument against progressive taxation: capital formation and investment.

A major component of the Great Inflation of the 1970s was stagnant-to-falling productivity. The Business Roundtable blamed this on falling investment in more efficient equipment and machinery, in addition to regulation (pollution regulation, mostly). There was a "capital shortage." Labor union leaders agreed that there was a capital shortage, although they assigned a different cause: the early 1970s witnessed the end of controls on capital outflow, and companies began to invest their capital overseas, not in the United States, beginning our long era of offshoring production.[74]

One of the planks in Carter's 1976 campaign had been tax reform. He had run on closing loopholes that allowed the wealthy and well connected to avoid taxation, which (he argued) would enable simplification of the tax code and lower overall rates. He targeted one "loophole" in particular: the tax code's preference for capital gains. Since 1921, capital gains had been taxed at a lower rate than the so-called ordinary income that most Americans get from wages. Carter intended to tax capital gains at the same rate as ordinary income. At the time, capital gains were taxed at a maximum of 49 percent, while the top ordinary income bracket was 70 percent. Lowering the top tax bracket to 50 percent, and eliminating loopholes to pay for it, seems to have been his thinking.[75] But that's not the tax reform that he signed in 1978. Instead, the Revenue Act lowered the capital gains rate substantially.

A moderate Republican congressman from Wisconsin, William Steiger, introduced the amendment for the capital gains cut, convinced by an electronics industry lobbyist that it would raise more "venture capital." Steiger's proposal attracted many Democratic votes, and when Carter recognized he was losing on the issue, he had congressional allies modify the amendment, setting the rate at 35 percent instead of the 25 percent Steiger had sought. They finally settled on 28 percent.[76] But Carter wanted the tax reform to be revenue neutral; this was accomplished by abandoning middle-class tax relief. Between inflation and a scheduled Social Security tax increase, the 1978 Revenue Act increased the middle-class tax burden.[77]

Lowering the capital gains tax didn't solve the productivity problem, however, because (as union leaders feared) its beneficiaries for the most part didn't invest in the United States. Instead, they moved their monies abroad: overseas investment nearly tripled during the Carter years.[78] Another common tax instrument, the investment tax credit, could have been expanded to ensure reinvestment in the United States, but it wasn't. Cutting the capital gains tax didn't generate a great flood of new venture capital, but it did substantially benefit those who already had spare assets to invest in the stock market. Whatever Carter's intent, the 1978 Revenue Act helped to bring an end to the era in which the gap between the wealthiest and poorest Americans had shrunk, and to launch a new gilded age of inequality.

ECONOMISTS HAVE COME to credit Carter's choice for chairman of the Federal Reserve in 1979 with finally ending inflation. After a cabinet shakeup in July that moved the incumbent Fed chairman, G. William Miller, to the Treasury Department, Carter chose Paul Volcker, president of the New York Federal Reserve Bank.[79] Volcker (no relation to the Volker Fund) was already widely known to support "price stability," and he would use the Fed's control of interest rates to rein in inflation. But Volcker, who occasionally dined with Kahn to commiserate over the challenge of the task, would turn out to be willing to go well beyond tweaking interest rates.[80]

A major consequence of placing the Federal Reserve in charge of the nation's economy was that it made the pursuit of low inflation, rather than low unemployment, the nation's primary economic goal. In 1926, the economist Irving Fisher had noticed the inverse relationship between inflation and unemployment, so a policy preference for low inflation meant a policy preference for higher unemployment.[81] This had been widely accepted by the 1950s. In 1955, William McChesney Martin, whom President Truman had appointed to the post of chairman of the Federal Reserve Board of Governors in 1951, made the classic statement of the Fed's role in this respect: "The Federal Reserve . . . is in the position of the chaperone who has ordered the punch bowl removed just when the party was really warming up."[82] If unemployment got too low, the Fed would raise interest rates to reverse its potentially inflationary effects (or, as many economists prefer to say it, to restore "price stability"). This, of course, benefited employers who hoped to keep down wages, but it hurt workers looking for jobs. But if unemployment got too high, the Fed could lower interest rates to stimulate the economy to produce more jobs. At least in theory, the Fed role was symmetrical. But in practice, it didn't generally work that way.

In 1956, the Federal Open Market Committee (a committee of the Federal Reserve) members had discussed using their power to control interest rates to help industry suppress union wage demands, suggesting that the Fed in the 1950s was not an unbiased foreman of the nation's economy and that its tendencies aligned more with management than with labor.[83] By the 1960s, there was another argument that influenced the Fed to focus more on inflation than unemployment, and it came from Milton Friedman.

In a 1967 speech to the American Economic Association, Friedman argued that the basic policy choice U.S. leaders had been making since the Depression—trading unemployment against inflation—was no choice at all. "There is always a temporary trade-off between inflation and unemployment; there is no permanent trade-off," he said.[84] Inflating the economy to improve employment would only work temporarily, because people would begin to anticipate future inflation and price it into everything. That's what happened in union negotiations during the 1970s. Despite Kahn's exhortations to restrain wage demands during negotiations, unions asked for, and often got, wage increases beyond the inflation targets he had wanted.[85]

By 1978, many economists took Friedman's 1967 argument as a prediction that had come true, leading some of them, including Volcker, to conclude that controlling inflation was more important than lowering unemployment.[86] In his confirmation hearings, he nearly used Friedman's words, commenting that "the perceived 'trade-off' between unemployment and inflation would only be worsened" by premature fiscal or monetary efforts to stimulate the economy. Volcker set out to destroy the expectation of inflation. His first attempts, almost as soon as he started the new job in August 1979, came via the Fed's traditional mechanism of raising short-term interest rates. Perhaps because financial markets had expected him to do much more, it had no effect.[87] It took Volcker time to convince enough of the other Fed governors to do what he thought necessary: to target the money supply directly.

The Federal Reserve traditionally influenced the creation of new money by private banks by manipulating interest rates: higher interest rates were supposed to reduce demand for bank loans, the principal way new money is injected into the nation's economy. But Volcker's predecessor had been raising interest rates to no avail. It was evidently not enough to get Wall Street's attention after a decade of high inflation, so Volcker targeted the money supply's growth rate and enforced it by manipulating the reserve requirement, the amount of capital that commercial banks had to park in the Fed's twelve regional banks.[88] Raising the reserve requirement would remove money from the economy; reducing it would put money back in. Volcker intended the change in policy to send a message to the entire financial system that the Fed was going to be much more aggressive in its efforts to suppress inflation. That change in policy would be the shock to the economy needed to drive out inflationary expectations.

Volcker may have targeted the psychology of investors, the financial markets, and union leaders, but he hit hundreds of millions of people beyond that. The Fed's new policy drove interest rates up to 14.5 percent by election day 1980. In December, commercial bank interest rates peaked at 21.5 percent and drove the United States into a recession that lasted well into the next administration. By 1982 the unemployment rate reached a new postwar high of 10.8 percent. The thrift industry was thrown deeper into crisis. Housing construction and car sales reached postwar lows.[89] The Volcker Shock triggered financial crises in several other countries as well, and a debt crisis that would destroy lives around the globe, and among people who knew nothing of the arcana of intertwined global financial markets.[90] Eventually inflation did subside, but at a high cost to many.

In the short term, Carter's efforts to follow the standard conservative nostrum of fiscal austerity failed to vanquish inflation. The reforms that he, Kahn, and their congressional supporters implemented were anti-inflationary in the long run but, to paraphrase John Maynard Keynes, in the long run they were dead—or at least out of office.[91] In the 1980 presidential election, Carter lost to the juggernaut of market fundamentalism, Ronald Reagan.

AFTER CARTER'S DEFEAT, Alfred Kahn returned to Cornell. He remained a Democrat, and still believed that economic liberalism required a conscience. "Traditional liberalism has achieved its greatest triumphs by marrying the quest for social justice with the promotion of economic growth," he wrote in 1981. "We cannot, by neglecting the second of these, afford to entrust our national destinies to people who seem not to care at all about the first." Kahn's fear was that the Reagan administration would respond to continuing inflation "in ways that almost totally dissolve the social contract. His methods may alienate large groups in our society, and flout our conceptions of social justice and equity."

The contrast between what Carter and Reagan did is important to understand. Kahn's vision of economic deregulation meant restoring the power of price signals to produce greater efficiency and productivity, enabling the economic growth necessary to pay for "continued progress in humanizing our society," but it did not mean throwing workers (and consumers) to the wolves.[92] Kahn remained a key champion of competition and would continue to testify before Congress on tele-communications and utility regulation matters, as well as teach and write papers, until he died in 2010—a happy Obama Democrat, he told an interviewer shortly before his passing. He also continued to believe that market forces had to be tempered with social conscience. Kahn, the quasi-institutionalist, understood that markets did not exist unto themselves, but that states shaped markets, and he used his public service to reshape American markets in ways that he believed would be broadly beneficial.

We might call what Carter and Kahn did *marketization*—the creation of competitive markets where they did not previously exist—or market liberalization, removing controls that were counterproductive or no longer justified, or simply price decontrol. Most people, however, just called it deregulation, and under that moniker Ronald Reagan would pursue a very different program. The Carter administration had focused on the deregulation of *prices*—ideally as means to lower them—but the Reagan administration would expand the concept to cover a much wider range of changes, from aggressive de-unionization to the weakening of environmental, health, and safety statutes. In other words, precisely what Kahn had warned against.

CHAPTER 13

Magical Thinking

"Government is not the solution to our problem; government is the problem." So declared Ronald Reagan as he launched his administration in January 1981, with a speech that would have warmed the heart of Herbert Hoover. The crisis of the moment was the Great Inflation, still raging despite the Fed's aggressive actions beginning more than a year earlier, but the speech wasn't really about the current crisis. Reagan had been using antigovernment rhetoric since the 1950s, and now, finally, his moment had come to shape national reality. He would popularize an ideological framework that deified markets and demonized government. He would promise to "get the government off our backs" (while actually only removing it from the backs of businessmen).[1] It was the framework that NAM had been promoting since the 1930s, and that Hayek and Friedman had made respectable— the inseparability of political and economic freedom—encapsulated by Reagan's winning slogan: "the magic of the marketplace."

Like the "Gipper" he had played in a Hollywood film, Reagan was a team player, and even before winning the presidency he had a shadow cabinet writing reports and white papers outlining the framework for the new administration. That shadow was the network of conservative and libertarian think tanks that had developed in the 1970s to promote ideas that the business community had been pushing since the earliest days of the debate over child labor and workplace death and disability, repackaged for the late twentieth century. Together, Reagan and his allies in American business would persuade us to loathe government and love the "Free Market."

THE EXPLOSIVE GROWTH of right-wing think tanks was the product of a conscious plan, articulated in a 1971 memo by then lawyer and soon-to-be Supreme Court justice Lewis Powell.[2] Powell addressed his memo to Eugene B. Sydnor, the chairman of the Education Committee of the U.S. Chamber of Commerce. Journalist Bill Moyers has called the memo a "call-to-arms for corporations."[3] It exhorted business leaders to build a set of institutions to push back against the growing influence of liberals. In language reminiscent of Lemuel Boulware, Powell asserted: "Business must learn the lesson . . . that political power is necessary; that such power must be assiduously cultivated; and that when necessary, it must be used aggressively and with determination—without embarrassment and without the reluctance which has been so characteristic of American business."[4] Businessmen would need to take the long view and put their money where their ideology was: "strength lies in organization, in careful long-range planning and implementation, in consistency of action over an indefinite period of years, in the scale of financing available only through joint effort, and in the political power available only through united action and national organizations."[5]

Powell's claim that business had been a reluctant partner in politics was ridiculous: from NELA and NAM to Harold Luhnow and Lemuel Boulware, American business leaders had actively sought to shape both public opinion and government policy. The businessmen we have tracked in this story aggressively worked to bend the federal government to their will, pushing back against policies designed to protect citizens against unethical labor practices, unsafe workplaces, and the anticompetitive effects of corporate monopolies and oligopolies. But Powell's call to arms represented a new, more ambitious, and even more aggressive chapter.

The crescendo of Powell's memo returned to a familiar argument. The captains of industry were not "economic royalists," as FDR had tagged them; they were defenders of freedom. The free-enterprise capitalism they had helped to build was the bulwark of liberty. "The threat to the enterprise system is not merely a matter of economics. It also is a threat to individual freedom," Powell declared.[6] Business leaders would not be fighting for their self-interest; they would be fighting for freedom, both economic and political. For "whatever the causes of diminishing economic freedom may be, the truth is that freedom as a concept is indivisible. As the experience of the socialist and totalitarian states demonstrates, the contraction and denial of economic freedom is followed *inevitably* by governmental restrictions on other cherished rights. It is this message, above all the others, that must be carried home to the American people."[7] It was the indivisibility thesis, the road to serfdom, restated for a new generation.

The Powell memo was dated August 23, 1971. Two months later, President Nixon nominated Powell to the Supreme Court. The following year, NAM moved its headquarters from New York to Washington in recognition that "the thing that affects business most today is government."[8] The year 1972 also saw the creation of the Business Roundtable, which would help to make CEOs into a culturally visible and influential force. Companies opened public affairs offices in Washington, many of which would run antiregulatory ad campaigns. (It was around this time that Mobil began its program of weekly "advertorials"—advertisements formatted to look like op-ed pieces—in the *New York Times*, intended to weaken public support for environmental policies, a practice that continued when the company became ExxonMobil.)[9] Corporations also began to hire lobbyists in force, and to create Political Action Committees (PACs). And they began to fund (and in some cases even to create) "third-party" allies—organizations that appeared independent, but often had intricate ties to corporate patrons.[10] Higher education was also a target: in 1974, the chairman of Hewlett-Packard demanded that his corporate colleagues stop supporting colleges and universities that promoted anticapitalist views (or even capitalist-neutral views) and focus instead on funding institutions that contributed "in some specific way to our individual companies or to the general welfare of our free-enterprise system."[11]

Also around this time, the Chamber of Commerce became a leading force in American politics, participating in efforts to undermine antipollution statutes, weaken workplace safety, block action on climate change, and pressure universities and their faculty on numerous fronts. They filed or participated in countless amici briefs.[12] But as the Powell memo directed, NAM, the Chamber of Commerce, the Business Roundtable, and their allies did not seek simply to influence specific government policies. They sought to turn the American people toward business and against government.

Much of this work would be done through the antigovernment think tanks, foundations, and "philanthropies" that proliferated in the 1970s and '80s—heavily financed by American corporations and billionaire industrialists. These included the American Enterprise Institute, founded in 1943 but reinvigorated in the 1970s; the Heritage Foundation, established in 1973 to "build and promote conservative public policies"; the Wall Street–friendly American Council for Capital Formation, also founded in 1973; the Cato Institute, founded in 1977 by businessman Edward Crane, an early proponent of the privatization of Social Security; the George C.

Marshall Institute, founded in 1984 to defend Ronald Reagan's Strategic Defense Initiative but soon converted into an anti-climate-science organ; the Heartland Institute, also founded in 1984 and a major force of climate-change denial; and the Acton Institute, founded in 1990 to promote the "benefits of a limited government, [and] the beneficent consequences of a free market." By 1981 there were so many of these antigovernment think tanks that they needed a new group, the Atlas Network, to serve as an umbrella; by 1990 there were an estimated fifty such groups.[13] Meanwhile, liberal nongovernmental organizations and foundations focused on specific issues, like education or the environment, not realizing that their opponents had set much more capacious and integrative goals.[14]

These think tanks produced books, journals, and newsletters, such as *Regulation*, the magazine of the Cato Institute which, despite its name, argues against regulation. They developed generous programs and fellowships to nurture conservative intellectuals and advance their ideas and careers. And they supported spin-off organizations, such as the Federalist Society (founded in 1982). The latter became particularly significant: with abundant funding from far-right groups including the Olin Foundation, the Scaife Foundation, the Koch Family Foundation, and the Mercer Family Foundation—as well as companies, including Google and Chevron—the Federalist Society would quickly spread through American universities and law schools, promoting an originalist and textualist interpretation of the Constitution. According to the *Washington Post*, as of 2019 six of the nine Supreme Court justices were or had been members; Amy Coney Barrett, appointed in 2020, was a member as well.[15]

While these organizations were diverse in tone, they were nearly uniform in message, offering some version of the Heritage mission statement: "to formulate and promote public policies based on the principles of free enterprise, limited government, [and] individual freedom."[16] Many of these groups explicitly promoted the indivisibility thesis. And while frequently accusing environmentalists of alarmism, they promoted an alarmist vision of capitalism under siege. The rise of right-wing think tanks helped spread the pro-market, antigovernment gospel across the country and insert what had been decidedly niche views into the mainstream. William Baroody Sr. of the American Enterprise Institute called it "public attitude formation," and it worked.[17]

In 1980, Ronald Reagan rode into office on a horse that this network of think tanks and organizations had groomed and saddled. Perhaps most influential in helping to frame Reagan's antiregulatory narrative was the 1980 Heritage report *Mandate for Leadership*, written explicitly as a handbook for the new administration. Its premise was that America faced a "crisis of overregulation" threatening to "destroy the private competitive free-market economy it was originally designed to protect."[18] This was exaggeration fused with misdirection. In the Carter years, both Democrats and Republicans had agreed that some New Deal–era regulations needed to be revisited, and Carter, together with Alfred Kahn, had worked to reduce regulation where the factual case for doing so was strong. But if there was a crisis in the American economy, there was little if any evidence for a cause in "overregulation." Moreover, to say that the *purpose* of regulation was to protect the "free-market economy" was perverse. The lion's share of the regulations that business had spent decades opposing were not designed to protect the free-market economy, but to address and redress its failures. As for those regulations that had been designed to protect competition—such as the Sherman and Clayton antitrust statutes—they had been the target of organized conservative efforts to undermine.

"Overregulation" was a libertarian construct, linked to the myth of the indivisibility thesis and the metaphor of the road to serfdom. (In the 1980s, many European countries would fare better economically than the United States, even though they were by many measures more regulated.)[19] Still, many voters agreed that America was in crisis, and blaming it on a single thing—overregulation—rather than a complex nexus of social, historical, and economic factors proved to be an election-winning strategy. With the election of Ronald Reagan, market fundamentalists finally had the opportunity to put their ideology into practice, whether it was supported by facts or not.

DURING THE PRESIDENTIAL campaign, Reagan had promised his top priority would be to reduce the federal deficit. In his 1981 inaugural speech he stood by that promise. "For decades we have piled deficit upon deficit, mortgaging our future and our children's future for the temporary convenience of the present."[20] Carter had blamed the nation's financial ills on the public for spending too much and saving too little. Reagan flipped the script, making spending government's fault.

The U.S. government was (and still is) effectively an insurance company with an army.[21] This was the most obvious effect of the New Deal and the creation of the Cold War economy. In 1932, defense represented 13 percent of the federal budget and only 1.1 percent of GDP; the federal government in toto comprised 8.4 percent of GDP.[22] Carter's 1981 budget request would have 21.5 percent of federal spending, or about 4.6 percent of GDP, go to military outlays, while the federal budget had grown to around 19 percent of GDP. Carter tried to cut the budget—his anticipated deficit of $16 billion was quite a bit less than in prior years—but Congress only gave him some of the cuts he wanted, while the unanticipated recession of 1980 reduced federal tax receipts. The 1980 federal deficit ballooned to $73 billion.[23]

In that context, it wasn't unreasonable that Reagan wanted to cut federal spending. The argument was reinforced in Europe, where UK prime minister Margaret Thatcher and others were saying that high government spending as a percentage of GDP was a drag on economies.[24] But to be serious about cutting the federal budget, Reagan would have to address military spending. He refused. When he sent his budget plan to Congress, its centerpiece was a huge tax cut: a 30 percent across-the-board decrease, phased in over three years.

The inspiration for Reagan's tax cuts came from New York congressman Jack Kemp, who had tried to pass something similar in 1978.[25] The idea itself was still older. Dating back at least to Andrew Mellon, secretary of the treasury from 1921 to 1932, it was called "trickle-down economics," and it was what NAM had advocated since the 1930s. Cutting the highest tax rates, the theory went, would allow the wealthy to invest more in production, which would generate new jobs and therefore new tax revenues, so despite the cut in tax rates, tax revenues would stay the same or even grow. In the 1970s, the idea gained a new name, "supply-side economics," because it would stimulate the economy not through government spending or increased consumer demand, but by boosting production. The theory crisply rejected the Keynesian economics that had dominated for the previous five decades. Mid-century Keynesians had abandoned supply-side solutions, since they had failed either to prevent the Great Depression or to help the economy recover from it. Half a century later, Keynesianism was on the back foot.

The resurrection of supply-side economics did not come from NAM, however, but from a new economic guru: Arthur Laffer. A professor of business economics at the University of Chicago, Laffer moved in 1976 to the University of Southern California, where he worked on behalf of Proposition 13, a measure to amend California's state constitution to drastically limit property taxes.[26] Laffer's work supporting large tax cuts had come to the attention of *Wall Street Journal* editor and conservative commentator Jude Wanniski, who arranged a meeting between Laffer and future vice president Dick Cheney.[27] Popular lore has it that, at a restaurant in Washington, D.C., Laffer pitched his idea with a drawing on a napkin.[28] The "Laffer Curve" was a graphical argument for a Goldilocks approach to taxation: rates that were too high would prevent investment in new production and/or suppress the desire to work hard; rates that were too low would be inadequate to finance necessary government functions like law enforcement and national defense. Somewhere between these two extremes was the optimal tax rate.

Few would argue there isn't a balance to be struck between funding government services and letting people retain their earned wealth. But Laffer's claim went much further than that general premise: he (and his followers) said the optimal rate would maximize productive investment, maximize growth, and generate so much additional income that cutting the marginal tax rate would cause no loss of government revenues. It was practically magic: lower rates yield higher revenues.

The catch was that the model presupposed that growth was closely correlated with net investment, which it might or not be. Even if the premise were correct, Laffer had no evidence to show where the optimal rate sat.[29] This led to decades of academic arguments; meanwhile, conservatives simply latched on to the assertion—which was certainly Laffer's own belief—that the United States was on the way-too-high side of the tax rate curve.[30] Wanniski was sure Laffer was right; he promoted the idea aggressively in his columns and then in a book modestly entitled *The Way the World Works*. (According to the *New York Times*, George Will once said of Wanniski, "I wish I was as confident about something as he is about everything.")[31]

It's not clear when Reagan first heard of the Laffer Curve, but he was briefed on it in 1978 when Wanniski's book came out. It resonated. Reagan had railed for decades against the American income tax system, telling an anecdote about turning down movie roles because he'd make too much money and wind up in a higher tax bracket. (So he claimed; it is hard to believe he really would have turned down a good role that paid well.) Now, Reagan had more than an anecdote to justify his views. He had a (seemingly) respectable academic theory, and it became the basis for the economic recovery program he submitted to Congress in February 1981.

The Economic Recovery Tax Act (ERTA) cut the top tax rate by 20 percent, while the other tax brackets were chopped 23 percent.[32] Tax brackets were also indexed to inflation to eliminate "bracket creep," and estate taxes were dramatically reduced. Corporate tax rates were also cut, and the depreciation schedule for business assets was restructured. ERTA reduced the capital gains tax rate to 20 percent, too. It passed Congress, and Reagan signed it in early August 1981.[33] The potential revenue loss from ERTA was colossal: $750 billion over five years. Unless accompanied by comparable spending cuts, this would explode the federal debt.[34] Enter supply-side economics. Reagan's revisions to Carter's fiscal year 1982 budget had revenue rising from $600 billion in 1981 to $650 billion in 1982. Under this projection, the budget would be balanced in fiscal year 1984.[35]

David Stockman, the director of the Office of Management and Budget (OMB), was worried; he thought serious budget cuts were still necessary. Even before inauguration day, Stockman was having regular breakfasts with William Greider, then an editor at the *Washington Post*, about his efforts to reform the budget. Stockman had been pushing for $40 billion in cuts and wanted it known that he was trying to alter expectations—in this case, expectations for endless budget growth. He told Greider that he wanted to weed out "weak claims" to federal largesse. The problem was that there simply were not enough weak claimants. Reagan had run on a pledge to increase military spending, and much of the rest of the budget involved direct benefits that were more or less mandated by law. Nor could Congress stop paying the interest on the federal debt. That left two small wedges: grants to state and local governments (fifteen cents on the dollar) and everything else (nine cents). President Reagan proposed cuts to both, but even he admitted that he could only reduce the growth rate of those functions, not shrink them. So Stockman didn't have much to work with.[36] Stockman added what he called a "magic asterisk," an unspecified set of additional reductions to be determined later, totaling $44 billion.[37] It was this budget—with the "magic asterisk"—that Congress had approved.

With military spending sacrosanct and discretionary spending just not that big a piece of the pie, Stockman said, the only thing left to cut was Social Security. This was a sleight of hand, because the program was independently financed: Social Security benefits were paid out of Social Security taxes, and from its inception in 1937 through 1974 the program overall had run in the black. Until the 1970s, there had never been more than two years in a row when the program had to draw on the Treasury. It was true that demographics now posed a challenge to the program's long-term solvency: from 1975 to 1980, it ran annual deficits, which was not sustainable, so adjustments needed to be made. (One obvious potential remedy was to index the Social Security tax to inflation, since benefits were so indexed.) Either way, an objective observer could reasonably suggest that the structural problems within the Social Security program had little to do with the annual federal deficit.[38] But Social Security was still part of the federal budget, so when the program was in deficit, it contributed to the bottom-line federal deficit. Stockman saw that cutting benefits would make the federal deficit appear smaller. Congress, however, had other ideas.

In March 1981, a bipartisan group of senators met with President Reagan to propose adjusting the formula used to determine Social Security cost-of-living adjustments (COLA). By reducing COLA, total Social Security spending could be constrained. But to minimize the political exposure, they intended to phase in the changes over years. They estimated saving $10 billion in the first year and $25 billion by the fifth. Stockman, working with Reagan's chief of staff, James Baker, blocked this proposal: Baker because he believed touching Social Security would be politically disastrous, and Stockman because he was holding out for larger cuts. Stockman wanted to slash early retirement and disability payments immediately. In May, Stockman pitched his plan to Reagan, and the president agreed.[39]

Democrats were jubilant. Stockman had handed them their 1982 campaign theme: "It's not fair ... It's Republican."[40] Horrified Republicans realized they needed to do something, so they passed the baton to a "blue-ribbon" committee led by Alan Greenspan, formerly chairman of the Council of Economic Advisers under Gerald Ford. (In 1974, when he was sworn in, Greenspan invited three people to the ceremony: his mother, Ayn Rand, and Rand's husband.)[41] The panel was divided as to whether the system was really broken, as Greenspan and others claimed, or just needed adjustment; they settled on the latter, by modest reductions in benefits and increases in the Social Security tax.[42] Reagan signed the resulting Social Security Reform Act on April 20, 1983. Within a few years, Social Security was back on track.[43]

Because Social Security was both extremely successful and popular, opponents of Big Government were bound to target it whether it worked or not. But it did work, and with modest adjustments it would continue to work. The Republican desire to dramatically decrease benefits—or even to privatize the program—was, if anything, rooted in this success, because it refuted Reagan's core claim that government was dead weight. His administration had to insist that Social Security was "broken," when—like any fifty-year-old thing—it just needed some maintenance and repair.[44] Many people know Senator Daniel Patrick Moynihan's quip that "everyone is entitled to his own opinion, but not to his own facts." Fewer know that he coined it during this debate over Social Security.[45]

WALL STREET HAD never believed the rosy supply-side forecasts emanating from the White House. They saw exploding deficits, not surging revenue, and to 1980s investors, deficits meant inflation.[46] When the tax bill passed in August 1981, markets dropped, interest rates increased, and the economy entered the deepest recession since the Great Depression. The investment boom that was supposed to follow the supply-side tax cut never came. The economy would not recover until late in 1983, when—as any Keynesian would have expected—consumer spending recovered, and the downside of the business cycle ended.

At least one person had anticipated this: Federal Reserve chairman Paul Volcker, who at the time was deep into his crusade to combat inflation through monetary policy.[47] He accepted that reducing taxes would stimulate the economy to some degree, as any infusion of money would; no Keynesian of the past half-century could fault that logic. However, tax cuts and deficit spending could also trigger inflation, which he was trying to prevent. For the first few months of 1981, Volcker gave talks about the risk of the new tax-cut plan. However, as it became clear that he had lost the political initiative, he confined his criticism to private discussions with members of Congress. In May, an apparent surge in the money supply caused the Fed to stomp on the brakes, interest rates soared to over 19 percent, and the economy fell back into recession.[48] The recession caused tax receipts to fall even farther, the deficit exploded, and Volcker would become a major thorn in the administration's side, arguing for the rest of Reagan's first term in office that the White House and Congress needed to get the deficit under control.

In 1982, several of the 1981 corporate tax cuts would be quietly repealed, but that did not stem the hemorrhage.[49] The deficit for fiscal year 1982 would be $110 billion, rising to $195 billion for fiscal year 1983.[50] Reagan continued raising taxes, albeit without the fanfare with which they had previously been reduced. The 1982 Tax Equity and Fiscal Responsibility Act raised taxes by about 1 percent of GDP—the largest peacetime tax increase in American history—and ten more tax increases would follow.[51] All in all, one analyst observed, Reagan "took back about half the 1981 tax cut with subsequent tax increases."[52] The deficit would peak in 1986 at $221 billion and only begin to decline after another large tax hike. The Reagan administration added more than a trillion dollars to the federal debt; Stockman later wrote a book decrying the Washington politics that had defeated his crusade.[53]

Politics were of course a large part of the story, particularly the refusal of both Democrats and Republicans even to consider the option of military cuts. But there was a larger, deeper issue: Republican leadership's resistance when their ideology was confronted with facts that didn't fit. Just as they refused to accept the reality that Social Security did work, they refused to accept that supply-side economics didn't. With that failure, the supply-side story that tax cuts would finance themselves should have been seriously reevaluated, if not thrown out completely. Instead, conservative (and even many moderate) Republicans continued to insist that taxes needed to be cut and that doing so would stimulate the economy, so we could have our economic cake and eat it, too.

In 1980, competing with Reagan for the Republican presidential nomination, George H. W. Bush had called supply-side "voodoo economics."[54] Bush was acknowledging the awkward truth: tax cuts do not pay for themselves. Even Stockman allowed that the whole thing was "premised on faith. On a belief about how the world works."[55] There's nothing wrong with testing a theory, but when the theory fails, it's time to move on. That is not what happened. Within a few years, tax cuts to stimulate the economy had become Republican gospel. When Bush became Reagan's vice president, he would claim he had only been "kidding" when he called supply-side economics "voodoo"; later he would deny ever having made the comment at all.[56]

When Bush ran for president at the end of Reagan's second term, he tried to solidify his support among the conservative benches in the party while embracing a bit of Reagan's swagger with his famous promise: "Read my lips. No new taxes."[57] Economic adviser Richard Darman advised against it, calling a pledge of that sort "stupid and dangerous," more helpful in winning than governing.[58] Events would vindicate Darman: Bush came from behind to win the presidency, but when he signed a budget that raised taxes, he lost the support of conservatives and went down to a crushing second-term defeat. That was the last time any major leader of the Republican Party questioned the wisdom of cutting the marginal tax rate.

Supply-side economics—now referred to as Reaganomics—didn't produce an American investment boom or surging tax receipts; neither did it produce the vaunted "trickle-down" effect. What it did demonstrably do was explode income inequality. A 1986 Congressional Budget Office analysis of the 1981 tax cut's effects found that the income of the top 1 percent had soared. They now made so much money that, despite the 20 percent cut in their tax rate, the total they owed had increased. Meanwhile, the bottom 50 percent of taxpayers saw their incomes decline. Based on the 1981–1983 data, the budget office authors found: "During this period, the real after-tax income per return in the bottom half of the income distribution declined by almost 3 percent and remained virtually constant for returns in the next highest 25 percent of the income distribution. For the top percentile of returns, the increase in real after-tax income per return was almost 23 percent."[59] The rich got richer, the poor got poorer, and the middle class treaded water.

Supply-side economics was a shell game. The theory had been tested and failed. In a rational world, this should have discredited the idea and the economists who preached it. Instead, conservatives doubled down.[60] Since the 1980s, the centrality of tax cuts has been the single most consistent theme in the Republican Party catechism. Ronald Reagan cut taxes, George W. Bush cut taxes, Donald Trump cut taxes. And in every case tax revenue as a share of GDP fell and the federal budget deficits got bigger.[61] In 2019, this refuted theory earned Arthur Laffer the Presidential Medal of Freedom.[62]

ANOTHER ONGOING CHALLENGE in the Reagan administration's early years was the foundering savings and loan system. The Depository Institutions Deregulation and Monetary Control Act of 1980 had left a fundamental problem unresolved: the mismatch between the interest rates thrifts needed to pay on savings accounts to stay competitive versus the income they could earn from mortgages. There was a substantive argument that existing regulations needed to be updated, even overhauled. But for the Reagan administration, the solution to the saving and loan crisis was not to update the regulatory system; it was to neuter the regulator.

Reagan's team took office knowing trouble was coming.[63] In 1981, the savings and loan industry suffered losses of $4.6 billion. One hundred and twelve thrifts were insolvent, with many more on the verge.[64] One available option was to permit insolvent institutions to merge with solvent ones. In 1981, 34 thrifts failed, but 269 others were authorized to merge. In many cases, this meant making up the difference between assets and liabilities with funds from the Federal Savings and Loan Insurance Corporation (FSLIC). But the FSLIC had $6.2 billion in assets, while the at-risk assets totaled $19.5 billion. Following this strategy, the FSLIC would go bust.

The Treasury Department came up with an alternative: instead of consuming the FSLIC's assets by pledging them in these mergers, it would issue federal certificates drawn on the Treasury as IOUs to cover the difference. Under the federal government's accounting practices, however, these would then appear on the government's own books as debt, increasing the (apparent) federal deficit. The White House had the Office of Management and Budget (OMB) change the accounting rules so these certificates wouldn't count against the deficit, temporarily sweeping the problem under the rug.[65]

Meanwhile, the Federal Home Loan Bank Board (FHLBB) made additional changes. Previously, stockholder-owned thrifts were required to have at least four hundred shareholders, 75 percent of whom had to live within the thrift's market area. To bring new owners and capital into the industry, these restrictions were eliminated.[66] This was designed to buy time, while regulators awaited two expected developments. The first was a decline in interest rates, which would allow thrifts to offer lower rates on deposits, improving their balance sheets. Lower interest rates would also help the economy to recover, which would tend to increase the value of the properties in their loan portfolios. The Reagan administration also worked with Congress to permit the thrifts to expand in riskier but more lucrative directions. The result was the Garn-St. Germain Depository Institutions Act of 1982, which allowed thrifts to make real estate development loans for up to 100 percent of appraised value, and to expand beyond mortgages into educational, business, and personal loans.[67]

The new law essentially abandoned the concept of a thrift as a local bank chartered to help families get home mortgages. It also allowed the thrifts to exchange their state charters for federal charters.[68] By rechartering, thrifts in states with strict regulations could operate under more lax federal rules. But because state-based deposit insurance programs depended on income from their state-chartered institutions, states now had little choice but to deregulate, too. The classic case was California, which effectively repealed its regulations.[69] The Garn-St. Germain Act created a regulatory race to the bottom; the consequences would end up costing taxpayers billions. But by this time, Reagan had largely defined his "revolution" as deregulation, comparing it to the revolution against taxation and undemocratic governance that had motivated American independence from England. "Today we are working to bring about another revolution, this time against the intolerable burdens [of] over-regulation . . . and over-taxation."[70]

In addition to weakening regulatory statutes, Reagan had another, less visible trick up his sleeve: decreasing the number of regulators. A particular target was the

FHLBB, funded directly by Congress but subject to personnel ceilings that OMB could lower.[71] One post-hoc analysis argued that "OMB zealously promoted deregulation, reductions in government personnel and reports required of the business. OMB was determined to control the Board's operations and displayed an intransigent attitude toward the Board's budget and staff size."[72]

At first, Garn-St. Germain seemed to be successful. The savings and loan industry saw a huge influx of funds and hundreds of new institutions were chartered. But 10 percent of the industry was still insolvent under traditional accounting rules, and those insolvent thrifts held 35 percent of industry assets.[73] In 1983, interest rates did come down, but the economic recovery didn't salvage the situation. If anything, it made things worse: the influx of new investment resulted in over-building commercial real estate, depressing prices, and asset values. Low oil prices compounded the problem in oil-producing states: Texas would be the state with the largest number of failed thrifts, and California would also take a big hit.

The insolvent thrifts that regulators allowed to keep operating created additional problems. To finance their operations, these "zombie banks" kept their deposit interest rates high to keep attracting deposits, which forced other banks to do the same. The result was a competitive spiral that undermined everyone's profitability. Worse, bad banks drove out good. "Their presence in the marketplace contributed to the overall decline in bank lending standards during the 1980s," a later analysis by the Federal Deposit Insurance Corporation (FDIC) found.[74]

Soon things began to unravel. Penn Square Bank, a commercial bank in Oklahoma City, failed in 1982, endangering a much larger commercial bank, Continental Illinois National Bank and Trust Company. The FDIC bailed out Continental Illinois to the tune of $4.5 billion, establishing the principle that certain banks were too big to fail.[75] Meanwhile a big problem was brewing at the Home State Savings Bank of Cincinnati, which came to a head in March 1985. The thrift had been the victim of a securities fraud that cost it around $150 million. When the *Cincinnati Enquirer* reported on the losses, there was a run on the bank. The governor of Ohio closed seventy state-chartered thrifts and gained a promise from the Federal Reserve to provide funds to shore up the state's depleted reserves.[76] A month later, the Federal Reserve noticed excessive borrowing by a Maryland thrift and warned the governor that a failure was imminent there. The state attorney general launched a criminal investigation, triggering a run on Maryland's thrifts.[77] By mid-1986, there were 445 insolvent (but still operating) thrifts with $112 billion in assets.

The Reagan administration would witness the largest number of bank and thrift failures since the Great Depression. The expected cost of salvage was $23.5 billion.

The administration's first idea was to recapitalize the FSLIC. Its reserves had fallen below $2 billion; a General Accounting Office (GAO) audit of the corporation suggested it might even have a substantial negative net worth. The Treasury proposed to infuse the system with private funds, setting up a new financing corporation for the purpose. A GAO review concluded this would not be the least expensive solution, but it would keep the cost off the government's books.[78]

Bills to do this passed both houses of Congress, but the two versions were never reconciled. The banking committees took up the problem again in March 1987.[79] Current and former thrift owners, all from the economically struggling oil states, testified to the FHLBB's performance. Several witnesses complained that the board's examiners were poorly trained. Another contended the board—with only three members—was too small and should be expanded to cope with their growing duties.[80] But this small size was not accidental: the OMB had been suppressing hiring in the name of shrinking government.

These witnesses blamed the crisis in part on the board and asked for reform, particularly of "regulatory forbearance" practices. The Treasury IOUs used earlier in the decade were one form of forbearance; another under standard accounting practice was simply called "goodwill." Regulators could assign goodwill values if, in their opinion, an institution was otherwise well managed. This pattern was fundamental to many of the complaints the committee heard: goodwill could be seen as an appropriate exercise of professional discretion or as an inappropriate exercise of unaccountable power. Witnesses wanted Congress to codify the various forms of forbearance, and to force compliance with general accounting principles. Not one witness asked for an end to regulation. They all believed regulation was necessary; they simply wanted it to be fair, appropriate, and consistently enforced.

In 1987, Congress passed the Competitive Equality Banking Act, intended to resolve the savings and loan crisis. Reagan signed it, claiming that, from the outset, his administration's "guiding principle in working with the Congress on this bill has been to avoid a taxpayer bailout—as was the case in both Ohio and Maryland—for an industry that has the wherewithal to help itself."[81] But a bailout was just what they got. The industry had a vested interest in making the problem appear smaller than it was—because thrifts paid the insurance premiums that funded the FSLIC—and they did not want to pay more to resolve these problems. That's why witnesses had pressed for forbearance: it was a form of capital that wouldn't have to be repaid.[82] It was also in Reagan's interest to make the problem look smaller. As signed, the law authorized $10.8 billion in borrowing authority over three years for the new financial entity that was to recapitalize FSLIC. It wasn't enough—not according to the GAO's own study the year before, and not in light of what actually happened.

The administration and Congress's actions made the situation worse, and not just by failing to provide proper regulation earlier in the decade or use taxpayer funds to resolve the crisis sooner. The 1981 tax cut contained a real estate tax shelter that was at least partly responsible for a construction boom that went bust in 1985. The 1986 Tax Reform Act paid for its income tax cut in part by repealing the tax shelter, but that depressed real estate values even more, reducing the value of the thrifts' assets. The net effect of the Competitive Equality Banking Act was to make the ultimate resolution even more expensive.

SOME OF THE activities that led to the savings and loan crisis were criminal, but those crimes were enabled by lax regulation. The most famous case involved Charles Keating, who purchased Lincoln Savings and Loan, a thrift in Irvine, California, in 1984. Keating invested heavily in high-risk securities, most purchased from "junk bond" king Michael Milken. Keating routinely violated basic regulations, including legal limits on direct investments and on loans made to a single purchaser. He also engaged in a long-banned practice of "loan swapping," trading mortgages back and forth with another friendly thrift in Texas to drive up the apparent value and create the impression of greater profits. The collapse of his empire cost taxpayers $3 billion; Keating served four and a half years of a twelve-year sentence for his crimes. Meanwhile, thousands of his investors lost their funds entirely, as many of the securities Keating had sold them were uninsured.[83]

How did this happen? In 1987, regulators in San Francisco had realized that something was amiss at Lincoln Savings and Loan and concluded it should be seized and closed, but no action was taken. One reason, perhaps, is that Keating had helped purchase a relaxed regulatory climate. It was widely reported that he had "friends" in the White House, and Reagan had tried to appoint a Keating ally, an Atlanta real estate developer, to the FHLBB.[84] Although this gambit failed when the developer's link to Keating was exposed, Keating had meanwhile given about $1.4 million to several senators, Democratic and Republican: Alan Cranston of

California, Dennis DeConcini and John McCain of Arizona, John Glenn of Ohio, and Donald Riegel of Michigan. In April 1987, these senators intervened on Keating's behalf; the following September the FHLBB removed the San Francisco office's investigatory authority. But even without congressional interference, the FHLBB was hamstrung by underfunding, and the weakening of regulatory agencies made it difficult to stop fraud even when regulators saw it.

In the end, criminal activity was not the main problem. A report to Congress contended that losses to taxpayers due to fraud were 10 to 15 percent of net losses—a huge amount of money in absolute terms, but a small fraction of the total.[85] Far more significant to the crisis was the interest rate mismatch between deposits and loans—a side effect of earlier deregulation—and the inability of regulators to close the zombie banks that resulted.[86]

The beginning of the end of the crisis would finally come under President George H. W. Bush. The Financial Institutions Reform, Recovery, and Enforcement Act of 1989 eliminated the FHLBB and handed saving and loan management to the FDIC, which served the same function for commercial banks but was independent of the OMB. The FDIC forced thrifts to comply with some of the same safeguards under which national banks already operated; it also created a new entity, the Resolution Trust Corporation, to take on and dispose of insolvent thrifts' assets. When the initial bill was announced, its price tag was expected to be $50 billion. It took six months to pass, though, and by the time it did, more thrifts had failed. Some couldn't meet the new capital requirements; others failed because the law repudiated the goodwill that FSLIC had been using in lieu of cash to facilitate mergers.[87]

A 1999 study published in *FDIC Banking Review* estimated the direct cost to taxpayers of the savings and loan crisis at $124 billion. (It cost the industry another $29 billion to resolve failed thrifts via their insurance premiums, for a total of approximately $153 billlion. It's unclear what individual investors lost.) A total of 1,043 thrifts failed and had to be sold off.[88] Other estimates of the total cost, including interest payments on the bonds sold to finance the bailout, ranged as high as $480 billion.[89]

"It must be concluded that the savings and loan crisis reflected a massive public policy failure," the official history of the FDIC later stated.[90] And that failure was a failure of underregulation. What was needed were stronger, more independent regulators with adequate resources to do their job. Reviewing the episode, banking attorney and journalist Martin Lowy returned to an insight Adam Smith had offered two hundred years earlier: "We can't have free markets because the world is too complex and interdependent to let everyone run around doing whatever he or she wants to do. As a society, we have to regulate conduct when it interferes with other people's freedoms or when it threatens damage to other people's properties."[91] Unregulated banks risk other people's money, which is, of course, what Adam Smith argued—and the Chicago school did its best to downplay.

REAGAN'S BUDGET DISASTER and savings and loan catastrophe would be at least partly repaired by later administrations. But one area in which Reagan did truly lasting damage was environmental protection. He established a pattern— persistent to this day—of Republican rejection of facts that got in the way of their story.

In the first half of the twentieth century, environmental protection was a GOP cause. Theodore Roosevelt, John D. Rockefeller, Gifford Pinchot, and other Republicans sought to preserve and protect America's natural resources, in part by creating special areas—particularly in the western states—set aside from daily use and development. Their environmentalism was classist, sexist, and racially problematic—they considered it essential that upper-class men have rugged places to hunt and fish, and they framed Indigenous people's lands as "empty"—but the national parks and forests they helped create proved to be popular with Americans of many sorts.[92] While their goals sometimes clashed with those of corporate America—particularly the timber industry—these clashes tended to be local.[93]

In the 1950s and '60s, this changed, as Americans became concerned about the health effects of pollution—particularly urban air pollution. Aesthetic environ-mentalism, which had focused on preserving places of exceptional beauty or unique natural features, was now supplemented and to some degree displaced by regulatory environmentalism, focused on protecting health. Both Democratic and Republican Congress members recognized the compelling public interest in clean air and clean water, and passed several sweeping protective statutes by wide margins, including the Clean Air Act (1970), the National Environmental Policy Act (1970), the Clean Water Act (1972), and the Endangered Species Act (1973).[94] In 1970, Republican president Richard Nixon established the U.S. Environmental Protection Agency (EPA).[95] He also appointed Russell Train, a brilliant Republican conservationist, as head of the newly created Council on Environmental Quality (CEQ).

Almost immediately, there was pushback from the private sector, including the U.S. Chamber of Commerce, the Business Roundtable, and NAM.[96] Nixon was not a great environmentalist; he was a savvy politician who recognized an issue of public concern, and having created the EPA then acted behind the scenes in ways that undermined it.[97] In 1974, for example, without consulting either the EPA or the CEQ, the administration proposed amendments intended to weaken the Clean Air Act.[98] Train was outraged; the proposal blew up; and with little support in Congress, the proposed changes faded away. But the message was clear: conservative Republicans had not embraced environmental protection, at least not fully, and not if vested in the federal government.[99] They were still primarily on the side of business opposition.

By the time Reagan was elected in 1980, corporate conservatives were pressuring him to reduce the federal role in environmental protection, saying it was both ineffective and too expensive. A report by the Business Roundtable, for example, claimed that the Clean Air Act had created "substantial burdens of unnecessary costs without improving air quality."[100] In a powerful rhetorical move, the administration and its allies began to talk of "regulatory relief." In the 1930s, "relief" had meant help for beleaguered Americans who had lost their jobs; now it mean help for (allegedly) beleaguered businessmen.

Conservative economists meanwhile offered theoretical arguments about why regulation was not the best answer, even if positive effects sometimes ensued. Among them was Charles Wolf Jr., a senior economic adviser at the RAND Corporation and senior fellow at the Hoover Institution. In 1979 he published a long and influential article in the Chicago school vehicle the *Journal of Law and Economics*, arguing that one should not assume the remedy to market failure was government action. To his credit, Wolf did not deny the reality of market failure; he recognized the "voluminous" literature documenting cases where markets could not produce "either economically optimal or socially desirable outcomes."[101] The question was what to do about it. The nineteenth-century utilitarian economist Henry Sidgwick had encapsulated the problem: "It does not follow that whenever laissez-faire falls short government interference is expedient, since the inevitable drawbacks of the latter may, in any particular case, be worse than the shortcomings of private enterprise."[102]

How should nations determine when government interference was expedient—or perhaps even urgent—and when it was not? As a utilitarian, Sidgwick had an easy answer: by evaluating the relative benefits of government action versus inaction. A utilitarian would not *presume* which was preferable but would try to determine empirically which produced the greatest happiness for the greatest number. Wolf had a different answer: to compare market failure with nonmarket (which is to say government) failure.

Like many Chicago scholars, Wolf began with a fair point: the reality of market failure should not create a presumption that all government responses will succeed. But his analysis seemed to presume the opposite: that in most cases the government remedy would fail. "Where the market's 'hidden hand' doesn't 'turn private vices into public virtues,' it may be hard to construct visible hands that effectively turn nonmarket vices into public virtues," he asserted.[103] Wolf offered a number of reasons for this, such as the difficulty of defining the output or evaluating the quality of a nonmarket intervention, and the fact that nonmarket outputs are often produced by a single entity (for example, at the time, space travel), making it impossible to compare performance. Furthermore, in the political arena, constituents may demand government action, but once a law or statute is passed, legislators may move on with little attention to how well the intervention worked.[104] These were valid points, but while Wolf offered reasons why government interventions *might* fail, he presented no *evidence* to show that they regularly did fail.

Wolf's theory was thought-provoking—as all good theories should be. His suggestion that scholars should pursue "implementation studies" to see how remedies worked in practice was an excellent one. (Such an analysis of the Reagan tax cuts would have been instructive!) But his paper suggested that general skepticism about government remedies was justified, and this suggestion hinged on a fundamental asymmetry in the argument: "Juxtaposing the market failure to be remedied, and the nonmarket failure *to be anticipated* from the intended remedies, would permit an assessment that has been rare in previous policy studies."[105]

Wolf equated *actual* market failures with "*anticipated*" nonmarket failures and proposed that the latter were as severe as the former, when in fact they were—at least in this presentation—simply *theorized*. Wolf provided no evidence that these "anticipated" nonmarket failures occurred, much less that they were routine or severe. He cited only anecdotes, including a story about West German public television based on a conversation with a colleague, and another about the post office based on an article in a newspaper—nothing to prove the existence of what he called "the frequent tendency of implemented policies to result in higher costs and lower benefits, as well as different consequences, from those calculated in conventional policy studies."[106] Toward the end of the paper, Wolf's pro-market, antigovernment bias broke open: "The existing theory of market failure provides a useful corrective to the theory of perfectly functioning markets," and "the theory of nonmarket failure . . . is intended as a corrective for the implicit theory of perfectly functioning governments."[107] It seems highly unlikely that many people assume perfectly functioning governments. But many economists *do* begin their work with the assumption of perfectly functioning markets.

IF REGULATION WASN'T the solution to the most widely recognized market failure of the time, then what was? "Cornucopian" economists led by Julian Simon had an answer: combat pollution with growth. Human resourcefulness and innovation would remedy whatever problems arose, so in most cases regulations would prove superfluous.[108] Never mind that air pollution statutes had become necessary *because* of growth—particularly as cars had come to dominate American life—and that despite decades of opportunity, the market had failed to remedy—much less prevent—the deadly air pollution in London, Los Angeles, and elsewhere.[109]

Defenders of existing statutes allowed that they might be better, more equitably, or more rationally enforced. After a decade of experience with the Clean Air Act, for example, EPA staff had begun to experiment with flexible regulatory approaches, such as offsets that permitted a polluter to expand in an area that was out of compliance so long as any resulting pollution increase was offset by equivalent or larger reduced emissions elsewhere.[110] But offsets were a question of implementation—not *whether* statutes should be enforced, but how best to achieve their goals. In a review mandated by Congress, the bipartisan National Commission on Air Quality concluded in 1981 that the Clean Air Act had so far "generally worked well," and was unlikely to hinder the nation's energy development in the future.[111] The commission also concluded that the federal approach to air quality standards made sense because the states lacked the capacity to set and enforce standards of their own.[112]

Meanwhile, public support for environmental protection remained strong. Opinion polls consistently showed a clear majority in favor, even "at the risk of curbing economic growth."[113] (In 1984—the only Reagan year surveyed—61 percent of Americans prioritized the environment, 28 percent prioritized the economy, and the rest were undecided.)[114] Congressional sentiment was similar. Though Republicans controlled the Senate—and the 1980 election had narrowed the Democratic majority in the House—Reagan did not have the votes to repeal any significant environmental statute.

What he did instead was undermine enforcement, just as he had with the savings and loan regulatory regime. Reagan decreased funding for the EPA, CEQ, and other agencies involved in environmental protection, reducing staffing levels and hiring people based more on ideological fealty than technical expertise. Crucially, he appointed leaders at odds with the environmental components of their agency missions. Many of his appointees had overt conflicts of interest, such as having been employees of or lawyers for the industries they were supposed to be regulating.[115]

The most egregious example was Secretary of the Interior James Watt, a pro-development corporate lawyer who had worked for the U.S. Chamber of Commerce and then served as the founding president and chief legal officer of the Mountain States Legal Foundation, a libertarian "public interest" law firm. (The foundation describes itself today as being "focused on defending the Constitution, protecting property rights, and advancing economic liberty.")[116] In the new administration, Watt vowed, "We will mine more, drill more, cut more timber."[117]

Environmentalists despised Watt. One popular joke at the time: "What is James Watt's idea of wilderness?" Answer: "A parking lot without lines." And Watt was aggressive. Early in his tenure, he declared that he would be on a crusade to "undo fifty years of bad government." He pushed for commercial development on federal lands, including coal mining and oil and gas drilling; promoted oil drilling off the California coast; and placed a moratorium on land purchases to expand national parks.[118] Five months into the administration, the *Washington Post* reported that "no member of the Reagan team with the possible exception of Secretary of State Alexander M. Haig Jr. has stirred quite so much unease among his allies and antagonism among his opponents."[119] But the coal industry loved him; the president of the National Coal Association described his compatriots as "deliriously happy."[120] A second joke went around: "How much power does it take to stop a million environmentalists? One Watt."[121]

Another antienvironmental appointee was Anne Gorsuch (mother of current Supreme Court justice Neil Gorsuch), who was named head of the EPA in 1981. She had spent four years in the Colorado state legislature, where she was part of the self-professed "Crazies," passionate opponents of federal environmental protection. She also had extensive industry ties, most notably to libertarian beer magnate Joseph Coors, who in 1973 had helped to create the Heritage Foundation.[122] At EPA Gorsuch took numerous steps that undermined environmental protection via selective or weak enforcement of the law, or none at all.

Political scientist Judith Layzer has described the strategy as exploiting agency discretion. Administrators have substantial leeway in how they interpret and implement statutes (and until recently, courts often deferred to agency discretion).[123] Gorsuch weaponized this, applying minimalist interpretations of what statutes required, delaying adoption of new rules required by law, impeding implementation of existing rules, and reducing penalties for violations.[124] Perhaps because support for environmental protection was so strong—both in Congress and in the country as a whole—Gorsuch framed her efforts not as decreasing enforcement, but as increasing "pragmatism," "efficiency," "rationality," "economic realism," and "economic discipline." Statutes that had been passed by large bipartisan margins were critiqued for imposing an undue economic or "regulatory burden"; environmentalists were cast as unrealistic extremists.[125]

In June 1981, the administration proposed changes to weaken the Clean Air Act, in part by turning over enforcement to the states, something the National Commission on Air Quality had explicitly advised against. A Harris poll showed that Americans strongly opposed this: 86 percent supported a statute as strong as or stronger than the existing one. Louis Harris himself told a congressional committee that, in his twenty-five years of polling, "the desire on the part of the American people to battle pollution" was "one of the most overwhelming and clearest" he had recorded.[126] Yet a spokesman for NAM concluded happily that the proposed changes were "right in line with the things we asked for."[127] In the face of congressional opposition—including from many Republicans—the administration reframed its proposals, but NAM was still content. "There is not anything missing that was a major priority for us."[128]

Political scientist Phillip Cooper has concluded that the most serious and lasting impact of the weakening of federal environmental agencies was that overburdened agencies were more likely to make mistakes, contributing to an impression of inconsistent or even arbitrary choices, thus rendering their decisions more vulnerable to legal challenge. In a self-fulfilling prophecy, industry attacks on agency competence thus became more credible.[129] Among other things, Cooper's argument sheds light on the 1984 comedy *Ghostbusters*.[130] The movie's principal villain is not a monster, a ghost, or even Manhattan-crushing Gozer the Destroyer in the form of a giant marshmallow. It is a *government scientist*. An inspector from the Environmental Protection Agency unleashes disaster by shutting down an unlicensed paranormal energy storage facility, believing the ghostbusters are con artists selling a nonexistent product. In *Ghostbusters*, government was the problem. Entrepreneurs were the solution.

THE REAGAN ADMINISTRATION's gutting of regulatory agencies undermined trust in science at the worst possible moment. By the early 1980s, the set of emerging environmental issues differed from the problems that had primarily motivated the Clean Air and Clean Water acts. They did not affect public health in the immediate way that urban air pollution did, nor kill birds and fish the way an oil spill did. They did not cause a river to catch on fire. Yet they were serious and seemed to demand a forceful federal (or even international) government response.

By the early 1980s, scientists had identified several major environmental threats—acid rain, the ozone hole, and anthropogenic climate change—that many economists identified as market failures. A company could spew carbon dioxide into the atmosphere, leading to deadly heat waves and damaging droughts, storms, and sea level rise, yet these costs appeared on no one's balance sheet. These problems were not merely "nuisances," as the law often characterized them, or "neighborhood effects," in Milton Friedman's dismissive framing. They were serious threats to health, well-being, and property, and they crossed state and national boundaries. Acid rain from power plants in the American Midwest affected lakes, rivers, and infrastructure in Canada. Lead from gasoline was found in Antarctica. The nonhuman world was negatively impacted, too; the destruction of stratospheric ozone threatened the very existence of life on Earth. Lord Nicholas Stern, a former chief economist at the World Bank, would later call climate change the "greatest and most wide-ranging market failure" ever seen.[131]

This was a potentially fatal blow to the idea of the "magic of the marketplace." At minimum it showed there were potentially enormous sacrifices associated with business as usual, evading the conventional cost-benefit analyses conservatives demanded to justify regulation. At maximum, it suggested that capitalism as practiced threatened the future of life on Earth.[132]

Rather than admit that the ideology was wrong, or at least incomplete—that markets could not solve all our problems, and that in cases of market failure government might be an essential part of the solution—the Reagan administration responded by misrepresenting or disparaging the relevant science. In attempt to minimize the significance of acid rain, Reagan falsely claimed that Mount St. Helens—the volcano in Washington State that erupted in 1980, killing fifty-seven people—had released more sulfur dioxide than a decade's worth of cars.[133] (Republicans would later blame volcanoes for global warming.)[134] On another occasion, he said "trees cause more pollution than automobiles do."[135] And in a full-bore attack on scientific integrity, the Reagan White House science adviser instructed the chair of a scientific panel on acid rain to alter its report—after the other panel members had signed off—to make the evidence appear less certain than the scientists had concluded it was.[136]

This pattern of disdain for information that didn't fit a political agenda, of rejecting inconvenient truths, and finally of denying reality was the (il)logical endpoint of market fundamentalism, epitomized in a now-familiar phrase. In speech after speech, Reagan declared that trusting "the magic of the marketplace" would solve everything. Following in Milton Friedman's footsteps, Reagan presented markets not merely as a place where people expressed their interests and satisfied their desires, but as the embodiment of freedom.

In a 1986 domestic radio address, Reagan applauded a recent decline in oil prices as "a triumph not of government, but of the free market; and not of political leaders, but of freedom itself." The speech was a short one—the transcript is under two pages—but he used the words "free," "freedom," or "freeing" seven times, an average of once every paragraph. Ignoring the central role of OPEC, a cartel, in controlling supply—as well as the widespread use of subsidies to stimulate oil and gas production—Reagan proclaimed the solution to high oil prices was to let "freedom solve the problem through the magic of the marketplace." Oil was flowing again, the price had fallen, but "the government didn't perform any of these miracles; freedom did, the marketplace did, the entrepreneurs and businessmen and women of America did." Government just had to sit back and watch "the gushers blow."[137]

A key rhetorical element in many of Reagan's speeches was equating market-forward economic policies with freedom and, conversely, reducing freedom to market-oriented policies. In memos sent from the Treasury Department, the State Department, and other parts of the administration, we see terms such as "commitment to market forces," working to "promote market forces and flexibility," "enhancing the market environment," and, in one case, establishing the "market-oriented conditions which maximize the efficiency of resource allocation."[138] Reagan would have none of that jargon. In a 1986 speech at an International Monetary Fund (IMF) meeting, he reduced all these ideas to three sentences and a single word: "We've heard many names given to these rediscovered economic insights—names describing policies of taxation, regulation, government spending, monetary management and trade. But all those names—and the many theories with which they are associated—come down in the end to one name, one theory, one word. The word is freedom."[139]

By 1987, Reagan had so honed his message that he could put the word *free* or *freedom*, as well as the word *magic*, more than once into a single sentence. Defending Robert Bork's nomination to the Supreme Court, Reagan reminded his audience that his entire administration was founded on a "policy of cutting back government while giving free markets and free people a chance to work their magic. And the results have been economic magic."[140] At a 1988 fund-raiser, he reduced the argument even further: "Get government out of the way, and the free people in a free economy work their magic."[141]

Magic, magic, magic. Reagan brandished the word so frequently that in 1984 one aide objected to its use in a draft speech that read: "The 'magic' of rewarding hard work and risk taking has given birth to an American renaissance. Born in the safe harbor of freedom, economic growth has gathered force, and rolled out in a rising tide that has reached distant shores." The aide scratched out "the magic of," writing in the margin, "This cliché needs to be replaced." Someone suggested instead a line invoking the indivisibility thesis: "No nation can have prosperity and successful development without economic freedom. Nor can it preserve personal and political freedoms without economic freedom." Reagan liked that line, but he also wanted to keep the cliché. One aide noted: "Pres. Has used before, wants it in." The "magic of rewarding hard work" stayed.[142]

On a second occasion, a speechwriter again took issue with "magic," writing in the margin of a draft speech: "MUST either drop this phrase which will dominate the PRESS, <u>OR</u> WE can explain what it means, as a method of allocating resources." The explanation was added: "Millions of individuals, making their own decisions in the marketplace, have, can, and always will allocate resources better than any centralized planning system." (Later the "have, can" was deleted, so it affirmatively asserted: "will always.")[143] If that were what Reagan meant by his favored phrase, it wouldn't have been entirely unreasonable: the argument for bottom-up market efficacy generally holds when compared with the inefficiencies of top-down centralized planning. "We who live in free market societies believe that growth, prosperity, and ultimately human fulfillment are created from the bottom up, and not the government down," an early draft of his 1981 IMF speech read.[144] But was that really what he meant? After all, who in the United States in the 1980s was seriously arguing for centralized planning?[145]

After Reagan had invoked the "magic of the marketplace" in the 1981 IMF speech, the press had indeed focused on the phrase. The *Washington Post* reported that the president had "told the world's poor nations to 'believe in the magic of the marketplace' as the route to achieving economic progress and a higher standard of living," and to rely not on foreign aid but on building "the free enterprise system" at home.[146] The article noted that this was part of a "determined American effort to reshape both the IMF and the World Bank," which it was. The Reagan administration wanted these institutions to focus less on antipoverty efforts—which the administration considered "socialistic" and "redistributionist"—and more on economic growth through market-forward policies.[147] Countries that were benefiting from World Bank and IMF help should give "a warmer welcome to private business."[148] The *Christian Science Monitor* business editor called it the "free enterprise gospel."[149]

These messages were developed primarily in the context of foreign aid and the developing world's debt crisis, but they comported with Reagan's domestic agenda. In the 1984 speech in which the word *magic* was questioned, one suggested alternative was "what united [them] was a willingness to trust the people—to believe in rewarding hard work and legitimate risk."[150] Reagan would use that formulation many times, but did he trust the American people?

Despite his aw-shucks manner and his insistence that markets reflected the popular will—"millions of people making decisions," in effect, voting with their dollars—Reagan often rejected the wisdom of the American people, who (polls showed) wanted environmental protection, approved of Medicare, and were horrified by the thought of privatizing Social Security. A draft of the 1986 IMF speech had Reagan saying that "centrally planned economies have been discredited as nations around the globe turn increasingly to the private sector."[151] That was fair, but it didn't mean the world shouldn't want the private sector to be well regulated. It didn't mean that there weren't important questions to be asked about how capitalism worked, not just in theory, but in practice.

Chile was a case in point. In 1973, with CIA support, the Chilean military overthrew democratically elected socialist president Salvador Allende and installed a brutal, violent dictatorship. The United States backed the dictatorship, as did Milton Friedman, on the grounds that its market-friendly policies would enhance freedom; a group of economists influenced by the Chicago school and nicknamed the "Chicago Boys" served as consultants for the regime.[152] But Chileans under General Augusto Pinochet were not free; they were terrorized. Taiwan and Singapore were also following market-forward policies of which the administration approved, but they were not democracies, either. Meanwhile, Japan had used export-led industrial policies to achieve high growth rates; the visible hand of government policy had played a significant role in its postwar economic success.

Reagan offered Japan and South Korea as "classic examples of nations rising from the ashes of war to set standards of economic prosperity that dazzle the world." Americans should let go of protectionist impulses and "recognize Japanese and Korean efficiency for what it is," because "that's what the magic of the marketplace is all about."[153] This was just plain wrong. Japanese and Korean companies may have been efficient, but their successes were heavily government-led. Samsung, the most successful Korean company selling to Americans, had risen to prominence on the back of tax breaks, preferential bank loans, export credits, and other forms of government favoritism. Koreans even had a name for the large conglomerates, like Samsung, that had prospered from their strong ties with government agencies: chaebols. (A chaebol is literally a "rich clan," sometimes also translated as a "wealth clique" or "money clan".)[154] The pattern of Asian development that Reagan loved to tout did not support his claims.

The president continued to equate market-forward economic policies with freedom writ large, and to repeat the leitmotif of the "magic of the marketplace." Sometimes he added "the magic of hard work" and of risk-taking, or reprised Leonard Read's theme of capitalism as a miracle. International development was a favorite topic for these themes, but they appear in his discussions of domestic issues as well. In a 1982 domestic radio address on tuition tax credits and interest rates, Reagan lauded one of the major auto manufacturers for lowering its interest rates on auto financing, closing his speech, "You know, there really is something magic about the marketplace when it's free to operate."[155]

The speeches in which Reagan credited economic success to the "magic of the marketplace"—regardless of the historical and economic facts—were many. Prosperity, wherever it was found, was the uncomplicated outcome of letting the market do its magic. In contrast, economic failures were the product of the dead weight of government intervention.[156] Or sometimes just the dead weight of government itself.[157] In a different context, Reagan famously invoked a Russian maxim: "Trust, but verify."[158] But when it came to markets, he simply told us to trust.

THE 1987 HOLLYWOOD film *Wall Street* captured the Reagan zeitgeist. Directed by Oliver Stone and starring Michael Douglas, the movie focused on a business strategy that became popular in the 1980s: corporate takeovers—sometimes hostile, sometimes not—when the pieces of a company could be dismantled and sold separately for more than the whole was worth.[159] In the process, unions might be destroyed, communities undermined, benefit packages cut. But defenders of these practices insisted that they would make American business (and therefore America) more competitive and profitable—leaner and meaner. Michael Douglas's character, Gordon Gekko, explained:

> I am not a destroyer of companies. I am a liberator of them! The point is, ladies and gentlemen, that greed—for lack of a better word—is good. Greed is right. Greed works. Greed clarifies, cuts through, and captures the essence of the evolutionary spirit. Greed, in all of its forms—greed for life, for money, for love, knowledge—has marked the upward surge of mankind. And greed—you mark my words—will not only save Teldar Paper, but that other malfunctioning corporation called the USA.[160]

Gekko tells his protégé—the son of a union worker who is being "downsized"—that the "richest one percent in American control half the wealth and consequently make the rules."[161] In the mid-twentieth century, that had not been the case. In 1948, the top 10 percent held about 30 to 35 percent of American wealth.[162] By the end of the century, life would imitate art: the top 10 percent held 70 percent of the wealth, and the top 1 percent had not quite but almost half of everything.[163] And, it would become increasingly clear, the preferences of the rich were setting the policy agenda.[164]

The idea that corporations had obligations to no one except their shareholders had been aggressively promoted in the Reagan era by Milton Friedman. In *Capitalism and Freedom*, he had argued that "there is one and only one social responsibility of business—to use its resources and engage in activities designed to increase its profits so long as it stays within the rules of the game."[165] In 1981, Friedman's axiom was further distilled when an accounting professor, Alfred Rappaport, came up with the label "shareholder value." The concept took off.[166] The managers' task was to maximize return to shareholders, as adjudicated by the stock market, and nothing else. From there it was common sense that a company "worth" more in pieces than as a whole should be taken apart.

This idea was epitomized in Reagan's old haunt, General Electric, where a new CEO, Jack Welch, brought the fetish of shareholder value to the giant manufacturing conglomerate in 1981. Known as "Neutron Jack"—after the neutron bomb, which destroyed people but left buildings intact—Welch shrank the GE workforce by more than a third, shuttered dozens of domestic plants while moving manufacturing overseas, and eliminated the basic research portfolio—the innovation machine that Reagan had proudly pitched in the 1950s to tens of millions of Americans.[167]

Neutron Jack's GE was Reagan's America in microcosm. But the Reagan Revolution was not quite over. It would take another decade, and another Democratic president, to complete it.

CHAPTER 14

Apotheosis

If Jimmy Carter began the Reagan Revolution, Bill Clinton completed it. Both Carter and Reagan worked to deregulate large swaths of the American economy, but Clinton in some ways went further, with dramatic deregulation of telecommunications and financial markets. In 1996, he declared that the "era of Big Government is over."[1]

Clinton's rise to power—and embrace of deregulation—can partly be traced to the 1978 midterm elections, in which both Democrats and moderate Republicans suffered substantial losses. *Newsweek* magazine declared that a new politics had emerged in which "Democrats talk like Republicans to survive,"[2] trumpeting a "no longer partisan agenda for the nation—a consensus on inflation as the primary target and tax-and-spend government as the primary villain," Liberal Republican senator Charles Percy of Illinois encapsulated: "We've had it with overregulation."[3]

The claim that a political program demonizing government was nonpartisan was absurd; corporate America, mostly aligned with the Republican Party, had been vilifying government since the New Deal. Equally wrong was the implication that there was a consensus on overregulation as villain. Opinion polls in the late 1970s revealed no surge in antigovernment conservatism among voters, who by and large continued to support Social Security, Medicare, environmental protection, and civil rights enforcement.[4] What *was* true was that after Jimmy Carter lost his 1980 reelection bid, some Democrats began to think about how their party should respond.

Between 1968 and 1980, only one Democrat had won the presidency, and he was a centrist. The reliably liberal candidates Hubert Humphrey and George McGovern had both gone down to defeat, McGovern crushingly so. It wasn't unreasonable to think the party needed to restrategize. In 1980, a group including Tennessee senator Al Gore, Colorado senator Tim Wirth, Missouri representative Richard Gephardt, and others from what we would now call purple states created the Democratic

Study Group to consider the question.[5] This evolved into a self-named Democratic Leadership Council (DLC). Looking back on that period, Wirth argues that the DLC's focus was not on moving to the center, per se, but on finding policies to "grow the economy" as Bill Clinton would soon put it. Rather than focus on redistribution, it would be better to make the pie bigger so everyone could have a larger slice. Alfred Kahn would certainly agree.

These Democrats considered a variety of approaches to stimulate economic growth, including access to education, investment in research and development, and worker retraining. But the drama of the moment was elsewhere. Wirth recalled Alfred Kahn "waving the deregulatory flag" in his colorful and persuasive congressional testimonies, telling his audiences that the economy was being hamstrung by "a lot of old rules," particularly in telecommunication.[6] Meanwhile, Democrats lost again in 1984 and 1988, when two additional reliably liberal candidates—Walter Mondale and Michael Dukakis—suffered defeat. For many Democrats, whether old or new, it seemed obvious that the party needed to move to the right. Since the right had defined its territory as pro-market—and Kahn (a Democrat) had made the case—many Democrats embraced deregulation as a framework for stimulating economic growth. When 1992 finally brought a Democrat back to Pennsylvania Avenue, it was a "New Democrat" who would champion a set of market-friendly principles that came to be viewed as neoliberal.

It was said that Margaret Thatcher carried "Hayek in her handbag," but his views were still mostly known in the United States only among a cadre of intellectual conservatives.[7] Ludwig von Mises was by now mostly forgotten, except perhaps by historians of economics. However, "neoliberalism"—largely divorced from its Mont Pèlerin roots—was becoming the term of art for a portfolio of pro-market policies, particularly those centering international trade. Under Bill Clinton (and in the UK, Labour leader Tony Blair), these ideas now became mainstream.

Clinton was in many ways a neo-neoliberal. He did not embrace the indivisibility thesis. He did not think government activity in the marketplace would put us onto the slippery slope to socialism. And his declaration in 1996 that the "era of Big Government" was over wasn't true. Clinton governed from the center-left, defending Social Security and Medicare. His administration had already triggered a giant fight when he attempted to create national health insurance, and his vice president, Al Gore, was the strongest environmental champion the White House had seen since Theodore Roosevelt. In 1999, as the sun set on the Clinton presidency, the

libertarian Independent Institute would lament that big government remained
"firmly in place."[8]

On the other hand, under Clinton federal spending fell to about 18 percent of
GDP, its lowest level since the Eisenhower administration, and Clinton (unlike
Reagan) succeeded at balancing the federal budget.[9] Moreover, the tenor of the
times had changed, both in the United States and the world at large. The Soviet
Union had collapsed at the end of 1991, the United Kingdom under Thatcher (from
1979 to 1990) had privatized many state enterprises, and more than a few economists had concluded that high public spending relative to GDP—particularly in
the European social democracies—had contributed to the destructively high inflation of the 1970s and '80s.[10] Even in the People's Republic of China, economic liberalization was gaining ground. All this gave a big boost to capitalism's global image.

Intellectuals—particularly but not only conservative ones—advanced the case,
announcing the hand-in-glove triumph of deregulated capitalism and liberal
democracy. Most notable was political scientist Francis Fukuyama, with his theory
that the Soviet Union's demise marked not merely the end of the Cold War, but
the end of *history*: market capitalism and liberal democracy had permanently
triumphed. (After 9/11, George Will would dryly observe that "history had returned
from vacation.")[11]

Clinton discerned this momentum and rode it. He competed with Republicans
on their terms, delivering on two key components of his promise to "reinvent
government": market deregulation and trade liberalization. This was by no means
all bad: trade liberalization in the 1990s and 2000s would help create a large,
emerging middle class in many parts of the world, particularly Asia. There were
(and continue to be) substantial global benefits to liberal trade. But there have also
been substantial harms, particularly to workers and the environment. And, as had
happened to both Jimmy Carter and Ronald Reagan, market deregulation did not
work out as Clinton intended. On the contrary, in telecommunication it ended up
decreasing competition, and in financial markets it laid the foundations for the
worst economic collapse since the Great Depression.

TELECOMMUNICATION DEREGULATION WAS already under way when Bill
Clinton came to office. The Cable Communications Policy Act of 1984 deregulated
the cable television industry, and in 1987 the Fairness Doctrine was abolished,

eliminating the requirement that licensed broadcasters provide balanced coverage of public affairs.[12] Prior to 1984, cable was regulated at the state and, often, local level. Rates were set by negotiations with the towns and cities being served. The Cable Communications Policy Act preempted local and state rules, handing regulation to the Federal Communications Commission (FCC). At the same time, the Act limited how the FCC could regulate the industry.[13]

Within a few years, it was evident that deregulation was not working the way its advocates had hoped. The expected increase in competition had not occurred, while municipalities had lost their ability to regulate now-skyrocketing rates.[14] In 1992, a coalition of consumer groups, public interest advocates, and even some cable companies lobbied for the Cable Television Consumer Protection and Competition Act (passed over President George H. W. Bush's veto), which attempted to protect consumers through rate regulation and the creation of a "basic tier" of local and educational channels that providers would have to offer at a relatively low rate—what came to be known as basic cable.[15] But even this act affirmed the primacy of the market approach, which was further reinforced in the Telecommunications Act of 1996.

The 1996 act was a major overhaul—the first since the 1930s—designed to provide a framework for a new technological era that now included not just cable television, but also cell phones and the internet. The goal was to improve service and lower prices by encouraging competition, "to let anyone enter any communications business—to let any communications business compete in any market against any other." The FCC would play its role by "creating fair rules for this new era of competition."[16] Technological change made it obvious that at least some rethinking of existing frameworks was in order, and the bill was wildly popular: it would pass the House 414–6 and the Senate 91–5. Among the few who opposed it were Senator John McCain and then-Representative Bernie Sanders.

The new law promised a lot. It would "promote competition and reduce regulation in order to secure lower prices and higher quality services . . . and encourage the rapid deployment of new telecommunications."[17] Among its provisions: obligating the "incumbent local exchange carriers"—the existing local phone companies—to allow other companies to connect with their networks; allowing the regional Bell operating companies (the "Baby Bells" that had been created by the breakup of AT&T) to compete in the long-distance markets; eliminating the cap on radio station ownership and easing restrictions on ownership of other media;

and promising universal internet access (although without stipulating how that would occur).[18] Like the 1984 act, it let the FCC preempt state and local regulations, but at the same time permitted regulation of obscene content.

Clinton hailed the bill as not only providing "the key to opening new markets and new opportunities" but also inaugurating the next episode in technological modernity. "It will help connect every classroom in America to the information superhighway by the end of the decade," while still protecting "consumers by regulating the remaining monopolies for a time and by providing a roadmap for deregulation in the future."[19] Many consumer groups and even some economists were skeptical, because the bill offered few provisions to prevent monopolization, but the administration claimed there was no need to fear.[20] Pointing to its pursuit of antitrust cases against Microsoft, Intel, and American Airlines, Clinton assured skeptics of his commitment to competition; he would resist any tendencies toward monopoly.[21]

But the administration would have a hard time pressing antitrust cases in the face of skeptical judges and Federal Trade Commission (FTC) appointees.[22] The American Airlines case would be dismissed by federal judge J. Thomas Marten—a Clinton appointee—who concluded the airline had engaged "only in bare, but not brass, knuckle competition."[23] The Intel case was even less reassuring. In 1993, an FTC investigation of the company found "no evidence . . . to support charges of anticompetitive behavior."[24] Perhaps they hadn't looked very hard, because after more complaints from more companies, the FTC investigated again and in 1999 found that Intel had indeed engaged in wrongful behavior; a settlement required Intel to refrain. (Intel would be repeatedly investigated, including in Europe, in Korea, and in New York State. In 2009, the company would pay $1.25 billion to a rival company, Advanced Micro Devices, which had first brought a complaint against it in 1991.)[25]

The Microsoft case was the least reassuring of all. In 1992, the FCC deadlocked over whether Microsoft had engaged in anticompetitive practices by "bundling": providing its operating system to computer manufacturers at cost as long as they excluded any other operating system. The Clinton Justice Department pursued the matter, leading to a 1995 consent decree. In 1998, the Department of Justice, joined by twenty state attorneys, took Microsoft to court, again for bundling—this time, for requiring that manufacturers include the company's web browser, Internet Explorer, with the operating system.[26] Microsoft lost and the presiding judge ordered its breakup. But Microsoft appealed, and in 2001 the government and Microsoft settled, leaving the company intact and in control of the operating system environment. The Microsoft suit illustrated just how difficult it was to protect consumers from anticompetitive practices, in part because many judges had been influenced by Chicago school arguments that monopolistic behavior was both rare and rarely bad.

In 1999, the Independent Institute published, as a full-page advertisement in the *New York Times* and *Washington Post*, "An Open Letter to President Clinton from 240 Economists on Antitrust Protectionism," maintaining that these prosecutions did not serve the public interest. It was Robert Bork's argument, lock, stock, and barrel. It didn't matter if Microsoft was a monopoly: "Consumers of high technology have enjoyed falling prices, expanding outputs, and a breathtaking array of new products and innovations . . . many of the proposed interventions will weaken successful U.S. firms and impede their competitiveness abroad."[27] The erstwhile defenders of the competitive free market now defended anticompetitive practices. Markets, in whatever manner they functioned, could just about do no wrong.

But markets *did* do wrong. Airline deregulation had mixed results: for most customers, prices got better but service got worse. Telecom deregulation performed even more poorly. With the development of cellular networks, competition proved evanescent as the new regulatory structure permitted a panoply of mergers and acquisitions. *Consumer Reports* summarized the situation in 2013: "[T]he Telecommunications Act of 1996 has failed to produce the consumer benefits policy makers promised because competition has failed to take hold across the communications industry . . . The fundamental problem is that the huge companies that dominate telephone and cable TV prefer mergers and acquisitions to competition. They have refused to open their markets by dragging their feet in allowing competitors to interconnect, refusing to negotiate in good faith, litigating every nook and cranny of the law, and avoiding head-to-head competition like the plague . . . *The answer is to insist on effective competition—demonopolization—before deregulation.*"[28] Even economists agreed that telecom deregulation had not delivered on its promises. At New York University Stern School of Business, Nicolas Economides stated plainly: "More than three years after the passage of the act, there is very little entry and competition in the local exchange markets . . . [instead] there has been a wave of mergers."[29]

Corporate conservatives had long insisted what they wanted was competition, but the telecom and airline experiences belied that claim: what corporate America wanted was to control their business practices with little federal constraint, and, if possible, to control their markets, too. Consumer advocates were not arguing for centralized planning—they wanted genuine competition—but they received no support from corporate-funded think tanks. And Economides was not quite right: in telecom, there had been entry, but most of the newcomers were quickly bought up, creating behemoths.

The Telecommunications Act also misinterpreted what future technology would bring. The internet would become essential to our lives, and in principle any business could find its place online; the internet was not a "natural" monopoly. Yet it would quickly be monopolized by two companies: Google and Microsoft.[30] The same would prove true of social media, as Facebook—founded in 2004— took over the world it helped create.[31] The tendency toward monopolization—recognized a century earlier by the Sherman Anti-Trust Act—had not gone away. On the contrary, by 2020 it had become routine to say that monopoly was in the tech industry's "DNA."[32] A for the promised internet superhighway, come the twenty-first century the United States had some of the highest-priced broadband and the slowest speeds of any wealthy nation.[33]

CONSERVATIVES LIKE TO remind liberals that regulations—even if well intentioned—can have unintended negative consequences. Telecom deregulation proved that the opposite was true as well. The goals of expanding service and decreasing cost were good ones, but the costs in terms of media consolidation and polarization were enormous. They were not just financial. They were cultural and political, too.

In the early days of cable television, broadcast networks were not permitted to own cable channels. In 1992, the FCC relaxed the restrictions.[34] This decision, elevated into statute in the 1996 Telecommunications Act, effectively consolidated broadcast, film, and cable channels into a single visual-media content market.[35] It also enabled the creation of multimedia empires, such as Time Warner and Fox News Media, which would go on to control huge segments of the media market. Today, the Walt Disney Company owns the ESPN, Lifetime, History, A&E, and FX cable/satellite channels. It also owns the ABC broadcast network, 20th Century

Fox (rebranded as 20th Century Studios), Marvel, Pixar, Lucasfilm, Hollywood
Records, and the Hulu and Disney Plus streaming services.[36] In 2017, for $52 billion,
Disney bought National Geographic.[37] Before telecom deregulation, such a mega-
media conglomerate would have been illegal.

Deregulation has also enabled the growth of overtly partisan, propagandistic
news networks that have helped to create and sustain our current polarized society.[38]
The most obvious example is Roger Ailes's cable-based Fox News, which since its
founding has been a reliable Republican organ. (Ailes was a longtime media consultant to Republican leaders, including Presidents Nixon, Reagan, and George H. W.
Bush, and would later advise Donald Trump.) A less well-known but perhaps even
more consequential conglomerate is the Sinclair Broadcast Group, which has
bought huge numbers of local stations—by 2020 it owned 294.[39] Sinclair describes
itself as "one of the largest and most diversified television broadcasting companies
in the country," but from a political standpoint it is anything but diversified. The
New York Times has described it as a "conservative TV giant" that uses its network
"to advance a mostly right-leaning agenda."[40]

During the 2004 presidential election, Sinclair ordered local affiliates to run a
"documentary" that promoted the "swift-boating" of Senator John Kerry: the false
claim that Kerry, a decorated war veteran, had misrepresented his military record.
Around the same time Sinclair ordered some affiliates not to run an episode of
Nightline—one of the most popular news programs at the time—in which anchor
Ted Koppel read the names of every American soldier lost in Iraq.[41] In 2017, *Politico*
reported that Donald Trump's son-in-law Jared Kushner had boasted "that
the campaign had struck a deal with Sinclair to secure better coverage in the
states where they needed spots most."[42] Michael Copps, a former FCC chairman
appointed by George W. Bush, has described Sinclair as "the most dangerous
company most people have never heard of."[43]

Conservatives have defended Fox and Sinclair by pointing to the counter-
partisanship of MSNBC.[44] But that is hardly a defense, as partisanship on either
side contributes to information polarization that can reinforce political and social
division. Even if liberals owned as many radio and television stations as conservatives did—even if partisanship were equal and opposite—that would not be a good
situation. And liberals do not own as many stations, nor do they reach as many
people. Right- and left-wing media may be balanced in their opposing political

directions, but they are anything but equal in magnitude and reach: overtly left-wing television stations are much less abundant than overtly right-wing ones. This should come as little surprise: corporate America tends to be either centrist, right-leaning, or overtly right-wing, and it is corporate America that has been able to develop media conglomerates. There aren't many communists in America, and so far as the evidence goes, none owns a radio station, much less hundreds of them.

Equally if not more impactful have been the evangelical radio empires that now saturate the airwaves. It had always been possible for religious leaders to own a radio station, and in the mid-twentieth century several did. The first woman to own a radio station in the United States was Aimee Semple McPherson, an evangelical preacher in Los Angeles. But she didn't own a network, and under the rules of her era she would have been limited to seven stations if she'd tried. James Fifield and his associate Clarence Manion had religious shows, distributed to the nation's radio networks and independent station owners via syndication, but the law would not have allowed them to control networks. Prior to the 1980s, there was no shortage of religious programming on the airwaves, but most of it was broadcast on commercial stations amid other offerings—music, news, sports, the miscellany of secular life. Religious radio was not a world unto itself.

That changed with telecommunication deregulation. White evangelicals wanted their own networks, and relaxed laws made it possible. Cable provided the beginnings of that opportunity, with Pat Robertson turning his small, Virginia-based Christian Broadcasting Network (CBN) into a satellite-based cable channel in 1977. CBN sought the end of the Fairness Doctrine and the lifting of ownership limits. (Some have interpreted the dissolution of the Fairness Doctrine as President Reagan's reward to evangelicals for their support; it permitted demonization of homosexuality, abortion, and feminism without restraint or right of response.)[45] Under the Clinton administration, radio empires were enabled by the removal of national ownership limits, and several nationwide conservative evangelical networks resulted, including Salem Media Group, Bott Radio Network, and American Family Radio, part of the fundamentalist American Family Association. By 2020, Salem owned 119 radio stations in the United States, while the American Family Association network held 159. The largest, though, was the innocently named Educational Media Foundation, owning 434 stations. Nearly all listed their format as "Christian Contemporary."[46]

Why did an act intended to increase competition, and with it, consumer choice, end up decreasing both? It was not a matter of drift: consolidation, particularly in radio, began as soon as the ink on the bill was dry. (Between 1996 and 1998, 4,000 of the nation's 11,000 radio stations changed hands, according to an analysis published in 2003. In that year, the newly consolidated Clear Channel—a merger of Clear Channel Communications and Jacor Communications—was operating 1,225 stations; before the act, it had 36.)[47] The answer is that the act deregulated rates, market access, and to some extent content, while containing no provision to stop consolidation.[48] A cynic might conclude this was the real intent, but the historical context suggests something a bit less cynical, although perhaps more unnerving: that even liberal and moderate Democrats had been persuaded that all government needed to do was stand back and let markets do their magic. It didn't work out that way in telecommunication, and it wouldn't work out that way in financial markets, either.

THE GLASS-STEAGALL ACT refers to four provisions of the United States Banking Act of 1933 intended to reduce financial practices that were thought to have contributed to the 1929 stock market crash, particularly banks' habit of investing depositors' savings in risky securities. The act separated commercial banking from investment banking by preventing securities and investment firms from taking deposits, and by preventing commercial banks from trading, under-writing, or distributing nongovernmental securities to themselves or customers. It also created the now-familiar FDIC to guarantee depositors' monies and prevent future bank runs. And it required all FDIC-participating banks to be part of the Federal Reserve system.[49] Like workmen's compensation, which is funded by employers, deposit insurance would be financed by premiums paid by participating banks; all national banks would have to participate.[50]

By most accounts, Glass-Steagall was successful. According to the FDIC, "No depositor has ever lost a penny of insured deposits since the FDIC was created in 1933."[51] Nearly all banks participate, the main exception being state banks, which are insured by those states. But the financial industry hated Glass-Steagall, and almost as soon as it passed they began trying to weaken or repeal it. By the 1990s it had already been considerably diluted, either by statute or by loose interpretation and enforcement.[52]

Many economists alleged that Glass-Steagall was hurting competition, even asserting that the era before Glass-Steagall had not been so bad.[53] Others said the problems of the past were past, that financial institutions had learned their lessons. One article by two Chicago economists, published in the *American Economic Review*, posed the question: "Is the Glass-Steagall Act justified?" No, they answered, because the act presumed that "conflicts of interest induce commercial banks to fool the public into investing in securities that turn out to be of low quality." Their research found no evidence of that. Rather, they concluded, "the public appears to have rationally accounted for the possibilities of conflicts of interest, and this appears to have constrained banks to underwrite high-quality securities."[54] If the law was unnecessary, then why have it? For conservatives who believed regulation hurt business, Glass-Stegall was an obvious target.

In 1999, Congress passed the Financial Services Modernization Act, also known as the Gramm-Leach-Bliley Act, repealing the Glass-Steagall provisions that had established a firewall between commercial and investment banking. Commercial banks, investment banks, securities firms, and insurance companies would be allowed to affiliate and merge.

Wall Street had been lobbying for this for years, but according to law professors Lissa Broome and Jerry Markham, the impetus for the act was in part to legalize something that had already happened: the merger between Citicorp and the Travelers Group to form Citigroup. The merger took advantage of a provision of the Bank Holding Company Act that grants a two-year grace period to any company that becomes a bank holding company by virtue of an acquisition. Citigroup was taking a chance that within two years "financial modernization legislation" would be passed to render what they had done legal. Whether they had inside information, had been lobbying Congress, or had other reason to believe this was a good gamble, they were right: Citicorp merged with Travelers in April 1998 and Gramm-Leach-Bliley was enacted in November 1999. Under the new act, the merger was now legal; some critics called it the "Citigroup Relief Act."[55] Others noted that the Clinton administration had a giant conflict of interest. In 1999, Robert Rubin resigned his position as Clinton's treasury secretary. Less than a week after the administration and Congress agreed on the bill, Rubin joined Citicorp as a board member.[56] In announcing Rubin's move to Citicorp, the *New York Times* noted that Gramm-Leach-Bliley removed "many of the restrictions preventing banks, securities firms and insurance companies from buying one another or engaging in one another's businesses," and that both "Mr. Rubin and Citigroup strongly supported the bill, which would greatly benefit the company."[57] (Before joining the administration, Rubin had worked for twenty-six years at Goldman Sachs.)[58]

Gramm-Leach-Bliley didn't just rescue Citigroup from a legally precarious situation, it also left the Securities and Exchange Commission (SEC) without authority to regulate the investment conglomerates that would now form. This was the second time in the 1990s that a major market was deregulated on the premise that it would encourage competition and offer more consumer choice, but without giving the government tools to ensure these positive effects. This was in keeping with the corporate conservative push toward deregulation. The sponsors—Phil Gramm, Jim Leach, and Thomas J. Bliley—were all Republicans, and the initial congressional vote left the Senate on strict party lines, with a vote of 54–44. In the House, Democrat John Dingell presciently warned that the new law would permit the creation of financial service groups that were "too big to fail," and the American taxpayer would end up bailing them out.[59] In the Senate Paul Wellstone reiterated the point, arguing that, absent legal constraints, financial institutions would resume the risky practices that had prompted regulation in the first place.[60] But with Clinton's backing, the bill passed both houses.

At the White House signing ceremony, the president invited co-sponsors Gramm and Leach to speak, along with the new secretary of the treasury, Lawrence Summers. They stressed the forward-looking character of the act, asserting that Glass-Steagall no longer fit the needs of the times. But freedom was another major theme. Gramm declared:

> In the 1930s, at the trough of the Depression, when Glass-Steagall became law, it was believed that government was the answer. It was believed that stability and growth came from government overriding the functioning of free markets. We are here today to repeal Glass-Steagall because we have learned that government is not the answer. We have learned that freedom and competition are the answers. We have learned that we promote economic growth, and we promote stability, by having competition and freedom.[61]

Leach reiterated the argument, declaring with massive redundancy: "[This bill] is competitive. It advances competition at home. And it increases our competitive ability to compete abroad."[62]

But if Republicans got on base with the Gramm-Leach-Bliley Act, it was the Democratic president who brought the runners home. "You heard Senator Gramm characterize this bill as a victory for freedom and free markets," Clinton whole-heartedly agreed. Glass-Steagall was "no longer appropriate for the economy in which we live." That law had "worked pretty well for the industrial economy, which was highly localized . . . But the world [today] is very different."[63]

The world had changed in sixty years, to be sure, but Glass-Steagall was about financial practices; if there was a coherent argument for why it mattered whether money was earned locally or globally, the president did not offer it. It was simply time for change, he implied. "[T]oday what we are doing is modernizing the financial services industry, tearing down these antiquated laws and granting banks significant new authority," Clinton proclaimed. It would save consumers "billions of dollars a year through enhanced competition."[64] But the new law did *not* save the American people billions of dollars, because the relaxed regulatory framework did not enhance competition, at least not in the way the president promised. Instead, it permitted a huge wave of mergers and acquisitions, with no means to regulate the new financial conglomerates that had emerged.

By 2000, the subprime loan market was worrying many observers. Some thought the Fed or the SEC might have informal authority to do something about subprime mortgages, and in 2000, Federal Reserve governor Edward Gramlich asked Fed chairman Alan Greenspan to send examiners to investigate. But Greenspan—a libertarian and Ayn Rand acolyte—refused.[65] Nor would he raise margin require-ments (minimum down payments) on lending for the purpose of buying stock. The Fed had a long history of imposing such requirements, so it was well within Greenspan's authority to do so, and as the stock market climbed to unprecedented heights some observers felt he should. He demurred. Greenspan also refused to investigate the proliferation of complex and opaque financial instruments, including the so-called collateralized debt obligations, which pooled millions of subprime mortgages and then sliced and diced them in ways that advocates insisted were safe (on the theory that the risk was being spread) but that turned out to be anything but when the housing market subsequently went bust.

Greenspan worked with Robert Rubin and others within the Clinton administration to prevent the Commodity Futures Trading Commission from regulating
these new financial instruments.[66] The sudden bankruptcy and bailout of the hedge
fund Long-Term Capital Management in 1998 didn't slow the deregulatory train.
Rubin (at that point still treasury secretary) and Summers (at that time Rubin's
deputy secretary) insisted that "market discipline" should be relied upon to prevent
problems, not federal regulation—in other words, the same self-regulation that
hadn't worked before. Then, Congress went further, making it *illegal* to regulate
most kinds of financial derivatives. This was achieved through the Commodity
Futures Modernization Act, which Clinton signed in December 2000.

The head of the Commodity Futures Trading Commission had argued for a
requirement that these new instruments be traded on public exchanges as commodities are. Exchanges require public disclosure of risks and finances, obviating the
opaqueness and risks related to it. They're not perfect, but they can reduce risk.
Greenspan rejected even that modest proposal.[67]

The Commodity Futures Modernization Act was followed by the collapse of one
of the stars of the "new economy." Enron had built its business trading unregulated
energy securities and investing in worldwide energy infrastructure. Along with
others, it gamed the newly deregulated California electricity market, earning high
profits while saddling the state and its utilities with debt and its citizens with black-
outs.[68] California quickly undid electricity deregulation, effectively ending a big
industry-led push for nationwide energy market deregulation. And its windfall
profits didn't really help Enron, either. The company had paid no attention to
its investment income—growth was the only metric valued within its internal
culture—and eventually it couldn't pay its bills. Its implosion should have given
further lie to the myth of "self-regulation." Somehow it didn't. Neither did the savings
and loan crisis of the 1990s, which by this time had already been largely forgotten.

In 2008, SEC chair Christopher Cox excoriated both the Gramm-Leach-Bliley
Act and the voluntary regulatory framework, concluding that it was "abundantly
clear that voluntary regulation does not work. When Congress passed [the Act,] it
created a significant regulatory gap by failing to give to the SEC or any agency the
authority to regulate large investment bank holding companies, like Goldman
Sachs, Morgan Stanley, Merrill Lynch, Lehman Brothers, and Bear Stearns."[69] But
his complaint was more than a day late and a dollar short; it was billions of dollars
short. By then, the United States was immersed in the greatest financial crisis since

the Great Depression. To stabilize the markets and stave off a complete economic collapse, the Fed bought billions of dollars in government securities, allowed banks to borrow more than $50 billion at subsidized interest rates, and lent bond dealers more than $200 billion to stabilize the bond market. Political commentator James Carville later quipped that if he were ever reincarnated, he wanted to come back as the bond market: "You can intimidate everyone."[70]

Chicago school economists had said the public would ascertain conflicts of interest and reject crappy securities, but it was not just "the public" who had been fooled; it was financial institutions as well. Under the Troubled Assets Relief Program (TARP), the American taxpayer bailed out banks and other financial institution to the tune of $500 billion.[71] And that was only a slice of the problem—a tranche, if you will. American households lost breathtaking amounts of net worth from the stock market plunge, real estate foreclosures, business bankruptcies, and other knock-on effects.[72]

In 2018, the Federal Reserve Board of San Francisco concluded that, a decade on, the U.S. economy remained "significantly smaller than it should be based on its pre-crisis growth trend. One possible reason lies in the large losses in the economy's productive capacity following the financial crisis. The size of those losses suggests that the level of output is unlikely to revert to its pre-crisis trend level. This represents a lifetime present-value income loss of about $70,000 for every American."[73] In total: about $23 *trillion*.

Economists and historians still argue over the causes of the Great Depression, so it's not surprising that the debate over the causes of the Great Recession continues. But many believe the repeal of Glass-Steagall, along with other initiatives that decreased regulatory oversight and encouraged fraudulent activity, played a significant role.[74] Columbia economics professor, Nobel Memorial Prize laureate, and one-time World Bank chief economist Joseph Stiglitz argues that the Glass-Steagall repeal—"the culmination of a $300 million lobbying effort by the banking and financial-services industries"—was determinative. "The proponents said, in effect, Trust us: we will . . . make sure that the problems of the past do not recur." But the problems did recur.[75] Financial regulation—like telecom regulation—needed retooling for the twenty-first century. But instead of updating the relevant regulations Congress and the Clinton administration gutted them. The Gramm-Leach-Bliley Act effectively removed the guardrails that for six decades had done the job they were built to do. When they were removed, the system crashed.

Stiglitz thinks the biggest effect of the Glass-Steagall repeal was cultural: commercial banks, previously known for their pinstriped conservatism, were encouraged to shed their stodgy skins. Investment banks typically handled the money of wealthy clients with a high tolerance for risk, and when they merged with commercial banks, "the investment bank culture came out on top."

Stanford Business School professor Anat Admati stresses that the enormous 2008 bank bailouts shared elements with the earlier Savings and Loans crisis. She argues that, in financial crises and inefficiencies, the culprit is invariably the excessive use of debt—money borrowed and owed to depositors and other creditors—to take risks and obscure them in poor disclosures and complex "off balance sheet" structures. When the 2008 crisis hit, policymakers felt compelled to prevent defaults, which implicitly rewarded the banks' excessive borrowing and unreasonable risk taking.[76] Either way, the bailout represented a huge subsidy to banks, investment houses, and insurance companies. Profits had accrued privately, but the losses were socialized.

LIKE TELECOM AND financial deregulation, the North American Free Trade Agreement (NAFTA) had roots in the Reagan years but would be realized under Clinton. When Reagan ran for election in 1979, his platform included free trade among Canada, Mexico, and the United States—the first time a major political figure advanced such a position. "We live on a continent whose three countries possess the assets to make it the strongest, most prosperous and self-sufficient area on earth," Reagan said. "Within the borders of this North American continent are the food, resources, technology, and undeveloped territory which, properly managed, could dramatically improve the quality of life of all of its inhabitants."[77] In a speech during his presidency, Reagan would insist that one of his key goals had been "a new era of free and fair trade."[78] Perhaps not incidentally, that particular speech was delivered at the annual meeting of the National Association of Manufacturers.

Neither Canadian prime minister Pierre Trudeau nor Mexican president José López Portillo was interested, however, and once in office, Reagan's record included a fair amount of protectionism.[79] The Cato Institute noticed the gap between rhetoric and reality—particularly the 1987 imposition of a 100 percent tariff on Japanese electronics—and objected. *Washington Post* columnist Mark Shields had criticized "Reagan's blind devotion to the doctrine of free trade"; Cato retorted that if the president was so devoted, then he was indeed blind, because most of his actions had been "off the mark . . . Only short memories and a refusal to believe one's own eyes would account for the view that President Reagan is a free trader."[80]

Cato's complaints aside, Reagan did sign the Canada–United States Free Trade Agreement in 1988, and it laid the groundwork for NAFTA, which was negotiated during the administration of George H. W. Bush and signed into law by Clinton.[81] During the Bush years, the business community lobbied heavily for lowering trade barriers, but public support remained weak and labor opposition strong. Business leaders redoubled their efforts. In 1993, the Business Roundtable wrote a memo encouraging its member CEOs to coax their employees to write letters in support of NAFTA. One particularly active corporation was Wal-Mart, which lobbied heavily for congressional passage—promoting both the benefits of its collaborations with Mexican suppliers and the opportunity for American producers to sell to Mexican consumers—and asked its suppliers to weigh in as well.[82] The National Retail Federation also got involved, "pushing members to pressure their employees to write and fax Congress."[83]

Congress passed NAFTA in 1993 with more Republican than Democratic support.[84] The treaty Clinton signed created the world's largest market, valued at an estimated $6 trillion, encompassing more than 365 million people.[85] NAFTA eliminated about half of all existing tariff barriers in agriculture, manufacturing, and the service industry, with the goal of phasing out most of the rest over ten to fifteen years. It also sought to eliminate most or all nontariff barriers, such as licensing requirements for trucks crossing the U.S.–Mexico border.[86]

Clinton embraced NAFTA as he embraced marketplace deregulation, insisting it was the way of the future: "We cannot stop global change," he declared. "We cannot repeal the international economic competition that is everywhere. We can only harness the energy to our benefit." Concerns about NAFTA eliminating U.S. jobs, he maintained, were unfounded: "To the men and women of our country who were afraid of these changes and found in their opposition to NAFTA an expression of that fear—what I thought was a wrong expression and what I know was a wrong expression but nonetheless represented legitimate fears—the gains from this agreement will be your gains, too."[87]

Clinton was wrong: many of the fears were founded. NAFTA did some good; many experts believe it helped the U.S., Canadian, and Mexican economies, albeit by a small amount. According to Lorenzo Caliendo of Yale and Fernando Parro of the Federal Reserve, the deal yielded a 0.08 percent increase in net economic welfare. Mexico benefited the most, with a gain of 1.31 percent, and Canada lost a marginal 0.06 percent.[88] Clearly, the net beneficial effect was far smaller than its advocates had promised.[89] But like most economic policies, this one affected some people and some sectors more than others.

The most obvious harm came to American manufacturing jobs. NAFTA did not kill American manufacturing, as is sometimes alleged. Those jobs as a percentage of total nonfarming employment had been declining since the 1950s, and they continued to decline at roughly the same rate after NAFTA. But the treaty did severely affect workers in some parts of the country. A 2016 study coauthored by economists Shushanik Hakobyan of the International Monetary Fund and John McLaren of the University of Virginia concluded that the hardest hit were blue-collar workers in California, Texas, New York, Michigan, and Ohio; the most affected industries were automobile manufacturing, textiles and footwear, and computers and electrical appliances.[90] (By 2000, there were about 3,600 maquiladoras—U.S.-owned factories operating in Mexico to produce goods primarily for U.S. consumers—the vast majority of which had developed when factories north of the border were shrunk or shuttered and U.S. workers laid off.)[91] This study concluded that the aggregate positive effects of NAFTA were small, but negative local effects were large. Blue-collar workers in "NAFTA-vulnerable" industries—such as shoe manufacturing, which lost prior protections—experienced large declines in wage growth, quickly falling behind industries that had never been protected in the first place. "For an important minority of workers, the effects [were] very negative."[92]

NAFTA also had substantive indirect effects on U.S. blue-collar household income. Many U.S. employers—like General Electric—sang a new variation on an old song: threatening to move. In the 1950s, GE had moved many of its facilities to "right-to-work" states; now many companies threatened to move to Mexico. Between 1993 and 1995, 64 percent of U.S. manufacturing firms in key industries used the threat of moving plants to Mexico to weaken unions and depress wages; by 1999 the figure was 71 percent. This created downward wage pressure in NAFTA-vulnerable industries—even when the companies stayed in place—and the effect rippled outward: Hakobyan and McLaren found that service industry wages in NAFTA-impacted regions fell significantly as well. "The blue-collar diner worker in the footwear town is hurt by the agreement, as is the blue-collar footwear-factory worker in a town dominated by insurance companies. Worst hit of all is the blue-collar footwear worker in a footwear town, particularly if that worker never finished high school." College-educated workers, however, "skate away mainly unharmed."[93]

Other analysts have come to similar conclusions. North of the border, American workers lost jobs and real wage growth; south of the border, Mexican farmers were driven out of business, maquiladora workers were exploited, and the Mexican environment deteriorated as the competitive pressures of NAFTA led farmers to use more fertilizers and pesticides and to cut down trees in search of more land.[94] Former Clinton labor secretary Robert Reich, who was a proponent of NAFTA, experienced a conversion and became a vocal opponent of the subsequent Trans-Pacific Partnership, which he characterized as a "Trojan horse in a global race to the bottom."[95]

While defenders insisted that NAFTA would not result in weakening environmental or labor protections, in fact it did. Among other things, it prevented Canada from enacting some of its commitments under the Paris Climate Accords when they were agreed to in 2015 and overrode a key article of the Mexican constitution that prevented Indigenous communal landholdings from being sold or privatized. Under NAFTA this provision was viewed as a barrier to investment; its overturning contributed to the 1994 Zapatista revolt in Chiapas, in which Indigenous rebels and their supporters formally declared war on the federal government.[96] During the twelve-day uprising, buildings were occupied, 230 prisoners were released, land records were destroyed, and more than one hundred thousand people marched in Mexico City in solidarity. By the end, three hundred people had died.

In many ways, NAFTA was a model of unfairness, with a small proportion of American workers and many Mexicans bearing the brunt of loss while others gained. The inequities on the U.S. side could have been remedied by a program of direct grants to the adversely affected workers or by improving educational opportunities. During the 1992 presidential campaign, independent candidate Ross Perot had imagined "a giant sucking sound" of jobs being vacuumed up and sent to Mexico, but the real sucking sound was income being pulled from the pockets of working-class Americans.[97]

It has long been established by economists that trade policy in general tends to be characterized by large redistributional effects.[98] Conservatives often rail against "income redistribution," particularly if achieved by progressive taxation, but they essentially endorsed income redistribution away from blue-collar workers and toward the middle and upper classes when they supported NAFTA. This was the treaty's largest documented effect. Free-trade advocates may argue this was an unintended consequence, but it should not have come as a surprise.

THE IDEAS THAT animated NAFTA—as well as financial and telecom deregulation—came together in the 1990s under the rubric of the "Washington Consensus," endorsed in the United States by Bill Clinton and in the United Kingdom by Prime Minister Tony Blair.[99] Economist John Williamson had originally coined the term in 1989 to refer to a far more specific matter. Williamson was concerned with Latin America—a region that at the time was crippled by debt burden—and was trying to identify a conceptual framework of reforms that "more or less everyone in Washington would agree were needed more or less everywhere in Latin America." He identified ten:

1. Fiscal discipline
2. Reordering public expenditure priorities
3. Tax reform
4. Liberalizing interest rates
5. A competitive exchange rate
6. Trade liberalization
7. Liberalization of inward foreign direct investment
8. Privatization
9. Deregulation
10. Property rights

Together, these principles comprised the serious intellectual case for "disciplined macroeconomics, the use of markets, and trade liberalization."[100] Perhaps because there were ten items in Williamson's list, many people came to read the list as the ten commandments of market fundamentalism.

Development experts Robin Broad and John Cavanaugh—who emphasize that they were never part of the alleged consensus—characterized its key tenets as "free trade, free investment, deregulation, and privatization." The framework, they lamented, displaced a previous way of thinking that feared the effect of "unfettered markets in a world of unequal nations." A "once vibrant debate about development all but disappeared as the consensus took on almost religious qualities." Because many debt-ridden countries were dependent on the World Bank and IMF, they often had little choice but to accept their dictates. Economists who tried to object—for example, to argue that different countries might need different policies—were treated as "heretics."[101] Worse, citizens of the countries where these policies were being applied had little or no place at the table, even as they pointed to mounting evidence that market-oriented policies were increasing inequality and worker mistreatment, causing massive environmental destruction, and driving traditional small farmers and Indigenous peoples off their lands. Workers in wealthy countries complained too, as evidence mounted that export-oriented jobs in the global south were hurting workers in the global north. By 1998, 58 percent of Americans felt that free trade was "bad for the U.S. economy."[102]

In 2004, looking back on his work, Williamson stressed that he had *not* intended the framework as a "pseudonym for market fundamentalism," even if it had often been taken that way.[103] Nor was it (he wrote) "neoliberalism." Williamson found that term useful to refer to the doctrines of the Mont Pelerin Society, but in any other context it appeared to be little "more than an intellectual swear word."[104] Williamson also distanced himself from the initiatives of the Reagan administration and the Thatcher government, including monetarism, supply-side economics, and minimal government; these had been "discarded as impractical or undesirable fads...no trace of them can be found in what I labeled the 'Washington Consensus,'" he wrote.[105]

Williamson took pains to point out several ways in which the reforms he had articulated had been misrepresented or misinterpreted. On fiscal discipline, Williamson said he was talking about poor countries with large deficits that drove high inflation, which (he believed) hurt the poor more than the rich (because they had less to buffer them). On reordering public expenditure, the operative word was *reordering*—away from "things like nonmerit subsidies" and toward "basic health and education and infrastructure." In other words, public expenditure should focus on common goods like roads and education, which benefit society but are unlikely to be adequately supplied by free markets. His was not a general call to "starve the beast." Williamson was emphatic that the Washington Consensus "did *not* call for all the burden of achieving fiscal discipline to be placed on expenditure cuts." Nor was it an attack on big government. "On the contrary, the intention was to be

strictly neutral about the desirable size of the public sector." On financial liberalization, he regretted not having paid more attention to Stiglitz's warning that, without
supervision (which is to say, regulation), it would likely "lead almost inexorably to
financial crisis"—which, in 2008, it did.[106]

Williamson's views—at least as expressed in 2004—are far removed from Mont
Pelerin–style neoliberalism, much less Thatcherist or Reaganite market fundamentalism. Maybe this is why the Washington Consensus is more famous than its
author. As with Smith and Hayek, Williamson's nuanced analysis was flattened by
the cheerleaders of deregulation into the suggestion that markets could be stripped
of protective regulations. The Washington Consensus was not a brief for minimal
government, but it was mobilized as one.

Amid the collapsing of the Soviet Bloc and the opening of the Berlin Wall, 1989
was the perfect year for free-marketeers to misread Williamson. With the dichoto-
mous logic that had characterized neoliberal thought since Ludwig von Mises,
triumphalist ideologues would interpret the failure of communism to mean the
only thing left standing was capitalism, and if capitalism was the superior economic
system, then the best version of it was its purest one.[107] In this context, it was easy to
ignore the lessons of history and read the Washington Consensus as a brief for the
return of laissez-faire.

To Williamson, it seemed plausible that some had deliberately attempted to
discredit the Washington Consensus by bundling it with "a raft of ideas that deserve
to be consigned to oblivion."[108] He also found it "preposterous" to associate Bill
Clinton—who enthusiastically embraced the consensus—with the key neoliberal
tenets of "supply-side economics, monetarism, or minimal government." That was
true, so what did it mean for Clinton to espouse the Washington Consensus as he did?

Clinton adopted a broadly "pro-market" stance, stressing the importance of
competition in his advocacy of financial and telecommunications deregulation.
This was not the same as market fundamentalism. As Williamson noted, "[o]ne
does not have to be some sort of market fundamentalist who believes that less
government is better government and that externalities can safely be disregarded in
order to recognize the benefits of using market forces to coordinate activity and
motivate effort."[109] Quite so, and Bill Clinton is best understood as attempting to
do just this. But because the idea of harnessing market forces had become so tied
rhetorically and intellectually with the idea of "small" government, Clinton and his

advisers seem to have fallen into the trap into which Williamson concedes he also fell: underappreciating that liberalization only works if coupled with effective governance.

Whether the Washington Consensus was neoliberal or not—and whether the term neoliberal even had (or has) a coherent meaning—by the mid-1990s the framework of trade liberalization, deregulation, privatization, and low taxation had taken hold and would inform American administrations, both Democratic and Republican. In 2006, Larry Summers declared that "any honest Democrat will admit that we are now all Friedmanites."[110] Many problems that previously would have been considered the terrain of government were now viewed as more appropriately addressed in the marketplace, even in the face of clear evidence of market failure or inequitable redistribution. Some, following in Leonard Read's footsteps, went further, virtually deifying the marketplace, to the point that (as we have seen) a leading intellectual could say, without sarcasm, "it's not crazy to worship markets."[111]

Yet the Washington Consensus—whatever it meant—was never really a consensus, at least not a social, cultural, or political one. In many ways, it was more of an imposition. In 1997, the IMF responded to a currency crisis afflicting South Korea by imposing drastic austerity measures—privatization of industries, massive job cuts in the public and banking sectors—in return for stabilization loans. These measures created mass unemployment and further damaged the nation's economy. "In 1996, 63.7 percent of South Koreans identified as middle class; by 1999 that number was down to 38.4 percent."[112] Suddenly, twenty million people were thrown back into poverty. Other Asian nations similarly suffered, generating massive protests. In a 1982 edition of *Capitalism and Freedom*, Milton Friedman had theorized that "Only a crisis—actual or perceived—produces real change. When that crisis occurs, the actions that are taken depend on the ideas that are lying around." He saw it as the job of intellectuals (like himself) to keep ideas in circulation until "the politically impossible becomes politically inevitable."[113] Naomi Klein framed it differently: "Crises are, in a way, democracy-free zones—gaps in politics as usual when the need for consent and consensus do not seem to apply."[114] Radical, undemocratic change can be imposed during crises—and that's what the IMF did, ordering off the menu that Friedman had helped to design.

The World Trade Organization (WTO), created in 1995 out of the older General Agreement on Tariffs and Trade, suffered a big setback of its own in 1999. Meeting in Seattle to launch a new round of trade liberalization (this time, with a modicum of attention paid to labor and environmental rights that had been ignored for decades), the WTO discovered how unpopular it was when the international delegates were greeted by massive but peaceful protests. However, a small group of anarchists began damaging property, and the city sent riot police to "control" the situation.[115] Police violence expanded the problem, and it became a days-long television spectacle.

The WTO meeting came to no new agreement. Delegates weren't particular concerned with the street violence, but with the demands from the Clinton administration and other countries for environmental and labor protections, even weak ones. The WTO had long been corporatist in its outlook, and many delegates rejected even a suggestion that labor and environmental standards should become part of the institution's rules. The Seattle protests simply "brought home" to the U.S. audience what was being done in its name to other countries. It also brought home the fact that the WTO was profoundly undemocratic, given huge power with little or no public oversight.

LUDWIG VON MISES had insisted that economics should be a science; Milton Friedman's advocacy of "positive" economics was another way of saying the same thing. But as Oxford economist Ha-Joon Chang has shown, there is scant empirical evidence to support the policies the WTO tried to impose. Actually, history suggests the opposite: developing countries' performance was generally better when their development was state-led, and worse when they undertook market-oriented reform.[116] Free-trade agreements typically redistribute wealth (even while their advocates decry redistribution achieved through other means). They also impose on developing nations terms that rich nations did not follow in their own histories. Often these terms hurt poor countries by making it hard or even impossible for them to protect infant industries and nurture home-grown innovation. Thus, in a latter-day version of colonialism, they become permanent provisioners of raw materials for wealthier countries.

"Dead presidents don't talk," Chang writes. "But if they could, they would tell Americans and the rest of the world how the policies that their successors promote today are the exact opposite of what they used to transform a second-rate agrarian economy dependent on slave labor into the world's greatest industrial power."[117] To highlight these facts is not to advocate communism, socialism, or any other -ism. It is simply to underscore a problem at the root of many economic discussions: crucial arguments are asserted or assumed rather than tested and confirmed.

With a degree of candor rare in economics, Williamson admits that the belief among nearly all contemporary economists in the "benefits of using market forces to coordinate activity and motivate effort" is more of an axiom than a tested and proven theory. "This proposition is such a basic part of economic thinking that it is actually rather difficult to think of a work that conclusively established its truth."[118]

Any physicist could point to key experiments that proved the theory of relativity; most biologists could describe the work that demonstrated the double-helix structure of DNA; and geologists can easily explain the evidence supporting plate tectonic theory. But here is one of the world's leading economists frankly admitting that he *cannot think of a work that establishes the truth of economists' most basic foundational belief.*

The fundamental requirement of science is that theories be tested by evidence and modified in accordance with the results, but many neoliberal or market fundamentalist assertions have either never been properly tested, have yielded ambiguous results, or have been tested and failed. Yet, their advocates cling to them. Indeed, they insist. Williamson offers weakly that there have been good indirect confirmations of market beneficence and efficacy, "from the universal acclaim that meets the abandonment of rationing to the success of emissions trading in reducing pollution."[119] This is absurd. For one thing, price systems *are* rationing systems—they simply allocate larger rations to people with more money and smaller ones to people with less. The fact that people welcomed the abandonment of government-imposed rationing, as they did after World War II, does not prove that rationing was *inefficient*; it just proves that people didn't like it. As for emissions trading—much beloved by many economists for its market orientation—that is a form of rationing, too.

In emissions trading systems, a government sets an annual emissions cap—in effect a ration—which it divides into permits and auctions off. Economists claim that this rationing by price is the most efficient means of allocating what is now a scarce resource (the right to pollute), but that's unproven. It may even be a circular argument: in several well-documented examples, emissions trading was embraced because it proved more politically feasible to institute than the alternatives. Why was it politically feasible? Because economists had persuaded people of its efficiency![120] Emissions trading can work—it successfully reduced acid rain in both

Europe and the United States and dramatically cleared the air in Southern California—but that does not prove it works better than alternatives.

There is an old joke: A physicist, an engineer, and an economist are stranded on a desert island with nothing but canned food. The physicist proposes to make a fire and heat the can until it bursts. The engineer proposes to climb to a local ridge and drop the can, which will burst on landing. The economist says: "Assume a can opener."

IN THE 1990S, as capitalism was being declared triumphant in many quarters, scientists had proved that man-made climate change was under way.[121] Climate change was textbook market failure. It arose from everyday economic activity—using fossil fuels—but was about to impose a huge external cost, inundating major coastal cities around the globe, making hurricanes and cyclones even more deadly than they already were, and dislocating tens or even hundreds of millions of people. It was also textbook environmental injustice, as poor people would almost certainly bear the brunt of a problem created by the rich.

But it also had a textbook answer: putting a price on carbon. Economists called this solution a "Pigouvian tax"—after the Cambridge economist Arthur Pigou, who in the early twentieth century had helped develop the concept of negative externalities. (Pigou also suggested it would be reasonable for governments to subsidize activities that had "positive externalities," such as education.) The idea of pricing social and environmental costs of carbon was hardly radical; Pigou was firmly mainstream, a respected scholar at Cambridge University, a leading figure in what came to be known as the Cambridge school of economics.[122] The obvious benefit of the Pigouvian approach was that it remedied the market failure directly by embedding information—in this case scientific information—into the price of fossil fuels. Then consumers could decide for themselves whether or not to buy more expensive fossil fuels, and producers of alternatives could compete on a level playing field.

The Clinton administration proposed to address climate change through a Pigouvian tax, the so-called "BTU" tax (referring to the heat content of fuels as measured in British Thermal Units).[123] But it was opposed—indeed, ridiculed—by a broad coalition of conservatives, including, the Chamber of Commerce, the American Petroleum Institute, and virtually every right-wing think tank in America.[124] The notorious Global Climate Coalition, a network of fossil fuel producers and users that in the 1990s successfully prevented the U.S. Congress from ratifying the Kyoto protocol to the U.N. Framework Convention on Climate Change, was originally established as a committee of the National Association of Manufacturers. Even though the idea of putting a price on carbon was a mainstream economic approach to market failure, Republicans framed it as just another example of Democrats' penchant to "tax and spend." The *Wall Street Journal* mocked it as Al Gore's "favorite tax."[125]

In his 1979 paper on nonmarket failure, economist Charles Wolf had slipped into his conclusion the idea that one cause of nonmarket failure was "premature but politically effective demands for government action."[126] In the 1990s, many Republicans picked up on this theme, arguing that it was premature to act on climate change. Even at the time, that was wrong: scientists already had a consensus that man-made climate change was under way and likely to be very costly.[127] To act in the 1990s would have been appropriate. It would have been timely. But Clinton was unable to generate congressional support for action; Republican opposition made it clear that any proposal to put a price on carbon would be dead on arrival. In 1999, when Vice President Al Gore ran for president on a platform prioritizing climate change, journalist Gregg Easterbrook (brother of Judge Frank Easterbrook) embarrassed him on the campaign trail with a false story that his mentor—climate champion Roger Revelle—had experienced a deathbed conversion and died thinking climate change was not a serious problem.[128] (He had not.)

As the 1990s became the 2000s—and scientists declared the evidence "unequivocal"—market fundamentalist did not adjust their views. To the contrary, their opposition hardened.[129] In 2006, Lord Nicholas Stern, former chief economist of the World Bank, concluded on behalf of the UK government that, yes, fixing climate change would be expensive—perhaps as much as 1 percent of global GDP per annum—but not fixing it would cost much more: at least 5 percent and perhaps as much as 20 percent.[130] Here was a solid argument from a man who could scarcely be accused of being any kind of -ist other than an economist. In response, conservatives dug in deeper. Senator Ted Cruz promoted the canard that global warming had stopped; Senator James Inhofe called it a liberal conspiracy to bring down capitalism.[131] No matter what solutions were proposed—market-friendly or not—the right wing found reasons to oppose them. The science wasn't settled (they claimed). It would be too expensive to fix. We could just adapt. It was all a hoax. Often these claims were couched in libertarian terms, as when in 2011 former House Speaker

Newt Gingrich deemed the push to address climate change "the newest excuse to take control of lives."[132]

The singular exception to climate denial in Republican Party leadership was Senator John McCain. He and conservative Democrat Joe Lieberman introduced Climate Stewardship acts in 2003, 2005, and 2007 to address the carbon dioxide emissions that drive climate change by creating an emissions trading system—a proven mechanism, albeit more complicated than a Pigouvian tax. But when given the chance to use it to address climate change, Republicans refused.[133] The 2003 bill failed on mostly party lines, with a few Democrats and nearly all Republicans in opposition. But it was a closer call than many expected, and soon Congress faced intense lobbying pressure against climate legislation, particularly from NAM and the U.S. Chamber of Commerce. The 2005 version came to a vote and failed 60–38, with only a handful of Republicans voting yea.[134] Two years after that, McCain could not even persuade Republican leaders to bring a climate bill to the Senate floor.[135]

In 2009, Congress tried once more, with the American Clean Energy and Security Act (better known as Waxman-Markey, for its primary sponsors, Massachusetts representative Ed Markey and California representative Henry Waxman). For the fourth time in a decade, Congress had the opportunity to address climate change using a market mechanism, and for the fourth time rejected it. The bill barely passed the Democratic-led House; nearly all Republicans voted against, as did Democrats from fossil-fuel-producing states (and a few Democrats who found the bill too weak). The Senate never brought it to a vote. Democrats concluded they could not overcome the "wall of opposition" they faced from their Republican colleagues, opposition fortified by fierce lobbying.[136] One analysis concluded that, in the eighteen months between January 2009 and June 2010, electric utilities, oil and gas companies, trade associations, and think tanks spent at least $500 million against climate change legislation.[137] Another study tracing anti-climate lobbying back to 2003 places the figure at closer to $1 billion.[138]

THE FOSSIL FUEL industry's economic interests in preventing climate action have always been obvious; less understood is how it has camouflaged those interests. No one ever said, "I am denying climate change to protect corporate profits." They said they were protecting jobs, protecting the economy, and protecting free markets from government "encroachment." They said they were fighting for capitalism and freedom.

But historically, capitalism has never been just one thing: Adam Smith's eighteenth-century vision of a democratic, distributed marketplace populated by small bankers and businessmen was a far cry from the industrial capitalism that developed in early nineteenth-century England and Germany—with its cruel "Satanic mills"—or the monopolies and managerial capitalism that came to dominate America in the late nineteenth century, much less the globally financed capitalism that emerged at the end of the twentieth century. China has liberalized its markets while continuing to oppress and even murder its ethnic and religious minorities. There are many capitalisms. American market fundamentalists fight for a form of capitalism that is both brutal and ignorant: that brushes aside market failure, anticompetitive practices, and external costs, in part by denying the facts of science, the facts of history, and the necessary role of government in making capitalism work.[139]

The question is not whether government should set limits that prevent individual autonomy from producing collective harm, the question is where we draw the lines. That is not an economic question, it is a political one. Market fundamentalists have managed to distract from the political aspects of these decisions and frame them as questions of "economic freedom." Thus, a reasonable response to climate change is rejected as unreasonable "government encroachment."

All this may make one wonder: was this ever *really* about capitalism? Or freedom? Or was it all just one long, semi-continuous, shape-shifting defense of the prerogatives of big business? Of freedom for capital and capitalists? Or had the market fundamentalists spent so much time defending the magic of the marketplace that they simply couldn't accept market failure on a global scale? To accept the enormity of what climate change portended for civilization was to accept that capitalism, as practiced, was undermining the very prosperity it was supposed to deliver. And not just in some distant future, but *now*.

PART IV

Beyond the Myth

CHAPTER 15

The High Cost of the "Free" Market

As a novel virus crisscrossed the globe in early 2020, the *Economist* ran an editorial acknowledging the urgent need for a "Big Government" response but demanding that government shrink back as soon as the crisis had passed. Even in an hour of darkest need, the century-long campaign to implant the myth of the free market had succeeded in making government "encroachment" seem as scary as a deadly pathogen. But the Covid-19 crisis has made crystal clear why some problems demand substantive governmental solutions, and why many of them can't just be temporary.[1]

For decades, scientists have known that an emerging virus could cause a pandemic and they warned that America was woefully underprepared. In 1988, the Institute of Medicine—renamed the National Academy of Medicine in 2015—suggested that the risk justified an expanded federal government role in public health. The states could and should do most of the day-to-day work of public health, but epidemics were different. "Only the federal government can focus attention and resources that such a health problem demands," because the federal government is "*structured* in a way that allows [for a] clearly defined national focus point."[2]

In 2019, in a meeting that now seems clairvoyant, experts at the Center for Health Security at Johns Hopkins University addressed "preparedness for a high-impact respiratory pathogen pandemic." Among their recommendations: countries should improve their core public health competencies; draw up national action plans, with strategies to make decisions quickly when needed and prepare for supply interruptions; and develop the capacity for "surge manufacturing in crisis."[3] Obviously, their advice was ignored.

Over the past thirty years, scientists' counsel on a wide range of issues—from pandemic preparedness to climate change—has been widely discounted and sometimes rejected outright. A major reason is the influence of the thinking that insists on limiting the power and reach of the federal government and relying on markets to solve our problems. Most damagingly, the market-oriented framework of recent decades has resisted any facts—scientific, historical, sociological, or otherwise— that suggest a need for a strong, centralized, or otherwise coordinated governmental response.

In some countries, concentrated central power may be a threat to liberty, but the United States is not one of them, in part because the country was set up with that concern in mind. The conservative preoccupation with constraining government power has left us with a federal government too weak and too divided to handle big problems like Covid-19 and climate change. Even as the pandemic raged, millions of Americans refused to get vaccinated in large part because of distrust of "the government," and the lion's share of those Americans were political conservatives.

The steps necessary to avoid the worst effects of an emergent disease—stockpiling supplies, educating people about hand-washing and social distancing, developing accurate tests and implementing them equitably, and sustaining the research infrastructure that can kick in to develop a vaccine—are not readily undertaken by the private sector. There's not much of a business case for stockpiling a billion face masks.[4] Nor can we rely on the private sector to step up when a new virus emerges, because by then it is too late. The "just in time" supply model that dominates in business is efficient for many purposes, but it does not work in the face of a pandemic.[5]

For any problem that has a scientific, medical, or technological component, the challenge is not simply to mobilize resources when they are needed, but to have them ready in advance. It takes a year or more to build a laboratory; it takes a decade to train a cadre of scientists and engineers. We could no more muster on demand the needed expertise and infrastructure to fight a pandemic than we could suddenly raise a professional military, replete with aircraft carriers and their air wings, within weeks of an attack. Nearly all conservatives acknowledge the need for military preparedness, yet they have been loath to allow that government is needed to address a wide range of problems—and not just scientific ones—that markets can't or won't solve on their own.

The United States's Covid-19 experience compared to that of other countries—as well as the comparative experience of the United States before and after the 2020 election—proves that when a well-organized national government acts efficiently on robust information and technical expertise, big problems can be tackled and outcomes substantially improved. Government can be more or less efficient, but it will certainly be inefficient if it lacks the wherewithal to act, and if it is hobbled by people who see it as their role to restrict government power at all times, rather than use it judiciously and appropriately. This is what we saw in the American response to Covid-19. A Republican administration denied the crisis, while its political appointees deliberately undermined the nation's public health officials. Hostility to federal action was recapitulated on the state level, as Republican governors flouted public health advice, refused to impose mask mandates, and insisted—even as the scope of the crisis became brutally clear—that the decision to mask or not to mask was a personal choice.

As we write these words, more than a million Americas have died, and many of these lives could have been saved with a more resolute and rapid governmental response. Countries that mounted a strong, coordinated response—South Korea, Germany, China, New Zealand, Vietnam—did a far better job containing the virus and suffered far fewer deaths. (Most of these countries have suffered less economic damage as well, for the obvious reason that "The Economy" is constituted by the people who work and invest in it; if people can't work, the economy can't work.)[6] A 2021 study published in the *Lancet*—the world's premier medical journal— concluded not only that the policies and actions of the Trump administration actively contributed to the viral spread, but that 40 percent of American Covid-related deaths could have been prevented had the United States adopted policies more like those of other wealthy, democratic nations.[7] A more recent study comparing the United States and Australia suggested the figure could be as high as 90 percent. In other words, as many as *nine hundred thousand deaths* may have been entirely avoidable. The biggest difference between the two countries was trust: in science, in institutions, and in each other.[8]

The *Lancet* authors argued that the fault lay not just in the mismanagement of the previous four years, but in the prior forty years of public health neglect; Donald Trump's actions are best understood as an "aggressive acceleration of neoliberal policies" that had already undermined access to health care and created substantive health disparities.[9] But if the U.S.-Australia comparison is valid, it suggests that the problem goes back even farther, into the long history of efforts to undermine trust in government (including government science) that we have recounted here.

Things changed in America when Joe Biden was elected and mobilized the capacities of the federal government to expedite vaccine production and distribution and to assist state-based vaccination efforts. But by then, damage had been done. Many conservative Americans—egged on by Republican governors and right-wing media—resisted the vaccine even after its safety and efficacy were demonstrated. As the pandemic raged, fueled in part by the scientifically predictable emergence of new variants, dying patients demanded Ivermectin, a drug that does nothing for Covid patients but was promoted in right-wing circles.[10] In South Dakota, patients in their final hours thought nurses were lying when they told them they were dying from Covid-19.[11]

According to a 2020 paper by former treasury secretary Lawrence Summers and economist David Cutler, the total cost to the United States of the Covid-19 crisis may reach $16 trillion.[12] This does not include the mental health costs, or the incalculable personal losses in sadness and suffering. Nor does it include the lost value of the "missing Americans"—the friends, family members, and elders without whose company and wisdom we now go forward. Moreover, whatever the United States *has* done to get the pandemic under control has not been thanks to the magic of the marketplace. It has been thanks to science, which provided the basis for vaccine development; to government purchase agreements that removed much of the risk from vaccine development; and to the collaborative efforts of the federal, state, and local governments, nonprofits, and the private sector to get vaccines distributed to the American people. To be sure, the private sector stepped up to the plate, but the 2021 U.S. vaccine development was much closer to the New Deal war mobilization model than the market fundamentalist one.

THE COVID-19 PANDEMIC has shown us how expensive overreliance on the "free" market can be. Yet, as bad as it has been, the failures of American political economy go well beyond it. In domain after domain after domain, overreliance on markets and underreliance on government have cost the American people dearly. And this has been the case during both Democratic and Republican administrations since Bill Clinton.

Consider the opioid crisis. In 2019, 49,860 Americans died of opioid overdoses.[13] According to the Centers for Disease Control and Prevention, total deaths from opioids, both prescription and illicit, in the years 1999 to 2019 approached 500,000.[14] That number is likely an underestimate, as many death certificates attribute a drug-related death to heart or respiratory failure. Nor does this figure include many opioid-related deaths, such as suicide in children of addicted parents. One study suggests that such suicides are sufficiently common as to help explain the recent overall increase in adolescent suicide.[15]

This staggering death rate is matched by a comparable economic burden: $78.5 billion.[16] Yet only twenty years ago, few Americans died from opioid overdose; in 1999, the number was less than eight thousand. Like all social problems, this one is complex, but an important cause is inadequate regulation. When synthetic opioids came on the market, they were falsely sold by their manufacturers as unlikely to cause addiction. A weak (and arguably captured) federal agency, the U.S. Food and Drug Administration, declined to control them the way it controls morphine, heroin, and other highly addictive drugs, allowing manufacturers to market aggressively, particularly in regions of the country where disability from workplace injury was known to be high. In Europe, where these drugs are better regulated—and there is generally greater state support for injured or addicted individuals—there is no opioid crisis.[17]

Or consider gun violence. According to the CDC, in 2019, 39,707 Americans died from firearm injuries, more than died in the Korean War.[18] One analysis concludes that in the years 1999 to 2015, 519,338 people died from firearms.[19] In Canada, the equivalent number (normalized for population) is about 180,000.[20] Across the globe, deaths by firearms are far less frequent than in the United States, and these lower death rates generally correlate with stricter gun regulation and lower rates of gun ownership. In the United States, the rate of gun ownership per 100,000 inhabitants is 120.5; in France it is 19.6.[21] Switzerland has relatively high gun ownership rates for a European country—one estimate places it as high as 41 per 100,000—but all guns must be permitted, and no one with a history of mental health problems can get one. The Swiss have not had a mass shooting since 2001.

Obesity causes heart disease, cancer, and stroke, the leading killers of Americans. In the 1950s, only about 10 percent of Americans were obese; today 70 percent of us are overweight or obese.[22] Like the opioid crisis, the causes of obesity are complex, but manufactured food plays a major role. Or consider endocrine-disrupting chemicals, which mimic the structure and sometimes the function of hormones. These chemicals—found legally in a breathtakingly long list of consumer products including paint, carpets, hand sanitizers, shampoo, sunscreen, and lipstick—have been associated with an astonishing array of adverse effects. These include prostate and breast cancer, infertility, endometriosis, diabetes, cardiopulmonary disease, and more. The cost of this disease burden is huge, in the United States perhaps as much as $340 billion *each year*.[23]

Inadequate oversight also enables fraud. There was plenty of it during the Reagan-Bush–era savings and loan debacle, and more during the run-up to the 2008 financial collapse and Great Recession. But it didn't end there and wasn't confined to the financial sector. One example is the implosion of Theranos, the Silicon Valley startup whose basic idea—a complete health diagnosis from a drop of blood—sounded amazing. The company raised $700 million in venture capital funding on the promise of "disrupting" the nation's health care system (and of course making Theranos investors very wealthy), at one point reaching a valuation of nearly $10 billion. Except the technology didn't exist. Silicon Valley's hyped-up investment culture was one problem. Another, according to John Carreyrou, the *Wall Street Journal* reporter who broke the story, was failure of both the corporate board of directors and federal regulators to provide adequate oversight.[24] The now-defunct company's founder and CEO, Elizabeth Holmes, was convicted of fraud, and hundreds of millions lost will likely never be recovered.[25]

Theranos attracted some very wealthy and famous investors, and we might not feel too sorry for rich people who failed to do their due diligence. But at the other end of the spectrum are ordinary citizens who not only have no money to invest but can't make ends meet despite working full time. At Disneyland—the "happiest place on Earth"—73 percent of workers can't afford to live nearby and more than a few live in their cars.[26] And then there are untold older Americans, staying in the workplace past seventy because of the decline of pension programs.[27] One consequence of deregulation has been that when companies went bankrupt—or were bought, sold, or merged—they often escaped obligations to their workers, including paying out pension benefits. Many airline workers, for example, received only pennies on their promised pension dollars. Other Americans never earned enough to cover their bills and also save for retirement, while Social Security benefits failed to keep pace with inflation. There is now a large mobile cohort of retirees who work part-time—often living in their cars and campers—because they cannot afford permanent homes on meager fixed incomes.[28] As the 2021 film *Nomadland* highlighted, some of these Americans like this lifestyle, but this does not obviate the fact that others have been forced into it.

The problem of "retirees" who can't retire is of course linked to income inequality.[29] We all know the problem of the "top 1 percent"; what many people don't know is that income inequality is associated with a variety of ills across the board, including poor physical and mental health, higher rates of crime, and shorter life expectancy.[30] The two countries with the lowest levels of income inequality—Finland and Sweden—lead the world in most measures of well-being. In contrast, the United States, which is very wealthy but very unequal, trails many much poorer countries in health, education, life expectancy, and many other measures.[31] Income inequality also decreases social mobility, which means that many Americans simply can't improve their situations, even if they really want to. The American Dream becomes a receding horizon.[32]

As Thomas Piketty and others have shown, income inequality is intrinsic to capitalist systems, a result of markets working as they "should." But blaming the problem on "capitalism" writ large hides the crucial fact that the growing inequality of the past forty years has been driven by changes in the rules of how our capitalism operates.[33] They include changes to our tax structure and forms of deregulation that hugely favor the wealthy, and these changes have been justified—in some quarters even celebrated—as "letting the market do its magic."

The inequality capitalism creates can be readily remedied through progressive taxation. In the past this was done: in the 1950s the top marginal tax rate in America was 91 percent, and the economy did as well as or better than in most other decades. Not many people actually paid that rate, of course; the median male wage earner made $3,400 in 1955 and had a marginal tax rate of 22 percent.[34] But that's the point. The superrich can afford to pay super-high taxes, and the moderately rich can afford to pay moderately high taxes. It doesn't wreck the economy, much less lead us down the road to serfdom. Today, the top marginal tax rate on the income of the wealthiest Americans is only 37 percent, and because of tax loopholes and lower rates on capital gains their effective tax rates are far lower.[35] Billionaire Warren Buffett has more than once noted that he pays tax at a lower rate than his secretary. Many profitable corporations pay no taxes at all.[36]

While a proven effective remedy for inequality is easily at hand, business conservatives have consistently dug in against it. In fact, they have been doing so for as long as we have had that remedy at our disposal. When the federal income tax was first established, conservatives opposed it as a "socialistic confiscation of wealth."[37] At its 1924 convention, the National Association of Manufacturers declared its opposition to "the use of the taxing power for purposes of economic equalization."[38] NAM lost the argument for decades, until, in the 1980s, it won. This is where things have largely remained, thanks to the work of libertarian think tanks, conservative economists, Republican political and business leaders who demonized taxation as "theft," and Democrats who were unwilling, unable, or too craven or captured to fight back.

Clearly a tax rate that starved consumers of disposable income and businesses of profit would be bad in many ways. Sweden gets a lot of negative press for its high marginal tax rate—these days 57 percent—but it has a thriving economy and offers its citizens "the best in class [in] public facilities and infrastructure."[39] The idea that we generate prosperity by cutting taxes on the rich is not just unethical, it's untrue.

We might call it criminal when a hardworking Disneyland employee can't afford a home, and courts have found illegality in the ways that prescription opioids were marketed and sold. But many market failures involve products and activities that are perfectly legal, yet whose outcomes are disturbing. Tobacco, a legal product, kills eight million people worldwide every year.[40] Air pollution kills nine million.[41] Oil, gas, and coal are legal products, yet their unrestricted use is now threatening to drown a good deal of the globe and to burn up much of the rest.

The novelist Kim Stanley Robinson has summed it up: "the invisible hand never picks up the check."[42] Today, an awful lot of checks have come due. The biggest one is climate change.

TO ACCEPT THE reality of climate change is to accept that big negative externalities cannot be dismissed as mere "neighborhood effects." Credible estimates place the economic damages from fossil fuel use between 0.5 and 4.0 percent of GDP per year. (For comparison, the catastrophic 2011 Tohoku earthquake and resulting tsunami and nuclear plant meltdown in Fukushima cost Japan about 3 percent of GDP in the year it occurred.) A 2019 analysis finds that, if present trends continue, the impacts of hurricane damage, real estate losses, energy costs, and water costs in the United States will carry a price tag of *$1.9 trillion per year* (in today's dollars), or 1.8 percent of U.S. GDP by 2100.[43] This does not include a plethora of hard-to-quantify ill effects, such as losses of cultural heritage; the psychic costs of losing one's home, community, or livelihood; species extinctions; or the sadness of solastalgia.

Because these costs are huge, nearly all independent studies conclude that fixing climate change is a good economic bet.[44] The IMF, the World Bank, and most mainstream economists recommend government action to account for the true costs of using carbon-based fuels. Typically, this means "putting a price on carbon," either by taxing it directly or by creating markets to buy and sell carbon under an emissions trading scheme. Yet, despite this, few conservative political leaders have supported it. Indeed, an absurd number of them are still denying that climate change is serious. The Foundation for Economic Education (FEE)—the group that helped bring Austrian economics to America—has long insisted that climate "skeptics" are more likely to be right than the world's thousands of climate scientists, and argued that even if the scientists are right "we'll do best simply to adapt."[45] The Cato Institute has argued that adapting to climate change will be cheaper than preventing it.[46] Almost no scientist believes this. As John Holdren, former science adviser to President Obama, has stressed, without mitigation, climate adaptation is a euphemism for suffering.[47] But the wealthy donors who fund FEE and the Cato Institute most likely won't bear the brunt of that suffering. The rest of us will.

Groups like FEE and the Cato Institute tout the virtues of free markets, but energy markets are hugely subsidized. According to the IMF, the world spent $5.3 trillion on energy subsidies in 2015, subsidies that mainly go to fossil fuels. The lion's share of this subsidy is the unpaid costs of environmental damage and harms to human health.[48] One hundred ninety-one nations have ratified the Paris Climate Accords (also called the Paris Agreement), pledging to stop climate change, but most of these countries continue to subsidize fossil fuels.[49] Electricity from renewable energy is now cheaper in most countries than from oil, gas, or coal, yet renewables struggle to compete because energy markets are weighted in favor of incumbents, and the political arena is freighted by the power of the fossil fuel industry.

Climate change is a problem for markets, because the "free" choices I make impose costs on other people, but it is only one example (albeit an existential one). This is why all societies accept some limitations on the actions of others: without such limits, there would be no civil society. We establish limits based on our judgment of potential risks and harm, so when it comes to economic activity, the question is whether markets are working as we want them to, and, if not, whether we need to adjust the rules under which they operate. It wasn't always illegal to dump toxic chemicals in lakes and rivers, but now it is. Once upon a time it was legal to buy and sell people.

In hindsight, we can see slavery as a theft of labor, and in many ways, climate change is a theft, too: from citizens and communities who are now paying its costs, from farmers losing crops and livestock to drought, from people who have lost their homes to wildfires or floods. Future generations will likely find it as shocking that people were allowed to freely dump carbon pollution into the atmosphere as we find it that people were once allowed to buy and sell other people. Just as we ended slavery, we *will* find a way to stop climate change, but the longer we deny the problem (or insist that markets will solve it "on their own") the greater the costs will be.

The solution to climate change will have to involve better and novel technologies, and here there is some good news: there is a long history of effective government support of science and technological innovation. Nearly all the large-scale transformative technologies from the late nineteenth to the early twenty-first centuries—railroads, electricity, telephone, radio, aviation, television, feedback control systems, space travel, digital computing, and microwave technology—were developed as public-private partnerships. As economist Mariana Mazzucato has observed, the U.S. federal government has been highly entrepreneurial, often taking risks that the private sector would not.[50] The internet owes its existence to scientists and engineers organized and funded by the federal government and to the government's vast background investment in electronics and computer science in the Cold War.[51] But libertarian Silicon Valley executives whitewash this history, foregrounding instead the role of entrepreneurs, bold "disruptors," and young guys in hoodies moving fast and breaking things.[52]

IT IS NOT government's job to *make* us happy, but it is government's job to facilitate the conditions that help us to pursue happiness.[53] So perhaps the clearest evidence that something is amiss in America is that we are much less happy than people in most other wealthy countries.[54]

The Nordic countries are the happiest. Finland, Denmark, Norway, Sweden, and Iceland consistently place in the top ten (despite their cold climate and potentially depressing winter darkness). Their high level of happiness coincides with high levels of democracy and political rights, lack of corruption, trust among citizens and between citizens and government, social cohesion, gender equality, and income equality, and their people feel themselves to have a high level of freedom. The

United States, however, despite its exceptional wealth, consistently falls outside the top ten—typically ranking between fifteenth and twentieth.[55]

What makes Nordic folks happy? One reason that can be ruled out is ethnic homogeneity. The 2018 edition of the World Happiness Report specifically addressed this question. It found that the proportion of immigrants within a country has *no effect* on the average level of happiness of those locally born.[56] Rather, the Nordic countries are caught up in "a virtuous cycle, where well-functioning and democratic institutions provide citizens extensive benefits and security, so that citizens trust institutions and each other, which leads them to vote for parties that promise to preserve the welfare model." A key element of this virtuous cycle is the institutions that provide citizens with "generous and effective social welfare benefits"—the very thing NAM and the opponents of the New Deal, Hayek and Friedman, and Reagan Republicans all railed against.

The report also found there was nothing particularly Nordic about this Nordic exceptionalism: the other countries regularly ranked at the top of international comparisons of life satisfaction—Switzerland, the Netherlands, New Zealand, Canada, and Australia—"have most of the same elements in place." There is no "secret sauce specific to Nordic happiness that is unavailable to others," the Happiness Report happily concluded. "There is rather a more general recipe for creating highly satisfied citizens: Ensure that state institutions are of high quality, non-corrupt, able to deliver what they promise, and generous in taking care of citizens in various adversities." In other words, happy people in happy countries are cared for by state institutions.[57] The United States of late, with its emphasis on individual choice and personal (rather than social) responsibility, simply does not care for its people in the way these other countries do.

Study after study has shown that people are happiest not when they are most "free"—however that might be assessed—but when they live in societies with strong social safety nets and robust family and community ties. Typically that means living in a country with good health provision, with protections to buffer unemployment, and where work is not so all-consuming as to leave inadequate time for family and friends.[58] Money plays a role—wealthy people tend to be happier than poor people—but a smaller one than many Americans assume, and research shows that young people who aspire to be rich are less likely to end up happy than those who focus on other goals.[59] Crucially, the differences between the United States and these other countries are, to a substantial degree, the result of government policies.[60]

As historian Tony Judt put it, the experiences of the European social democracies prove that "government can play an enhanced role in our lives without threatening our liberties," and since "the state is going to be with us for the foreseeable future, we would do well to think about what sort of a state we want."[61]

It's not just happiness that is in scarce supply in America these days, it's also life itself. In France, Switzerland, Germany, the Netherlands, and many other countries, the historic pattern of increased life expectancy has continued in recent decades, but in the United States the picture is starkly different. In the 1990s, cause-specific mortality began to increase.[62] One of these specific causes was suicide: since 1999, the U.S. suicide rate has increased a staggering 33 percent (while the global suicide rate fell almost 30 percent).[63] In 2010, a variety of cause-specific increases combined to produce an increase in all-cause adult mortality. And in 2015, for the first time since World War I, American life expectancy fell, driven in large part by suicide, drug overdoses, and liver disease linked to alcoholism and obesity—what sociologists call "deaths of despair."[64]

In 1809, Thomas Jefferson concluded that the "care of human life and happiness and not their destruction is the first and only legitimate object of good government." In the late twentieth century, we lost this insight, and our government largely stood by as ordinary Americans became sicker and more unhappy (and the top 1 percent ran away with all the prizes). Conservatives in the White House, in Congress, and in state legislatures refused to turn to the authority of the federal (and in some cases even the state) government to address these issues. Instead, like Margaret Thatcher, they brandished Hayek (or Milton Friedman), proclaiming "this is what we believe."

We can't blame Adam Smith for this; he believed that an excessive focus on accumulating wealth could undermine the very qualities in us that capitalism needed to flourish, what Smith called our "moral sentiments." Among other things, these sentiments tell us that people deserve to be paid not simply what the market will bear, but a sufficient wage on which to base a decent life. Already in the eighteenth century it was clear that markets often failed to meet that standard, and more than two hundred years later little has changed. What *did* change in the late twentieth century—as we have shown in this book—is what we believe about markets.

Why did we change what we believed about what markets—and governments—can and cannot do? Because of the drumbeat of market fundamentalism. Because of the dominant rhetoric to which we were exposed, and many of us came to accept.

The market fundamentalists told us to love "the free market" and loathe the government. And because we heard that argument so many times, in so many ways, and from so many sources, we began to believe it. We lost the caveats. We forgot the lessons of history. And we bought the myth that the invisible hand could do things even Adam Smith didn't think it could do.

AT THIS POINT we may interject, did the men and women in this story *really* believe in liberty?[65] Put another way, whose freedom were they defending? While NAM and Lemuel Boulware and Ronald Reagan propagandized competition, much of the American capitalism they defended wasn't competitive at all. NAM was founded to defend protectionism. NELA fought to prevent competition from municipal utilities. GE built its business on government electricity contracts while rigging electricity markets.[66] J. Howard Pew and Rose Wilder Lane worked to ban an economics textbook they didn't like. Ayn Rand glorified freedom while writing censorship codes and condoning violence so long as it was undertaken by "superior" people.

Milton Friedman and his Chicago school colleagues were skeptical of antitrust enforcement, seeing it as "government interference" in a competitive system that had "naturally" produced winners and losers. But their own work was made possible by business interference in the academic marketplace of ideas. Harold Luhnow and Jasper Crane picked Hayek and Friedman and worked to make them winners. And when it comes to antitrust, without competition—protected where necessary by government enforcement—we have no way of differentiating who deserves to win from who has advanced by cheating.[67]

It is also revealing what these men and women defended in the name of "freedom." That word, for them, meant freedom to expropriate native lands, to exploit children, to sustain unsafe workplaces, to pay workers as little as businessmen could, to pollute with impunity, to engage in anticompetitive practices. It meant, above all, an absolute right to property, the asserted foundation of freedom for the American Liberty League, Rose Wilder Lane, and generations of conservatives after them, including the Chicago school adherents who preached against antitrust statutes and environmental protections on property-rights grounds. But their property was largely taken from other people. And their framework sheltered a multitude of sins against others. As Lincoln said, "for some the word liberty . . . may mean for some men to do as they please with other men, and the product of other men's labor." In its day, slavery—the ultimate denial of liberty—was a property-rights cause too.

DISHONESTY AND DENIAL of evidence are perhaps the most consistent elements running through the story we have told here, and they link this book to our earlier work on anthropogenic climate change. In *Merchants of Doubt*, we showed how climate-change denial was rooted in market fundamentalism. The original "merchants" were in some sense buyers: men who bought the myth that market economies were a bulwark against tyranny and that government regulations threatened our freedom. What we didn't know when we wrote that book was where this myth had come from and why it had so much traction. Now we know. We also know how toxic the myth is, because fundamental to market fundamentalism is the anti-intellectual denial of facts that might disrupt the ideology. Hayek argued that the key to deciding whether a government intervention was warranted was to consider the scale and gravity of the social ill or unmet social need to which the intervention was addressed. That implies an honest evaluation of those ills and needs. One didn't have to be a socialist to want to combat the Great Depression, and one doesn't have to be a socialist to want to combat the failures of capitalism we face today. But one does have to confront the facts of market failure, and that is what market funda-mentalists consistently refuse to do.

How do intelligent, even well-informed people manage to deny obvious facts? One way is to deny the import of one's own epistemic privilege. If a system is working for you, it is easy to see its successes and harder to discern its failures. It is also easy to exaggerate your ability to judge information and put it in context. Philosopher José Medina puts it this way: it is "not uncommon for members of unjust societies to have distorted images of themselves as knowers . . . interiorizing a superiority complex . . . with negative epistemic consequences."[68] Among these negative consequences is arrogance, which diminishes openness to facts that challenge your worldview and impedes meaningful reflection and self-correction.[69] Epistemic arrogance can also lead to a kind of "cognitive immaturity"—as when grown-ups engage in magical thinking. Such immaturity can become patho-logical "when the subject becomes absolutely incapable in acknowledging any mistake."[70]

That sort of ideology as pathology was on vivid display after the 2008 financial meltdown and again in the Trump administration's behavior during the Covid-19 crisis. It continues to be on display among climate-change deniers who insist that technological innovation—led by the private sector with little or no government role—will solve the problem. A 2021 piece in the *Wall Street Journal* asserted that there was no one "of serious judgment who didn't privately pooh-pooh the idea that humanity will control CO_2 by means other than the mostly unregulated progress of markets and technology."[71] Man-made climate change has been underway since the 1980s, and "the unregulated progress of markets and technology" has not responded in a manner remotely commensurate with the scale of the problem. Still, the market fundamentalists counsel faith, in what the sociologist Charles Mills calls a "closed circuit of epistemic authority," impervious not only to moral suasion, but also to evidence.[72] Like Joe McCarthy insisting he had the names of communists inside the State Department, the strategy works by invoking unnamed people of "serious judgment" without telling us who they are, making the claim not only immune to refutation but impervious even to examination.

These rhetorical strategies help to explain how market fundamentalism proves resilient despite the abundant evidence that refutes it. Its advocates have been in positions of privilege—socially, politically, financially—that enable them both to promote their preferred views and to shield those views from critique. Living in a world of privilege, they often just don't see the evidence of failure. (It is easy to believe in magic when the magic is working for everyone you know, including the magician.)[73] Most people tend to mingle with the like-minded, but the rich and powerful have far more opportunity to build around themselves an entire world of like-mindedness. (And if they are powerful, as the rich often are, people around them who discern the problems in their worldview may be loath to speak up.) Only the superrich can shield themselves from seeing the consequences of poor health care, inadequate transportation, and other societal failures. Only the superrich can afford to build a network of self-reinforcing institutions devoted to spreading and defending their ideological preferences. Were these men and women to acknowledge the realities of what their worldview has wrought, they would have to abandon their self-image as superior "truth-tellers."[74] Some might even have to abandon their self-image as Christians.

The wealthy businessmen whose story we have told here were able to support those who agreed with them, to construct institutional arrangements to reinforce their views, and to pay to produce books, films, radio and television shows, and other products. Their goal was not only to out-compete other potential players but also to stymie genuine debate.

The story we have told here supports the work of journalist Jane Mayer and historian Nancy MacLean, who have further documented how corporate leaders have attempted to control not merely what the American government did, but what the American people thought.[75] MacLean adds the important insight that because libertarians have *always* been outnumbered—and have known this to be the case— they have actively sought ways to keep majoritarian democracy at bay.[76] The same might be said about the rich in general. In a true democracy, the rich would not be able to establish rules that disproportionately benefit themselves. To preserve their position of privilege, they frequently fight democracy.

Milton Friedman argued that it was a benefit of capitalism that a rich man had the freedom to fund an academic like himself, but what about the poor man with a good idea? What about ordinary people for whom the system is not delivering on its promises? In Friedman's world, intellectual competition is a rich man's game: survival of the fittest becomes the triumph of the richest. Then, in circular logic, the survivors credit their survival to their own superiority, rather than, as Darwin would have stressed, the randomness of inherited wealth, inherited racial privilege, and inherited social position.

There is also a kind of naïveté or disingenuousness in market fundamentalist claims. North Carolina senator Thom Tillis once explained why he didn't think government should require employees to wash their hands after using the bath-room: companies should be able to decide for themselves what was right for their businesses and customers. "I don't have any problem with Starbucks if they choose to opt out of this policy as long as they post a sign that says, 'We don't require our employees to wash their hands after they use the restroom' . . . The market will take care of that."[77] Sure, but who will require Starbucks to put up the sign?

MARKET FUNDAMENTALISTS AREN'T wrong about everything. Markets can be more flexible than governments, and competition can spur innovation, leading to better products at lower prices. Market fundamentalists are also right that all action risks unintended consequences, so when addressing a large and complex issue it makes sense to be judicious. Sometimes the right answer to a problem is to do nothing—or at least to wait until we have better information. And reformers do sometimes go too far. It is not a coincidence that Democrat Al Smith was motivated to make common cause with the reactionary American Liberty League over Prohibition. Alcohol abuse was (and still is) a terrible problem in the United States, but Prohibition was at least in some ways a cure worse than the disease. A decade of study of conservative thinking—both serious and propagandist—has persuaded us the best solution to any problem is the smallest one that does the job.

But competition doesn't mean we don't have rules. Football, soccer, baseball, and basketball are supremely competitive sports; they all have rules. Without rules there *is* no game; there are just people running around with a ball. Moreover, when the rules in sports are properly enforced, athletes have to be better because they can't cheat, and both athletes and spectators end up with a better game. Nearly all human activities have rules; without them we just get chaos.

Experience shows that unconstrained competition can lead to a race to the bottom, as manufacturers reduce quality to reduce costs and treat workers as disposable components rather than humans deserving of dignity. Both history and our present moment demonstrate that markets can devolve into destructive monopolies; markets need governance to protect competition. And by definition markets do not account for external costs such as workplace injury and pollution. Markets may respond eventually—as they are now starting to do for climate change—but in the interim consequential problems go unaddressed, people are hurt, and injustice festers. Delay can also make a problem effectively insoluble: if the West Antarctic ice sheet disintegrates, no "market mechanism" will bring it back. The Americans who have died in the opioid epidemic, or from gun violence, or from the Trump administration's malevolent response to Covid-19, will not come back, either. For these people, conservative admonitions to let the market do its "magic" offer neither solution nor solace.

The late Immanuel Wallerstein encapsulated the problem this way. Conservatives counsel caution, and with some warrant. "The heart of conservatism as a modern ideology is the conviction that the risks of conscious collective intrusion into existing social structures that have historically and slowly evolved are very high . . . There is no doubt good historical reason for such skepticism . . . one can see how intelligent, caring people might conclude that in general it is best to go slowly with political change, lest things become even worse than they are presently." Prudence, judiciousness, and respect for established institutions are not wrongheaded ideals. The problem with "such honest conservatism is that it represents the position (and the interests) of those who are better off at the moment in terms of their economic and social position . . . What this position leaves for all those less well off, and especially for those really badly off, is merely a counsel of patience . . . But since, by virtue of the conservative doctrine, the patience required is in some sense without any time limits (and conservatives are often wont to talk about the inevitability of social hierarchy and therefore of permanent social inequality), it offers little improvement that is concrete in their lifetimes for the majority of the world's people, and little that is concrete even in their children's lifetimes."[78] Injustices remain unremedied, victims are left to suffer, and rewards are promised in the hereafter.

Wallerstein wrote those lines in 1998 and since then the problem has become far worse. The extra twist, in our times, is that so many conservatives are not simply counseling patience. They are denying that the problems exist at all.

FOR MANY AMERICAN conservatives, Friedrich von Hayek remains a hero and *The Road to Serfdom* their bible, despite all the evidence that refutes its central claim. Bruce Bartlett, a political adviser to Ronald Reagan and George H. W. Bush, wrote in the *New York Times*: "The big problem for those who continue to cite *The Road to Serfdom* as a guide"—or, we might add, who look to markets to solve social problems—"is that they must essentially ignore everything that happened after 1944."[79] Events since 1944—a point at which, Bartlett wrote, "it looked as if the United States were traveling in the same direction as Europe, and Hayek's thesis was not implausible given recent history"— have proven both that economic liberalization does not necessarily lead to political liberalization, and that government actions to address market failure do not put a country on the road to serfdom.[80] The European social democracies after World War II all developed strong social safety nets and none became communistic or even seriously socialist. Of course, it did not take the events of the postwar period to show this: the United States was capitalist in the first half of the nineteenth century while nearly 15 percent of its population was enslaved.[81] Capitalism doesn't protect freedom.

Loose talk about "free markets," "free market forces," or, most egregiously, "*The Free Market*" creates the erroneous impression that markets have a native state. From there it follows that governments should not interfere with their (supposedly) natural functioning.[82] But markets have always operated under rules—sometimes

tacit and informal, other times explicit and formalized. This is what the rule of law
is: we set boundaries for human activities based on our assessment of how they
affect both participants and bystanders. We do not allow theft. We do not permit
murder. We forbid fraud and lying under oath, but we permit advertisers to make
exaggerated claims. We recognize property rights, but we also have zoning laws. As
Robert Reich has put it, the decisions we make about how markets should (and
shouldn't) operate don't "intrude" on the market, they define it, just as the rules of
football define the game.[83]

Hayek acknowledged that whether any specific government action is warranted
is always a matter of judgment, and such judgments are made through public debate
and political processes. Some of FDR's proposed New Deal reforms were blocked
by Congress because they went too far. Some environmental regulations may be too
strict—but others might not be strict enough. These are all questions that can and
should be mooted. But in the past four decades, reasonable discussion has been
hamstrung by economists who have presumed, as an *axiom*, that markets are efficient and the public sector inefficient, and by conservative politicians, pundits, and
business leaders, who out of self-interest have blocked reforms and claimed there is
no cure for social ills that would not be worse than the disease.[84]

But are markets consistently efficient? More important: are government
programs doomed to inefficiency, if not outright failure? Must we simply tolerate
social ills and market failures? The answer is no. We have many examples in the
United States of successful government programs and public-private partnerships, some of which have proved truly transformative, like rural electrification,
the interstate highway system, space-based telecommunication, and, of course, the
internet.

If we expand our purview to the world at large, we have many examples of social
welfare programs that work well in democratic countries; and by many measures,
the European social democracies are *more* democratic than the United States. (The
Economist's Democracy Index 2022 placed the United States at twenty-six, behind
all the European social democracies, as well as Japan, South Korea, Uruguay, Costa
Rica, and post-Pinochet Chile.)[85] Government remedies to social costs and market
failure don't always work, but experience shows that they can work and are not only
compatible with democracy but help to sustain it. Conversely, there are many examples of business failure, but we do not take them as a general indictment of
capitalism.

Which brings us to the central mendacity—and resulting immorality—in the market fundamentalist view, what Lewis Lapham has called the "dark side of the American moon."[86] Whether deliberately or inadvertently, market fundamentalists become advocates for the interests of the people with the most money. In a market economy, money does the talking, and the more money one has, the more one gets to talk. Milton Friedman embraced this unabashedly, praising how inequality gives wealthy individuals the means to buy advocacy for their minority views. This idea extends into the metaphor of buying as voting: the claim that markets are fundamentally democratic because people express their will through their purchases. In the 1970s, Carter economic adviser Charles Schultze went so far as to claim that markets were a form of "unanimous consent arrangement."[87] In the 1990s, shamelessly usurping a civil rights slogan, Citibank CEO Walter Wriston declared that "markets are voting machines" that give "power to the people."[88] But who exactly is consenting to the arrangements worked out in markets? To which people do markets give power? The obvious answer is that markets give power to people with the money to participate, and the more money they have, the more power they have.

Markets don't operate under the rule of "one man, one vote." They operate by the rule of "one dollar, one vote," so the rich (or profligate) will *always* have more say in a market-based system than the poor or middle class.[89] The wealthy not only have more *purchasing* power, they also have more *cultural* power, because among the things they can buy are academics and other intellectuals. Put less crudely, the rich have the wherewithal to find, cultivate, and promote smart people to help them articulate their views and garner them attention they frequently do not deserve. And, as marketers know well, if you bombard people with a message—particularly a well-packaged one—people will start to believe it even if it is untrue. Money may not buy happiness, but it does buy the intellectual packaging that can make lies appear true and half-truths seem like the whole truth.

The cheerleaders of the "free market" refuse to acknowledge this. They also refuse to acknowledge that government can serve the common good in part because they reject the notion of a common good. Rather, they see goods as solely a matter of individual preference, which markets satisfy. In the real world, however, many needs go unmet by markets, because (with rare exceptions) markets don't address needs that can't be satisfied at a profit, typically a very big profit.

We have seen how in the 1920s the profit-driven electricity industry did not bring electricity to rural Americans, despite their clear preference to have electricity.

In the 1930s, "The Market" did not bring jobs to millions of Americans who clearly preferred to work. Today, there is a large body of academic literature on how the profit-oriented pharmaceutical industry does not provide medicines for diseases that mostly afflict the poor.[90] Yet it did provide dangerous opioid drugs that have killed hundreds of thousands of Americans. The industry accomplished this through an enormous exaggeration, followed by a lie. The exaggeration was that there was an "epidemic of untreated pain"; the lie was that synthetic opioids could safely treat that pain with little or no risk of addiction. Scholars who have looked at the matter have concluded that the "epidemic of pain" was largely an invention of opioid manufacturers, and we know now that these drugs were highly addictive, and deadly.[91]

Five hundred thousand dead from opioids, over a million dead from Covid-19, massive inequality, rampant anxiety and unhappiness, and the well-being of us all threatened by climate change: these are the true costs of the "free" market.

Conclusion

"Of course they take the smart ones away."

"Who takes them?" I asked.

"Why, our dirty rotten government, of course," my mother answered.

I said nothing, just looked up at the ceiling. It has been
my experience throughout life that the people who have been given
the most by our government—education, food, rent subsidies—
are the ones who are most apt to find fault with the whole
idea of government. I understand this in a way.

—ELIZABETH STROUT, *MY NAME IS LUCY BARTON*

Judge Richard A. Posner is one of America's most distinguished conservative jurists and for many years a leader of the law and economics movement. This movement, which originated at the University of Chicago, holds that the law is best viewed as a tool to promote economic efficiency and that economic analysis can and should can guide legal practice.[1] Posner spent most of his career displaying a jaundiced view of government regulation and he influenced many a young jurist to do the same; one analysis finds him to be the most cited law writer of the second half of the twentieth century.[2] His jurisprudential philosophy—which substantially equated justice with economic efficiency—provoked one critic to snarl that "Maximum Wealth, badly distributed, does not lead to maximum happiness."[3]

In 2009, Posner undertook an analysis of the 2008 financial crisis, which caused him to rethink his views. A "rational decision-maker starts with a prior probability," Posner wrote in *A Failure of Capitalism: The Crisis of '08 and the Descent into Depression*, "but adjusts that probability as new evidence comes to his attention." The near collapse of the world's banking system offered a raft of evidence about the reality of market failure and the need for government regulation, particularly in financial markets. "Behavior that generates large external costs," he tartly observed, "provides an apt occasion for government regulation."[4] What he had learned from the crisis was that "we need a more active and intelligent government to keep our model of a capitalist economy from running off the rails. The movement to deregulate the financial industry went too far by exaggerating the resilience—the self-healing powers—of laissez-faire capitalism."[5] The responsibility for building the guard rails that capitalism has proven itself to require has to rest with government, because there isn't any other institution to do it.[6]

The 2008 collapse should have hit "economic libertarians in their solar plexus," Posner observed, because the crisis was the result of underregulation, a consequence of the "innate limitations of the free market."[7] But if the economic libertarians were hit by the 2008 crisis, they refused to flinch. In conservative circles and the offices of K-street lobbyists, trade associations, and think tanks, and on the pages of the *Wall Street Journal*, as well as in much academic economics, free-market ideology remained largely in place.

THE TIDE MAY be finally turning, or at least trying to turn.[8] In June 2021, some Republicans joined the Democratic-led U.S. House Judiciary Committee to approve new antitrust bills aimed largely at Silicon Valley.[9] In April 2022, Assistant Attorney General Jonathan Kanter delivered the keynote address at the University of Chicago Antitrust and Competition Conference—held in no less an inner sanctum of the anti-antitrust movement than the George Stigler Center—where he declared that "the era of lax enforcement is over, and the new era of vigorous and effective antitrust law enforcement has begun." Previously Kanter had stated the purpose of antitrust enforcement "is not to decide what is maximally efficient, but to enforce the law";[10] at the Stigler Center he reiterated that "[t]he Purpose of Antitrust [law] Is to Protect Competition."[11] It is a measure of the unreasonable influence of the Chicago school and the ways in which the ideals of "economic efficiency" have come to be taken for granted, even outside the precincts of economics, that Kanter's position—that his role as an assistant attorney general is to enforce the law—is considered radical.[12]

Some leading economists are also rethinking their positions. Paul Romer, once a reliable free-market scholar, has recently admitted he no longer believes in the magic of the market. Romer built a name for himself arguing against federal regulation of "tech" companies on Chicago school grounds. "Economists taught, 'It's the market. There's nothing we can do,' " Romer told the *New York Times*. Now he says: "That's really just so wrong."[13]

What changed? The *Times* quoted Yale economist Fiona Scott Morton explaining, "We've all changed because what really happened is an expansion of the evidence."[14] That's ridiculous. The evidence has been plain to see for a long time (if one were willing to look). The Sherman Anti-Trust Act was passed in 1890, in recognition of the reality that corporations tended toward monopoly, with destructive economic and political effects. When the Sherman Act proved too weak (and was applied in ways its authors did not intend), it was strengthened in 1914 by the Clayton Act.

What changed in the mid-twentieth century was not the evidence but its interpretation—or, better, the reinterpretation of reality. The antitrust project at the University of Chicago reinterpreted monopoly as the legitimate outcome of competition rather than the illegitimate outcome of anticompetitive practices. Ignoring the adverse political effects of concentrated corporate power, Aaron Director, Milton Friedman, and Robert Bork insisted that monopolies were often beneficial, so long as they were privately held. A generation of economists (and lawyers) then built their reputations on that interpretation. As economic historian Michael Bernstein argued two decades ago—and as we have underscored here—many of these economists cast their lot with the people who could afford to fund their programs, in effect becoming "privy councillors to private wealth."[15] Citing the earlier work of the great historian William Appleman Williams, Bernstein noted that "laissez-faire" really meant "laissez-*nous* faire"—letting the captains of industry do what they wanted with little or no government oversight.[16] The outcome was a Second Gilded Age that generated vast wealth for a few Americans but made life nastier, more brutish, and shorter for a far greater number.

A handful of economists now recognize that the Chicagoans sold them an interpretation based not so much on evidence, but on a background of hostility to government and even to political democracy.[17] But this realization has been slow in coming. After all, as Posner argued, the lessons of the 2008 financial collapse were plain to see more than a decade ago. They told us that self-regulation doesn't work, at least not in financial markets. History has shown that it doesn't work in telecommunications or energy markets, either.[18] Actually, there aren't many contexts where it does work, as Paul Romer learned when he went to Burning Man, touted by its organizers as "a city wherein almost everything that happens is created entirely by its citizens, who are active participants in the experience." That sounds bottom-up—maybe even libertarian—but as Romer observed, even this bacchanal of individualism has a central planning committee.[19] Someone has to figure out where water and fire extinguishers go and make sure there are enough toilets.

Despite Romer's and Posner's conversions, the myth of the "free market" continues to dominate the pages of the *Wall Street Journal*, *Fortune*, and *Forbes*, and finds its place in the pages of the *New York Times* and the *Washington Post*, as well. It also still resounds in the halls of American business schools. Consider Rebecca Henderson, a Harvard business professor and admirable advocate for corporate responsibility and climate action. In her book *Reimagining Capitalism in a World on Fire*, Henderson points to many promising signs of business leaders rejecting the notion that corporate managers' only obligation is to increase shareholder value. The Friedman framework makes no sense, she argues, amid climate change and other existential threats, and so corporations are increasingly committing to social and environmental responsibility. Yet even as Henderson articulates a new vision organized around a capacious conception of corporate responsibility that includes workers, consumers, and even the planet, she perpetuates two traditional business myths. One is the idea that markets are magic, or at least have magical capabilities. Throughout her book, she uses the term *free market* without scare quotes or irony. Her caveat is that "[f]ree markets only work their magic when prices reflect all available information, when there is genuine freedom of opportunity, and when the rules of the game support genuine competition."[20] Which is precisely never. There has never been a time in human history when markets met these conditions, and there is no reason to think that such conditions ever could exist.

Henderson suggests our current situation is not the fault of business leaders, because they have only done what "we" told them to do. "When we told the leaders of firms that their sole duty was to focus on shareholder value," she writes, "we gave them permission to turn their backs on the health of the institutions that have historically balanced concentrated economic power."[21] But who is this "we"? It wasn't union leaders. Or consumers. And it certainly wasn't history professors. It was Milton Friedman, backed by Harold Luhnow and the other corporate leaders who funded the Mont Pelerin Society and the Chicago school's Free Market Project. It was GE's

Jack Welch, continuing that corporation's tradition of trying to convince workers, consumers, and regulators that what was good for GE was good for Americans. And it was business schools at Harvard and other universities, all the way back to the days of NELA financial support and influence, that promoted antiregulatory, laissez-faire ideology. The fact is: *we* didn't tell business leaders this, *they* told *us*.

In any case, to focus on Milton Friedman and shareholder value is to miss the larger point we have raised in this book. The market fundamentalists didn't simply deify the marketplace; they also demonized government and this second half of their framework is arguably the more important. As Binyamin Appelbaum has recently noted, the biggest issue facing us today is not the behavior of corporations—as important as that may be—but the role of the state.[22] After all, it wouldn't matter if corporations didn't contribute to women's tennis or the opera if those activities were fully funded by the public purse. It wouldn't matter if workers didn't have medical "benefits" and retirement plans if they could count on a national health service and a solid system of social security. And we wouldn't have to beg corporations not to destroy the planet if we had strong laws, vigorously enforced, that forbade it.

WE HAVE SHOWN in this book how business leaders and conservative intellectuals worked for more than a century to build a myth that, in the past forty years, has come to dominate American thinking and discourse. History is not easily undone. Even if Harvard Business School professors and the *New York Times* are now beginning to question the market fundamentalist framework, across America the Big Myth lives on. It is the myth that markets are efficient and governments are inefficient. That markets work and public policies fail. It is the myth that we do best when government "gets out of the way," and lets the market do its "magic."

The Big Myth has a tenacious hold. Polls show that in many domains, Americans trust the private sector more than they trust "The Government."[23] Many continue to carry the Reaganite vision that government is a threat to freedom and prosperity, ready at any time to take away both. This hostility makes many Americans resistant to any robust governmental response, even to an existential threat like climate change. It makes them refuse to get vaccinated against Covid-19, or even to accept a painless and inexpensive countermeasure like wearing a mask. And it makes the *Wall Street Journal* argue that the only "serious" approach to climate change is to rely on "the unregulated progress of markets and technology."

These views especially prevail among conservatives, but they are not restricted to "red states." You can find the Gadsden flag—"Don't Tread on Me"—waving in northern New Hampshire and in California's Central Valley to suggest that the government is ever on the verge of denying individual freedom. In its more extreme form, antigovernment sentiment animated the rioters who stormed the Capitol on January 6, 2021, at least some of whom intended to kidnap and murder.[24] ("The government did this to us," one rioter declared.[25] He evidently felt entitled to do "this" back.) And many Republican leaders support them, or at least their claim that the 2020 election was stolen. Some on the right wing who—like J. Howard Pew, Rose Wilder Lane, and Milton Friedman—disdain democracy have gone so far as to try to rebrand the events of that day as "tourism," instead of the violent insurrection that they were.[26]

The rioters were extremists, but their actions were sanctioned by the complicity of conservative political and business leaders who endorse their antigovernment stance. Throughout the country, you can find plenty of highly educated people who will tell you with a straight face that the best way to solve a social problem is just to let everyone pursue their own self-interest, because the "invisible hand" will sort it out. And they "know" they are right because they read it in the *Wall Street Journal,* or learned it at Wharton.

IT'S IMPOSSIBLE TO say what form and scale of government is best in any absolute sense. People in Norway have different expectations of their government than in Singapore; the French have different attitudes about childcare than Americans; and it may be that American regional differences are so great that the best solutions to our problems will be found in a new form of federalism.[27] However, when we compare outcomes across different U.S. states, we find that the evidence falls strongly on the side of higher levels of taxation and stronger degrees of regulation, rather than less.

One way to measure how people are doing is the Human Development Index (HDI). Created by the United Nations as a counterweight to GDP, HDI is a metric that tries to track how people are faring in terms of health, education, life expectancy, and overall standard of living. The U.S. state that conservatives most love to hate—for its high taxes and nanny-state mentality—Massachusetts—ranks number one on the HDI, closely followed by Connecticut, Minnesota, and New

Jersey. In contrast, the bottom eight are all states whose voters tend to lean against government: Mississippi, West Virginia, Alabama, Arkansas, Kentucky, Louisiana, South Carolina, and Tennessee.[28]

The heavily taxed and regulated states do better economically as well.[29] (One result of this is that the blue states, paying more in federal taxes, subsidize red states.[30]) This is not because wealthy people tend to vote Democratic; overall, wealthy people mostly vote Republican.[31] Nor is it that liberals have fled red states and moved to blue ones; if anything the demographics trend the other way.[32] No, the evidence suggests that the sorts of policies that business conservatives and libertarians tout—low taxes and little regulation—are not good for people and not even good for the economy.

Utah is an exception that helps to prove the rule. It is a very conservative state, with a flat personal income tax rate of 4.95 percent, low property taxes, and a thriving economy.[33] But the expansion of its "Silicon Slopes"—the tech companies that have driven its strong economy and booming housing market in recent years—was built on Salt Lake City's role as one of the original nodes in ARPANET, the U.S. government precursor to the internet. The Salt Lake region has also proved attractive to young professionals because of its easy access to great outdoor recreation—particularly its world-class skiing—almost all of which takes place on federally protected lands. And, because Utah has historically been a rural state, many young professionals recruited to the Slopes are eligible for U.S. Department of Agriculture mortgages that require little or no down payment.[34] The Utah experience suggests that where red states thrive, they have not left matters to the "magic of the marketplace" but have invested in infrastructure, built strong public-private partnerships, and benefited from federal lands and other largesse.

The evidence is strong that "small government" does not yield better economic outcomes. As policy analyst Jeff Madrick concluded in his 2008 book *The Case for Big Government*, "History offers no lesson about the values of minimal government . . . To the contrary, the evidence shows that government typically contributed vitally to growth."[35] That was true in the past and remains true today. E. J. Dionne concludes that history has demonstrated both the need for "regular fine-tuning to a market system . . . and adjustments to spread the riches it produces more fairly."[36] But it's more than fine-tuning. The histories of the internet, the interstate highway system, and rural electrification are histories of government taking a leading role where the market did not.

REPUBLICANS SINCE REAGAN have railed against "Big Government," but that term was invented by American captains of industry as a counter to "Big Business." That was a neat rhetorical trick, for it enabled them to displace crucial political, economic, and moral questions into a fight over the *size* of government. Even if we accept the premise that the size of our government is a pertinent concern, the reality is that the American federal government is small by comparison with governments of other wealthy nations, and the evidence belies any assertion that bigger govern- ment threatens democracy, per se. Most western European governments are by many measures "bigger" than the American government—for example, in levels of taxation and provision of social services—but they are at least as democratic.

One way to measure the size of a government is by considering central govern- ment spending as a proportion of GDP. In recent decades, total U.S. federal govern- ment spending, not including the national debt, has hovered around 20 to 25 percent of GDP. In 1990, the figure was 23 percent, but it fell to a low of 18 percent in 2000. Then it went back up, peaking at 26 percent in 2010. From 2010 to 2020, the figure ranged from 23 to 26 percent. These numbers are lower than in many other nations, and lower than nearly all highly industrialized nations.[37]

If we look at the world at large, we find that, generally, wealthy industrialized countries spend more than poor, non-industrialized and developing countries. Since 1990, the European Union countries have on average spent about 35 to 40 percent. Germany is a bit lower, around 30 percent. France is higher, hovering since 1990 around 45 percent.[38] Developing nations typically spend less: since 1990 India has held steady around 15 percent; spending in Argentina has increased steadily, averaging around 20 percent, with a local peak in 2016 of 26 percent. Peru is similar to Argentina: over the past forty years it has annually spent between 15 and 20 percent of GDP. Poor nations are more variable—some have high levels of government expenditures—but they typically spend less than 20 percent. As a share of national GDP, U.S. government spending in the past decades has looked more like that of a developing nation than a wealthy, long-industrialized one. In America we are rich, but when it comes to public spending we act as if we are poor.

What about the relationship between public spending and inflation? In the 1970s and '80s, many argued that public spending drove inflation, but in hindsight, the evidence is mixed. For one thing, as Jeff Madrick points out, U.S. federal spending in the early 1970s (when inflation was sky high) was only one percentage point higher as a proportion of GDP than it had been in the early 1960s.[39] The slow economic growth in Europe in that period was blamed by some on "excessive" public spending, but after the 1980s the economies of the United Kingdom, the United States, and Germany all rebounded, even as public spending continued to increase.[40]

Comparing the United States to other wealthy nations, America spends even less on public goods than the numbers might indicate, because so much American federal outlay goes to military spending and interest on the national debt. Opinion polls consistently show that Americans approve of Social Security, Medicare, and paying veterans their promised benefits, but what about military spending?[41] The same antigovernment conservatives who repeatedly attack "federal spending" almost never question this, the single biggest component of the discretionary budget.[42] Ronald Reagan could not deliver on his promise to balance the federal budget primarily because he refused to consider military cuts.

In 2019, 51 percent of federal discretionary budget ($676 billion) went to military spending.[43] In 2020, the figure was $714 billion (although a smaller percentage, due to the spike in non-defense spending from Covid-19).[44] Before losing the 2020 election, President Trump had called for 55 percent of the 2021 discretionary budget to go to military spending, increasing to 62 percent by 2030.[45] But it's not just Republican administrations who have pushed high levels of military spending. Since 2000, the highest level of military spending as a percentage of GDP occurred under President Obama. President Biden's 2022 budget request of $715 billion for the Pentagon was increased by the Democratic-led Congress to $768 billion.[46] This heavy spending carries a huge carbon footprint. In fact, the carbon footprint of the U.S. military is bigger than most nations.[47]

Conservatives decry "throwing money" at problems, yet decade after decade both Democratic and Republican presidents have thrown money at the military with unclear return. One result of this enormous military spending is that Americans get far less bang for our buck in government spending than people in other countries do.[48] Perhaps this is why so many of us accept the argument that government is inefficient: much of our tax dollar *is* wasted, not on "wasteful" social programs, but on wasteful militarism.

In 1953, Dwight Eisenhower, one of the few men in Washington (then or now) who had fought and won a war, reminded the American people that "This world in arms is not spending money alone. It is spending the sweat of its laborers, the genius of its scientists, the hopes of its children." Since that time American expenditures on armaments have only grown. No country in the world spends as much on weaponry as we do; the United States spends more money on "defense" that the next ten countries combined.[49] Americans argue ad infinitum about taxes, but even a modest cut in the military budget would permit us to fix our infrastructure and address our national needs without raising taxes at all.

ONE OF THOSE national needs is to acknowledge our own cognitive blind spots. In his analysis of the 2008 financial collapse, Richard Posner noted that the limits of self-interest are precisely why we need governance. In strictly financial terms, he argued, it is rational to be indifferent to the consequences of one's business or behavior to others so long as the direct consequences are profitable for oneself; the problem is that those indirect consequences can severely hurt others, as they did with financial deregulation. "Government has a duty," Posner concluded, "to do more than prevent fraud, theft, and other infringements on property and contract rights, which is the only duty that libertarians believe government has. Without stronger financial regulation than that, the rational behavior of law-abiding financiers and consumers can precipitate an economic crisis . . . rational maximization by businessmen and consumers, all pursuing their self-interest more or less intelligently within a framework of property and contract rights, can set the stage for economic catastrophe."[50]

Finance is not the exception that proves the rule, it is the rule. Self-interest can drive business activities in good ways, but it can also create huge social costs. Nearly all the activities that have led to disruptive climate change represent the rational self-interest of some party. Most of the activities that have led to the opioid crisis, the sale of endocrine-disrupting chemicals, and income inequality were rational in this (narrow) sense, too. A framework focused on individual self-interest is *not* rational, because we don't live as individuals; we live as part of a world and that world is being massively damaged by inadequately regulated capitalism. Untempered self-interest does not serve our interests, not collectively and in many cases not even individually.

OUR CHOICES ARE not confined to oppressive communism or heartless capitalism. To suggest that they are is a dangerous failure of vision. But that is precisely what market fundamentalism has achieved: it has blinded its adherents to the realities around them, while making it hard for all of us to see the range of options that have worked in the past and could work again in the future. Unions were never perfect, but they were an important tool with which workers could level the playing field and ensure that their interests were fairly represented, and they helped to build the American middle class. Workmen's compensation aided injured workers and their families and created incentives for managers to make workplaces safer for all. The federal government programs of the New Deal went a long way toward getting Americans back to work during the Great Depression, and they may have saved the American economy from a collapse that could well have led to totalitarianism.

Many government programs of the postwar period—Medicare, Medicaid, Pell Grants, state support for public universities, and more—worked to make our society safer, fairer, and—as the name Social Security suggests—more secure. Markets can work very well—they are powerful tools which we would be silly to abandon entirely—but they need supervision. Think of it this way: No sane person would set a machine saw in motion without attending to it. Or turn on a car's engine and send the car down the road on its own. Regulations need to be updated to account for social and technological change (and one day our cars will drive themselves), but to conflate that with discarding regulation makes no sense. After all, as Joseph Stiglitz observed, the invisible hand is invisible because it doesn't actually exist.[51]

Market fundamentalism is rooted in the myth that markets can operate (or even exist) on their own—without government oversight. Without rules of the road. But that would be like arguing—as one of the reasonable neoliberals put it back in the 1940s—that cars should just drive in any direction. A stop sign is a regulation. So is the controlled entry onto a freeway. In exchange for stop signs, we get to drive without crashing into each other, and in exchange for controlled entries onto freeways, we get to drive fast. Regulations don't just protect us; in many cases they *enable* us to do things we could not otherwise do. The same is true of taxes. Regulations and taxes are tools to make our economic system work better, treat people fairly, and permit them to live with dignity, while protecting the natural world on which we all depend for our health, our well-being, and ultimately our survival.

One way to recover a positive vision of regulation is through the concept of biological regulation: the mechanisms that enable organisms to survive in response to changing external conditions. From warm-blooded animals maintaining their body temperature to a single-celled organism controlling its internal chemistry, regulation is essential to life; it is nature's way of making things work. Without (biological) regulation, there is no life. Some scientists have described regulation as an "architecture of functional relationships."[52] Markets are no different from other systems, organic or inorganic, natural or human-built: remove regulation and (sooner or later) their functional relationships break down.

THE DEIFICATION OF markets and demonization of government has deprived us of the tools and the insights we need to address the challenges before us: to live long and healthy lives, to generate prosperity, and to coexist in concord with each other and with the nonhuman inhabitants of our planet. It is time we rejected the myth of market fundamentalism and re-embraced the proven tools we have at our disposal. It takes governance to address the problems that people, pursuing our self-interest, create. One does not have to be a socialist to come to this conclusion. Only an observer.

Ronald Reagan was wrong. Our most consequential problems have arisen not because of too much government, but because of too little. Government is not the solution to all our problems, but it is the solution to many of our biggest ones.

ACKNOWLEDGMENTS

This book is Tim Wirth's fault. Several years ago, after *Merchants of Doubt* was published, the former senator and president of the United Nations Foundation hosted an elegant dinner party in Naomi's honor in Washington, D.C. Around the table were some very serious people, including the science adviser to the president. The dinner, however, was not just a social event. It was an occasion for the group to apply their collective wisdom to determining the subject of our next book. *Merchants of Doubt* explained why so many otherwise intelligent people were refusing to take climate change seriously. The next book, Tim said, should tell us what to do about it. No big deal. Just write the book that would break the logjam and save humanity from climate catastrophe.

For a long time, we thought that would be a book about technology, specifically large-scale technological change. We focused our attention on what the history of technology could tell us about the origins of transformative technologies. We wrote several book proposals that we threw away, because we kept coming up against a central stumbling block: that the best technology imaginable would do us little good if people didn't think we needed it, and governments didn't put the policies in place to support its widespread uptake. The more we thought about the problem, the more we realized that the world already had most of the technologies needed to stop further climate change. We didn't need a new miracle technology. We didn't need a "breakthrough." At least not a technological breakthrough. After all, by the mid-2010s America already had electric cars—Erik was driving one and it was fabulous—but the country lacked an adequate charging infrastructure. America (and most of the world) also had competitively priced renewable energy, but in many states utilities were blocking their uptake. And so on.

We realized that what our country (and the world) needed was the right *policies* to support a rapid and thoroughgoing transition to a green energy economy. Something similar to what the nation had done when it electrified the country in the first place, during the New Deal. But to do that, we needed to break through the mentality that told us, as the *Wall Street Journal* put it, that climate change would only be solved by the "unregulated progress of markets and technology." And so we began to try to answer the question: Why do so many people believe this? Why do people have so much faith in the "magic of the marketplace," when history shows that *none* of the major technological transformations of the past century or longer was the product of the progress of unregulated markets? Not the railroads; not the telegraph, telephone, or radio; not civilian aviation or space travel; and above all, not the internet and all the astonishing technological transformations that have followed in its wake.

This book is the answer to that question.

Like all books, this one has led us to incur many debts. Our agent, Ayesha Pande, encouraged us to take the time we needed to write a "worthy successor to *Merchants of Doubt*." Nancy Miller at Bloomsbury Publishing expressed the belief in the project that we needed to believe in it ourselves. The Guggenheim Foundation funded the project and made it possible for Erik to get crucial time away from his day job, as did Harvard University's generous leave policies, which have periodically enabled Naomi to live her perfect life of writing and skiing. Finally, our smart and savvy editor, Ben Hyman, our associate editor, Morgan Jones, our production editor, Barbara Darko, our copy editor, Janet McDonald, our proofreader, Katherine Kiger, and our indexers, Peter Brigaitis and Marie Nuchols, made it all come together.

At Harvard, we had the tremendous benefit of a team of crazy-smart, hard-working, and breathtakingly knowledgeable research assistants. Connor Chung, Hannah Conway, Gustave Lester, Aaron van Neste, Erik Baker, and Charlie Tyson read and commented on draft chapters, watched episodes of *GE Theater*, listened to episodes of *The American Family Robinson*, dug out references, spotted errors, checked and formatted footnotes, and, most important, held our feet to the fire when we were on the verge of overgeneralizing historical claims, oversimplifying answers to complex questions, or saying something nice about John Locke. Any remaining mistakes and oversimplifications are assuredly our own fault. We are doubly indebted to Hannah Conway, who did most of the grunt work of getting the manuscript prepared: when we submitted the first version, when we submitted subsequent revisions, and when we copyedited the final text.

We are also indebted to colleagues friends, family, and with whom we discussed our arguments, or who read and commented on all or part of the manuscript: James Antal, Harry Collins, Ellen Darion, Mott Greene, Dale Jamieson, Ed Larson, John Mashey, Jane Mayer, Harro Maas, Nancy MacLean, Melanie Mitchell, Michael

Oreskes, Gus Speth, Nick Stern, and undoubtedly someone dear to us who we are forgetting here and to whom we apologize in advance. The team of authors who wrote the book *The Disinformation Age* helped us to think through many issues regarding regulation and deregulation. The 2020 Princeton workshop on myths in American history, organized by Julian Zelizer and Kevin Kruse, helped us situate our project in the context of American political narratives. (The papers from that workshop can be found in the 2022 volume *Myth America: Historians Take On the Biggest Legends and Lies about Our Past*.) Hilary Lane played the role of "lay reader"—without her advice this book would have been much longer and more boring.

No work of history can be undertaken without access to archives. Covid-19 reduced that access and we are therefore doubly indebted to colleagues whose work we have relied on more heavily than would otherwise have been the case—particularly Kim Phillips-Fein, Wendy Wall, and Gary Gerstle—and hope that we have cited them sufficiently. Pre-pandemic we were able to work at the Reagan Presidential Library, the Hagley Library, and the archives of the Harvard Business School; we are grateful to their staff, particularly Lucas Clawson at the Hagley, who helped us enormously both when we were at the archives and later when we found gaps in our note-taking. We're also grateful to John Jackson Jr. of Michigan State University, who provided difficult-to-get copies of *Christian Economics* and *Faith and Freedom*.

We are, of course, indebted to our families—Ken, Hannah and Clara, Andrea and Alexander—who have come to accept that writing a book is not an event but a way of life.

This book is not a sequel to *Merchants of Doubt*, but it might be the prequel. Sequels are never as good as the original, but we hope that this book manages to enlarge the conversation we started in *Merchants of Doubt*. And if it's no good or not convincing, we'll just blame Tim Wirth.

NOTES

INTRODUCTION

1. George Soros, *The Crisis of Global Capitalism: Open Society Endangered* (London: Public Affairs, 1998); see also George Soros, "The Capitalist Threat," *Atlantic*, February 1997, https://www.theatlantic.com/magazine/archive/1997/02/the-capitalist-threat/376773/; and Fred Block and Margaret R. Somers, *The Power of Market Fundamentalism: Karl Polanyi's Critique* (Cambridge, MA: Harvard University Press, 2014), 3.

2. Fred Singer and Kent Jeffreys, *The EPA and the Science of Environmental Tobacco Smoke*, Alexis De Tocqueville Institution, University of Virginia, 1994, Bates Number: TICT0002555, Legacy Tobacco Documents Library, http://www.legacy.library.ucsf.edu, quoted in Naomi Oreskes and Erik M. Conway, *Merchants of Doubt: How a Handful of Scientists Obscured the Truth on Issues from Tobacco Smoke to Global Warming*, pbk. ed. (New York: Bloomsbury, 2011), 249.

3. Soros, "The Capitalist Threat."

4. Zachary D. Carter, "The End of Friedmanomics," *New Republic*, June 17, 2021, https://newrepublic.com/article/162623/milton-friedman-legacy-biden-government-spending. The speech is "The Fragility of Freedom," by Milton Friedman, in *Milton Friedman in South Africa*, ed. Meyer Feldberg, Kate Jowell, and Stephen Mulholland (Cape Town and Johannesburg: Graduate School of Business of the University of Cape Town, 1976), 3–10.

5. Although, as historian Ruth Schwartz Cowan has shown, labor-saving electrical appliances often did not actually save (net) female labor, as expectations for home cleanliness increased. *More Work for Mother: The Ironies of Household Technology from the Open Hearth to the Microwave* (New York: Basic Books, 1983).

6. Glenn Beck, "Glenn Beck -6/8/2010- The Road to Serfdom," Youtube, March 9, 2012, https://www.youtube.com/watch?v=CMk5_4pBlfM; Glenn Beck, "The Road to Serfdom," *Fox News*, March 25, 2015, https://www.foxnews.com/story/the-road-to-serfdom; Daniel Hannan, *The New Road to Serfdom: A Letter of Warning to America*, 1st ed. (New York: Harper, 2010); Bernard Harcourt, "How Paul Ryan Enslaves Friedrich Hayek's The Road to Serfdom," *Guardian*, September 12, 2012, http://www.theguardian.com/commentisfree/2012/sep/12/paul-ryan-enslaves-friedrich-hayek-road-serfdom; and Rush Limbaugh, "Rush Limbaugh on Brooks, Hayek & Obama," *Taking Hayek Seriously* (blog), February 25, 2009, accessed March 23, 2022, http://hayekcenter.org/?p=360.

7. On the Mont Pelerin Society, see Philip Mirowski and Dieter Plehwe, eds., *The Road from Mont Pèlerin: The Making of the Neoliberal Thought Collective* (Cambridge, MA: Harvard University Press, 2009). Other books important to our analysis include Wendy L. Wall, *Inventing the "American Way": The Politics of Consensus from the New Deal to the Civil Rights Movement* (Oxford: Oxford University Press, 2008); Kim Phillips-Fein, *Invisible Hands: The Businessmen's Crusade Against the New Deal* (New York: W. W. Norton, 2010); Michael Perelman, *Railroading Economics: The Creation of the Free Market Mythology* (New York: Monthly Review Press, 2006); Richard A. Posner, *A Failure of Capitalism: The Crisis of '08 and the Descent into Depression* (Cambridge, MA: Harvard University Press, 2009); and Mariana Mazzucato, *The Entrepreneurial State: Debunking Public vs. Private Sector Myths*, rev. ed. (London: Anthem Press, 2015). See also Ngaire Woods, "The Case Against Free-Market Capitalism," *Project Syndicate*, October 12, 2017, www.project-syndicate.org

/commentary/free-market-capitalism-neoliberalism-debate-by-ngaire-woods-2017-10
?barrier=accessreg.

8. Hobart Rowen, "Free-Market Proponent at University of Chicago," *Washington Post*, October 21, 1982, https://www.washingtonpost.com/archive/business/1982/10/21/free-market -proponent-at-university-of-chicago/37c6b377-5d6c-41c4-9ed6-38a18f2777ee/.

9. In June 2021, for example, a federal judge threw out a Department of Justice complaint against Facebook on grounds that echoed many of Bork's arguments; see chapter 9. Cecilia Kang, "Judge Throws Out 2 Antitrust Cases Against Facebook," *New York Times*, June 28, 2021, https://www.nytimes.com/2021/06/28/technology/facebook-ftc-lawsuit.html.

10. Kevin M. Kruse, *One Nation Under God: How Corporate America Invented Christian America* (New York: Basic Books, 2015), 11–34.

11. Gwenda Blair, "How Norman Vincent Peale Taught Donald Trump to Worship Himself," *Politico*, October 6, 2015, www.politico.com/magazine/story/2015/10/donald-trump-2016 -norman-vincent-peale-213220/.

12. Harriet Rubin, "Ayn Rand's Literature of Capitalism," *New York Times*, September 15, 2007, https://www.nytimes.com/2007/09/15/business/15atlas.html.

13. "Ayn Rand," FEE: Foundation for Economic Education, accessed May 12 2022, https://fee .org/people/ayn-rand/.

14. Rubin, "Ayn Rand's Literature of Capitalism."

15. Ibid.

16. "Everything Wrong with the Reagan Administration," Libertarianism.org (Cato Institute), April 9, 2019, https://www.libertarianism.org/everything-wrong-presidents/everything-wrong -reagan-administration.

17. Jane Mayer, *Dark Money: The Hidden History of the Billionaires Behind the Rise of the Radical Right*, 1st ed. (New York: Anchor, 2016); and Thomas Medvetz, *Think Tanks in America* (Chicago: University of Chicago Press, 2012). On conservative versus liberal philanthropy, see Sally Covington, "Moving a Public Policy Agenda: The Strategic Philanthropy of Conservative Foundations," National Committee for Responsive Philanthropy, July 23, 1997, accessed July 12, 2021, https://www.ncrp.org/publication/moving-public-policy-agenda. See also David Callahan, "$1 Billion for Ideas: Conservative Think Tanks in the 1990s," National Committee for Responsive Philanthropy, March 18, 1999, accessed July 12, 2021, https://www .ncrp.org/publication/1-billion-ideas; and Jeff Krehely, Meaghan House, and Emily Kernan, "Axis of Ideology: Conservative Foundations and Public Policy," National Committee for Responsive Philanthropy, March 2004, accessed July 12, 2021, https://www.ncrp.org/wp -content/uploads/2016/11/AxisofIdeology.pdf.

18. "Survey: What the Factory Worker thinks about Free Enterprise (A Survey)," Folder: What the Factory Worker thinks about Free Enterprise, Box 847, Series III, National Association of Manufacturers Records, accession 1411, Hagley Museum and Library, Wilmington, DE 19807.

19. Ronald Reagan, "Inaugural Address" (Washington, D.C., January 20, 1981), https://www .reaganfoundation.org/ronald-reagan/reagan-quotes-speeches/inaugural-address-2/.

20. The exception to this is the notion of Pareto efficiency in economics, which aims to maximize net welfare. "Three Normative Models of the Welfare State," *Public Reason* 3, no. 2 (2011): 13–43; and Elizabeth Popp Berman, *Thinking Like an Economist: How Efficiency Replaced Equality in U.S. Public Policy* (Princeton, NJ: Princeton University Press, 2022),

21. Quoted in Tony Judt, *Ill Fares the Land* (London: Penguin Books, 2011).

22. David Brooks, "Fracking and the Franciscans," *New York Times*, June 23, 2015, www.nytimes .com/2015/06/23/opinion/fracking-and-the-franciscans.html.

23. Eduardo Porter, "Climate Change Calls for Science, Not Hope," *New York Times*, June 23, 2015, https://www.nytimes.com/2015/06/24/business/combating-climate-change-with-science -rather-than-hope.html.

24. Joseph Aldy, quoted in "A Blessing to Slow Climate Change," *Harvard Gazette*, June 18, 2015, https://news.harvard.edu/gazette/story/2015/06/a-blessing-to-slow-climate-change/.

25. Naomi Klein, *This Changes Everything: Capitalism vs. The Climate* (New York: Simon & Schuster, 2014); Andreas Malm, *Fossil Capital: The Rise of Steam Power and the Roots of Global Warming* (London: Verso Books, 2016); and Andreas Malm, *How to Blow Up a Pipeline: Learning to Fight in a World on Fire* (London: Verso Books, 2021).

26. Tim Worstall, "Nick Stern Is Wrong; Climate Change Is Not the Largest Market Failure the World Has Ever Seen," *Forbes*, January 25, 2015, https://www.forbes.com/sites/timworstall/2015/01/25/nick-stern-is-wrong-climate-change-is-not-the-largest-market-failure-the-world-has-ever-seen/.

27. Conny Olovsson, "The CO_2 Market Failure: It's Free to Emit but Has Costly Consequences," *LSE Business Review*, October 15, 2020, https://blogs.lse.ac.uk/businessreview/2020/10/15/the-co2-market-failure-its-free-to-emit-but-has-costly-consequences/.

28. Eric R. Wolf, *Pathways of Power: Building an Anthropology of the Modern World* (Berkeley and Los Angeles: University of California Press, 2001), 385. See also Wolf, "Distinguished Lecture: Facing Power—Old Insights, New Questions," *American Anthropologist* 92, no. 3 (September 1990): 586–96.

29. Timothy Mitchell, *Carbon Democracy: Political Power in the Age of Oil* (London and New York: Verso Books, 2013) argues that the notion of "the economy" does not emerge until the twentieth century. The FTC first established an economic division in 1915 (Berman, *Thinking Like an Economist*, 28). The Hoover administration was the first to collect systematically the sort of data that could be used to analyze "the economy" as we now understand it.

CHAPTER 1: THE SOCIAL COSTS OF CAPITALISM

1. John Fabian Witt, *The Accidental Republic: Crippled Workingmen, Destitute Widows, and the Remaking of American Law* (Cambridge, MA: Harvard University Press, 2006), 3.

2. "USA War Losses," International Encyclopedia of the First World War, October 8, 2014, https://encyclopedia.1914-1918-online.net/article/war_losses_usa. According to the International Encyclopedia of the First World War's estimates of war losses, 2.5 percent of American soldiers died and another 6.8 percent became sick or injured while serving. For American industry overall, 2 percent of the workforce were killed or disabled for at least four weeks each year in industrial accidents during the War years. Witt, *The Accidental Republic*, 23.

3. Witt, *The Accidental Republic*, 22–24.

4. On the recent resurgence of black lung disease in the United States, see PBS *Frontline*, "Coal's Deadly Dust," January 22, 2019, https://www.pbs.org/wgbh/frontline/film/coals-deadly-dust/.

5. Witt, *The Accidental Republic*, 3. Also Jeffrey Helgeson, "American Labor and Working-Class History, 1900–1945," *Oxford Research Encyclopedia of American History*, August 31, 2016.

6. As late as 1890 "firms did not develop an insurance product marketable to the class of Americans most subject to the vicissitudes of the new industrial economy. Life insurance policies for the working man . . . were considered 'bad risks.'" Witt, *The Accidental Republic*, 73.

7. On the rise of cooperative societies and the exclusion of most workers from private insurance, see Witt, *The Accidental Republic*, 3.

8. The concept of contributory negligence held that if it could be shown that the worker had made a mistake of any kind, then even if the employer had been negligent, he was generally absolved of responsibility. Ibid., chap. 2.

9. Cited by Witt, Ibid., 118. Also discussed on Witt, 44–45.

10. Ibid., 7.

11. Gregory P. Guyton, "A Brief History of Workers' Compensation," *Iowa Orthopaedic Journal* 19 (1999): 106–10.

12. Massachusetts Bureau of Statistics of Labor, "Annual Report of the Bureau of Statistics of Labor Embracing the Account of Its Operations and Inquiries from March 1, 1872 to March 1, 1873" (Boston: Wright and Potter Printing Co., State Printers, 1873), 282–83.

13. Witt, *The Accidental Republic*, 10.

14. Ibid.

15. Ibid., 116.

16. Ibid., 4; J. S. Haller, "Industrial Accidents: Worker Compensation Laws and the Medical Response," *Western Journal of Medicine* 148, no. 3 (March 1988): 341–48.

17. Michael McGerr, *A Fierce Discontent: The Rise and Fall of the Progressive Movement in America, 1870–1920* (Oxford: Oxford University Press, 2005), 109–12; and Steven J. Diner, *A Very Different Age: Americans of the Progressive Era* (New York: Hill and Wang, 1998). This is not to say that progressives were perfect; their movement, like most of American history, was marred by racism and sexism. Thomas C. Leonard overstates the relation between racism, eugenics, and the progressive movement, but there was a relationship. See *Illiberal Reformers: Race, Eugenics, and American Economics in the Progressive Era* (Princeton, NJ: Princeton University Press, 2016).

18. Cited in "Child with a Hoe," *Harvard Crimson*, February 8, 1941, https://www.thecrimson.com/article/1941/2/8/child-with-a-hoe-pb-but-if/. For Holmes's argument see his dissent in *Hammer v. Dagenhart*, 247 U.S. 251 (1918), https://www.lexisnexis.com/community/casebrief/p/casebrief-hammer-v-dagenhart; see also https://www.britannica.com/event/Hammer-v-Dagenhart. Some contemporary neoliberals have tried to reopen this argument, suggesting that child labor is not necessarily wrong, particularly if the children's earnings help the family overall. See, for example, James Warren, "Judge Richard A. Posner Stuns in Ruling on Child Labor," *New York Times*, July 14, 2011, https://www.nytimes.com/2011/07/15/us/15cncwarren.html.

19. The Progressive Era argument against child labor was linked to the argument for expanded public education, since a child working in a factory was obviously not attending school. By 1918, in major American cities, most children were attending school at least until the age of fifteen. In Boston, 83.4 percent of children aged fourteen and fifteen were still in school, but that dropped to 43 percent for the sixteen- and seventeen-year-old cohort. In New York, the numbers were a bit lower: 94 percent of children were still in school at thirteen, but only 78.7 percent of fourteen- and fifteen-year-olds and only 28.5 percent of those aged sixteen and seventeen. Elaine Chao and Kathleen Utgoff, "100 Years of U.S. Consumer Spending: Data for the Nation, New York City, and Boston" (U.S. Department of Labor and U.S Bureau of Labor Statistics, 2006). Education rates were lower in rural areas, in part because farm families were likely to expect their children to work on the farm, and in part because of general resistance to state-sponsored schooling. See Paul Theobald, *Call School: Rural Education in the Midwest to 1918* (Carbondale: Southern Illinois University Press, 1995). See also McGerr, *A Fierce Discontent*.

20. McGerr, *A Fierce Discontent*, 109.

21. Holmes was vindicated when *Dagenhart* was overturned in *United States v. Darby*, 312 U.S. 100 (1941). *Darby* upheld the Fair Labor Standards Act of 1938, which for the first time established a federal minimum wage and the right to overtime, and prohibited most forms of child labor. "[T]hese principles of constitutional interpretation have been so long and repeatedly recognized by this Court as applicable to the Commerce Clause, that there would be little occasion for repeating them now were it not for the decision of this Court twenty-two years ago in *Hammer v. Dagenhart*, 247 U.S. 251 (1918) . . . In that case, it was held by a bare majority

of the Court over the powerful and now classic dissent of Mr. Justice Holmes setting forth the fundamental issues involved . . . The conclusion is inescapable that *Hammer v. Dagenhart* was a departure from the principles which have prevailed in the interpretation of the Commerce Clause both before and since the decision, and that such vitality, as a precedent, as it then had, has long since been exhausted. It should be, and now is, overruled."

22. Julia C. Ott, "'The Free and Open People's Market': Political Ideology and Retail Brokerage at the New York Stock Exchange, 1913–1933," *Journal of American History* 96, no. 1 (June 1, 2009): 44–71.

23. Opposition was especially vitriolic toward a graduated income tax. "Any government, whatever name it may assume, is a despotism, and commits acts of flagrant spoliation," popular writer and former Internal Revenue Commissioner David Wells declared in the late nineteenth century, "if it grants exemptions or exacts a greater or lesser rate of tax from one man than from another." Legal scholar Ajay Mehrotra argues that Wells and his supporters thought "progressive taxes of any sort were a form of emasculating charity." See Ajay K. Mehrotra, "Envisioning the Modern American Fiscal State: Progressive-Eva Economists and the Intellectual Foundations of the U.S. Income Tax," Symposium: Rethinking Redistribution; Tax Policy in an Era Rising Inequality, *UCLA Law Review* 52 (2004–5): 1844.

24. McGerr, *A Fierce Discontent*, 109. Pierre Du Pont was still making this argument in the 1930s. Kim Phillips-Fein, *Invisible Hands: The Businessmen's Crusade Against the New Deal* (New York: W. W. Norton, 2010), 4.

25. Hammer v. Dagenhart, 247 U.S. 251 (1918).

26. The federal government argued that it was within its rights to ban interstate commerce in products produced by child labor, citing previous cases where courts had allowed prohibitions on commerce of impure foods and drugs, of women for the purposes of prostitution, of alcohol, and the sale of lottery tickets. But the court held that these other cases "rested upon the character of the particular subjects dealt with," which were manifestly evil. The Keating-Owen bill, however, dealt with goods that were "of themselves, harmless." Holmes argued in dissent that the power to regulate necessarily includes the power to prohibit. There were several precedents in which courts had upheld this power, including the case of oleomargarine, where "Congress levied a tax upon the compound when colored so as to resemble butter that was so great as obviously to prohibit the manufacture and sale." Similarly, Congress had imposed taxes on foreign banks with the purpose of driving them out of business, and had used the Sherman Anti-Trust Act to break up trusts, "using the power to regulate commerce as a foothold." On Congress using a recognized power in previously unrecognized ways, see Gary Gerstle, *Liberty and Coercion: The Paradox of American Government from the Founding to the Present*, rev. ed. (Princeton, NJ: Princeton University Press, 2015), 5–6.

27. National Child Labor Committee (U.S.) and Owen Reed Lovejoy, *Annual Report* (New York, 1916), 4–5.

28. Ibid.

29. Ibid.

30. Owen R. Lovejoy, *Thirteenth Annual Report of the General Secretary of the National Child Labor Committee, for the fiscal year ending September 30, 1917* (New York: National Child Labor Committee, 1918), 148.

31. The same argument was used later in the twentieth century against state anti-pollution laws, and more recently in the context of controlling greenhouse gas emissions. See William R. Lowry, *The Dimensions of Federalism: State Governments and Pollution Control Policies* (Durham, NC: Duke University Press, 1991); Wolfgang Keller and Arik Levinson, "Pollution Abatement Costs and Foreign Direct Investment Inflows to U.S. States," *Review of Economics and Statistics* 84, no. 4 (November 2002): 691–703; and Dallas Burtraw et al., "Ancillary

Benefits of Reduced Air Pollution in the U.S. from Moderate Greenhouse Gas Mitigation Policies in the Electricity Sector," *Journal of Environmental Economics and Management* 45, no. 3 (May 1, 2003): 650–73.

32. James Lynn Barnard, *Factory Legislation in Pennsylvania: Its History and Administration*, University of Pennsylvania Series in Political Economics and Public Law 19 (pub. for the University, 1907), 14.

33. Fred Rogers Fairchild, "The Factory Legislation of the State of New York," *Publications of the American Economic Association* 6, no. 4 (1905): 45.

34. Hammer v. Dagenhart, 247 U.S. 251 (1918) at 62.

35. Here is the whole text: "Section 1. The Congress shall have power to limit, regulate, and prohibit the labor of persons under eighteen years of age. Section 2. The power of the several states is unimpaired by this article except that the operation of state laws shall be suspended to the extent necessary to give effect to legislation enacted by the Congress." "Proposed Amendments Not Ratified by the States," Constitution Annotated, accessed May 12, 2022, https://constitution.congress.gov/browse/essay/intro.4/ALDE_00000026/. In 1933, the "lame duck" amendment, which moved the start of the presidential and vice-presidential terms from March to January, became the Twentieth Amendment to the Constitution.

36. Jennifer A. Delton, *The Industrialists: How the National Association of Manufacturers Shaped American Capitalism* (Princeton, NJ: Princeton University Press, 2020), 19.

37. Noel Sargent, ed., *Open Shop Encyclopedia for Debaters*, 3rd ed. (New York: National Association of Manufacturers, 1922).

38. Philip G. Wright, "The Contest in Congress Between Organized Labor and Organized Business," *Quarterly Journal of Economics* 29, no. 2 (1915): 250.

39. "The Clayton Antitrust Act," U.S. House of Representatives: History, Art and Archives, accessed July 2, 2019, https://history.house.gov/Historical-Highlights/1901-1950/hh_1914_10_15_clayton_antitrust/.

40. Wright, "The Contest in Congress." Wright claimed that unions' entry into politics was a response to the activities of NAM and other industrial groups.

41. A. K. Steigerwalt, "The NAM and the Congressional Investigations of 1913: A Case Study in the Suppression of Evidence," *Business History Review* 34, no. 3 (1960): 335–44. Archival materials show that Steigerwalt was a paid consultant to NAM, and that he became angry with NAM after he wrote a paper that entirely vindicated NAM and excoriated the congressional investigations, but NAM failed to pay him what he thought he had been promised. According to the documents, he was paid $8,650.80 for writing the article. Chuck Sligh, "Letter from Chuck Sligh to A.K. Steigerwalt," National Association of Manufacturers, July 21, 1960, box 42, series I, National Association of Manufacturers Records, accession 1411, Hagley Museum and Library, Wilmington, DE 19807. See also Wright, "The Contest."

42. Phillips-Fein, *Invisible Hands*.

43. James A. Emery, *An Examination of the Proposed Twentieth Amendment to the Constitution of the United States (Being the So-Called Child Labor Amendment)*, August 1924, folder NAM Industrial Relations Division Child Labor, 1923–43 box 135, National Association of Manufacturers Records, accession 1411, Hagley Museum and Library, Wilmington, DE 19807.

44. This is tricky language because the labor force could include sharecropping.

45. This was a hypocritical argument, because the numbers were dropping, no thanks to NAM (or other business leaders), but because of the impact of compulsory education laws.

46. Marjorie Cruickshank, *Children and Industry: Child Health and Welfare in North-West Textile Towns During the Nineteenth Century* (Manchester, UK: Manchester University Press, 1981).

47. See Alan Derickson, "Making Human Junk: Child Labor as a Health Issue in the Progressive Era," *American Journal of Public Health* 82, no. 9 (September 1992): 1280–90; Russell Freedman, *Kids at Work: Lewis Hine and the Crusade Against Child Labor* (New York: Houghton Mifflin Harcourt, 1994); and Tom McCunnie, "Regulation and the Health of Child Workers in the Mid-Victorian Silk Industry," *Local Population Studies* 74 (2005): 54–74.

48. Emery, "An Examination," 4.

49. Ibid.

50. Ibid. The income tax was also devised with an intentional social function: to distribute fiscal burdens more equitably. NAM's Trojan horse argument ignores the intentions of the Sixteenth Amendment's advocates and designers. See Mehrotra, "Envisioning the Modern American Fiscal State."

51. James Madison, quoted in Emery, "An Examination," 12. The original is James Madison, 1788. Amendment X, *Federalist*, no. 45, 313–14.

52. Gerstle, *Liberty and Coercion*, 54. Gerstle notes that this was often used to argue for expansive police powers being retained by the states, including the right to do many things that were prohibited to the federal government, such as establishing religion, which, in the early years of the republic, many states did.

53. Emery, "An Examination: Child Labor in the United States" (National Association of Manufacturers, n.d.), 2, folder NAM Industrial Relations Division Child Labor, 1923–43, box 135, National Association of Manufacturers Records, accession 1411, Hagley Museum and Library, Wilmington, DE 19807. Local responsibility was a theme conservatives would return to again and again: see Gerstle, *Liberty and Coercion*.

54. Emery, "An Examination," 8.

55. Discussed in Noel Sargent, "Pending Child Labor Amendment to the United States Constitution Should Be Rejected: Address before City Club of Albany," National Association of Manufacturers, January 16, 1934, 4, folder NAM Industrial Relations Division Child Labor, 1923-43, box 135, National Association of Manufacturers Records, accession 1411, Hagley Museum and Library, Wilmington, DE 19807. An interesting paper demonstrating parental "non-altruism" is Donald O. Parsons and Claudia Goldin, "Parental Altruism and Self-Interest: Child Labor Among Late Nineteenth-Century American Families," *Economic Inquiry* 27, no. 4 (1989): 637–59.

56. One of the contradictions of anti-progressive rhetoric was that it accepted limitations on personal freedom when imposed by state government while rejecting the same limitations when imposed by the federal government. The generous interpretation of this, offered by Gerstle, is that advocates of expansive state police powers assumed that the states were closer to the will of the people and therefore less likely to prove tyrannical than the federal government. For majorities in many states, this was true, but it also led to disregard of the rights of minorities, and ultimately to the Fourteenth Amendment extension of the Bill of Rights to the states. See Gerstle, *Liberty and Coercion*, especially 22–23 and 80–82.

57. Ibid., 20.

58. "The Brandeis Brief—in Its Entirety," Louis D. Brandeis School of Law Library, accessed July 2, 2019, https://louisville.edu/law/library/special-collections/the-louis-d.-brandeis-collec tion/the-brandeis-brief-in-its-entirety.

59. Florence Kelley, "Speaks Out on Child Labor and Woman Suffrage," Philadelphia, PA, July 22, 1905, https://www.infoplease.com/us/speeches-primary-documents/speaks-out-child -labor-and-woman-suffrage; "Florence Kelley (1859-1932): Social Reformer, Child Welfare Advocate, Socialist and Pacifist," Social Welfare History Project, April 3, 2008, https:// socialwelfare.library.vcu.edu/people/kelley-florence/.

60. Emery, "An Examination," 20. In point of fact, it was the Rand School of Social *Science*, although admittedly it was socialist in orientation.

61. McGerr, *A Fierce Discontent*. Leonard, *Illiberal Reformers*, stresses that many progressives rejected racial equality and were at best ambivalent about the poor.

62. Emery, "An Examination," 21.

63. Ibid., 21.

64. Some eugenicists made this argument. Daniel J. Kevles, "From Eugenics to Patents: Genetics, Law, and Human Rights," *Annals of Human Genetics* 75, no. 3 (2011): 326–33.

65. Emery, "An Examination," 22–23.

66. Ibid., 24.

67. Ibid., 25.

68. "The Child Labor Amendment," *Social Service Review* 9, no. 1 (1935): 107.

69. William Kessen, "The American Child and Other Cultural Inventions," *American Psychologist* 34, no. 10, Psychology and Children: Current Research and Practice (October 1979): 815–20. Reformers drew on sentimental tropes from British and continental literature, especially Elizabeth Barrett Browning's poem "The Cry of the Children." While putting a face to child labor, these writings also gave ammunition to opponents of reform who argued that reformers were being overly dramatic. James D. Schmidt, *Industrial Violence and the Legal Origins of Child Labor* (Cambridge: Cambridge University Press, 2010), 71.

70. "Child Labor in the United States" (National Association of Manufacturers, n.d.), folder NAM Industrial Relations Division Child Labor, 1923–43, box 135, National Association of Manufacturers Records, accession 1411, Hagley Museum and Library, Wilmington, DE 19807. On the Clark-Connery bill, see Fred L Kuhlmann, "Child Labor Amendment or Alternative Legislation?" n.d., 7. See also "Child Labor Legislation: Its Past, Present, and Future," *Fordham Law Review* 7, no. 2 (1938): 23. And "Child Labor Bill Fought; Measure Advocated by Manufacturers' Group Is Challenged," *New York Times*, February 8, 1937, https://www.nytimes.com/1937/02/08/archives/child-labor-bill-fought-measure-advocated -by-manufacturers-group-is.html.

71. Noel Sargent, "Why Employers are Opposed to the Twentieth Amendment," (National Association of Manufacturers, reprinted from American Industries, February 1925), folder Socialism, box 6, series I, National Association of Manufacturers Records, accession 1411, Hagley Museum and Library, Wilmington, DE 19807. Butler was the longest-serving president of Columbia, from 1902 to 1945. In 1917, he had dismissed without hearing two Columbia faculty, the writer Henry Wadsworth Longfellow Dana and the psychologist James McKeen Cattell, on grounds of disloyalty when they failed to support U.S. involvement in World War I. The historian Charles A. Beard resigned in protest; all three would go on to distinguished careers. See Today in Civil Liberties History, "Columbia University Fires Two 'Disloyal' Faculty," accessed January 31, 2022, http://todayinclh.com/?event=columbia -university-fires-two-disloyal-faculty. Beard became one of the most prominent historians of his generation and was well known for his pioneering economic interpretation of the U.S. Constitution; see Encyclopaedia Britannica, s.v. "Charles A. Beard," accessed January 31, 2022, https://www.britannica.com/biography/Charles-A-Beard.

72. George H. Haynes, "Review of *True and False Democracy* by Nicholas Murray Butler; *The Citizen's Part in Government* by Elihu Root; *Political Problems of American Development* by Albert Shaw," *American Political Science Review* 2, no. 3 (1908): 485–90.

73. Mary Tourek, "Ernest Hemingway Denied Pulitzer Prize for 'For Whom the Bell Tolls,'" *Today in Civil Liberties History* (blog), July 30, 2013, http://todayinclh.com/?event=ernest -hemingway-denied-pulitzer-prize-for-for-whom-the-bell-tolls.

74. Noel Sargent, "The Case Against Socialism, with Particular Analysis of the Views of Norman Thomas," National Association of Manufacturers, April 18, 1933, folder Socialism, box 6, series I, National Association of Manufacturers Records, accession 1411, Hagley Museum and Library, Wilmington, DE 19807.

75. Elizabeth Balanoff, "Norman Thomas: Socialism and the Social Gospel," *Religion Online*. Originally published in *Christian Century*, January 30, 1985, 101–2. https://www.religion -online.org/article/norman-thomas-socialism-and-the-social-gospel/.

76. Sargent, "The Case Against Socialism."

77. Ibid., 11.

78. Robert C. Bannister, *Sociology and Scientism: The American Quest for Objectivity, 1880–1940* (Chapel Hill: University of North Carolina Press, 1991), 88. Sumner and his student Albert Keller are also mentioned in Thomas C. Leonard, "Origins of the Myth of Social Darwinism: The Ambiguous Legacy of Richard Hofstadter's Social Darwinism in American Thought," *Journal of Economic Behavior and Organization* 71, no. 1 (July 2009): 37–51. Leonard notes that "social Darwinism" is a complex topic, often reduced to platitudes, but it is still broadly correct to consider Sumner a social Darwinist, even if he did not use that term.

79. Bannister, *Sociology and Scientism*.

80. William Graham Sumner, *What Social Classes Owe to Each Other* (New York: Arno Press, [1883] 1972).

81. Bannister, *Sociology and Scientism*, 88. Sargent insists that his views have a "scientific basis," (e.g., p. 14), suggesting a reference to eugenic notions of inequality among social classes. For more on eugenics and class, see Garland E. Allen, "The Eugenics Record Office at Cold Spring Harbor, 1910–1940: An Essay in Institutional History," *Osiris* 2 (1986): 225–64; Garland E. Allen, "Eugenics and Modern Biology: Critiques of Eugenics, 1910–1945," *Annals of Human Genetics* 75, no. 3 (May 2011): 314–25; and Diane B. Paul, *Controlling Human Heredity: 1865 to the Present*, repr. ed. (Amherst, NY: Humanity Books, 1995).

82. Sargent, "The Case Against Socialism."

83. Which is both ironic and circular, given that Darwin had been heavily inspired by the economic ideas of Thomas Malthus.

84. "Arthur T. Hadley," The History of Economic Thought, accessed July 2, 2019, https://www .hetwebsite.net/het/profiles/hadley.htm. Lest anyone think we are picking on Yale and Columbia, Harvard president emeritus A. Lawrence Lowell also opposed the amendment, saying in 1934 that he opposed child labor, but thought the amendment gave federal authorities too much power over an issue that rightly belonged to parents. "The child labor amendment, 1924–1934," *Editorial research reports 1934*, 1 (1934), http://library.cqpress.com /cqresearcher/cqresrre1934030300. This argument would be taken up by the Chicago school of economics, particularly the jurist Robert Bork. See chapters 9 and 14.

85. John Stuart Mill, "On Liberty," in *Collected Works of John Stuart Mill Volume XVIII*, ed. J. M. Robson (Toronto: University of Toronto Press, 1977), 223. Hadley framed it in terms of the problem of *interference*—which, of course, is a form of harm.

86. Arthur Twining Hadley, *The Conflict Between Liberty and Equality*, Raymond F. West Memorial Lectures (Boston and New York: Houghton Mifflin Company, 1925).

87. *The Conflict Between Liberty and Equality*, 787–88.

88. Ibid., 788.

89. Ibid. Sargent, "The Case Against Socialism," 12, directly quotes Hadley, *The Conflict Between Liberty and Equality*. For a contemporary review, see F. H. Hankins, *Journal of Social Forces* 3, no. 4 (1925): 786–88. Hadley was an economist known mostly for his analysis and defense of property rights; see Melvin L. Cross and Robert B. Ekelund Jr., "A. T. Hadley: The

American Invention of the Economics of Property Rights and Public Goods," *Review of Social Economy* 39, no. 1 (April 1981): 37–50.

90. Floyd Parsons, "Everybody's Business," American Liberty League, 1934, 7, folder advertising, selling, 1934, Longwood Manuscripts, Group 10, series A, Papers of P. S. DuPont, File 881 1929–1948, Hagley Museum and Library, Wilmington, DE 19807.

91. Later NAM would also be investigated by Congress for violating the free speech rights of workers; see U.S. Congress, Senate, Committee on Education and Labor, *Violations of Free Speech and Rights of Labor: Report of the Committee on Education and Labor Pursuant to S. Res 266: Labor Policies of Employers' Associations Part III: The National Association of Manufacturers*, 76th Congress, 1st Session, August 14, 1939 (Washington, D.C.: U.S. Government Printing Office, 1939). In congressional hearings, it was revealed that NAM had turned to the public relations firm Hill and Knowlton to promote their case—the same company that would later create the framework of tobacco industry deception. See Naomi Oreskes and Erik M. Conway, *Merchants of Doubt: How a Handful of Scientists Obscured the Truth on Issues from Tobacco Smoke to Global Warming*, pbk. ed. (New York: Bloomsbury, 2011). As part of its investigation of NAM activities, Congress issued a subpoena to Hill and Knowlton.

92. Sargent, "The Case Against Socialism."

93. "In 1902 Maryland became the first state to pass a law providing accident compensation regardless of fault, but the law was declared unconstitutional in 1904 by the state supreme court." "Progressive Ideas," U.S. Department of Labor, accessed May 12, 2022, https://www .dol.gov/general/aboutdol/history/mono-regsafepart06. Wisconsin was the first state to pass a comprehensive program, in 1911, the same year as the infamous Triangle Shirtwaist Factory fire. New York State and many other states soon followed suit. Price V. Fishback and Shawn Everett Kantor, "The Adoption of Workers' Compensation in the United States, 1900–1930," *Journal of Law and Economics* 41, no. 2 (1998): 305–42. See also Witt, *The Accidental Republic*, 10; Robert F. Wesser, "Conflict and Compromise: The Workmen's Compensation Movement in New York, 1890s–1913," *Labor History* 12, no. 3 (June 1, 1971): 346.

94. Wesser, "Conflict and Compromise," 347.

95. Ibid., 347.

96. Witt, *The Accidental Republic*, 264n80.

97. Wesser, "Conflict and Compromise," 353.

98. Ibid., 370.

99. Guyton, "A Brief History of Workers' Compensation"; and Haller, "Industrial Accidents."

100. It was only partial protection: workers still had to prove that the railroad was at least partly at fault. See "Federal Employers' Liability Act: Introduction," Villanova University Charlest Widger School of Law LibGuides, March 3, 2022, https://libguides.law.villanova.edu/FELA.

101. Wesser, "Conflict and Compromise," 354.

102. Ibid., 367. The National Civic Federation situated itself as a moderate group attempting to promote harmony between labor and capital, and was criticized by NAM for being too soft on labor. However, it was dominated by business leaders and was fiercely antisocialist. See "Biographical/Historical Information," National Civic Federation Records 1894–1989, The New York Public Library Archives & Manuscripts, https://archives.nypl.org/mss/2101.

103. Haller, "Industrial Accidents." The new laws often also compelled physicians to testify when called by a workmen's compensation board or commission.

104. Ibid. The American Medical Association went far beyond this, actively undermining community health clinics and prepaid health insurance systems whether they were public or privately managed, or funded by local or state government. See Alice Sardell, *The U.S. Experiment in*

Social Medicine: The Community Health Center Program, 1965–1986 (Pittsburgh: University of Pittsburgh Press, 1989), 62–63, 93–95, 203.

105. Edward F. McSweeney, quoted in Haller, "Industrial Accidents." Original is in E. F. McSweeney, "Industrial Accident Insurance," *Trans Mass Medico-Legal Soc.* 4 (1914): 55–62.

106. The American Bar Association also opposed the Child Labor Amendment; see footnote 6 in James Barclay Smith, "A Child Labor Amendment Is Unnecessary," *California Law Review* 27, no. 1 (November 1938): 15, https://doi.org/10.2307/3476320.

107. Smith, "Child Labor." Smith argued that child labor was not a crisis and therefore not a legitimate basis for amending the Constitution.

108. Abraham Lincoln, "Address at a Sanitary Fair," Baltimore, MD, April 18, 1864, The American Presidency Project, https://www.presidency.ucsb.edu/documents/address-sanitary-fair-baltimore-lecture-liberty.

109. Isaiah Berlin, *The Crooked Timber of Humanity* (Princeton, NJ: Princeton University Press, 1959).

110. Isaiah Berlin, *Four Essays on Liberty* (Oxford: Oxford University Press, 1969), xlv. For an interesting discussion of this by libertarians, who don't generally like to admit the latter part of this quotation, see Murray Rothbard, "Isaiah Berlin on Negative Freedom," in *The Ethics of Liberty* (Ludwig van Mises Institute, 1982), https://mises.org/library/isaiah-berlin-negative-freedom. See also Ian Carter, "Positive and Negative Liberty," in *Stanford Encyclopedia of Philosophy*, ed. Edward N. Zalta, Summer 2018 (Metaphysics Research Lab, Stanford University, 2018), https://plato.stanford.edu/archives/sum2018/entries/liberty-positive-negative/, which says the famous essay was first published in 1958, and then republished in 1969.

CHAPTER 2: POWER PLAYS AND PROPAGANDA

1. Ruth Schwartz Cowan argues that many of these appliances did not save labor, but just changed its character. Cowan, *More Work for Mother: The Ironies of Household Technology from the Open Hearth to the Microwave* (New York: Basic Books, 1985).

2. David E. Nye, *Electrifying America: Social Meanings of a New Technology, 1880–1940* (Cambridge, MA: MIT University Press, 1990).

3. Nye, *Electrifying America*. The British model remained decentralized and unstandardized, in part because of tension between the Labor and Conservative parties over the issue of centralization. On views of electricity in countries other than the United States at that time, see Harold Evans, "The World's Experience with Electrification," *Annals of the American Academy of Political and Social Science* 118 (1925): 30–42.

4. Ibid.

5. Sarah Phillips, *This Land, This Nation: Conservation, Rural America, and the New Deal* (Cambridge: Cambridge University Press, 2007), 26.

6. Nye, *Electrifying America*, 287.

7. Ibid., 297.

8. Gifford Pinchot, "Governor Pinchot's Message of Transmittal," in Giant Power Survey Board, Pennsylvania, *Report of the Giant Power Survey Board to the General Assembly of the Commonwealth of Pennsylvania* (Harrisburg, PA: Telegraph Printing Co., 1925), iii.

9. Ibid., iv.

10. Ibid., xiii.

11. *Muncie* [Indiana] *Morning Star*, March 17, 1935, 3, quoted in Nye, *Electrifying America*, 339.

12. Pinchot, "Message of Transmittal," xii.

13. Gifford Pinchot, "Pinchot Argues for Super Power," *New York Times*, August 3, 1924, https://www.nytimes.com/1924/08/03/archives/pinchot-argues-for-super-power.html.

14. *Encyclopaedia Britannica*, s.v., "supply and demand," accessed December 17, 2019, https://www .britannica.com/topic/supply-and-demand. One of the classic statements is Alfred Marshall, *Principles of Economics*, first published in 1890, https://oll.libertyfund.org/title/marshall -principles-of-economics-8th-ed#Marshall_0197_857.

15. Marshall compares the equilibrating forces to gravity returning a disturbed spring to its natural position, hence suggesting a parallel with the laws of physics. We can argue whether the laws of natural systems are in fact laws, any more than the laws of economics are, insofar as they all represent ideal situations. See Nancy Cartwright, *How the Laws of Physics Lie* (Oxford: Oxford University Press, 1983).

16. In the 1990s, ATSF merged with Burlington Northern to create BNSF; today BNSF and Union Pacific have a duopoly on all rail freight travel in the United States.

17. Richard White, *Railroaded: The Transcontinentals and the Making of Modern America* (New York: W. W. Norton, 2011).

18. The slaughter of bison has been the subject of many academic works, but it is most powerfully portrayed in John Williams's novel *Butcher's Crossing* (New York: Macmillan, 1960). See Naomi Oreskes, "The Bloody Autumn of *Butcher's Crossing*," in "Books that Matter," ed. Arien Mack, special issue, *Social Research* 89, no. 2 (2022).

19. Ronald Kline, *Consumers in the Country: Technology and Social Change in Rural America* (Baltimore: Johns Hopkins University Press, 2000), 132. Kline notes that in 1922, there were only three thousand municipal plants, but the number was growing, causing concern in the private electricity industry. The quotation in the text comes from William J. Hausman and John L. Neufeld, "How Politics, Economics, and Institutions Shaped Electric Utility Regulation in the United States 1879–2009," in *The Economic and Social Regulation of Public Utilities: An International History*, ed. Judith Clifton, Pierre Lanthier, and Harm Schröter (New York: Routledge, 2013), 69.

20. Kline, *Consumers*, 72.

21. Ibid. Also see discussion in Thomas Hughes, *Networks of Power: Electrification in Western Society, 1880–1930* (Baltimore: Johns Hopkins University Press, 1993).

22. In 1935, Congress passed the Public Utility Holding Company Act, which limited their activities to a single state so that they would fall under the jurisdiction of state regulators. This act was repealed in 2005.

23. Hausman and Neufeld, "How Politics."

24. Char Miller, *Gifford Pinchot and the Making of Modern Environmentalism* (Washington, D.C.: Island Press, 2001).

25. W. S. Murray and others, "A Superpower System for the Region between Boston and Washington," U.S. Geological Survey GS Professional Paper 123 (Washington, D.C.: Department of the Interior, 1921), https://pubs.er.usgs.gov/publication/pp123.

26. Kendrick A. Clements, *Hoover, Conservation and Consumerism: Engineering the Good Life* (Lawrence: University Press of Kansas, 2000), 249, note 35.

27. Jean Christie, *Morris Llewellyn Cooke: Progressive Engineer* (New York: Garland Publishing, 1983), 72–73. See also Bayla Singer, "Power Politics," *IEEE Technology and Society Magazine* 7, no. 4 (1988): 20–27.

28. Pinchot, "Message of Transmittal," viii.

29. Ibid.

30. Ibid.

31. Gifford Pinchot, "Introduction," *Annals of the American Academy of Political and Social Science* 118, 1 (1925): viii. This introduction to this special issue on "Giant Power, Large Scale Electrical Development as a Social Factor" is almost the same as his message of transmission of the report of the Giant Power Survey Board. Several essays in the volume touch on the

theme of drudgery, and the idea that Giant Power will free women from it. See esp. Mary Pattison, "The Abolition of Household Slavery," 124–27.

32. Gifford Pinchot, quoted in Christie, *Morris Llewellyn Cooke*, 73.

33. Ibid., 243. See also Pinchot, "Introduction," viii.

34. Giant Power Survey Board, *Report*, 3–4.

35. Pinchot, "Introduction," ix.

36. Cooke similarly argued that what was needed was not public ownership but the provision of public benefit. See Christie, *Morris Llewellyn Cooke*, 57. Christie argues that Cooke had seen enough of government, and how easily it was corrupted, to be skeptical of any idea for government takeover of electricity. Yet, Christie also notes that not all members of the original advisory committee agreed on this point: some wanted public ownership, others abhorred the idea. Giant Power was a compromise. See Christie, *Morris Llewellyn Cooke*, 74–75.

37. Christie, *Morris Llewellyn Cooke*.

38. Ibid., 46.

39. Ibid., 1. Christie also says Cooke was influenced by Walter Lippman's 1914 book *Drift and Mastery: An Attempt to Diagnose the Current Unrest* (Madison: University of Wisconsin Press), a book that advocates scientific planning while rejecting grand theories. This was written before Lippman's turn to the right and rejection of both scientific and economic planning.

40. Ibid., 23, 49–50.

41. Ibid., 11.

42. Ibid., 11, 23–37.

43. Ibid., 33, 79. Underscoring this point, when Cooke and Pinchot proposed Giant Power, many engineering clubs invited opponents of the plan to speak, but not supporters.

44. Ibid., 33.

45. Ibid., 47.

46. Morris Llewellyn Cooke, "Forward," *Annals of the American Academy of Political and Social Science* 118 (1925): v.

47. Pinchot, "Introduction," xi.

48. On the accusation that Pinchot was communistic, see Christie, *Morris Llewellyn Cooke*, 79. On Cooke's views, particularly the idea that he took "capitalism as a given," see Christie, *Morris Llewellyn Cooke*, 239.

49. Chap. 1 of the *Annals* special issue on "Giant Power, Large Scale Electrical Development as a Social Factor" is a discussion of electricity in the United Kingdom which argues that the problem there is not the lack of municipal power, but the lack of engineers' involvement in the UK government's electricity plan. Heber Blankenhorn, "Power Development in Great Britain," *Annals of the American Academy of Political and Social Science* 118 (1925): 1–9.

50. Christie, *Morris Llewellyn Cooke*, 71.

51. Ibid., 76.

52. Pinchot, "Message of Transmittal," vii.

53. Ibid., viii.

54. Ibid., v.

55. Ibid., viii; Giant Power Survey Board, *Report*, i.

56. An interesting detail of the Canadian scheme was that famers who lived along the roads where lines were built be required to "assist in the construction . . . at a suitable rate of wage." Giant Power Survey Board, *Report*, 135.

57. Kline, *Consumers*, 132. See also Keith Fleming, *Power at Cost: Ontario Hydro and Rural Electrification, 1911–1958* (Montreal: McGill–Queens University Press, 1992). For a very useful, contemporary assessment, see Frederick A. Gaby, "Electrical Development in the Dominion of Canada," *Annals of the American Academy of Political and Social Science* 118 (1925): 21–29.

58. Ernest Gruening, *The Public Pays: A Study of Power Propaganda* (New York: Vanguard Press, 1931); Nye, *Electrifying America*.

59. Gruening, *The Public Pays*, xv and 28–29.

60. Gruening, *The Public Pays*; Nye, *Electrifying America*; Hughes, *Networks of Power*; and Judson King, *The Challenge of the Power Investigation to American Educators: Address to the American Political Science Association Convention* (National Popular Government League, 1929). On the founding of NELA, see "General Historical Review of the National Electric Light Association," in *The Electrical World* XIX, no 9 (New York: The W. J. Johnston Company, 1892), 133.

61. Herbert Hoover, quoted in Christie, *Morris Llewellyn Cooke*, 61.

62. Jill Lepore, *These Truths: A History of the United States* (New York: W. W. Norton, 2018).

63. Herbert Hoover, "Muscle Shoals Veto Message," Congressional Record 74, no. 7, 1931, http://college.cengage.com/history/ayers_primary_sources/vetoesmuscle_shoalsbill_1931.htm;.

64. Kline says two other presidents also vetoed bills that "would have created an Ontario-like yardstick" for private utilities in the United States, but he is not specific about what those bills were. Kline, *Consumers*, 133.

65. Hughes, *Networks of Power*; Gruening, *The Public Pays*.

66. Gruening, *The Public Pays*, 28.

67. Ibid., xi.

68. Hausman and Neufeld, "How Politics"; see also Kline, *Consumers*, 133.

69. Hausman and Neufeld, "How Politics," 74.

70. Nye, *Electrifying America*, 340.

71. Kline, *Consumers*, 133 (underhanded) and 139 (unethical).

72. King, *Challenge*, 5.

73. Ibid. King was also a friend and associate of Morris Llewellyn Cooke. See Christie, *Morris Llewellyn Cooke*, 59.

74. King, *Challenge*, 3.

75. Ibid.

76. Ibid.

77. Ibid., 10.

78. Ibid., 5.

79. Gruening, *The Public Pays*, xiii.

80. Ibid., 211. See also King, *Challenge*. Gruening was the governor of the Alaska Territory from 1939 until 1953 and a United States senator from Alaska from 1959 (after Alaska became a state) until 1969.

81. Gruening, *The Public Pays*, 180.

82. Nye, *Electrifying America*, 340.

83. CPI Inflation Calculator, https://www.in2013dollars.com/us/inflation/1945?amount=1000000.

84. Gruening, *The Public Pays*, 181.

85. Ibid., 181.

86. Ibid., 174.

87. Ibid., 19.

88. Ibid., xiii. NELA also used film; see Paul Monticone, "'Useful Cinema,' of What Use? Assessing the Role of Motion Pictures in the Largest Public Relations Campaign of the 1920s," *Cinema Journal* 54, no. 4 (2015): 43, http://www.jstor.org/stable/43653129.

89. Ibid., 237.

90. Fleming, *Power*, 104. See also Gruening, *The Public Pays*, xxiii.

91. Gruening, *The Public Pays*; Robert F. Hirsch, *Powering American Farms: The Overlooked Origins of Rural Electrification* (Baltimore: Johns Hopkins University Press, 2022). See also E. A. Stewart, Red Wing Project on Utilization of Electricity in Agriculture (1928), https://agris.fao.org/agris-search/search.do?recordID=US201300356783.

92. Gruening, *The Public Pays*, 72; also Fleming, *Power*, 104–5.

93. Gruening, 72–73; also Fleming, 105–6.

94. Gruening, 74–75.

95. Ibid, 198.

96. Fleming, *Power*, 105. Fleming argues that Stewart's report was not as biased as the Ontario Hydro-Electric Power Commission claimed, but it was misleading in one central respect. Rather than compare the cost of Ontario hydroelectric power to a private utility serving rural customers in a comparable setting, Stewart compared it to an "ideal performance rating, and then demonstrated how far short of that ideal the Commission fell." (106) Stewart also claimed that the true cost was underestimated by opponents of Ontario Hydro-Electric Power because of costs that fell on Canadian taxpayers. As far as we can determine, this argument was unsupported, because Ontario Hydro-Electric Power was financed by bonds and the commission supplied power to municipalities at cost, which included the cost of debt finance. See Gaby, "Electrical Development," 28, and discussion in Christie, *Morris Llewellyn Cooke*, 58.

97. Gruening, *The Public Pays*, 46, 70.

98. Ibid., 67.

99. Ibid., 68.

100. Ibid., xxv and 65.

101. Kline, *Consumers*, 136–37, notes that other industry groups, such as the Committee on the Relation of Electricity to Agriculture (an industry confederation that, ironically, included NELA), took the opposite view: that if farmers could be persuaded to use large amounts of electricity, this could create enough demand to make rural regions financially attractive to the utilities. Among other things, they persuaded some utilities to hire home economists to help expand the domestic market. A large part of this work was to promote the use of electrical appliances in the home, on the grounds of their promised labor-saving effects. One professor who worked with CREA, Eloise Davison, later became the chief home economist for NELA. See also Cowan, *More Work for Mother*.

102. Gruening, *The Public Pays*, 65.

103. Ibid., 83.

104. Ibid., 84.

105. Ibid., 87–88.

106. Ibid., 85.

107. Ibid., 90.

108. Ibid., 90–91.

109. Ibid., 91.

110. Ibid., 89.

111. Ibid., 92.

112. "Public Utilities Propaganda in the Schools, June 28, 1928," *Editorial Research Reports 1928*, vol. II, https://library.cqpress.com/cqresearcher/document.php?id=cqresrre1928062800.

113. Gruening, *The Public Pays*, 87.

114. "Public Utilities Propaganda."

115. Gruening, *The Public Pays*, 83–84; "Public Utilities Propaganda."

116. Ibid., 102; "Public Utilities Propaganda."

117. Ibid., 105; "Public Utilities Propaganda."

118. Gruening, *The Public Pays*, 93.

119. Ibid., 94–95.

120. Ibid., 105.

121. "Public Utilities Propaganda."

122. Gruening, *The Public Pays*, 107.

123. Ibid., 106.

124. "Public Utilities Propaganda."

125. Ibid.

126. Ibid.

127. Ibid., 26–27. Gruening, *The Public Pays*, 117.

128. "Letter from the Chairman of the Federal Trade Commission in Response to Senate Resolutions Nos. 83 and 112, Exhibit 1432 to 2575," 70th Congress, 1st session (Washington, D.C.: U.S. Government Printing Office, 1930), 797.

129. NELA, "Proceedings of the 49th Convention," 1926, 310, folder 12, box 15, Clyde Orval Ruggles Papers, HBS Archives, Baker Library Historical Collections, Harvard Business School. The speaker here is the chairman of the Committee on Cooperation with Educational Institutions. He was giving remarks to the 1926 NELA convention.

130. Quoted in "Public Utilities Propaganda."

131. Gruening, *The Public Pays*, 64.

132. Ibid., 145.

133. Ibid., 223–24.

134. Ibid., 69; "Public Utilities Propaganda."

135. Groening, *The Public Pays*, 63.

136. Wendy L. Wall, *Inventing the "American Way": The Politics of Consensus from the New Deal to the Civil Rights Movement* (Oxford: Oxford University Press, 2008); see also Christie, *Morris Llewellyn Cooke*, 53.

137. "Letter from the Chairman of the Federal Trade Commission," 380.

138. Gruening, *The Public Pays*, 40.

139. "Letter from the Chairman . . . Exhibits 1435 to 2575," 379.

140. Ibid., 53.

141. Ibid., 71–72.

142. Naomi Oreskes, "Jeffrey Epstein's Harvard Connections Show How Money Can Distort Research," *Scientific American*, September 1, 2020, https//www.scientificamerican.com/article/jeffrey-epsteins-harvard-connections-show-how-money-can-distort-research/.

143. Gruening, *The Public Pays*, 81.

144. King, *Challenge*, 69.

145. "Notes from Speech to the Association of Electragists," May 29, 1928, pg. 2, folder 24, carton 1, Philip Cabot Papers, HBS Archives, Baker Library Historical Collections, Harvard Business School.

146. "FTC Report," pg. 625, Harvard Business School, "National Electric Light Association Education Survey, 1927," folder 12, box 15, Clyde Orval Ruggles Papers, HBS Archives, Baker Library Historical Collections, Harvard Business School. Ruggles seems to have copied pages (622–38) of the FTC report relating to Harvard and placed them in his personal papers, which are now organized within this folder. National Electric Light Association, *National Electric Light Association Bulletin* VIII (New York: National Electric Light Association, 1921). On the salary question, see National Electric Light Association, *Nation Electric Light Association Bulletin* XII (New York: National Electric Light Association, 1925), 716–17: "In October, 1925, it was reported that this work [HBS research funded by NELA] was progressing satisfactorily. The staff [Cabot and his assistant] and two hundred students had collected, and were studying

two hundred cases, the intention being to examine a thousand cases and select about two hundred of them to be used in the regular course [Cabot's HBS course]."

147. "FTC Report."

148. Quoted in Ibid., 625.

149. Cabot, Public Utilities Fortnightly, 1933, "The Dangers of Rigid Rate Fixation, or A Critical Period" 8/17/33 written 7/5/33, on p. 9, folder 46, carton 1, Philip Cabot Papers, HBS Archives, Baker Library Historical Collections, Harvard Business School. See also "Prof. Philip Cabot of Harvard Dead," *New York Times*, December 26, 1941, https://timesmachine .nytimes.com/timesmachine/1941/12/26/109599957.pdf.

150. He also argued for state rather than federal regulation, using the railroads as his model, a preposterous position given the well-known failures of state-based railroad regulation. See Philip Cabot, "The Public Utilities or Little Red Riding Hood," *New York Sun*, January 4, 1936, folder 46, carton 1, Philip Cabot Papers, HBS Archives, Baker Library Historical Collections, Harvard Business School.

151. Ibid.

152. "Public Utilities Propaganda."

153. King, *Challenge,* 47–48.

154. News clipping, *Washington Herald*, May 10, 1928, folder 27, box 1, Clyde Orval Ruggles Papers, HBS Archives, Baker Library Historical Collections, Harvard Business School.

155. Ibid.

156. "Data from the Replies of Educators Concerning the Cooperation of the Utility Industry and Educational Institutions," folder 12, box 15, Clyde Orval Ruggles Papers, HBS Archives, Baker Library Historical Collections, Harvard Business School.

157. Ruggles, "Data from the Replies of Educators," 3.

158. The NEA reported that, in October 1927, a national survey of public utility teaching was undertaken under the direction of Dean Ruggles, who was granted a salary of fifteen thousand dollars a year while engaged on this work. If this figure is correct, it would be equivalent to being paid about a quarter of a million dollars today, according to https://www .in2013dollars.com/us/inflation/1929?amount=15000.

159. Clyde Ruggles to George Rightmire, May 14, 1928, folder 13, box 15, Clyde Orval Ruggles Papers, HBS Archives, Baker Library Historical Collections, Harvard Business School.

160. "Public Utilities Propaganda."

161. Ibid.

162. United States. Federal Trade Commission. *Reprint of official report of proceedings before the Federal Trade Commission in the matter of investigation of public utility corporations under Senate resolution number 82 . . . Public hearings at Federal Trade Commission building, 2004 D Street, Washington, D.C.* (New York [state]: National Electric Light Association, 1928).

163. *Boston Post*, May 12, 1928, and *New York American*, May 1, 1928. The *Boston Post* noted that within the FTC investigation "a sharp distinction has been drawn between financial contributions to the colleges . . . and the textbook 'surveys' and public school government ownership 'catechisms' which have also played a part in the educational efforts of the power group." Clipping, Clyde Orval Ruggles Papers, HBS Archives, Baker Library Historical Collections, Harvard Business School.

164. Gruening, *The Public Pays*, 43, italics in original.

165. *Harvard Business School Alumni Bulletin* VI, July 1929–November 1930, "Public Utilities: A Survey of the [NELA] Committee on Cooperation with Educational Institutions of the National Electric Light Association." Business folder 10, carton 7, Philip Cabot Papers, HBS Archives, Baker Library Historical Collections, Harvard Business School. The committee in

question is NELA's Committee on Co-operation with Educational Institutions. The quotations are on pages 13 and 16, respectively.

166. Ibid.

167. Nye, *Electrifying America*, 340.

168. Christie, *Morris Llewellyn Cooke*, 86.

169. J. V. Deyo, "Papers of Morris L. Cooke, 1914–1953, Description of Material," courtesy of the Franklin D. Roosevelt Library, Hyde Park, NY, 12538, accessed July 23, 2021, https://www.fdrlibrary.org/documents/356632/390886/findingaid_cooke.pdf/10837c86-580e-4ef8-bbe8-055ab9b99fbe.

170. Hughes, *Networks of Power*, 312.

171. Climate Investigations Center, "Edison Electric Institute," accessed July 23, 2021, https://climateinvestigations.org/trade-association-pr-spending/edison-electric-institute/; Daniel Tait, "Tom Fanning Floats Misleading Updated Greenhouse Gas Goal," Energy Policy Institute, April 16, 2020, https://www.energyandpolicy.org/tom-fanning-floats-misleading-updated-greenhouse-gas-goal-in-podcast-interview/.

172. American Public Power Association, "Stats and Facts," accessed July 31, 2021, https://www.publicpower.org/public-power/stats-and-facts.

173. Troy Segal, "Enron Scandal: The Fall of a Wall Street Darling," Investopedia, January 19, 2021, https://www.investopedia.com/updates/enron-scandal-summary/; Peter Bondarenko, s.v. "Enron scandal," *Encyclopaedia Britannica*, October 7, 2019, https://www.britannica.com/event/Enron-scandal.

174. Matt Stevens and Matthew Haag, "Jeffrey Skilling, Former Enron Chief, Released After 12 Years in Prison," *New York Times*, February 22, 2019, https://www.nytimes.com/2019/02/22/business/enron-ceo-skilling-scandal.html.

175. Early reports grossly understated the deaths; see Natalie Neysa Alund, "How Did at Least 86 People Die in the Austin Area During Texas Freeze? It Remains a Mystery," *Austin American-Statesman*, February 26, 2021, https://www.statesman.com/story/news/2021/02/25/texas-power-outage-death-toll-medical-examiner-processing-86-cases/6808150002/; and Umair Irfan, "Why Every State is Vulnerable to a Texas-Style Power Crisis," *Vox* March 11, 2021, https://www.vox.com/22308149/texas-blackout-power-outage-winter-uri-grid-ercot. Later estimates were an order of magnitude higher: "Data-driven Report Says 700 Died in Texas' February Power Outages, Not the 151 Reported by the State," *San Antonio Current*, May 27, 2021, https://www.sacurrent.com/the-daily/archives/2021/05/27/data-driven-report-says-700-died-in-texas-february-power-outages-not-the-151-reported-by-the-state. On the monetary costs, see Garret Golding, Anil Kumar, and Karel Mertens, "Cost of Texas' 2021 Deep Freeze Justifies Weatherization," Federal Reserve Bank of Dallas, April 15, 2021, https://www.dallasfed.org/research/economics/2021/0415.aspx.

176. Robert Walton, "Xcel, Boulder to Settle Lawsuit: City Agrees to Dissolve Utility," Utility Dive, May 24, 2019, https://www.utilitydive.com/news/xcel-boulder-to-settle-lawsuit-city-agrees-to-dissolve-utility/555523/.

177. In the 1930s, when the U.S. federal government took up rural electrification, it was accused of taking up planning of the entire social order (see chapter 3), an accusation that was also later made by the tobacco industry and its supporters. We explored this in Naomi Oreskes and Erik Conway, *Merchants of Doubt: How a Handful of Scientists Obscured the Truth on Issues from Tobacco Smoke to Global Warming*, pbk. ed. (New York: Bloomsbury, 2011), esp. 163–65. This argument is also made by libertarian opponents of climate action.

178. Michael A. Bernstein, *A Perilous Progress: Economists and Public Purpose in Twentieth-Century America* (Princeton, NJ: Princeton University Press, 2001). For an opposing view,

see Raj Chetty, "Yes, Economics Is a Science," *New York Times*, October 20, 2013, https://www
.nytimes.com/2013/10/21/opinion/yes-economics-is-a-science.html.

CHAPTER 3: FIGHTING THE NEW DEAL

1. Online Stock Trading Guide, "1928–1954 Stock Chart Pre Thru Post Great Depression Era,"
   accessed March 28, 2021, http://online-stock-trading-guide.com/1928-1954-stock-chart.html.
   The crash didn't happen out of the blue. The market had peaked in August and had been
   sliding downward for several weeks; many insiders noted that the stock market was unusually
   volatile and weak. But they did not predict a crash. Nor did they anticipate that it would take
   twenty-five years for the market to recover.
2. Gilder Lehrman Institute of American History, "Herbert Hoover on the Great Depression,"
   accessed March 28, 2021, https://www.gilderlehrman.org/history-resources/spotlight-primary
   -source/herbert-hoover-great-depression-and-new-deal-1931%E2%80%931933.
3. David E. Hamilton, "Herbert Hoover: Domestic Affairs," UVA Miller Center, accessed
   March 28, 2021, https://millercenter.org/president/hoover/domestic-affairs.
4. Donald Worster, *Dust Bowl: The Southern Plains in the 1930s* (New York: Oxford University
   Press, 2004); and William E. Leutenberg, *Herbert Hoover: The American President's Series:
   The 31st President, 1929–1933* (New York: Times Books, 2009), 115.
5. Leutenberg, *Hoover*, 108.
6. Ellis W. Hawley, *The Great War and the Search for a Modern Order: A History of the American
   People and Their Institutions 1917–1933*, 2nd ed. (Prospect Heights, IL: Waveland Press, 1997),
   chap. 11.
7. Terry Golway, *Frank and Al: FDR, Al Smith, and the Unlikely Alliance that Created the
   Modern Democratic Party* (New York: St. Martin's, 2018), 224–26.
8. Franklin D. Roosevelt, "Address Accepting the Presidential Nomination at the Democratic
   National Convention in Chicago," *American Presidency Project*, ed. Gerhard Peters and
   John T. Woolley, accessed March 28, 2021, https://www.presidency.ucsb.edu/node/275484.
9. Ibid. The theme of sunlight may have come from Louis Brandeis; see "Brandeis and the
   History of Transparency," Sunlight Foundation, May 26, 2009, https://sunlightfoundation
   .com/2009/05/26/brandeis-and-the-history-of-transparency/.
10. Ibid.
11. Eric Rauchway, *Winter War: Hoover, Roosevelt, and the First Clash Over the New Deal* (New
    York: Basic Books, 2018), chap. 7.
12. Federal Reserve History, "Bank Holiday of 1933," November 22, 2013, https://www
    .federalreservehistory.org/essays/bank-holiday-of-1933.
13. "Proceedings Platform of the American Industry Committee for 1928," Folder: Conventions,
    Platform of American industry 1924 [*sic*], box 137, series I, National Association of
    Manufacturers Records, accession 1411, Hagley Museum and Library, Wilmington, DE,
    19807.
14. Rauchway, *Winter War*, 232.
15. Ralph F. De Bedts, *The New Deal's SEC: The Formative Years* (New York: Columbia
    University Press, 1964).
16. On the trusts, see Thomas K. McCraw, *TVA and the Power Fight, 1933–1939* (Philadelphia:
    Lippincott, 1971), especially chap. 1.
17. Richard D. Cudahy and William D. Henderson, "From Insull to Enron: Corporate (Re)
    regulation after the rise and fall of two energy icons," *Energy Law Journal* 26, no. 1 (March
    2005): 35, https://www.repository.law.indiana.edu/facpub/308.
18. Forrest McDonald, "Samuel Insull and the Movement for State Utility Regulatory
    Commissions," *Business History Review* 32, no. 3 (Fall 1958): 241–54; and Philip J. Funigiello,

Toward a National Power Policy: The New Deal and the Electric Utility Industry, 1933–1941 (Pittsburgh: University of Pittsburgh Press, 1973), 25.

19. Franklin D. Roosevelt, Address in Portland, Oregon, September 21, 1932, in Franklin D. Roosevelt, "The Great Communicator," Master Speech Files, Series 1, file No. 518, accessed March 28, 2021, http://www.fdrlibrary.marist.edu/_resources/images/msf/msf00530.

20. McCraw, *TVA*. On Willkie, see Samuel Zipp, "When Americans Fell in Love with the Ideal of 'One World,'" *Zócalo Public Square* (blog), March 29, 2020, https://www.zocalopublic square.org/2020/03/29/true-history-wendell-willkie-one-world/ideas/essay/.

21. De Bedts, *The New Deal's SEC*, 112–43.

22. It is known today as Southern Company, and it played a major role in fighting the Obama administration's Clean Power Plan. See Union of Concerned Scientists, "Who's Fighting the Clean Power Plan and EPA Action on Climate Change?" April 12, 2016, https://www.ucsusa .org/global-warming/fight-misinformation/whos-fighting-clean-power-plan-and-epa-action -climate; and News Documents, "Pushing an Attorney General to Move Legislation—and Sue," *New York Times*, December 6, 2014, https://www.nytimes.com/interactive/2014/12 /07/us/politics/5-pushing-an-attorney-general-to-move-legislation-and-sue.html#document /p9/a191261. The company has also funded climate change denial: see Kert Davies, "Willie Soon Harvard Smithsonian Documents Reveal Southern Company Scandal," *Climate Investigations Center*, February 21, 2015, https://climateinvestigations.org/willie-soon-harvard -smithsonian-documents-reveal-southern-company-scandal/; Gabe Elsner and Matt Kasper, "Willie Soon Secret Fossil Fuel Funding Revealed for Paper Denying Man-Made Climate Change," *Energy and Policy Institute*, February 21, 2015, https://www.energyandpolicy.org /willie-soon-secret-fossil-fuel-funding-revealed-for-papers-denying-man-made-climate -change/.

23. McCraw, *TVA*, 51.

24. On business-government relations in World War I, see chapter 1 in Mark R. Wilson, *Destructive Creation: American Business and the Winning of World War II* (Philadelphia: University of Pennsylvania Press, 2016).

25. McCraw, *TVA*, 108.

26. Wendell L. Willkie, "Government and the Public Utilities," *Vital Speeches of the Day* 1, no. 10 (February 11, 1935): 297.

27. Ibid.

28. Ibid. This was also disingenuous, insofar as business leaders consistently fought regulation.

29. Wendell L. Willkie, "Sober Second Judgment," *Vital Speeches of the Day* 2, no. 7 (December 30, 1935): 201.

30. On Willkie, see Zipp, "When Americans Fell in Love with the Ideal of 'One World.'"

31. "Semantic notes related to N.I.I.C. Program," folder Program Semantics 1943, Box 846, Series III, National Association of Manufacturers Records, accession 1411, Hagley Museum and Library, Wilmington, DE 19807.

32. Indeed, the creation of open public roads and waterways was a key development in European capitalism.

33. George Wolfskill, *The Revolt of the Conservatives: A History of the American Liberty League, 1934–1940* (Boston: Houghton Mifflin, 1962), chap. 9.

34. William A. Gregory and Rennard Strickland, "Hugo Black's Congressional Investigation of Lobbying and the Public Utility Holding Company Act: A Historical View of the Power Trust, New Deal Politics, and Regulatory Propaganda," *Oklahoma Law Review* 29 (1976): 554.

35. Ibid., 559.

36. Ibid., 568. On the Farmer's Independent Council, see "Anti-New Dealers Backed Farm Group; Industrialists of Liberty League Helped Finance Independence Council. Called

Republican Ally Black Committee Holds Testimony of an Organizer Shows Political Partisanship," *New York Times*, April 15, 1936, https://www.nytimes.com/1936/04/15/archives /antinew-dealers-backed-farm-group-industrialists-of-liberty-league.html?scp=1.

37. On Cooke's role at REA, see "Morris L. Cooke, Engineer, Dies," *New York Times*, March 6, 1960, https://www.nytimes.com/1960/03/06/archives/morris-l-cooke-engineer-dies-first -administrator-of-rea.html.

38. McCraw, *TVA*, 86–87.

39. David E. Nye, *Electrifying America: Social Meanings of a New Technology, 1880–1940* (Cambridge, MA: MIT Press, 1990), 316. Such lines were called "spite lines," as in "to spite the REA."

40. Carl Kitchens and Price Fishback, "Flip the Switch: The Spatial Impact of the Rural Electrification Administration 1935–1940," *Journal of Economic History* 75, no. 4 (2015): 1161–95.

41. Bruce Edward Walker, "Tyranny Afoot: Arthur Koestler's Communist Chronicles," *Foundation for Economic Education*, September 21, 2011, https://fee.org/articles/tyranny -afoot-arthur-koestlers-communist-chronicles/.

42. Wendell L. Willkie, "Five Minutes to Midnight," *Saturday Evening Post*, June 22, 1940, 10–11, 72, 75. Also see Lawrence B. Glickman, *Free Enterprise: An American History* (New Haven: Yale University Press, 2019), 9. Unlike many Republicans of his era, Willkie was an internationalist, and after the election FDR appointed Willkie to be his personal ambassador to Britain, Middle Eastern nations, the USSR, and China. Willkie then had a brief career as a civil rights attorney. He tried again to gain the Republican party nomination in 1944 but by then he was seen (ironically) as far too liberal. He died after a series of heart attacks late that year.

43. Frederick Rudolph, "The American Liberty League, 1934–1940," *American Historical Review* 56, no. 1 (Oct. 1950): 19–33.

44. David Farber, *Everybody Ought to Be Rich: The Life and Times of John J. Raskob, Capitalist* (Oxford: Oxford University Press, 2013), 4–5. On the DuPont takeover of GM see George W. Stocking, "The Du Pont–General Motors Case and the Sherman Act," *Virginia Law Review* 44, no. 1 (January 1958): 1–40, https://www.jstor.org/stable/1070959?seq=1.

45. Encyclopaedia Britannica, s.v. "John Jakob Raskob, American financier," March 15, 2021, https://www.britannica.com/biography/John-Jakob-Raskob.

46. Wolfskill, *The Revolt of the Conservatives*, 38–39; Farber, *Everybody*, 229.

47. GM president Alfred P. Sloan didn't want GM to be seen as partisan, so when Raskob agreed to run Smith's presidential campaign, he was forced to step down from GM—highly ironic in light of Sloan's own activities. Farber, *Everybody*, 240.

48. Farber, *Everybody*, 8.

49. Pierre du Pont, quoted in Robert Frederick Burk, *The Corporate State and the Broker State: The Du Ponts and American National Politics, 1925–1940* (Cambridge, MA: Harvard University Press, 1990), 37.

50. Wolfskill, *The Revolt*, 55.

51. Burk, *Corporate State*.

52. Irénée du Pont to Pierre S. du Pont, July 10, 1934, folder American Liberty League, box 1294, The Longwood Manuscripts—group 10, series A, file 771, Papers of P. S. du Pont, Hagley Museum and Library, Wilmington, DE, 19807.

53. "Certificate of the Formation of the Union Asserting the Integrity of Persons and Property," folder American Liberty League, box 1294, The Longwood Manuscripts—group 10, series A, file 771, Papers of P. S. du Pont, Hagley Museum and Library, Wilmington, DE, 19807.

54. Ibid.

55. S. M. DeBrul to Donaldson Brown, June 19, 1934, folder July 1934, file 61, John J. Raskob Papers, accession 0473, Hagley Museum and Library, Wilmington, DE 19807. Members of the League repeatedly invoked "the first ten amendments"—rather than referring to "Bill of Rights"—to underscore the idea that they did not agree with subsequent amendments.
56. See Burk, *Corporate State*, 289.
57. Pierre du Pont, quoted in Burk, *Corporate State*, 287.
58. Burk, *Corporate State*, 66.
59. The Foundation for Economic Education would attack the speech as a "perversion," because it omitted "freedom from the State." James Bovard, "The 'Four Freedoms' Speech: FDR's Worst Perversion of Freedom," *Foundation for Economic Education*, January 27, 2019, https://fee.org/articles/the-four-freedoms-speech-fdr-s-worst-perversion-of-freedom/.
60. C. M. Chester, Pauline Morton Sabin, Alfred E. Smith, and Jouett Shouse, "Report to the Executive Committee of the American Liberty League," December 20, 1934, folder Organization and Charter 1934, file 671, John J. Raskob Papers, accession 0473, Hagley Museum and Library, Wilmington, DE 19807.
61. Edward L. Bernays to C. M. Chester, December 28, 1934, folder December 1934, file 671, John J. Raskob Papers, accession 0473, Hagley Museum and Library, Wilmington, DE 19807.
62. Mark Crispin Miller, introduction to *Propaganda*, by Edward L. Bernays (New York: IG Publishing, 2009), 27.
63. Allan M. Brandt, *The Cigarette Century* (New York: Basic Books, 2007), 85.
64. "Hits AAA Regimentation: Liberty League Asserts Act Reduces Farmers to Peasants," *New York Times*, December 2, 1935, https://www.nytimes.com/1935/12/02/archives/hits-aaa-regimentation-liberty-league-asserts-act-reduces-farmers.html.
65. The terminology here can be confusing. The National Industrial Recovery Act (NIRA) created the National Recovery Administration (NRA), not to be confused with the National Rifle Association.
66. Hebert Hoover, *The Challenge to Liberty* (New York: Charles Scribner's Sons, 1934), 197–204.
67. Ibid.
68. Edward L. Bernays, *Propaganda* (New York: IG Publishing, 2009), 52.
69. Ibid.
70. One leader in advocating central planning in the context of business operations was George Eastman, who went so far as to plan his own death. Eastman Museum, "About George Eastman," accessed April 4, 2021, https://www.eastman.org/about-george-eastman.
71. See, for example, "Liberty League Warns of Peril in Dictatorship: Fears Present Trend Will Thwart Constitution," *Chicago Daily Tribune*, December 16, 1935.
72. Wolfskill, *The Revolt*, 109.
73. Ibid., 108.
74. Robert H. Jackson, *That Man: An Insider's Portrait of Franklin D. Roosevelt* (New York: Oxford University Press, 2004.)
75. S. M. DeBrul to Donaldson Brown, June 19, 1934, folder July 1934, file 61, John J. Raskob Papers, accession 0473, Hagley Museum and Library, Wilmington, DE 19807, italics added.
76. Advocates of the gold standard see it as a way of limiting government spending, insofar as it prevents governments from printing money unless backed by gold. Some commentators have noted that a return to the gold standard now would be physically impossible, as there simply is not enough gold in the world to match all the money that has been printed, but this does not stop some extreme conservatives from advocating it.
77. Wolfskill, *The Revolt*, 141.
78. "'Nonpartisan' Fight on Roosevelt Is Opened by the Liberty League," *New York Times*, July 1, 1936, 17, https://timesmachine.nytimes.com/timesmachine/1936/07/01/issue.html.

79. Michael Hiltzik, "They Tried to Call FDR and the New Deal 'Socialist' Too. Here's How He Responded," *Los Angeles Times*, February 13, 2019, https://www.latimes.com/business/hiltzik/la-fi-hiltzik-socialism-20190213-story.html.

80. Ibid.

81. James MacGregor Burns, *Roosevelt: The Soldier of Freedom (1940–1945)* (New York: Open Road Media, 2012); and William E. Leuchtenburg, *Franklin D. Roosevelt and the New Deal: 1932–1940* (New York: Harper Perennial, 2009), chap. 5.

82. Wolfskill, *The Revolt*, chap. 9, covers this in detail.

CHAPTER 4: THE TRIPOD OF FREEDOM

1. Kim Phillips-Fein, *Invisible Hands: The Businessmen's Crusade Against the New Deal* (New York: W. W. Norton, 2010), 13; Richard S. Tedlow, "The National Association of Manufacturers and Public Relations During the New Deal," *Business History Review* 50, no. 1 (1976): 29, https://doi.org/10.2307/3113573; Jennifer A. Delton, *The Industrialists: How the National Association of Manufacturers Shaped American Capitalism* (Princeton, NJ: Princeton University Press, 2020), 108.

2. Tedlow, "The National Association of Manufacturers," 25–45.

3. Ibid., 18. Tedlow describes the organization as having a "single-minded determination to stamp out unionization."

4. Ibid.

5. Robert L. Lund, quoted in Tedlow, "The National Association of Manufacturers," 31.

6. "A Frank, Straight Answer to an Honest Question," folder Publications, box 115, series I, National Association of Manufacturers Records, accession 1411, Hagley Museum and Library, Wilmington, DE 19807. This title seems to presage the tobacco industry's 1954 advertisement "A Frank Statement to Cigarette Smokers." See Allan M. Brandt, *The Cigarette Century* (New York: Basic Books, 2007), 170–1.

7. They called it "public relations," but we follow here the usage of the Hagley Library, where the NAM records are kept. According to the *New Oxford American Dictionary*, propaganda is "information, especially of a biased or misleading nature, used to promote or publicize a particular political cause or point of view." The NAM campaign was clearly that. See Hagley Library, "The National Association of Manufacturers and Visual Propaganda," September 22, 2014, https://www.hagley.org/librarynews/research-national-association-manufacturers-and-visual-propaganda.

8. Wendy L. Wall, *Inventing the "American Way": The Politics of Consensus from the New Deal to the Civil Rights Movement* (Oxford: Oxford University Press, 2008), 49.

9. "Survey: What the Factory worker thinks about Free Enterprise (A Survey)," Folder: What the Factory Worker thinks about free enterprise, box 847, series III, National Association of Manufacturers Records, accession 1411, Hagley Museum and Library, Wilmington, DE 19807.

10. Lawrence B. Glickman, *Free Enterprise: An American History* (New Haven, CT: Yale University Press, 2019), 19.

11. "Terminology concerning electric power and light," folder Semantics, box 847, Series III NIIC Records, National Association of Manufacturers Records, accession 1411, Hagley Museum and Library, Wilmington, DE 19807. This document also recommended replacing "public power" with "political power" and "public ownership" with "political management."

12. American industrialists had long fought demands for government-led social welfare reform. Some of the more enlightened had enacted employer-provided benefits, although at the same time still insisting that the nation's prosperity depended on the freedom of businessmen to run their businesses as they judged best. For a general discussion, see Jennifer Klein, *For All These*

Rights: Business, Labor, and the Shaping of America's Public-Private Welfare State (Princeton, NJ: Princeton University Press, 2006),

13. Richard S. Tedlow, "The National Association of Manufacturers and Public Relations During the New Deal," 27–28, 32. Historian Jennifer A. Delton also sees NAM as a largely modernizing force. See Jennifer Delton, *The Industrialists: How the National Association of Manufacturers Shaped American Capitalism* (Princeton, NJ: Princeton University Press, 2020).

14. Colleen Ann Moore, "The National Association of Manufacturers: The Voice of Industry and the Free Enterprise Campaign in the Schools, 1929–1949" (PhD diss., University of Akron, 1985), 272.

15. Folder Community Program, box 111, series I, National Association of Manufacturers Records, accession 1411, Hagley Museum and Library, Wilmington, DE 19807.

16. Moore, "The National Association of Manufacturers," 298–300.

17. NIIC statement in undated memo, p. 2., Folder Key Documents, 1942–1945, box 844, National Association of Manufacturers Records, accession 1411, Hagley Museum and Library, Wilmington, DE 19807.

18. "The National Association of Manufacturers and Visual Propaganda," Hagley, June 16, 2016, https://www.hagley.org/librarynews/research-national-association-manufacturers-and -visual-propaganda.

19. *Our Material Progress*, "You and Industry Booklet" series, 4/7/1943, spinning wheel quotation on p. 14, folder Our Material Progress, box 137, series I, National Association of Manufacturers Records, accession 1411, Hagley Museum and Library, Wilmington, DE 19807.

20. Speech to the Chautauqua Institution, July 29, 1949, folder A businessman looks at the national economy, box 115, National Association of Manufacturers Records, accession 1411, Hagley Museum and Library, Wilmington, DE 19807.

21. This theme would be reiterated in 1961, in a brochure with the title "Perils of Centralized Government," folder Publications, box 137, National Association of Manufacturers Records, accession 1411, Hagley Museum and Library, Wilmington, DE 19807.

22. Speech to the Chautauqua Institution, July 29, 1949, folder: A businessman looks at the national economy, box 115, National Association of Manufacturers Records, accession 1411, Hagley Museum and Library, Wilmington, DE 19807.

23. Civil Action No 381-48, *National Association of Manufacturers and Kenneth R Miller v Howard J McGrath*, Plaintiffs Trial brief, Desk stamp: 20 November 1931, p. 49, folder Lobbying, box 79, National Association of Manufacturers Records, accession 1411, Hagley Museum and Library, Wilmington, DE 19807. Note that this lawsuit recounts activities from the late 1930s and 1940s.

24. Folder Public Relations Posters, box 111, series I, National Association of Manufacturers Records, accession 1411, Hagley Museum and Library, Wilmington, DE 19807, original emphasis.

25. Folder Public Relations: Service for Plant Publications, July 1935–December 1940, box 111, series I, National Association of Manufacturers Records, accession 1411, Hagley Museum and Library, Wilmington, DE 19807.

26. Folder Making America Strong Clip Sheets, box 111, series I, National Association of Manufacturers Records, accession 1411, Hagley Museum and Library, Wilmington, DE 19807.

27. "Pamphlet explaining NAM 1946 public relations program (NIIC)," folder Publications: Plain Speaking . . . , box 137, series I, National Association of Manufacturers Records, accession 1411, Hagley Museum and Library, Wilmington, DE 19807. The 1946 budget was $3 million.

28. Tedlow, "The National Association of Manufacturers," 33.

29. Delton, *The Industrialists*, 108.

30. U.S. Congress, Senate, Committee on Education and Labor, *Violations of Free Speech and Rights of Labor: Report of the Committee on Education and Labor Pursuant to S. Res 266: Labor Policies of Employers' Associations Part III: The National Association of Manufacturers*, 76th Congress, 1st Session, August 14, 1939 (Washington, D.C.: U.S. Government Printing Office, 1939), 160–63.

31. Burton St. John III, "A View That's Fit to Print: The National Association of Manufacturers' Free Enterprise Rhetoric as Integration Propaganda in *The New York Times*, 1937–1939," *Journalism Studies* 11, no. 3 (June 1, 2010): 380.

32. U.S. Congress, Senate, Committee on Education and Labor, *Labor Policies of Employers' Associations Part III: The National Association of Manufacturers*, 162.

33. "Opinions Backed by Facts on Wasteful Public Spending," folder Opinions Backed by Facts 1941, box 137, series I, National Association of Manufacturers Records, accession 1411, Hagley Museum and Library, Wilmington, DE 19807.

34. St. John, "A View," 378.

35. St. John, "A View," 381. St. John did not examine *Times* coverage before 1937, but the NAM platforms are available in the NAM archives. The 1934 platform is particularly interesting: it supported Social Security so long as it did not become "extravagant" but opposed any form of "compulsory unemployment insurance or reserves." It also called on states to pass laws to prohibit blacklisting, boycotts, sympathetic strikes, general strikes, and lockouts. See "Platform and Resolutions, 1934," folder Conventions: Platform of American Industry, box 137, series I, National Association of Manufacturers Records, accession 1411, Hagley Museum and Library, Wilmington, DE 19807.

36. St. John, "A View," 388.

37. Louis Stark, "Chester Predicts Big Business Rise," *New York Times*, January 21, 1938, 1–2. St. John concludes that while journalists had been savvy about and wary of propaganda after World War II, NAM's success effectively reversed that trend: "The information, data and commentary provided by propagandists increasingly became views that were fit to print as news—a dynamic that persists to this day. Accordingly, since the days of NAM's campaign, American society has become steeped in integration propaganda, often embedded within news stories." St. John, "A View," 378.

38. Quoted in Richard W. Gable, "A Political Analysis of an Employers' Association: the National Association of Manufacturers" (PhD diss., University of Chicago, 1950), 333.

39. Ibid., 334. See also U.S. Congress, Senate, Committee on Education and Labor, *Labor Policies of Employers' Associations Part III: The National Association of Manufacturers*, 163. St. John offers a different estimate: "322 papers daily with a circulation of more than 5 million" (380). Either way, millions of Americans saw the Uncle Abner cartoons without knowing they were produced by NAM.

40. U.S. Congress, Senate, Committee on Education and Labor, *Violations of Free Speech and Rights of Labor: Hearings Before a Subcommittee of the Committee on Education and Labor, United States Senate, 75th Congress, 2nd Session, Part 16 "Citizens" Committees*, November 19, 1937 (Washington, D.C.: U.S. Government Printing Office, 1938), 7464.

41. Richard L. Neuberger, "Hooverism in the Funnies," *New Republic*, July 11, 1934, 234–35.

42. Ibid., 234.

43. U.S. Congress, Senate, Committee on Education and Labor, *Part 16 'Citizens' Committees*, 7477.

44. Ibid., 7466.

45. Herman Schnurer, "Notes on the Comic Strip," *Antioch Review* (Summer 1941): 142–55.

46. Schnurer, "Notes on the Comic Strip," 154.

47. Walter R. Courtenay, "The Road Ahead," published in the *Presbyterian Tower*, a newsletter of the Presbyterian Church, delivered on Lincoln's birthday, February 12, 1949, folder Socialism ½ (nd), box 6, series I, N National Association of Manufacturers Records, accession 1411, Hagley Museum and Library, Wilmington, DE 19807. In congressional hearings, La Follette pressed NAM on the impact of their activities; the NAM representative claimed not to have data to answer that point. Perhaps they assumed that these materials—if designed right—must have an impact. Or perhaps they lied.

48. John T. Flynn, *The Road Ahead: America's Creeping Revolution*, Special Ed Dist by Committee (New York: Devin-Adair Company, 1949). The "behind the mask" quotation appears on p. 67. See also pp. 9, 15, 29, 33 and 67 for key elements of the argument.

49. Thomas W. Evans, *The Education of Ronald Reagan: The General Electric Years and the Untold Story of His Conversion to Conservatism* (New York: Columbia University Press, 2006), 54.

50. Evans, *The Education of Ronald Reagan*, 98.

51. Ibid., 99.

52. Courtenay, "The Road Ahead."

53. Ibid.

54. Folder Robey Textbook Survey 1939–1944, box 847, National Association of Manufacturers Records, accession 1411, Hagley Museum and Library, Wilmington, DE 19807.

55. Letter, June 20, 1940, includes abstracts of objectionable paragraphs from textbooks, folder Robey Textbook Survey 1939–1944, box 847, National Association of Manufacturers Records, accession 1411, Hagley Museum and Library, Wilmington, DE 19807.

56. Paul F. Gemmill and Ralph Hamilton Blodgett, *Economics: Principles and Problems* (New York: Harper & Brothers, 1937).

57. Letter, "Mobilization for Understanding Private Enterprise," May 27, 1940, folder Robey Textbook Survey 1939–1944, box 847, National Association of Manufacturers Records, accession 1411, Hagley Museum and Library, Wilmington, DE 19807.

58. Memo, July 25, 1940, folder Robey Textbook Survey 1939–1944, box 847, National Association of Manufacturers Records, accession 1411, Hagley Museum and Library, Wilmington, DE 19807.

59. S. Alexander Rippa, "The Textbook Controversy and the Free Enterprise Campaign, 1940–1941," *History of Education Journal* IX, no. 3 (1958): 49–58.

60. Ibid., 52.

61. Ibid., 58.

62. Folder Textbook, 1944–1945, box 847, National Association of Manufacturers Records, accession 1411, Hagley Museum and Library, Wilmington, DE 19807; see also folder How We Live, On Plans for a Textbook, box 844, series III NIIC, National Association of Manufacturers Records, accession 1411, Hagley Museum and Library, Wilmington, DE 19807.

63. The name was later changed to the National Small Business Association. "National Small Business Association Backgrounder," accessed April 26, 2021, https://nsba.biz/docs/nsba_backgrounder.pdf.

64. "This Business of Name Calling," *Spectrum*, February 13, 1947, LXI, No. 16, 2, https://library.ndsu.edu/ir/bitstream/handle/10365/19766/nds-1947-02-13-0.pdf.

65. Elizabeth Fones-Wolf, "Creating a Favorable Business Climate: Corporations and Radio Broadcasting, 1934 to 1954," *Business History Review* 73, no. 2 (1999): 223. See also John Dunning, *On the Air: The Encyclopedia of Old-Time Radio* (New York: Oxford University Press, 998), 30–31.

66. Fones-Wolf, "Creating a Favorable Business Climate," 230.

67. Phillips-Fein, *Invisible Hands*, 13–15.

68. Folder Public Relations Community Program Services. Box 111, series I, National Association of Manufacturers Records, accession 1411, Hagley Museum and Library, Wilmington, DE 19807.

69. Fones-Wolf, "Creating a Favorable Business Climate," 231. William L. Bird Jr., *"Better Living": Advertising, Media, and the New Vocabulary of Business Leadership, 1935–1955* (Evanston, IL: Northwestern University Press, 1999), 54.

70. Memo, March 23, 1943, folder NIIC objectives 1943–45 (1/2), box 845, series III, National Association of Manufacturers Records, accession 1411, Hagley Museum and Library, Wilmington, DE 19807.

71. James P. Selvage, the NAM's vice president for public relations, attempted to pitch the series to NBC without success. See Bird, *"Better Living,"* 58–9.

72. J. Hillis Miller, introduction to *The Swiss Family Robinson*, by Johann D. Wyss, trans. William Goodwin (New York: Signet, 2004).

73. Ibid., xvi–xvi.

74. For the discussion of *The American Family Robinson* that follows, we have used MP3 recordings of radio broadcasts preserved on The Old Time Radio Catalog, available online at www.otrcat.com/p/american-family-robinson. This source has preserved many episodes, but without episode titles or airtime dates; therefore we list our references by episode number. We quote from the following episodes in order of reference: episode 68, episode 3, episode 2, episode 40, episode 52, episode 8, episode 71, episode 6, episode 46, episode 53, episode 56, episode 51, episode 43, episode 2, episode 39, episode 52, and episode 55.

75. Thomas Hughes, *Networks of Power: Electrification in Western Society, 1880–1930* (Baltimore: Johns Hopkins University Press, 1993); see discussion in chapter 2.

76. Old Time Radio Catalog (see n74).

77. *Frontiers of the Future (A Screen Editorial with Lowell Thomas)*, produced by Audio Productions, Inc. in collaboration with the National Industrial Council, 1937, https://www.youtube.com/watch?v=eofZ5w82Efo.

78. Like the 1930s and '40s radio programs and films, *Industry on Parade* was distributed free of charge to local stations, to schools, and to community groups. It ran for the entire decade 1950–60 and aired over five hundred episodes. In 1954 it won a Peabody Award for public service, prompting objections from the American Federation of Labor and Congress of Industrial Organizations (AFL-CIO), who briefly produced a program of their own.

79. Burton St. John III and Robert Arnett, "The National Association of Manufacturers' Community Relations Short Film *Your Town*: Parable, Propaganda, and Big Individualism," *Journal of Public Relations Research* 26, no. 2 (2014): 103–16.

80. "Shooting continuity," Your town: The story of America [Screenplay], box 113, series I, National Association of Manufacturers Records, accession 1411, Hagley Museum and Library, Wilmington, DE 19807.

81. Audio Productions Inc., *Your Town: A Story of America* (National Association of Mnanufacturers, 1940), http://archive.org/details/YourTown1940. See discussion of the "big individualism" theme in St. John and Arnett, "The National Association of Manufacturers' Community Relations Short Film *Your Town*," 111–12.

82. St. John and Arnett, "The National Association of Manufacturers' Community Relations Short Film *Your Town*," 110.

83. Ibid., 105.

84. Wall, *Inventing the "American Way,"* 47.

85. Frank Morn, *"The Eye that Never Sleeps": A History of the Pinkerton National Detective Agency* (Bloomington: Indiana University Press, 1982).

86. On Blankenhorn, see "Guide to the Heber Blankenhorn Papers 1919–1937," ULS Archives and Special Collections, University of Pittsburgh, https://digital.library.pitt.edu/islandora/object/pitt%3AUS-PPiU-ais196615/viewer.

87. U.S. Congress, Senate, Committee on Education and Labor, *Hearings Before a Subcommittee of the Committee on Education and Labor United States Senate Seventy-Fourth Congress Second Session on S. Res. 266*, April 10, 11, 14, 15, 16, 17, 21, and 23, 1936 (Washington, D.C.: U.S. Government Printing Office, 1936), 5–6.

88. Ibid., Madden Testimony, 2.

89. Ibid., Blankenhorn Testimony, 272.

90. Statement of NAM with reference to S 1970, A Bill to Eliminate Certain Oppressive Labor Practices, May 25, 1939. *Oppressive Labor Practices Act: Hearings Before a Subcommittee of the Committee on Education and Labor, United States Senate, Seventy-Sixth Congress, First Session, on S. 1970, a Bill to Eliminate Certain Oppressive Labor Practices Affecting Interstate and Foreign Commerce, and for Other Purposes* (Washington, D.C.: U.S. Government Printing Office, 1939), 201ff.

91. Various press clippings, 1938, including Somerset (PA) *Daily American*, March 10, 1938, and Newport News (VA) *Daily Press*, March 7, 1938, folder La Follette Committee, box 79, series I, National Association of Manufacturers Records, accession 1411, Hagley Museum and Library, Wilmington, DE 19807.

92. Tedlow, "The National Association of Manufacturers," 43.

93. Statement of NAM with reference to S 1970, A Bill to Eliminate Certain Oppressive Labor Practices, May 25, 1939. *Oppressive Labor Practices Act: Hearings Before a Subcommittee of the Committee on Education and Labor, United States Senate, Seventy-Sixth Congress, First Session, on S. 1970, a Bill to Eliminate Certain Oppressive Labor Practices Affecting Interstate and Foreign Commerce, and for Other Purposes.* (Washington, D.C.: U.S. Government Printing Office, 1939), 201ff.

94. Ibid. See, in particular, discussions of mass picketing on p. 201, and sit-down strikes on p. 208.

95. Ibid., 208 on civil rights.

96. Tedlow, "The National Association of Manufacturers," 43.

97. Quoted in Wall, *Inventing the "American Way,"* 59. This is from 1939.

98. This was a particular point for Rose Wilder Lane; see chapter 3.

99. Quoted in Wall, *Inventing the "American Way,"* 59.

100. "Declaration of Principles Relating to the Conduct of American Industry Adopted by the Congress of American Industry," December 8, 1939, folder National Association of Manufacturers 1939–40, box 2, J. Howard Pew Papers (Acc. 1634), Hagley Museum and Library, Wilmington, DE 19807.

101. Ibid.

102. Ibid., 3.

103. Ibid., 12.

104. "The American Family Robinson," Reports, The National Association of Broadcasters, vol. 7, no. 32, August 11, 1939, folder 32: Public Relations-radio-The American Family Robinson, 1939, box 143, series I, National Association of Manufacturers Records, accession 1411, Hagley Museum and Library, Wilmington, DE 19807.

105. Pamphlet: "Meet the American Family Robinson," folder 30: Public Relations- The American Family Robinson, 1940 June, box 143, series I, National Association of Manufacturers Records, accession 1411, Hagley Museum and Library, Wilmington, DE 19807.

106. H. W. Prentis Jr., quoted in Phillips-Fein, *Invisible Hands*, 59. See also Wall, *Inventing the "American Way,"* 59. This was a misrepresentation of religion, as well: Judaism is not founded

on the "sacredness of the individual." In Judaism, what is sacred is God, Torah, and the Sabbath. The story of Passover explains that the Jews were freed from Egypt *not* as individuals, but as a people. This becomes a metaphor for salvation in general.

107. "The Role of the NAM Public Information Program," unpublished memorandum, box 112, series I, National Association of Manufacturers Records, accession 1411, Hagley Museum and Library, Wilmington, DE 19807, quoted in St. John, "A View," 379. St. John also refers to this framework as the inseparability of "democracy and capitalism" (379). We agree that that is the underlying message, but generally the formulation is not democracy and capitalism: it is capitalism and freedom.

108. H. W. Prentis Jr., quoted in Wall, *Inventing the "American Way,"* 59.

109. H. W. Prentis Jr., quoted in Phillips-Fein, *Invisible Hands*, 60.

110. Phillips-Fein, *Invisible Hands*, 106.

111. Fones-Wolf, "Creating a Favorable Business Climate," 33–4.

112. Tim McMahon, "Inflation and CPI Consumer Price Index 1940–1949," InflationData.com, 2015, https://inflationdata.com/articles/inflation-consumer-price-index-decade-commentary /inflation-cpi-consumer-price-index-1940-1949/.

113. Robert R. Watson, "Now—Let's Free America!" speech before the American Legion, October 3, 1946, San Francisco, CA. Copy in folder Now Let's Free America!, box 136, series I, National Association of Manufacturers Records, accession 1411, Hagley Museum and Library, Wilmington, DE 19807.

114. Delton, *The Industrialists*, 62–82.

115. Gable, "A Political Analysis of an Employers' Association," 441. See also Elizabeth Fones-Wolf, *Selling Free Enterprise: The Business Assault on Labor and Liberalism, 1945–1960* (University of Illinois Press, 1994), 42–5.

116. On the continuation of wartime propaganda activities by the Advertising Council see Robert Griffith, "The Selling of America: The Advertising Council and American Politics, 1942–1960," *Business History Review* 57, no. 3 (Autumn 1983): 388–412; and Wall, *Inventing the "American Way,"* chap. 6.

117. "NAM Finds 11 Fallacies," 1941, p. 15. Quoted in St. John and Arnett, "The National Association of Manufacturers," 103–16.

118. St. John and Arnett, "The National Association of Manufacturers," 103–16.

119. Civil Action No 381-48, National Association of Manufacturers and Kenneth R. Miller v. Howard J. McGrath, Plaintiffs Trial brief, Desk stamp: 20 November 1951, p. 59, folder Lobbying, box 79, National Association of Manufacturers Records, accession 1411, Hagley Museum and Library, Wilmington, DE 19807. On the Federal Regulation of Lobbying Act, see Belle Zeller, "American Government and Politics: The Federal Regulation of Lobbying Act," *American Political Science Review* 42:2 (April 1948): 239–71. Inspired by utility company activities, it was the first federal statute to regulate lobbying. Among other things it required lobbyists to register and to disclose their funding sources. According to Zeller, one specific inspiration was the problem of people who did not visit Capitol Hill, but who "initiate propaganda from all over the country in the form of letters and telegrams, many of which have been based entirely on misinformation."

120. Flynn, *The Road Ahead*, 152–58.

121. See for instance Texas governor Rick Perry, whose 2012 presidential campaign launch speech argued, "It is time to believe again in the potential of private enterprise, set free from the shackles of an overbearing federal government." Rick Perry, "Rick Perry Presidential Announcement," http://www.4president.us/websites/2012/perry081311website.htm.

122. Noel Sargent, "The Case Against Socialism, with Particular Analysis of the Views of Norman Thomas," National Association of Manufacturers, April 18, 1933, folder Socialism, box 6,

series I, National Association of Manufacturers Records, accession 1411, Hagley Museum and Library, Wilmington, DE 19807.

123. "Workplace Safety," National Association of Manufacturers, accessed July 7, 2021, http://documents.nam.org/Nam.org_Web_Archive/www.nam.org/Issues/Workplace-Safety/index .html. NAM argues that "rigid work rules . . . make it impossible for some companies to succeed." On climate change, see, for example, Chevron et. al. v. Oakland et. al., Brief amicus curiae of National Association of Manufacturers, May 17, 2019, http://climatecasechart.com/wp-content /uploads/sites/16/case-documents/2019/20190517_docket-18-16663_amicus-brief-5.pdf.

124. Interoffice Memo Dec 18, 1944, folder Key Documents, 1942–1945, box 844, series III NIIC, National Association of Manufacturers Records, accession 1411, Hagley Museum and Library, Wilmington, DE 19807.

125. St. John argues that this is the very essence of propaganda: "It is a process that attempts to reinforce a public's understanding that it is acting out of self-interest, while it is actually being subtly called to align itself to the concerns of a privileged interest whose agenda may not actually be in concert with large sectors of the public." St. John, "A View," 387.

CHAPTER 5: "A STRINGENT, CRYSTALLINE VISION OF THE FREE MARKET"

1. Gary Gerstle, *Liberty and Coercion: The Paradox of American Government from the Founding to the Present*, rev. ed. (Princeton, NJ: Princeton University Press, 2015), 63, quoting fellow historian Louis Hartz. We are indebted to Gerstle for this entire discussion and hope that we have paraphrased sufficiently so as not to seem guilty of plagiarism: otherwise we would have had to cite the lion's share of his p. 63.

2. Also discussed in Gerstle, *Liberty and Coercion*.

3. Ibid., 62.

4. David I. Spanagel, *DeWitt Clinton and Amos Eaton: Geology and Power in Early New York*, 1st ed. (Baltimore: Johns Hopkins University Press, 2014).

5. Gerstle, *Liberty and Coercion*, 64.

6. Kim Phillips-Fein, *Invisible Hands: The Businessmen's Crusade Against the New Deal* (New York: W. W. Norton, 2010), 13–15.

7. Ken Alder, *Engineering the Revolution: Arms & Enlightenment in France, 1763-1815* (Chicago: University of Chicago Press, 1997).

8. David A. Hounshell, *From the American System to Mass Production, 1800–1932: The Development of Manufacturing Technology in the United States* (Baltimore: Johns Hopkins University Press, 1985).

9. On militias, see Gerstle, *Liberty and Coercion*; on the railroads, see Richard White, *Railroaded: The Transcontinentals and the Making of Modern America* (New York: W. W. Norton, 2012).

10. "Slave Code for the District of Columbia, Articles and Essays, Slaves and the Courts, 1740–1860, Digital Collections, Library of Congress," web page, Library of Congress, Washington, D.C. 20540, accessed April 2, 2021, https://www.loc.gov/collections/slaves-and-the-courts -from-1740-to-1860/articles-and-essays/slave-code-for-the-district-of-columbia/.

11. Paul Finkelman, "Slavery in the United States: Persons or Property?" in *The Legal Understanding of Slavery: From the Historical to the Contemporary*, ed. Jean Allain (Oxford: Oxford University Press, 2012), 114.

12. Hamilton's economic plan was for an economy strongly supported by the federal government. One of the main purposes of the Constitution was to give the federal government more power in supporting the nation's fledgling economy.

13. George Washington, "First Annual Address to Congress," January 8, 1790, American Presidency Project, University of California Santa Barbara, https://www.presidency.ucsb .edu/documents/first-annual-address-congress-0.

14. John Chester Miller, *The Federalist Era, 1789–1801*, 1st ed. (New York: Waveland Press, 1960), 15–19; and Douglas A. Irwin, "The Aftermath of Hamilton's 'Report on Manufactures,'" *Journal of Economic History* 64, no. 3 (Sept 2004): 800–21.

15. Lewis L. Gould, *Grand Old Party: A History of the Republicans* (New York: Oxford University Press, 2012), 10–11. The American system in many ways reflects Hamilton's vision of protective tariffs combined with internal improvements like roads, canals, and eventually railroads. He also envisioned a form of regulation that wouldn't be enacted until Teddy Roosevelt's administration: government quality inspection of products. Ron Chernow, *Alexander Hamilton* (New York: Penguin, 2005), 378.

16. Ha-Joon Chang, *Kicking Away the Ladder: Development Strategy in Historical Perspective* (London: Anthem Press, 2002).

17. Ibid., 36. That is to say, 45 percent of the value of the imported object.

18. Paul Bairoch, *Economics and World History: Myths and Paradoxes*, 1st ed. (Chicago: University of Chicago Press, 1995), 32–33.

19. Quentin R. Skrabec Jr., *William McKinley: Apostle of Protectionism* (New York: Algora Publishing, 2007). This particular tariff debate illustrates how complicated the issue could become: McKinley wanted to lower tariffs on imported tin, but so as to protect and support an infant tinplate industry in the United States. In general, manufacturers wanted low tariffs on imported goods but high tariffs on manufactured goods, for obvious reasons.

20. "Republican Party Platform of 1896," American Presidency Project, https://www.presidency .ucsb.edu/documents/republican-party-platform-1896.

21. Gould, *Grand Old Party*, chap. 6.

22. William G. Roy, *Socializing Capital: The Rise of the Large Industrial Corporation in America*, later printing ed. (Princeton, NJ: Princeton University Press, 1999), chap. 3. White, *Railroaded*. For a recent example of corruption—or at least questionable labor practices—see Patrick Dorrian and Erin Mulvaney, "Union Pacific Disability Bias Class Scrapped by 8th Cir. (2)," Bloomberg Law, March 25, 2020, https://news.bloomberglaw.com/daily-labor -report/union-pacific-disability-bias-class-scrapped-by-eighth-circuit.

23. Folder NICC slide show May 11, 1944, Box 845, Series III, National Association of Manufacturers Records, accession 1411, Hagley Museum and Library, Wilmington, DE 19807.

24. Wendy L. Wall, *Inventing the "American Way": The Politics of Consensus from the New Deal to the Civil Rights Movement* (Oxford: Oxford University Press, 2008), 39.

25. Wall, *Inventing the "American Way,"* 18.

26. Labor leaders had their own version of the indivisibility thesis, which argued that if you weakened workers' freedoms, such as the right to unionization and collective bargaining, then other aspects of democracy would be threatened. See Wall, *Inventing the "American Way,"* 46.

27. Richard M. Ebeling, "The Life and Works of Ludwig von Mises," *Independent Review* 13, no. 1 (Summer 2008), 101, https://www.independent.org/publications/tir/article.asp?id=692. One of the many ironies of this story is that Mises, who was adamant that economics must be scientific, was himself throughout his career funded by business interests who were not concerned with the objective appraisal of the impacts of economic policies, but were unabashed advocates for pro-business policies. (One notes that Ebeling did not make that claim about the political motivation of the Chamber of Commerce as a criticism!) Hayek similarly seems unperturbed when events do not bear out his predictions, as in the foreword to the 1956 American edition of *The Road to Serfdom*, in which he acknowledges that "six years of socialist government in England have not produced anything resembling a totalitarian state." This might seem to falsify his central claim, but he evades it with the vague,

unverified, and possibly unverifiable assertion that "the most important change which extensive government control produces is a psychological change, an alteration in the character of the people." Friedrich A. Hayek, *The Road to Serfdom: Text and Documents*, edited with a foreword and introduction by Bruce Caldwell (Chicago: University of Chicago Press, 2003), 48. And this from a man who claimed to resent being known more for "a pamphlet" than for his "strictly scientific work." Hayek, *The Road to Serfdom*, 55.

28. Karen I. Vaughn, *Austrian Economics in America: The Migration of a Tradition* (Cambridge: Cambridge University Press, 1998), chap. 4.

29. Ludwig von Mises, *Socialism: An Economic and Sociological Analysis* (Indianapolis, IN: Liberty Fund, 2012).

30. Ibid. For a discussion of Mises's fascist sympathies from someone sympathetic to Mises, see Ralph Raico, "Mises on Fascism, Democracy, and Other Questions," *Journal of Libertarian Studies* 12, no. 1 (1996): 1–27, https://mises.org/library/mises-fascism-democracy-and-other-questions.

31. Encyclopaedia Britannica, s.v., "Engelbert Dollfuss," accessed February 17, 2021, https://www.britannica.com/biography/Engelbert-Dollfuss. See also Ludwig von Mises, "The Middle of the Road Leads to Socialism," University Club of New York, April 18, 1950, https://mises.org/library/middle-road-leads-socialism.

32. Angus Burgin, *The Great Persuasion: Reinventing Free Markets since the Depression*, 1–3, quote on the End of Laissez Faire on p 3; and Zachary D. Carter, *The Price of Peace: Money, Democracy, and the Life of John Maynard Keynes* (New York: Random House, 2020), 150–52. See also Mark Hendrickson, *American Labor and Economic Citizenship: New Capitalism from World War I to the Great Depression* (New York: Cambridge University Press, 2013). Hendrickson stresses that Herbert Hoover did not promote laissez-faire individualism, but "voluntary corporatism."

33. Vaughn, *Austrian Economics*, 66. Dieter Plehwe formulates it nicely in terms of the late 1930s: the "core message [of] the superiority of the market economy over state intervention [was] a principle that was (to say the least) leaning against the wind in the depths of the Great Depression." Dieter Plehwe, introduction to *The Road from Mont Pèlerin: The Making of the Neoliberal Thought Collective*, ed. Philip Mirowski and Dieter Plehwe (Cambridge, MA: Harvard University Press, 2009). In the early 1940s, the situation had not much changed in that regard.

34. Ebeling, "The Life and Works of Ludwig von Mises," 104. This was a major departure from nineteenth-century theories, especially labor theories of value. See Mariana Mazzucato, *The Value of Everything: Making and Taking in the Global Economy*, first U.S. edition (New York: Public Affairs, 2018).

35. Peter J. Boettke, "The Significance of Mises's 'Socialism,'" Foundation for Economic Education, September 1, 2016, https://fee.org/articles/the-significance-of-misess-socialism/. The Foundation for Economic Education (FEE) summarizes the argument this way: "Without a market for the means of production, there will not be monetary prices established on the market [and] without monetary prices, reflecting the relative scarcities of different goods and services, there will be no way for economic decision-makers to engage in rational economic calculation. . . . Without the ability to engage in rational economic calculation, economic decision-makers will be stumbling and bumbling in the dark." Therefore, there cannot be rational economic planning, because you cannot make rational decisions when you lack the information on which those decisions must be based. "Socialism as a rational economic system," Mises therefore concludes, is "impossible." Yet, what socialism cannot achieve, "capitalism achieves every day," through the mechanism of markets. So the theory goes.

36. Ibid.
37. Gregory Teddy Eow, "Fighting a New Deal: Intellectual Origins of the Reagan Revolution, 1932–1952" (PhD diss., Rice University, 2007), 140.
38. Bettina Bien Greaves, "Remembering Henry Hazlitt," *Freeman*, July 27, 2007, https://mises .org/library/remembering-henry-hazlitt.
39. Donald J. Boudreaux, "An Interview with Henry Hazlitt [Full Edition of Vol. 5, No. 1]," *Austrian Economics Newsletter* 5, no. 1 (Spring 1984), https://mises.org/library/interview -henry-hazlitt-full-edition-vol-5-no-1; and Greaves, "Remembering Henry Hazlitt."
40. Several of his contemporaries, including Henry D. Dickinson and Oskar Lange, argued that the difference between a planned economy and a free market came down to who was responsible for matching prices to values. If there was a surplus or shortage of goods, it could signal to the planners that the price should be adjusted—just as it did in a free market. The real issue would not be information, but flexibility, adaptability, and responsiveness: planning could work if the planners were paying attention to what was happening on the ground and responding to it. (In essence, Lange was advocating what in environmentalism would come to be known as adaptive management.) One could also say that it would depend on honesty; in the Soviet Union, political pressure led to dishonest reporting of economic output. Planning would necessarily fail in the face of such dishonesty. For more on Lange, and Hayek's response, see Bruce Caldwell, "Hayek and Socialism," *Journal of Economic Literature* 35, no. 4 (1997): 1862–63.
41. This problem seems to us so obvious that we are a bit baffled by why it is not highlighted in discussions of Mises, but then again much of the literature on Mises is written by his defenders. This criticism of Mises (and of Milton Friedman) can be found in the Wikipedia entry on "Authoritarian Socialism," *Wikipedia*, February 25, 2021, https://en.wikipedia.org /w/index.php?title=Authoritarian_socialism.
42. It is also interesting that Mises, who is writing in the early 1920s, and was part Jewish, ignores Zionism and the kibbutz movement. The early kibbutzim were socialist, but they were not centrally planned. And while the Zionist-socialist vision did not persist in the way that its founders had imagined, the reasons had little or nothing to do with inefficiency, much less "impossibility." (On the history of the kibbutz movement, see Ran Abramitzky, *The Mystery of the Kibbutz: Egalitarian Principles in a Capitalist World* [Princeton, NJ: Princeton University Press, 2018]; and Aviva Halamish, *Kibbutz: Utopia and Politics: The Life and Times of Meir Yaari, 1897–1987*, trans. Lenn Schramm, illustrated ed. [Boston: Academic Studies Press, 2017]). Another variant that Mises and his followers ignored was the religious socialism, sometimes also called Protestant socialism, of Paul Tillich. Tillich developed his ideas around the same time as Mises, beginning with his experience of World War I. See Gary Dorrien, "Religious Socialism, Paul Tillich, and the Abyss of Estrangement," *Social Research: An International Quarterly* 85, no. 2 (2018): 425–52; Kaci Norman and Austin Bess-Washington, "Tillich and Socialism," Paul Tillich Resources, accessed February 18, 2021, https://people.bu.edu/wwildman/tillich/resources/popculture_tillichandsocialism.htm; and John R. Stumme, *Socialism in Theological Perspective: A Study of Paul Tillich, 1918–1933* (Missoula, MT: Scholars Press, 1978).
43. Gary Dorrien, *Economy, Difference, Empire: Social Ethics for Social Justice* (New York: Columbia University Press, 2010), 87.
44. Dorrien, *Economy*, 88.
45. Ibid., 89. While hostile to organized religion, Eugene Debs saw his socialism as an expression of Christian values. See Eugene Debs, "Eugene Debs on the Real Religion of Jesus," letter written in December 1914, reprinted at *Jacobin*, December 25, 2020, https://www.jacobinmag .com/2020/12/eugene-debs-christmas-jesus-prisoner-letter; "Inmate No. 9756," The Terre

Haute Tribune, December 17, 1914, 4. Jacob H. Dorn, "'In Spiritual Communion': Eugene V. Debs and the Socialist Christians," *Journal of the Gilded Age and Progressive Era* 2, no. 3 (2003): 303–25.

46. Dorrien, *Economy*, 90.

47. Thomas believed that essential industries and national monopolies should be nationalized, but that nonessential industries should remain in private hands (Dorrien, *Economy*, 104). In many respects, Thomas's early policy positions on domestic issues were not dramatically different from those of Teddy Roosevelt. However, on foreign policies—particularly World War I—they differed radically, with Roosevelt pushing for the United States to join the war in Europe and Thomas encouraging draft resistance by American workers. Thomas remained antiwar throughout his life, although he reluctantly accepted the U.S. acceptance into World War II as necessary to prevent the spread of fascism, and then again in Korea as necessary to address communist expansion in Asia (Dorrien, *Economy*, 105–6).

48. Dorrien, *Economy*, 88. Others would of course disagree with this. Dorrien notes that a number of prominent socialists in fact became New Dealers (93). Thomas felt that the New Deal "used public money and federal government power to shore up private enterprises for the sake of private profit," a complaint with which Mises might have agreed. However, unlike Mises, Thomas believed that the New Deal shored up capitalism when it should have transformed it in the public interest (94–95). After World War II, Thomas became a voice for a "progressive anticommunism" (104).

49. Particularly prominent among this movement were Father Coughlin, Charles Lindbergh, and their followers. Also see Phillip Roth's 2004 novel *The Plot Against America*, which, although fictional, was based in large part on historical personages. Coughlin's broadcasts were sympathetic to both Hitler and Japanese emperor Hirohito. The radio program and Coughlin's newsletter were finally canceled by the Roosevelt administration in 1939 after war broke out in Europe, but this, again, had more to do with the war than with central planning.

50. "Charles Lindbergh and the Rise of 1940s Nazi Sympathizers," *Smithsonian*, accessed March 11, 2021, https://www.smithsonianmag.com/videos/charles-lindbergh-and-the-rise -of-1940s-nazi-s/. On the thought that Americans in the 1930s were more likely to turn to fascism than to communism, see Dorrien, *Economy*, "Chapter 5: Norman Thomas and the Dilemma of American Socialism."

51. Folder Public Relations Publications August 28, 1939, Box 111, Series I, National Association of Manufacturers Records, accession 1411, Hagley Museum and Library, Wilmington, DE 19807.

52. Noel Sargent, "The Case Against Socialism, with Particular Analysis of the Views of Norman Thomas," National Association of Manufacturers, April 18, 1933, 4, folder Socialism, box 6, series 1, National Association of Manufacturers Records, accession 1411, Hagley Museum and Library, Wilmington, DE 19807.

53. Ebeling, "The Life and Works of Ludwig von Mises," 103.

54. Eow, "Fighting a New Deal," 135–42.

55. Jörg Guido Hülsmann, *Mises: The Last Knight of Liberalism* (Auburn, AL: Ludwig von Mises Institute, 2007), 822–23.

56. Linton Weeks, "The 1940 Census: 72-Year-Old Secrets Revealed," NPR.org, April 2, 2012, https://www.npr.org/2012/04/02/149575704/the-1940-census-72-year-old-secrets-revealed.

57. "He was recalled [from service during World War I in London and Berlin] to the United States by Herbert Hoover where, as a principal member of the U.S. Food Administration, he coordinated the purchasing and distribution of over $5 billion (nearly 34 metric tons) of American-produced food to western and eastern European allies, and to Russia. Mullendore wrote the official history and detailed the intricate documentation of this reconstructive

period in a book, *The History of the U.S. Food Administration*, published in 1921." "William C. Mullendore Papers, 1930–1968," Archives West, accessed February 5, 2021, http://archives west.orbiscascade.org/ark:/80444/xv02410#historicalID.

58. James McKay, "Crusading for Capitalism: Christian Capitalists and the Ideological Roots of the Conservative Movement" (PhD diss., University of Wisconsin–Madison, 2015), 88. See also Eow, "Fighting a New Deal," 114–17; and Tibor Machan, "A Rare and Insightful Interview with Leonard Read," *Reason*, April 1975, https://infinitebanking.org/banknotes/a -rare-and-insightful-interview-with-leonard-read/.

59. McKay, "Crusading for Capitalism," 143.

60. "William C. Mullendore Papers, 1930–1968."

61. In 1946, Hazlitt would publish a free-market polemic: *Economics in One Lesson* (New York: Harper and Brothers, 1946). Missing from this early staff list for the Foundation for Economic Education is Ayn Rand. Rand was a militant atheist who rejected FEE's embrace of Christian libertarianism. See Eow, "Fighting a New Deal," 154–55; Jennifer Burns, *Goddess of the Market: Ayn Rand and the American Right* (Oxford: Oxford University Press, 2009); and chapter 8.

62. George A. Lopez, et al., eds., *The Conservative Press in Twentieth-Century America* (Westport, CT: Greenwood Publishing Group, 1999), 321–23. See also McKay, "Crusading for Capitalism," 84–85; and Phillips-Fein, *Invisible Hands*, 97–104, and chapter 11.

63. Phillips-Fein, *Invisible Hands*, 27; and McKay, "Crusading for Capitalism," 87.

64. Hülsmann, *Mises*, 823. He elaborates: "Read . . . was much impressed by what he had seen and heard. A year later he would move to New York and eventually establish the mother of all libertarian think tanks in collaboration with Mises. The association would last for the rest of Mises's lifetime." Hülsmann, *Mises*, 826. In 1945 or thereabout, Read had tired of some business groups which he saw as committed to hearing "both sides" of issues. Read wasn't interested in the "other side." He wanted to win the argument against government intervention, and the way to do that was not by listening but by talking and writing. It was this conviction that led him, in 1946, to set up FEE. The purpose of FEE would be to promote the "freedom thesis"—that political freedom and economic freedom went hand in glove—and a key partner in this work was Mises. The pamphlets that FEE distributed and conferences that they organized would promote the thinking of Mises and other "champions of classical liberalism."

65. Hülsmann, *Mises*, 851.

66. Eow, "Fighting a New Deal," 133–34. Among other things, Sumner, who had died in 1910, had been an opponent of the Enlightenment concept of natural rights, writing, "Before the tribunal of nature a man has no more right to life than a rattlesnake; he has no more right to liberty than any wild beast; his right to pursuit of happiness is nothing but a license to maintain the struggle for existence." William Graham Sumner, *Earth-Hunger and Other Essays* (New York: HardPress Publishing, 2013; original Yale University Press, 1913), 234.

67. Eow, "Fighting a New Deal," 132.

68. Eow, "Fighting a New Deal," 146.

69. Hülsmann, *Mises*, 846.

70. Hülsmann, *Mises*, 846 fn 17; and George H. Nash, *The Conservative Intellectual Movement in America Since 1945*, 30th anniv. ed. (Wilmington, DE: Intercollegiate Studies Institute, 2006), 13, 351. See also Charles H. Hamilton, '*The Freeman*: The Early Years,' in *The Conservative Press in Twentieth-Century America*, ed. R. Lora and W. H. Longton (London: Greenwood, 1999).

71. Vaughn, *Austrian Economics in America*, 64; and Gary North, "Leonard E. Read's Small-Tent Strategy," *LewRockwell* (blog), August 7, 2002, https://www.lewrockwell.com/2002/08 /gary-north/the-small-tent-strategy/.

72. Ebeling, "The Life and Works of Ludwig von Mises," 100. See also David Gordon, review of *"Austrian Economics in America: The Migration of a Tradition*, by Karen Vaughn," *Mises Review* 1, no. 3 (Fall 1995), https://mises.org/library/austrian-economics-america-migration -tradition-karen-vaughn. As Karen Vaughn notes in *Austrian Economics in America*, in the 1950s and '60s "Mises's New York University seminar became more a focus point for conservative and libertarian" thinkers "than a training ground for contemporary economists."

73. The academic position was particularly important give that by 1948, NAM had tired somewhat of Mises. His two-volume study *The American Individual Enterprise System*, published in 1946, may have been a bit too academic for their taste. Mises's strict anti-inflationary views may have felt off-key, given that inflation was never a central concern for NAM. But the end of his relationship with NAM was by no means the end of Mises's influence in the United States, thanks in large part to Hazlitt and Read.

74. Wendell L. Willkie, "Five Minutes to Midnight," *Saturday Evening Post*, June 22, 1940.

75. Hülsmann, *Mises*, 822. Hazlitt had been aware of Mises for some time and had been espousing his views since early or mid-1930s, so it is possible that the NAM arguments were influenced by Mises before he came to America. Still, the available evidence seems to suggest that NAM executives did not come to their views *because* of Mises. Rather, they found in Mises someone intellectually compatible, who could make their arguments appear to be more than simply self-serving.

76. Kemper Fullerton, "Calvinism and Capitalism: An Explanation of the Weber Thesis," in *Protestantism and Capitalism: The Weber Thesis and Its Critics*, ed. Robert W. Green (Boston: D. C. Heath and Company, 1959), 6–20.

77. Weber had also developed a theory of the economic calculation problem similar to Mises's. So perhaps history would not have been so different had Hayek made it to Germany and studied with Weber before he died. See Max Weber, *Economy and Society: An Outline of Interpretive Sociology*, ed. Guenther Roth and Claus Wittich (Berkeley: University of California Press, 1978), 100–103.

78. Ebeling, "The Life and Works of Ludwig von Mises," 141. Hayek had already been exposed to Austrian economics, in part because his grandfather, Franz von Juraschek, was an economist and friend of Eugen von Böhm-Bawerk, considered along with Carl Menger to be the cofounder of the Austrian school. (Hayek was also a cousin of Wittgenstein.) When Menger retired, he was replaced at the University of Vienna by Friedrich von Wieser, who introduced Hayek to Mises. Von Wieser was Hayek's research adviser, but it was Mises who most clearly influenced his work.

79. Ebeling, "The Life and Works of Ludwig von Mises," 100.

80. Friedrich A. von Hayek et al., *The Collected Works of F. A. Hayek* (Chicago: University of Chicago Press, 1989), 202. See also discussion in Hayek, "Letters to the Editor: Liberal pact with Labour," *Times* (London), March 31, 1977, 15. Hayek is concerned that government planning could increase monopolistic practices, yet strangely nonchalant about the actual monopolies that developed in the United States in the late nineteenth and early twentieth centuries with little or no help from government. See Hayek, *The Road to Serfdom*, 93.

81. It still exists today as "the leading institute for applied empirical economic research in Austria." "Mission und Leistungsspektrum: WIFO," accessed February 23, 2021, https://www.wifo.ac .at/jart/prj3/wifo/main.jart?rel=de&reserve-mode=active&content-id=1579496417859.

82. On Hayek's move to the London School of Economics, see Hayek, *The Road to Serfdom*, 3. Caldwell notes in the foreword that 1931 was a frightening year in the United Kingdom, as the Depression deepened, the government abandoned the gold standard, the labor government collapsed, and protectionist tariffs were imposed. In hindsight it seems that conservative economists were right to have argued against the retreat to protectionism.

83. Kimberly Amadeo, "Compare Today's Unemployment with the Past," The Balance, accessed February 23, 2021, https://www.thebalance.com/unemployment-rate-by-year-3305506.

84. Roger Middleton, "British monetary and fiscal policy in the 1930s," *Oxford Review of Economic Policy* 26, no. 3 (Autumn 2010): 414–41.

85. Milton Friedman, interview by Gene Epstein, *Barron's*, August 24, 1998, https://mises.org /library/business-cycles. Economists have argued as to whether the empirical evidence supports or refutes the Austrian school argument, but across the political spectrum, from John Quiggin and Paul Krugman to Milton Friedman and Gottfried von Haberler, they have critiqued Austrian business-cycle theory for its incompleteness and accession to the inevitability of cyclical financial collapse.

86. The essays in Hayek's *Collectivist Economic Planning* signal the larger critique of central planning that Hayek presents in *The Road to Serfdom*. See Friedrich A. Hayek et al., *Collectivist Economic Planning*, ed. Friedrich A. Hayek (Auburn, AL: Mises Institute, 2009).

87. Douglas French, "Hayek and Mises," in *Hayek: A Collaborative Biography: Part 1 Influences, from Mises to Bartley*, ed. Robert Leeson, Archival Insights into the Evolution of Economics Series (London: Palgrave Macmillan UK, 2013), 83. See also Mirowski and Plehwe, *The Road from Mont Pèlerin*, 11–12.

88. Which is not to imply that the Nobel is somehow apolitical. See Nathan Tankus, "The Economics 'Nobel' Prize is Central Bank Fiscal Policy," Substack, October 31, 2020, https:// nathantankus.substack.com/p/the-economics-nobel-prize-is-central, and the Nobel committee cited both his economic and his "inter-disciplinary work." See Carter, *The Price of Peace*; and Carter's 2021 declaration that Friedmanomics is finally dead, having left "a legacy of ruin." Zachary D. Carter, "The End of Friedmanomics," *New Republic*, June 17, 2021, https:// newrepublic.com/article/162623/milton-friedman-legacy-biden-government-spending.

89. R. W. Garrison, "F. A. Hayek as 'Mr. Fluctooations': In Defense of Hayek's 'Technical Economics,'" *Hayek Society Journal* (LSE) 5, no. 2 (2003): 1.

90. "In order to achieve their ends, the planners must create power—power over men wielded by other men—of a magnitude never before known. Democracy is an obstacle to this suppression of freedom which the centralized direction of economic activity requires. Hence arises the clash between planning and democracy." Friedrich A. Hayek, *The Road to Serfdom: Reader's Digest Condensed Version* (Trowbridge: Cromwell Press, 1999), 32. For more discussion and on how Friedman takes up the argument, so that he calls it the Hayek–Friedman hypothesis, as well as a discussion of why Friedman can tolerate authoritarianism as he did in Chile, see Christoph Michael Hindermann, *The Impact of Economic Freedom on State Legitimacy: An Empirical Investigation* (New York: Springer Gabler, 2018), 175.

91. Willkie, "Five Minutes to Midnight."

92. Hayek, *The Road to Serfdom*, 136.

93. Among the many influenced by this argument are David Bloor, one of the founders of science studies. Inspired by Mises, he argued that scientific terms and theories do not have "real" meaning outside the context of their uses: "The notion of the 'real meaning' of a concept or a sign deserves the same scorn as economists reserve for the outdated and unscientific notion of the 'real' or 'just' price of a commodity," Bloor writes. "The only real price is the price paid in the course of real transactions as they proceed *von Fall zu Fall*. There is no standard outside these transactions." David Bloor, *Wittgenstein, Rules and Institutions* (London; New York: Routledge, 1997), 76–77. See also David Bloor, *The Enigma of the Aerofoil: Rival Theories in Aerodynamics, 1909–1930* (Chicago: University of Chicago Press, 2011); and Erik Baker and Naomi Oreskes, "It's No Game: Post-Truth and the Obligations of Science Studies," *Social Epistemology Review and Reply Collective* 6, no. 8 (2017): 1–10. We agree that there are no

absolute values in economics and no absolute truths in science, but we fail to see how this leads to the conclusion that governments should not intervene in markets to protect workers, forbid child labor, prevent noncompetitive business practices, forbid false advertising, address climate change, or otherwise remedy market failure.

94. Hayek, *Road to Serfdom*, 110.

95. Friedrich A.Hayek, foreword to the 1956 American pbk. ed., in Bruce Caldwell, *The Road to Serfdom: Text and Documents* (Chicago: University of Chicago Press, 2003), 50. Scholars have argued over the meaning of the word "inevitable" in Hayek's writing, and whether passages like this should be read as warning or prediction. We agree with the argument that Hayek's claims should not be read as predictions in the formal sense—he certainly thinks there is still time to change course; in this sense his work is clearly intended as warning. On the other hand, both in *Road* and elsewhere, he argued that even modest interventions in the economy along social democratic lines place us on the road to serfdom, and this is how most of his followers, rightly or wrongly, have interpreted him. For entry into this discussion, see Andrew Farrant and Edward McPhail, "Hayek, Samuelson, and the logic of the mixed economy?" *Journal of Economic Behavior and Organization* 69 (2009): 5–16.

96. Caldwell, introduction to *The Road to Serfdom: Text and Documents*, 8.

97. Henry Hazlitt, "Economic Planning as Panacea," *New York Times*, August 1, 1937, 82.

98. Raphaël Fèvre, "Denazifying the Economy: Ordoliberals on the Economic Policy Battlefield (1946–1950)," *History of Political Economy* 50, no. 4 (2018): 679–707.

99. Caldwell notes that during the War years, when most of his LSE colleagues were asked to assist the government, Hayek was not, much to his chagrin (Caldwell, "Introduction," 10). This is reminiscent of foreign scientists in the United States, such as Harald Sverdrup. See Naomi Oreskes, *Science on a Mission: How Military Funding Shaped What We Do and Don't Know about the Ocean* (Chicago: University of Chicago Press, 2021). Sverdrup ended up returning to Norway; Hayek, it appears, ended up resentful, which could explain a few things.

100. Caldwell, introduction to *The Road to Serfdom*, 30.

101. Caldwell discusses this critique, pp. 24–27; in particular, the criticisms of "market socialists." He suggests that the reason Hayek did not lay out the arguments against market socialism in *The Road to Serfdom* is that the book was not primarily aimed at economists. This is consistent with our reading that *Road* is primarily political, not economic. Caldwell also rejects the idea that Hayek is insisting on some sort of inevitability thesis, but Hayek's own words belie that interpretation. Hayek had written in the original edition that "[T]he close interdependence of all economic phenomena makes it difficult to stop planning just where we wish and that, once the free working of the market is impeded beyond a certain degree, the planner will be *forced* to extend his controls until they become all-comprehensive" (page 137, italics added). Thus, while Hayek clarifies that he considers the rise of totalitarianism to be in most cases an unintended consequence of socialist policies, to the extent that he equates socialism with central planning, he reaffirms the inevitability that Caldwell insists he did not mean.In the preface to the 1976 edition, Hayek insists that he had never contended that "any movement in the direction of socialism is bound to lead to totalitarianism." But this claim is refuted by his line about the "inevitable consequences of socialist planning," cited above in his foreword to the 1956 edition. Hayek also claims in the 1976 edition that at the time he was writing, the word *socialism* "meant unambiguously the nationalization of the means of production and the central economic planning which made this possible and necessary." (p. 54) That claim is plainly false, and makes one wonder if Hayek was arguing in good faith or not. Perhaps he was simply trying to come up with a plausible account of why he—a man who prided himself on the scientific character of his work and whose views on science had

been changed by his friendship with Karl Popper—was clinging to an argument that by 1976 had been shown to be false. (On Hayek and Popper see Jeremy Shearmur, "Popper, Hayek, and Classical Liberalism," February 1, 1989, https://fee.org/articles/popper-hayek-and-classical -liberalism/.

102. Ralf Ptak, "Neoliberalism in Germany: Revisiting the Ordoliberal Foundations of the Social Market Economy," in *The Road from Mont Pèlerin: The Making of the Neoliberal Thought Collective*, ed. Philip Mirowski and Dieter Plehwe (Cambridge, MA: Harvard University Press, 2009), 98.

103. This said, the Nazis in the 1930s *were* directing the German economy, and many German and Austrian "ordoliberals"—who argued for an essential state role to protect competition in a market economy—were troubled by what they saw as a weakening of institutional separation of different spheres of action. Historian Harro Maas notes that "regulation is not the same as intervention. But with (Keynesian) interventionism, such an institutional separation is violated, and there we are on our slippery slope" (Harro Maas, email communication, May 22, 2021). This concern increased—rather than lessened—after World War II, when it appeared that many European countries, particularly the United Kingdom, were moving in the direction of increased government action in the marketplace and decreased institutional distinction between governmental and nongovernmental domains. See Raphaël Fèvre, "Denazifying the Economy: Ordoliberals on the Economic Policy Battlefield (1946–1950)," *History of Political Economy* 50, no. 4 (2018): 679–707. This may help to explain why Hayek focuses so much of his attention on *national* socialism, and why his U.S. followers took pains to insist that that term was no misnomer, but that Nazism really was a form of socialism (a position that those on the left rejected utterly, and that perhaps seemed more confusing to American audiences than to European ones).

104. Seymour Martin Lipset and Gary Marks, "How FDR Saved Capitalism," Hoover Institution, January 30, 2001, https://www.hoover.org/research/how-fdr-saved-capitalism. Lipset and Marks write: "The economic crisis of the 1930s was more severe in the United States than in any other large society except Germany. It presented American radicals with their greatest opportunity to build a third party since World War I, but the constitutional system and the brilliant way in which Franklin Delano Roosevelt co-opted the left prevented this. The Socialist and Communist Parties saw their support drop precipitously in the 1940 elections. America emerged from the Great Depression as the most antistatist country in the world." This is an interesting point, but probably untrue. American antistatism gains serious traction only after Richard Nixon. See part III of this book for our discussion of the rise of Republican anti-statism.

105. Hayek, *The Road to Serfdom*, 86.

106. Ibid., 85.

107. Ibid., 86–87.

108. Ibid., 118.

109. Ibid.

110. This, then, explains why later conservatives try to deny or downplay the social costs of a problem like climate change.

111. Hayek, *The Road to Serfdom*, 147–48.

112. Hayek, *The Road to Serfdom*, 148–49. Hayek tries to clarify what he sees as the distinction between legitimate and illegitimate demands for economic security. The gist seems to be that while truly unexpected and exceptional temporary hardship might merit government intervention, the normal ups and downs of a competitive system do not. General wage differentials, for example, are to be necessary in a competitive system. Dislocation due to automation is just life—sad, even "tragic"—but not necessarily cause for government intervention. And

any system of guaranteed income would remove the necessary incentives of a competitive system (149–51). Here the argument for the importance of a price system arises: if jobs did not pay differently, workers would not know what jobs society most valued. True, but this assumes that workers have the freedom, the knowledge, and the general wherewithal to change jobs, which in 1944 was often not the case (and still might not be the case today). It also assumes that the price system accurately reflects value to society, which, when one compares teachers and cosmetic plastic surgeons, might not be a defensible assumption.

113. Ibid., 88, italics added.

114. Ibid.

115. Ibid.

116. FEE used this argument to explain why Hayek would have opposed the Affordable Care Act of 2010. See Brittany Hunter, "Hayek Warned Us About Obamacare," October 20, 2017, https://fee.org/articles/hayek-warned-us-about-obamacare/.

117. Hayek, *The Road to Serfdom*, 102.

118. John Ranelagh, *Thatcher's People* (London: Flamingo, 1992), ix.

119. Glenn Beck, "The Road to Serfdom," Fox News Network, June 8, 2010, https://www.youtube.com/watch?v=CMk5_4pBlfM; Glenn Beck, "The Road to Serfdom," *Fox News*, published January 1, 2009, updated May 25, 2015, https://www.foxnews.com/story/the-road-to-serfdom; Daniel Hannan, *The New Road to Serfdom: A Letter of Warning to America*, 1st ed. (New York: Harper, 2010); Bernard Harcourt, "How Paul Ryan Enslaves Friedrich Hayek's *The Road to Serfdom*," *Guardian*, September 12, 2012, http://www.theguardian.com/commentisfree/2012/sep/12/paul-ryan-enslaves-friedrich-hayek-road-serfdom; Rush Limbaugh, "Rush Limbaugh on Brooks, Hayek & Obama," *Taking Hayek Seriously* (blog), February 25, 2009, accessed March 23, 2022, http://hayekcenter.org/?p=360; and "Ted Cruz: GOP Did 'Weepingly Terrible Job' Defining Itself to Hispanics, Minorities," accessed February 16, 2021, https://www.cruz.senate.gov/?p=news&id=391.

120. Jeffrey M. Berry and Sarah Sobieraj, *The Outrage Industry: Political Opinion Media and the New Incivility* (New York: Oxford University Press, 2016), 112. See also Donald J. Boudreaux, "Learning to Love Insider Trading," *Wall Street Journal*, October 24, 2009, https://www.wsj.com/articles/SB10001424052748704224004574489324091790350.s

121. "NR's List of the 100 Best Non-Fiction Books of the Century," *National Review*, March 17, 2011, https://web.archive.org/web/20110317101120/http://old.nationalreview.com/100best/100_books.html.

122. See also Harvey Cox, *The Market as God* (Cambridge, MA: Harvard University Press, 2016). It's not just ideologues who cite Hayek as sources of influence and inspiration. When Hayek received the U.S. Presidential Medal of Freedom in 1991, President George H. W. Bush called *The Road to Serfdom* a book that "still thrills readers everywhere." Gabriel Heaton, "F.A. Hayek and the Presidential Medal of Freedom," Sothebys, March 8, 2019, https://www.sothebys.com/en/articles/f-a-hayek-and-the-presidential-medal-of-freedom. A few years earlier, Ronald Reagan had welcomed Hayek to the White House and presented him with a set of presidential cuff links. Larry Summers, president emeritus of Harvard University and former U.S. treasury secretary under Barack Obama, has compared Hayek to Adam Smith, suggesting that the most important lesson of economics is that "the invisible hand" of the marketplace "is more powerful than the hidden hand" of government intervention. What is it that Summers learned from Hayek? "Things will happen in well-organized efforts without direction, controls, plans. That's the consensus among economists. That's the Hayek legacy." Summers is quoted in Bruce G. Carruthers and Sarah L. Babb, *Economy/Society: Markets, Meanings, and Social Structure* (New York: SAGE Publications, 2013), 175. In fact, the Hayek legacy is much more complex than that. Besides its use to justify extreme libertarian views, the ex-libertarian Niskanen Center invokes

Hayek to argue for a universal basic income—which, ironically, Milton Friedman also supported. Matt Zwolinski, "Hayek, Republican Freedom, and the Universal Basic Income," Niskanen Center, November 6, 2019, https://www.niskanencenter.org/hayek-republican -freedom-and-the-universal-basic-income/. See another Niskanen reappraisal of Hayek here: Jacob T. Levy, "The Shortcut to Serfdom," Niskanen Center, May 16, 2017, https://www .niskanencenter.org/the-shortcut-to-serfdom/.

123. The complete quotation is: "I[t] certainly has become true over the [recent] decades of American conservatism, where, you know, you read *Road to Serfdom*, you read Hayek or von Mises. You attend a couple of lectures at Cato and you think you're a libertarian and you've got the world figured out as kind of this seamless theory of everything. Next thing you know, you're arguing to privatize the sidewalks . . ." Freddy Gray, "Tucker Carlson: 'We Aren't Very Good at Talking about Death,'" *Spectator*, March 27, 2020, https://spectator.us/life/tucker -carlson-interview-good-talking-death/.

124. Nicholas Wapshott, *Keynes Hayek: The Clash That Defined Modern Economics* (New York: W. W. Norton, 2011), 291; Harcourt, "How Paul Ryan Enslaves Friedrich Hayek's *The Road to Serfdom*."

125. Bruce Caldwell also makes this point in the introduction to his 2003 edition of Hayek's *Road to Serfdom*.

126. Caldwell, introduction to *The Road to Serfdom*, 2, offers an answer in the fact that Hayek amended his views in later years and in many ways became more "reactionary." No doubt that is true, but it seems to us more important to consider which version of Hayek reached the most people. Lanny Ebenstein, in *Chicagonomics: The Evolution of Chicago Free Market Economics* (New York: St. Martin's, 2015) suggests on p. x that both Friedman's and Hayek's later views should be "discarded for their younger and more moderate opinions." Ebenstein may be right, but it is interesting that while most people become more moderate with age, these two became less so.

127. Ebenstein, *Chicagonomics*, 16.

128. David P. Ramsey, "The Role of the Supreme Court in Antitrust Enforcement" (PhD diss., Baylor University, 2010), 135.

129. Caldwell, introduction to *The Road to Serfdom*, 1. To gain an American audience, the editors felt they needed a prominent conservative to write the foreword, asking first the conservative journalist and social commentator Walter Lippman and then Wendell Willkie. Both declined; Chicago settled on John Chamberlain, who in the 1930s had been the *New York Times*'s leading book reviewer.

130. Phillips-Fein, *Invisible Hands*, 41.

131. Henry Hazlitt, "An Economist's View of 'Planning'; Regimentation on the Fascist Model, Says Dr. Hayek, Can Evolve from It: *The Road to Serfdom* by Friedrich A. Hayek. With a Foreword by John Chamberlain. 250 Pp. Chicago: University of Chicago Press. $2.75. 'Planning,'" *New York Times*, September 24, 1944.

132. Insofar as Hayek's argument took a predictive form, it is fair to point out that only a few years after *Road* was published, Sweden and other European countries would experiment with socialism—and indeed, many people would consider Sweden socialistic—but they did not end up murdering their people.

133. George Orwell, "Review of the Road to Serfdom by F. A. Hayek, Etc," in *George Orwell: As I Please, 1943–1945, The Collected Essays, Journalism and Letters of George Orwell*, Vol. 3, 1st ed. (San Diego: Harcourt, 1968), 3.

134. Hayek, *The Road to Serfdom*, 136.

135. Hayek does not address FDR's notion of an "industrial dictatorship."

136. This discussion is particularly ironic because elsewhere Hayek insists that "It may be bad to be a cog in an impersonal machine; but it is infinitely worse if we can no longer leave it . . ."

But that was precisely the complaint of American workers in company towns. Hayek, *The Road to Serfdom*, 138.

137. Caldwell, introduction to *The Road to Serfdom*, 23–24. See also John Maynard Keynes, *The Collected Writings*, ed. Donald Moggridge, vol. 27: Activities, 1940–46 (London: Macmillan, 1980), 385–88.

138. Caldwell, introduction to *The Road to Serfdom*, 24.

139. Ibid., 2.

140. Ibid., 17.

141. Ibid., 23. Some have suggested that Hayek held a "night watchman" view—the minimalist position that the state's role is to protect citizens against violence, theft, and other forms of encroachment by other citizens, and nothing more. The "night watchman" framework was developed in the 1970s by Robert Nozick in his influential book *Anarchy, State, and Utopia*, which is often understood as a rebuttal of his Harvard colleague John Rawls. One of Nozick's key arguments is that if people don't like the situations in which they find themselves, they can always pick up and move, an argument that Milton Friedman also makes, and the arrogance of which is astonishing. In any case, Hayek's defense of social insurance and preventing pollution refutes the night watchman interpretation.

142. This is a point that was made strongly in the 1970s by economist Paul Samuelson; see Andrew Farrant and Edward McPhail, "Hayek, Samuelson, and the logic of the mixed economy?" *Journal of Economic Behavior and Organization* 69 (2009): 5–16.

143. Phillips-Fein, *Invisible Hands*, 282. She is referring here more generally to free-market philosophy in the late 1940s, but Hayek's book was the most notable expression of that philosophy at that time.

144. According to his biographer, Mises's relationship with NAM began in 1943, and he then worked for them as a consultant. If this is the earliest connection, NAM developed the indivisibility thesis at least six years (1937) before Mises began to consult for them, and NAM's use of Hayek is in that sense an intellectual marriage of convenience. On the other hand, it is possible that members of NAM were aware of Mises's arguments via Henry Hazlitt. Mises's book *Socialism* was published in English in 1936. Hazlitt reviewed it for the *New York Times* in 1938, so it is likely that Hazlitt discussed these ideas with associates at NAM during those years. For Hazlitt's work on Mises, see Boettke, "The Significance of Mises's 'Socialism.'" The Mises Institute stresses the relationship between Hazlitt and Mises but does not give a year for when they met. "Henry Hazlitt," Text, Mises Institute, June 20, 2014, https://mises.org/profile/henry-hazlitt. "While at the *New York Times*, he met the émigré economist Ludwig von Mises, whose work Hazlitt had admired. Hazlitt and Mises became friends, and Mises was thrilled at Hazlitt's editorial blasts against government planning and often consulted Hazlitt on editorial matters and contemporary politics. It is said that Hazlitt even prepared, at Mises's request, a version of *Human Action* as a journalist would have written it. Mises thanked him, but rejected most of the changes." Hazlitt was later one of the founders of the Mises Institute. Probably Hazlitt and Mises met in 1940: https://reason.com/1984/12/01/interview-with-henry-hazlitt/

145. Caldwell, introduction to *The Road to Serfdom*, 19.

146. Encyclopaedia Britannica, s.v., "Max Eastman, American Writer," January 8, 2021, https://www.britannica.com/biography/Max-Eastman.

147. J. Y. Smith, "DeWitt Wallace, 91, Dies," *Washington Post*, April 1, 1981, https://www.washingtonpost.com/archive/local/1981/04/01/dewitt-wallace-91-dies/617d74dc-4f2a-49d5-899a-d22389f33b12/.

148. Caldwell, introduction to *The Road to Serfdom*, 19. On the low expectations for the book at the University of Chicago Press, see Phillips-Fein, *Invisible Hands*, 41.

149. The troops fighting Franco were many things, but they were not fascists. On German communists and the Thaelmann Battalion, which fought against the fascists in the Spanish Civil

War, see "Thaelmann Battalion," Spartacus Educational, accessed March 11, 2021, https://
spartacus-educational.com/SPthaelmann.htm. Among the many folk songs of the Spanish
Civil War was "Freiheit!," which celebrated the Thaelmann Battalion. Pete Seeger and Group,
Songs of the Spanish Civil War, vol. 1 (Folkways Records, 1961), https://folkways-media.si.edu
/liner_notes/folkways/FW05436.pdf. One verse went:

> Beat the drums, ready the bayonets (charge)
> Forward, march, victory our reward.
> With our scarlet banner, smash their columns.
> Thaelmann Battalion. Ready, forward march.

Irwin Silber and Fred Silber, *Folksinger's Wordbook* (New York: Oak Publications, 1973), 304.
150. Hayek, *The Road to Serfdom: Reader's Digest Condensed Version*, 2.
151. Ibid., 19.
152. Ibid., 13.
153. Ibid., 2.
154. Ibid., 14 and 4.
155. Ibid., 12. The idea that freedom is especially Anglo-Saxon goes a long way back: it can be found in Jefferson, in Ralph Waldo Emerson, and in Albert Beveridge, to name a few. But that pedigree did not make it true. To the extent that democracy traces its roots (as well as its name) to ancient Greece, the concept of free citizens cannot be said to be particularly Anglo-Saxon.
156. Hayek, *The Road to Serfdom*, 156.
157. The federal Fair Labor Standards Act of 1938—widely considered the last major legislative accomplishment of the New Deal—provided for a forty-hour workweek, outlawed child labor, and set a minimum wage of twenty-five cents per hour which increased to forty cents over a seven-year period. One might argue that a minimum wage is interfering with competition, but this is not true as long as the minimum wage is applied equitably.
158. Caldwell, introduction to *The Road to Serfdom*, 20.
159. For Hayek's views on these matters, see Naomi Beck, *Hayek and the Evolution of Capitalism* (Chicago: University of Chicago Press, 2018), 5.
160. Hayek, *The Road to Serfdom: Reader's Digest Condensed Version*, 111. The original discussion is in Hayek, *The Road to Serfdom*, chap. 11. How ironic that Hayek included a critique of propaganda, only to be enrolled as a propagandist of capitalism! Perhaps Hayek anticipated that he might be critiqued on this apparent hypocrisy, because he goes on to explain that it is *totalitarian* propaganda that is objectionable, because "in a totalitarian state . . . all propaganda serves the same goal." (171). Still, much of what Hayek says applies fully to NAM, such as the idea that the "process of creating a myth to justify his action need not be conscious" (173). Yet, as we saw in chapter 3, for NAM it was indeed conscious.
161. "The Essence of the Road to Serfdom (in Cartoons!)," August 7, 2015, https://fee.org/articles /the-essence-of-the-road-to-serfdom-in-cartoons/. If Hayek was distressed by the simplification of his argument, it did not stop him from continuing to work with NAM. In 1961, he participated in a conference NAM sponsored on the "Spiritual and Moral Significance of Free Enterprise." See: "Proceedings of a Symposium with Felix Morley, Herrell deGraff, F.A Hayek, John Davenport," December 6, 1961, Folder Publications Spiritual and Moral Significance of Free Enterprise, Box 142, Series I, National Association of Manufacturers Records, accession 1411, Hagley Museum and Library, Wilmington, DE 19807. See also F.A. Hayek, "The Moral Element in Free Enterprise," Foundation for Economic Education, July 1, 1962, https://fee.org/articles/the-moral-element-in-free-enterprise/.

162. "The Road to Serfdom in Cartoons," originally published in *Look* magazine, 1945, reproduced from a booklet published in Detroit by General Motors, in the "Thought Starter" series (no. 118), https://cdn.mises.org/Road%20to%20Serfdom%20in%20Cartoons.pdf.

163. The ironies are endless and heartrending. When we were writing this book, we noted that FEE illustrates the site where they discuss the *Look* cartoon with Picasso's *Guernica*. (This no longer seems to be the case.) Picasso was, of course, a leftist who hated Franco and his industrialist allies. "The Essence of the Road to Serfdom (in Cartoons!)," August 7, 2015, https://fee.org/articles/the-essence-of-the-road-to-serfdom-in-cartoons/.

164. Caldwell, introduction to *The Road to Serfdom*, 22.

165. Ibid.

166. Ibid., italics added.

167. Robert Manduca, "Selling Keynesianism," *Boston Review*, December 9, 2019, http://bostonreview.net/class-inequality/robert-manduca-selling-keynesianism.

168. Plehwe, introduction to *The Road from Mont Pèlerin*, 16.

169. Albert Hunold, "How Mises Changed My Mind," *Mont Pelerin Quarterly* III, no. 3 (October 1961): 16, https://mises.org/library/how-mises-changed-my-mind.

170. George H. Nash, quoted in Plehwe, introduction to *The Road from Mont Pèlerin*, 16. Nash would go on to write *The Conservative Intellectual Movement in America Since 1945*. See also Nancy MacLean, *Democracy in Chains: The Deep History of the Radical Right's Stealth Plan for America* (New York: Viking, 2017).

171. Phillips-Fein, *Invisible Hands*, 45.

172. Janek Wasserman, *The Marginal Revolutionaries: How Austrian Economists Fought the War of Ideas* (New Haven, CT: Yale University Press, 2019), 197.

173. Ibid.

174. Quoted in Plehwe, introduction to *The Road from Mont Pèlerin*, 16.

175. Plehwe, introduction to *The Road from Mont Pèlerin*, 22–24. This is edited for brevity.

176. Here we can see one element of conservative hostility to the "administrative state" and "agency deference." This also sheds additional light on the Republican refusal to hold hearings on President Barack Obama's nomination of Judge Merrick Garland to the U.S. Supreme Court in 2016. While Democrats defended Garland as a moderate, which in most respects he was, he was also a strong advocate of agency deference. James B. Stewart, "On Business Issues, Republicans Might Want a Justice Garland," *New York Times*, March 24, 2016, sec. Business, https://www.nytimes.com/2016/03/25/business/on-business-issues-republicans-might-want-a-justice-garland.html. On the other hand, the Republican actions suggested that they would have refused to hold hearings on any Obama nominee. Right-wing hostility to agency deference also played a major role in *West Virginia v. EPA*, which denied the agenda's authority to regulate greenhouse gases. See https:///www.supremecourt.gov.opinions.21pdf/20-1530_n758.pdf.

177. Plehwe, introduction to *The Road from Mont Pèlerin*, 24–25.

178. Ibid., 25.

179. Ibid., 28.

180. Plehwe suggests that the key shared values were economic freedom and individualism, the affirmation of moral standards, and "possibly surprising for many critiques: social minimum standards." What was notably missing were rights traditionally valued by liberals, such as the right to form coalitions and freedom of the press. Plehwe, introduction to *The Road from Mont Pèlerin*, 25–26.

181. Wasserman, *The Marginal Revolutionaries*, 197. According to Caldwell, Luigi Einaudi—at the time a governor of the Bank of Italy—was scheduled to attempt the first meeting, but for

some reason did not. (Bruce Caldwell, Mont Pèlerin, 1947, chapter 6 in the Mont Pelerin Society 1980–2020, a Special Meeting of the Hoover Institution, https://www.hoover.org /sites/default/files/research/docs/mps_caldwell.pdf). However, in 1951, by which time he had been elected president of Italy, he joined as a member, belying the society's claim (as Dieter Plehwe notes) to a "draconian renunciation of political activism." (Plehwe, introduction to *The Road from Mont Pèlerin*, 22.)

182. Nine Earhart Foundation fellows have won the Nobel Memorial Prize in Economic Sciences, and several others, including Milton Friedman and George Stigler, had Earhart support of some kind. The foundation closed in 2016. At one point its assets were $95 million. Kari Barbic, "Harry Earhart," Philanthropy Roundtable, accessed March 13, 2021, https://www .philanthropyroundtable.org/almanac/people/hall-of-fame/detail/harry-earhart. Earhart believed that "the free, competitive American enterprise system, based upon the Christian ethic, was the highest form of social organization in history." They supported scholars who argued, with respect to AIDS, "[t]hat the value of government intervention and medical research is often overstated, especially as the epidemic is largely limited to 'homosexual men' and intravenous drug abusers." Avner Ahituv, V. Joseph Hotz, and Tomas Philipson, "Will the AIDS Epidemic Be Self-Limiting? Evidence on the Responsiveness of the Demand for Condoms to the Prevalence of AIDS," Working Papers (Harris School of Public Policy Studies, University of Chicago, January 1994), https://ideas.repec.org/p/har/wpaper/9401 .html. The Earhart Foundation has also been a major supporter of the American Enterprise Institute, and the George C. Marshall Institute. "ExxonSecrets Factsheet: George C. Marshall Institute," Exxon Secrets, accessed March 13, 2021, https://exxonsecrets.org/html /orgfactsheet.php?id=36. For a full discussion of the Marshall Institute, see Oreskes and Conway, *Merchants of Doubt*.

183. Plehwe, introduction to *The Road from Mont Pèlerin*, 15.

184. Phillips-Fein, *Invisible Hands*, 44.

185. Ibid.

186. Ibid.

187. See Plehwe, introduction to *The Road from Mont Pèlerin*, 22, on Hayek's renunciation of political goals. Also see Phillips-Fein, *Invisible Hands*, for more on the political goals of Crane, Luhnow, et al.

188. Wasserman, *The Marginal Revolutionaries*, 199.

189. Nash, in *The Conservative Intellectual Movement*, argues that traditionalism often clashed with market fundamentalism, as markets can be disruptive and even inimical to traditional values. See also Burgin, *The Great Persuasion*, introduction.

190. Jacob S. Hacker and Paul Pierson, *American Amnesia: How the War on Government Led Us to Forget What Made America Prosper* (New York: Simon & Schuster, 2016), 348.

191. Quinn Slobodian, *Globalists: The End of Empire and the Birth of Neoliberalism* (Cambridge, MA: Harvard University Press, 2018), 2.

192. Ibid., 15. Slobodian argues that this is tied to decolonization, and the imperative to prevent popular will from prevailing in newly liberated post-colonial states. It can also help to explain the authoritarian tendencies of people like Rose Wilder Lane, and why Hayek and Friedman supported the military dictator Augusto Pinochet in Chile.

193. Ralf Ptak, "Neoliberalism in Germany," in *The Road from Mont Pèlerin: The Making of the Neoliberal Thought Collective*, ed. by Philip Mirowski and Dieter Plehwe (Cambridge, MA: Harvard University Press, 2009), 101.

194. Keith Tribe, "Liberalism and Neoliberalism in Britain, 1930–1980," in *The Road from Mont Pèlerin: The Making of the Neoliberal Thought Collective*, ed. Philip Mirowski and Dieter Plehwe (Cambridge, MA: Harvard University Press, 2009), 68–69.

195. François Denord, "French Neoliberalism and Its Divisions: From the Colloque Walter Lippmann to the Fifth Republic," in *The Road from Mont Pèlerin: The Making of the Neoliberal Thought Collective*, ed. Philip Mirowski and Dieter Plehwe (Cambridge, MA: Harvard University Press, 2009), 49. On Lippman's influence on Hayek, see Carter, *The Price of Peace*.

196. Denord, "French Neoliberalism," 49.

197. See Tribe, "Liberalism and Neoliberalism," 75, on this point. He argues that the key difference is the inversion of the relationship between politics and economics: classical liberalism vested liberty in individual rights. Neoliberalism sees liberty as guaranteed by the "impersonality of market forces."

198. Denord, "French Neoliberalism," 49.

199. Burgin, *The Great Persuasion*, 9–11.

200. Vinod Thomas, "The Danger of Dismissing Market Failures," *Brookings* (blog), July 12, 2017, https://www.brookings.edu/blog/future-development/2017/07/12/the-danger-of-dismissing -market-failures/. For a recent example of denying or brushing away market failure, see Tim Worstall, "Nick Stern Is Wrong; Climate Change Is Not the Largest Market Failure the World Has Ever Seen," *Forbes*, January 25, 2015, https://www.forbes.com/sites/timworstall /2015/01/25/nick-stern-is-wrong-climate-change-is-not-the-largest-market-failure-the-world -has-ever-seen/. Worstall argues that climate change is not a market failure, because no market exists for emissions. Therefore it is not a market failure, it is a "market absence." That is sophistry. Markets, operating under legal conditions, created a problem that markets have not solved; this is the very definition of market failure. There is no market for emissions because there is no demand for them; emissions have no positive value. They are an external cost, as identified by Pigou and Coase decades ago. Call it a market failure or a failure of markets, it amounts to the same thing, particularly if the solution is for governments to intervene to create carbon markets. Failures of capitalism are often dismissed with arguments that the capitalism wasn't pure enough, that it was crony capitalism, ethno-capitalism, or statist capitalism. In other words, they aren't actually capitalism. So the failures are in effect attributed to heresy.

201. Denord, "French Neoliberalism," 49.

202. Cox, *The Market as God*, 15.

203. Jonathan Haidt, quoted in James Hoggan and Grania Litwin, *I'm Right and You're an Idiot: The Toxic State of Public Discourse and How to Clean it Up* (Gabriola Island, BC: New Society Publishers, 2016), 39.

204. Cox, *The Market as God*, 15.

205. Margaret Atwood, *Payback: Debt and the Shadow Side of Wealth Management* (Toronto: House of Anansi Press, 2008), 180.

206. Hacker and Pierson, *American Amnesia*, 170.

207. Burgin, *The Great Persuasion*, 11.

208. Naomi Oreskes, *Science on a Mission*.

209. Our argument here therefore complements, but to some extent also critiques, previous studies, which have almost always noted the financial support of Luhnow and Crane but presented it as part of the "background" of the story.

CHAPTER 6: THE BIG MYTH GOES WEST

1. Herbert Hoover Presidential Library and Museum, "The Rose Wilder Lane Collection," March 13, 2020, https://hoover.archives.gov/research/collections/lane.

2. Roger Lea MacBride, introduction to *The Discovery of Freedom: Man's Struggle Against Authority*, by Rose Wilder Lane, reprinted ed. (New York: Laissez Faire Books, 1984 [1943]), v.

3. MacBride, introduction to *The Discovery of Freedom*, v. In her 1936 article "Credo," Lane claims that she was once a communist; MacBride claims that she never actually succumbed, but had been influenced and tempted. Jennifer Burns calls Lane's political vision "an individualist philosophy that stopped just short of anarchy." Jennifer Burns, "The Three 'Furies' of Libertarianism: Rose Wilder Lane, Isabel Paterson, and Ayn Rand," *Journal of American History* 102, no. 3 (December 2015): 761.

4. Caroline Fraser, *Prairie Fires: The American Dreams of Laura Ingalls Wilder* (New York: Metropolitan Books, 2017), 386.

5. Fraser, *Prairie Fires*, 386.

6. Burns, "Three 'Furies,'" 752.

7. A Grain Trader, "Wheat and the Great American Desert," *Saturday Evening Post*, 206, no. 13, September 23, 1933, 10.

8. Christine Woodside, *Libertarians on the Prairie: Laura Ingalls Wilder, Rose Wilder Lane, and the Making of the Little House Books* (New York: Arcade Publishing, 2016), 78.

9. Fraser, *Prairie Fires*, 401.

10. Rose Wilder Lane, "Credo," *Saturday Evening Post*, March 7, 1936, 6.

11. Rose Wilder Lane, *Give Me Liberty*, rev. ed. (Caldwell, ID: Caxton Printers, 1954), 42. The full context of this is interesting, as (like Hayek, later) she recognizes income inequality as a problem: "There is still far too much economic inequality; the gap between rich and poor has not been sufficiently narrowed. Something certainly should be done to distribute wealth, to raise the general standard of living, to improve living conditions for the poor and to give everyone a more abundant life. But that is precisely what this anarchy of individualism has been doing . . ." (34). Her solution, however, is more individualism.

12. Lane, *Give Me Liberty*, 49.

13. Fraser, *Prairie Fires*, 2, 489.

14. Herbert Hoover Presidential Library and Museum, "Rose Wilder Lane Collection," March 13, 2020, https://hoover.archives.gov/research/collections/lane. The finding aid notes that the Lane papers are among the most heavily used materials in the presidential collection.

15. The astonishing persistence of the myth of free land is amply illustrated in a recent piece in the *New York Times* on building on "free or inherited" land. Alyson Krueger, "Living on Free Land," *New York Times*, June 12, 2020, https://www.nytimes.com/2020/06/12/realestate/homesteading-free-land-programs.html. Most of the featured locales are in the American West, in areas where lands were forcibly taken from Indigenous peoples.

16. Frederick Jackson Turner, *The Frontier in American History* (Tucson: University of Arizona Press, 1986 [1920]), 1.

17. Native American resistance of course continued in diverse ways, but Wounded Knee was the last large organized armed resistance until the 1970s. Nick Estes, *Our History Is the Future: Standing Rock Versus the Dakota Access Pipeline, and the Long Tradition of Indigenous Resistance* (London: Verso, 2019), 133; and David Treuer, *The Heartbeat of Wounded Knee: Native America from 1890 to the Present* (New York: Riverhead Books, 2019).

18. Turner, *The Frontier*, 21–22.

19. Fraser, *Prairie Fires*, 61.

20. Fraser, *Prairie Fires*, 60. For a history of the Osage, see Robert Allen Warrior, *The People and the Word: Reading Native Nonfiction* (Minneapolis: University of Minnesota Press, 2005), 49–94.

21. Fraser, *Prairie Fires*, 72.

22. Ibid., 75–77.

23. Ibid., 80.
24. Ibid., 80.
25. Ibid., 88.
26. Ibid., 97.
27. Congress reduced the mandated cultivation period from ten to eight years in 1874 and in 1878 cut the acreage requirement to ten. The Timber Culture Act of 1873 was repealed in 1891. C. Barron McIntosh, "Use and Abuse of the Timber Culture Act," *Annals of the Association of American Geographers* 65, no. 3 (September 1975): 347–62.
28. Summarized from Fraser, *Prairie Fires*, 143–8.
29. Ibid., 153.
30. Ibid., 154–55.
31. Ibid., 104.
32. Clara Sue Kidwell, *The Choctaws in Oklahoma: From Tribe to Nation, 1855–1970* (Norman: University of Oklahoma Press, 2007), 137. See also Richard White, *Railroaded: The Transcontinentals and the Making of Modern America* (New York: W. W. Norton, 2011), 62–66, 489.
33. Fraser, *Prairie Fires*, 106.
34. Richard Maxwell Brown, "The Enduring Frontier: The Impact of Weather on South Dakota History and Literature," *South Dakota History* 15 (1985): 36.
35. The existing accounts of this birth are unclear: the local newspaper recorded the birth as July 11, 1889, but Laura later claimed August 5. Given the tragedy of this whole summer, one suspects Laura's memory was faulty. Fraser, *Prairie Fires*, 159.
36. Ibid., 250.
37. Woodside, *Libertarians on the Prairie*, 58.
38. Ibid., 58–61.
39. Laura Ingalls Wilder, *Little House in the Big Woods*, rev. ed. (New York: HarperCollins, 1953).
40. Woodside, *Libertarians on the Prairie*, 67.
41. Laura Ingalls Wilder, *Farmer Boy*, in *The Little House Books*, vol. 1, ed. Caroline Fraser (New York: Library of America, 2012), 117.
42. Wilder, *Farmer Boy*, 180.
43. Later, this simple view of accumulation through labor is undermined by a story in which Father explains interest to Almanzo as the easiest way to make money (though he doesn't explain where interest comes from).
44. Wilder, *Farmer Boy*, 183.
45. Wilder, *Farmer Boy*, 262.
46. The Boyhood Home of Almanzo Wilder near Malone, NY, operated by the Almanzo and Laura Ingalls Wilder Association, was listed on the National Register of Historic Places in 2014. Thus the site of a fictionalized account becomes a piece of "history." On a cultural level, that makes sense, but if visitors understand the site as accurately represented in the fictional works, that is another matter: https://almanzowilderfarm.com/support/about-our-association/. "Literary Landmark: Wilder Homestead," United for Libraries, accessed May 12, 2022, https://www.ala.org/united/products_services/literarylandmarks/landmarksbyyear/2015/.
47. Anita Clair Fellman, *Little House, Long Shadow: Laura Ingalls Wilder's Impact on American Culture* (Columbia: University of Missouri Press, 2008), 95–96.
48. Wilder, *The Little House on the Prairie* (New York: HarperCollins, 1953), 220–21.
49. John C. Weaver writes of Locke's "doctrine of Improvement" that "comparable beliefs were on the lips of frontiersmen everywhere . . . Around the world, colonizers who pleaded for

access to territory or enhanced property rights articulated common arguments." Weaver, *The Great Land Rush and the Making of the Modern World, 1650–1900* (Montreal: McGill–Queen's University Press, 2003), 81.

50. Wilder, *Little House*, 171.

51. Fellman, *Little House, Long Shadow*, 99. Fellman emphasizes that this story wasn't true either. Neighbors had been caught in the blizzard, not Charles Ingalls.

52. Woodside, *Libertarians on the Prairie*, 99.

53. Fraser, *Prairie Fires*, 387.

54. Laura Ingalls Wilder, *The Long Winter*, in *The Little House Books*, vol. 2, ed. Caroline Fraser (New York: Library of America: 2012), 321.

55. Wilder, *The Long Winter*, 347.

56. Ibid., 348.

57. Text quoted in Fraser, *Prairie Fires*, 460.

58. Jim Powell, "Rose Wilder Lane, Isabel Paterson, and Ayn Rand: Three Women Who Inspired the Modern Libertarian Movement," Foundation for Economic Education, May 1, 1996, https://fee.org/articles/rose-wilder-lane-isabel-paterson-and-ayn-rand-three-women-who-inspired-the-modern-libertarian-movement/; and Jim Powell and Lawrence Reed, "3 Women Who Inspired the Modern Libertarian Movement," Learn Liberty, March 12, 2017, https://www.learnliberty.org/blog/3-women-who-inspired-the-modern-libertarian-movement/.

59. Burns, "Three 'Furies,'" 746.

60. MacBride, introduction to *Discovery of Freedom*, vi.

61. Ibid., 202–3. Perhaps she meant the Seventeenth Amendment, which allowed for the direct election of senators.

62. Ibid., 158, 175.

63. Ibid., 42-45, emphasis in original. Her arguments echo Isabel Paterson's ideas in *The God of the Machine* (1943). Jennifer Burns notes that for a time, Paterson, Lane, and Rand were friends, but perhaps unsurprisingly these radical individualists all eventually fell out. See Burns, "Three 'Furies,'" 768, 773.

64. Lane, *Discovery of Freedom*, 39. In later years, Lane acknowledged that there were mistakes in the book, but she seemed to view the mistakes as problems in the argument, not errors of fact. See MacBride, introduction to *Discovery of Freedom*, xi.

65. Lane, *Discovery of Freedom*, 5–6.

66. Lane uses the term "pagan superstition" several times in the book.

67. Ibid., 16.

68. Ibid., ix.

69. Ibid., 270.

70. Ibid., 38.

71. Ibid., 27–8.

72. Ibid., 28–9.

73. Ibid., 29.

74. Lane does not address the question of defining "Bad Men." She seems to restrict it to those who rob and kill, although killing native people was presumably acceptable in her view.

75. Ibid., 32.

76. Ibid., 37.

77. Ibid., 178.

78. James Madison, "The Federalist Papers: No. 10 The Union as a Safeguard against Domestic Faction and Insurrection" from the New York Packet, Friday, November 23, 1787, available from the Avalon Project of Yale Law School Lillian Goldman Law Library, https://avalon.law.yale.edu/18th_century/fed10.asp.

79. For a recent survey of scholarly debates on Madison's political thought, see Peter S. Onuf, "Federalist Republican: Michael Zuckert's James Madison," *American Political Thought* 8, no. 2 (Spring 2019): 258–70; and Jedediah Britton-Purdy, "The Republican Party Is Succeeding Because We Are Not a True Democracy, *New York Times*, January 3, 2022, https://www.nytimes.com/2022/01/03/opinion/us-democracy-constitution.html

80. Lane, *Discovery of Freedom*, 179.

81. Presenting a coherent interpretation of Lane is a challenge, because at times she seems to approve of the Constitution as representing the will of the people, but at other times to reject representative democracy altogether. See Lane, *Discovery of Freedom*, 196–203. She repeatedly makes clear her disdain for majority rule. In her introduction, she suggests that America was on track for about eighty years (see xix and also her discussion on 196–203, esp. 201): "The American revolutionists solved" the problem of tyranny "not only by dividing and checking the government's use of force, but also by dividing and checking the majority"—in other words, by preventing majority rule.

82. Lane, *Discovery of Freedom*, 189–90.

83. Ibid., 149.

84. Ibid., 180.

85. Ibid., 183.

86. Ibid., 178.

87. Ibid., 203, italics added.

88. Ibid.

89. Ibid., 206. Here Lane invokes Prohibition and other social reforms.

90. Ibid., 207.

91. Ibid., 213.

92. This was a common talking point among the defenders of capitalism, including the *Economist* magazine in the nineteenth century. See Adam Tooze, "What the Economist Doesn't Tell You," *Prospect,* March 30, 2020, https://www.prospectmagazine.co.uk/magazine/what-the -economist-doesnt-tell-you-liberal-democracy-populism-review

93. Lane, *Discovery of Freedom*, 63.

94. Ibid., 64.

95. Hans F. Sennholz, foreword to Lane, *Discovery of Freedom*, viii.

96. Jörg Guido Hülsmann, *Mises: The Last Knight of Liberalism* (Auburn, AL: Ludwig von Mises Institute, 2007), 838. See also George H. Nash, *The Conservative Intellectual Movement in America Since 1945*, 30th anniv. ed. (Wilmington, DE: Intercollegiate Studies Institute, 2006).

97. Hülsmann, *The Last Knight*, 838.

98. For Lane's correspondence with Crane, see Roger Lea MacBride, ed., *The Lady and the Tycoon: The Best of Letters between Rose Wilder Lane and Jasper Crane* (Caldwell, ID: Caxton, 1973).

99. Powell, "Rose Wilder Lane, Isabel Paterson, and Ayn Rand."

100. Paterson would criticize the Chamber of Commerce for having sold out on the New Deal; she complained in a letter to Rand that "the Chamber of Commerce never put out anything that wouldn't be quite suitable for publication in the *New Masses* or the *Daily Worker*." The context of this quotation suggests that she believed that Leonard Read was also soft. Quoted in Burns, "Three 'Furies,'" 767.

101. Burns, "Three 'Furies,'" 748.

102. Ibid., 766.

103. Lane, *Discovery of Freedom*, 245.

104. Burns, "Three 'Furies,'" 766.

105. Ibid., 769.

106. Ibid., 766.

107. For accounts of this episode, see Sandra J. Peart and David M. Levy, "F. A. Hayek and the 'Individualists,'" in *F. A. Hayek and the Modern Economy*, ed. Sandra J. Peart and David M. Levy (New York: Palgrave Macmillan, 2013), 29–56; G. C. Harcourt, "Lorie Tarshis, 1911–1993: In Appreciation," in *50 Years a Keynesian and Other Essays* (London: Palgrave Macmillan UK, 2001), 114–30; and Zachary D. Carter, *The Price of Peace: Money, Democracy, and the Life of John Maynard Keynes* (New York: Random House, 2020), 375–81.

108. Admittedly, Keynes once described his approach as "liberal socialism" and imagined that the government would direct two thirds of total investment in the economy, so from the libertarian point of view, Keynes's ideas did pose a real threat. Still, they were not centralized planning in the Soviet sense. John Maynard Keynes, "Democracy and Efficiency," *New Statesman and Nation*, January 28, 1939. Quoted in Carter, *The Price of Peace*, 350. See also James Crotty, *Keynes Against Capitalism: His Economic Case for Liberal Socialism* (London: Routledge, 2019).

109. Pew to Lane, August 5, 1948, folder Rose Wilder Lane Correspondence, box 17, J. Howard Pew papers, accession 1634, Hagley Museum and Library, Wilmington, DE, 19807.

110. Burns, "Three 'Furies,'" 771.

111. During the Depression, Harvard had purged its economics department of faculty who were perceived to be too left-wing. As a result of this, John Kenneth Galbraith was advised by his mentor to look for work elsewhere. See chap. 10 in Zachary D. Carter, *The Price of Peace*; and Richard Parker, *John Kenneth Galbraith: His Life, His Politics, His Economics* (New York: Farrar, Straus and Giroux, 2005), 104–7. Harvard president James Conant denied that they were "discharged because of their liberal sentiments and sympathies with organized labor," but the specificity of his denial suggested otherwise. (He also suggested that they should be grateful for the "valuable experience" they had gained teaching at Harvard. See Special to the *New York Times*, "Dr. Conant Denies Ban on Liberals," *New York Times*, April 13, 1937, https://www.nytimes.com/1937/04/13/archives/dr-conant-denies-ban-on-liberals-harvard-did-not-drop-drs-j-r-walsh.html. A similar purge occurred again in the 1960s. Jeremy S. Bluhm, "Radical Economics: How Not to Get Tenure at Harvard," February 16, 1973, https://www.thecrimson.com/article/1973/2/16/radical-economics-how-not-to-get-tenure/. Contemporary conservatives love to complain about discrimination in academia against them, but we know of no documented cases of conservative economists being purged at Harvard, or for that matter anywhere.

112. Catherine Lawson, "The 'Textbook Controversy': Lessons for Contemporary Economics," *AAUP Journal of Academic Freedom* 6 (2015), 1–14; Samuelson himself believed the campaign against Tarshis was to his benefit. See Paul A. Samuelson, "Credo of a Lucky Textbook Author," *Journal of Economic Perspectives* 11, no. 2 (Spring 1997): 153–60.

113. Michael Bernstein, *A Perilous Progress: Economists and Public Purpose in Twentieth-Century America* (Princeton, NJ: Princeton University Press, 2001), 5. Binyamin Appelbaum agrees that "critiques of capitalism that remained a staple of mainstream debate in Europe were seldom heard" in American economics departments. *The Economists' Hour: False Prophets, Free Markets, and the Fracture of Society* (New York: Little Brown, 2019), 17.

114. Lane to Mises, July 5, 1947, quoted in Hülsmann, *The Last Knight*, 859n43.

115. Hülsmann, *The Last Knight*, 1025, quoting Mises writing to Bruno Leono.

116. Ibid., 1025–6.

117. Ludwig von Mises, quoted in Hülsmann, *The Last Knight*, 1026.

118. Powell and Reed, "3 Women Who Inspired the Modern Libertarian Movement."

119. For a detailed analysis of how Lane infused the Little House books with libertarian ideas (whether unconsciously or not), see Woodside, *Libertarians on the Prairie, passim.*

120. Christine Woodside, "How 'Little House on the Prairie' Built Modern Conservatism," *Politico*, September 11, 2016, https://www.politico.com/magazine/story/2016/09/little-house-on-the-prairie-conservatism-214237.

121. Lizzie Skurnick, "In Promoting the 'Myth of White Self-Sufficiency,' the 'Little House' Books Rewrite History," PBS, December 23, 2020, https://www.pbs.org/wnet/american masters/in-promoting-the-myth-of-white-self-sufficiency-the-little-house-books-rewrite -history/16545.

122. The television show was co-produced by Roger Lea MacBride, the "adopted" grandson of Rose Wilder Lane, who ran for president of the United States in 1976 on the Libertarian ticket. Fraser, *Prairie Fires*, 5, 504.

123. Internet Movie Database user review, October 8, 2020, https://www.imdb.com/review /rw6156930/?ref_=tt_urv.

124. Fraser, *Prairie Fires*, 504.

125. Ibid., 5.

126. Ibid., 2.

CHAPTER 7: A QUESTIONABLE GOSPEL

1. Kevin Michael Kruse, *One Nation Under God: How Corporate America Invented Christian America* (New York: Basic Books, 2015), 4–5; and James McKay, "Crusading for Capitalism: Christian Capitalists and the Ideological Roots of the Conservative Movement" (PhD diss., University of Wisconsin–Madison, 2015), 16–17.

2. Matthew 19:24, italics added.

3. This was not usual at the time. President Calvin Coolidge embodied the amalgamation of liberal Congregationalism with right-wing politics. Conversely, many conservative Christians, such as William Jennings Bryan, were politically progressive. See Edward J. Larson, *Summer for the Gods: The Scopes Trial and America's Continuing Debate over Science and Religion* (New York: Basic Books, 2006).

4. Kruse, *One Nation*, chap. 1.

5. James W. Fifield Jr. with Bill Youngs, *The Tall Preacher* (Los Angeles: Pepperdine University Press, 1977), p. 34.

6. McKay, "Crusading for Capitalism," 19.

7. Associated Press, "Church Group Asks Profit System End; Planned Social Economy Is Urged by Congregational and Christian Seminar," *New York Times*, June 27, 1934, http://times machine.nytimes.com/timesmachine/1934/06/27/94545698.html.

8. The full quotation is more nuanced and less dismissive: "Religious suffering is, at one and the same time, the expression of real suffering and a protest against real suffering. Religion is the sigh of the oppressed creature, the heart of a heartless world, and the soul of soulless conditions. It is the opium of the people." This is found in his 1843 "Contribution to the Critique of Hegel's Philosophy of Right," posthumously published as Karl Marx, *Critique of Hegel's Philosophy of Right*, ed. Joseph O'Malley (Cambridge: Cambridge University Press, 1970).

9. William Ernest Hocking, *Freedom of the Press: A Framework of Principle* (Chicago: University of Chicago Press, 1947), 70.

10. McKay, "Crusading," 11.

11. The son of a Congregational minister, Millikan was a parishioner in Fifield's First Congregationalist Church of Los Angeles and was also active in Pasadena's Neighborhood

Church, where he was a trustee. He was also a trustee of the Human Betterment Foundation, which was devoted to eugenics research and to the promotion of eugenics-based policies, including forced sterilization. He would support Fifield and Spiritual Mobilization until 1952, when Fifield began propagandizing against the United Nations. Millikan chose to support the internationalism of science instead. See Edward B. Davis, "Robert Andrews Millikan: Religion, Science, and Modernity" in *Eminent Lives in Twentieth-Century Science & Religion*, ed. Nicolaas A. Rupke (New York: Peter Lang GmbH, 2009), 253–74; Letter, R. A. Millikan to J. W. Fifield, June 2, 1952, box 39, folder 39.14 Fifield, James W., Papers of Robert A. Millikan, Archives, California Institute of Technology; and Nidhi Subbaraman, "Caltech Confronted Its Racist Past. Here's What Happened," *Nature* 599 (November 10, 2021), 194–98.

12. "Minister Sees Dictator Trend," *Los Angeles Times*, October 3, 1938.

13. Ibid., 8.

14. McKay, "Crusading," 56.

15. "A Suggested Answer to Hitler Paganism," *Los Angeles Times*, June 15, 1940, 20.

16. "Spiritual Mobilization Plan Reported Making Rapid Gains," *Los Angeles Times*, June 17, 1940.

17. "Industry Congress to Look to Future," *New York Times*, December 8, 1940. The oil industry had a history of supporting fundamentalist Christianity; in the 1910s Union Oil had funded booklets titled "The Fundamentals: A Testimony to Truth," a riposte to liberal theology.

18. Franklin D. Roosevelt, "State of the Union Address: The Four Freedoms," Washington, D.C., January 6, 1941, https://voicesofdemocracy.umd.edu/fdr-the-four-freedoms-speech-text/.

19. James J. Fifield Jr. to J. Howard Pew, August 21, 1943, folder 5, box 4, Papers of J. Howard Pew, accession 1634, Hagley Museum and Library, Wilmington, DE 19807.

20. Ibid.

21. Alfred P. Haake to J. Howard Pew, November 13, 1943, folder 5, box 4, Papers of J. Howard Pew, accession 1634, Hagley Museum and Library, Wilmington, DE 19807.

22. Ibid.

23. McKay, "Crusading for Capitalism," 50.

24. Folder S 1945, box 8, Papers of J. Howard Pew, accession 1634, Hagley Museum and Library, Wilmington, DE 19807.

25. "Hoover Warns Against Communist Trend Sweeping Over Old War," *Los Angeles Times*, August 12, 1945, 1–2; McKay, "Crusading," 54.

26. Ibid.

27. The OPA was dismantled in 1947.

28. Fifield, "Confidential Memorandum from the Director," n.d. but circa early 1945, folder Spiritual Mobilization, box 8, Papers of J. Howard Pew, accession 1634, Hagley Museum and Library, Wilmington, DE 19807, italics added.

29. Rev. John Evans, "Unitarians Rip Church Group's 'Pagan' Tenets," *Chicago Tribune*, August 23, 1944.

30. Reinhold Niebuhr, "As Others See Us," *Christianity and Crisis* 6, no. 21 (December 9, 1946): 5. McKay gives a much different interpretation of this. McKay, "Crusading, for Capitalism" 63.

31. Niebuhr, "As Others See Us," 4–6.

32. McKay, "Crusading," 59.

33. Carol V. R. George, *God's Salesman: Norman Vincent Peale and the Power of Positive Thinking*, 2nd ed. (New York: Oxford University Press, 2019), 100.

34. Norman Vincent Peale, "Perils to Freedom," October 12, 1947, copy in folder P 1947, box 14, Papers of J. Howard Pew, accession 1634, Hagley Museum and Library, Wilmington, DE 19807.

35. The founders' junking of their original plan of government for a quite different one is an admission that they, and their designs, were imperfect. They retained the right to fix a failing government—and so do we.

36. United States Constitution, First and Fifth Amendments, italics added.

37. In practice, speech often has been curtailed, most famously when courts have judged that speech to constitute to be a "clear and present danger." For discussion, see Lee C. Bollinger and Geoffrey R. Stone, "Dialogue," in *The Free Speech Century*, ed. Lee C. Bollinger and Geoffrey R. Stone (New York: Oxford University Press, 2019), 1–12; on hate speech and pornography, see Elena Kagan, "Regulation of Hate Speech and Pornography after *R.A.V.*," *University of Chicago Law Review* 60, no. 3–4 (1993): 873–902. For a classic analysis of the First Amendment, see Thomas I. Emerson, "Toward a General Theory of the First Amendment," *Yale Law Journal* 72, no. 5 (April 1963): 877–956.

38. Norman Vincent Peale, "Sermon: Perils to Freedom," New York, Marble Collegiate Church, October 12, 1947, 4.

39. Congress, courts, and lawyers have argued for centuries over what the founders actually meant by "property." There's an enormous body of law built on this one phrase now, and it must be updated when "innovators" create a new kind of property for which they want to secure rights. Engineered genes, to take a modern example, only became "property" when Congress updated patent laws to make them a form of intellectual property. See, for example, Myles Jackson, *The Genealogy of a Gene: Patents, HIV/AIDS, and Race* (Cambridge, MA: MIT Press, 2015).

40. Norman Vincent Peale, *The Power of Positive Thinking* (New York: Touchstone, 2015, repr. ed.). See also Gwenda Blair, "How Norman Vincent Peale Taught Donald Trump to Worship Himself," *Politico*, October 6, 2015, https://www.politico.com/magazine/story/2015/10/donald-trump-2016-norman-vincent-peale-213220.

41. Paul Schwartzman, "How Trump Got Religion—and Why His Legendary Minister's Son Now Rejects Him," *Washington Post*, January 21, 2016, https://www.washingtonpost.com/lifestyle/how-trump-got-religion—and-why-his-legendary-ministers-son-now-rejects-him/2016/01/21/37bae16e-bb02-11e5-829c-26ffb874a18d_story.html.

42. McKay, "Crusading," 66.

43. Ibid., 67–69.

44. Peale had introduced this argument as well in his Columbus Day sermon, "Perils to Freedom."

45. E.g., James W. Fifield, "Peace on Earth," *Faith and Freedom* 3, no. 3 (March 1951): 8.

46. McKay makes this point very well in "Crusading for Capitalism," 71.

47. Quoted in Ibid., 71.

48. McKay, "Crusading for Capitalism," 75.

49. Ibid., 76.

50. Frederick B. Pew to J. Howard Pew, January 9, 1957, folder James Fifield, box 54, Papers of J. Howard Pew, accession 1634, Hagley Museum and Library, Wilmington, DE 19807.

51. Amy C. Wallhermfechtel, "Shaping the Right to Work: The Cecil B. DeMille Foundation's Role in State and National Right to Work Campaigns" (PhD diss., Saint Louis University, 2014). DeMille was viewed by Fifield and Pew as a linchpin in the effort. See J. Howard Pew to James W. Fifield, May 24, 1951, folder Committee to Proclaim Freedom, box 28, Papers of J. Howard Pew, accession 1634, Hagley Museum and Library, Wilmington, DE 19807.

52. Kruse, *One Nation*, 27–28.

53. Kruse, *One Nation,* 33–34; and "'Freedom Under God' Will Feature July 4th Events," *Los Angeles Times,* July 2, 1951, 25.

54. Lloyd M. Harmon, "Swan Song of Coastal Sardine," *Los Angeles Times,* June 18, 1951.

55. James W. Fifield, "Dr. Fifield's Farewell," *Faith and Freedom* 5, no. 1 (1959).

56. Correspondence in folder James Fifield 1957, box 54, Papers of J. Howard Pew, accession 1634, Hagley Museum and Library, Wilmington, DE 19807. Fifield passed away in 1977: "Dr. James W. Fifield, Fiery Preacher, Succumbs at 78," *Los Angeles Times,* February 26, 1977.

57. McKay, "Crusading," 64, tells this story a bit differently. Also see James W. Fifield to Norman Vincent Peale, May 9, 1949; and James W. Fifield to J. Howard Pew, May 20, 1949, folder Spiritual Mobilization, box 23, Papers of J. Howard Pew, accession 1634, Hagley Museum and Library, Wilmington, DE 19807; Norman Vincent Peale, *The Art of Living* (Garden City, NY: Garden City Press, 1949, repr. ed.).

58. J. Howard Pew to Jeremiah Milbank, June 20, 1957, folder Christianity Today, box 53, Papers of J. Howard Pew, accession 1634, Hagley Museum and Library, Wilmington, DE 19807.

59. McKay, "Crusading for Capitalism," 195; and Glenn Fowler, "H. E. Kershner, 98, A Longtime Worker in Children's Causes," *New York Times,* January 3, 1990.

60. Robert McAfee Brown, "Is It 'Christian Economics'?" *Christianity and Crisis* 10, no. 20 (November 27, 1950): 155. *Christianity and Crisis* closed in 1993. Peter Steinfels, "Influential Christian Journal Prints Last Issue," *New York Times,* April 14, 1993.

61. Brown, "'Christian Economics,'" 155–156.

62. Ibid., 157.

63. Ibid., 156, 157.

64. Ibid., 158; Norman Vincent Peale, "Let the Church Speak Up for Capitalism," *Reader's Digest,* September 1950, 126–31.

65. Ibid., 128.

66. Brown, "'Christian Economics,'" 158.

67. McKay, "Crusading for Capitalism," 196.

68. Ibid., 235.

69. McKay, "Crusading for Capitalism," 204.

70. Ibid., 215.

71. "Billy Graham's Star Was Born at His 1949 Revival in Los Angeles," *Los Angeles Times,* September 2, 2007.

72. Darren Grem locates the origin with Graham and evangelical leader Harold Ockenga, but at virtually the same time. See Darren E. Grem, "'Christianity Today,' J. Howard Pew, and the Business of Conservative Evangelicalism," *Enterprise & Society* 15, no. 2 (June 2014): 337–79.

73. J. Howard Pew, quoted in McKay, "Crusading," 215.

74. Billy Graham to J. Howard Pew, April 13, 1955, folder Christianity Today, box 42, Papers of J. Howard Pew, accession 1634, Hagley Museum and Library, Wilmington, DE 19807.

75. Ibid.

76. J. Howard Pew to Billy Graham, April 7, 1955, folder Christianity Today, box 42, Papers of J. Howard Pew, accession 1634, Hagley Museum and Library, Wilmington, DE 19807.

77. Grem, "'Christianity Today.'"

78. "Outline for Christian Magazine," n.d. but by context March–April 1955, folder Christianity Today, box 42, Papers of J. Howard Pew, accession 1634, Hagley Museum and Library, Wilmington, DE 19807.

79. The Pew papers at the Hagley Museum and Library contain both a handwritten version on hotel letterhead and a typescript dated November 29, 1956. See "Declaration of Principles for Christianity Today," folder Christianity Today, box 42, Papers of J. Howard Pew, accession 1634, Hagley Museum and Library, Wilmington, DE 19807.

80. "Our History," *Christianity Today*, https://www.christianitytoday.org/who-we-are/our
-history/.

81. Irving E. Howard, "Christ and the Libertarians," *Christianity Today*, March 17, 1958.

82. Irving E. Howard, "Christian Approach to Economics," *Christianity Today*, August 18, 1958, 8.

83. Noel Sargent, "The Case Against Socialism, with Particular Analysis of the Views of Norman Thomas," National Association of Manufacturers, April 18, 1933, folder Socialism, box 6, series I, National Association of Manufacturers Records, accession 1411, Hagley Museum and Library, Wilmington, DE 19807.

84. Ibid., 6.

85. "Title VII of the Civil Rights Act of 1964," Clipping from the Charlotte, NC, *Observer*, October 15, 1964, folder: NAM Industrial Relations Division, Clinic, box 135, National Association of Manufacturers Records, accession 1411, Hagley Museum and Library, Wilmington, DE 19807.

86. Sargent, "The Case Against Socialism," 2.

87. Ibid., 10. By "scientific," Sargent was referring to eugenicist and social-Darwinist arguments, such as the work of W. J. Hickson, director of the Psychopathic Laboratory of the Chicago Municipal Court, which investigated genetic sources of criminality. Sargent agreed with the sentiment that it was urgent for America "to restore the balance of political power to where it belongs—to the better endowed mentally."

88. Franz Boas, *Changes in Bodily Form in Descendants of Immigrants* (Final Report of the Immigration Commission) (Washington, D.C.: Government Printing Office, 1911); Franz Boas, "Eugenics," *Scientific Monthly* 3, no. 5 (1916): 471–78.

89. Margaret Mead, "The Methodology of Racial Testing: Its Significance for Sociology," *American Journal of Sociology* 31, no. 5 (March 1926): 657–67.

90. Pius XI, *Casti connubii,* encyclical letter, Vatican, December 31, 1930.

91. Matthew 20:13–16.

92. Theology of Work Project, "The Parable of the Talents (Matthew 25:14–30), https://www
.theologyofwork.org/new-testament/matthew/living-in-the-new-kingdom-matthew-18-25
/the-parable-of-the-talents-matthew-2514-30. One website calls this "one of the most abused texts in the New Testament." Carla Works, "Commentary on Matthew 25:14–30," *Working Preacher*, November 13, 2011, https://www.workingpreacher.org/commentaries/revised-common
-lectionary/ordinary-33/commentary-on-matthew-2514-30-3#.

93. Sargent, "The Case Against Socialism," 12.

94. Ibid., 41.

95. Irving E. Howard, "Christian Approach to Economics," 8.

96. Harold John Ockenga, "Laborers with God," *Christianity Today*, August 18, 1958, 9.

97. The teamsters were also largely Catholic, which no doubt also contributed to Henry's animus.

98. Carl F. H. Henry, "Future of the American Worker," *Christianity Today*, May 13, 1957, 22.

99. Ibid.

100. Norman C. Hunt, "Christians and the Economic Order," *Christianity Today*, September 2, 1957.

101. See Kim Phillips-Fein, *Invisible Hands: The Businessmen's Crusade Against the New Deal* (New York: W. W. Norton, 2010).

102. McKay, "Crusading for Capitalism," 92.

103. George H. Nash, *The Conservative Intellectual Movement in America Since 1945*, 30th anniv. ed. (Wilmington, DE: Intercollegiate Studies Institute, 2006), 27.

104. Leonard Read, "I, Pencil: My Family Tree as Told to Leonard E. Read," *Freeman* (December 1958, reprinted March 3, 2015), 7, https://fee.org/resources/i-pencil/.

105. Ibid., 8.

106. On the sacralization of the market, see Harvey Cox, *The Market as God* (Cambridge, MA: Harvard University Press, 2016), and Eugene McCarraher, *The Enchantments of Mammon: How Capitalism Became the Religion of Modernity* (Cambridge, MA: Harvard University Press, 2019).

107. Read, *I, Pencil* (repr. By the Foundation for Economic Education, March 2019), 8.

108. Cox, *The Market as God*, 9.

109. Ibid., 9.

110. Ibid., 10.

111. Ibid., 9. This extension is particularly notable when we remember that the term *invisible hand* barely even appears in *The Wealth of Nations*, is nothing even close to a central metaphor in that book, and that historian Emma Rothschild suggests that Smith may have even intended it as a bit of a joke. Emma Rothschild, "Adam Smith and the Invisible Hand," *American Economic Review* 84, no. 2 (May 1994): 319–22.

112. National Labor Relations Board, "National Labor Relations Act," https://www.nlrb.gov/guidance/key-reference-materials/national-labor-relations-act.

113. Some recent observers have gone so far as to claim that modern capitalism is planned—by *Walmart*—and this could be a model for a future form of socialism. See Leigh Phillips and Michal Rozworski, *The People's Republic of Walmart: How the World's Biggest Corporations are Laying the Foundation for Socialism* (London: Verso Books, 2019).

114. John Quiggin, *Economics in Two Lessons: Why Markets Work So Well, and Why They Can Fail So Badly* (Princeton, NJ: Princeton University Press, 2019), 324.

115. Milton Friedman, "Afterword," in Leonard E. Read, "I, Pencil: My Family Tree as Told to Leonard E. Read," *Freeman* (December 1958, reprinted March 3, 2015), 12.

116. Daniel Stedman Jones, *Masters of the Universe: Hayek, Friedman, and the Birth of Neoliberal Politics* (Princeton, NJ: Princeton University Press, 2012), 329.

CHAPTER 8: NO MORE *GRAPES OF WRATH*

1. Murray Schumach, *The Face on the Cutting Room Floor: The Story of Movie and Television Censorship* (New York: Wolff, 1964), 139.

2. Lary May, *The Big Tomorrow: Hollywood and the Politics of the American Way* (Chicago: University of Chicago Press, 2000), 55–100.

3. May, *The Big Tomorrow*, 43–5.

4. Raymond Durgnat and Scott Simmon, *King Vidor, American* (Berkeley: University of California Press, 1988), 148–50.

5. Joseph McBride, *Searching for John Ford* (Jackson: University Press of Mississippi, 2011), 90.

6. Ibid., 210–11.

7. On the Depression in California see Kevin Starr, *Endangered Dreams: The Great Depression in California* (New York: Oxford University Press, 1996). Use of the Los Angeles Police Department to try to close the state's borders is on p. 177.

8. McBride, *Searching for John Ford*, 310.

9. "Ford uses this memory box," writes Graham Cassano, "to locate Ma Joad as an iconic American mother." Cassano, "Radical Critique and Progressive Traditionalism in John Ford's *The Grapes of Wrath*," *Critical Sociology* 34, no. 1 (2008): 99–116, 103.

10. On the film's visual style, see Vivian C. Sobchack, "*The Grapes of Wrath* (1940): Thematic Emphasis Through Visual Style," in *Hollywood as Historian: American Film in a Cultural Context*, rev. ed., ed. Peter C. Rollins (Lexington: University of Kentucky Press, 1983), 68–87.

11. McBride, *Searching for John Ford*, 313.

12. Rick Wartzman, *Obscene in the Extreme: The Burning and Banning of John Steinbeck's* The Grapes of Wrath (New York: PublicAffairs, 2008). Sales figure from Starr, *Endangered Dreams*, 256.

13. "'Grapes of Wrath' Linked to Propaganda of Reds," *New York Herald Tribune*, July 23, 1940.

14. For a more extensive count of the film's reception, see Stephen J. Whitfield, "Projecting Politics: *The Grapes of Wrath*," *La Revue LISA* 7, no. 1 (2009): 122–47; Terry Christensen, *Reel Politics: American Political Movies from* Birth of a Nation *to* Platoon (New York: Blackwell, 1987), 52; Starr, *Endangered Dreams*, 246–71.

15. The review was written by Whittaker Chambers, "Cinema: Grapes of Wrath," February 12, 1940, text available at https://whittakerchambers.org/articles/reviews/grapes-of-wrath/.

16. Louis Molnar, "Accuracy of 'Grapes of Wrath,'" *Washington Post*, April 5, 1940. An amusing episode suggests the limitations of this conservative fear that the film would lend succor to Communists. In 1948, *The Grapes of Wrath* was shown in Soviet cinemas as proof of the misery that flourished under the world's most advanced capitalist system. But a few weeks later the film was withdrawn in a hurry: Soviet audiences couldn't help but notice that even America's most impoverished denizens had cars. Whitfield, "Projecting Politics," 123.

17. Clayton R. Koppes and Gregory D. Black, *Hollywood Goes to War: How Politics, Profit, and Propaganda Shaped World War II Movies* (New York: Free Press, 1987).

18. *The Battle of Midway* (1942), directed by John Ford, U.S. Navy Film and 20th Century Fox, www.youtube.com/watch?v=Jr4YgpKU8ak.

19. Frank Capra, *The Name Above the Title: An Autobiography* (New York: Macmillan, 1971), 326.

20. Peter C. Rollins, "Frank Capra's *Why We Fight* Series and Our American Dream," *Journal of American Culture* 19, no. 4 (1996): 81–86, 83.

21. Koppes and Black, *Hollywood Goes to War*, 123–24; and Rollins, "Frank Capra's *Why We Fight*," 83.

22. Ibid., 84.

23. On NAM's involvement with *An American Romance*, see folder NIIC National Industrial Information Committee, box 842, Administrative Files, National Association of Manufacturers Records, accession1411, Hagley Museum and Library, Wilmington, DE 19807. This folder contains the complete script for the film, and correspondence about it.

24. Koppes and Black, *Hollywood Goes to War*, 146–50.

25. Ibid., 154.

26. Durgnat and Simmon, *King Vidor, American*, 221–34.

27. Walter H. Brooks to Holcombe Parkes, May 10, 1947, NIIC National Industrial Information Committee, Box 843, NIIC Records Subject Files, National Association of Manufacturers Records, accession1411, Hagley Museum and Library, Wilmington, DE 19807. For negotiations on use, see letter from MGM to Robert Oaks, March 13, 1947, NIIC National Industrial Information Committee, Box 843, NIIC Records Subject Files, National Association of Manufacturers Records, accession 1411, Hagley Museum and Library, Wilmington, DE 19807.

28. "Plain Speaking: Concise Facts about NAM's 1946 Public Relations Program (NICC)," NIIC National Industrial Information Committee, box 137, Publications, National Association of Manufacturers Records, accession 1411, Hagley Museum and Library, Wilmington, DE 19807.

29. Nelson Lichtenstein, *Labor's War at Home: The CIO in World War II* (Philadelphia: Temple University Press, 2003).

30. Jennifer Burns, *Goddess of the Market: Ayn Rand and the American Right* (Oxford: Oxford University Press, 2009), 9–38.

31. Burns, *Goddess*, 68.

32. Jennifer Burns, "The Three 'Furies' of Libertarianism: Rose Wilder Lane, Isabel Paterson, and Ayn Rand," *Journal of American History* 102, no. 3 (December 2015): 759.

33. Ibid.

34. Gregory Teddy Eow, "Fighting a New Deal: Intellectual Origins of the Reagan Revolution, 1932–1952" (PhD diss., Rice University, 2007), 153–54. For more on Rand, see Burns, *Goddess of the Market*.

35. Burns, "'Three Furies,'" 759. Rose Wilder Lane was invited in 1945 to testify before Congress regarding the proposed Bretton Woods agreement which established the World Bank, the IMF, and fixed exchange rates. Lane of course knew nothing about, and had no expertise in, the problems of currency and foreign exchange. Burns, 770.

36. Ibid., 765.

37. "The Motion Picture Alliance for the Preservation of American Ideals, Statement of Principles," Hollywood Renegades Archive, accessed December 22, 2019, http://www .cobbles.com/simpp_archive/huac_alliance.htm.

38. Burns, *Goddess of the Market*, 123.

39. Ayn Rand, "Screen Guide for Americans," reprinted in *Film Manifestos and Global Cinema Cultures*, ed. Scott MacKenzie (Berkeley: University of California Press, 2014), 422–32. Emphasis in original.

40. Ibid., 423–28.

41. Bosley Crowther, "The Screen in Review," *New York Times*, November 22, 1946, https://www .nytimes.com/1946/11/22/archives/the-screen-in-review-at-the-laffmovie.html.

42. John Sbardellati, *J. Edgar Hoover Goes to the Movies: The FBI and the Origins of Hollywood's Cold War* (Ithaca, NY: Cornell University Press, 2012), 100.

43. Ibid., 101.

44. Ayn Rand, quoted in Sbardellati, *J. Edgar Hoover Goes to the Movies*, 137.

45. Oliver Carlson, quoted in Sbardellati, *J. Edgar Hoover Goes to the Movies*, 139.

46. A variety of entities supplied names to be blacklisted, including the American Legion and a *Los Angeles Times* columnist named Hedda Hopper. The American Business Consultants published a pamphlet called *Red Channels* (the so-called bible of blacklisting) which identified entertainment-industry figures suspected of communist sympathies; another publication called *Counterattack*, published by Aware, Inc., was also devoted to naming communists. See Victor S. Navasky, *Naming Names* (New York: Viking Press, 1980), 87–89.

47. Schumach, *The Face on the Cutting Room Floor*. A famous case that helped bring an end to the practice of blacklisting was the 1957 film *The Bridge on the River Kwai*, based on a novel by Pierre Boulle. He won the Academy Award for best adapted screenplay, but practically everyone in Hollywood, including the FBI, knew it was the work of two blacklisted writers— Michael Wilson and Carl Foreman. Boulle didn't even speak English.

48. Murray Schumach points out that the studios weren't just responding to HUAC's pressure. The American Legion threatened boycotts over the alleged red in Hollywood, potentially affecting studio revenue.

49. Karl F. Cohen, *Forbidden Animation: Censored Cartoons and Blacklisted Animators in America* (Jefferson, NC: McFarland, 1997), 167.

50. Sbardellati, *J. Edgar Hoover Goes to the Movies*, 194.

51. May, *The Big Tomorrow*, 204.

52. Ayn Rand, *The Fountainhead* (New York: Signet, 1996), 683.

53. Sbardellati, *J. Edgar Hoover Goes to the Movies*, 162.

54. J. Hoberman, *An Army of Phantoms: American Movies and the Making of the Cold War* (New York: New Press, 2011), 98.

55. Rand, *The Fountainhead*, 680.

56. Burns, *Goddess of the Market*, 121. Also see Sbardellati, *J. Edgar Hoover Goes to the Movies*, 162.

57. John McCarten, "The Current Cinema," *New Yorker*, July 16, 1949, 47.

58. Bosley Crowther, "The Screen in Review; Gary Cooper Plays an Idealistic Architect in Film Version of 'The Fountainhead,'" *New York Times*, July 9, 1949; see also Crowther, "In a Glass House: Reckless Ideas Spouted by 'The Fountainhead,'" *New York Times*, July 17, 1949, https://www.nytimes.com/1949/07/09/archives/the-screen-in-review-gary-cooper-plays-an -idealistic-architect-in.html.

59. Reviews from the *Hollywood Reporter*, *Variety*, *Cue*, and the *Daily Worker* are quoted in Hoberman, *Army of Phantoms*, 98.

60. Quoted in Lisa Duggan, *Mean Girl: Ayn Rand and the Culture of Greed* (Oakland: University of California Press, 2019), 58.

61. Quoted in Ibid., 59.

62. Whittaker Chambers, "Big Sister Is Watching You," *National Review* 4, no. 25 (December 28, 1957), 594–96.

63. "Atlas Shrugged Franchise Movies at the Box Office," Box Office Mojo, accessed May 2, 2021, https://www.boxofficemojo.com/franchise/fr407342853/?ref_=bo_frs_table_281.

64. On Chambers, see George H. Nash, *The Conservative Intellectual Movement in America Since 1945*, 30th anniv. ed. (Wilmington, DE: Intercollegiate Studies Institute, 2006), esp. chap. 9.

65. Hiss was a consummate Washington insider: after attending Harvard Law School he had clerked for Supreme Court justice Oliver Wendell Holmes, traveled to Yalta in 1945 as an adviser to President Roosevelt, and in 1946 become president of the Carnegie Endowment for International Peace. Encyclopaedia Britannica, s.v., "Alger Hiss," accessed March 11, 2021, https://www.britannica.com/biography/Alger-Hiss.

66. Ezra Klein, "Romney's Theory of the 'Taker Class' and Why It Matters," *Washington Post*, September 17, 2012, https://www.washingtonpost.com/news/wonk/wp/2012/09/17/romneys -theory-of-the-taker-class-and-why-it-matters/.

67. Chambers, "Big Sister is Watching," 120–22.

68. Ibid.

69. Ibid.

70. Burns, *Goddess of the Market*, 175.

71. Michael Shermer, "The Unlikeliest Cult in History," *Skeptic* 2, no. 2 (1993), www.skeptic.com /reading_room/the-unlikeliest-cult-in-history/.

72. Harriet Rubin, "Ayn Rand's Literature of Capitalism," *New York Times*, September 25, 2007, www.nytimes.com/2007/09/15/business/15atlas.html.

73. Michael Shermer, personal correspondence with authors, December 26, 2021.

74. Richard Slotkin, *Gunfighter Nation: The Myth of the Frontier in Twentieth-Century America* (New York: Atheneum, 1992), 343.

75. Cecil B. DeMille, quoted in Alan Nadel, "God's Law and the Wide Screen: The Ten Commandments as Cold War 'Epic,'" *PMLA* 108, no. 3 (May 1993), 415–30, 417.

76. Peter Lev, *Transforming the Screen, 1950–1959* (New York: Scribners, 2000), 164.

77. Summarized from Amy C. Wallhermfechtel, "Shaping the Right to Work: The Cecil B. DeMille Foundation's Role in State and National Right to Work Campaigns" (PhD diss., Saint Louis University, 2014.)

78. McBride, 461–62; see also Scott Eyman, *Print the Legend: The Life and Times of John Ford* (New York: Simon & Schuster, 1999), 360–63.

79. Robert Griffith, "The Selling of America: The Advertising Council and American Politics, 1942–1960," *Business History Review* 57, no. 3 (1983): 388–412.

80. Wall, *Inventing the "American Way,"* 3.

81. Ibid., 194–200.

82. Caroline Jack, "Fun and Facts about American Business: Economic Education and Business Propaganda in an Early Cold War Cartoon Series," *Enterprise and Society* 16, no. 3 (September 2015): 491–520.

83. Robbie Maxwell, "'A Shooting Star of Conservatism': George S. Benson, the National Education Program and the 'Radical Right,'" *Journal of American Studies* 53, no. 2 (May 2019): 372–400.

84. Alfred P. Sloan, quoted in Jack, "Fun and Facts," 500.

85. Jack, "Fun and Facts," 515.

86. *Make Mine Freedom* (1948) [Film], U.S.: John Sutherland Productions, https://www.youtube.com/watch?v=mVh75ylAUXY.

87. *Going Places* (1948) [Film], U.S.: John Sutherland Productions, www.youtube.com/watch?v=moMdcdKFBwo.

88. He was likely referring the 1948 decision in the case of *United States v. Paramount Pictures, Inc.*, which forced film studios to divest their theater chains.

89. Jack, "Fun and Facts," 508.

90. Ibid.

91. A sixth film, *Fresh Laid Plans* (March 1951), finally broke the alliance. *Fresh Laid Plans* told the story of a town of chickens that came under the wing of an owl, who introduced production controls, farm subsidies, and high taxes. The chickens all bought feed on the black market and wound up in prison. MGM agreed to wide release, but it brought Sutherland and Benson under fire: farmers didn't like being presented as "gullible chickens." Nor did they care for the attack on farm subsidies. The controversy made the front page of the *New York Times* on March 18, 1951 (Ibid., 513). Neither Sutherland nor Benson minded—after all, in Hollywood, all publicity is good publicity—but the Sloan Foundation was shaken. Foundation officers took a much closer look at two more films in the pipeline. *Dear Uncle* and *The Devil and John Q* were produced, but they were rejected by MGM for large-scale distribution, and that ended the series.

92. *It's Everybody's Business* (1954) [Film], U.S.: John Sutherland Productions, https://youtu.be/nHDyE95414U. For information about the film's sponsors, see "It's Everybody's Business (1954)": Film Notes, *National Film Preservation Foundation*, www.filmpreservation.org/preserved-films/screening-room/it-s-everybody-s-business-1954.

93. Maxwell, "Shooting Star," 377–78.

94. Ahead of it in the rankings were the *Ed Sullivan Show* and *I Love Lucy*. Jacob Weisberg, "The Road to Reagandom," *Slate*, January 8, 2016, https://slate.com/news-and-politics/2016/01/ronald-reagans-conservative-conversion-as-spokesman-for-general-electric-during-the-1950s.html.

95. "Population of Voting Age and Votes Cast for President, 1964 and 1960, for States and Counties," United States Census Bureau, November 1990, www.census.gov/data/tables/time-series/demo/voting-and-registration/p23-168.html.

96. Quoted in Tomas Kellner, "Lights, Electricity, Action: When Ronald Reagan Hosted 'General Electric Theater,'" General Electric, February 17, 2019, www.ge.com/news/reports/ronald-reagan-ge.

97. Thomas Evans, *The Education of Ronald Reagan: The General Electric Years and the Untold Story of His Conversion to Conservatism* (New York: Columbia University Press, 2006), 58. According to Evans, fifty Academy Award winners appeared on the show.

98. McKay, "Crusading for Capitalism," 85.

99. Evans, *The Education of Ronald Reagan*, 58.

100. William Boddy, *Fifties Television: The Industry and Its Critics* (Urbana: University of Illinois Press, 1990), 158.

101. Ibid., 157–59.

102. Timothy Raphael, *The President Electric: Ronald Reagan and the Politics of Performance*, illus. ed. (Ann Arbor: University of Michigan Press, 2009), 167, discusses the overall GE strategy, first developed in the 1930s by advertiser Bruce Barton.

103. See for example "General Electric Theater," Decades TV Network, https://www.youtube.com/watch?v=-A2k81oZhjQ.

104. The flashbulb was the Power Mite M2, 1955. The episode (which features Natalie Wood) was "Feathertop," *General Electric Theater* [TV program], CBS, December 4, 1955.

105. Obituaries of Welch claim the "shareholder value model" as the CEO's legacy. See Scott Tong, "Jack Welch's legacy: value for shareholders, but not necessarily for workers," *Marketplace*, March 2, 2020, www.marketplace.org/2020/03/02/jack-welchs-legacy-value-for-shareholders-but-not-necessarily-for-workers/; and Joe Nocera, "Jack Welch Was a CEO Idol Who Damaged American Capitalism," *Financial Review*, March 3, 2020, www.afr.com/work-and-careers/leaders/jack-welch-inflicted-great-damage-on-corporate-america-20200303-p546bw.

106. "No Hiding Place," *General Electric Theater* [TV program], CBS, April 6, 1958, https://www.youtube.com/watch?v=vavWBsDA2xI.

107. "Tippy-Top," *General Electric Theater* [TV program], CBS, December 17, 1961, www.youtube.com/watch?v=UJDCKQutWnU.

108. "We're Holding Your Son," *General Electric Theater* [TV program], CBS, December 3, 1961, www.youtube.com/watch?v=oIxghOrzkoo.

109. "I'm a Fool," *General Electric Theater* [TV program], CBS, November 14, 1954, www.youtube.com/watch?v=1NwB4IhvKFg.

110. "The Clown," *General Electric Theater* [TV program], CBS, March 27, 1955, www.youtube.com/watch?v=lSg78kC9OB4.

111. "The Iron Silence," *General Electric Theater* [TV program], CBS, September 24, 1961, www.youtube.com/watch?v=GnRIIHdZeLI.

112. Boddy, *Fifties Television*, 198.

113. Ibid., 199.

114. In later years, this role would be played to some extent by public television, chartered in 1967 by the Public Broadcasting Act. But public television did not exist during the run of *General Electric Theater*, and even once it did, it never had the funding to match private-sector entertainment. And of course, public television has been a favorite target of free-marketeers. On the history of public television, see Patricia Aufderheide, "Public Television and the Public Sphere," *Critical Studies in Mass Communication* 8, no. 2 (1991): 168–83. For an assessment of how cable television failed to serve the public interest, see Aufderheide, "Cable Television and the Public Interest," *Journal of Communication* 42, no. 1 (March 1992): 52–65.

115. Yochai Benkler, Robert Faris, and Hal Roberts, *Network Propaganda: Manipulation, Disinformation, and Radicalization in American Politics* (New York: Oxford University Press, 2018). See also Benkler, "A Political Economy of the Origins of Asymmetric Propaganda in American Media," in *The Disinformation Age: Politics, Technology, and Disruptive Communication in the United States*, ed. W. Lance Bennett and Steven Livingston (Cambridge: Cambridge University Press, 2021), 43–66,

116. The full quotation: "The conscious and intelligent manipulation of the organized habits and opinions of the masses is an important element in democratic society. Those who manipulate

this unseen mechanism of society constitute an invisible government which is the true ruling power of our country. We are governed, our minds are molded, our tastes formed, our ideas suggested, largely by men we have never heard of." Edward L. Bernays, *Propaganda* (New York: Liveright, 1928), 9.

CHAPTER 9: STEERING THE CHICAGO SCHOOL

1. Friedrich A. Hayek, *The Road to Serfdom: Text and Documents*, edited with foreword and introduction by Bruce Caldwell (Chicago: University of Chicago Press, 2003), 99.
2. Kim Phillips-Fein, *Invisible Hands: The Businessmen's Crusade Against the New Deal* (New York: W. W. Norton, 2010), 41.
3. Ibid., 29, italics added. See also George H. Nash, *The Conservative Intellectual Movement in America Since 1945*, 30th anniv. ed. (Wilmington, DE: Intercollegiate Studies Institute, 2006).
4. Phillips-Fein, *Invisible Hands*, 29, italics added.
5. Gregory Teddy Eow, "Fighting a New Deal: Intellectual Origins of the Reagan Revolution, 1932–1952" (PhD diss., Rice University, 2007), puts it this way: "A closer look at the origins of the Chicago school, however, reveals that political activism rather than scholarship first led to the creation of this school of thought" (9).
6. Nash, *Conservative Intellectual Movement*, 11.
7. Phillips-Fein, *Invisible Hands*, 31.
8. Ibid., 30.
9. Actually, there were two snags. Phillips-Fein, *Invisible Hands*, 43, notes that Crane did have some reservations: he feared that Hayek was Jewish and would share the characteristic Jewish sympathy for collectivism, and that Hayek was too willing to compromise on matters such as minimum wage. But then he learned that Hayek was not Jewish, and the other concerns evidently receded.
10. Phillips-Fein, *Invisible Hands*, 40–52, quotation on 42.
11. Robert Van Horn and Philip Mirowski, "The Rise of the Chicago School of Economics and the Birth of Neoliberalism," in *The Road from Mont Pèlerin: The Making of the Neoliberal Thought Collective*, ed. Philip Mirowski and Dieter Plehwe (Cambridge, MA: Harvard University Press, 2009), 141.
12. Ibid., 149–50.
13. Ibid., 150. Caldwell concludes that it was on Hayek's 1945 book tour that seeds of "Chicago school of economics" were sown. This claim depends on how one defines the Chicago school, given that Knight, Simons, and Viner were already there, and Milton Friedman, Aaron Director, and Rose Friedman (at that time Rose Director). It is certainly true that under Luhnow's influence, the Chicago School moved in a more doctrinaire and overtly political direction.
14. Bruce Caldwell, introduction to Friedrich A. Hayek, *The Road to Serfdom: Text and Documents*, edited with a foreword and introduction by Bruce Caldwell (Chicago: University of Chicago Press, 2013), 20.
15. Van Horn and Mirowski, "Rise," 141.
16. On Simons, see "Biographical Note," Guide to the Henry C. Simons Papers 1925–1972, University of Chicago Library, accessed April 6, 2021, https://www.lib.uchicago.edu/e/scrc/findingaids/view.php?eadid=ICU.SPCL.SIMONS. Simons shared Knight's dim view of the New Deal, but—and in contrast with the hypocrisy of many of his colleagues—Simons was concerned with all forms of concentrations of power, including corporations and trade organizations, as well as large unions and monopolies (see Van Horn and Mirowski, "Rise," 142–43; and Eow, "Fighting a New Deal," 76–78). He also accepted that laissez-faire did not

mean "government inactivity," but government to protect and sustain competition, and he accepted that income redistribution might at times be justifiable (Eow, 76, 79). Simons's tone, however, was often stunningly intemperate. See, for example, Henry C. Simons, *A Positive Program for Laissez Faire: Some Proposals for a Liberal Economic Policy,* Public Policy Pamphlet No. 15 (Chicago: University of Chicago Press,1934), 14–16, which Eow characterizes as "an undisguised polemic" (Eow, 74). By 1936, Simons would insist that the only choices were "between a competitive system and authoritarian collectivism" (Eow, 84).

17. Eow, "Fighting a New Deal," 96–98.

18. Ibid., 99, notes that the University of Chicago at first balked at the idea of an overtly political and partisan think tank. Why they agreed the second time—whether because of Luhnow's money or the idea to put it in the Law School—is not clear.

19. Van Horn and Mirowski, "Rise," 165, citing John Nef, *Search for Meaning: The Autobiography of a Nonconformist* (Washington, D.C.: Public Affairs Press, 1973).

20. Ibid., 151.

21. Lanny Ebenstein, *Chicagonomics: The Evolution of Chicago Free Market Economics* (New York: St. Martin's Press, 2015), 76.

22. Henry Simons, quoted in Ebenstein, *Chicagonomics*, 145. Eow, "Fighting a New Deal," notes that at Harvard, Joseph Schumpeter continued to trumpet laissez-faire, but he was increasingly isolated. "In fact, the triumph of the idea of economic planning was so pronounced in the 1930s that historian Sidney Fine identified the period as the end of a fifty-year battle between proponents of laissez-faire and supporters of the welfare state" (8). Fine's report of the death of laissez-faire was premature.

23. Robert Van Horn, "Henry Simons's Death," *History of Political Economy* 46, no. 3 (Sept 2014): 529.

24. Cowles Foundation for Research in Economics, "About Us," accessed April 6, 2021, https://cowles.yale.edu/about-us. On the Cowles commission, see Ebenstein, *Chicagonomics*, chap. 6; Michael A. Bernstein, *A Perilous Progress: Economists and Public Purpose in Twentieth-Century America* (Princeton, NJ: Princeton University Press, 2001), 95–100.

25. Van Horn and Mirowski, "Rise," 164.

26. Ibid.

27. Eow, "Fighting for a New Deal," 99.

28. This sowed the seeds of what became the program in Law and Economics: see Steven G. Medema, "Chicago Law and Economics," in *The Elgar Companion to the Chicago School of Economics* (Cheltenham, UK: Edward Elgar Publishing, 2010), 160-174. Among its prominent members were Richard Posner, Ronald H. Coase, and Gary Becker. All three were uncompromising advocates of the powers of the free market and critics of government regulation. (Although in later years Posner took more seriously the problem of market failure.) Particularly important for our purposes is Coase, who attempted to refute Pigou's argument. Building on Friedman, Coase stressed the risks to property rights from a Pigouvian approach, arguing that a tax on pollution "diverts attention from those other changes in the system which are inevitably associated with the corrective measure, changes which may well produce more harm than the original deficiency" (43). R. H. Coase, "The Problem of Social Cost," *Journal of Law and Economics* 3 (October 1960): 1–44.

29. Van Horn notes that in early discussions, Aaron Director suggested that they should discuss both the benefits and limits of the free market, but it is clear that Luhnow had no interest in delineating the latter. See Van Horn, "Henry Simons's Death," 529.

30. Van Horn and Mirowski, "Rise," 152.

31. Ibid.

32. In later years, George Stigler would note that the history of economics was the "last unsubsidized research area in economics." Yet he evinced no interest in considering how the sources of those subsidies influenced what work was done. See Nathan Rosenberg, "Adam Smith's Best Friend," *Journal of Political Economy* 101, no. 5 (Oct 1993): 833.

33. Van Horn and Mirowski, "Rise," 146.

34. Ibid., 152–53.

35. Ibid. 154.

36. On Luhnow's meeting with Hutchins, see Van Horn and Mirowski, "Rise," 165. On the relation of this setback to Henry Simons's death, see Van Horn, "Henry Simons's Death."

37. Howard S. Miller, *Dollars for Research: Science and Its Patrons in Nineteenth-Century America* (Seattle: University of Washington Press, 1970). In some fields, funding also came from state agencies, such as state geological surveys supporting research by academic geologists, or state public health services.

38. Dieter Plehwe points out that neoliberals often view themselves as "independent" if they don't take money from the state yet have seen little or no problem with taking money from private patrons with explicit political agendas. Dieter Plehwe, introduction to *The Road from Mont Pèlerin: The Making of the Neoliberal Thought Collective*, ed. Philip Mirowski and Dieter Plehwe (Cambridge, MA: Harvard University Press, 2009), 31–32. The logic is that the state is all-powerful—or at least potentially so—whereas businessmen are a diverse group with diverse interests and so cannot—or are not likely to—work with the kind of singular aim that a government can. This ideal is belied by the story told here, as well as by the quotidian disorganization and infighting of most governments. Plehwe also notes that the Chicago school grotesquely violated the focus Hayek and the Mont Pelerin Society (MPS) maintained on the rule of law when it began to argue the law-and-economics perspective that judges apply a rule of "economic reason." This was the very sort of subjective discretion that the original MPS statement singled out for approbation. On the influence of the Chicago school argument of the "rule of reason" in the enforcement (or nonenforcement) of antitrust law, see Sam J. Ervin and Clark Ramsey, *The Role of the Supreme Court: Policymaker or Adjudicator?* (Washington, D.C.: American Enterprise Institute for Public Policy Research, 1970).

39. Plehwe, introduction to *The Road from Mont Pèlerin*, 21; Van Horn and Mirowski, "The Rise of the Chicago School of Economics," in *The Road from Mont Pèlerin*, 158–63.

40. Caldwell, introduction to *The Road to Serfdom*, 20.

41. On the hiring of George Stigler, see Binyamin Appelbaum, *The Economists' Hour: False Prophets, Free Markets, and the Fracture of Society* (New York: Little, Brown, 2019), 140.

42. Plehwe, introduction to *The Road from Mont Pèlerin*, 29.

43. F. A. Hayek, quoted in Caldwell, introduction to Hayek, *The Road to Serfdom*, 20. The Chicago school also became far more antiunion than most European neoliberals (Plehwe, introduction to *The Road from Mont Pèlerin*, 30). Given the strong antiunion attitudes of Crane, Luhnow, and their associates—and the way they had insisted that unions were a form of monopoly, no different from a railroad or utility—it seems reasonable to conclude that their influence played some role in this development.

44. For full treatments, see Ebenstein, *Chicagonomics*; Appelbaum, *Economists' Hour*; and Daniel Stedman Jones, *Masters of the Universe: Hayek, Friedman, and the Birth of Neoliberal Politics* (Princeton, NJ: Princeton University Press, 2012).

45. The Nobel Prize, "George J. Stigler: Facts," May 1, 2021, https://www.nobelprize.org/prizes/economic-sciences/1982/stigler/facts/.

46. A 1966 facsimile edition was published in two volumes, each over five hundred pages: Adam Smith, *An Inquiry into the Nature and Causes of the Wealth of Nations* (New York: Augustus M. Kelley, 1966).

47. Smith, *Wealth*, book 1, chap. 2, 21–22.

48. Smith, *Wealth*, 250, italics added. This passage is particularly significant because it is one of the few places where Smith uses the word "restraint" in a positive context; most of his discussion of restraints, e.g., in the context of mercantilism in book 4, is critical. See particularly book 4, chap. 3, where he discusses the "unreasonableness" of mercantilist restraints on trade. We are indebted to Ronald F. Hoffman, former staff member of the Council of Economic Advisers under President Nixon, for calling our attention to this passage. It discussed as well in Tahany Naggar, "Adam Smith's Laissez Faire," *American Economist* 21, no. 2 (1977): 36, and Jacob Viner, "Adam Smith and Laissez Faire," *Journal of Political Economy* 35, no. 2 (April 1927): 224–25.

49. Smith, *Wealth*, 224. This passage is also quoted by Amartya Sen to argue that Smith emphasizes the necessity of virtues other than self-interest for the market economy to function, much less society as a whole. See Amartya Sen, "Uses and Abuses of Adam Smith," *History of Political Economy* 43, no. 2 (Summer 2011): 266.

50. Smith, *Wealth*, 229.

51. Ibid., 228–30.

52. Ibid., 233–34.

53. Ibid., 247.

54. Ibid., 248–49.

55. Ibid., 250.

56. Sen, "Abuses," 259. Sen observes that Smith was impressed by the power and dynamism of markets, and he gives a compelling account of "how that dynamism" worked, but that is a far cry from viewing markets as comprehensive, and there is nothing in Smith to indicate that he believed in the self-sufficiency of the market economy.

57. Viner, "Adam Smith," 227.

58. Smith, *Wealth*, 61.

59. Ibid., 62.

60. On variations in wages, see Ibid., 86–101.

61. Adam Smith, quoted in Emma Rothschild, "Adam Smith and Conservative Economics," *Economic Historical Review* 45, no. 1, (1992):74–96; Smith, *Wealth*, 70. See also Jules Steinberg, *"To Be Themselves Tolerably Well Fed, Cloathed, and Lodged": Liberalism, The Humanization of Labor, and Adam Smith's Protests Against the Injustice of Working Class Poverty and Misery* (St. Petersburg, FL: BookLocker.Com, Inc, 2019).

62. Smith, *Wealth*, 71.

63. Adam Smith, quoted in Rothschild, "Adam Smith"; Smith, *Wealth*, 70. See also Steinberg, *"To Be Themselves."* This passage reminds us of the important point, stressed as well by Sen, that even though capitalism was in its infancy in 1776, many of its failures were already becoming clear. "Even to Adam Smith . . . the huge limitations of relying entirely on the market economy and only on the profit motive were absolutely clear." (Sen, "Abuses," 260.) Sen sees in this the explanation for how Marx could admire Smith yet revile John Stuart Mill. Dennis C. Rasmussen argues that Smith saw commercial society as the best of a menu of bad options. See Rasmussen, *The Problems and Promise of Commercial Society: Adam Smith's Response to Rousseau* (University Park, PA: Penn State University Press, 2008).

64. Smith, *Wealth*, 73.

65. Ibid., 73–74.

66. Adam Smith, quoted in Sen, "Abuses," 262. Sen stresses that Smith believed that self-interest was a powerful and useful motivator of economic activity, but by no means did he think it was the only valid—or even only existing—motivation for human action, as many latter-day libertarians have bizarrely insisted.

67. Rothschild, "Adam Smith," 84.

68. Sen, "Abuses," 262.

69. Ibid., 625.

70. Ibid., 634–35.

71. For example: Michael Huemer, "Is Taxation Theft?" Libertarianism.org, accessed April 7, 2021, https://www.libertarianism.org/columns/is-taxation-theft.

72. Smith, *Wealth*, 634.

73. Ibid., 625. We are not Marx scholars, but the language is so close that it seems reasonable to ponder whether Marx got his famous phrase ("from each according to his ability, to each according to his needs") from Smith.

74. Stigler's selective vision is evident not least in his attitude toward race. In 1962 he wrote an astonishing piece blaming the plight of African Americans on themselves, including this passage: "The Negro boy is excluded from many occupations by the varied barriers the prejudice can raise, . . . [B]ut he is excluded from more occupations by his own inferiority as a worker . . . Consider the Negro as a neighbor. He is frequently repelled and avoided by the white man, . . . because the Negro family is, on average, a loose, morally lax, group, and brings with its presence a rapid rise in crime and vandalism." The contrasting experience of Jews and Blacks, Stigler held, proved that the problems of the latter were mostly of their own making. George Stigler, "The Problem of the Negro," *New Guard* 1960, reprinted: *https://www.bradford-delong.com/2019/05/weekend-reading-george-stigler-in-1962-on-the-problem-of-the-negro.html.* The potential refutations of this position are numerous. One obvious one is the 1921 Tulsa massacre; another is the driving out of Black homeowners and businesspeople and the seizure of their property in Manhattan Beach, California. See: Jacey Fortin, "This Black Family Ran a Thriving Beach Resort 100 Years Ago. They Want Their Land Back," *New York Times*, March 11, 2021. This is exemplary of what sociologist Woody Doane notes as the tendency of privileged classes to support "an interpretative framework in which whites' explanations for inequality focus upon the cultural characteristics (e.g., motivation, values) of subordinate groups . . . Politically, this blaming of subordinate groups for their lower economic position serves to neutralize demands for anti-discrimination initiatives or for a redistribution of resources." Quoted in Charles W. Mills, "White Ignorance," in *Agnotology: The Making and Unmaking of Ignorance*, ed. Robert N. Proctor and Londa Schiebinger (Stanford, CA: Stanford University Press: 2008), 230–49.

75. Viner, "Adam Smith," 228.

76. Viner, "Adam Smith," 231, also quoted in Naggar, "Adam Smith's Laissez Faire," 37.

77. Viner, "Adam Smith," 218.

78. Viner, "Adam Smith," 218. Original italics. Viner also notes that, at times, Smith seems to suggest that government is part of the natural order and not a distortion of it—an idea that his later venerators rejected adamantly!

79. Smith's hostility to Oxford dons may have been linked to his hostility to established religion, since the universities and colleges at this time were all ecclesiastical institutions. On Smith's views of established religion, see Rothschild, "Adam Smith," 91. Or, it may simply be that he was ill and unhappy while at Oxford. See John Rae, *Life of Adam Smith* (New York: Macmillan, 1895).

80. George J. Stigler, *Selections from The Wealth of Nations Smith* (Wheeling, IL: Harlan Davidson, Inc., 1957), 108–9.

81. Ibid., 113.

82. Stigler, *Selections*, 110.

83. There is of course a regulatory solution to this, which Smith hints at: The state could mandate tranferability of credits, and/or the transportability of scholarships.

84. Searching Google Books reveals several additional uses of the verb "regulate," but no other use of the noun "regulation," accessed April 7, 2020, https://www.google.com/books/edition

/Selections_from_The_Wealth_of_Nations/hPNjBAAAQBAJ?hl=en&gbpv=1&bsq
=regulation.

85. Rosenberg, "Adam Smith's Best Friend"; Sherwin Rosen, "George J. Stigler and the Industrial Organization of Economic Thought," *Journal of Political Economy* 101, no. 5 (Oct 1993): 809–17.

86. Rothschild, "Adam Smith."

87. For an excellent short summary, see Adam Smith Institute, "The Theory of Moral Sentiments," accessed April 7, 2021, https://www.adamsmith.org/the-theory-of-moral-sentiments.

88. Sen emphasizes that for Smith, the market was an important societal institution but by no means the only one. Nonmarket institutions play a crucial role in providing public goods, while the state has a unique role in regulating markets when needed. See Sen, "Abuses," 258–59.

89. Sen, "Abuses," 258.

90. Craig Freedman, "Was George Stigler Adam Smith's Best Friend? Studying the History of Economic Thought," *Journal of the History of Economic Thought* 29, no. 2 (June 2007): 173.

91. Sen, "Abuses," 258.

92. Ibid.

93. Eow, "Fighting a New Deal," 83.

94. Sen, "Abuses," 258.

95. One can dive deeper. Smith does not tell us how to define safety and security, nor ponder how small the minority need be to justify infringing its liberty on behalf of others. Nor does he anticipate, much less answer, the problem of what to do when the actions of the present generation threaten the future. But these further questions would not be posed by students reading Stigler's Smith, for they would not have known that Smith accepted the need for infringements on liberty at all.

96. Indeed, as Van Horn and Mirowski point out, for capitalists these men were surprisingly insouciant about their contractual obligations! Van Horn and Mirowski, "Rise," 166.

97. John McGee quoted in Tim Wu, *The Curse of Bigness: Antitrust in the New Gilded Age*, illus. ed. (New York: Columbia Global Reports, 2018), 85. This is often referred to as the "efficient market hypothesis." For a critical discussion, see Harvey Cox, *The Market as God* (Cambridge, MA: Harvard University Press, 2016), 29.

98. Edmund W. Kitch, "The Fire of Truth: A Remembrance of Law and Economics at Chicago, 1932–1970," *Journal of Law and Economics* 26, no. 1 (1983): 183.

99. As Friedman would later put it, "A liberal is fundamentally fearful of concentrated power." Milton Friedman, *Capitalism and Freedom* (Chicago: University of Chicago Press, 1962). But the Chicago school was not fearful of concentrations of private power, only government power.

100. For a recent discussion of Bork and his role in undermining antitrust enforcement, see Appelbaum, *Economists' Hour*, 149–54. Appelbaum agrees that Bork's theory required the rewriting of history. He aptly calls Bork's position "protrust."

101. "Economist, Hoover Fellow Aaron Director Dies at 102," Stanford University, September 22, 2004, http://news.stanford.edu/news/2004/september22/obit-director-922.html.

102. Mark Sherman, Associated Press, "Bork: Nixon Offered Next High Court Vacancy in '73," *Seattle Times*, February 26, 2013, https://www.seattletimes.com/seattle-news/politics/bork-nixon-offered-next-high-court-vacancy-in-73/.

103. This argument would be invoked in 2021 by the federal judge who rejected the U.S. Department of Justice case against Facebook, in part on the grounds that, because Facebook was free, no argument could be made that its monopolistic position "cost" customers anything. See: Cat Zakrzewski and Rachel Lerman, "Court Says FTC Hasn't Provided Evidence Facebook Is a Monopoly, Dismisses Lawsuit," *Washington Post*, June 28, 2021,

https://www.washingtonpost.com/technology/2021/06/28/ftc-facebook-antitrust-complaint-dismissed/.

104. This point was stressed in 2022 by Assistant Attorney General Jonathan Kanter, when he announced a renewed commitment at the Department of Justice to antitrust enforcement: "[F]or years scholars and pundits have expended enormous energy debating the meaning of words that do not appear in the statute: the ephemeral 'consumer welfare standard.' By my count, 831 academic articles have been written invoking the consumer welfare standard, with more than 200 since 2020. It is the academic gift that keeps on giving." But it was not just an academic gift; it was a gift to the industries engaged in predatory practices, who justified their potentially illegal activity by claiming it benefited consumers. Jonathan Kanter, "Antitrust Enforcement: The Road to Recovery," keynote at the University of Chicago Stigler Center, Chicago, Illinois, April 21, 2022, https://www.justice.gov/opa/speech/assistant-attorney-general-jonathan-kanter-delivers-keynote-university-chicago-stigler#_ftn1.

105. Robert H. Bork, "Legislative Intent and the Policy of the Sherman Act," *Journal of Law and Economics* 9, no. 1 (January 1966): 7–48; a fuller discussion is in Bork, *The Antitrust Paradox* (New York: Basic Books, 1978).

106. It is only very recently that it has been seriously challenged, e.g., Lina M. Khan, "Amazon's Antitrust Paradox," *Yale Law Journal* 126, no. 3 (2017): 564–907.

107. Richard Hofstadter, "The Paranoid Style in American Politics," *Harper's Magazine*, November 1964: 199–200. Also see Wu, *The Curse of Bigness*; and Robert H. Lande, "Wealth Transfers as the Original and Primary Concern of Antitrust: The Efficiency Interpretation Challenged," *Hastings Law Journal* 34, no. 1 (September 1982): 65–151.

108. John Sherman, quoted in U.S. Congressional Record, S. 2460, 51st Congress, 1st session, Vol. 21, Part 12, March 21, 1890, italics added.

109. Ibid.

110. Ibid.

111. This point is elaborated in Richard White, *Railroaded: The Transcontinentals and the Making of Modern America* (New York: W. W. Norton, 2011).

112. Wu, *The Curse of Bigness*, 89.

113. Friedman, *Capitalism and Freedom*, 2.

114. See discussion in chapter 8.

115. Wu, *The Curse of Bigness*, 91. To be fair, there were some on the left who defended monopoly as well, as when John Kenneth Galbraith suggested that government could direct private monopoly to serve public interests. Matt Stoller, *Goliath: The 100-Year War Between Monopoly Power and Democracy* (New York: Simon & Schuster, 2019).

CHAPTER 10: THE AMERICAN *ROAD TO SERFDOM*

1. Friedman was famous for promoting "positive economics"—by which he meant an economics that was scientific, separated from normative economics. Mises had also stressed the idea that economics had to be scientific, which meant empirical rather than normative. See Robert Van Horn and Philip Mirowski, "The Rise of the Chicago School of Economics and the Birth of Neoliberalism," in *The Road from Mont Pèlerin*, ed. Philip Mirowski and Dieter Plehwe (Cambridge, MA: Harvard University Press, 2009), 140. Yet the whole Free Market Project, as well as a good deal of the Austrian economics that inspired it, was built on a normative positions.

2. The National Archives, "Fifties Britain," accessed July 17, 2021, https://www.nationalarchives.gov.uk/education/resources/fifties-britain/

3. Peter Lewin, "Rediscovering Friedman's *Capitalism and Freedom*," FEE Stories, Foundation for Economic Education, December 11, 2017, https://fee.org/articles/rediscovering-friedman -s-capitalism-and-freedom/ (accessed April 10, 2021).

4. "Samuelson and Friedman to Write for Newsweek," *New York Times*, September 4, 1966, https://www.nytimes.com/1966/09/04/archives/samuelson-and-friedman-to-write-for -newsweek.html

5. Friedman's defenders question how connected Friedman was to the Chilean dictatorship; see Megan McArdle, "Milton Friedman and Chile," *Atlantic*, July 15, 2008, https://www .theatlantic.com/business/archive/2008/07/milton-friedman-and-chile/3841/. This misses the point that he was unquestionably sympathetic to the Pinochet regime, brushed aside criticisms of it, and argued that the economic policies it had adopted were good ones, in part because they would (allegedly) increase freedom. It also misses the point that, irrespective of how much time Friedman may have spent with Pinochet himself, economists influenced by the Chicago school played a major role in constructing the regime's policies. For Friedman's own rationale, see Milton Friedman, "Interview," October 1, 2000, https://www.pbs.org /wgbh/commandingheights/shared/minitextlo/ufd_reformliberty_full.html.

6. George H. Nash, *The Conservative Intellectual Movement in America Since 1945*, 30th anniv. ed. (Wilmington, DE: Intercollegiate Studies Institute, 2006), 267. This is based on interviews Nash undertook in the 1970s.

7. Milton Friedman, *Capitalism and Freedom* (Chicago: University of Chicago Press, 1962), 17.

8. Ibid.

9. Ibid., 19.

10. F. A. Hayek, *The Road to Serfdom*, 1956 American pbk. ed. (Chicago: University of Chicago Press, 1956), 45.

11. For the role of wealth in controlling political voice, see Kay Lehman Schlozman, Henry E. Brady, and Sidney Verba, *Unequal and Underrepresented: Political Inequality and the People's Voice in the New Gilded Age* (Princeton, NJ: Princeton University Press, 2018).

12. Johann J. Go, "Structure, Choice and Responsibility," *Ethics and Behavior* 30, no. 3 (2020): 230–46.

13. On the workings of patronage in science, see Naomi Oreskes, *Science on a Mission: How Military Funding Shaped What We Do and Don't Know About the Ocean* (Chicago: University of Chicago Press, 2021).

14. Friedman, *Capitalism and Freedom*, 2.

15. Leon H. Keyserling, "Review: Milton Friedman, with the assistance of Rose D. Friedman. *Capitalism and Freedom*," *Annals of the American Academy of Political and Social Science* 350 (1963): 195–96.

16. Friedman, *Capitalism and Freedom*, 4.

17. Ibid., 5.

18. Ibid., 12.

19. Ibid., 13.

20. Ibid.

21. Ibid., 15.

22. Ibid., 8.

23. This is yet another example of how Friedman slips into his argument some very misleading bits and pieces. He has a point here—denial of travel is denial of travel—but the quotation ends: "because of his political views." But Americans were not denied the right to travel in Russia during the Cold War because of *their* political views. They were denied the right because of their government's views.

24. Friedman, *Capitalism and Freedom*, 8.

25. Ibid., 9.

26. Ibid.

27. Ibid., viii.

28. Ibid., 2.

29. Ibid.

30. Ibid., 6.

31. Ibid., 23.

32. Ibid., 15. Nice argument, but then why doesn't he support proportional representation in government? And, of course, the tie case is trivial; what if the issue is something more important, like health care or housing, and the market doesn't offer affordable choices? Or in some cases any choices?

33. Ibid., 24.

34. Ibid., 25.

35. Ibid.

36. Ibid., 26.

37. Ibid., 27.

38. Ibid.

39. Ibid., 199. Public health does appear in his conclusion, as a rare area of governmental success.

40. Discussed in Keyserling, "Review."

41. Van Horn and Mirowski, "Rise," 8.

42. Friedman, *Capitalism and Freedom*, 28.

43. Ibid, 32. Emphasis added. This passage foreshadows what Ronald Coase would soon argue about environmental protection and social costs: that any protective regulation had to be weighed against the loss of property rights that would ensue. See R. H. Coase, "The Problem of Social Cost," *Journal of Law and Economics* 3 (1960): 1–44. It also helps to explain the Republican/conservative turn first against environmental regulation, and then against science, since it is science that proves the monetary and health costs of pollution.

44. Friedman, *Capitalism and Freedom*, 28.

45. Friedman, *Capitalism and Freedom*. Friedman also hugely discounts the positive neighborhood effects of conservation. Thus, he argues that national parks, like Yellowstone, are unjustified, because we can identify who uses the parks and charge them admission. This of course was undertaken in the Reagan administration. But Friedman insists that "if the public wants this kind of activity enough to pay for it [i.e., a national park] private enterprises will have every incentive to provide such parks" (31). In fact, the national parks were created because private enterprises were set to destroy them through logging, unbridled tourism, and other forms of commercial development. It also misses the point that the public wants these things and pays for them through our tax dollars; public opinion polls consistently show that Americans support the National Park Service. See Roper Center For Public Opinion Research, "See America First: Public Opinion and National Parks," accessed April 10, 2021, https://ropercenter .cornell.edu/see-america-first-public-opinion-and-national-parks. In a poll taken in 2001, 29 percent said if offered a free, all-expenses-paid trip to various locations, they would choose "an outdoor attraction such as the Grand Canyon or Yellowstone Park," trailing a cruise at 31 percent but substantially ahead of a major theme park, New York City, or a spa in the country. One poll showed 95 percent of the American people wanting the federal government to protect the parks for the future: National Parks Conservation Association, "New Poll of Likely Voters Finds Unity in Public Support for National Parks," August 7, 2012, https://www.npca.org /articles/693-new-poll-of-likely-voters-finds-unity-in-public-support-for-national-parks.

46. Van Horn and Mirowski, "Rise," 8.

47. The World Health Organization has estimated that air pollution causes seven million premature deaths each year (https://www.who.int/health-topics/air-pollution#tab=tab_2). Recent research suggests that the number may be even higher, perhaps more than eight million, which is one in five deaths worldwide each year: https://www.hsph.harvard.edu/c-change/news/fossil-fuel-air-pollution-responsible-for-1-in-5-deaths-worldwide/. Tobacco, which continues to be legal, kills about six million. Robert N. Proctor, *Golden Holocaust: Origins of the Cigarette Catastrophe and the Case for Abolition* (Los Angeles: University of California Press, 2012).

48. Nash, *Conservative Intellectual Movement*, chap. 9, asserts that by the late 1960s the argument was becoming increasingly empirical, as rigorous academic studies had shown that many government programs did not work, or at least did not work as intended. Perhaps, but *Capitalism and Freedom* predated most of the studies that Nash cites. Our point, in any case, is not that government programs always work. Of course they don't. But private-sector initiatives don't always work either, and our observation is that conservatives beat their chests over the former and mostly ignore or outright deny the latter.

49. Friedman, *Capitalism and Freedom*, 13.

50. On the history of state coercion, see Gary Gerstle, *Liberty and Coercion: The Paradox of American Government from the Founding to the Present*, rev. ed. (Princeton, NJ: Princeton University Press, 2015). Gerstle explains: "The Bill of Rights was liberal in the eighteenth-century sense, meaning that it was intended to identify a core area of human freedom, assert its inviolability, and protect it from the exercise of arbitrary government power … In eighteenth-century America, however, the import of the Bill of Rights was limited by the decision to exempt state governments from its strictures … As such, while the First Amendment barred Congress from limiting freedom of religion, states that wanted to limit this freedom, such as Massachusetts and South Carolina, were able to do so." (22–23) On Thomas Jefferson's views on states establishing religion, see Thomas Jefferson Foundation, "Thomas Jefferson and Religious Freedom," accessed July 17, 2021, https://www.monticello.org/site/research-and-collections/thomas-jefferson-and-religious-freedom.

51. Ibid., 20.

52. Friedman, *Capitalism and Freedom*, 21.

53. Trumbo did not officially win full credit from the Writers Guild of America for the 1953 movie *Roman Holiday* until 2011—thirty-five years after he had died.

54. Ellen Schrecker, *No Ivory Tower: McCarthyism and the Universities* (Oxford: Oxford University Press, 1986), discusses academics whose careers were destroyed. On aerospace generally, see Jessica Wang, *American Science in an Age of Anxiety: Scientists, Anticommunism, and the Cold War* (Chapel Hill: University of North Carolina Press, 1999); for specific impacts on a corner of the aerospace industry, see Fraser MacDonald, *Escape from Earth: A Secret History of the Space Rocket* (New York: Public Affairs, 2019).

55. Friedman, *Capitalism and Freedom*, 133. Friedman later developed this idea further, in a very influential *New York Times* piece from September 13, 1970, "The Social Responsibility of Business Is to Increase Its Profits," https://timesmachine.nytimes.com/timesmachine/1970/09/13/223535702.html?pageNumber=379. Some executives who now reject the argument describe themselves and their colleagues as having been "brainwashed." "It influenced—I'd say brainwashed—a generation of C.E.O.s who believed that the only business of business is business," Marc Benioff, interviewed in "A Free Market Manifesto that Changed the World, Reconsidered," DealBook, *New York Times*, September 11, 2020, https://www.nytimes.com/2020/09/11/business/dealbook/milton-friedman-doctrine-social-responsibility-of-business.html. Binyamin Appelbaum argues that rather than fight about corporate responsibility, we would be better off fighting Friedman on his view of the state. We agree. Appelbaum, "50 Years of Blaming Milton Friedman. Here's Another Idea," *New York Times*,

September 18, 2020, https://www.nytimes.com/2020/09/18/opinion/milton-friedman -essay.html.

56. Friedman, *Capitalism and Freedom*, 133, quoting Adam Smith, *An Inquiry into the Nature and Causes of the Wealth of Nations* (New York: Augustus M. Kelley, 1966). On the Management Laboratory Press edition, which we draw upon, it is 345.

57. One of our students says that "this alone is hardly an indictment; nearly every economist in history has done it." If so, that does not speak well of the discipline.

58. Friedman, *Capitalism and Freedom*, 135. This leads to an argument for the abolition of corporate taxes because they encourage corporations to make gifts on behalf of their shareholders, which should be the decision of the shareholders themselves.

59. Ibid. This helps to explain his jaundiced view of democratic governance: he thinks it is unlikely to represent the full range of individual opinion.

60. This could explain how Friedman could defend Pinochet: Friedman doesn't actually believe in democracy—just individualism—so if he sees Pinochet's pro-market policies as advancing individualism, along with economic freedom, he is satisfied. In Friedman's framework, like Jeffrey Epstein, would be perfectly justified in supporting science, but the federal government has no business creating a National Science Foundation. On Epstein's funding of disreputable genetic determinism, see Naomi Oreskes, "Jeffrey Epstein's Harvard Connections Show How Money Can Distort Research," *Scientific American*, September 1, 2020, https://www .scientificamerican.com/article/jeffrey-epsteins-harvard-connections-show-how-money-can -distort-research/.

61. Mariana Mazzucato, *The Entrepreneurial State: Debunking Private vs. Public Sector Myths*, rev. ed. (London: Anthem Press, 2015).

62. Friedman, *Capitalism and Freedom*, 3.

63. Greg Nokes, "Black Exclusion Laws in Oregon," *Oregon Encyclopedia*, July 6, 2020, https:// oregonencyclopedia.org/articles/exclusion_laws/#.Xo1yJNNKhTY.

64. Paul Samuelson, *Economics* (1970 edition). For a discussion (and reproduction) of this chart, and of Samuelson's views of Hayek, see Andrew Farrant and Edward McPhail, "Hayek, Samuelson, and the logic of the mixed economy?" *Journal of Economic Behavior and Organization* 69 (2009): 5–16.

65. Paul Samuelson, "My life philosophy," *American Economist* 27: 5–12, quoted in Andrew Farrant and Edward McPhail, "Hayek, Samuelson, and the logic of the mixed economy?" *Journal of Economic Behavior and Organization* 69 (2009): 12.

66. Friedman, *Capitalism and Freedom*, 10.

67. Ibid., 9–10.

68. Sometimes Friedman writes as if capitalism were a necessary condition for freedom. But in this section, he makes clear that he does not believe that, viz: "History only suggests that capitalism is a necessary condition for political freedom. Clearly it is not a sufficient condition . . . The relation between political and economic freedom is complex and by no means unilateral." Ibid., 10.

69. Friedman notes this, with some satisfaction, in the preface to the 1982 edition.

70. Joan Davies, "Back to Free Enterprise," *Tribune* (London), February 15, 1963, 10.

71. Oscar Handlin, "Review: Milton Friedman with Rose D. Friedman, 'Capitalism and Freedom,'" *Business History Review* 37, no. 3 (Fall 1963), 315.

72. C.W., "Review [Untitled], Reviewed Work: *Capitalism and Freedom* by Milton Friedman," *Ethics* 74:1 (October 1963), 71.

73. Keyserling, "Review," 195–6.

74. William Henry Chamberlin, "The Bookshelf: University of Chicago Economist States Case for True Liberals," *Wall Street Journal*, October 8, 1962, 12.

75. "A Tract for the Times," *Economist*, February 16, 1963, 611.
76. Keyserling, "Review," 196.
77. Leland H. Jenks, "Review: *Capitalism and Freedom*," *American Sociological Review*, 28, no. 3 (June 1963), 491.
78. Milton Friedman, "The Negro in America," *Newsweek*, December 11, 1967, 89, https://miltonfriedman.hoover.org/internal/media/dispatcher/214014/full.
79. Dwight R. Lee, "*Capitalism and Freedom*: A 50th-Anniversary Tribute to Milton Friedman," *Freeman* (October 2012): 10–13.
80. Andrew Ross Sorkin, introduction to "A Free Market Manifesto that Changed The World Reconsidered," *New York Times*, September 11, 2020, https://www.nytimes.com/2020/09/11/business/dealbook/milton-friedman-doctrine-social-responsibility-of-business.html.
81. Dwight Lee, an admirer, recalls that in the 1960s most economics courses were still Keynesian and Friedman's ideas were largely "dismissed as ridiculous." Lee, "Tribute."
82. Rainer Zitelmann, "Bob Chitester: The Champion of Freedom Who Made Milton Friedman a Household Name," Foundation for Economic Education, June 6, 2021, https://fee.org/articles/bob-chitester-the-champion-of-freedom-who-made-milton-friedman-a-household-name/.
83. Ibid.
84. Free to Choose Network, "Tribute to Our Founder, Bob Chitester," accessed July 17, 2021, https://www.freetochoosenetwork.org/.
85. *Free to Choose—The Original 1980 TV Series*, accessed July 17, 2021, https://www.amazon.com/Free-Choose-Original-1980-TV/dp/B07FSV4Y8T.
86. Tom New, email communication with authors, July 6, 2021. On our request, New, president and CEO, WQLN PBS NPR, Erie, PA, found this information in a January 1979 article on the series in the WQLN "Year in Review."
87. *Free to Choose, Volume 1: The Power of the Market*, directed by David Filkin, PBS, 1980, https://www.youtube.com/watch?v=f1Fj5tzuYBE.
88. Harrington appears in Vol. 11, *The Power of the Market*.
89. Thomas Sowell, "The Day Cornell Died," Hoover Institution, October 30, 1999, https://www.hoover.org/research/day-cornell-died.
90. Sorkin, introduction to "A Free Market Manifesto."
91. Marc Benioff, interviewed in "A Free Market Manifesto that Changed the World, Reconsidered," DealBook, *New York Times*, September 11, 2020, https://www.nytimes.com/2020/09/11/business/dealbook/milton-friedman-doctrine-social-responsibility-of-business.html.
92. *Free to Choose, Volume 1: The Power of the Market*, PBS, 1980.
93. Kim Phillips-Fein, "Business Conservatives and the Mont Pèlerin Society," in *The Road from Mont Pèlerin: The Making of the Neoliberal Thought Collective*, ed. Philip Mirowski and Dieter Plehwe (Cambridge, MA: Harvard University Press, 2009), 297. In the preface to the 1956 edition of *The Road to Serfdom*, Hayek addresses the issue of the welfare state, which he describes as that "hodgepodge of ill-assembled and often inconsistent ideals which . . . has largely replaced socialism as the goal of reformers." He allows that some of its aims may be "practicable and laudable," but they need "very careful sorting out if its results are not to be very similar to those of full-fledged socialism" (Hayek, *Road*, 44). Unfortunately, he does not explain what form that sorting might take. Rather, he quickly returns to the warning regarding "measures [that] can destroy the basis of an economy based on the market and gradually smother the creative powers of a free civilization." In this same section, he explains why he is not a conservative: "A conservative movement, by its very nature, is bound to be a defender of established privilege and to lean on the power of government for the protection of privilege" (Hayek, *Road*, 45). This makes it that much more perplexing that Hayek and his

followers do make common cause with American conservatives, and that Hayek is more concerned with the threat of the loss of freedom than the reality of how the protection of privilege perpetuates inequity and suffering and often stymies competition. On the relation of conservatism and the problem of privilege, see Immanuel Wallerstein, *Utopistics: Or Historical Choices of the Twenty-First Century* (New York: New Press, 1998); and discussion in chapter 15.

94. Ebenstein, *Chicagonomics*, 1–19, 184–93, and *passim*.

CHAPTER 11: A LOVE STORY ABOUT CAPITALISM

1. Timothy Rives, "Eisenhower, the Frontier, and the New Deal: Ike Considers America's Frontier Gone, Embraces, Adds to FDR's Legacy," *Prologue* (Fall 2015), 8.

2. Ibid.

3. Daniel J. Kevles, *The Physicists: The History of a Scientific Community in Modern America,* rev. ed. (Cambridge, MA: Harvard University Press, 1995); Rebecca S. Lowen, *Creating the Cold War University: The Transformation of Stanford* (Berkeley: University of California Press, 1997); Naomi Oreskes, *Science on a Mission: How Military Funding Shaped What We Do and Don't Know About the Ocean* (Chicago: University of Chicago Press, 2021; and Mariana Mazzucato, *The Entrepreneurial State: Debunking Public vs. Private Sector Myths*, rev. ed. (London: Anthem Press, 2015).

4. This was a point that NAM officials often acknowledged; hence they needed to change how Americans viewed "The Government."

5. Bruce L.R. Smith and James D. Carroll, "Reagan and the New Deal: Repeal or Replay?" *PS* 14, no. 4 (1981): 765. Reagan's election—often attributed to his charismatic personality—did not represent the irrelevance of interest groups, but rather indicates "that one set of interest groups has out-organized and out-gunned its rivals." Many analysts have seen fundamentalist Christians, social conservatives, independent-minded westerners, and "Reagan Democrats"— blue-collar workers who had previously mostly voted Democrat—as key to the Reagan coalition. That may explain his electoral success, but the interest groups whose interest is most clearly reflected both in his politics and his rhetoric is the conservative network that we have tracked in the previous chapters.

6. Tim Raphael, "The Body Electric: GE, TV, and the Reagan Brand," *TDR/The Drama Review* 53, no. 2 (June 2009): 113–38; Thomas W. Evans, *The Education of Ronald Reagan: The General Electric Years and the Untold Story of His Conversion to Conservatism* (New York: Columbia University Press, 2008). On Reagan's faltering acting career before he went to GE, see Timothy Raphael, *The President Electric: Ronald Reagan and the Politics of Performance*, illus. ed. (Ann Arbor: University of Michigan Press, 2009), 160.

7. Ronald Kline, "Electricity and Socialism: The Career of Charles P. Steinmetz," *IEEE Technology and Society Magazine* 6, no. 2 (June 1987): 9–17; and David Loth, *Swope of GE: The Story of Gerard Swope and General Electric in American Business* (New York: Arno Press, 1976).

8. Richard Rudolph and Scott Ridley, *Power Struggle: The Hundred-Year War Over Electricity* (New York: Harper & Row, 1986), 56.

9. Myron W. Watkins, "Electrical Equipment Antitrust Cases—Their Implications for Government and for Business," *University of Chicago Law Review* 29, no. 1 (October 1, 1961): 97–110, 97.

10. GE also paid hundreds of millions in civil damages; Evans, *Education of Ronald Reagan*, 214.

11. Watkins, "Electrical Equipment Antitrust Cases," 100.

12. Ibid., 103.

13. Ibid.

14. Ibid., 110.
15. Ibid., 100. See also Richard A. Whiting, "Antitrust and the Corporate Executive," *Virginia Law Review* 47, no. 6 (October 1961): 929–87.
16. Watkins, "Electrical Equipment Antitrust Cases," 101.
17. Robert F. Kennedy, quoted in John G. Fuller, *The Gentlemen Conspirators: The Story of the Price-Fixers in the Electrical Industry* (New York: Grove Press, 1962), 176. Fuller states that the comment was made by Kennedy in "a television interview on CBS-TV," but does not include a citation to the original interview (the book does not include any citations). However, Kennedy's concern with price-fixing in the electricity industry is documented in Kenneth Keating, "Interview of the Honorable Robert F. Kennedy," *Let's Look at Congress*, March 19, 1961, transcript available at https://digitalcollections.lib.rochester.edu/ur/interview-honorable-robert-f-kennedy-attorney-general-united-states-senator-kenneth-b-keating-0; and Robert F. Kennedy, "Vigorous Antitrust Enforcement Assists Business," speech before the Economic Club of New York, November 13, 1961, transcript available at U.S. Department of Justice, https://www.justice.gov/sites/default/files/ag/legacy/2011/01/20/11-13-1961.pdf.
18. Robert F. Kennedy, quoted in Fuller, *Gentlemen Conspirators*, 176.
19. Watkins, "Electrical Equipment Antitrust Cases," 104.
20. Kimberly Phillips-Fein, "American Counterrevolutionary: Lemuel Ricketts Boulware and General Electric, 1950–1960," in *American Capitalism: Social Thought and Political Economy in the Twentieth Century*, ed. Nelson Lichtenstein (Philadelphia: University of Pennsylvania Press, 2006), 250–52.
21. Phillips-Fein, "American Counterrevolutionary."
22. Ibid.; see also discussion in chapter 10 of this book.
23. Joan Cook, "Lemuel Ricketts Bouwlare, 95, Headed Labor Relations for G.E.," *New York Times*, November 8, 1990, https://www.nytimes.com/1990/11/08/us/lemuel-ricketts-boulware-95-headed-labor-relations-for-ge.html.
24. Rick Perlstein, "Boulwarism," *New Republic*, April 1, 2007.
25. T.C.C., "Labor Law: General Electric's 'Overall Approach' to Bargaining Held a Violation of Good Faith," *Duke Law Journal* 1965 (1965): 661–67.
26. Evans, *The Education of Ronald Reagan*, 137.
27. T.C.C., "Labor Law," 664. Original emphasis.
28. Phillips-Fein, "American Counterrevolutionary," 255–56.
29. T.C.C., "Labor Law," 664. The name of the case was *National Labor Review Board v. General Electric Company*, 418 F. 2d 736 (Court of Appeals, 2nd Circuit 1969).
30. T.C.C., "Labor Law," 666.
31. This is one of many examples of American reactionaries doing precisely what they vilified the Soviets for: indoctrination. See chapters 1 and 2.
32. In 2004, one of us (Oreskes) published the first peer-reviewed study analyzing the scientific consensus on climate change. For this, she was accused of being economically illiterate. At the time, the complaint seemed like a non sequitur. The Alfred P. Sloan Foundation today fosters "economic and financial literacy" through the Council for Economic Education. See, for example, Council for Economic Education, "News and Information, Category: Alfred P. Sloan," accessed August 3, 2021, https://www.councilforeconed.org/category/alfred-p-sloan/. See also Council for Economic Education, "Take the Quiz," accessed August 3, 2021, https://www.councilforeconed.org/economic-literacy-quiz/.
33. Lemuel Boulware, "Salvation Is Not Free," cited in Evans, *The Education of Ronald Reagan*, 230.
34. Sargent had made this argument back in the 1930s, in Noel Sargent, "The Case Against Socialism, with Particular Analysis of the Views of Norman Thomas," National Association

of Manufacturers, April 18, 1933, 13, folder Socialism, box 6, series 1, Hagley Museum and Library, Wilmington, DE, 1980?.

35. Lemuel Boulware, "Salvation," quoted in Evans, *Education of Ronald Reagan*, 230.

36. Ibid., 231.

37. Ibid., 233.

38. Ibid., 232.

39. Ibid., 233.

40. Phillips-Fein, "American Counterrevolutionary," 254.

41. Lemuel Boulware, quoted in Evans, *Education of Ronald Reagan*, 234–35. Phillips-Fein notes that the argument that socialism was more dangerous—because we did not fear it—was one that Boulware used in many speeches. See Phillips-Fein, "American Counterrevolutionary," 263.

42. Boulware, quoted in Evans, *Education of Ronald Reagan*, 236–37.

43. Evans, *Education of Ronald Reagan*, 50.

44. Ibid., 51.

45. Ibid., 53.

46. Ibid.

47. On the role of government contracts in companies that also worked against government, see Jane Mayer, *Dark Money: The Hidden History of the Billionaires Behind the Rise of the Radical Right* (New York: Anchor, 2016); and Thomas Medvetz, *Think Tanks in America* (Chicago: University of Chicago Press, 2012).

48. Evans, *Education of Ronald Reagan*, 52.

49. "Lawrence W. Fertig," Mises Institute, April 7, 2016, https://mises.org/profile/lawrence-w-fertig. Also see chapter 5.

50. Evans, *Education of Ronald Reagan*, 104–5. On Hazlitt and Hayek as influences, see Marcus Witcher, "Everything Wrong with the Reagan Administration," Libertarianism.org (Cato Institute), April 9, 2019, https://www.libertarianism.org/everything-wrong-presidents/everything-wrong-reagan-administration.

51. Boulware, "The Truth About Boulwarism," in Evans, *Education of Ronald Reagan*, 1. Climate change "skeptics" in the 1990s, for example, would accuse climate scientists of having a hidden "socialist agenda," and even of being part of a global conspiracy to bring down global capitalism. Naomi Oreskes and Erik M. Conway, *Merchants of Doubt: How a Handful of Scientists Obscured the Truth on Issues from Tobacco Smoke to Global Warming*, pbk. ed. (New York: Bloomsbury, 2011).

52. Evans, *Education of Ronald Reagan*.

53. Ibid., 69.

54. Mises Institute, "Books: *Economics of the Free Society*" blurb, accessed January 23, 2022, https://mises.org/library/economics-free-society-1; Wilhelm Röpke, *Economics of the Free Society* (Mises Institute, 1963).

55. Evans, *Education of Ronald Reagan*. Evans does not provide details of how GE used the book groups to canvass employee opinions.

56. Phillips-Fein, "American Counterrevolutionary," 258.

57. Evans, *Education of Ronald Reagan*, 69.

58. Ibid. See also "The Harvard of Corporate America," *Fortune*, August 12, 1991, https://archive.fortune.com/magazines/fortune/fortune_archive/1991/08/12/75364/index.htm.

59. Evans, *Education of Ronald Reagan*, 72.

60. Ibid., 73.

61. Quoted in Evans, *Education of Ronald Reagan*, 74.

62. Ibid., 87–88.

63. "The Powerhouse," *Time*, January 12, 1959, 66–77.

64. In part for legal reasons, GE had to insist that these efforts were educational. But as Evans notes on page 93 of *The Education of Ronald Reagan*, GE executives freely admitted in private that their views were far closer to those of the Republican Party than the Democratic. Evans is a Reagan admirer, but he allows that the effort to create a "better business climate" was "virtually a code" for activities that supported the Republican Party (96).

65. For an analysis of the lecture tours as performance, see Raphael, "The Body Electric."

66. Lemuel Boulware, quoted in Evans, *Education of Ronald Reagan*, 232.

67. Sources give various numbers for the number of factories and number of states, but most likely reliable are the figures provided by historian Phillips-Fein, "American Counterrevolutionary," 250.

68. Evans, *Education of Ronald Reagan*, 58–59.

69. Ibid., 61.

70. Ibid., 67.

71. Jacob Weisberg, "The Conservative Conversion of Ronald Reagan, GE Pitchman," *Slate*, January 8, 2016, https://slate.com/news-and-politics/2016/01/ronald-reagans-conservative -conversion-as-spokesman-for-general-electric-during-the-1950s.html. See also Evans, *Education of Ronald Reagan*, 58–59. George Nash, "Ronald Reagan's Road to Conservatism," *Imaginative Conservative* (blog), November 7, 2018, https://theimaginativeconservative.org /2018/11/ronald-reagan-road-conservatism-george-nash.html.

72. Evans, *Education of Ronald Reagan*, 63. Citing Reagan's autobiography, Evans asserts that this is what Reagan "found" but there is no way to verify that as no materials from this period are available.

73. Ibid., 66. In 1986, Reagan would say that he well remembered the "antitrade frenzy in the late twenties that produced the Smoot-Hawley tariffs." Reagan was born in 1911, so in the late twenties he would have been in his late teens. It's possible that he did remember the debate over protectionism, but one wonders. Ronald Reagan, "Remarks to the Annual Meeting of the National Association of Manufacturers," https://www.reaganlibrary.gov /archives/speech/remarks-annual-meeting-national-association-manufacturers-0. In reviewing a draft of this speech, Jeff Eisenbach at the Office of Management and Budget queried this, writing "Smoot-Hawley greased the skids for the descent into World War II?" The bit about World War II was deleted, but it ended up reinstated. This is a pattern in many Reagan speeches: someone queries a claim, it gets deleted, but then it ends up back in the final version. Reagan almost never cited sources, but his speechwriters were consulting conservative sources, including Friedman, Hayek, and Peter Drucker. In preparation for the 1986 address to NAM, speechwriter Joshua Gilder wrote a memo on Hayek's book *The Constitution of Liberty*. Gilder later went on to create a strategic communications consulting firm, the White House Writers Group, made up at first of former speechwriters; clients included Philip Morris and R. J. Reynolds. At one point Robert Bork was also a member of the group. Gilder would also blog for the American Enterprise Institute. "Joshua Gilder," *American Enterprise Institute/AEI* (blog), accessed April 13, 2021, https://www.aei.org/profile/joshua-gilder/; and "White House Writers Group: Josh Gilder," White House Writers Group, accessed April 13, 2021, https://www.whwg.com/joshua-gilder.

74. One outstanding example of the latter is the late Malcolm Forbes, scion of the Forbes publishing empire, who collected motorcycles, hot-air balloons, and Fabergé eggs. Abram Brown, "Jewels, Eggs, and Empires: The Story of Forbes and Faberge," *Forbes*, September 19, 2017, https://www.forbes.com/sites/abrambrown/2017/09/19/forbes-faberge/?sh=26a25da14ccf.

75. Lemuel Boulware, "Salvation is not Free Speech" reproduced in Evans, *Education of Ronald Reagan*, speech on. pp 229–37, quotation on 235.

76. Ronald Reagan, quoted in Evans, *Education of Ronald Reagan*, 67.

77. Ibid., 89.

78. Ibid., 91. Raphael, "The Body Electric," 135, cites seven hundred thousand employees.

79. Evans, *Education of Ronald Reagan*, 92–93.

80. Evans, *Education of Ronald Reagan*, 177. On the Christian Anti-Communism Crusade, see "About CACC & the Schwarz Report," The Schwartz Report: A Publication of the Christian Anti-Communism Crusade, 2021, https://www.schwarzreport.org/about; and "Guide to the Christian Anti-Communism Crusade Collection ARS.0079," Online Archive of California, accessed April 13, 2021, https://oac.cdlib.org/findaid/ark:/13030/kt0p3034cc/entire_text/.

81. Evans, *Education of Ronald Reagan*, 113–16.

82. Ibid., 115.

83. Ibid., 68.

84. Nash, "Ronald Reagan's Road to Conservatism."

85. Evans, *Education of Ronald Reagan*, 67.

86. Kurt Vonnegut, *Mother Night* (New York: Random House, 1962), v.

87. Dino Felluga, "Modules on Althusser: On Ideology," *Introductory Guide to Critical Theory*, January 31, 2011, Purdue University, accessed April 13, 2021, http://www.purdue.edu/guide totheory/marxism/modules/althusserideology.html.

88. Robert A. Schadler, "Reaganomics Revealed," *American Enterprise Institute* (blog), February 8, 2007, https://www.aei.org/articles/reaganomics-revealed/.

89. Raphael, "The Body Electric," 133.

90. Ibid., 135.

91. Ibid.

92. Ibid., 115.

93. In *The Education of Ronald Reagan*, Thomas Evans notes on p. 201 that in later years, when asked who wrote Reagan's speeches, one Reagan speechwriter answered, "Reagan. They were pretty much the speeches he had given when he worked for General Electric."

94. Martin Fridson, "Republicans Reverse History with TVA Defense," *Forbes*, May 3, 2013, https://www.forbes.com/sites/investor/2013/05/03/republicans-reverse-history-with-tva -defense/.

95. Garry Wills, *Reagan's America: Innocents at Home* (Garden City, NY: Doubleday, 1988), 317–18, 324. See also Raphael, "The Body Electric," 134, citing Wills, *Reagan's America*. The deal was this: In exchange for giving actors residuals (which at the time no other production company did), MCA would have the exclusive right to represent SAG members in television. Besides being anti-competitive, the agreement embedded a conflict of interest; MCA would now both produce television shows and represent the actors appearing in them. Ten years later, MCA controlled "over 40 percent of all primetime television and 60 percent of the entertainment industry as a whole," a degree of growth and control that attracted the attention of the Department of Justice, which launched eight investigations, including of the sweetheart agreement.

96. Evans, *Education of Ronald Reagan*, 194.

97. Rick Perlstein, *Before the Storm: Barry Goldwater and the Unmaking of the American Consensus* (New York: Bold Type Books, 2009), 256.

98. Perlstein, *Before the Storm*, 33–35.

99. Perlstein, *Before the Storm*, 48, and Phillips-Fein, *Invisible Hands*, 129.

100. Perlstein, *Before the Storm*, 499–501.

101. Barry M. Goldwater, *The Conscience of a Conservative* (Shepherdsville, KY: Victor Publishing Company, 1960).

102. Ibid., 24–25.

103. Ronald Reagan, *Ronald Reagan Speaks Out Against Socialized Medicine*, LP, 1961; Eric Zorn, *Zorn Delivered* (blog), *Chicago Tribune*, September 2, 2009, https://blogs.chicagotribune.com/news_columnists_ezorn/2009/09/ronald-reagan-on-medicare-circa-1961-prescient-rhetoric-or-familiar-alarmist-claptrap-.html.

104. David Mikkelson, "Norman Thomas on Socialism," Snopes, September 26, 2009, https://www.snopes.com/fact-check/norman-thomas-on-socialism.

105. Jeffrey St. Onge, "Operation Coffeecup: Ronald Reagan, Rugged Individualism, and the Debate Over 'Socialized Medicine,'" *Rhetoric and Public Affairs* 20, no. 2 (Summer 2017): 223–51.

106. Biographer Garry Wills focuses on the importance of executives associated with MCA; we think it odd that he does not pay more attention to Reagan's supporters from GE. *Reagan's America*.

107. He would later direct Volunteers for Nixon-Agnew. On Wuerthner's ties to Nixon, see "Memo Wuerthner to Citizen's Staff, RNC Staff, New York Staffs, Citizen's Field Operation and GOP Leaders Re: Progress Report on Enlisting 5 Million Volunteers, with Attachments. 5 Pages," September 25, 1968, Box 36, Folder 7, Richard Nixon Presidential Library White House Special Files Collection, Richard Nixon Presidential Library and Museum, Yorba Linda, CA.

108. Evans, *Education of Ronald Reagan*, 167. On the role of both Cordiner and Boulware in the Goldwater campaign, and on Boulware's later support for Reagan, see Phillips-Fein, "American Counterrevolutionary," 264–65.

109. Ibid., 102. Thus, in some ways, Nixon's infamous Southern strategy had already been partially enacted as a GE strategy. On GE's decision to move facilities to right-to-work states, and its role as a tool to discipline workers, see Phillips-Fein, "American Counterrevolutionary," 261–62.

110. Evans, *Education of Ronald Reagan*, 174–75.

111. "Notes on People; Revival of Conservatism Surprises Schlesinger," *New York Times*, June 23, 1981, https://www.nytimes.com/1981/06/23/nyregion/notes-on-people-revival-of-conservatism-surprises-schlesinger.html. See also William A. Rusher, *The Rise of the Right*, rev. ed. (New York: National Review, 1993), 307.

112. The question of Friedman's racial views is a complex one, but certainly his comments about civil rights, housing, as well as his assertion that discrimination is a "taste," are both ahistorical and ethically problematic. See, for example, John Jackson, "Milton Friedman's Economic Racism," *Evonomics* (blog), June 20, 2019, https://evonomics.com/milton-friedmans-economic-racism/; and Stuart Rosenbaum, "Milton Friedman, American Economist and Liberal (1912–2006)," *Race, Justice and American Intellectual Traditions*, 41–49. https://link.springer.com/chapter/10.1007/978-3-319-76198-5_5.

113. Racially restrictive covenants were widespread, including in many Northern cities. See Michael Jones-Correa, "The Origins and Diffusion of Racial Restrictive Convenants," *Political Science Quarterly*, 115 (4) (January 2001): 541–68; also "1920s–1948: Racially Restrictive Covenants," Boston Fair Housing, accessed April 13, 2021, https://www.bostonfairhousing.org/timeline/1920s1948-Restrictive-Covenants.html; and Jackson, "Milton Friedman's Economic Racism."

114. Rick Perlstein, *Nixonland: The Rise of a President and the Fracturing of America*, illus. ed. (New York: Scribner, 2009), 91; also see Ryan Reft, "Reagan's 1966 Gubernatorial Campaign Turns 50: California, Conservatism, and Donald Trump," KCET, August 19, 2016, https://www.kcet.org/shows/lost-la/reagans-1966-gubernatorial-campaign-turns-50-california-conservatism-and-donald-trump.

115. Ryan Reft, "How Prop 14 Shaped California's Racial Covenants," KCET, September 20, 2017, https://www.kcet.org/shows/city-rising/how-prop-14-shaped-californias-racial-covenants.

Reagan's efforts at welfare reform, and his inveighing against "welfare queens" during his presidential campaigns, can be similarly interpreted as racially motivated, given the false perception that most welfare recipients were people of color. See Marguerite Ward, "How Decades of U.S. Welfare Policies Lifted Up the White Middle Class and Largely Excluded Black Americans," *Business Insider*, August 11, 2020, https://www.businessinsider .com/welfare-policy-created-white-wealth-largely-leaving-black-americans-behind-2020 -8. On Reagan's "successful" welfare reform efforts as governor, see Evans, *Education*, 182–83.

116. Wills, *Reagan's America*, chap. 33.
117. Bruce Bartlett, "Reagan's Forgotten Tax Record," *Tax Notes* 130, no. 8 (February 2011): 966.
118. Bartlett, "Reagan's Forgotten Tax Record," 966. Also discussed in Evans, *Education of Ronald Reagan*, 182.
119. Wills, *Reagan's America*, 373.
120. Ronald Reagan, "What Ever Happened to Free Enterprise?" Ludwig von Mises Memorial Lecture at Hillsdale College, Hillsdale, MI, November 10, 1977, https://www.americanrhet oric.com/speeches/ronaldreaganhillsdalecollege.htm.
121. Ibid.

CHAPTER 12: THE DAWN OF DEREGULATION

1. John F. Kennedy, "4 April 1962, Special Message on Transportation," John F. Kennedy Presidential Library and Museum, accessed May 9, 2020, https://www.jfklibrary.org/asset -viewer/archives/JFKPOF/050/JFKPOF-050-015.
2. Daniel K. Williams, *The Election of the Evangelical* (Lawrence: University Press of Kansas, 2020).
3. Rick Perlstein, *The Invisible Bridge: The Fall of Nixon and the Rise of Reagan* (New York: Simon & Schuster, 2014), xiv.
4. Investopedia, "Stagflation," August 2, 2021, https://www.investopedia.com/terms/s/stag flation.asp. On the slowing of economic growth in the 1970s, and how it was used to justify deregulation, see Jeff Madrick, *The Case for Big Government* (Princeton, NJ: Princeton University Press, 2008), 88.
5. Dennis L. Weisman, "Fred Kahn at 100: A Brief Look Back at the Man and the Principles He Championed," *Electricity Journal* 30, no. 7 (August–September 2017): 67–71.
6. Elizabeth Popp Berman, *Thinking Like an Economist: How Efficiency Replaced Equality in U.S. Public Policy* (Princeton, NJ: Princeton University Press, 2022).
7. Richard F. Hirsh, *Technology and Transformation in the American Electric Utility Industry* (Cambridge: Cambridge University Press, 2003), 46–51, calls this the "grow and build" strategy. Also see Thomas K. McCraw, *Prophets of Regulation: Charles Francis Adams, Louis D. Brandeis, James M. Landis, Alfred E. Kahn* (Cambridge, MA: Harvard University Press, 1984).
8. McCraw, *Prophets of Regulation*, 240.
9. Ibid., 225.
10. Judith Stein, *Pivotal Decade: How the United States Traded Factories for Finance in the Seventies*, Kindle edition (New Haven, CT: Yale University Press, 2010), chap. 2.
11. There is a universe of argument about the gold standard, far beyond the scope of our expertise.
12. Meg Jacobs, *Panic at the Pump: The Energy Crisis and the Transformation of American Politics in the 1970s* (New York: Hill and Wang, 2017), 155.
13. Williams, *The Election of the Evangelical*, 199–238.

14. Jimmy Carter, "Our Nation's Past and Future," Speech, Madison Square Garden, New York City, July 15, 1976, https://www.jimmycarterlibrary.gov/assets/documents/speeches/accep tance_speech.pdf.

15. Jacobs, *Panic at the Pump*, 4, 74–76.

16. Milton Friedman, "Gas Crisis: Weather or Washington?" *Newsweek*, February 28, 1977.

17. Naomi Oreskes and Erik M. Conway, *Merchants of Doubt: How a Handful of Scientists Obscured the Truth on Issues from Tobacco Smoke to Global Warming*, pbk. ed. (New York: Bloomsbury Press, 2011).

18. Jimmy Carter, "Address to the Nation on Energy," Speech, Washington, D.C., April 18, 1977, https://millercenter.org/the-presidency/presidential-speeches/april-18-1977-address-nation -energy

19. Jacobs, *Panic at the Pump*, 170–86; see also Stuart E. Eizenstat, *President Carter: The White House Years* (New York: St. Martin's, 2018), 170–203.

20. W. Carl Biven, *Jimmy Carter's Economy: Policy in an Age of Limits*, new edition (Chapel Hill: University of North Carolina Press, 2002), 177; Jacobs, *Panic at the Pump*, 198; and Eizenstat, *President Carter*, 237.

21. Jacobs, *Panic at the Pump*, 189.

22. On studies of transportation deregulation in the Nixon and Ford administrations, see Matt Stoller, *Goliath: The 100-Year War Between Monopoly Power and Democracy* (New York: Simon & Schuster, 2019), chap. 12.

23. Richard H. K. Vietor, *Contrived Competition: Regulation and Deregulation in America* (Cambridge, MA: Harvard University Press, 1994), 51.

24. U.S. Senate, Committee of the Judiciary, "Oversight of Civil Aeronautics Board Practices and Procedures," 94th Congress, 1st sess., vol. 1 (Washington, D.C.: Government Printing Office, February 6, 1975), 1.

25. Ibid., 2.

26. Ibid., 3.

27. U.S. House of Representatives, Committee on House Administration, *The Presidential Campaign, 1976: The Debates* (Washington, DC: U.S. Government Printing Office, 1978), 235–36, https://books.google.com/books?id=q_3IaSPCA-UC.

28. Jimmy Carter, "Airline Industry Regulation Message to the Congress," March 4, 1977, cour-tesy of the American Presidency Project, University of California Santa Barbara, https://www .presidency.ucsb.edu/documents/airline-industry-regulation-message-the-congress.

29. Eizenstat, *President Carter*, 368. On pro-consumer groups promoting anti-government rhetoric from a consumers' rights position, see Paul Sabin, *Public Citizens: The Attack on Big Government and the Remaking of American Liberalism* (New York: W. W. Norton, 2021).

30. Thomas Petzinger Jr., *Hard Landing: The Epic Contest for Power and Profits that Plunged the Airlines into Chaos* (Redfern, New South Wales, Australia: Currency Press, 1996), 82.

31. "Regulatory Reform in Air Transportation: Hearings Before the Subcommittee on Aviation of the Committee on Commerce," United States Senate, 94th Congress, 2nd sess. (Washington, D.C.: U.S. Government Printing Office, 1976), quoted from 510. Also see Vietor, *Contrived Competition*, 54.

32. "U.S. Airline Traffic & Capacity," Airlines.org, May 8, 2020, https://www.airlines.org /dataset/annual-results-u-s-airlines-2/.

33. McCraw, *Prophets of Regulation*, 287.

34. Estimate from Kenneth Button, "A Book, the Application, and the Outcomes: How Right Was Alfred Kahn in *The Economics of Regulation* About the Effects of the Deregulation of

the U.S. Domestic Airline Market?" *History of Political Economy* 47, no. 1 (March 1, 2015): 1–39.

35. Alfred Kahn, quoted in McCraw, *Prophets of Regulation*, 278.

36. David Card and Lisa Saunders, "Deregulation and Labor Earnings in the Airline Industry," in *Regulatory Reform and Labor Markets*, ed. James Peoples, 183–247 (Dordrecht: Springer Netherlands, 1998).

37. Andrew R. Goetz and Timothy M. Vowles. "The Good, the Bad, and the Ugly: 30 Years of U.S. Airline Deregulation," *Journal of Transport Geography* 17 (July 1, 2009): 251–63. PBGC had been created in 1974 to absorb the pension responsibilities of failed manufacturers, financed partly by whatever assets remained from a company's retirement assets and by a per-worker fee charged on insured companies.

38. Micheline Maynard, "United Air Wins Right to Default on Its Employee Pension Plans," *New York Times*, May 11, 2005.

39. U.S. v. AMR Corp., 335 F.3d 1109 (10th Cir. 2003). The case was brought by the Justice Department, and Vanguard Airlines filed an amicus brief.

40. Alfred E. Kahn, "American and Predatory Pricing," *Wall Street Journal*, June 16, 1999, A27.

41. Easterbrook had gone to the University of Chicago Law School and taught as a lecturer there before being appointed to the Seventh Circuit. Judge Easterbrook continues to serve today and he has authored many notable decisions, including a 2020 decision that upheld voting restrictions in Wisconsin. Overturning a lower court that had found the restrictions unconstitutional, Easterbrook held that they were acceptable because they had an overt political intent—to disenfranchise Democrats—rather than a racial basis. Todd Richmond, "Appeals Court Reinstates Some Voting Restrictions in Wisconsin," WUWM 89.7 FM, Milwaukee's NPR, June 30, 2020, https://www.wuwm.com/politics-government/2020-06 -30/appeals-court-reinstates-some-voting-restrictions-in-wisconsin.

42. See footnote 9 of the opinion in *U.S. v AMR Corp.*, 2003.

43. This was problematic on another count: the argument was that high prices now were the consequences of excessively low earlier prices, prices that had driven out the would-be competitor. To frame the evidence solely in terms of currently high prices was thus misleading.

44. The citations (omitted from the main text for brevity) are to: Frank H. Easterbrook, "Predatory Strategies and Counterstrategies," *University of Chicago Law Review* 48 (1981), 263, 264; Richard J. Pierce Jr., "Is Post-Chicago Ready for the Courtroom? A Response to Professor Brennan," *George Washington Law Review* 69 (2001), 1103, 1106; the decision in Matsushita Elec. Indus. Co. v. Zenith Radio Corp., 475 U.S. 574, 589 (1986); and Brooke Group Ltd. v. Brown & Williamson Tobacco Corp., 509 U.S. 209, 226 (1993).

45. Edwin McDowell, "Five Questions for Alfred E. Kahn; He Freed the Airlines. But What to Do Now?" *New York Times*, May 16, 1999, https://www.nytimes.com/1999/05/16/business /five-questions-for-alfred-e-kahn-he-freed-the-airlines-but-what-to-do-now.html.

46. McDowell, "Five Questions for Alfred E. Kahn."

47. Robert H. Bork, "This Antitrust Theory Won't Fly," *Wall Street Journal*, May 17, 1999, https://www.aei.org/articles/this-antitrust-theory-wont-fly/.

48. Alfred E. Kahn, "American and Predatory Pricing," *Wall Street Journal*, June 16, 1999, http://www.wsj.com/articles/SB929482757852350778.

49. Jonathan L. Rubin, "The Premature Post-Chicagoan: Alfred E. Kahn." *Antitrust* 25, no. 3 (2011). For a recent example of how high the bar is to prove harm, see David S. Evans and Richard Schmalensee, "The Role Of Market Definition in Assessing Anticompetitive Harm in Ohio v. American Express," *Competition Policy International*, June 25, 2019, https://www .competitionpolicyinternational.com/the-role-of-market-definition-in-assessing-anticompe titive-harm-in-ohio-v-american-express/.

50. Shane Hamilton, *Trucking Country: The Road to America's Wal-Mart Economy* (Princeton, NJ: Princeton University Press, 2008), chaps. 3 and 4.

51. Richard White, *Railroaded: The Transcontinentals and the Making of Modern America* (New York: W. W. Norton, 2011).

52. Hamilton, *Trucking Country*, 8.

53. Ibid., 19–20.

54. Ibid., 18–19.

55. Ibid., 212.

56. Quoted from Ibid., 215.

57. Jimmy Carter, "Trucking Industry Deregulation Message to the Congress Transmitting Proposed Legislation," June 21, 1979, courtesy of the American Presidency Project, https:// www.presidency.ucsb.edu/documents/trucking-industry-deregulation-message-the-congress -transmitting-proposed-legislation.

58. U.S. House of Representatives, "Examining Current Conditions in the Trucking Industry and the Possible Necessity for Change in the Manner and Scope of its Regulations, part 1," Hearings Before the Subcommittee on Surface Transportation of the Committee on Public Works and Transportation, 96th Congress, first sess. (Washington, D.C.: United States Government Printing Office, 1980), 393.

59. Jimmy Carter, quoted in Dorothy Robyn, *Braking the Special Interests: Trucking Deregulation and the Politics of Policy Reform*, 1st ed. (Chicago: University of Chicago Press, 1987), 56.

60. Carter, "Trucking Industry Deregulation Message."

61. Robert W. Hahn and John A. Hird, "The Costs and Benefits of Regulation: Review and Synthesis," *Yale Journal on Regulation* 8 (1991): 233–78.

62. Clifford Winston, "The Success of the Staggers Rail Act of 1980," AEI-Brookings Joint Center for Regulatory Studies, October 15, 2005, https://www.brookings.edu/research/the -success-of-the-staggers-rail-act-of-1980/.

63. James M. MacDonald and Linda C. Cavalluzzo, "Railroad Deregulation: Pricing Reforms, Shipper Responses, and the Effects on Labor." *Industrial and Labor Relations Review* 50, no. 1 (October 1996): 80–91.

64. Hamilton, *Trucking Country*, 229-23.

65. Ibid., 229–30.

66. Michael H. Belzer, *Sweatshops on Wheels: Winners and Losers in Trucking Deregulation*, 1st edition (New York: Oxford University Press, 2000), 65–75.

67. U.S. House of Representatives, "Current Conditions in the Trucking Industry," 397.

68. Richard L. Florida, "The Political Economy of Financial Deregulation and the Reorganization of Housing Finance in the United States," *International Journal of Urban and Regional Research* 10, no. 2 (June 1986): 207–31.

69. Greta R. Krippner, "The Social Politics of U.S. Financial Deregulation," in *Capitalizing on Crisis: The Political Origins of the Rise of Finance*, ed. Greta R. Krippner, (Cambridge, MA: Harvard University Press, 2011), 80.

70. Florida, "The Political Economy of Financial Deregulation."

71. Jimmy Carter, "Financial Reform Legislation Message to the Congress Proposing the Legislation," May 22, 1979, courtesy of the American Presidency Project, https://www .presidency.ucsb.edu/documents/financial-reform-legislation-message-the-congress-propos ing-the-legislation.

72. Kathleen Day, *Broken Bargain: Bankers, Bailouts, and the Struggle to Tame Wall Street* (New Haven, CT: Yale University Press, 2019), 139.

73. Charles R. McNeill and Denise M. Rechter, "Depository Institutions Deregulation and Monetary Control Act of 1980," *Federal Reserve Bulletin* 66, no. 80 (June 1980): 444–53.

74. Stein, *Pivotal Decade*, 122.

75. Ibid., chap. 8.

76. Office of the Secretary of the Treasury Office of Tax Analysis, *Report to Congress on the Capital Gains Tax Reducations of 1978* (September 1985), https://home.treasury.gov/system /files/131/Report-Capial-Gains-Reduction-1978.pdf.

77. Ibid., 202.

78. Ibid., 204.

79. Biven, *Carter's Economy*, 237.

80. Susan E. Dudley, "Alfred Kahn, 1917–2010: Remembering the Father of Airline Deregulation," *Regulation* 34, no. 1 (Spring 2011), 5.

81. This relationship is generally referred to as the Phillips Curve, after New Zealand economist William Phillips, but see Irving Fisher, "A Statistical Relation between Unemployment and Price Changes," *International Labour Review* 13:6 (1926), 785–92.

82. William McChesney Martin, quoted in David Stein, "Containing Keynesianism in an Age of Civil Rights: Jim Crow Monetary Policy and the Struggle for Guaranteed Jobs, 1956– 1979," in *Beyond the New Deal Order: U.S. Politics from the Great Depression to the Great Recession*, ed. Gary Gerstle, Nelson Lichtenstein, and Alice O'Connor (Philadelphia: University of Pennsylvania Press, 2019), 127.

83. Ibid., 128.

84. Quoted in Paul Krugman, "Who Was Milton Friedman?" *New York Review of Books*, February 15, 2007.

85. Biven, *Carter's Economy*, 194.

86. In 1960, no mainstream economist would have accepted Friedman's statement. In 1980, it became accepted, but the 2010s saw many years of high employment and no inflation. So, the idea that there is a simple relationship between inflation and employment had broken down. See Kristie Engemann, "What's the Phillips Curve & Why Has It Flattened?" Federal Reserve Bank of St. Louis, January 14, 2020, https://www.stlouisfed.org/open-vault/2020 /january/what-is-phillips-curve-why-flattened.

87. Eizenstat, *President Carter*, 341. William Greider, *Secrets of the Temple: How the Federal Reserve Runs the Country* (New York: Simon & Schuster, 1989), 77.

88. William L. Silber, *Volcker: The Triumph of Persistence*, 1st ed. (New York: Bloomsbury, 2012), 174.

89. Data from U.S. Federal Reserve, FRED database, https://fred.stlouisfed.org/.

90. Naomi Klein, *The Shock Doctrine: The Rise of Disaster Capitalism* (New York: Picador, 2007), 199–210.

91. John Maynard Keynes, *A Tract on Monetary Reform* (London: Macmillan, 1923), 80.

92. Alfred E. Kahn, "Liberals Must Face the Facts," *Challenge* 24, no. 5 (November 1, 1981): 25–32.

CHAPTER 13: MAGICAL THINKING

1. In 1994 the tobacco industry would draw on this phrase in a major campaign to fight federal tobacco control. See Dorie E. Apollonio and Lisa A. Bero, "The Creation of Industry Front Groups: The Tobacco Industry and 'Get Government Off Our Back,'" *American Journal of Public Health* 97, no. 3 (March 2007): 419–27.

2. Lewis F. Powell Jr. to Eugene B. Sydnor Jr., "Confidential Memorandum: Attack on American Free Enterprise System," August 23, 1971, courtesy of the Washington and Lee University School of Law Scholarly Commons, accessed July 12, 2021, https://scholarlycommons.law .wlu.edu/powellmemo/1/.

3. Bill Moyers, introduction to "The Powell Memo: A Call-to-Arms for Corporations," BillMoyers.com, September 14, 2012, accessed July 12, 2021, https://billmoyers.com/content/the-powell-memo-a-call-to-arms-for-corporations/.
4. Powell, "Confidential Memorandum," 25–26.
5. Ibid., 11.
6. Powell, "Confidential Memorandum," 32.
7. Ibid., 33, italics added.
8. Burt Raynes, quoted in Jacob S. Hacker and Paul Pierson, *Winner-Take-All-Politics: How Washington Made the Rich Richer—and Turned Its Back on the Middle Class* (New York: Simon & Schuster, 2010), 116. An excerpt of this section is posted on Bill Moyers's website: https://billmoyers.com/content/the-powell-memo-a-call-to-arms-for-corporations/.
9. Geoffrey Supran and Naomi Oreskes, "Assessing ExxonMobil's Climate Change Communications, 1977–2014," *Environmental Research Letters* 12, 084019 (2017); and "Addendum to 'Assessing ExxonMobil's Climate Change Communications, 1977–2014' Supran and Oreskes (2017)," *Environmental Research Letters* 15, 119401 (2020).
10. Judith Layzer, *Open for Business: Conservatives' Opposition to Environmental Regulation* (Cambridge, MA: MIT Press, 2012), 50.
11. Quoted in Bethany Moreton, *To Serve God and Wal-Mart: The Making of Christian Free Enterprise* (Cambridge, MA: Harvard University Press, 2009), 152. Moreton does not identify the CEO who is speaking, but the president of HP at that time was William Hewlitt.
12. On the amici briefs, see "Federal Amicus," U.S. Chamber of Commerce Litigation Center, https://www.chamberlitigation.com/what-we-do/federal-amicus. On the U.S. Chamber of Commerce's legal activities in general, see Layzer, *Open for Business*, 58, particularly her discussion of the creation of the Pacific Legal Foundation, the first conservative public-interest law firm.
13. Brad Lips, *The Freedom Movement: Its Past, Present, and Future* (Arlington, VA: Atlas Network, 2020), 21.
14. Sally Covington, "Moving a Public Policy Agenda: The Strategic Philanthropy of Conservative Foundations," National Committee for Responsive Philanthropy, July 23, 1997, accessed July 12, 2021, https://www.ncrp.org/publication/moving-public-policy-agenda. See also David Callahan, "$1 Billion for Ideas: Conservative Think Tanks in the 1990s," National Committee for Responsive Philanthropy, March 18, 1999, accessed July 12, 2021, https://www.ncrp.org/publication/1-billion-ideas; and Jeff Krehely, Meaghan House, and Emily Kernan, "Axis of Ideology: Conservative Foundations and Public Policy," National Committee for Responsive Philanthropy, March 2004, accessed July 12, 2021, https://www.ncrp.org/wp-content/uploads/2016/11/AxisofIdeology.pdf.
15. David Montgomery, "Conquerors of the Courts," *Washington Post Magazine,* January 2, 2019, https://www.washingtonpost.com/news/magazine/wp/2019/01/02/feature/conquerors-of-the-courts/. See also Eric Lipton and Jeremy W. Peters, "In Gorsuch, Conservative Activist Sees Test Case for Reshaping the Judiciary," *New York Times,* March 18, 2017, https://www.nytimes.com/2017/03/18/us/politics/neil-gorsuch-supreme-court-conservatives.html.
16. The Heritage Foundation, "About Heritage," https://www.heritage.org/about-heritage/mission.
17. Phillips-Fein, *Invisible Hands*, 166. David Callahan suggests that by 1999 these organizations had spent $1 billion to shape "the framework of national deliberations" and that this exceeded the amount spent by Republican Party "soft money." Callahan, "$1 Billion for Ideas."
18. Layzer, *Open for Business*, 87.

19. United Nations, "World Economic and Social Survey Archive: 1980–1989," accessed January 16, 2022, https://www.un.org/development/desa/dpad/publication/world-economic-and-social-survey-archive-1980-1989/.

20. Ronald Reagan, "Inaugural Address 1981," Ronald Reagan Presidential Library, accessed July 12, 2021, https://www.reaganlibrary.gov/archives/speech/inaugural-address-1981.

21. This comment is often attributed to economist Paul Krugman, but Krugman says it originated from Under Secretary of the Treasury Peter Fisher in 2002. Mark Thoma, "Who First Said the U.S. Is 'An Insurance Company with an Army?'" *Economist's View* (blog), January 17, 2013, https://economistsview.typepad.com/economistsview/2013/01/who-first-said-the-us-is-an-insurance-company-with-an-army.html. But Krugman himself had written a column making a similar claim in 2001. See Paul Krugman, "Reckonings; Outside the Box," *New York Times*, July 11, 2001, http://www.nytimes.com/2001/07/11/opinion/reckonings-outside-the-box.html.

22. Author calculation from the 1932 budget and GDP data from FRED. Defense spending in 1932, not including veterans' payments, was $658 million real year dollars; the federal budget was $5.006 billion, and GDP is estimated at $59.522 billion.

23. "The Budget of the United States Government Fiscal Year 1981," January 28, 1980; and White House Office of Management and Budget, "Historical Tables," accessed June 28, 2020, https://www.whitehouse.gov/omb/historical-tables/.

24. Anthony Barnes Atkinson and Nicholas Stern, "Tony Atkinson on Poverty, Inequality, and Public Policy: The Work and Life of a Great Economist," *Annual Review of Economics* 9, no. 1 (2017): 1–20.

25. Milton Friedman, "The Kemp-Roth Free Lunch," *Newsweek*, August 7, 1978, Collected Works of Milton Friedman Project, Hoover Institution Library and Archives, accessed July 12, 2021, https://miltonfriedman.hoover.org/objects/56703/the-kemproth-free-lunch.

26. On Laffer, see "Feature on Dr. Laffer, The Father of Supply-Side Economics: Proposition 13 [Part 4]," interview by Hanako Cho, The Liberty Web, September 30, 2020, accessed July 12, 2021, http://eng.the-liberty.com/2020/8030/. On impacts, see, e.g., Manuel Pastor, "After Tax Cuts Derailed the 'California Dream,' Can the State Get Back on Track?" KQED, November 1, 2017, accessed July 12, 2021, https://www.kqed.org/news/11624431/after-tax-cuts-derailed-the-california-dream-can-the-state-get-back-on-track; and Christopher Hoene, "Fiscal Structure and the Post-Proposition 13 Fiscal Regime in California's Cities," *Public Budgeting and Finance* 24, no. 4 (2004): 51–72. Also see Binyamin Appelbaum, *The Economists' Hour: False Prophets, Free Markets, and the Fracture of Society*, illus. ed. (New York: Little, Brown, 2019), 100–2.

27. Douglas Martin, "Jude Wanniski, 69, Journalist Who Coined the Term 'Supply-Side Economics,' Dies," *New York Times*, August 31, 2005, https://www.nytimes.com/2005/08/31/business/jude-wanniski-69-journalist-who-coined-the-term-supplyside.html.

28. Haynes Johnson, *Sleepwalking Through History: America in the Reagan Years* (New York: W. W. Norton, 2003), 99.

29. Appelbaum, *The Economists' Hour*, 100–2. For the optimality argument see Michael Bernstein, *A Perilous Progress: Economists and Public Purpose in Twentieth-Century America* (Princeton, NJ: Princeton University Press, 2001), 165–66.

30. Ibid.

31. Martin, "Jude Wanniski."

32. Congressional Budget Office, "Effects of the 1981 Tax Act on the Distribution of Income and Taxes Paid," August 1986, accessed July 12, 2021, https://www.cbo.gov/sites/default/files/99th-congress-1985-1986/reports/doc20a-entire.pdf.

33. "H.R. 4242—97th Congress (1981-1982): Economic Recovery Tax Act of 1981," August 13, 1981, accessed July 13, 2021, https://www.congress.gov/bill/97th-congress/house-bill/4242.

34. William Greider, *Secrets of the Temple: How the Federal Reserve Runs the Country* (New York: Simon & Schuster, 1989), 398. The original tax-cut plan had been for $540 billion in cuts but the usual "horse-trading" in Congress drove the cost far higher.

35. Congressional Budget Office, "An Analysis of President Reagan's Budget Revisions for Fiscal Year 1982" (Washington, D.C.: Government Printing Office, March 1981), xiii.

36. "Fiscal Year 1982," *Budget of the United States Government* (Washington, D.C.: Government Printing Office, January 15, 1981), 8, accessed July 13, 2021, https://fraser.stlouisfed.org/title/budget-united-states-government-54/fiscal-year-1982-19036.

37. William Greider, "The Education of David Stockman," *Atlantic*, December 1981, accessed July 13, 2021, https://www.theatlantic.com/magazine/archive/1981/12/the-education-of-david-stockman/305760/.

38. "Trust Fund Operations," Social Security, accessed April 14, 2021, https://www.ssa.gov/history/tftable.html.

39. Lou Cannon, *President Reagan: The Role of a Lifetime* (New York: PublicAffairs, 2000), 210–13.

40. Tim Wirth, interview with Naomi Oreskes, January 29, 2021, 3:45–5:00 P.M. on Zoom.

41. A few years later, Greenspan would argue that it had become "conventional wisdom that the [S]ocial [S]ecurity system, as currently constructed, will not be fully viable after the so-called baby boom generation starts to retire in about fifteen years." In hindsight it is clear that his ideological commitments blinded him to the reality that the program was viable, it just needed to be run right. Alan Greenspan, "Remarks by Chairman Alan Greenspan," Federal Reserve, December 6, 1996, accessed July 13, 2021, https://www.federalreserve.gov/board docs/speeches/1996/19961206.htm. On Greenspan inviting Rand to his swearing-in as chairman of the CEA under Ford, see Appelbaum, *Economists' Hour*, figure captions opposite 217.

42. Cannon, *President Reagan*, 214; also "Trust Fund Operations"; Paul C. Light, "The Crisis Last Time: Social Security Reform," *Brookings* (blog), March 2, 2005, https://www.brookings.edu/opinions/the-crisis-last-time-social-security-reform/. David Shribman, "Don't Alter the Basics of Social Security, Panel Advises," *New York Times*, January 21, 1983, https://www.nytimes.com/1983/01/21/us/don-t-alter-the-basics-of-social-security-panel-advises.html.

43. John A. Svahn and Mary Ross, "Social Security Amendments of 1983: Legislative History and Summary of Provisions," *Social Security Bulletin* 46, no. 7 (July 1983): 46. On NAM see "Should Congress Adopt the Recommendations of the National Commission on Social Security Reform? Pro," *Congressional Digest* 62, no. 4 (April 1983): 106. As one of the commission's members, NAM president Alexander Trowbridge helped broker the compromise recommendations. Edward Cowan, "Compromise Arises on Social Security," *New York Times*, December 9, 1982, https://www.nytimes.com/1982/12/09/us/compromise-arises-on-social-security.html.

44. In later years, this would be recast as the system being broke—a fake claim that is still so widely believed that many websites are dedicated to refuting it: Boston College Center for Retirement Research, "Social Security Is Not Going Bankrupt!" *Stanford Center on Longevity* (blog), June 27, 2018, https://longevity.stanford.edu/social-security-not-going-bankrupt/. *Forbes* even calls the claim fake news: John F. Wasik, "Fake News: Why Social Security Isn't Going Broke," *Forbes*, June 8, 2018, https://www.forbes.com/sites/johnwasik/2018/06/08/fake-news-why-social-security-isnt-going-broke/. *Forbes* notes that Social Security is "the nation's most successful annuity program" and the claim that it "is going bust is a lie." Yet Fox

News continues the canard that "Social Security is broke," John Stossel, "Social Security Is Going Broke," Fox News, August 14, 2018, https://www.foxnews.com/opinion/john-stossel -social-security-is-going-broke; Wasik, "Fake News."

45. There's ambiguity about the exact context, but in 1982 Greenspan quoted Moynihan as saying it, just on the heels of their having worked together on Social Security. Lindsey Bever, "This GOP Senator Just Attributed a Well-Known Liberal Quote to Ronald Reagan," *Washington Post*, March 15, 2017, https://www.washingtonpost.com/news/the-fix/wp/2017/03/15/this -gop-senator-just-attributed-a-well-known-liberal-quote-to-ronald-reagan/.

46. Greider, "The Education of David Stockman."

47. See William L. Silber, *Volcker: The Triumph of Persistence*, 1st ed. (New York: Bloomsbury, 2012), 205–9, and Greider, *Secrets of the Temple*, 352–404.

48. Ibid., 387–93. Greider says that the recession was probably a "mistake." The "monetary aggregate" known as M1 was in flux due to rapid changes in the financial system produced by both deregulation and new financial innovations. The Fed misread movement of money from a different monetary aggregate (M2) into M1 and overreacted.

49. Silber, *Volcker*, 211–15.

50. Data from FRED: U.S. Bureau of Economic Analysis, "Federal Government Budget Surplus or Deficit (-)," FRED, Federal Reserve Bank of St. Louis (November 4, 2020), https://fred .stlouisfed.org/series/M318501A027NBEA.

51. Bruce Bartlett, "Reagan's Forgotten Tax Record," *Tax Notes* 130, no. 8 (February 2011): 965–66; Catherine Rampell, "The Other Way George H. W. Bush's Passing Was the End of an Era," *Washington Post*, December 3, 2018, https://www.washingtonpost.com/opinions /george-hw-bush-was-the-last-of-his-kind—a-republican-who-didnt-believe-in-voodoo -economics/2018/12/03/25aa090a-f740-11e8-8c9a-860ce2a8148f_story.html.

52. Bartlett, "Reagan's Forgotten Tax Record."

53. David Stockman, *The Triumph of Politics: Why the Reagan Revolution Failed* (New York: Harper, Row, 1986).

54. "Reagonomics or 'Voodoo Economics'?" BBC, June 5, 2004, http://news.bbc.co.uk/2/hi /americas/270292.stm.

55. Greider, "The Education of David Stockman."

56. Helen Thomas, "Vice President George Bush Was Only 'Kidding' Reporters When . . . ," UPI, February 10, 1982, https://www.upi.com/Archives/1982/02/10/Vice-President-George -Bush-was-only-kidding-reporters-when/3128382165200/.

57. *1988 Flashback: George H. W. Bush Says, "Read My Lips: No New Taxes"* (NBC News, 1988), https://www.youtube.com/watch?v=AdVSqSNHhVo; *Read My Lips* (History Channel), accessed April 14, 2021, https://www.history.com/topics/us-presidents/read-my-lips-video.

58. Richard Darman, *Who's in Control? Polar Politics and the Sensible Center* (New York: Simon & Schuster, 1996), 193. See also John Robert Greene, *The Presidency of George H. W. Bush*, 2nd ed. (Lawrence: University Press of Kansas, 2015), 37.

59. Congressional Budget Office, "Effects of the 1981 Tax Act," viii.

60. Steve Forbes, the publisher of *Forbes* magazine, continues to push the flat-tax idea, which is not necessarily coupled with a low overall tax rate, but in Republican circles almost always is. Steve Forbes, "Is a Flat Tax the Stimulus Americans Need?" *Forbes,* October 1, 2020, https://www.forbes.com/sites/steveforbes/2020/10/01/is-a-flat-tax-the-stimulus-americans -need/.

61. For the effect of tax cuts on federal revenues, see "Historical Tables," White House Office of Management and Budget, accessed April 14, 2021, https://www.whitehouse.gov/omb /historical-tables/.

62. Jim Tankersley, "Trump to Give Arthur Laffer, Tax-Cut Champion, the Presidential Medal of Freedom," May 31, 2019, https://www.nytimes.com/2019/05/31/business/trump-arthur -laffer-medal-of-freedom.html.

63. Kathleen Day, *Broken Bargain: Bankers, Bailouts, and the Struggle to Tame Wall Street* (New Haven, CT: Yale University Press, 2019), 141.

64. Federal Deposit Insurance Corporation (FDIC), *History of the Eighties: Lessons for the Future*, vol. 1, *An Examination of the Banking Crises of the 1980s and Early 1990s* (Washington, D.C.: FDIC, 1997), 168, accessed July 14, 2021, https://www.fdic.gov/bank/historical /history/vol1.html.

65. Day, *Broken Bargain*, 143.

66. FDIC, *History of the Eighties*, vol. 1, 173–74.

67. Gillian Garcia, "Financial Deregulation: Historical Perspective and Impact of the Garn-St. Germain Depository Institutions Act of 1982, Staff Study 83-2," in *Working Papers (Federal Reserve Bank of Chicago)* (March 1983), accessed July 14, 2021, https://fraser.stlouisfed.org/title /working-papers-federal-reserve-bank-chicago-5285/financial-deregulation-574908, 10–12.

68. Ibid.

69. FDIC, *History of the Eighties*, vol. 1, 176–77.

70. Ronald Reagan, "Proclamations, Messages & Executive Orders, March 24, 1981," Ronald Reagan Presidential Library, accessed July 14, 2021, https://www.reaganlibrary.gov/research /speeches/32481a.

71. U. S. Congress. Senate Committee on Banking, Housing, and Urban Affairs, *Final Oversight Hearings on the Savings and Loan Industry in the 100th Congress: Hearings Before the Committee on Banking, Housing, and Urban Affairs, United States Senate, One Hundredth Congress, Second Session . . . August 2 and 3, 1988* (Washington, D.C.: U.S. Government Printing Office, 1989), 310.

72. Norman Strunk and Fred Case, *Where Deregulation Went Wrong: A Look at the Causes Behind Savings and Loan Failures in the 1980s* (Washington, D.C.: United States League of Savings Institutions, 1988), 141.

73. FDIC, *History of the Eighties*, vol. 1, 180.

74. Ibid., 185.

75. Day, *Broken Bargain*, 122.

76. Ibid., 21.

77. Ibid., 26.

78. U.S. General Accounting Office (GAO), "The Treasury/Federal Home Loan Bank Board Plan for FSLIC Recapitalization," GAO/GGD-87-46BR (Washington, D.C.: U.S. General Accounting Office, March 3, 1987), https://www.gao.gov/products/ggd-87-46br.

79. Martin Lowy, *High Rollers: Inside the Savings and Loan Debacle*, 1st ed. (New York: Praeger, 1991), 186–87.

80. Summarized from U.S. House of Representatives, Committee on Banking, Finance, and Urban Affairs, "Federal Savings and Loan Insurance Corporation Recapitalization Act of 1987" (Washington, D.C.: House of Representatives), 475–522.

81. Quoted in Day, *Broken Bargain*, 150.

82. Lowy, *High Rollers*, 179.

83. Kitty Calavita, Henry N. Pontell, and Robert M. Tillman, *Big Money Crime: Fraud and Politics in the Savings and Loan Crisis* (Berkeley: University of California Press, 1997).

84. Nathaniel C. Nash, "Showdown Time for the Bank Board's Danny Wall," *New York Times*, July 9, 1989, https://www.nytimes.com/1989/07/09/business/showdown-time-for-danny-wall .html.

85. Ibid.

86. Will Kenton, "Savings and Loan Crisis—S&L Crisis Definition," Investopedia, May 16, 2019, https://www.investopedia.com/terms/s/sl-crisis.asp, and "Garn-St. Germain Depository Institutions Act," Investopedia, November 9, 2021, https://www.investopedia.com/terms/g/garn-st-germain-depository-institutions-act.asp.

87. Summarized from Lowy, *High Rollers*, 222–26.

88. Timothy Curry and Lynn Shibut, "The Cost of the Savings and Loan Crisis: Truth and Consequences," *FDIC Banking Review* 13, no. 2 (2000): 26–45.

89. Robert A. Rosenblatt, "GAO Estimates Final Cost of S&L Bailout at $480.9 Billion," *Los Angeles Times*, July 13, 1996, https://www.latimes.com/archives/la-xpm-1996-07-13-fi-23615-story.html.

90. Alane Moysich, "The Savings and Loan Crisis and Its Relationship to Banking," in FDIC, *History of the Eighties*, vol. 1, 187.

91. Lowy, *High Rollers*, 245; see also discussion in chapter 9.

92. Monica Rico, *Nature's Noblemen: Transatlantic Masculinities and the Nineteenth-Century American West* (New Haven, CT: Yale University Press, 2013); and Polly Welts Kaufman, *National Parks and the Woman's Voice: A History*, updated edition (Albuquerque: University of New Mexico Press, 2006). See also Isaac Kantor, "Ethnic Cleansing and America's Creation of National Parks," *Public Land and Resources Law Review* 28 (2007): 42–64.

93. Timothy Egan, *The Big Burn: Teddy Roosevelt and the Fire That Saved America*, repr. ed. (Boston: Mariner Books, 2010).

94. The Clean Water Act was passed over Nixon's veto. See Ellen Simon, "The Bipartisan Beginnings of the Clean Water Act," *Waterkeeper*, January 30, 2019, https://waterkeeper.org/news/bipartisan-beginnings-of-clean-water-act/.

95. He did this through administrative reorganization. See Layzer, *Open for Business*, 34.

96. Krystal L. Tribbett, "RECLAIMing Air, Redefining Democracy: A History of the Regional Clean Air Incentives Market, Environmental Justice, and Risk, 1960–Present" (PhD diss., University of California San Diego, 2014).

97. Layzer, *Open for Business*, 37–41.

98. Ibid., 41.

99. Ibid., chap. 3; Train's objections to changes to the Clean Air Act are discussed on 41.

100. Ibid., 84.

101. Charles Wolf Jr., "A Theory of 'Non-Market Failure': Framework for Implementation Analysis," (Santa Monica, CA: RAND Corporation, January 1978): 4, https://www.rand.org/pubs/papers/P6034.html. He recognizes four categories: externalities and public goods; cases of increasing returns with declining marginal costs, which lead to inefficient outcomes and therefore tend toward monopoly; market imperfection (a potentially very broad category!); and distributional inequity, although he notes that "most economists exclude distributional effects from market failure strictly defined." Ibid., 8.

102. Ibid., 4. Quotation is in the first footnote of the text; it essentially summarizes the problem. Wolf presumably puts it in a footnote because he would not agree with Sidgwick's answer.

103. Ibid., 10. Here Wolf is quoting Smith, but without citing, presumably because these lines from Smith are so well known to economists that they need no attribution.

104. Wolf had a point about the failure of government institutions to follow up on outcomes; one of us once reviewed this question with respect to environmental modeling. One example that would support Wolf: the Army Corp of Engineers counted the success of beach replenishment projects by whether the appropriate amount of sand was placed on the intended beach by the intended deadline, and at the intended price. Whether or not the sand actually stayed on the beach was a different matter, and often it did not. See Naomi Oreskes and Kenneth Belitz,

"Philosophical Issues in Model Assessment," in *Model Validation: Perspectives in Hydrological Science*, ed. M. G. Anderson and P. D. Bates (Hoboken, NJ: John Wiley, 2001), 23–41.

105. Wolf, "A Theory of 'Non-Market Failure,'" 45, italics added.

106. Ibid., 50. In fact, studies have often shown lower costs and greater benefits than anticipated. See Imad A. Moosa and Vikash Ramiah, *The Costs and Benefits of Environmental Regulation* (Cheltenham, UK: Edward Elgar, 2014).

107. Ibid., 38. For further discussion, see Brian Dollery, "Perspectives on Wolf's Theory of Nonmarket Failure," *University of New England Working Papers in Economics*, no. 11 (July 1994): 1–17.

108. Julian L. Simon, *The Resourceful Earth: A Response to Global 2000*, ed. Herman Kahn (New York: Blackwell, 1984).

109. Ibid.

110. Ibid., 78 and 84–85.

111. Ibid., 87, 94.

112. Ibid., 94.

113. Ibid., 372. Since 1984, the Gallup organization has asked the question: "With which one of these statements about the environment and the economy do you most agree? Protection of the environment should be given priority even at the risk of curbing economic growth, or economic growth should be given priority, even if the environment suffers to some extent?" Between 1974 and 2000, consistently more than 60 percent chose the first. Priority for environmental issues slipped significantly in the 2000s, dipping to a low of 38 percent in 2010, but then rose again, and by 2019 was back to 65 percent. In 2022, the figures were 53 vs. 42 in favor of the environment. However, during this time, the percentage prioritizing the economy never exceeded 53 percent. So at worst, Americans over the last half-century have been divided on the issue, but for most of the time have prioritized the environment over the economy; see https://news.gallup.com/poll/1615/environment.aspx. That said, the question is problematic, because many studies now show that environmental protection tends, in general, to be good for the economy overall, even if it hurts individual industries. See Steve Cohen, "Economic Growth and Environmental Sustainability," *State of the Planet* (blog), January 27, 2020, https://news.climate.columbia.edu/2020/01/27/economic-growth-environmental-sustainability/.

114. Gallup, "Environment."

115. Layzer, *Open for Business*, 101. On the budget cutting, see 104. Reagan tried to zero out CEQ, which under his leadership effectively ceased to function.

116. "About Us," Mountain States Legal Foundation, accessed April 22, 2022, https://mslegal.org/.

117. Cannon, *President Reagan*, 469.

118. Bill Prochnau, "The Watt Controversy," *Washington Post*, June 30, 1981, https://www.washingtonpost.com/archive/politics/1981/06/30/the-watt-controversy/d591699b-3bc2-46d2-9059-fb5d2513c3da/.

119. Ibid.

120. Ibid.

121. Ibid.

122. Douglas Martin, "Anne Gorsuch Burford, 62, Reagan E.P.A. Chief, Dies," *New York Times*, July 22, 2004, https://www.nytimes.com/2004/07/22/us/anne-gorsuch-burford-62-reagan-epa-chief-dies.html.

123. Layzer, *Open for Business*, 23–26. As a judge, Attorney General Merrick Garland was known for the defense of agency discretion. See James B. Stewart, "On Business Issues, Republicans Might Want a Justice Garland," *New York Times*, March 24, 2016, https://www.nytimes.com/2016/03

/25/business/on-business-issues-republicans-might-want-a-justice-garland.html, and Hannah Belitz, "The Supreme Court Vacancy and Labor: Merrick Garland," *OnLabor* (blog), February 23, 2016, https://onlabor.org/the-supreme-court-vacancy-and-labor-merrick-garland-2/.

124. Lazyer, *Open for Business*, foreword and 110.

125. Quoted in ibid., ix. See also Alex John Boynton, "Confronting the Environmental Crisis: Anti-Environmentalism and the Transformation of Conservative Thought in the 1970s" (PhD diss., University of Kansas, 2015). Gorsuch argued for a states' rights framework that would devolve enforcement to the states, despite the fact that most states had inadequate funding and infrastructure to undertake enforcement, and that the EPA had been created in part because of the acknowledged need for federal standards and enforcement in pollution control.

126. Lazyer, *Open for Business*, 95.

127. Ibid.

128. Ibid., 96.

129. Phillip J. Cooper, *The War Against Regulation: From Jimmy Carter to George W. Bush* (Lawrence: University Press of Kansas, 2009).

130. J. Hoberman, *Make My Day: Movie Culture in the Age of Reagan* (New York: New Press, 2019), 204.

131. Nicholas Stern, *The Economics of Climate Change: The Stern Review* (Cambridge: Cambridge University Press, 2006).

132. Naomi Klein, *This Changes Everything: Capitalism vs. The Climate* (New York: Simon & Schuster, 2014).

133. Joanne Omang, "Reagan Criticizes Clean Air Laws and EPA as Obstacles to Growth," *Washington Post*, October 9, 1980, https://www.washingtonpost.com/archive/politics/1980 /10/09/reagan-criticizes-clean-air-laws-and-epa-as-obstacles-to-growth/abed4cf4-b16e -47e9-8e35-5f7e67c49fb6/.

134. Alex Park, "Surprise! This GOP Senator's Theory about Volcanoes and Climate Change Is Totally Wrong," *Grist*, November 7, 2014, accessed July 16, 2021, https://grist.org/politics /surprise-this-gop-senators-theory-about-volcanoes-and-climate-change-is-totally-wrong/. Volcanoes contribute to transient climate effects, but these are typically cooling; Murkowski was blaming volcanoes for global warming.

135. Tim Radford, "Do Trees Pollute the Atmosphere?" *Guardian*, May 13, 2004, http://www .theguardian.com/science/2004/may/13/thisweekssciencequestions3.

136. Naomi Oreskes and Erik M. Conway, *Merchants of Doubt: How a Handful of Scientists Obscured the Truth on Issues from Tobacco Smoke to Global Warming*, pbk. ed. (New York: Bloomsbury, 2011), chap. 3.

137. Ronald Reagan, "Radio Address to the Nation on Oil Prices," April 19, 1986, https://www .reaganlibrary.gov/archives/speech/radio-address-nation-oil-prices.

138. Memo 12 Sept 1984, from Christopher Hicks, Treasury Dept to Robert M Kimmett NSC and Ben Elliott, speechwriter, folder International Monetary Fund and World Bank, (Elliott/ White) (6), box 178, Ronald Reagan Presidential Library, Simi Valley, CA 93065. See also "A domestic approach to the world economy, International Economic Policy Under the Reagan Administration, by Henry R Nau, George Washington University," folder International Monetary Fund and World Bank, September 25, 1984 (7), box 178, Ronald Reagan Presidential Library, Simi Valley, CA 93065.

139. Folder: Joint Meeting of the World Bank and IMF [1 of 6] September 30, 1986. (Judge, White). The drafts go back and forth between that version, and one in which he adds "in this case economic freedom." Box 295, Ronald Reagan Presidential Library, Simi Valley, CA 93065.

140. Ronald Reagan, "Radio Address to the Nation on Volunteerism and the Supreme Court Nomination of Robert H. Bork," October 3, 1987, https://www.presidency.ucsb.edu /documents/radio-address-the-nation-voluntarism-and-the-supreme-court-nomination -robert-h-bork

141. Ronald Reagan, "Remarks at the Annual Republican Congressional Fundraising Dinner," May 11, 1988, https://www.reaganlibrary.gov/archives/speech/remarks-annual-republican -congressional-fundraising-dinner-0.

142. "Draft Speech, September 21, 1984, with KW changes," folder International Monetary Fund and World Bank, (Elliott/White) September 25, 1984 (3), box 178, Ronald Reagan Presidential Library, Simi Valley, CA 93065. It is not clear who KW was. There are two aides at this time with last name beginning with W, Faith Whittlesey and Richard Wirthlin: Sam Roberts, "Faith Whittlesey, Conservative Voice and Reagan Aide, Dies at 79," *New York Times*, May 24, 2018, https://www.nytimes.com/2018/05/24/obituaries/faith-whittlesey -conservative-voice-and-reagan-aide-dies-at-79.html; Adam Clymer, "Richard Wirthlin, Pollster Who Advised Reagan, Dies at 80," *New York Times*, March 18, 2011, https://www .nytimes.com/2011/03/18/us/politics/18wirthlin.html. Given other materials in this folder, in particular the distribution lists, it seems most likely that the "K" was an R with the top cut off and this was Wirthlin. Reagan's handwriting is distinct, so it is fairly certain that it is RR who reinstates the "cliché." For the line about the indivisibility thesis and the comment "Pres. Has used before, wants it in," see folder International Monetary Fund and World Bank (Elliott/White) Sept 25, 1984, folder 2 of 7, box 178, Ronald Reagan Presidential Library, Simi Valley, CA 93065. The line about prosperity was used again many times.

143. Folder: OAS Caribbean Basin Initiative Coalition Celebration July 21, 1982 (Elliott), box 46, Ronald Reagan Presidential Library, Simi Valley, CA 93065.

144. Folder: Speech Annual Meeting of the International Monetary Fund & World Bank Group. [Elliott] September 19, 1981, box 17, Ronald Reagan Presidential Library, Simi Valley, CA 93065. Interestingly, the chief speechwriter for this one was Bently T. Elliott, who previously had worked for the Chamber of Commerce.

145. Folder: 09/29/1987 Joint Meeting of the World Bank/ IMF (10 of 10), box 343, Ronald Reagan Presidential Library, Simi Valley, CA 93065.

146. Hobart Rowan, "Stress Free Enterprise, Reagan Tells Poor Lands," *The Washington Post*, September 30, 1981, https://www.washingtonpost.com/archive/politics/1981/09/30/stress -free-enterprise-reagan-tells-poor-lands/d4b692a1-70c0-43e0-9d0d-c70beb8d55f7/.

147. Robert L. Ayres, "Clausen and the Poor," *New York Times*, July 1, 1981, sec. Opinion, https://www.nytimes.com/1981/07/01/opinion/clausen-and-the-poor.html. A clipping of this piece is found in folder World Bank Speech 9/29/81, box 22, Ronald Reagan Presidential Library, Simi Valley, CA 93065.

148. Folder World Bank Speech 9/29/81, box 22, Ronald Reagan Presidential Library, Simi Valley, CA 93065.

149. "Reagan Touts Capitalism to IMF," *The Christian Science Monitor*, September 30 1981, https://www.csmonitor.com/1981/0930/093019.html.

150. Folder International Monetary Fund and World Bank (Elliott/ White) September 25, 1984 (1 of 7), box 178, Ronald Reagan Presidential Library, Simi Valley, CA 93065.

151. Folder 09/29/1987 Joint Meeting of the World Bank/ IMF (10 of 10), box 343, Ronald Reagan Presidential Library, Simi Valley, CA 93065.

152. For a contemporaneous critique, see TNI, "The Chicago Boys in Chile: Economic Freedom's Awful Toll," accessed August 2, 2021, https://www.tni.org/my/node/12111. For a historical perspective, see "Hayek in Chile," chap. 23 in Grégoire Chamayou, *The Ungovernable Society* (Cambridge: Polity Press, 2021).

153. Ronald Reagan, "Radio Address to the Nation on the President's Trip to Indonesia and Japan," November 12, 1983, https://www.reaganlibrary.gov/archives/speech/radio-address-nation-presidents-trip-indonesia-and-japan. Protectionism was tricky territory for the administration, because while most conservatives opposed it, some manufacturers supported it. When preparing for a 1986 address to NAM, one memo noted, "We're making an effort to bring this organization [NAM] closer to the W.H. Sandy Trowbridge has been helpful." Trowbridge was the president of NAM and a former secretary of commerce (under Lyndon Johnson). But another memo noted that NAM was "with us on trade but not on tax reform (manufacturers don't want to lose breaks) and with us on the budget." Presumably NAM was also not entirely with the president on eliminating protections for U.S. manufacturing. Folder 05/29/1986 Address National Association of Manufacturers (6 of 6), box 267, Ronald Reagan Presidential Library, Simi Valley, CA 93065.

154. Peter Pham, "What Is South Korea's Secret Weapon?" *Forbes*, May 31, 2018, https://www.forbes.com/sites/peterpham/2018/05/31/what-is-south-koreas-secret-weapon/; and Carlos Tejada, "Money, Power, Family: Inside South Korea's Chaebol," *New York Times*, February 17, 2017, https://www.nytimes.com/2017/02/17/business/south-korea-chaebol-samsung.html.

155. Ronald Reagan, "Radio Address to the Nation on Taxes, Tuition Tax Credit, and Interest Rates," April 24, 1982, https://www.presidency.ucsb.edu/documents/radio-address-the-nation-taxes-the-tuition-tax-credit-and-interest-rates

156. For example, see Ronald Reagan, "Radio Address to the Nation on United States–Soviet Relations," September 29, 1984, https://www.reaganlibrary.gov/research/speeches/92984a

157. Ronald Reagan, "Remarks to Brokers and Staff of the New York Stock Exchange in New York," New York, March 28, 1985, https://www.reaganlibrary.gov/research/speeches/32885a. In one formulation it was the economic growth itself that was "almost dead" from "a government that taxed too much and spent even more than it taxed." Ronald Reagan, "Address to the Nation on the Federal Budget and Deficit Reduction," April 24, 1985, https://www.reaganlibrary.gov/research/speeches/42485b.

158. Ronald Reagan, "Remarks on Signing the Intermediate-Range Nuclear Forces Treaty," December 8, 1987, https://www.reaganlibrary.gov/archives/speech/remarks-signing-intermediate-range-nuclear-forces-treaty. It is better in Russian: "Dovorey no provorey."

159. A brief discussion of this takeover wave in manufacturing appears in Jennifer Delton, *The Industrialists: How the National Association of Manufacturers Shaped American Capitalism* (Princeton, NJ: Princeton University Press, 2020), chap. 11.

160. "Gordon Gekko: Address to Teldar Paper Stockholders," American Rhetoric: Movie Speeches, accessed July 15, 2021, https://www.americanrhetoric.com/MovieSpeeches/moviespeechwallstreet.html.

161. Quoted in J. Hoberman, *Make My Day*, 309.

162. Thomas Piketty, *Capital in the Twenty-First Century* (Cambridge, MA: Harvard University Press, 2017), 32.

163. Christopher Ingraham, "The Richest 1 Percent Now Owns More of the Country's Wealth than at Any Time in the Past 50 Years," *Washington Post*, December 6, 2017, https://www.washingtonpost.com/news/wonk/wp/2017/12/06/the-richest-1-percent-now-owns-more-of-the-countrys-wealth-than-at-any-time-in-the-past-50-years/.

164. Benjamin I. Page, Larry M. Bartels, and Jason Seawright, "Democracy and the Policy Preferences of Wealthy Americans," *Perspectives on Politics* 11, no. 1 (March 2013): 51–73.

165. Milton Friedman, quoted in Justin Fox, *The Myth of the Rational Market: A History of Risk, Reward, and Delusion on Wall Street* (New York: Harper Business, 2009), 159–60.

166. Justin Fox, *Myth of the Rational Market*, chap. 9.

167. Timothy Aeppel and Alwyn Scott, "'Neutron Jack' Welch, Who Led GE's Rapid Expansion, Dies at 84," Reuters, March 2, 2020, accessed July 15, 2021, https://www.reuters.com/article /us-people-jackwelch-idUSKBN20P20T; Steve Lohr, "Jack Welch, G.E. Chief Who Became a Business Superstar, Dies at 84," *New York Times*, March 2, 2020, accessed July 15, 2021, https://www.nytimes.com/2020/03/02/business/jack-welch-died.html

CHAPTER 14: APOTHEOSIS

1. William J. Clinton, "State of the Union Address," Washington, D.C., January 23, 1996, https://clintonwhitehouse4.archives.gov/WH/New/other/sotu.html. One should note that the next sentence was "But we cannot go back to the time when our citizens were left to fend for themselves." The second sentence is less often quoted.

2. Quoted in Judith A. Layzer, *Open for Business: Conservatives' Opposition to Environmental Regulation* (Cambridge, MA: MIT Press, 2012), 75.

3. Ibid.

4. William F. Grover and Joseph G. Peschek, "Bill Clinton and the Neoliberal Presidency," in *The Unsustainable Presidency: Clinton, Bush, Obama, and Beyond*, ed. William F. Grover and Joseph G. Peschek, The Evolving American Presidency Series (New York: Palgrave Macmillan U.S., 2014), 5.

5. Tim Wirth, interview with Naomi Oreskes, January 29, 2021, 3:45–5:00 P.M. on Zoom.

6. Ibid.

7. John Micklethwait and Adrian Wooldridge, *The Wake-Up Call: Why the Pandemic Has Exposed the Weakness of the West, and How to Fix It* (London: Short Books, 2020), 42.

8. Robert Higgs, "The Era of Big Government Is Not Over," *Good Society* 9, no. 2 (1999): 97.

9. Timothy Canova, "Legacy of the Clinton Bubble," *Dissent*, Summer 2008, https://www .dissentmagazine.org/article/the-legacy-of-the-clinton-bubble.

10. Anthony Barnes Atkinson and Nicholas Stern, "Tony Atkinson on Poverty, Inequality, and Public Policy: The Work and Life of a Great Economist," *Annual Review of Economics* 9, no. 1 (2017): 1–20. See also discussion in Micklethwait and Wooldridge, *Wake-Up Call*.

11. Paraphrased by Francis Fukuyama, "History Is Still Going Our Way," *Wall Street Journal*, October 5, 2001, http://www.wsj.com/articles/SB1002238464542684520. For the original, see George F. Will, "The End of Our Holiday from History," September 12, 2001, *Washington Post*, https://www.washingtonpost.com/archive/opinions/2001/09/12/the-end-of-our -holiday-from-history/9da607fd-8fdc-4f33-b7c9-e6cda00453bb/.

12. For an overview, see Victor Pickard, "The Strange Life and Death of the Fairness Doctrine: Tracing the Decline of Positive Freedoms in American Policy Discourse," *International Journal of Communication*, 12 (2018): 3434–53.

13. Jennifer Holt, *Empires of Entertainment: Media Industries and the Politics of Deregulation, 1980–1996* (New Brunswick, NJ: Rutgers University Press, 2011), 66. According to Holt, the cable-telecommunication cross-ownership ban was first an FCC rule in 1970 and was codified by Congress in the CCA in 1984. FCC/Congress wanted to protect the young cable industry from being bought out by telecommunications companies that already had the infrastructure. The new law created a set of "Baby Bells"—regional pieces of AT&T that retained control of the phone lines, even while Ma Bell held on to long-distance service—and barred the Baby Bells from entering the cable market.

14. John M. Myers and Daniel P. Schuering, "Cable Television Franchise Renewals: A Primer," *Illinois Municipal Review* January 1991, 21–22, https://www.lib.niu.edu/1991/im910121.html.

15. Brian Caterino, "Cable Television Consumer Protection and Competition Act of 1992," *First Amendment Encyclopedia*, accessed July 17, 2021, https://mtsu.edu/first-amendment/article

/1058/cabletelevision-consumer-protection-and-competition-act-of-1992; and Holt, *Empires of Entertainment*, 168.

16. "Telecommunications Act of 1996," Federal Communications Commission, June 20, 2013, https://www.fcc.gov/general/telecommunications-act-1996.

17. Telecommunications Act of 1996, Pub. LA. No. 104-104, 110 Stat. 56 (1996).

18. The Act is not particularly precise, but it does lay out a set of actions to be taken to achieve universal internet access.

19. David McCabe, "Bill Clinton's Telecom Law: Twenty Years Later," *The Hill*, February 7, 2016, https://thehill.com/policy/technology/268459-bill-clintons-telecom-law-twenty-years-later.

20. Manfred B. Steger and Ravi K. Roy, *Neoliberalism: A Very Short Introduction* (Oxford: Oxford University Press, 2010), 62–63.

21. Ibid.

22. David A. Balto, "Antitrust Enforcement in the Clinton Administration," *Cornell Journal of Law and Policy* 9, no. 1 (1999): 73.

23. Laurence Zuckerman and Stephen Labaton, "American Airlines Is the Winner in a U.S. Antitrust Case," *New York Times*, April 28, 2001, https://www.nytimes.com/2001/04/28/business/american-airlines-is-the-winner-in-a-us-antitrust-case.html.

24. Network World staff and IDG News Service, and John Brodkin, "Intel and Antitrust: A Brief History," *Network World*, December 9, 2009, https://www.networkworld.com/article/2239461/intel-and-antitrust—a-brief-history.html.

25. Ibid.

26. Nicholas Economides, "The Microsoft Antitrust Case," *NYU Center for Law and Business Research Paper No. 01-003* (April 2, 2001). Available at SSRN: https://ssrn.com/abstract=253083 or http://dx.doi.org/10.2139/ssrn.253083.

27. David J. Theroux, "Open Letter on Antitrust Protectionism," Independent Institute, June 2, 1999, https://www.independent.org/news/article.asp?id=483.

28. Consumer Reports, "Lessons from 1996 Telecommunications Act: Deregulation Before Meaningful Competition Spells Consumer Disaster," February 2000, https://advocacy.consumerreports.org/wp-content/uploads/2013/03/lesson.pdf.

29. Nicholas Economides, "The Telecommunications Act of 1996 and Its Impact," *Japan and the World Economy* 11, no. 4 (December 1999): 455–83.

30. Robert W. McChesney, *Digital Disconnect: How Capitalism Is Turning the Internet Against Democracy*, illus. ed. (New York: New Press, 2013).

31. Fortune 500, "Facebook Company Profile," *Fortune*, December 30, 2020, https://fortune.com/company/facebook/fortune500/.

32. For example, A. O. Scott, "The Oscars Are a Mess. Let's Make Them Messier," *New York Times*, January 27, 2021, https://www.nytimes.com/2021/01/27/movies/oscars-2021-changes.html.

33. Robert B. Reich, *Saving Capitalism: For the Many, Not the Few* (New York: Knopf, 2015), 31.

34. Holt, *Empires of Entertainment*, 136.

35. Ibid., chap. 6.

36. Talia Lakritz, "14 Companies You Didn't Realize Disney Owns," *Insider*, January 28, 2020, https://www.insider.com/companies-disney-owns. See also "Disney Ends the Historic 20th Century Fox Brand," *BBC News*, August 12, 2020, https://www.bbc.com/news/business-53747270.

37. Michael Zhang, "Disney to Buy National Geographic in $52 Billion Deal for Fox," PetaPixel, December 15, 2017, https://petapixel.com/2017/12/15/disney-buy-national-geographic-part-52-billion-deal-fox/.

38. On evidence that polarized media leads to polarized points of view, see Jonathan S. Morris, "The Fox News Factor," *Harvard International Journal of Press/Politics* 10, no. 3 (July 2005): 56–79; Gregory J. Martin and Ali Yurukoglu, "Bias in Cable News: Persuasion and Polarization," *American Economic Review* 107, no. 9 (September 2017): 2565–99.

39. Edmund Lee and Amie Tsang, "Tribune Ends Deal With Sinclair, Dashing Plan for Conservative TV Behemoth," *New York Times*, August 9, 2018, https://www.nytimes.com /2018/08/09/business/dealbook/sinclair-tribune-media.html; Gregory J. Martin and Josh McCrain, "Yes, Sinclair Broadcast Group Does Cut Local News, Increase National News and Tilt Its Stations Rightward," *Washington Post*, April 10, 2018, https://www.washing tonpost.com/news/monkey-cage/wp/2018/04/10/yes-sinclair-broadcast-group-does-cut -local-news-increase-national-news-and-tilt-its-stations-rightward/; and Gregory J. Martin and Joshua McCrain, "Local News and National Politics," *American Political Science Review* 113, no. 2 (May 2019): 372–84.

40. "Sinclair Broadcast Group: The Largest and Most Diversified Television Broadcasting Company in the Country Today," Sinclair Broadcast Group, accessed April 22, 2021, https:// sbgi.net/. On Sinclair's right-wing orientation: Cecilia Kang, Eric Lipton, and Sydney Ember, "How a Conservative TV Giant Is Ridding Itself of Regulation," *New York Times*, August 14, 2017, https://www.nytimes.com/2017/08/14/us/politics/how-a-conservative-tv -giant-is-ridding-itself-of-regulation.html; Sydney Ember, "Sinclair Requires TV Stations to Air Segments That Tilt to the Right," *New York Times*, May 12, 2017, https://www.nytimes .com/2017/05/12/business/media/sinclair-broadcast-komo-conservative-media.html.

41. Lucia Graves, "This Is Sinclair, 'The Most Dangerous U.S. Company You've Never Heard Of,'" *Guardian*, August 17, 2017, http://www.theguardian.com/media/2017/aug/17/sinclair -news-media-fox-trump-white-house-circa-breitbart-news.

42. Ibid.

43. Ibid. For Copps's full critique, see "Fmr. FCC Head: Sinclair Most Dangerous Media in U.S.," *CNN*, accessed April 22, 2021, https://www.cnn.com/videos/cnnmoney/2018/04/03 /michael-copps-sinclair-broadcasting-dangerous-sot-ctn.cnn.

44. Alex Shephard, "The Problem with MSNBC Isn't That It's Too Liberal," *New Republic*, August 6, 2020, https://newrepublic.com/article/158824/problem-msnbc-isnt-its-liberal. Fox also has far more viewers than MSNBC: Amy Watson, "Top Cable News Networks U.S. 2020, by Number of Viewers," Statista, February 5, 2021, https://www.statista.com/statistics /373814/cable-news-network-viewership-usa/.

45. Anne Nelson, *Shadow Network: Media, Money, and the Secret Hub of the Radical Right* (New York: Bloomsbury, 2019), 46; and Adam Piore, "A Higher Frequency," *Mother Jones*, December 2005, https://www.motherjones.com/politics/2005/12/higher-frequency/.

46. Data from Radio Lineup, accessed August 8, 2020, https://www.radiolineup.com.

47. Gregory M. Prindle, "No Competition: How Radio Consolidation Has Diminished Diversity and Sacrificed Localism," *Fordham Intellectual Property, Media, and Entertainment Law Journal* 14, no. 1 (2003): 49; Andrew Chadwick, *The Hybrid Media System: Politics and Power* (Oxford: Oxford University Press, 2013); Robert Britt Horwitz, *The Irony of Regulatory Reform: The Deregulation of American Telecommunications* (Oxford: Oxford University Press, 1991); and McChesney, *Digital Disconnect*.

48. The 1996 act attempted to both regulate and deregulate content. It included the Communications Decency Act, which would have restricted obscene content like pornography, but it was struck down by the Supreme Court on First Amendment grounds. But it also included Section 230, which says internet service providers (ISPs) and other platforms are not responsible for the content their users publish. Sara L. Zeigler, "Communications

Decency Act of 1996," *First Amendment Encyclopedia*, accessed July 18, 2021, https://www
.mtsu.edu/first-amendment/article/1070/communications-decency-act-of-1996.

49. Julia Maues, "Banking Act of 1933 (Glass-Steagall)," Federal Reserve History, November 22,
2013, https://www.federalreservehihysoo9tory.org/essays/glass-steagall-act.

50. "Deposit Insurance Fund," FDIC, July 14, 2021, https://www.fdic.gov/resources/deposit
-insurance/deposit-insurance-fund/

51. "FDIC: When a Bank Fails: Facts for Depositors, Creditors, and Borrowers," Federal Deposit
Insurance Corporation, accessed April 22, 2021, https://www.fdic.gov/consumers/banking
/facts/.

52. Corinne Crawford, "The Repeal of The Glass-Steagall Act and the Current Financial Crisis,"
Journal of Business and Economics Research 9, no. 1 (January 2011): 127–33.

53. "We attribute repeal of these prohibitions to the increasingly persuasive evidence from
academic studies of the pre–Glass-Steagall era, the recent favorable experience in the United
States following partial deregulation of banking activities, the experience of banking systems
abroad with broader scopes for banking activities, and rapid technological change in telecommunications and data processing." James Barth, R. Dan Brumbaugh Jr., and James A. Wilcox,
"Policy Watch: The Repeal of Glass-Steagall and the Advent of Broad Banking," *Journal of
Economic Perspectives* 14, no. 2 (2000): 191–204.

54. Randall S. Kroszner and Raghuram G. Rajan, "Is the Glass-Steagall Act Justified? A Study of
the U.S. Experience with Universal Banking before 1933," *American Economic Review* 84,
no. 4 (September 1994): 810.

55. Lissa Lamkin Broome and Jerry W. Markham, "The Gramm-Leach-Bliley Act: An
Overview," February 17, 2012, https://web.archive.org/web/20120217055223/http://www
.symtrex.com/pdfdocs/glb_paper.pdf. Some of the studies include: George W. Edwards,
"The Myth of the Security Affiliate," *Journal of the American Statistical Association*, 37,
no. 218 (June 1942), 225–32; William D. Jackson, "Glass-Steagall Act: Commercial vs.
Investment Banking" Congressional Research Service, June 29, 1987; George G. Kaufman
and Larry R. Mote, "Glass-Steagall: Repeal by Regulatory and Judicial Reinterpretation,"
Banking Law Journal 107 (1990), 388; Kroszner and Rajan, "Is the Glass-Steagall Act
Justified?" 810–32; and Eugene Nelson White, "Before the Glass-Steagall Act: An Analysis of
the Investment Banking Activities of National Banks," *Explorations in Economic History* 23,
no. 1 (1986): 33–55.

56. Joseph Kahn, "Former Treasury Secretary Joins Leadership Triangle at Citigroup," *New York
Times*, October 27, 1999, https://www.nytimes.com/1999/10/27/business/former-treasury
-secretary-joins-leadership-triangle-at-citigroup.html

57. Ibid.

58. "Robert E. Rubin (1995–1999)," U.S. Department of the Treasury, accessed April 22, 2021,
https://home.treasury.gov/about/history/prior-secretaries/robert-e-rubin-1995-1999.

59. "House Session, Part 2," C-SPAN video, 4:03:54, November 4, 1999, Program ID 153391-1,
accessed July 18, 2021, https://www.c-span.org/video/?153356-101/house-session-part-2. Event
begins at 03:02:11.

60. Crawford, "The Repeal of the Glass- Steagall Act and the Current Financial Crisis."

61. Ibid.

62. Ibid.

63. Ibid.

64. Ibid.

65. Canova, "Legacy of the Clinton Bubble."

66. Patrick J. Maney, *Bill Clinton: New Gilded Age President* (Lawrence: University of Kansas
Press, 2016), 230–35.

67. Sebastian Mallaby, *The Man Who Knew: The Life and Times of Alan Greenspan* (New York: Penguin, 2016), 543, 663, 678.

68. The Enron saga is well told in Bethany McLean and Peter Elkind, *The Smartest Guys in the Room: The Amazing Rise and Scandalous Fall of Enron* (New York: Portfolio, 2003).

69. "Press Release: Chairman Cox Announces End of Consolidated Supervised Entities Program," U.S. Securities and Exchange Commission, September 26, 2008, https://www.sec.gov/news/press/2008/2008-230.htm.

70. Liz Capo McCormick and Daniel Kruger, "Bond Vigilantes Confront Obama as Housing Falters," *Bloomberg News*, May 29, 2009, https://web.archive.org/web/20110805042208/http://www.bloomberg.com/apps/news?pid=newsarchive&sid=a6eMpGVUDeeE&refer=home.

71. Tam Harbert, "Here's How Much the 2008 Bailouts Really Cost," MIT Sloan, February 21, 2019, https://mitsloan.mit.edu/ideas-made-to-matter/heres-how-much-2008-bailouts-really-cost. Much of this was repaid but at least one credible study concludes that "the main winners were the large, unsecured creditors of large financial institutions."

72. "The Great Recession Definition," Investopedia, accessed April 22, 2021, https://www.investopedia.com/terms/g/great-recession.asp.

73. Regis Barnichon, Christian Matthes, and Alexander Ziegenbein, "The Financial Crisis at 10: Will We Ever Recover?" Federal Reserve Bank of San Francisco, August 13, 2018, https://www.frbsf.org/economic-research/publications/economic-letter/2018/august/financial-crisis-at-10-years-will-we-ever-recover/. Other estimates are similar: see Sarah Childress, "How Much Did the Financial Crisis Cost?" *Frontline*, May 31, 2012, https://www.pbs.org/wgbh/frontline/article/how-much-did-the-financial-crisis-cost/. Earlier reports said less, closer to $12 trillion, but the full impacts weren't clear yet: Stacy Curtin, "2008 Financial Crisis Cost Americans $12.8 Trillion: Report," Yahoo Finance (2012), https://finance.yahoo.com/blogs/daily-ticker/2008-financial-crisis-cost-americans-12-8-trillion-145432501.html.

74. Mark Sumner blames the repeal of Glass-Steagall for price manipulations that led to the California energy crash and the downfall of Governor Gray Davis, and for bringing about the 2008 crash by creating "too-big-to-fail" megabanks: Mark Sumner, "John McCain: Crisis Enabler," *The Nation*, September 21, 2008, https://www.thenation.com/article/archive/john-mccain-crisis-enabler/. See also Erin Coghlan, Lisa McCorkell, and Sara Hinkley, "What Really Caused the Great Recession?" Institute for Research on Labor and Employment, September 19, 2018, https://irle.berkeley.edu/what-really-caused-the-great-recession/.

75. Joseph E. Stiglitz, "Capitalist Fools," *Vanity Fair*, January 2009, https://www.vanityfair.com/news/2009/01/stiglitz200901-2. For a discussion of other financial safeguards that were removed, see Canova, "Legacy of the Clinton Bubble."

76. Anat Admati and Martin Hellwig, *The Bankers' New Clothes: What's Wrong with Banking and What to Do about It*, rev. ed. (Princeton, NJ: Princeton University Press, 2014); Anat R. Admati, "We're All Still Hostages to the Big Banks," *New York Times*, August 25, 2013, https://www.nytimes.com/2013/08/26/opinion/were-all-still-hostages-to-the-big-banks.html. Admati has led a multiyear campaign to explain how "capital regulations" intended to rein in the strong incentives in banking to borrow too much can be improved, and to debunk the misleading narratives used by industry lobbyists and policymakers to defend the existing system and fight better regulations. See https://www.gsb.stanford.edu/faculty-research/excessive-leverage and https://gsb-faculty.stanford.edu/anat-r-admati/advocacy/.

77. Ronald Reagan, quoted in Robert Lindsey, "Reagan, Entering Presidency Race, Calls for North American 'Accord'; 'Mankind Looks to Us,' " *New York Times*, November 14, 1979, https://www.nytimes.com/1979/11/14/archives/reagan-entering-presidency-race-calls-for-north-american-accord.html.

78. For example: Ronald Reagan, "Remarks to the Annual Meeting of the National Association of Manufacturers," May 29, 1986, courtesy of the Ronald Reagan Presidential Library and Museum, https://www.reaganlibrary.gov/archives/speech/remarks-annual-meeting-national -association-manufacturers-0.

79. Reagan put tariffs on Japanese semiconductors, arguing that Japan was engaging in anticompetitive behavior. (This flew in the face of his free-market rhetoric, but was consistent with a long history of American protectionism that in the nineteenth century NAM had wanted, and some members of its community still did.) On Reagan's protectionism, see Tom Meinderts, "The Power of Section 301: The Reagan Tariffs in an Age of Economic Globalization," *Globalizations* 17, no. 4 (May 18, 2020): 746–58; and Ronald Reagan, "Remarks at a White House Meeting With Business and Trade Leaders," September 23, 1985, https://www.reagan library.gov/archives/speech/remarks-white-house-meeting-business-and-trade-leaders. On the history of protectionism in the United States, see Ha-Joon Chang, *Kicking Away the Ladder: Development Strategy in Historical Perspective* (London: Anthem Press, 2002); Ha-Joon Chang, *Bad Samaritans: The Myth of Free Trade and the Secret History of Capitalism*, repr. edition (New York: Bloomsbury, 2009); Ha-Joon Chang, *23 Things They Don't Tell You About Capitalism*, repr. ed. (New York: Bloomsbury, 2012).

80. Donald Trump also noticed this, and used it to defend his own protectionist policies: Louis Jacobson, "Donald Trump Cites Ronald Reagan as a Protectionist Hero. Was He?" *Politifact*, July 1, 2016, https://www.politifact.com/article/2016/jul/01/donald-trump-cites-ronald -reagan-protectionist-her/.

81. Some Canadians had advocated for this for a long time, believing that removing tariffs would increase Canada's real GDP, while others worried increasing economic ties to the United States would hurt Canadian sovereignty. One of us (Oreskes) recalls attending a party in Canada at the time, where Canadians harangued her about the threat of a flood into their country of "cheap, American junk."

82. Bethany Moreton, *To Serve God and Wal-Mart: The Making of Christian Free Enterprise* (Cambridge, MA: Harvard University Press, 2009), 255.

83. Moreton, *To Serve God and Wal-Mart*, 259.

84. For a strong critique of Clinton policies, see Canova, "Legacy of the Clinton Bubble."

85. "North American Free Trade Agreement (NAFTA)," Inc.com, accessed April 23, 2021, https://www.inc.com/encyclopedia/north-american-free-trade-agreement-nafta.html.

86. On dispute resolution under NAFTA see David A. Gantz, "Dispute Settlement Under the NAFTA and the WTO: Choice of Forum Opportunities and Risks for the NAFTA Parties," *American University of International Law Review* 14, no. 4 (1999): 1025–106.

87. William J. Clinton, "December 8, 1993: Remarks on the Signing of NAFTA," UVA Miller Center, accessed July 19, 2021, https://millercenter.org/the-presidency/presidential-speeches /december-8-1993-remarks-signing-nafta. Independent Ross Perot ran against both Bush and Clinton in 1992, on a platform that included opposition to NAFTA—the only presidential candidate to do so. Perot got 19 percent, easily the strongest third-party performance in decades before or after, arguably underscoring how NAFTA was an example of how close the two major parties were in the early 1990s. "The 1992 Campaign; Transcript of 2d TV Debate Between Bush, Clinton and Perot," *New York Times*, October 16, 1992, accessed July 19, 2021, https://www.nytimes.com/1992/10/16/us/the-1992-campaign-transcript-of-2d-tv-debate -between-bush-clinton-and-perot.html. Bethany Moreton notes that before Bill Clinton got elected, Hillary Clinton had served on the Wal-Mart board. Moreton, *To Serve God and Wal-Mart*, 254–55.

88. Lorenzo Caliendo and Fernando Parro, "Estimates of the Trade and Welfare Effects of NAFTA," *Review of Economic Studies* 82, no. 1 (January 2015): 1–44.

89. Michael Hiltzik, "NAFTA Doesn't Count for Much Economically, but It's Still a Huge Political Football. Here's Why," *Los Angeles Times*, January 30, 2017, https://www.latimes.com/business/hiltzik/la-fi-hiltzik-nafta-politics-20170130-story.html; and Dani Rodrik, "What Did NAFTA Really Do?" *Dani Rodrik's weblog* (blog), January 26, 2017, https://rodrik.typepad.com/dani_rodriks_weblog/2017/01/what-did-nafta-really-do.html.

90. Shushanik Hakobyan and John McLaren, "Looking for Local Labor-Market Effects of NAFTA," *Review of Economics and Statistics* 98, no. 4 (October 1, 2016): 728–41, on 729.

91. "U.S. Trade with Canada and Mexico," Bureau of Transportation Statistics, December 27, 2011, https://www.bts.gov/archive/publications/north_american_trade_and_travel_trends/trade_can_mex#10.

92. Hakobyan and McLaren, "Looking for Local Labor-Market Effects of NAFTA," 729.

93. Hakobyan and McLaren, "Looking for Local Labor-Market Effects of NAFTA," 740–41.

94. Amadeo, "The Problems with NAFTA." Her analysis draws on work of the Economic Policy Institute, Robert E. Scott, "The high price of 'free' trade: NAFTA's failure has cost the United States jobs across the nation," November 17, 2003, https://www.epi.org/publication/briefingpapers_bp147/. See also U.S. unemployment: U.S. Department of Commerce, *Historical Statistics of the United States, part 1: Colonial times to 1970*, Bicentennial Edition (U.S. GPO, Washington, D.C., 1976), 126, and, on inflation, Federal Reserve Bank of Minneapolis, "Consumer Price Index 1913," https://www.minneapolisfed.org/about-us/monetary-policy/inflation-calculator/consumer-price-index-1913-.

95. Robert Reich, "Former Labor Secretary Robert Reich Takes on the Trans-Pacific Partnership," *CWA News*, Spring 2015, https://cwa-union.org/news/article/former_labor_secretary_robert_reich_takes_on_the_trans-pacific_partnership.

96. Frank Ackerman, et al., "NAFTA 2.0: For People or Polluters? A Climate Denier's Trade Deal versus a Clean Energy Economy," Oakland: Sierra Club, Council of Canadians, and Greenpeace Mexico, April 2018, https://www.sierraclub.org/sites/www.sierraclub.org/files/uploads-wysiwig/NAFTA%20and%20Climate%20Report%202018.pdf; and Subcomandante Insurgente Marcos, and Rafael Guillén Vincente, *Ya Basta! Ten Years of the Zapatista Uprising*, ed. Ziga Vodovnik (Oakland, CA: AK Press, 2004).

In 2018, the United States, Canada, and Mexico replaced NAFTA with the USMCA, or United States–Mexico–Canada Agreement, which contains some increased labor and environmental standards, prohibition of tariffs for digital content, increased enforcement measures, and tweaks some minor trade policy. "United States–Mexico–Canada Trade Fact Sheet: Modernizing NAFTA into a 21st Century Trade Agreement," Office of the United States Trade Representative, accessed April 23, 2021, https://ustr.gov/trade-agreements/free-trade-agreements/united-states-mexico-canada-agreement/fact-sheets/modernizing. The American Enterprise Institute considers NAFTA a victory of globalization over protectionism. James Pethokoukis, "Trump's Newish NAFTA Deal Shows the Power of Globalization vs. Populist Politics," *AEIdeas* (blog), Oct 1, 2018, https://www.aei.org/economics/trumps-nafta-deal-shows-the-power-of-globalization-vs-populist-politics/.

97. Ross Perot in presidential debate in St. Louis, Missouri, Aired on NBC October 11, 1992, https://www.youtube.com/watch?v=VRr6onmDyu4

98. Deeksha Kokas, Gladys Lopez Acevedo, and Jakob Engel, "Distributional Impacts of Trade," video, *The Distributional Impacts of Trade: Empirical Innovations, Analytical Tools, and Policy Responses*, May 19, 2021, https://www.worldbank.org/en/topic/trade/publication/distributional-impacts-of-trade-empirical-innovations-analytical-tools-and-policy-responses.

99. E. J. Dionne Jr., "The Big Idea," *Brookings*, August 9, 1998, https://www.brookings.edu/opinions/the-big-idea/. Blair and Clinton's approach is sometimes also referred to the "Third Way," but the meaning of that term is far more obtuse than the Washington Consensus,

which at least has the virtue of authorship. For a scathing critique of the Blair-Clinton approach see John Gray, "The End of a Dream," *New Statesman*, December 10, 2009, https://www.newstatesman.com/long-reads/2009/12/past-decade-world-western. To wit: "It is not often that large-scale crises are due to intellectual error, but a single erroneous belief runs through all of the successive delusions of the past decade." The erroneous belief in Gray's analysis was, the Washington consensus.

100. John Williamson, "A Short History of the Washington Consensus," PIIE, September 24, 2004, https://www.piie.com/commentary/speeches-papers/short-history-washington-consensus.

101. Robin Broad and John Cavanagh, "The Death of the Washington Consensus?" *World Policy Journal* 16, no. 3 (Fall 1999): 79–80.

102. Ibid., 82. Broad and Cavanagh note that, the Washington Consensus was criticized from the right by the Heritage Foundation and the Cato Institute, who were unhappy with the IMF for giving monies to governments who used them to bail out investors, thus undermining market discipline.

103. Williamson, "A Short History," 13.

104. Ibid., 2fn1.

105. Ibid., 2.

106. Ibid., 5.

107. Mary Elise Sarotte, *1989: The Struggle to Create Post–Cold War Europe* (Princeton, NJ: Princeton University Press, 2011); and Mary Elise Sarotte, *The Collapse: The Accidental Opening of the Berlin Wall* (New York: Basic Books, 2014).

108. Williamson, "A Short History of the Washington Consensus," 8.

109. Ibid., 10.

110. Lawrence H. Summers, "The Great Liberator," *New York Times*, November 19, 2006, https://www.nytimes.com/2006/11/19/opinion/19summers.html.

111. Jonathan Haidt, quoted in James Hoggan with Grania Litwin, *I'm Right and You're an Idiot: The Toxic State of Public Discourse and How to Clean It Up*, 2nd ed. (Gabriola Island, BC, Canada: New Society Publishers, 2016), 39. Harvey Cox, *The Market as God* (Cambridge, MA: Harvard University Press, 2016), gives many more examples.

112. Naomi Klein, *The Shock Doctrine: The Rise of Disaster Capitalism* (New York: Picador, 2007), 334–50, quote on p. 343.

113. Milton Friedman, *Capitalism and Freedom* (Chicago: University of Chicago Press, 1982), xiv.

114. Klein, *Shock Doctrine*, 174. Klein notes that the idea didn't originate with Friedman but with the radical left.

115. Margaret Levi and David Olson. "The Battles in Seattle," *Politics and Society* 28, no. 3 (September 2000): 309–29.

116. Chang, *23 Things They Don't Tell You About Capitalism*, 63.

117. Ibid., 68; Chang, *Bad Samaritans*. From the other side, some scholars have argued that pref-erential trading agreements undermine free trade more broadly. Jagdish Bhagwati, *Termites in the Trading System: How Preferential Agreements Undermine Free Trade* (Oxford: Oxford University Press, 2008). Chang and Bhagwati agree that free-trade agreements are often bad for the developing world.

118. Williamson, "A Short History of the Washington Consensus," 10.

119. Ibid.

120. Edward A. Parson, *Protecting the Ozone Layer: Science and Strategy* (Oxford: Oxford University Press, 2003); Krystal L. Tribbett, "RECLAIMing Air, Redefining Democracy: A History of the Regional Clean Air Incentives Market, Environmental Justice, and Risk, 1960– Present" (PhD diss., University of California San Diego, 2014); Elizabeth M. Bailey, et al., *Markets for Clean Air: The U.S. Acid Rain Program*, illus. ed. (New York: Cambridge

University Press, 2000); and Rachel Emma Rothschild, *Poisonous Skies: Acid Rain and the Globalization of Pollution* (Chicago: University of Chicago Press, 2019).

121. Nicholas Stern, *The Economics of Climate Change: The Stern Review* (Cambridge: Cambridge University Press, 2006).

122. On Pigou, see Nahid Aslanbeigui and Guy Oakeschap, "Chapter 49: Arthur Cecil Pigou," in *The Elgar Companion to John Maynard Keynes*, ed. Robert W. Dimand and Harald Hagemann (Cheltenham, UK; Northampton, MA: Edward Elgar, 2019), 309–16, https://doi.org/10 .4337/9781788118569.00060.

123. The Chicago school had criticized Pigou. In 1960, Chicago economist Ronald Coase had written what would become a widely cited paper insisting that just because pollution occurred, it did not necessarily follow that a Pigouvian tax should be imposed. True, but it did not necessarily follow that it should not, either. For the contemporary opposition, see Davis S. Hilzenrath, "Miscalculation, Lobby Effort Doomed BTU Tax Plan," *Washington Post*, June 11, 1993, https://www.washingtonpost.com/archive/business/1993/06/11/miscalculations-lobby-effort -doomed-btu-tax-plan/d756dac3-b2d0-46a4-8693-79f6f8f881d2/.

124. David Levy and Sandra Rothenberg, *Corporate Strategy and Climate Change: Heterogeneity and Change in the Global Automobile Industry*, E-99-13, Belfer Center for Science and International Affairs (November 1999), https://citeseerx.ist.psu.edu/viewdoc/summary? doi=10.1.1.25.6082. The GCC was first established as a committee of NAM, and then reorganized as an independent 501(C)(6) tax-exempt entity in 1991. See www.climatefiles.com/deni- al-groups/global-climate-coalition-collection/1991-interested-parties-information/. See also Robert J. Brulle, "Advocating Inaction: A Historical Analysis of the Global Climate Coalition," *Environmental Politics* 11 (April 11, 2022), https://doi.org/10.1080/09644016.2022.2058815.

125. "Al Gore's Favorite Tax," *Wall Street Journal*, March 14, 2000, http://www.wsj.com/articles /SB952995423722707163.

126. Charles Wolf Jr., "A Theory of Nonmarket Failure: Framework for Implementation Analysis," *Journal of Law and Economics* 22, no. 1 (April 1979): 138.

127. Naomi Oreskes, "The Scientific Consensus on Climate Change," *Science* 306, no. 5702 (December 3, 2004): 1686.

128. Naomi Oreskes and Erik M. Conway, *Merchants of Doubt: How a Handful of Scientists Obscured the Truth on Issues from Tobacco Smoke to Global Warming*, pbk. ed. (New York: Bloomsbury, 2011), 194–95.

129. "IPCC, 2007: Summary for Policymakers," in *Climate Change 2007: The Physical Science Basis. Contribution of Working Group I to the Fourth Assessment Report of the Intergovernmental Panel on Climate Change*, ed. S. Solomon et al. (Cambridge and New York: Cambridge University Press, 2007).

130. Stern, *The Economics of Climate Change*.

131. Chris Mooney, "Ted Cruz Keeps Saying That Satellites Don't Show Global Warming. Here's the Problem," *Washington Post*, January 29, 2016, https://www.washingtonpost.com /news/energy-environment/wp/2016/01/29/ted-cruz-keeps-saying-that-satellites-dont -show-warming-heres-the-problem/; and Kevin Cowtan and Stephan Lewandowsky, "Global Warming 'Hiatus' Is the Climate Change Myth That Refuses to Die," *DeSmog*, March 9, 2019, https://www.desmog.com/2019/03/09/global-warming-hiatus-climate-change-myth-refuses -die/; Stephan Lewandowsky, James S. Risbey, and Naomi Oreskes, "The 'Pause' in Global Warming: Turning a Routine Fluctuation into a Problem for Science," *Bulletin of the American Meteorological Society* 97, no. 5 (2016), 723–33; and Stephan Lewandowsky, James S. Risbey, and Naomi Oreskes, "On the definition and identifiability of the alleged 'hiatus' in global warming," *Scientific Reports* 5, article no. 16784 (2015), https://doi.org/10 .1038/srep16784.

132. Elspeth Reeve, "Mitt Romney Is a Lonely Global Warming Believer in the GOP Field," *Atlantic*, June 3, 2011, https://www.theatlantic.com/politics/archive/2011/06/mitt-romney -believes-humans-cause-global-warming/351428/

133. Jay Yarrow, "Inventor of Cap and Trade Says a Carbon Tax Is Better," *Business Insider*, August 13, 2009, https://www.businessinsider.com/inventor-of-cap-and-trade-says-a-carbon -tax-is-better-2009-8.

134. "U.S. Senate Roll Call Votes 109th Congress—1st Session," United States Senate, accessed April 24, 2021, https://www.senate.gov/legislative/LIS/roll_call_lists/roll_call_vote_cfm .cfm?congress=109&session=1&vote=00148.

135. Marianne Lavelle, "John McCain's Climate Change Legacy," *Inside Climate News*, August 26, 2018, https://insideclimatenews.org/news/26082018/john-mccain-climate-change-leadership -senate-cap-trade-bipartisan-lieberman-republican-campaign/.

136. Daniel J. Weiss, "Anatomy of a Senate Climate Bill Death," Center for American Progress, October 12, 2010, https://www.americanprogress.org/issues/green/news/2010/10/12/8569 /anatomy-of-a-senate-climate-bill-death/.

137. Ibid.

138. Robert J. Brulle, "Institutionalizing Delay: Foundation Funding and the Creation of U.S. Climate Change Counter-Movement Organizations," *Climatic Change* 122, no. 4 (February 2014): 681–94.

139. On the role of government in making capitalism work, see Reich, *Saving Capitalism*.

CHAPTER 15: THE HIGH COST OF THE "FREE" MARKET

1. Naomi Oreskes, "We Need Big Government to Save Us from the Pandemic," *Time*, April 17, 2020, https://time.com/5823063/we-need-big-government-pandemic/.

2. Institute of Medicine, *The Future of Public Health* (Washington, D.C.: National Academies Press, 1988).

3. Jennifer B. Nuzzo, Lucia Mullen, Michael Snyder, Anita Cicero, and Thomas V. Inglesby, *Preparedness for a High-Impact Respiratory Pathogen Pandemic* (Baltimore: Johns Hopkins Center for Health Security, 2019), "surge manufacturing" on p. 7.

4. Yuki Noguchi, "Not Enough Face Masks Are Made In America To Deal With The Coronavirus," *NPR*, March 5, 2020, https://www.npr.org/sections/health-shots/2020/03/05 /811387424/face-masks-not-enough-are-made-in-america-to-deal-with-coronavirus.

5. Nicholas Kulish, Sarah Kliff, and Jessica Silver-Greenberg, "The U.S. Tried to Build a New Fleet of Ventilators. The Mission Failed," *New York Times*, March 29, 2020, https://www .nytimes.com/2020/03/29/business/coronavirus-us-ventilator-shortage.html.

6. On the invention of "The Economy" as a Ding an sich, see Timothy Mitchell, *Carbon Democracy: Political Power in the Age of Oil* (London: Verso, 2013).

7. Steffie Woolhandler et al., "Public Policy and Health in the Trump Era," *Lancet*, February 21, 2021, The Lancet Commissions, 39 (10275): 705–53. https://www.thelancet.com/journals /lancet/article/PIIS0140-6736(20)32545-9/fulltext.

8. Damien Cave, "How Australia Saved Thousands of Lives while Covid Killed a Million Americans," *New York Times*, May 15, 2022. https://www.nytimes.com/2022/05/15/world /australia/covid-deaths.html.

9. Ibid.

10. Ann W. Latner, JD, "Hospitalized Covid-19 Patient Demands Therapy with Ivermectin," *Clinical Advisor*, December 15, 2021, https://www.clinicaladvisor.com/home/my-practice /legal-advisor/covid-patients-demands-ivermectin-therapy/.

11. Paulina Villegas, "South Dakota Says Many Patients Deny the Coronavirus Exists—Right Up Until Death," *Washington Post*, November 16, 2020, https://www.washingtonpost.com /health/2020/11/16/south-dakota-nurse-coronavirus-deniers/.

12. David M. Cutler and Lawrence H. Summers, "The Covid-19 Pandemic and the $16 Trillion Virus," *JAMA* 324, no. 15 (October 12, 2020): 1495–96, https://jamanetwork.com/journals /jama/fullarticle/2771764. $7.6 trillion of the total was the Congressional Budget Office's estimated cost of lost economic output over the next decade; $4.4 trillion was the economic cost of premature deaths, with a value of $7 million per life.

13. "Overdose Death Rates," National Institute on Drug Abuse, January 29, 2021, https://www .drugabuse.gov/drug-topics/trends-statistics/overdose-death-rates.

14. "Opioid Overdose," Centers for Disease Control and Prevention, March 10, 2021, https://www.cdc.gov/drugoverdose/data/analysis.html.

15. David A. Brent, Kwan Hur, and Robert D. Gibbons, "Association Between Parental Medical Claims for Opioid Prescriptions and Risk of Suicide Attempt by Their Children," *JAMA Psychiatry* 76, no. 9 (May 22, 2019): 941–47.

16. "Opioid Overdose Crisis," National Institute on Drug Abuse, March 11, 2021, https://www .drugabuse.gov/drug-topics/opioids/opioid-overdose-crisis.

17. Jan van Amsterdam, Mimi Pierce, and Wim van den Brink, "Is Europe Facing an Emerging Opioid Crisis Comparable to the U.S.?" *Therapeutic Drug Monitoring* 43, no. 1 (February 2021): 42–51, https://journals.lww.com/drug-monitoring/Abstract/2021/02000/Is_Europe_Facing _an_Emerging_Opioid_Crisis.6.aspx; and "Lessons from Abroad: How Europeans have Tackled Opioid Addiction and What the U.S. Could Learn from Them," *North Carolina Health News*, accessed July 20, 2021, https://www.northcarolinahealthnews.org/lessons-from -abroad-how-europeans-have-tackled-opioid-addiction-and-what-the-u-s-could-learn-from -them/.

18. "National Center for Health Statistics," Centers for Disease Control and Prevention, April 9, 2021, https://www.cdc.gov/nchs/fastats/injury.htm.

19. Louis Jacobson, "More Americans Killed by Guns Since 1968 than in All U.S. Wars, Columnist Nicholas Kristof Writes," *Politifact*, August 27, 2015, http://www.politifact.com /punditfact/statements/2015/aug/27/nicholas-kristof/more-americans-killed-guns-1968-all -wars-says-colu/.

20. Brooklyn Neustaeter, "More than Half of Ontario Gun Deaths are from Self-Harm, Majority in Older Men in Rural Areas, Study Finds," *CTV News*, October 19, 2020, https://www .ctvnews.ca/canada/more-than-half-of-ont-gun-deaths-are-from-self-harm-majority-in -older-men-in-rural-areas-study-finds-1.5150002.

21. "United States—Gun Fact, Figures, and Law," GunPolicy.org, accessed April 2, 2020, https://www.gunpolicy.org/firearms/region/united-states; and "France—Gun Facts, Figures and the Law," GunPolicy.org, accessed April 28, 2020, https://www.gunpolicy.org/firearms /region/france.

22. David Meyer, "Obesity in America Keeps Getting Worse, Says New CDC Report," *Fortune*, October 13, 2017, https://fortune.com/2017/10/13/obesity-in-america/; Sara Police, "How Much Have Obesity Rates Risen Since 1950?" livestrong.com, accessed July 24, 2021, https://www.livestrong.com/article/384722-how-much-have-obesity-rates-risen-since -1950/.

23. "Endocrine Disruptors Cost U.S. More than $340 Billion in Health and Other Costs," AACC, November 17, 2016, https://www.aacc.org/cln/cln-stat/2016/november/17/endocrine -disruptors-cost-us-more-than-340-billion-in-health-and-other-costs. A study of the costs to the EU places them at €157 billion. Linda G. Kahn et al., "Endocrine-Disrupting Chemicals: Implications for Human Health," *Lancet Diabetes and Endocrinology* 8, no. 8 (August 2020): 703–18, https://doi.org/10.1016/S2213-8587(20)30129-7. See also "Disease Burden and Costs Due to Endocrine-Disrupting Chemicals," NYU Langone Health, accessed July 21, 2021, https://med.nyu.edu/departments-institutes/pediatrics/divisions/environmental-pediatrics /research/policy-initiatives/disease-burden-costs-endocrine-disrupting-chemicals;

Teresa M. Attina et al., "Exposure to Endocrine-Disrupting Chemicals in the USA: A Population-Based Disease Burden and Cost Analysis," *Lancet Diabetes and Endocrinology* 4, no. 12 (December 2016): 996–1003; Christopher D. Kassotis, et al., "Endocrine-Disrupting Chemicals: Economic, Regulatory, and Policy Implications," *Lancet Diabetes and Endocrinology* 8, no. 8 (August 2020): 719–30.

24. Sachin Waikar, "What Can We Learn from the Downfall of Theranos?" *Insights by Stanford Business*, December 17, 2018, https://www.gsb.stanford.edu/insights/what-can-we-learn-downfall-theranos.

25. Michael Sheetz, "Secretary DeVos, Walmart heirs and other investors reportedly lost over $600 million on Theranos," CNBC, May 4, 2018, https://www.cnbc.com/2018/05/04/theranos-devos-other-investors-reportedly-lost-over-600-million.html; and Miles Cohen, "Theranos founder Elizabeth Holmes convicted on 4 counts of fraud," ABC News, January 3, 2022, https://abcnews.go.com/US/elizabeth-holmes-trial-jury-unable-unanimous-verdict-counts/story?id=82055043.

26. Hugo Martin, "Three-Quarters of Employees Surveyed at Disney's Anaheim Resort Say They Can't Afford Basic Living Expenses," *Los Angeles Times*, February 28, 2018, https://www.latimes.com/business/la-fi-disneyland-study-20180228-story.html.

27. Erin Botsford, *The Big Retirement Risk: Running Out of Money Before You Run Out of Time* (Austin, TX: Greenleaf Book Group Press, 2012); Ben Steverman, "Working Past 70: Americans Can't Seem to Retire," *Bloomberg*, July 10 2017, https://www.bloomberg.com/news/articles/2017-07-10/working-past-70-americans-can-t-seem-to-retire; and Jim Probasco, "The Rise of the Semi-Retired Life," *Investopedia*, January 3, 2021, https://www.investopedia.com/articles/retirement/080316/5-reasons-why-more-retirees-are-going-back-work.asp#ixzz59lmc60J4.

28. Spencer Woodman, "On the Road with the 'Workampers,' Amazon's Retirement-Age Mobile Workforce," *Vice*, January 12, 2015, https://www.vice.com/en/article/mv5dn8/in-the-prime-of-their-lives-0000544-v2n1.

29. Robert B. Reich, *Saving Capitalism: For the Many, Not the Few* (New York: Alfred A. Knopf, 2015).

30. Tony Judt, *Ill Fares the Land* (New York: Penguin, 2010), 18–20. See also Aaron O'Neill, "Life Expectancy in the United States, 1860–2020," *Statista*, February 3, 2021, https://www.statista.com/statistics/1040079/life-expectancy-united-states-all-time/. O'Neill writes: "Despite this overall increase, the life expectancy dropped three times since 1860; from 1865 to 1870 during the American Civil War, from 1915 to 1920 during the First World War and following Spanish Flu epidemic, and it has dropped again between 2015 and now. The reason for the most recent drop in life expectancy before 2020 was not a result of any specific event, but has been attributed to negative societal trends, such as unbalanced diets and sedentary lifestyles, high medical costs, and increasing rates of suicide and drug use." Life expectancy has now decreased further because of Covid-19. Allison Bell, "Covid-19 Reduces U.S. Life Expectancy," Treasury and Risk, July 22, 2021, https://www.treasuryandrisk.com/2021/07/22/covid-19-slashes-u-s-life-expectancy-at-age-65-411-25374/?slreturn=20210625114811.

31. Kate Pickett and Richard Wilkinson, *The Spirit Level: Why More Equal Societies Almost Always Do Better* (London: Allen Lane, 2009). Binyamin Appelbaum also focuses on the fall in life expectancy as evidence, as he puts it, that the "market revolution went too far." *The Economists' Hour: False Prophets, Free Markets, and the Fracture of Society* (New York: Little Brown, 2019), 6–8.

32. Hedrick Smith, *Who Stole the American Dream?* (New York: Random House, 2012).

33. Reich, *Saving Capitalism*; Thomas Piketty and Emmanuel Saez, "How Progressive Is the U.S. Federal Tax System? A Historical and International Perspective," *Journal of Economic*

Perspectives, American Economic Association 21, no. 1 (2007): 3–24; Facundo Alvaredo, et al., "The Top 1 Percent in International and Historical Perspective," *Journal of Economic Perspectives*, American Economic Association 27, no. 3 (2013), 3–20. Thomas Piketty, Emmanuel Saez, and Gabriel Zucman, "Distributional National Accounts: Methods and Estimates for the United States," *NBER* Working Paper, December 2016, http://piketty.pse .ens.fr/files/PSZ2016.pdf.

34. "Federal Income Tax Brackets (Tax Year 1955)," Tax-Brackets.org, accessed July 22, 2021, https://www.tax-brackets.org/federaltaxtable/1956. It could also be solved with a minimum basic income, which some libertarians from Milton Friedman to Andrew Yang have endorsed, but that idea has never gained real traction with conservatives or the business community.

35. Ellen Chang and Kemberley Washington, "2021–2022 Tax Brackets and Federal Income Tax Rates," *Forbes*, updated March 15, 2022, https://www.forbes.com/advisor/taxes/taxes-federal -income-tax-bracket/.

36. Chris Isidore, "Buffet Says He's Still Paying Lower Tax Rate than His Secretary," *CNN*, March 4, 2013, https://money.cnn.com/2013/03/04/news/economy/buffett-secretary-taxes /index.html. On corporations that don't pay tax, see "60 Fortune 500 Companies Avoided All Federal Income Tax in 2018 Under New Tax Law," Institute on Taxation and Economic Policy, April 11, 2019, https://itep.org/60-fortune-500-companies-avoided-all-federal-income -tax-in-2018-under-new-tax-law/.

37. "BRIA 11 3 b The Income Tax Amendment: Most Thought It Was a Great Idea in 1913," Constitutional Rights Foundation, accessed July 22, 2021, https://www.crf-usa.org/bill-of -rights-in-action/bria-11-3-b-the-income-tax-amendment-most-thought-it-was-a-great-idea -in-1913.html.

38. "The Republican and Democratic Platforms," folder Conventions: Platform of American Industry, 1924, box 137, series I, National Association of Manufacturers Records, accession 1411, Hagley Museum and Library, Wilmington, DE 19807.

39. Rahul M, "People in these countries pay the highest taxes," Yahoo Finance, January 21, 2021, https://in.finance.yahoo.com/photos/countries-that-pay-the-highest-taxes-in-the-world -093827810/. On the history of taxation in Sweden, see Magnus Henrekson and Mikael Stenkula, *Swedish Taxation Since 1862: An Overview*, IFN Working Paper No. 1052 (Research Institute of Industrial Economics, September 2015), https://www.ifn.se/wfiles/wp/wp1052 .pdf.

40. World Health Organization, "Tobacco," July 26, 2021, https://www.who.int/news-room /fact-sheets/detail/tobacco. See also Robert N. Proctor, *Golden Holocaust: Origins of the Cigarette Catastrophe and the Case for Abolition* (Los Angeles: University of California Press, 2012.)

41. Richard Fuller et al., "Pollution and Health: A Progress Update," *The Lancet Planetary Health* 6, no. 6: E535–E547 (2022), https://www.thelancet.com/journals/lanplh/article/PIIS2542 -5196(22)00090-0/fulltext.

42. Kim Stanley Robinson, *Fifty Degrees Below* (New York: Bantam, 2005), 368. The full quotation is: "However, since he had been elected with the help of big oil and everything transnationally corporate, and had done more than any previous presidents to strip-mine the nation and use it as a dumping ground, he did not appear to be as convincing as Phil. It was getting hard to believe his assertions that the invisible hand of the market would solve everything, because, as Phil put it, the invisible hand never picked up the check."

43. Ryan Nunn et al., "Ten Facts About the Economics of Climate Change and Climate Policy," *Brookings*, October 23, 2019, https://www.brookings.edu/research/ten-facts-about-the -economics-of-climate-change-and-climate-policy/; and Frank Ackerman and Elizabeth A. Stanton, *The Cost of Climate Change: What We'll Pay If Global Warming Continues Unchecked*

(New York: National Resource Defense Council, 2008), https://www.nrdc.org/sites/default /files/cost.pdf. See also Matthew E. Kahn, et al., "Long-Term Macroeconomic Effects of Climate Change: A Cross-Country Analysis," IMF Working Paper, International Monetary Fund, October 11, 2019, https://www.imf.org/en/Publications/WP/Issues/2019/10/11/Long -Term-Macroeconomic-Effects-of-Climate-Change-A-Cross-Country-Analysis-48691. From the abstract: "[A] persistent increase in average global temperature by 0.04°C per year, in the absence of mitigation policies, reduces world real GDP per capita by more than 7 percent by 2100."

44. William D. Nordhaus, *The Climate Casino: Risk, Uncertainty, and Economics for a Warming World* (New Haven, CT: Yale University Press, 2013); Nicholas Stern, *The Economics of Climate Change: The Stern Review* (Cambridge: Cambridge University Press, 2006); Nicholas Stern, *A Blueprint for a Safer Planet: How to Manage Climate Change and Create a New Era of Progress and Prosperity* (London: Bodley Head, 2009); and Nicholas Stern, *Why Are We Waiting? The Logic, Urgency, and Promise of Tackling Climate Change*, Lionel Robbins Lectures (Cambridge, MA: MIT Press, 2015).

45. Max Borders, "Climate Change: What if They're Right?" *Foundation for Economic Education*, January 1, 2007, https://fee.org/articles/climate-change-what-if-theyre-right/.

46. Swaminathan S. Anklesaria Aiyar, "Adapting to Climate Change is Less Costly Than Spending Trillions on Emission Targets," Cato Institute, November 7, 2012, https://www .cato.org/commentary/adapting-climate-change-less-costly-spending-trillions-emission -targets.

47. Elizabeth Gehrman, "Holdren talks back to skeptics of global warming," *Harvard Gazette*, November 8, 2007, https://news.harvard.edu/gazette/story/2007/11/holdren-talks-back-to -skeptics-of-global-warming/. Recently, a similar point has been made about Covid-19, that "herd immunity" is a euphemism for uncontrolled morbidity and mortality—in other words, suffering. John M. Barry, "What Fans of 'Herd Immunity' Don't Tell You," *The New York Times*, October 19, 2020, https://www.nytimes.com/2020/10/19/opinion/coronavirus-herd -immunity.html.

48. "IMF Survey: Counting the Cost of Energy Subsidies," International Monetary Fund, July 17, 2015, https://www.imf.org/en/News/Articles/2015/09/28/04/53/sonew070215a.

49. According to the UNFCCC webpage, 191 parties out of 197 parties to the United Nations Framework Convention on Climate Change are parties to the Paris Agreement. United Nations Climate Change, "Paris Agreement—Status of Ratification," accessed August 2, 2021, https://cop23.unfccc.int/process/the-paris-agreement/status-of-ratification.

50. Mariana Mazzucato, *The Entrepreneurial State: Debunking Public vs. Private Sector Myths*, rev. ed. (London: Anthem Press, 2015).

51. Janet Abbate, *Inventing the Internet* (Cambridge, MA: MIT Press, 1999).

52. Jonathan T. Taplin, *Move Fast and Break Things: How Facebook, Google, and Amazon Cornered Culture and Undermined Democracy* (New York: Little, Brown, 2017); and Max Chafkin, *The Contrarian: Peter Thiel and Silicon Valley's Pursuit of Power* (New York: Penguin, 2021).

53. Derek Bok, *The Politics of Happiness: What Government Can Learn from the New Research on Well-Being* (Princeton, NJ: Princeton University Press, 2010).

54. Frank Martela et al., "The Nordic Exceptionalism: What Explains Why the Nordic Countries Are Constantly Among the Happiest in the World?" in *World Happiness Report 2020*, ed. John F. Helliwell et al. (New York: Sustainable Development Solutions Network, 2020), 128-46, https://worldhappiness.report/ed/2020/the-nordic-exceptionalism-what-explains- why-the-nordic-countries-are-constantly-among-the-happiest-in-the-world/. See also Ben Schiller, "America, Desperate for Happiness, Is Getting Less and Less Happy," *Fast Company*,

March 16, 2018, https://www.fastcompany.com/40544341/america-desperate-for-happiness
-is-getting-less-and-less-happy; and "Self-Reported Life Satisfaction, 2018," Our World in
Data, accessed April 28, 2021, https://ourworldindata.org/grapher/happiness-cantril-ladder.
Americans are also less happy than Australians, New Zealanders, and Israelis. (This despite
the fact that Israelis live with a high degree of anxiety about their day-to-day physical safety.)
Jean M. Twenge, "The Sad State of Happiness in the United States and the Role of Digital
Media," in *World Happiness Report 2019*, ed. J. Helliwell, R. Layard, and J. Sachs (New York:
Sustainable Development Solutions Network, 2019), 86–96, https://worldhappiness.report/
ed/2019/the-sad-state-of-happiness-in-the-united-states-and-the-role-of-digital-media/.

55. Laura Begley Bloom, "The 20 Happiest Countries in the World in 2021 (Guess Where the
U.S. Is Ranked?)," *Forbes*, March 19, 2021, https://www.forbes.com/sites/laurabegleybloom
/2021/03/19/the-20-happiest-countries-in-the-world-in-2021/?sh=308a85c970a0.

56. The Nordic countries have higher levels of diversity than often imagined, but what they do
not have is "an underclass of slaves or cheap labor imported from colonies." And this, the
report concludes, is important in sustaining trust between ethnic groups. Martela et al., "The
Nordic Exceptionalism." See also: Jenny Gross and Johanna Lemola, "What Makes a Happy
Country?" *New York Times*, April 20, 2021, https://www.nytimes.com/2021/04/20/world
/europe/world-happiness-report-ranking.html.

57. Martela et al., "The Nordic Exceptionalism."

58. Bok, *Politics of Happiness*, 17.

59. Ibid., 166.

60. Ibid., 186.

61. Judt, *Ill Fares*, 5.

62. Steven H. Woolf and Heidi Schoomaker, "Life Expectancy and Mortality Rates in the
United States, 1959-2017," *JAMA* 322, no. 20 (2019): 1996–2016.

63. Uptin Saiidi, "U.S. Life Expectancy Has Been Declining. Here's Why," *CNBC*, July 9, 2019,
https://www.cnbc.com/2019/07/09/us-life-expectancy-has-been-declining-heres-why
.html.

64. Woolhandler et al., "Public Policy and Health in the Trump Era." Woolf and Schoomaker,
"Life Expectancy." On life expectancy in the United States vs. Europe: Carina Storrs and
Special to CNN, "Why Americans Don't Live as Long as Europeans," *CNN*, February 9,
2016, https://www.cnn.com/2016/02/09/health/american-life-expectancy-shorter-than
-europeans/index.html. Drawing on the research of Anne Case and Angus Deaton, Atul
Gawande has advanced the idea of an epidemic of despair in "Why Americans Are Dying
from Despair," *New Yorker*, March 16, 2020, https://www.newyorker.com/magazine/2020
/03/23/why-americans-are-dying-from-despair. Life expectancy continued to drop in 2021,
but a good deal of this weas driven by Covid-19 https://www.washingtonpost.com/health
/2022/04/07/life-expectancy-covid/. The framers of the concept of "Deaths of Despair"
explicitly link them to capitalism as practiced in the United States: Anne Case and Angus
Deaton, *Deaths of Despair and the Future of Capitalism* (Princeton: Princeton University
Press, 2020).

65. For a thought-provoking discussion of the relationship between neoliberalism and authoritarianism, or what he calls Authoritarian Liberalism, see Grégoire Chamayou, *The
Ungovernable Society* (Cambridge: Polity Press, 2021).

66. On wealthy corporations who fought "government" while profiting from government
contracts, see Jane Mayer, *Dark Money: The Hidden History of the Billionaires Behind the Rise
of the Radical Right* (New York: Anchor, 2016). On GE rigging electricity markets, see Frank
Browning and John Gerassi, *American Way of Crime: From Salem to Watergate, a Stunning
New Perspective on American History* (New York: Putnam, 1980).

67. John Sherman, the original sponsor of the Sherman Anti-Trust Act, explained in 1890 that the government had made a mistake in allowing the concentration of so much power in so few hands. U.S. Congressional Record, S. 2460, 51st Congress, 1st session, Vol. 21, Part 12, March 21, 1890. See also Ufuk Akcigit and Sina T. Ates, "Ten Facts on Declining Business Dynamism and Lessons from Endogenous Growth Theory," *National Bureau of Economic Research*, Working Paper 25755, (April 2019): 43. See chapter 14.

68. José Medina, "Active Ignorance, Epistemic Others, and Epistemic Friction," in *The Epistemology of Resistance: Gender and Racial Oppression, Epistemic Injustice, and the Social Imagination*, ed. José Medina (Oxford: Oxford University Press, 2013), 2. See also José Medina, "The Relevance of Credibility Excess in a Proportional View of Epistemic Injustice: Differential Epistemic Authority and the Social Imaginary," *Social Epistemology* 25, no. 1 (2011): 15–35.

69. Medina, "Active Ignorance," 5.

70. Ibid. A similar argument is made by sociologist Woody Doane, who notes the tendency of privileged classes to support "an interpretative framework in which whites' explanations for inequality focus upon the cultural characteristics (e.g., motivation, values) of subordinate groups . . . Politically, this blaming of subordinate groups for their lower economic position serves to neutralize demands for anti-discrimination initiatives or for a redistribution of resources." Quoted in Charles W. Mills, "White Ignorance," in *Agnotology: The Making and Unmaking of Ignorance*, ed. Robert N. Proctor and Londa Schiebinger (Stanford: Stanford University Press: 2008), 240.

71. Holman W. Jenkins Jr., "How a Physicist Became a Climate Truth Teller," *Wall Street Journal*, April 16, 2021, https://www.wsj.com/articles/how-a-physicist-became-a-climate-truth -teller-11618597216.

72. Mills, "White Ignorance," 245.

73. Medina, "Active Ignorance," 6.

74. Jenkins, "How a Physicist Became a Climate Truth Teller."

75. Nancy MacLean, *Democracy in Chains: The Deep History of the Radical Right's Stealth Plan for America* (New York: Viking, 2017); and Jane Mayer, *Dark Money*.

76. MacLean, *Democracy in Chains*; Nancy MacLean, "Since we are Greatly Outnumbered," in *The Disinformation Age: Politics, Technology, and Disruptive Communication in the United States*, ed. W. Lance Bennett and Steven Livingston (Cambridge: Cambridge University Press, 2020), 120–49; see also Bennett and Livingston's discussion of MacLean in *The Disinformation Age*, 19.

77. Humberto Sanchez, "Thom Tillis: Keep Government out of the Bathroom," Roll Call, February 3, 2015, https://www.rollcall.com/2015/02/03/thom-tillis-keep-government-out-of -the-bathroom/

78. Immanual Wallerstein, *Utopistics: Or Historical Choices of the Twenty- First Century* (New York: New Press, 1998), 5–6.

79. *The National Desk* (blog), "'Rick Perry Is an Idiot': The Politics of Name-Calling," *Los Angeles Times*, August 19, 2011, https://latimesblogs.latimes.com/nationnow/2011/08/rick -perry-is-an-idiot-the-politics-of-namecalling-.html; Bruce Bartlett, "Why Hayek Isn't Paul Ryan's Guru," *Economix* (blog), *New York Times,* August 28, 2012, https://economix.blogs .nytimes.com/2012/08/28/why-hayek-isnt-paul-ryans-guru/.

80. Bruce Bartlett, "Why Hayek Isn't Paul Ryan's Guru."

81. Kimberly Kutz Elliott, "African Americans in the Early Republic," Khan Academy, accessed July 22, 2021, https://www.khanacademy.org/humanities/us-history/the-early-republic /culture-and-reform/a/african-americans-in-the-early-republic.

82. Editorial Board, "The Task Ahead for Biden on Climate," *New York Times*, February 6, 2021, 2021, https://www.nytimes.com/2021/02/06/opinion/biden-climate-change-environment.html.

83. Reich, *Saving Capitalism*, slightly paraphrased from 9.

84. In fairness, many economists recognize that markets are often not efficient. Still, the dominant disciplinary discourse is that they are. As Appelbaum has stressed, economists express their faith in markets in the theory of "efficient markets." See *Economists' Hour*, 288–89. (For a discussion of some complexities and counter-examples, see Sebastian Mallaby, "How Economists' Faith in Markets Broke America," *Atlantic*, September 2019, https://www.theatlantic.com/magazine/archive/2019/09/nicolas-lemann-binyamin-appelbaum-economics/594718/.) In some ways it is worse than Appelbaum allows, because so many mainstream economists in the second half of the twentieth century worked not merely from an assumption of efficient markets, but from an assumption of *perfectly functioning* markets. As Tony Atkinson said of the textbook that he and Stiglitz published in 1980, "it locked in a lot of assumptions about perfectly functioning markets that should've been at the root of many discussions of policy itself." Were they to rewrite the textbook, he and Stiglitz would start instead "from a world in which there's monopolistic competition, imperfect information . . . and all sorts of things." Anthony Barnes Atkinson and Nicholas Stern, "Tony Atkinson on Poverty, Inequality, and Public Policy: The Work and Life of a Great Economist," *Annual Review of Economics* 9, no. 1 (2017), 13.

85. "Global Democracy Has Another Bad Year," *Economist*, January 22, 2020, https://www.economist.com/graphic-detail/2020/01/22/global-democracy-has-another-bad-year. For 2022 see https://www.armstrongeconomics.com/international-news/politics/the-democracy-index/.

86. Lewis H. Lapham, *Money and Class in America* (New York: OR Books, 2018), 157.

87. Charles Schultze, quoted in Daniel T. Rodgers, *Age of Fracture* (Cambridge, MA: Harvard University Press, 2012), 42.

88. Walter Wriston, quoted in Rodgers, *Age of Fracture*, 75. See also Jeff Madrick, *Age of Greed* (New York: Knopf, 2011), chap. 1.

89. Jacob S. Hacker and Paul Pierson, *American Amnesia: How the War on Government Led Us to Forget What Made America Prosper* (New York: Simon & Schuster, 2016), 195.

90. On medically distorting effects of profit in Big Pharma, see Catherine D. Deangelis, "Big Pharma Profits and the Public Loses," *Milbank Quarterly* 94, no. 1 (2016): 30–33.

91. Matthew Perrone and Ben Wieder, "Pro-Painkiller Echo Chamber Shaped Policy and Drug Epidemic," Center for Public Integrity, September 19, 2016, https://publicintegrity.org/politics/state-politics/pro-painkiller-echo-chamber-shaped-policy-amid-drug-epidemic/.

CONCLUSION

1. Brian Edgar Butler, "Law and Economics," Internet Encyclopedia of Philosophy, accessed May 12, 2022, https://iep.utm.edu/law-and-economics/. See also Richard Posner, "The Law and Economics Movement, Richard T. Ely Lecture," *The American Economics Review* 77, no. 2 (1987): 1–13.

2. Daniel T. Rodgers, *Age of Fracture* (Cambridge, MA: Harvard University Press, 2012), 58–59.

3. Cited in Ibid., 59.

4. Richard A. Posner, *A Failure of Capitalism: The Crisis of '08 and the Descent into Depression* (Cambridge, MA: Harvard University Press, 2009), 326.

5. Ibid., xii.

6. Ibid., 285.

7. Ibid., 306. See also Mehrsa Baradaran, "The Neoliberal Looting of America," *New York Times*, July 2, 2020, https://www.nytimes.com/2020/07/02/opinion/private-equity-inequality.html.

8. Some Democrats, most famously Bernie Sanders and Alexandria Ocasio-Cortez, openly declare themselves to be socialists, and many young people are questioning capitalism. While 60 percent of baby boomers have a very or somewhat favorable view of capitalism, only 49 percent of Gen Z do. Sixty-four percent of the latter say they would vote for a socialist; among millennials the figure is 70 percent. See Stef W. Kight, "70% of Millennials Say They'd Vote for a Socialist," Axios, October 28, 2019, https://www.axios.com/millennials-vote-socialism-capitalism-decline-60c8a6aa-5353-45c4-9191-2de1808dc661.html. See also Mike Konczal, *Freedom from the Market: America's Fight to Liberate Itself from the Grip of the Invisible Hand* (New York: New Press, 2021). But our concern is not with socialism, but with the prospects for adequately regulated capitalism.

9. Kai Ryssdal and Andie Corban, "Is Congress About to Regulate Big Tech?" *Marketplace*, June 24, 2021, https://www.marketplace.org/2021/06/24/is-congress-about-to-regulate-big-tech/.

10. Jonathan Kanter, Reponses to Questions for the Record, Committee on the Judiciary, October, 18 2021, https://www.judiciary.senate.gov/download/kanter-responses-to-questions-for-the-record.

11. Jonathan Kanter, "Antitrust Enforcement: The Road to Recovery," keynote at the University of Chicago Stigler Center, Chicago, Illinois, April 21, 2022, https://www.justice.gov/opa/speech/assistant-attorney-general-jonathan-kanter-delivers-keynote-university-chicago-stigler#_ftn1.

12. Ibid. As noted above, Kanter highlighted that academics had written 831 academic articles on the "consumer welfare standard"—the idea promoted by Robert Bork—even though that term appears nowhere in the statute.

13. Paul Romer, quoted in Steve Lohr, "Once Tech's Favorite Economist, Now a Thorn in Its Side," *New York Times*, May 20, 2021, https://www.nytimes.com/2021/05/20/technology/tech-antitrust-paul-romer.html.

14. Fiona Scott Morton, quoted in Lohr, "Once Tech's Favorite Economist."

15. Michael A. Bernstein, *A Perilous Progress: Economists and Public Purpose in Twentieth-Century America* (Princeton, NJ: Princeton University Press, 2001), 173.

16. Ibid. The original source is William Appleman Williams, *The Contours of American History* (Cleveland: World Publishing Company, 1961).

17. Zachary D. Carter, "The End of Friedmanomics," *New Republic*, June 17, 2021, https://newrepublic.com/article/162623/milton-friedman-legacy-biden-government-spending. At Harvard, George Serafeim is developing new methods of corporate accounting that include the effect of corporate products and operations on people and the environment, but he is an exception. See Saijel Kishan, "How Wrong was Milton Friedman? Harvard Team Quantifies the Ways," *Bloomberg*, December 1, 2020, https://www.bloomberg.com/news/articles/2020-12-01/how-wrong-was-milton-friedman-harvard-team-quantifies-the-ways.

18. Carter, "The End of Friedmanomics."

19. Emily Badger, "A Nobel-Winning Economist Goes to Burning Man," *New York Times*, September 5, 2019, https://www.nytimes.com/2019/09/05/upshot/paul-romer-burning-man-nobel-economist.html.

20. Rebecca Henderson, *Reimagining Capitalism in a World on Fire* (New York: PublicAffairs, 2020), 19.

21. Henderson, *Reimagining Capitalism*, 27.

22. Binyamin Appelbaum, 2020, "50 Years of Blaming Milton Friedman. Here's Another Idea," *New York Times*, September 18, 2020, https://www.nytimes.com/2020/09/18/opinion/milton-friedman-essay.html. See also the fuller argument in Binyamin Appelbaum, *The Economists' Hour: False Prophets, Free Markets, and the Fracture of Society* (New York: Little, Brown, 2019).

23. John Tures, "Americans Trust Businesses More Than Government—Except Social Media, Which They Hate," *Observer*, August 12, 2020, https://observer.com/2020/08/polls-americans-trust-businesses-more-than-government-except-social-media/.

24. Eric Bradner, "Trump's Big Lie About 2020 Results Suffers Legal and Political Blows in Key Swing States," *CNN*, June 27, 2021, https://www.cnn.com/2021/06/27/politics/2020-election-falsehoods-voting/index.html; Aaron Blake, "Trump's 'Big Lie' Was Bigger than Just a Stolen Election," *Washington Post*, February 12, 2021, https://www.washingtonpost.com/politics/2021/02/12/trumps-big-lie-was-bigger-than-just-stolen-election/; and Martin Pengelly, "Romney: Trump's Lie that He Lost 2020 Election from Voter Fraud 'Like WWF,'" *Guardian*, June 27, 2021, https://www.theguardian.com/us-news/2021/jun/27/mitt-romney-donald-trump-big-lie-2020-election.

25. Art Cullen, "How to Quash the Resentments that Cleave Us," *Washington Post*, January 8, 2021, https://www.washingtonpost.com/opinions/how-to-quash-the-resentments-that-cleave-us/2021/01/08/474f54b6-51f2-11eb-bda4-615aaefd0555_story.html.

26. Mitt Romney, "Romney Condemns Insurrection at U.S. Capitol," Press Releases, January 6, 2021, https://www.romney.senate.gov/romney-condemns-insurrection-us-capitol.

27. For a thought-provoking defense of the view that we do need a progressive version of states' rights, see Michael H. Shuman, "The Promise of a Million Utopias," in *New Systems Reader: Alternatives to a Failed Economy*, ed. James Gustave Speth and Kathleen Courrier (New York: Routledge, 2020), 20–36. On the question of whether the United States is too big to govern, see Neil Gross, "Is the United States Government Too Big?" *New York Times*, May 11, 2018, https://www.nytimes.com/2018/05/11/opinion/sunday/united-states-too-big.html.

28. Joachim Klement, "Red States, Blue States: Two Economies, One Nation," Enterprising Investor, March 13, 2018, https://blogs.cfainstitute.org/investor/2018/03/13/red-states-blue-states-two-economies-one-nation/. Overall, "blue" states have HDIs similar to the Netherlands, "red" states closer to Russia. See also Paul Chiariello, "8 Economic Indicators: Are Red or Blue States Better?" *Applied Sentience*, July 30, 2020, https://appliedsentience.com/2020/07/30/economics-are-red-or-blue-states-better/. On gun deaths, see Eugenio Weigend Vargas, "Gun Violence in America: A State-by-State Analysis," Center for American Progress, November 20, 2019, https://www.americanprogress.org/issues/guns-crime/news/2019/11/20/477218/gun-violence-america-state-state-analysis/.

29. Marc Muro and Jacob Whiton, "America Has Two Economies—and They're Diverging Fast," *Brookings* (blog), September 19, 2019, https://www.brookings.edu/blog/the-avenue/2019/09/10/america-has-two-economies-and-theyre-diverging-fast/. For an analysis of why key voting patterns have developed and persist, see also Andrew Gelman, *Red State, Blue State, Rich State, Poor State: Why Americans Vote the Way They Do* (Princeton, NJ: Princeton University Press, 2008). See also Hacker and Pierson, *American Amnesia*, 355–56.

30. If many Republicans are locked into the myth of small government, it is not because it is materially benefiting them, either economically or personally; the states that receive the most federal dollars give the highest electoral margins to Republicans. Dean Lacy notes that "The ratio of federal spending per dollar of tax revenue from a state is positively related to Republican margin: More federal spending per tax dollar is associated with a higher Republican vote." He notes that it is possible that Republicans know that their states receive

large amounts of federal funding, but dislike how those funds are spent, such as on federal water projects. Our experiences living, working, and traveling in the West suggest the answer is more likely to be broadly ideological: that many people in red states "just don't like" the federal government, and resent their dependence on it. Lacy also noted that "one implication of the federal fiscal paradox may be that Democrats in the Northeast, Great Lakes, and Pacific Coast may become advocates for states' rights and smaller federal government." We have often had this thought, but so far no real sign of that has emerged. Dean Lacy, "Why Do Red States Vote Republican While Blue States Pay the Bills?" Paper Presentation, Annual Meeting of the American Political Science Association, Toronto, Ontario, September 3–6, 2009, 14, 25, accessed July 23, 2021, https://papers.ssrn.com/sol3/papers.cfm?abstract_id =1451268.

31. Gelman, *Red State, Blue State*.

32. If anything, the demographics go the other way, with liberal-leaning easterners moving to places like Arizona, which have now become a lot more purple. See Gelman, *Red State, Blue State*; and Hacker and Pierson, *American Amnesia*.

33. "Utah Income Tax Calculator," SmartAsset, accessed July 23, 2021, https://smartasset.com /taxes/utah-tax-calculator.

34. "Programs and Services for Individuals," USDA Rural Development, accessed April 30, 2021, https://www.rd.usda.gov/programs-services/programs-services-individuals.

35. Madrick, *Big Government*, xv.

36. E. J. Dionne Jr., *Why the Right Went Wrong: Conservatism—from Goldwater to Trump and Beyond* (New York: Simon & Schuster, 2016), 444. Dionne's comment confirms an observation by political scientist Jonathan Schlefer, cited by Binyamin Appelbaum: "Cambridge, England, saw capitalism as inherently troubled; Cambridge, Massachusetts, came to see capitalism as merely in need of fine-tuning." Appelbaum, *The Economists' Hour*, 17.

37. In 2016 it was 22.7 percent of GDP; in 2019, it was 21 percent; in 2022 it was 33 percent, pushed up by Covid-related spending, https://ourworldindata.org/grapher/total-gov-expenditure -gdp-wdi?time=2019.

38. "Central government expenditure as share of GDP, 1972 to 2020," Our World in Data, https://ourworldindata.org/grapher/total-gov-expenditure-gdp-wdi?tab=chart&country =USA~PAN~PER~BTN~CAN~DNK~European+Union~DEU~FRA. Of the "big three" countries that first industrialized—the United Kingdom, Germany and the United States—the United States spends the least. Public spending in all three countries saw a huge spike during World War II, dropped back when the war ended, and then began a steady climb. Spending in the United Kingdom dropped dramatically during the years when Margaret Thatcher was prime minister, in part as a result of the influence of conservative economists, who blamed stagflation on this rise in public spending. Public spending may have been too high, but it was probably not a major factor in stagflation; a more likely explanation is that the economies were in their down cycle, and then inflation was triggered by the exogenous shock of dramatically increased oil prices. See Jeff Madrick, *The Case for Big Government* (Princeton, NJ: Princeton University Press, 2008), 6, and discussion in chap. 12.

39. Madrick, *Big Government*, 6.

40. Understanding the federal budget can be a challenge because most analyses distinguish between mandatory and discretionary spending. About 60 percent of all federal spending is "mandatory," determined by formulas written in law rather than by annual appropriations: Social Security, Medicare, Medicaid, and veterans' benefits. About 8 percent of the federal budget goes to interest in the debt. Of what's left, more than half (about 55 percent in most recent years) goes to military spending (of various sorts). What many of us think of as "government programs"—education, transportation, health care—are slivers: about 5 to 7 percent of

the discretionary budget each, or about 3 percent each of the total budget. For example, according to the Congressional Budget Office, total non-defense discretionary spending—the entire 2019 federal outlay for all non-mandated non-defense government programs—was $661 billion out of a total budget of $4.4 trillion. Put this way, it becomes easy to see why many people are susceptible to arguments about government waste and inefficiency. Most federal spending goes to things that are invisible in our day-to-day lives until we retire, and by then the lion's share of our voting days are behind us. And it's not clear what can be done about the national debt. See "How Does the Federal Government Spend Their Money?" in *Tax Policy Center's Briefing Book* (Urban Institute and Brookings Institution Tax Policy Center, 2020), accessed July 22, 2021, https://www.taxpolicy'scenter.org/briefing-book/how-does-federal -government-spend-its-money; and "The Federal Budget in 2019: An Infographic," Congressional Budget Office, April 15, 2020, https://www.cbo.gov/publication/56324.

41. For an overview of U.S. military spending as a percentage of GDP since 1960, see https://www .macrotrends.net/countries/USA/united-states/military-spending-defense-budgetary. Military spending as a percentage of GDP peaked in 1967 at 9.4 percent and then fell—with up and downs—to a low of 3.1 percent in 2000. Spending began an upward climb in 2001, peaking at 4.9 percent in 2010, and then stabilizing in the late 2010s around 3.5 percent.

42. For a concise discussion of the "conservative contradiction" of being unwilling to discuss the role of military spending in the federal budget, see Gary Gerstle, *Liberty and Coercion: The Paradox of American Government from the Founding to the Present*, rev. ed. (Princeton, NJ: Princeton University Press, 2015), 326–27. He notes that this is not just a contradiction in terms of the size of the federal government but also insofar as the federal government, through military procurement, effectively directs a major portion of the American economy.

43. "Discretionary Spending in 2019: An Infographic," Congressional Budget Office, April 15, 2020, https://www.cbo.gov/publication/56326.

44. Ibid.

45. Lindsay Koshgarian, "Trump's 2021 Budget Gives 55% to the Military," National Priorities Project, February 10, 2020, https://www.nationalpriorities.org/blog/2020/02/10/trumps -2021-budget-gives-55-military; the dollar value figure for 2020 was $714 billion. "Discretionary Spending in 2019: An Infographic."

46. Aaron Mehta and Joe Gould, "Biden requests $715B for Pentagon, hinting at administration's future priorities," Defense News, April 9, 2021, https://www.defensenews.com/breaking -news/2021/04/09/biden-requests-715b-for-pentagon-hinting-at-administrations-future -priorities/; Alexandra Jaffe, "Biden authorizes $768.2 billion in defense spending, percent increase," PBS.org, December 28, 2021, https://www.pbs.org/newshour/politics/biden -authorizes-768-2-billion-in-defense-spending-a-5-increase.

47. Sonner Kehrt, "The U.S. Military Emits More Carbon Dioxide Into the Atmosphere Than Entire Countries like Denmark or Portugal," Inside Climate News, January 18, 2022, https://insideclimatenews.org/news/18012022/military-carbon-emissions/; Niall McCarthy, "Report: The U.S. Military Emits more CO_2 Than Many Industrialized Nations," *Forbes*, June 13, 2019, https://www.forbes.com/sites/niallmccarthy/2019/06/13/report-the-u-s-military -emits-more-co2-than-many-industrialized-nations-infographic/?sh=4c482cbd4372.

48. As a percentage of GDP, as of 2021 the United States spends 3.5 on its military. In comparison, the United Kingdom spends 2.2, France is 1.9, Italy is 1.5, and Canada is 1.3. M. Szmigiera, "Military expenditure as percentage of gross domestic product in highest spending countries 2021," Statista, April 29, 2022, https://www.statista.com/statistics/266892/military-expendi ture-as-percentage-of-gdp-in-highest-spending-countries/.

49. "U.S. Defense Spending Compared to Other Countries," Peter G. Peterson Foundation, May 13, 2020, https://www.pgpf.org/chart-archive/0053_defense-comparison. See also

Szmigiera, "Military Spending"; Niall McCarthy, "The Countries with the Highest Military Expenditure in 2020," *Forbes*, April 28, 2021, https://www.forbes.com/sites/niallmccarthy/2021/04/28/the-countries-with-the-highest-military-expenditure-in-2020-infographic/?sh=32aad18b4e80.

50. Posner, *Failure of Capitalism*, 107–12.

51. The exact quotation is "Adam Smith's invisible hand—the idea that free markets lead to efficiency as if guided by unseen forces—is invisible, at least in part, because it is not there." Joseph Stiglitz, "There Is No Invisible Hand," *Guardian*, December 20, 2002, https://www.theguardian.com/education/2002/dec/20/highereducation.uk1. We like our version better.

52. Leonardo Bich, et al., "Biological Regulation: Controlling the System from Within," *Biology and Philosophy* (2015), https://hal.archives-ouvertes.fr/hal-01185296.

INDEX

A NOTE ON THE AUTHORS

NAOMI ORESKES is the Henry Charles Lea Professor of the History of Science and Affiliated Professor of Earth and Planetary Sciences at Harvard University. Her writing has appeared in the *New York Times*, the *Washington Post*, the *Los Angeles Times*, and elsewhere, and her TED Talk, "Why We Should Trust Scientists," has been viewed more than 1.5 million times. She is the author of *Why Trust Science?* (2019) and *Science on a Mission* (2021). ERIK M. CONWAY is a historian of science and technology and works for the California Institute of Technology. He is the author of seven books and dozens of articles and essays. Together, they are the authors of *The Collapse of Western Civilization* (2014) and the bestselling *Merchants of Doubt* (2010), which in 2014 was made into a feature-length documentary produced by Participant Media.